THE
FORGOTTEN
ARTS AND
CRAFTS

IN ASSOCIATION WITH

**THE
NATIONAL
TRUST**

IN ASSOCIATION WITH

THE
NATIONAL
TRUST

THE
FORGOTTEN
ARTS AND
CRAFTS

JOHN SEYMOUR

A Dorling Kindersley Book

The National Trust and Crafts

Perhaps more than most organizations, because of its dedication to conservation and the appearance of things, the National Trust often needs to foster the skills of craftsmen. There are stone walls to be repaired, hedges to be laid, and stiles, gates, and fences to be constructed. Thatching has to be carried out on anything from cottages in Somerset to Sir John Soane's model farm at Wimpole, in Cambridgeshire. A new iron gate may be forged by the local blacksmith. The Trust's concern for nature conservation means that copses are coppiced. Even boats are rebuilt – *Gondola*, the steam yacht on Coniston Water, and *Shamrock* on the Tamar. In general, the craftsmen can be found locally for all but the most abstruse tasks. The National Trust itself has set up several workshops across the country, and many of the old artifacts can be seen displayed, and preserved, at its properties.

The National Trust looks after a wealth of buildings housing fine examples of forgotten household crafts. There are dairies and butteries which show the amount of work involved in processing milk before the advent of modern machinery, and herb gardens where household medicines were grown. Apiaries, breweries, and home farms added to the contents of larders, and ice houses preserved food long before refrigerators were invented. Wells and laundries bear witness to the labour of washing by hand, and kitchens full of gleaming brass implements record the skills involved in preparing meals without present-day, labour-saving devices. Most Trust houses have examples of hand-sewn bed linen, chair covers or patchwork quilts testifying to many hours of patient needlework, and there are a number of costume collections showing how fine sewing and embroidery were applied to personal adornment.

Dorling DK Kindersley

LONDON, NEW YORK, SYDNEY, DELHI, PARIS,
MUNICH and JOHANNESBURG

For Angela

Combined Edition
Designer Wesley Richards **Project Editor** Jennifer Jones
Production Ruth Charlton and Julian Deeming
Senior Managing Editor Mary-Clare Jerram **Senior Managing Art Editor** Lee Griffiths

The Forgotten Arts first published in 1984 and *Forgotten Household Crafts* first published in 1987
by Dorling Kindersley Limited
Combined edition published in Great Britain in 2001
by Dorling Kindersley Limited
9 Henrietta Street, Covent Garden, London WC2E 8PS
In association with the National Trust

A CIP catalogue record for this book is available from The British Library.

ISBN 0 7513 2782 4

Colour reproduction by Colourscan, Singapore.
Printed in Slovakia by Neografia.

see our complete catalogue at
www.dk.com

Previous page:
Cider making in Wiltshire, and everybody helps with the cider press, which although old-fashioned, is extremely efficient.

CONTENTS

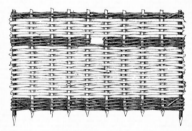

PART II
FORGOTTEN
HOUSEHOLD
CRAFTS 192

INTRODUCTION 194

KITCHEN CRAFTS 205

TEXTILES 174

DAIRY CRAFTS 257

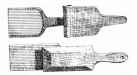

LAUNDRY CRAFTS 273

AROUND THE HOME 291

TEXTILE CRAFTS 331

DECORATIVE CRAFTS 361

FOREWORD

It is now more than 10 years since the first versions of these books were published, and sadly some of the craftsmen and friends I mention have now died. But I am very pleased that Dorling Kindersley has decided to produce a new "bumper" edition. There never was a time when it was more important for the health and wellbeing of humankind that men and women should start to make real things with their own hands again. For a human being to spend a life of pressing computer buttons, or doing boring and non-creative "jobs" in a factory, is to spend a life in hell.

As the huge multinational corporations close in on the world, fewer and fewer individuals find themselves in the position of being able to produce anything of use or beauty themselves – they are all just cogs in some huge money-making machine with its head office thousands of miles away and God knows where!

Apart from the fact that the huge global monstrosity is not sustainable and is due to come crashing down anyway, the intolerable aridness and boredom for most people will eventually become unbearable and we will all rebel. We will seize the right again to make things of utility and beauty for ourselves, with our own intelligence and our own hands, helped by simple, basic, and so often, beautiful tools.

As we reach the end of the Age of Plunder, as this our present age should be called, we will have to bring in a new age – the Age of Healing – and in this age our looted and wounded planet must be brought to health and wealth again, and we must fill our homes and our lives with beautiful things again and cast out the plastic and mass-produced rubbish that fills them now. This book is an attempt to show that such things are possible.

I wish to dedicate this book to Angela Ashe and to thank her for her invaluable help in researching much of the information it contains.

John Seymour
Killowen, 1999

Left: *Wiltshire basket maker Albert Eastbrook in his workshop in the 1950s.*

PART ONE

FORGOTTEN ARTS

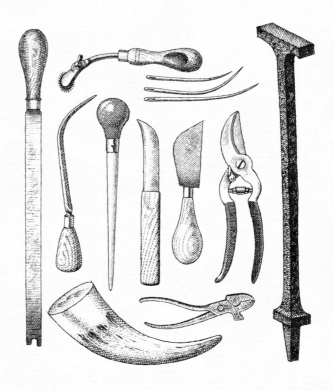

TYRING A WOODEN WHEEL
Wheelwrights quickly quench the hot tyre as soon as it has been positioned around the wooden rim of the wheel (see pp.86–93).

INTRODUCTION

RACTICALLY EVERY ARTIFACT A PERSON USES TODAY can easily be made from oil-derived plastic, in a large factory, by machine-minders whose chief quality is their ability to survive lives of intense boredom. Even the machine-minders are being replaced rapidly by robots who, we are told, don't get bored at all.

Artifacts so produced often do their jobs perfectly well. They are ugly, for beauty in an artifact depends on the texture of some natural material combined with the skill and loving care of an artisan; they are short-lived, so consequently our world is becoming choked with partly degraded, broken-down plastic objects, and their production is causing the pollution of our planet on a scale never before experienced. But, by and large, they work.

If everything we use is to be ugly and boring to make, what is the purpose of living at all? Was there once really something people called the quality of life? A good and satisfying quality of life that is. Could there be again? Or are we, as a species, doomed to live out the rest of our destiny doing boring jobs and surrounded by mediocrity and ugliness?

Now it is often said that it is mass production which makes it possible for so many of the members of our grossly distended human population to have as many objects as they do have. This argument begs two questions. The first is, do we need as many objects as we think? I often walk round local shops and look with amazement at the merchandise. I cannot see how the possession of nine-tenths of it could in any way add to a person's happiness or bring him nearer to what one could describe as the "good life" at all. Nine-tenths of it will quickly end up on the rubbish dump and prove that it should not have been made in the first place. The other question is, need we make people do with mass-produced rubbish when a growing proportion of the population of the "developed" world is unemployed? The only possible justification for producing the rubbish is that there are not enough workers to make good high-quality artifacts. But there *are* enough workers. Or there could be enough workers if young people were trained to do good, useful and interesting jobs.

Are we justified in using articles, no matter how convenient it may be for us to use them, that we know were produced in conditions which bored and even stultified the human beings who had to make them? It was in an attempt to be able to feel a little less culpable in this respect that I began to look around and do the research that led to the writing of this book. Surely, I thought, it must be possible to produce the things we really need without causing our fellow humans to live and work in such surroundings?

Well, thank God, I found that the Forgotten Arts are not completely forgotten at all. There is not a human skill that was ever developed that is not still practised somewhere on this planet. And, what's more, almost everywhere in the so-called developed world at least, there are the beginnings of a revival of the ancient arts and crafts. More and more people are demanding good craftsmanship.

The Chatti or the Debbie

Did I say that mass-produced objects can do their jobs perfectly well? If I did I was contradicting the great Bengali poet and mystic Rabindranath Tagore who, comparing a *debbie*, or four-gallon can once used for petrol, with a *chatti*, which is an earthenware pot created by a village craftsman, described the former object as *mean*. The *debbie*, he wrote, carried water just as well as the *chatti*, but while doing so the *debbie* looked ugly. The *chatti* not only did the job of carrying water just as well as the *debbie* but it did more – it delighted and pleased both the user and the onlooker. He could have added that even a pretty woman looks ugly carrying a *debbie* on her head – even quite a plain one looks graceful and beautiful carrying a *chatti*. He could also have added that the use of the *chatti* helps to give a living to a friend and neighbour in the village : the use of the *debbie* merely compounds the pollution and adds to the degradation of our planet.

The Discipline of Natural Materials

The use of artifacts made from natural materials gives a pleasure far in excess of the pleasure that we may derive from simply doing the job. The form, the texture, the subtle feel of such artifacts, together with an awareness of their origins – in trees, a crop growing in a field, part of the hide of an ox, part of the living rock – add greatly to the pleasure of seeing and using them. Wood, iron and steel (including that excellent material stainless steel), other metals both precious and base, beautiful gems and stones, stone, leather, natural fibres such as wool, hemp, flax, cotton, silk, jute and manilla, clay : these materials, shaped and put together by the hands of skilled human beings, provide all the artifacts that we should legitimately need. If something cannot be made with these natural materials I simply don't want it.

The very intractability of a natural material imposes a discipline that forces the craftsman to produce something beautiful as well as useful. It is the grain of wood with its liability to split along one plane and not the others, that forces the carpenter, the wheelwright, the cooper, the turner or the shipwright to fashion it in certain ways, to use the qualities of wood and overcome its disadvantages, that imposes a pattern of beauty on wooden objects. It also forces the craftsman in wood to learn the mystery of his craft and this elevates him high above the mere factory operative. Any fool can mould plastic; it has no grain at all.

It has been the limitations of stone as a building material which have forced the builder, over the centuries, to develop the great beauty of arch and vault, of column and arcade and flying buttress. Concrete, which, when reinforced, can be made to any shape, is rarely made into anything beautiful at all. Look at a modern skyscraper, you might say. Yes, but compare it to the fan-vaulted ceiling of Sherborne Abbey, in Dorset, a photograph of which is stuck to the side of my filing cabinet and which overcomes me with awe every time I look at it. The fact that one was built for the enrichment of mammon and the other for the glory of God might have something to do with the matter, too.

REAL COSTS

Hand-crafted goods often cost more than the mass-produced equivalent initially, but do they in the long term? Surely it is more economical to pay money to a friend and neighbour – a local craftsman – to make something good for you than to pay a little less money for some rubbishy item mass produced far away and God knows by whom? The money you pay your neighbour may come back to you. By helping to keep your neighbour in business you are enriching your own locality.

Furthermore, you are increasing the total sum of real enjoyment in the world, for your craftsman almost certainly enjoys making the article for you and you will certainly enjoy owning and using it. The operative in the factory may enjoy the wages he or she gets but the *work*, well, no.

Now people who seek for and demand articles made by craftsmen and women are often described as élitist. Well we are, of course – the charge is completely justified. And the nice thing about élitism is that anybody can be an élitist if he or she wants to be. Come and join us! There is plenty of room in this élite, room for all in fact. Nobody has to put up with

mass-produced rubbish. The stuff simply did not exist two hundred years ago and yet human beings got on perfectly well, and lived 'til they died, as we do today. There are people who can't afford to join our élite, I hear you say. Oh yes they can – all they have to do is make out with fewer unnecessary articles than they have come to believe they need now. The word élitist is used nowadays as if there is something shameful about being a member of an élite. I would find it shameful not to be a member of this particular one.

And so, slowly and steadily, I am ridding my home, as far as I can, of mass-produced rubbish, and either learning to do without certain things or else replacing them by articles made out of honest materials by people who enjoyed making them and who, by long diligence and training, have qualified themselves to make them superbly. This has brought me into contact with many crafts people in Ireland where I live, in Wales where I used to live, in England where I was born, in France, Germany, Austria, Italy and Greece, and even in the Middle East and in Africa. Some of these people were poor – some were struggling for a living, but poor or not they had one thing in common – they enjoyed their work. They took a great pride in it and, if you showed an intelligent interest, they loved to show what they were doing and how they did it.

REWARDS

The older craftsman still has that ancient attitude to the reward for work that used to be universal but is, alas, now seldom found. And that is the attitude that there should be a fair reward for good work. Nowadays the predominating attitude is "I charge what the market will bear." I will never forget the time I finally persuaded that great craftsman Mr Harry King, the boatbuilder of Pin Mill in Suffolk, to build me a 14-foot wooden dinghy. This was soon after the Second World War when it was hard to find craftsmen to make such an item. For a long time he refused but finally he relented.

"How much will you charge for her?" I asked. Later I learned that you do not ask such people how much they will charge, at least not in Suffolk.

"Three pun' a foot," he snapped.

"But, Mr King, everyone I have been to charges *four* pounds a foot! You must have made a mistake?"

"Three pun' a foot's my price. If you don't like it you can go somewhere else!" he replied. "I don't hev to build ye a dinghy!"

The real craftsman does not need more than enough. In our times of social mobility, everyone is after more than enough. We no longer ask "what is our product worth?" or "how much do I need?" but "how much can I get?" I have

known many young people who have tried a craft and given it up because they found that, although they could make enough, they could not make more than enough. And more than enough is what they feel they require. A planet on which every inhabitant tries to get more than enough is a planet that is in for a hard time. And in the final reckoning I am sure that having more than enough does not make us more happy. You can definitely have too much of a good thing. What makes a person happy is doing work that he or she loves doing, being fairly paid for it, and having it properly appreciated.

Apprenticeship

But to become superbly good at one of the crafts is not easy. Many a young person tries it and fails in the attempt. The old-fashioned apprenticeship system was the best system that there has ever been for young people, and for master crafts-men, too. The young person was subjected to pretty rigorous discipline, maybe in some cases too rigorous, but by this he was taught not only his craft but also the habit of hard work that would, later, enable him to enjoy life and prosper at his trade. For the master craftsman is a happy man. He glories in his skill and his work, drinks his wine or his beer with zest, looks forward to his food and sleeps well o' nights! Boredom he is a stranger to. If he looks back over his life surely he does not regret the hard apprenticeship that qualified him for being what he is? Surely it is better for a young person to be subjected to some pretty hard discipline, and earn low wages, for a few years, and then spend the rest of his life as a respected and self-respecting craftsman, than to tumble straight into a factory, no matter how good the wages are. I include here the "professions" in my assessment; a good doctor or a good dentist is a master craftsman too and should be treated as one, no more, no less. And there is nothing higher, on this planet at least, that man or woman can aspire to.

INTERDEPENDENCE OF CRAFTSMEN

During my researches I was struck by the *isolation* of many of the craftspeople I met. When I talked to the old people – some of whom were in their eighties and still working every day – I had the impression that in their younger days they were not isolated at all. At that time there seems to have been a great interdependence of craftsmen in the countryside. Each craftsman was dependent on his brother craftsmen of different trades in order to be able to carry on his own trade. The fisherman, for example, was dependent on the farmer who grew the flax for his nets, the net maker who made them, the basket maker to make his traps and pots, the boat builder who built his boat. The boat builder in turn was dependent

on the blacksmith who forged the chain plates, spider-bands, anchors, chains, and dozens of other items needed for a fishing boat, the woodsman who felled and carried the timber for the boat, the sawyer who cut it up, the oil-miller who made the linseed oil needed to preserve it, the flax spinners and weavers who made the canvas for the sails, the sail maker who made them, the rope maker who spun and twisted the hemp for the ropes, the iron founder who cast the pigs of ballast for the bilge – and so it went on and on. All these interdependent craftsmen once knew each other. Each could go to his supplier and discuss with him exactly what he wanted. Each saw the beginning and the end of what he had created and each one of them probably thought of his own

contribution as he ate the fish that the fisherman caught. But now such men are isolated. They make a good living because of the new interest in hand-crafted goods, but a lonely one.

And what of the few young people who want to enter the noble hand crafts? They, too, plough a lonely furrow. A hundred bureaucratic rules and regulations have made it almost impossible to find a craftsman willing to take on apprentices. The very few that do manage to learn a trade ultimately benefit hugely, because the products of the hand crafts are becoming scarcer and more sought after as every year goes by. A young man set up as a farrier near where I used to farm in Dyfed, in Wales. He makes his rounds in a

little van with a portable forge and anvil in it and shoes horses. I worked out how much money he must have been making once and was staggered at the amount.

Other young men and women manage to scramble their way into a craft without undergoing a formal apprenticeship. They are at a great disadvantage but some of them, by sheer determination, manage to reach near perfection in their trade. These are mostly very happy men and women. I believe more and more people will join their ranks and as this happens the world will become a much better place. I believe that as more and more craftspeople fight through, in town as well as country, something like the old community inter-relationships will waken and grow again.

PROGRESS

The dream of high industrial and technological civilization is fast turning into a nightmare. It may be "progress" for scientists to devise ever more sophisticated and complicated ways of making what we think we need, but it is hell for the men and women who have to drag themselves to the dreary places where they make these things to watch the dials and press the buttons, and it is hell for the men and women, increasing in numbers all the time, who are told they are "redundant". Redundant human beings? Mass industry has, from its inception, had a strong tendency to class its opera-tives as mere components of the machine. Like the machine the worker becomes just a means to an end. No, man is not a means; he is an end. He is, on this Earth, the end towards which all human production must be the means.

Whether mankind just gets fed up with a way of working which is boring, and sordid, and produces ugly things, or whether the constraints imposed by the dwindling resources of our planet finally halt the Gadarene rush to the cliff's edge, in the end, if mankind is to survive at any kind of level of true civilization, the craftsman must triumph.

The only whole and happy life possible to a woman or man on this planet is a life in which *work* – honest and noble *work* – is the greatest joy. Leisure yes, but leisure can only be a joy if it is true leisure, which means leisure from work. Just constant idleness – the idleness of the unemployed – is not leisure at all but is a corrosive and corrupting thing. That good craftsman, Eric Gill, once wrote: "Leisure is secular, work is sacred. The object of leisure is work, the object of work is holiness. Holiness means wholeness."

It was in search of wholeness that this book was written.

WOODLAND CRAFTS

At one time broad-leaved native woodland flourished and was used by rural communities to the full. The maiden trees – those grown from seed and intended to reach maturity a century or more later – were hardwood trees and were spaced so their boughs would grow big and wide. Their timber would eventually be cut and seasoned and used by workshop craftsmen. Between and eventually beneath the maiden trees, smaller trees and saplings proliferated and were cut and used every 10 or 15 years. This was known as the underwood, and it was divided into areas called cants and sold to woodsmen who lived by and mostly in the wood. They would cut and sort the wood, use whatever they needed for their own special woodland craft, and sell the rest. In this age of waste big trees are felled and taken to the sawyers, and all their tops and the underwood are piled into great heaps and burned.

COPPICING

F YOU CUT DOWN PRACTICALLY any well-established hardwood, particularly deciduous, tree just above ground level the stump will not die. Shoots will sprout up and you have perhaps a dozen smaller trees where you had one before – the basis of *coppicing*. If you cut the trees higher up the trunk similar new growth sprouts, out of the reach of cattle and horses. This is *pollarding*, which is practised where animals have access to the trees or where their appearance is considered important, as in streets or parks. Coppicing is chosen where grazing animals are totally excluded.

Coppicing is the most fundamental of woodland crafts. In Europe the most commonly coppiced trees are *hazel, ash, sweet* or *Spanish chestnut, oak, alder* and *sycamore*, each of which is made use of in different ways, as will become apparent in the rest of this section on woodland crafts. *Willow* will coppice readily and is used for basketry and sometimes hurdle-making, but it is cut annually whereas true coppice trees have anything up to a 20-year growing span

RIVING TOOLS
Light pieces of wood can be rived with a *froe*, while heavier pieces require a *beetle* and steel *wedges*.

FROE

CLEAVING-BRAKE FOR THIN SECTIONS OF WOOD

BEETLE OR BITTLE

WEDGES

before they are cut back and the wood used. The *rotation* of coppiced trees depends on the size of the wood required. Thus walking sticks grow in five or six years, hazel for spars in eight years, and sweet chestnut for hop poles and ash for hurdles in 15 years. The *stools*, as the cut-over stumps are called, may last a hundred years, although ash stools do not as a rule last this long. When a stool dies another tree should be planted.

Coppice-with-standards is an old and excellent system of woodland management. Here the coppice trees are grown fairly closely together (perhaps every four feet), but other trees or *standards* are interplanted 20 to 40 to the acre and allowed to grow to maturity to be felled for big timber. Oak is the favourite tree for this, although sweet chestnut, ash and larch are often used. Typically the standards are felled after a rotation time of about 10 times that of the coppice; say 120 years if the coppice is cut every 12. Where *grown crooks* (curved boughs) were needed for ship building (see p.118) coppice-with-standards was a very popular method, for the oaks sent forth side branches which provided the crooks. In the belief that wooden ship building will come into its own again, I am planting some coppice-with-standards near my home.

RIVING
Riving, or splitting wood, is a craft that is harder to master than it looks. A good woodman will rive plenty of straight-grained pieces out of a small tree trunk, where a less experienced person will waste more wood than he rives successfully. The reason for this is that the wood breaks out *across the grain* and the rive comes out of the side of the trunk instead of running true to the other end of it. The way to rive most coppice wood is to knock a blade into the end grain, and then push the blade while working it from side to side to open the grain.

HURDLE MAKING

WHEN I WAS A BOY I WORKED FOR A winter on a farm in the Cotswolds, uplands in the west of England, on which it was my duty to *fold* two hundred sheep behind hurdles. Folding is a sheep-farming technique which involves keeping the sheep within a rectangle made of hurdles, like small hingeless field gates, tied one to the other, on a crop that the sheep will eat. In my case the crop was turnips and swedes.

THE BUSINESS OF FOLDING SHEEP
Every day I had to move the sheep on to fresh turnips and, at the same time, shut them off from the land they had already been over. The sheep were enclosed in a square of hurdles and the first day they would happily eat the turnips within their enclosure. The next day I would come along with enough hurdles for another three sides and build an identical square enclosure on one of the sides of the original.

I would then take out one of the hurdles dividing yesterday's enclosure from today's and drive the sheep through on to fresh turnips. From then on, every day I had to take down three sides of yesterday's enclosure, carry the hurdles over or around today's enclosure and build tomorrow's. In this way the flock was directed over the field in an orderly manner and this did the sheep good and the land too: on land where the soil was light, their droppings took the place of the expensive imported fertilizers.

RIVEN ASH GATE HURDLES
The hurdles I had to carry forwards so laboriously were made of riven ash. They were expensive to buy new and took a lot of hard wear, so sometime in the spring the old man who was the local hurdle maker came out from the nearby village to go over them all and repair them. I watched him then and I also went with him to his place of work and saw how they were made.

MAKING A GATE HURDLE
If you have ever made an artifact in wood which is jointed and meant to be square, you will know how skilful it is to put the 14 mortice and tenon joints together that make an ash gate hurdle. An experienced hurdle maker relies solely on his eye and works surprisingly quickly.

1 *The first job is to remove the bark with a draw-knife from the heavy sections of ash set by for the uprights (known as heads). The hurdle maker then points them with a bill.*

2 *He sets each head in the fork of the brake (his clamp), marks the mortice slots, then bores three holes along each slot.*

He bought ash coppice every winter, felled the 12-year-old trees, and sawed them with a cross-cut saw into the lengths he required. Using a froe and a riving brake he rived these lengths into as many members as he could. Back in his little working area he had a *morticing machine*, or morticing engine as he called it. This was simply a chisel blade fixed near the fulcrum of a lever which could be driven downwards with great force by depressing the end of the lever. With this he cut mortices, or long narrow slots, in the short thick pieces of wood he had retained for the pairs of uprights, or *heads* of each hurdle. He then took the *bars*, or rails, of the hurdle – fairly light pieces of ash as long as the hurdle was to be wide – and tapered both ends of each with a draw-knife, holding the work in a *shaving horse* as he did so (see p.33). These ends formed taper-fit tenons that he then drove into the mortices in the uprights, holding them firm with small wire nails. The ash did not split as the nails were driven home because the wood was so green and full of sap. A light upright, not reaching the ground, was next nailed to the

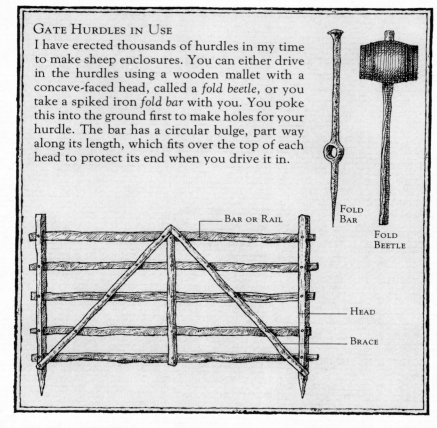

GATE HURDLES IN USE
I have erected thousands of hurdles in my time to make sheep enclosures. You can either drive in the hurdles using a wooden mallet with a concave-faced head, called a *fold beetle*, or you take a spiked iron *fold bar* with you. You poke this into the ground first to make holes for your hurdle. The bar has a circular bulge, part way along its length, which fits over the top of each head to protect its end when you drive it in.

FOLD BAR

FOLD BEETLE

BAR OR RAIL

HEAD

BRACE

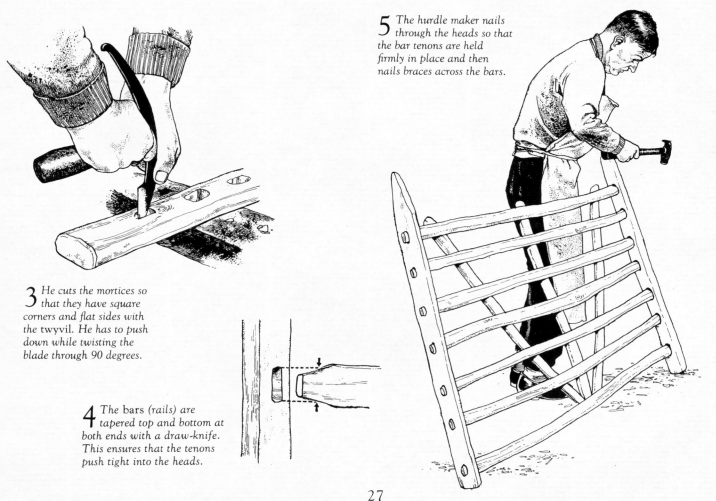

3 *He cuts the mortices so that they have square corners and flat sides with the twyvil. He has to push down while twisting the blade through 90 degrees.*

4 *The bars (rails) are tapered top and bottom at both ends with a draw-knife. This ensures that the tenons push tight into the heads.*

5 *The hurdle maker nails through the heads so that the bar tenons are held firmly in place and then nails braces across the bars.*

middles of the rails and then two slanting braces nailed on with their lower ends near the upright ends and their tops near the top of the centre upright. The hurdle was complete and looked very like a narrow field gate. But whereas a well-made field gate would be made in a carpenter's workshop, as I describe on page 148, with its heavy timbers squared, shaved and smoothed, the gate hurdle is left rough hewn and neither head is strong enough to last very long hinged to a gate post.

OTHER MEANS OF MORTICING
Not every hurdle maker has made or inherited a morticing engine, and those that do not, do as I do, and simply drill three adjacent holes with a one-inch bit in a brace and then ream out the long ragged hole with a chisel. A better tool than a chisel for this job is a specially made mortice-knife or a little tool called a *twyvil*. The difference between the tools is that the mortice-knife is two-handled whereas the twyvil has one. Both tools have a pointed blade with one edge straight and the other curved and sharpened on one face only. The blade of either of these will square off the edges of the mortices in the hurdle uprights admirably.

THE GOLDEN RULE OF GATE HURDLE MAKING
There is one trick that you quickly learn when you start making morticed gate hurdles, or field gates for that matter. That is to taper the *tenon* of the rail or horizontal

so that when you drive it in to the mortice the taper exerts pressure up and down and not sideways. If it exerts pressure sideways of course it splits the upright.

Riven ash hurdles are very strong and long-lasting but very heavy. I could carry six of them on my back by pushing a stake through them and getting my shoulder under it, but it was gruelling hard work, particularly as I always had to carry them over a rough muddy field and then over a fence of the same hurdles. A disadvantage also of the gate hurdle is that sheep can see through them. We never had trouble with the heavy old Cotswold ewes who would never try to get out, but we also kept some Border Leicester-Cheviots which were mountain animals and could jump like greyhounds. If a sheep can't see it won't go. These sheep, with these hurdles, could see, and they went.

WATTLES
Hurdles which do not have the disadvantage that sheep can see through them are used in the south and south-west of England. These are called *wattles*, and are usually woven with hazel rods, some left *in the round*, meaning not riven, and some riven once. I have seen these made in the West Country, around Dorset.

Wattle making was generally a summer task for which the coppice worker would set aside plenty of hazel of the right sort of thickness, firstly for the *sails*, or uprights of the wattle, and secondly for the long rods used to weave between them. His only

WATTLE HURDLE
The wattle hurdle is woven with hazel rods, some riven and some left in the round. The uprights are also of hazel and consist of two strong end shores with flimsier riven sails in between. When you need to move them, you put a pole through the holes in the middle of half a dozen or so such hurdles and heave them on to your shoulder.

THE MOULD
The wattle hurdle maker uses a mould to hold the shores and sails in place while he weaves the hazel. The mould is slightly curved to produce a weave that tightens when straightened.

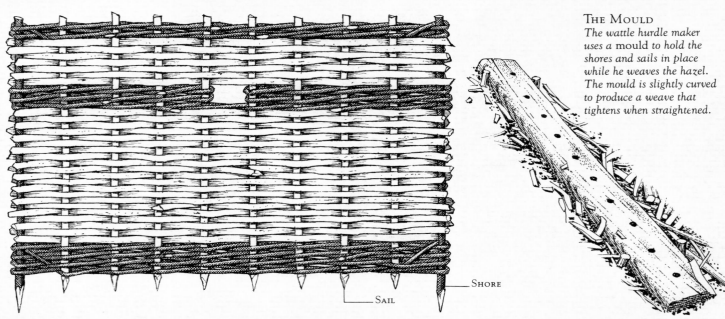

SHORE

SAIL

indispensable tool is a curved billhook. He also makes a rough framework of hazel, called the *gallows*, to stand his bundles of rods against, a measuring pole to keep all the sails to a common height, and a heavy log, riven in two so it will stand flat, used as a stand for the sails during the weaving and called the *mould*. This has 10 holes to take the 10 sails of a true sheep hurdle.

STRENGTHENING DEVICES

Hundreds of years of wattle weaving have produced one or two features that increase strength, given that the hurdler obviously wants to get the most hurdles from the least amount of precious hazel. If you look at the mould closely you will notice it is slightly curved, not because the hurdler had difficulty in finding a straight one, but because he wants a slightly curved wattle. They are stronger this way because stacking them to season will flatten them and so tighten the weave. Look at the hurdle itself closely and you will see that the hazel is left in the round for strength at points of weakness, such as the end sails and the top and bottom of the wattle, while the remaining sails and the bulk of the weaving rods are made from riven hazel.

Most of the wattles made today are not for folding sheep but are used to keep the neighbours from looking into suburban gardens. You can tell a proper sheep hurdle by the little hole left in the middle of the panel for the sheep folder to carry it by, putting a stake through half a dozen hurdles, just like I used to.

MAKING THE HURDLE
Watching a hurdle maker rive hazel with a hook, above, is worrying. It always looks as if he will slice through his hand; but he never does. The first few rows of weave, far left, are of hazel in the round, for added strength. Once the weave is above six inches or so high, the hurdle maker changes to riven weavers, twisting them around the end shores and tucking new rods into the weave, as shown near left.

RAKE MAKING

HE HAND RAKE WAS ONCE SO MUCH a part of the agricultural scene that every piece of lowland coppice would support at least one rake maker confident of the demand for new rakes.

Like so many other useful and pleasing country artifacts, the wooden rake is not difficult to make provided you have the right tools, a knowledge of wood and you know how! I know some people now who make the *tines* (the pegs) of wooden rakes out of machine-cut dowel. They simply buy dowel of the right diameter, cut it into the right lengths and sharpen these lengths slightly with a draw-knife. As most machined dowel is of pretty inferior soft wood the merry snapping sound of tines breaking off accompanies the first attempt to use the rake in a rough field.

MAKING LONG-LASTING TINES

The best material for rake tines is that tough wood, ash, although willow is used in some areas. A seasoned ash pole of about six inches diameter is ideal to start with. You saw the pole into tine-length logs. Each log has to be riven into as many potential tines as possible, and by far the best way of doing this is first to tie a piece of twine tightly around the log, close to one end. You can then put the log on a block and *rive* it in equal parallel cuts one way, and then at 90 degrees, using a froe and mallet (see p.25). The string holds the riven sections together and you are then left with a bunch of square-sectioned pieces of wood tied together with a piece of string.

There would be nothing to stop you from carving each of these square sections round with a pen-knife, but a much quicker way is to use a *tine-former*. This is a device that can be made by any good metal worker who has a lathe capable of cutting steel. It is a steel pipe with one end sharpened and tempered. The cutting end is as wide as the size you want the tines. The pipe sits in a stand and you place it over a hole in a bench. Sitting astride the bench, with a pile of square-section tines to hand, it is an easy and satisfying thing to place each tine over the sharpened end of the pipe and wallop it with a mallet.

HEADS AND STAILS

The remaining parts of a rake are the *head*, the block that holds the tines, and the handle, called the *stail* or the *haft*. It is in these parts and how they are joined that there are many regional variations depending on the sort of use to which the rake is traditionally put.

Welsh rakes, used on hillsides where you are most likely to come across stones in the hayfield and where a rake is expected to last, are made with heads only some 18 inches or so wide and set at 45 degrees to the haft. The joint between head and haft

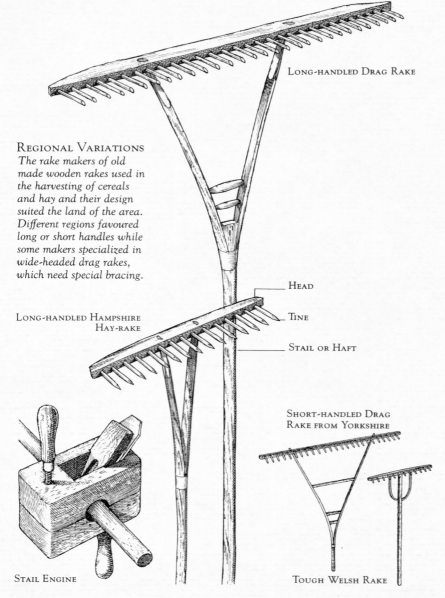

Long-handled Drag Rake

REGIONAL VARIATIONS
The rake makers of old made wooden rakes used in the harvesting of cereals and hay and their design suited the land of the area. Different regions favoured long or short handles while some makers specialized in wide-headed drag rakes, which need special bracing.

Long-handled Hampshire Hay-rake

Head

Tine

Stail or Haft

Short-handled Drag Rake from Yorkshire

Stail Engine

Tough Welsh Rake

is strengthened with a willow hoop. This is the sort I have used most and it is a different class of implement to most country rakes. These have much wider heads set at just less than 90 degrees to the haft and are made to gather grass which grows to a more luxuriant length. Some large drag rakes for gathering hay and corn have as many as 30 tines. The epitome of these lowland English rakes is the Hampshire hay-rake, where the haft is split or sawn part way down its length so that it can be divided and joined to the head in two places.

Ash can be used for the head, sycamore may be better, while elm has the advantage that it will not split. Rake makers of long-standing inherit or make a large upright *brake*, or clamp, to hold the head while it is

shaped and drilled for the tines. All such brakes I have seen use scrap-metal on a chain to weight the jaws and are obviously very effective. The rake maker will wet the ends of the tines before hammering them into the head so the ash or willow fibres swell to a tight fit.

Ash is easily the best wood for hafts. If you can find dead straight poles all the better, but most have to be set straight in the brake after steaming in a chest built over a water boiler. If you have ever used a rake for any length of time you will know how important a smooth haft is. To make the final smoothing there is one of those unique woodworking tools that must have developed over centuries of trial and error. It is called in some parts the *stail engine*, and is a double-bladed rotary plane (see opposite) that you twist down the ash pole.

FIXING THE HEAD
The durability of the rake depends on a good, strong fit between head and stail. Good rake makers bore out the head to take the split haft, judging the perfect, slightly acute angle by eye alone.

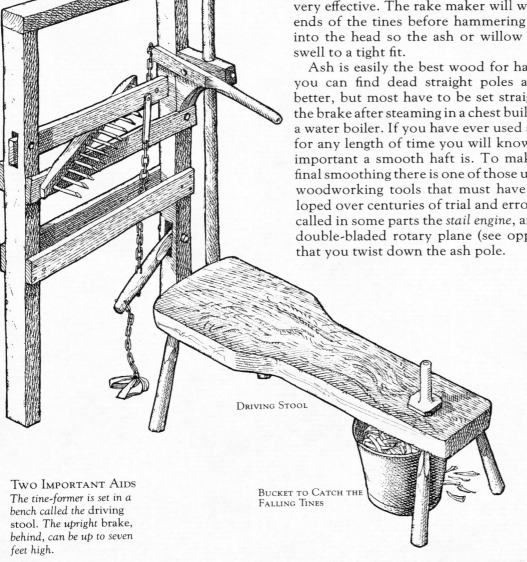

UPRIGHT BRAKE

DRIVING STOOL

BUCKET TO CATCH THE FALLING TINES

TWO IMPORTANT AIDS
The tine-former is set in a bench called the driving stool. *The* upright *brake, behind, can be up to seven feet high.*

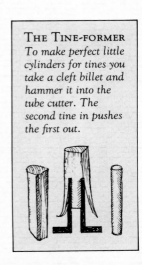

THE TINE-FORMER
To make perfect little cylinders for tines you take a cleft billet and hammer it into the tube cutter. The second tine in pushes the first out.

FORK MAKING

NEARLY EVERYBODY WHO WANTS A pitchfork nowadays goes to the ironmongers or agricultural co-op and buys a steel-pronged one. For heavy work, such as lifting hay or straw bales, such instruments are mandatory – a wooden pitchfork would break. But for pitching loose hay or straw the wooden version is ideal, a pleasure to work with and much safer to use when working in stables near horses.

In the Cévennes in France, pitchforks are grown, not made. Little trees are pruned to leave three or four branches, cut when they are ready and taken to a factory near St Hippolyte du Gard. Here, the handles are straightened if necessary by steaming and then sold to the local farmers. But I am lucky in that the same son-in-law who makes me rakes also makes me pitchforks.

CUT AND STEAMED FORK

SPACER

WEDGE

GROWN FORKS

JIG

TYPES OF FORK
For light work around the farm, a wooden hay fork can't be bettered. It is a pleasure to use and much safer than a metal tined one. Forks can either be grown, carefully shaping the living tree by judicious pruning, or cut from a straight trunk. To produce the elegant lines of the fork, the wood is first steamed and then placed in a mould for a few weeks.

MAKING A FORK
First of all he cuts down an ash tree that has a straight trunk for at least six feet and is about nine inches in diameter. This he rives into halves, quarters and perhaps eighths to produce the right-sized blanks. He then shapes each blank so that the intended head of the fork is wider than the handle. The handle he shapes carefully with draw-knife, spoke-shave and scraper. Holes must now be drilled at the point at which the *tines* (prongs) of the fork will meet the handle and a rivet inserted. His rivets are four-inch nails with a washer next to the head, cut off short so as to leave about quarter of an inch proud when pushed through the hole, and another washer popped on the cut end. He spreads the cut end of the nail over with a hammer.

I have known people rive out the tines with a froe but my son-in-law saws them out with a hand rip-saw. He then drills three holes where the *spreaders* are to go before putting the head in his steamer. This is simply an iron pipe propped at a slant with water in it, a plug at the bottom, a rag closing the top and a fire underneath to heat the water. He leaves the fork in for at least two hours, pulls it out and, while it is still hot, drives wooden wedges between the tines. He drives them until the tines are the right distance apart. He makes two, three and four tine forks so obviously he uses different sizes and combinations of wedges.

Using a draw-knife he prepares three rods of hardwood to act as spacers and pushes them through the different series of spacer-holes before pinning them in place with very small nails. The wood, being hot and wet, doesn't split. Now he returns the fork to the steamer, pushing the handle end in first this time, as far as it will go – the splayed-out tines will stop it going right in. After a few hours in the steamer he clamps the handle into the *jig* or mould, which is a standard part of his equipment. The bending, or shaping jig is responsible for producing those beautifully elegant lines of the wooden pitchfork. The work must be left in the jig for a couple of weeks before it is ready. For the last stage the fork is clamped in a shaving horse and the tines shaped with a spoke-shave and the whole fork sandpapered – ready for me to use.

BESOM MAKING

 HE MAKING OF BESOMS, OR "witches' brooms", was greatly simplified with the invention of wire. Or at least, when wire became cheap enough for *broom squires*, as besom makers are called, to afford it.

I watched a besom maker in the south of England. He sat at the end of a shaving-horse in the open right next to a huge stack of birch trimmings which he had cut the previous winter. On a peg stuck into a post near the far end of the horse hung a roll of soft galvanized wire. He quite simply bound up the butt ends of double handfuls of birch using three turns of the wire, each hauled tight against the grip of the horse.

FITTING THE HANDLE
The squire had a stack of handles which he had cut from young ash coppice, selecting them for straightness, and roughly trimming them with the draw-knife to a point. He shoved the point of one of these into the butt end of the wired birch bundle and rammed it hard home. This has the effect of even further tightening the bundle. The broom was done. I think the whole operation took 10 minutes to complete.

OLDER BINDING METHODS
Before the days of cheap wire, *withies* (see p.164) or hazel wands were used for binding the broom head materials. A heavy clamp with a circular mouth called a *besom-grip* was used, the closing joints crushing the twigs together while the binding was applied. The *bond-poker* was a curved concave blade which was pushed under the binding and allowed the final tying off. As a boy I remember watching an old man using the leg bone of a goose as a bond-poker.

WITHY BONDS
The traditional besom bond of hazel wands or willow rods does not clamp the broom handle quite so tightly as wire. Some squires pre-drill the handle and drive in a retaining peg through the bundle of birch twigs.

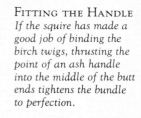

FITTING THE HANDLE
If the squire has made a good job of binding the birch twigs, thrusting the point of an ash handle into the middle of the butt ends tightens the bundle to perfection.

BINDING WITH WIRE
The squire I watched had a roll of wire hanging close to the end of his horse with one end passing through the jaws of the clamp. As he closed the jaws with his feet, he hauled backwards to tighten the bonds around the birch bundle.

HANDLE MAKING

SCYTHE

SLASHER

AXE

TYPES OF HANDLE
An ordinary stail *as on
the slasher can be trimmed
to shape from a still-green
ash sapling. An axe
helve is cut from a billet
of solid wood that has
some curve to the grain,
while a scythe snead needs
steaming and setting.*

USING A POLE LATHE
*One of the woodsman's
classic tools is the pole
lathe (see pp.41–2 and
104). The treadle is
connected by a cord or
strap, wrapped around the
work, to a springy pole set
up to bend above the head
of the operator. For turning
straight handles, the
framework of the lathe
must be wide enough to
accept the length of the
handle. With a pole lathe,
you only cut with the
chisel while you are
pushing down on the
treadle. As you let the pole
pull the treadle back up,
the work spins the wrong
way for cutting.*

OST TOOL HANDLES ARE MADE nowadays in small factories, or large ones in some cases. Ash trees are cut and brought into the integrated sawmill, billets sawn out with a circular rip-saw and turned on the lathe to make handles. But there are still many country people who make their own handles and they do not, as a rule, have a lathe.

For ordinary *stails* (the country word for straight handles), such as rake and hoe handles and the like, it is often possible to select and cut a straight ash sapling and to trim it down close to the finished shape, while still green, with the draw-knife. To straighten any bends you can clamp the green wood in some sort of holding device. You then leave the handle to season for a year or two, by which time it will have assumed the new straighter shape. After seasoning you can shape it again with the draw-knife, taking the wood down to its final shape and fairing down any irregularities. If the countryman owned, or could make or borrow such a thing as a *stail engine* (see p.30), his job was a lot easier. But patient work with a draw-knife and fine sandpaper can make a very good job.

Sneads (handles) for scythes have to be steamed and bent, but it is interesting that

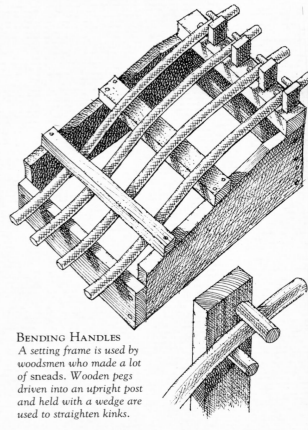

BENDING HANDLES
*A setting frame is used by
woodsmen who made a lot
of sneads. Wooden pegs
driven into an upright post
and held with a wedge are
used to straighten kinks.*

English and Welsh scythes have strongly curved handles, while those used in the Alps, for example, have quite straight ones.

The best axe handles, or *helves*, are cut from billets of solid wood riven from a log at least 10 inches thick, which has some curve to the grain that matches the curve of the finished helve. Hickory is the best possible wood, but it is rarely grown in Europe where we "make do" with ash. A good maker lays an existing axe helve sideways on the squared billet and draws round it. He can then clamp the wood and rough-shape the curved profile with a draw-knife before similarly copying the front to back plane. Copying an existing helve only gives you a square guide, mind you, and there is great skill in making the curves just right in the round. Then, if the wood is green, he seasons it for a few months.

After seasoning, the helve can be *fined* right down to the finished shape with a spoke-shave, and then a scraper and fine sandpaper for a glassy-smooth finish. The end that will go into the eye of the axe needs special care as it must be a perfect, cosy fit.

HOOP MAKING

N THE DAYS WHEN ANY AND EVERY-thing was packed in a barrel, the wooden hoops that bound the slack barrels (see p.102) used for storing dry-stuffs were needed in their thousands. They were a woodland product made by a craftsman called a *hooper*.

Coppice-grown hazel up to eight years old was the best wood for hoops, but chest-nut, ash and even oak were used. The wood was cut in spring and soaked in water for a while to soften. It was then riven into 2½- to 14-foot lengths, depending on the barrel size, with a *froe* (see p.25). To make the hoops easier to bend, the riven side of the

wood was then shaved with a draw-knife leaving the bark intact in a *brake*, or clamp. Willow rods (*withies*) can also be used for making hoops, and my friend Joe Shanahan showed me how. Using an in-genious instrument called a *cleave*, shaped like an egg with three fins carved in its end, Joe took a fairly stout withy and split the withy into three by simply pushing it against the fins. He next shaved the withy with a draw-knife and pushed it through a *bender*, a concave piece of wood with a heavy roller set adjacent to it. The two ends of the hoop were then nailed together to make a perfect circle.

THE HOOPER'S BRAKE
Hoopers had a curious shaving clamp, or brake that allowed them to trim right down the length of a long, whippy rod. This simple device clamped the wood in place by squashing it between a pivoting upright, counterbalanced by a weighted bucket and controlled by the work-man's knee, and a fixed cross member.

A HOOP BENDING EASEL
One method of coiling hoop lengths of riven hazel was to use an easel with six or more crossbars attached to the uprights into which were driven wooden pegs. The wood was simply coiled between the pegs, which were adjustable for different sizes of hoops, until it assumed its new shape.

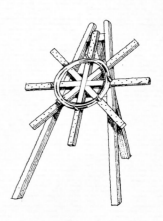

LADDER MAKING

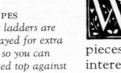

RIVEN OAK-RUNGED LADDER

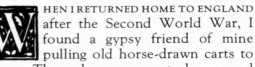

FRUIT PICKING LADDERS

BARN BEAM LADDER

AUSTRIAN HAY-LOFT LADDER

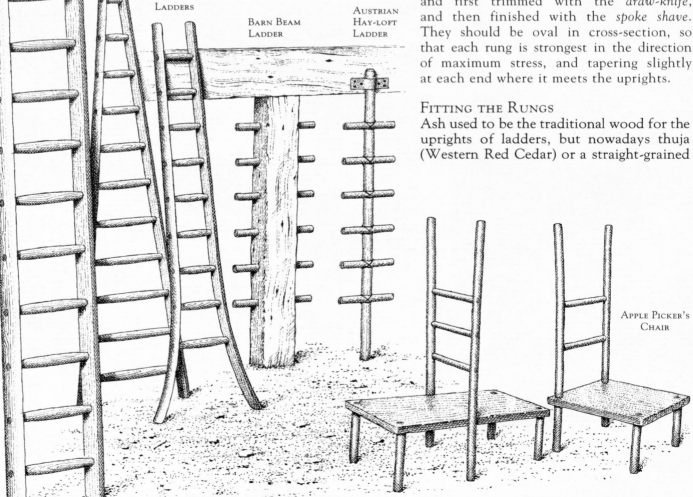

APPLE PICKER'S CHAIR

APPLE PICKER'S CHAIR LADDER FROM NEW ENGLAND

WHEN I RETURNED HOME TO ENGLAND after the Second World War, I found a gypsy friend of mine pulling old horse-drawn carts to pieces. The only components he seemed interested in were the spokes of the wheels. Curious, I asked him what he wanted these for, and he said "ladders". He showed me a ladder he was making, using the oak wheel spokes as rungs. I told him he ought to be pulling ladders to pieces to get the rungs out to make wheel spokes, but he did not seem to agree with this at all. "Them things is things of the past!" he said. When one sees the numbers of aluminium extension ladders about today one might be excused for thinking that wooden ladders were also things of the past but, fortunately for ladder makers, this is not quite so.

HEART OF OAK

The only wood fit to be trusted for ladder rungs, in Northern Europe at least, is heart of oak. I shouldn't be at all surprised if hickory is, or has been, used for this purpose in North America. And ladder rungs should always be cleft, or riven, never sawn. Rip-sawing always cuts across some of the grain of the wood, thus weakening it and letting the damp in, leading eventually to rot. Cloven wood, on the other hand, inevitably has the grain running true – for that is the nature of cleaving. Makers of wooden ladders (and any country carpenter can do it) saw heart of oak trunks into lengths a little in excess of the length of the completed rung, cleave the log in half, quarter it, and then cleave it into the three sizes required for the rungs. Then, in the *shaving horse* (see p.33), each rung is clamped and first trimmed with the *draw-knife*, and then finished with the *spoke shave*. They should be oval in cross-section, so that each rung is strongest in the direction of maximum stress, and tapering slightly at each end where it meets the uprights.

FITTING THE RUNGS

Ash used to be the traditional wood for the uprights of ladders, but nowadays thuja (Western Red Cedar) or a straight-grained spruce is preferred as being much lighter. The uprights have holes to receive the rungs drilled out with an auger and in the best ladders these holes are rasped out to give them an oval shape consistent with the oval shape of the rungs. To help ensure the ends of the rungs are all of an identical size, the ladder maker employs a shallow wooden gauge set to the same diameter as the holes drilled in the uprights. Holes and rung ends are so shaped that, when the rungs are driven in, pressure is applied up and down the ladder – that is, along the grain of the side pieces and not across the grain. Thus, the rungs will not split the uprights. This is the same principle that is always applied by woodworkers when driving the end of one piece of wood into another.

Now, trying to put a ladder together is something that can drive you mad unless you know how to do it. The secret is to drive all the rungs in, lightly, to one of the uprights, then to lay this on its side on the ground or, better still, across two tables. Next you take the other upright and, putting it nearly into position, place the first rung into its hole in this second upright. Then tie a piece of string around the two ends of the uprights. You can now engage rung after rung, starting from the first one, until you have all the rungs safely engaged. You are then home and dry and can knock all the rungs fully home using a mallet.

The way a ladder is constructed, it needs no glue, dowels, nails or anything else to hold it together. What it does need, however, is three pieces of wrought iron, threaded at both ends, pushed through small holes in the uprights and held in place with washers and nuts. Commonly, these iron rods are placed out of sight under rungs at the top, bottom and in the middle of the ladder. Now as long as the nuts are kept tight, so as to pull the two uprights of the ladder together, none of the rungs can come out of their holes or work loose. I have also seen ladders made without iron bracing rods but with three or four of the rungs longer than the others, so that they stick out a little. These have holes drilled through their ends and wedges driven into the holes to hold the uprights together.

Less sophisticated ladders can easily be made from a single upright pole to which are lashed simple, unshaped rungs. These are most often found in hay lofts where their light weight makes them ideal for propping in any convenient position.

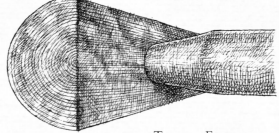

CONSTRUCTION
Putting the rungs and uprights of a ladder together is not easy. First, you support one upright and push all the rungs home, as the maker above is doing. Then you attempt to engage the other upright.

TAPERED FIT
The rungs are tapered at both ends. This ensures that all the joints tighten as the uprights close.

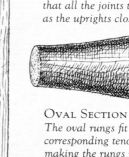

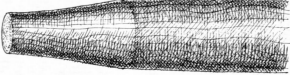

OVAL SECTION
The oval rungs fit corresponding tenons, making the rungs unlikely to split the uprights.

CRIB MAKING

OTHING IS WORSE THAN THROWING loose hay down in a wet field for sheep or cattle to feed on, only to find that much of it gets trodden into the mud. It is surprising how many people do this, and I must admit that I have done it myself.

It is puzzling to think that farmers continue to waste good hay in this manner when hay cribs are so easy to make. I used to make good hay cribs for cattle, and nothing could have been simpler. I simply built a big X shape at each end, forming the feet and the heads of the crib, with crosspieces joining them and slats at intervals of about four inches. A refinement would have been to have some structure at the bottom between the legs to collect the short bits of hay that fell through, but I never got round to that. This type of crib had a high centre of gravity, so needed to be firmly anchored in the ground or the cattle or sheep would have simply turned the whole thing over in their enthusiasm.

COMBINING SKILLS

In various parts of the south of England there is a craft of crib making, and the cribs are strong, good looking and, most important, very serviceable. One might say that this trade is a combination of the skills of the hurdle maker (see p.26) and those of the basket maker (see p.163).

The light rods of hazel or willow are bent round to form the ribs. These should be freshly cut and still green to avoid the problem of the wood cracking or splitting. Two long poles (about six to eight feet) are needed to form the base of the crib, drilled at nine-inch intervals. To hold the poles at the right distance from each other, larger cross-members are attached either end and then the bent ribs inserted in the drilled holes. With the basic frame complete it is just a matter of nailing on the long split rods that form the sides, and the crib is made. The farmer simply rolls it over with his foot, stuffs it with hay and turns it the right way round again. This design works fine for sheep, but for larger animals such as cattle a more substantial affair is necessary.

SHEEP CRIBS
Fresh-cut willow or hazel rods are bent to form the ribs, some makers shaping the rods so that they bend into a nice bow. Cribs are easy to make, look good, use renewable materials and don't leave rusting scrap in the fields when they finally do give up.

VARIATIONS ON A THEME
For this design of hay crib an old wagon wheel was used as a template. Riven hazel uprights are pushed into holes drilled on the flat edge of the rim and hazel in the round used as the weavers.

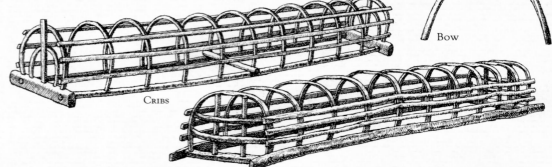

Bow

CRIBS

BROACHES & PEGS

HE ESSENCE OF THE WOODLAND crafts is making the best and thriftiest use of that most precious of raw materials – wood. But every craft – be it hurdle making, chair leg bodging, clogging, ladder or trug making – does generate waste, and so there are craftsmen ready to turn it to their gain.

Mr Firmin lives in the village of Honing in the Norfolk Broads country and makes his living out of *sways*, *liggers* and *broaches*, the fixings for thatched roofs. Sways are the hazel or willow poles used to hold the layers of thatch in place. Liggers are almost the same, but thinner and more decorative, and are used on the topmost layer of thatch at the apex of the roof. Broaches are sometimes called *thatching spars* and are used to hold the sways in place.

Mr Firmin works with his son, and to watch the two of them splitting and shaping broaches is an experience. The broaches are all two feet two inches long and are of riven or split hazel. Chestnut will do for this also and even green elm. Ash, however, cannot be used as it will rot. They each sit down on a wooden *horse*, which has a round piece of wood sticking up through it. They start the rive by knocking an adze into the wood and then shove the split on to the vertical piece of wood so as to widen the split. Very quickly they shove the hazel further and further into the upright wood, guiding the rive with slight twists of the blade of the adze. Out of a small piece of hazel they might extract a dozen broaches.

I tried the same technique with results that seemed hilarious to my teachers. Every time the rive simply split out at the side. I just did not seem able to guide the split straight from one end to the other.

Pegs

A gypsy man used to come and sit at my fireside in Wales and drink home-brewed beer and teach me how to make such things as clothes pegs, tent pegs and baskets. Gypsy clothes pegs are, alas, almost a thing of the past now – nearly everybody prefers spring pegs. The gypsy pegs served generations of washerwomen and I can never quite see why they should be unusable now. Perhaps they do not grip so well on plastic washing lines.

THATCHING BROACHES
Broaches are supplied to the thatcher in bundles. It is important to keep them soaking, as above, until they are needed for use because the thatcher bends them into a staple shape. The dampness of the wood helps to stop it splitting, as does a deft twisting action as the bend is made.

BROACHES COUNTED AND READY FOR BUNDLING

TWISTED AND BENT FOR USE

My friend John Jones used to take a stick of willow, cut it into suitable lengths (about six inches – his pegs were generous) with sharp blows with a finely-honed hatchet and fashion a head on one of the lengths by shaving the rest of the peg down with his pocket knife. He would then wrap a little strip of tin around the peg at the point up to which he was going to split it and tap a tiny nail through the two overlapping ends of tin and into the wood using the back of his chopper. He cut the tin out of old tinned cans with a pair of tin-snips. He then split the peg down from the end opposite the head with the blade of his knife.

Anybody can make a clothes peg. But to make them quick enough to earn a living – that's another matter! He used to make tent pegs, too, out of riven hazel. He did all the shaping with his knife (after the initial riving) except for the cut across the grain for the notch which he did with a little saw.

SPLIT PEG

TENT PEG

GYPSY PEGS
Split peg and tent peg making has been an important commercial activity of the gypsy community for many generations. The willow wood used for the pegs can be found almost anywhere in the country, growing unwanted in swamps or unused ground, and is there for the taking.

CLOG SOLE CUTTING

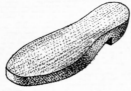

THE CLOG SOLE
Thick, unyielding pieces of alder wood, with shaped sole and heel, once kept the wet and cold from the feet of many farm and factory workers. The clog remains a most practical piece of footwear.

SOLE CUTTING KNIVES
The shaping of an oblong billet of wood to suit the form of the human foot is a skilled business taking many cutting strokes with different shapes of blade. The beauty of the levered knives used for this shaping is that you can exert great force on the blade while being able to move the wood to any angle.

LOG MAKERS WERE SETTLED PEOPLE with their own workshops (see pp. 140–1), while *cloggers* were itinerants who lived where their work was – in the woods, in camps among the trees that provided their livelihood. They provided rough-cut soles to individual clog makers, but the bulk of their work went to the clog making factories.

Their raw material was alder, willow, birch, sycamore or beech wood, preferably alder, since it is a quick growing, coarse-grained soft wood that is easy to cut. It is water resistant and makes a durable barrier against a wet factory floor or a muddy field.

BREAKING UP
The clogger would cut alder trunks up to two feet in diameter, and use it immediately

STOCK-KNIFE

GRIPPING KNIFE

while still green and easy to work. The first operation was to crosscut the trunks into shorter logs of four graded sizes – *men's, women's, children's* and *middles*. These logs were then riven into *sole blocks* with a *beetle* (a heavy wooden mallet) and wedge, then with an axe and finally with a *stock-knife* or *bench-knife* to the rough size and oblong shape of the finished sole. Cloggers called this part of the operation, *breaking up*.

The clogger's stock-knife is about 30 inches long, with a hook at one end which is slipped under a ring on a low bench, and a handle at the other. The knife is slightly curved, and has a lethal-looking blade four inches deep and about a foot long near the hook. By pushing down on the handle, great leverage is exerted on the blade. Grasping the handle with his right hand, the clogger would hold a sole block in his left and with a few deft strokes of the knife cut it out to the right shape, carving out the notch between heel and toe as he did so. Some cloggers went on to use a *hollowing knife*, similar to the stock-knife, to scoop out the instep, and then with a *gripping* or *shaping knife*, to cut the narrow groove around the side of the sole into which the clog maker would later fit the leather upper.

All this would take the clogger very few minutes indeed, for years of practice made him able to build a stack of soles twice as high as a man in a couple of days. He had to work fast to make a living.

Cloggers would work an alder grove until it was exhausted, then move on. Alder is a prolific grower in damp fertile soil so cloggers could follow riverside groves confident that new growth was establishing itself in the groves they had left.

SEASONING
Being a very sappy wood, alder needs to dry out for perhaps nine months before it can be used. The clogger built great conical stacks using the rough-cut soles like bricks, but being careful to space each sole so that there was a good circulation of air throughout the stack.

BODGING

 OT SO MANY YEARS AGO, THE beechwoods of England were populous with a class of men known as *chair bodgers*. In fact, these men were not "bodgers" at all but highly skilled craftsmen, and just how they came to be called by this rather misleading title is hard to understand.

Chair bodgers were one of three types of craftsmen associated with the making of traditional country chairs. The bodger was basically an itinerant woodland worker who specialized in the making of the legs and stretchers of the famous Windsor chairs. Even as late as the 1950s there were some chair bodgers, but unfortunately now there are none left. And so a craft going back at least five hundred years is no more.

In their heyday, however, they would purchase a stand of trees, clear a space to set up their temporary living quarters and go about the business of selecting just the right trees from which to make the chair legs and *stretchers*, or braces. Ideally, the beech trees had to be not overly old. They also had to be straight grained and rather *leggy*, meaning that they had grown a little too quickly. By only felling the right trees, gaps were left in the wood where new seedlings could grow, and by not cutting trees too young, they could be allowed to grow on and so extend the useful life of that paticular stand of trees. These people had a real awareness of their surroundings, nature if you like, which not many of us are privileged to experience nowadays.

The tools of the chair bodger were few and simple: an axe, draw-knife, saw and some chisels. This helps explain why the life of the bodger was so isolated – with so few tools it was much easier for the bodger to work the trees where they fell rather than haul logs back to a central workshop somewhere in a distant village. As the bodger was responsible for the turned parts of the chair, a lathe was also necessary.

After felling the tree, the bodger would haul or roll the trunk back to his woodland workshop, remove any side branches and saw the log into *billets*, pieces of wood approximately the right length for a chair leg. Next, a wedge was driven into the billet in order to split it into as many pieces as possible without causing undue waste. Depending on the size of the billet, anywhere from four to as many as sixteen legs could be split from the one piece of wood.

THE POLE LATHE
A pole lathe, *below, is powered by a tensioned ash or larch sappling up to 12 feet long secured firmly to the ground at one end and left unsupported at its other end over the lathe itself. Depressing the foot-operated treadle pulls down the pole by means of a piece of cord, or a leather thong, which looped around the work, as the piece of wood to be shaped is called, and twists the work in one direction. This allows the bodger to cut the work with a chisel supported on the tool rest. When the treadle is released, the bodger withdraws the blade as the pole springs back again, turning the work in the other direction. The lathe is adjusted to take different lengths of work by moving the puppets along the bed of the lathe.*

PREPARING THE CLEFT
Once the hewn wood has been sawn into billets and then split with mallet and cleaving axe, the cleft can be worked on by the bodger with a side-axe to trim it to the approximate shape of the finished leg.

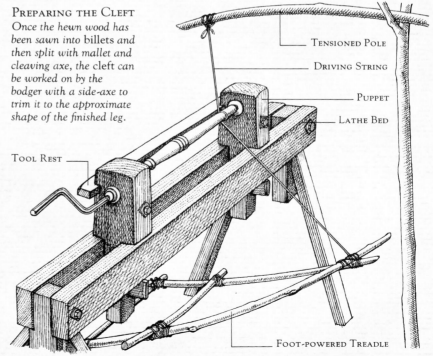

TENSIONED POLE

DRIVING STRING

PUPPET

LATHE BED

TOOL REST

FOOT-POWERED TREADLE

Now the bodger would use his side-axe, which was sharpened on one side only, to fashion the pieces into the approximate chair leg shape. The next refining stage involved the bodger's draw-knife. As with all draw-knives, this was a two-handed affair with handles set at right-angles to the blade. The bodger would draw the blade over the wood with such skill that the shape and proportion of the leg or stretcher were immediately discernible.

The final stage was the turning of the wood on the lathe. Now, despite our modern conception of what a lathe is, simple versions have been in use stretching back probably as far as the Iron Age. And I should reckon that the type used by the bodger would have been recognizable by our Iron Age ancestors. The bodger's *pole lathe* was a simple affair, made entirely from the rough products of the woodland. The *work*, as the piece of wood being shaped was called, was revolved a short distance in one direction by a treadle powered by nothing more than the bodger's foot, and then turned in the opposite direction by the action of a bent ash pole that acted as a spring. This ash pole could be as long as 12 feet. A piece of string ran from the foot treadle to the top of the pole, which was planted securely in the ground and further supported by the wall of the bodger's hut. The top of the pole was left unsupported to allow it to bend and whip back upright again. The pole lathe had one major draw-back – the actual cutting of the wood could only be done on the foot-powered turn of the lathe.

From this description it can be seen that the beechwood was cut, shaped and turned when still green. Green wood is not suitable for chair making, so the bodger would stack the finished legs and stretchers beside his hut for weeks until they were sufficiently seasoned. The length of time seasoning took was very much dependent on the weather. When this process was complete, the bodger would transport his work to one of the big chair-making centres such as High Wycombe in Buckinghamshire. Here, the other two types of craftsmen would take over – the *benchman*, who was responsible for all the sawn parts of the chair such as the seat and back, and the *framer*, who would assemble the chair and carry out any of the little finishing details. The framer would also make the steam-bent parts of the chair if this was required.

A Chair Bodger's Camp

Deep in the beechwood forests of England, when there were beechwood forests in England, the quiet was disturbed by the sounds of axe and chisel against wood wherever chair bodgers went about their work. The bodgers travelled light, sometimes alone, sometimes with a workmate, with the few tools necessary for their trade. They would set up camp, making a shelter to work and sleep in through the spring and summer months. The results of their industry were pro-lific. Cleft wood soon piled up waiting to be cut to shape at the shaving horse, and then to be turned at the bodger's pole lathe. The lathe was made of hewn wood components and designed to be dis-mantled and carried from camp to camp. The clear-ing and any shelter would quickly be covered in wood chips and shavings amidst the stacks of seasoning chair legs. Such itinerant work is now a thing of the past, for the last chair bodger left the forest more than twenty years ago, and what woodland there is echoes to very different sounds now.

CHARCOAL BURNING

 O MAKE CHARCOAL YOU BURN wood in conditions with insufficient oxygen for complete combustion. In the past I have helped to make charcoal for such diverse purposes as burning bricks and powering a Model T Ford with a *producer gas* engine. In Africa the technique was to dig out a large trench perhaps six yards long, two yards deep and a yard and a half wide, with the *spoil* dug out piled on each side of the trench. You then took an ox wagon load of dry wood, cut it into small pieces and threw it into the pit, leaving a little space at one end for a boy to climb down into to light the fire and then get out pretty quickly!

To stand near the trench soon became well-nigh impossible, but stand there we did holding pieces of rusty corrugated iron until, on command, we flung the iron on to the flames and then shovelled mightily to pile the spoil from the trench on top. A week later the earth would be dug off, the iron removed, and there, in the pit, mixed with ashes and earth would be the charcoal.

THE KILN METHOD

Years later, back in Suffolk, in a wood near Bury St Edmunds, I came across a more professional way of making charcoal. The charcoal burner, who came from the south of England, was living in a small trailer-caravan on the edge of the wood. A great many large trees had been felled in the wood the year before and the *tops*, or branches, left behind. It was these that he was sawing up into quite short lengths with a circular saw driven by an old tractor, and splitting with an axe, for charcoal making. He used a kiln which was formed of steel rings, each about two feet deep and five feet in diameter. He packed one ring with wood and then hauled another ring on top of it until three rings full completed the kiln. He covered it with a steel roof with a vent in it, which could be opened or closed. He lit the fire at a vent in the bottom of the kiln and, when the fire had well and truly taken, closed the vents. It was several days before the kiln was burnt out and cool enough for the burner to open and dismantle, raking out the charcoal and throwing it on a *riddle* which sieved the dust and ashes out. He could then shovel it into bags. He showed me how you could test the quality of the charcoal by throwing a piece down on a board. It should make a ringing sound as it strikes the hard surface.

PRIMITIVE SHELTER
The charcoal burners of old lived out in the woods during the summer months, building their own makeshift shelters. These had a wooden framework, lashed together, which was roughly thatched, as shown right, or covered in turf. Inside, there was room for a couple of improvised bunks above the bare earth.

THE TRADITIONAL METHOD

In the days before the introduction of the steel ring kiln, charcoal burners built their wood into conical stacks, covering them first with straw and then with ashes and earth. The old English charcoal burners were, we are told, a race apart. Before the discovery that you could smelt iron ore with coke made from coal, which happened in the early eighteenth century, these wild men of the woods were the basis of most industry. Their product was used for iron making, glass making, and in gunpowder. All summer (for the burning was done in the summer when winds were not too ferocious) they lived in conical shelters made from sticks with a turf or thatch covering, often far from their homes and in very primitive conditions. They were true men of the woods. They used tools with esoteric names, such as the *mare*, which was a kind of framework barrow for carrying wood. Then there was the *loo* (a country way of saying lee), which was a screen to keep the wind off. The rake used – a curious one – was called the *corrack*, and the long-handled shovel, the *shool*.

The burning took considerable skill and the old charcoal burners were secretive about their methods. It is known, however, that the work started by building a vertical chimney of logs. Around this core a stack was carefully built up of logs (from two to four feet long) up to about the height of a man. This was then covered with bracken, straw or other vegetation and then very carefully covered with ashes and earth to form a *clamp*. Burning charcoal was dropped down the chimney at the centre of the clamp, followed by dry tinder on top to ignite the wood. Then, when the fire had spread out through the stack to the burner's satisfaction the hole at the top was plugged with mud. The burner then watched the clamp for about a week. If a strong wind got up the smouldering fire within would *break out*, and if this happened the whole batch was lost. More earth was added to *dress* any weak places.

Nowadays charcoal, made in sophisticated retorts, has a hundred uses in modern industry, but the days of the smoke-blackened men, wise in the ways of the woods, are over. Even so, I saw it made in clamps in Mallorca in 1955 or thereabouts, and it is still being made in this way in Mediterranean countries where much cooking and heating is done with charcoal.

BUILDING THE STACK

The success of the traditional woodland method of charcoal burning depends on the skill with which the stack is built. Too much air circulating in the wood reduces it to ashes, while excluding air completely results in charcoal of variable quality. The way an old woodsman from Sussex used to stack the wood is shown below.

1 *The burner builds a chimney of billets, triangular in fashion, in the middle of the area cleared for the stack.*

2 *He stacks billets against the three sides of the chimney, working out to a circular shape with the clear space of the chimney at its centre.*

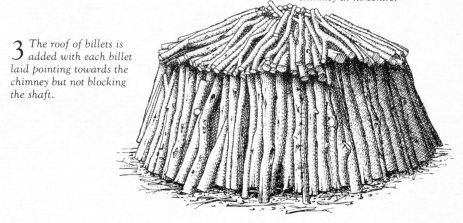

3 *The roof of billets is added with each billet laid pointing towards the chimney but not blocking the shaft.*

CHARCOAL BURNING IN PORTUGAL
The traditional method of charcoal burning is still alive and kicking in some Mediterranean regions, as this recent picture of a Portuguese clamp shows.

OAK BASKET MAKING

ASKETS MADE OF SPLIT OAK COME IN many different sizes and shapes and are designed to carry a wide variety of produce in countries as wide ranging as England, Scandinavia and America. One such is the Sussex *trug*. The name comes from *trog*, which is an old name for a boat. The little basket is boat-shaped, is light, strong and handy, and any girl in a garden is improved by having one, filled with flowers, hanging from her arm.

The trug is a member of that large family of containers woven, not of round wood, but of flat slats of material. I have seen charming African women catching tiny fish in a shallow lagoon by tramping forwards in a line, holding baskets below the water. The baskets they used were made just as a Sussex trug is made, with thin slats of wood slightly overlapping and making an escape-proof trap for the small fish.

MAKING A TRUG

The Sussex trug maker takes two straight wands of ash or chestnut and splits them in half. He steams them, then bends them around jigs – both into round-cornered oblong shapes, one with the bark inside the ring and one with the bark outside. The hoops are held with small nails. The two are then fitted together – the one with the bark inside vertically to act as the handle for the trug, the one with the bark outside horizontally to act as the rim. The strips used for the body of the trug are best made of oak, split as thinly as possible. They must then be *faired down* – made wider in the middle and narrower at each end.

TRUG MAKING

To make a trug you need a draw-knife and shaving horse, wood steamer and some improvised jigs. The frame and handle are set in jigs (1), and then tacked together with the main split-oak slat (2). The rest of the slats are filled in and the feet added to complete the trug (3).

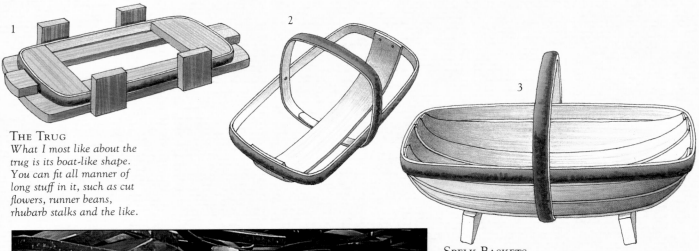

THE TRUG

What I most like about the trug is its boat-like shape. You can fit all manner of long stuff in it, such as cut flowers, runner beans, rhubarb stalks and the like.

SPELK BASKETS

Spelk, or swill baskets, are made by weaving thin slats of oak around a stout hoop or bow of ash or hazel wood. The strips are obtained by boiling oak poles and riving them while they are still hot. You use the stoutest strips for the warp of the basket and save the lighter ones to weave through them. The result is a basket in which you can hold fine materials, even flour.

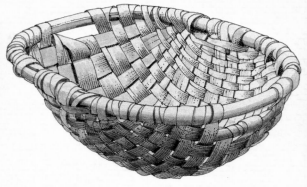

A wider central strip is then nailed to the rim at both ends, being bent round into the necessary boat shape. The rest of the strips are simply bent round and nailed at each end to the rim so that they form the *planks*, as it were, of the boat. Really, nothing could be simpler. The little nails used must, of course, be clenched over. As in so many examples of what I call "engineering in wood", every piece that makes up the trug is under tension – it is *sprung*. And it is this springing that gives the trug its strength.

SPELK BASKETS

These oddly named baskets are true baskets (unlike trugs) in that they are woven with a *warp* and a *weft*. They are built round a hoop (often called a *bow* or *bool* in the north of England) made of ash or hazel. The *spelks*, as the weaving elements are called, are made by boiling oak poles from four to six inches in diameter, and riving them while still hot. The stouter spelks are nailed to the bow as the warp and lighter spelks woven into them as the weft. These lighter spelks are sometimes called *chisies* or *ribands* in different parts of the country. It is important to keep the spelks soft and so they are immersed in hot water until used so that they will bend without breaking.

If such baskets are to be used for carrying, say, coal, coke or firewood, the warp of the basket is often made with round wood such as hazel. If it is to hold small stuff, both warp and weft are of spelks.

In some parts of Sweden you may be lucky enough to see elaborate split oak basketry. Some of these baskets are made in much the same way as the spelk, with slivers of oak being used to weave a container. Some Swedish baskets have a stiff wooden frame with split oak weaving filling the gaps. In America, too, there is a long tradition of split-oak basket making. Baskets of many different designs were (and still are) made by the Indians.

AMERICAN BASKETS
Most of the baskets from the Appalachian Mountains of the USA are made of split oak, some, like the Tennessee-made basket shown below, using white oak coloured with vegetable dyes. Regional differences account for the many varying designs and the uses to which the baskets are put.

SWEDISH BASKET
Traditional wooden-weave baskets from Sweden, like the one made in 1866 illustrated bottom, were ornately painted and used to carry gifts of bread and other produce on feast days.

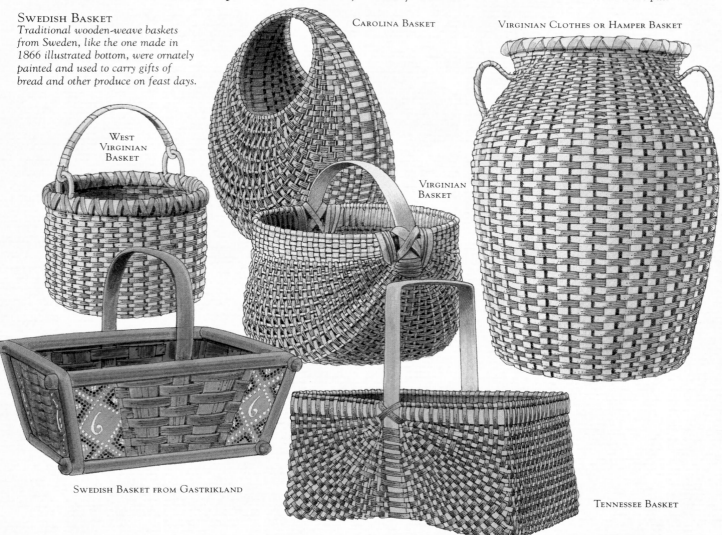

WEST VIRGINIAN BASKET

CAROLINA BASKET

VIRGINIAN CLOTHES OR HAMPER BASKET

VIRGINIAN BASKET

SWEDISH BASKET FROM GASTRIKLAND

TENNESSEE BASKET

BUILDING CRAFTS

At one time you could walk through a village and know in what part of the country you were by asking yourself a few questions about the type of building around you. Were the roofs thatched in straw or reed? Were the walls of clay or flint? There was a usage of local building materials and techniques that you could depend on. It would have been thought madness to pay for building materials to be hauled across the country when there were local materials that could be exploited for nothing but the sweat of your own brow, or for the price of an honest day's work by a local craftsman. If there was good stone in an area then houses were built of it. If timber was plentiful, fine timber homes resulted. Buildings were then sure to sit comfortably on the land and to look as if they should be there. Now there is a great uniformity of building. Materials are mass-produced and concrete reigns king among them. Local skills required by local materials are either lost or are now an expensive alternative.

WOODEN BUILDING

TYPE OF BUILDING I HAVE HELPED to construct, and have spent many comfortable months in, is what I call the archetypal African hut. In fact, the simple wooden construction is common in many parts of the world.

To build such a hut, you choose a flat site and scribe a perfect circle on the ground by using a piece of string tied to a central peg. You dig a narrow, deep trench around the circle, leaving a section undug for the doorway. Then you stand rough poles in the trench so that they touch each other right round, except for the door. These you lash together at the top with strips of bark or creepers, and then you trample the earth down hard around the base of the poles. This makes the wall, which you finish off by daubing liberally with mud. For the roof you make a circular framework of light poles on the ground nearby. It is best to make a simple cone shape, and this you thatch (see p.54) and lift on to the circular wall, securing it there with any convenient binding material. A family of Africans can build such a hut in a day. It should last for many years and when it does eventually rot, it only takes another day to build a new one while the old hut makes good firewood. The floor is of beaten earth and sometimes, for real luxury, smeared with cowdung. When a fire is burning in the middle of the floor you cannot stand up with comfort, but the moment you sit down you are below the smoke level, are warm and, most important, free of flies and mosquitoes. They don't particularly like smoke.

On a recent visit to old haunts in Kenya I was horrified to see the good old round hut being replaced by oblong buildings with corrugated iron roofs. They were hot inside, full of mosquitoes and most uncomfortable. Furthermore, the iron costs money that the owners could ill afford and would rust away rather quickly. But they look *modern* and have, therefore, status.

Log Cabins

I once spent a few nights in what the owners claim is the biggest log cabin in the world. It is not, as one might expect, in the Canadian wilderness but in Scotland, at a place called Lothlorien near the Galloway coast. The cabin is enormous and houses a large community, comprising several families, who, despite the physical drawbacks of the construction, find it a pleasant place.

The reason why the community chose logs to build with is because they were offered a large supply of very cheap, extremely long Douglas Fir trunks. I personally would not have chosen this method of construction. In the first place it is a very

Log Building in Finland
Finnish or Scandinavian log house builders have always made log homes to last with hard, seasoned red deal or pine. They interlock a number of rooms and the jointing of log to log is traditionally so precise that a thin layer of moss inserted between the logs during construction is all that is needed for a permanently weatherproof result.

lavish use of that splendid material – wood. The same logs ripped down into planks would have provided enough material to build an entire village, and the planks could have been tongued and grooved so as to keep out the wind. As it was, the inevitable chinks between the logs had to be bunged up with mortar (*chinking*, as it was called in the New World), which cracked and fell out at regular intervals.

THE AMERICAN TRADITION

The American backwoodsmen were said to carry their sawmills on their backs. The only tools they carried were an axe, a broadaxe, a crosscut saw and an auger bit. Together with these they needed a sheet of thin steel, to be made into a stove, and a small sack of nails for fixing *shingles* – the roof tiles made from wood. With this equipment they could build a cabin that would stand up to the fiercest winters. I gather from my early days as a reader of romantic novels that these hardy woodsmen would wait for the first frost and then throw buckets of water over their cabins. The water thus thrown would freeze and seal the building. Well, rather they than I!

The only disappointment with this romantic image is that there is nothing

NOTCHING

The crux of building with logs is to make good corner joints – a process known as notching. The beautifully intricate joints shown below required a master craftsman's skill. They are: the square notch (A); the furrow notch, with inclined side cut (B); the furrow notch with heel (C); and the dovetail notch, with its impossibly complex angles (D).

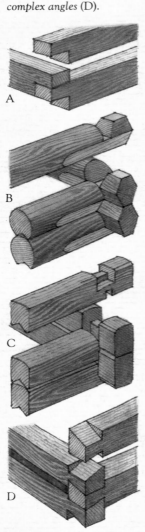

A

B

C

D

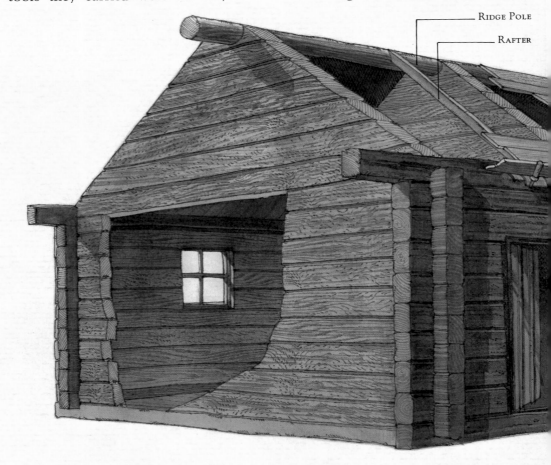

RIDGE POLE

RAFTER

SWEDISH LOG HOUSE

The cutaway illustration, above, shows a standard Swedish log house. It was the model for timber building in America for many settlers but whereas the American version was seen as a temporary home, the Scandinavian log house was built with great care and expected to last for generations. The logs were split and hewn as smooth as planed boards, and they were grooved so that they slotted together. The two-room plan consisted of the vardagstuga, the larger living, dining and sleeping room, and the gang, used for storage.

STONE FOUNDATIONS

If a timber home is intended to be permanent, it has to have dry feet. That means having a foundation that lifts the bottom timbers clear of the damp earth that will rot them. You might see a stone plinth used, especially where the cabin is built on uneven ground.

ROOFING
Roof construction was developed to a high degree and included layers of birch bark and moss with an outer layer of riven timber. One side of this layer was allowed to project over the ridge somewhat like a comb.

Moss

PLANKING

BIRCH BANK

EAVES BOARD

IRON FIXING
AND PEG

RIVEN LOG
OUTER LAYER

MOUNTAIN CABIN
An American log cabin of this type, with a wood and clay chimney, would have been built up to the end of the nineteenth century. The shingle roof (roof tiles of riven white oak) was fixed with nails – a very precious commodity.

CUTTING SHINGLES
I watched shingles being cut from pine and larch in Austria. In America, shingles are still made from white oak and red cedar in the East, and red-wood in the West. Some cutters call shingles shakes if they use the traditional method of riving them with a froe, as shown here. The average size of a shingle is approximately 8 by 12 inches.

really unique about the American log cabin. Its origins are very firmly rooted in Sweden and Finland. The first log cabins in America were introduced in the mid seventeenth century by Swedish and Finnish settlers who established colonies along the Delaware. But the proliferation of this type of building is probably due to the more wide-ranging Scots, Irish and German settlers. They built a version of pioneer cabin with an external chimney, made of wood and clay, stone or brick, against the gable end.

Although, theoretically, a log cabin could be built by one man, construction was more usually a community affair. After the trees had been felled they had to be hauled back to the building site and *notched*, or cut for the corner joints of the cabin, before being raised to their correct position. As the walls became higher, logs had to be hauled by ropes and pushed from below, using two other logs as a ramp. Only when the outer shell and roof were complete were the windows and doors cut out.

Contrary to popular belief, the American log cabin was never meant as a permanent home. It was more regarded as a temporary shelter until a family became established in its new settlement and a conventional timber or brick house became possible.

WALLING

IN MANY PARTS OF THE WORLD YOU will find houses, from simple huts to substantial and enduring two-storey cottages, made from locally available material such as clay and flint.

CLAY LUMP WALLING

Go to most villages in East Anglia and you will see many buildings with what are called locally *clay lump walls*. These are made of clay with a mixture of sand and other components, rammed moist into moulds and then turned out. There are thousands of clay lump houses still standing, none built later than the 1920s. So long as they are kept well covered with rendering and "their heads and feet dry" (that is built on an impervious foundation and roofed) they will stand for years.

COB WALLING

In the West Country *cob* walling is common, using unfired earth as a raw material. Either the walls are built up, a layer at a time, by placing a mixture of mud and straw on the layer below, after it has been allowed to dry, or *rammed earth* construction is employed. Rammed earth techniques require strong wooden shuttering to contain the mixture and heavy ramming from above. The soil used must have the right moisture content – too wet it bulges up each side of the ram, and too dry it does not knit together. Also,

the soil should consist of a mixture of graded particles for best results. Every sized particle from clay through coarse sand to small gravel can be used. All soil is improved for this purpose if five percent cement is added to it. Lime, too, makes a good stabilizer, though not as good as cement. Cob walling makes it possible for people to build lasting houses costing practically no money at all.

FLINT WALLING

Flints washed out of gravel beds or picked up from the beach are either round or oval shaped, they tend to be all about the same size and are a real headache to build with. The secret of success lies in the mortar. Nowadays, cement is used but traditionally it was a mixture of lime, left to mature in the damp for at least a month, and sand. The desired consistency was like butter.

The corners or *quoins* of flint-built houses are always of brick, as are the foundations and door and window surrounds. The flint, in fact, acts as in-filling only. Nearly all the churches in East Anglia are built principally of flint and several are still standing after 700 years. Modern flint building is expensive, but there is a lot of it still done in north Norfolk because this is the *flint coast* and for many miles around all the houses and barns are built of flint. It is a tradition which is being kept up.

Most buildings of flint were built, at least partly, of *knapped flint*. This is flint that has been struck with a hammer to make at least one face of it straight. Many such flints were knapped into cubes. Building with knapped flint is called *flush work* and much of it includes beautiful patterns.

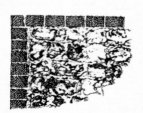

BRICK QUOINS

KNAPPED FLINT

FLINT HOUSES
Brick is used for the quoins or corners, foundations and door and window surrounds of flint houses, since flint by itself lacks the strength for such load-bearing positions and is too random in shape.

COB HOUSES
The walls of cob-built houses are built up of unfired earth layers of clay mud and straw, with chalk and grit added for strength. Each layer is up to two feet high and two feet across, depending on the wall that is being built, and must be left to dry before the next layer is placed on top.

LIME BURNING

 IME IS A MOST USEFUL COMMODITY for any rural community, conditioning its soil, whitewashing its walls and mortaring its stones. Every village within easy reach of either lime or coal used to have its own lime kiln, and lime production was once an important rural industry. Nowadays industrially produced lime has replaced locally produced material, but many old kilns still survive.

TYPES OF LIME

There are three types of lime. The first is rock limestone ground up in a mill. Often called *whitines*, it is used for neutralizing soil acidity and improving clay soils. From limestone rock we also get *quicklime*, or calcium oxide, produced by heating up lime in a kiln. This is a pretty ferocious substance and was much used in days of old for disposing of the bodies of criminals and others the authorities wanted to get rid of. If you leave quicklime about in the air for long enough, or chuck water on it, you will get *slaked lime*, or calcium hydroxide. This is quite a harmless and benign substance, but the act of slaking with water causes great heat, and should be done with care.

Slaked lime has been put on the fields of Europe, to *sweeten* acid soil, for at least two thousand years. Added to about three times its volume of sand and mixed with water, it makes a fine mortar which, though not as strong as cement mortar, has nevertheless stood up, in many a medieval castle or other buildings, for a thousand years or so.

Another important use of lime is for whitewash. To make this you merely have to mix slaked lime, very thinly, in water. A hundredweight of lime will whitewash a medium-sized house. Then you simply slosh the stuff on. The only disadvantage of this traditional whitewash is that it will rub off on your coat if you lean against it.

LIME KILNS

A lime kiln is a huge brick pot with an open top and a hole in the bottom of it. The bottom of the kiln is plugged with brushwood, and then layer upon layer of coal or, better still, anthracite, and broken limestone are piled on top, filling up the kiln. The brushwood is then ignited, and the thing left alone. Tramps used to love to

sleep on burning kilns in cold weather and occasionally one would be overcome by the fumes and not wake up again. After the kiln has burned out and cooled, the contents are raked out of the bottom hole of the kiln and the lime is slaked with water.

When the cost of imported cement was too high I burned lime in the open, in a heap. You lay brushwood on the ground, maybe two feet of it, then six inches of broken limestone on top, then another of brushwood, then a further layer of limestone, and so on to the height required. The object is to make a neatly rounded stack, which you then plaster thickly with mud, the thicker the better. You need to make a hole at the bottom of the mud on the windward side, and several small holes in a line at the top on the leeward side. The wood is then lit and left to burn and cool.

SRI LANKAN KILN
In Sri Lanka, rural kilns such as the one above, are still used today, This example is roofed against the tropical rains.

LOCATION
Kilns like this were often built next to a waterway for ease of transport.

THATCHING

HE FIRST ROOF ANY MAN SHELTERED under, apart from the roof of a cave, was of thatch. The traditional huts of tribal Africans are nearly always roofed with thatch. The conical framework of the roof is thatched by laying on grass with the heads of the grasses pointing downwards and lashing it down with bark strips. At the top the stems of the last round of grasses are tied tightly together with bark to form a sort of top-knot. I never knew one of these huts leak.

Sri Lankans have a magnificent form of thatch called *cadjan*. It is, I suppose, common to all tropical countries where palm trees will grow for it is thatch made from interwoven palm fronds. A good cadjan roof will keep the worst monsoon out.

EUROPEAN THATCH

In Europe we make do with such stuff as grass, heather, corn-straw or reed. Heather was, and is, used to roof the little "black houses" of the Outer Hebrides and other northern isles. In the West of Ireland oat or barley straw is still sometimes used to form a rather primitive kind of thatch. It only lasts two or three years but this is not a drawback when you can re-thatch yourself or when you can get the local thatcher to do it for the price of a bottle of whiskey.

The thatch of northern Germany, Denmark and England differs from African tribal thatch in that the *butts* (bottoms) of whatever vegetable material is used point downwards, not upwards. As the butts are thicker than the flowering tops, each strand

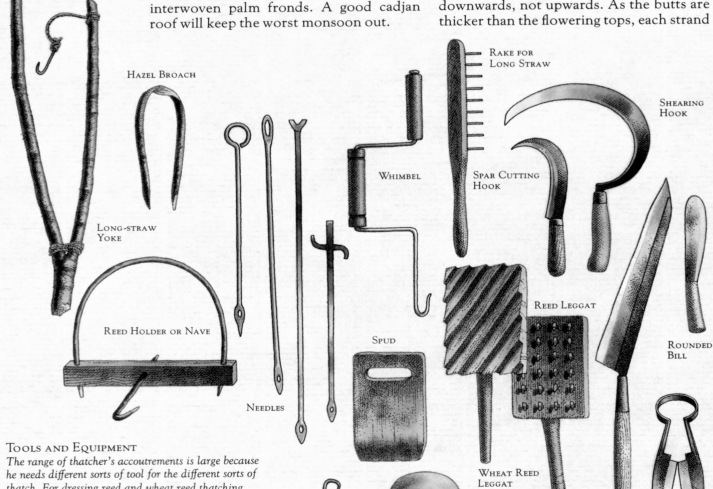

HAZEL BROACH

RAKE FOR LONG STRAW

SHEARING HOOK

LONG-STRAW YOKE

WHIMBEL

SPAR CUTTING HOOK

REED HOLDER OR NAVE

REED LEGGAT

ROUNDED BILL

SPUD

NEEDLES

WHEAT REED LEGGAT

IRON SECURING HOOK

KNEE AND ARM PADS

SHEARS

EAVES KNIFE

TOOLS AND EQUIPMENT

The range of thatcher's accoutrements is large because he needs different sorts of tool for the different sorts of thatch. For dressing reed and wheat reed thatching you need different sorts of leggat, whereas for long-straw thatching you do not need a leggat so much as a rake and a sharp shearing hook for trimming. Then different thatch holders are used for long straw and reed. All thatch is sewn to the rafters at points across the roof, using long needles and twine or straw rope twisted with a whimbel.

of thatch lies closer to the horizontal than you would think and so Northern European thatch tends to be very thick and requires a great deal of material to make a roof, combined with much labour and skill.

LONG-STRAW THATCHING

When I was a boy, in the Essex and Suffolk countryside, every farm labourer could thatch a rick, or a hay stack, and many an older man could, and often had, thatched his own house. The material they used in both cases is called *long straw*. This is simply corn straw – generally wheat but oats would do at a pinch and rye is excellent – which has passed through a threshing machine. The *drum*, as the old type of threshing machine is called, knocks out the grain and also breaks and mixes individual straws.

Old Bill Keeble, the foreman of a farm on which I worked in Essex, showed me how to prepare this straw for thatching. He

AT THE RIDGE
Whatever the thatching material at the ridge, you have to use a flexible material, such as sedge or long straw, to cap the apex.

LONG-STRAW THATCH
Once you have a little experience of thatch you will recognize the soft finish of long-straw thatching. Hefty yealms, or bundles, of straw are tied firmly to the battens nearest the eaves to start the job which continues up the roof to the ridge. The thatcher staggers the layers of thatch up the roof securing each layer with hazel rods pinned to the rafters with iron hooks.

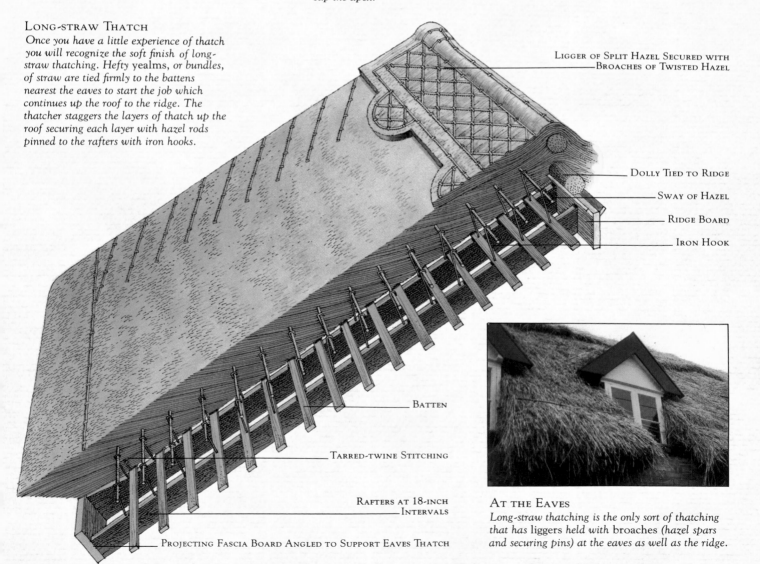

LIGGER OF SPLIT HAZEL SECURED WITH BROACHES OF TWISTED HAZEL

DOLLY TIED TO RIDGE

SWAY OF HAZEL

RIDGE BOARD

IRON HOOK

BATTEN

TARRED-TWINE STITCHING

RAFTERS AT 18-INCH INTERVALS

PROJECTING FASCIA BOARD ANGLED TO SUPPORT EAVES THATCH

AT THE EAVES
Long-straw thatching is the only sort of thatching that has liggers held with broaches (hazel spars and securing pins) at the eaves as well as the ridge.

*The wheat reed thatching,
above, is more than just
beautiful to look at. You
have to live under a thatch
to appreciate it fully. It
provides excellent thermal
insulation and keeps out a
lot of noise – not an
unimportant consideration
in these days of screaming
jet planes.*

ANCIENT ORIGINS
*The thatch shown here, with its turf ridge, is part of a
reconstruction of an ancient Saxon hut. It displays none
of the fine finish that a modern thatcher would take pride
in, but it shows how thatch has been an effective roof
covering since early times.*

called the process *drawing* but thatchers in
other parts of England call it *yealming*. The
object is to turn a mass of bent and broken
straw, all lying higgledy-piggledy, into
orderly bundles of straws all pointing more
or less the same way.

We would fork the loose straw into
layers. As Bill formed each layer it was my
job to fling a bucket of water over it to make
the straw less brittle. Then working from
the bottom of the pile Bill would pull
handfuls of straw out and lay them on the
ground. The wet straw would slip out easily
and slide straight as each handful was
pulled. When he had six bundles he would
lay these inside a forked stick which was
called a *yoke*. A piece of string closed the
mouth of the forked stick to keep the
yealms in. The yoke was then carried up the
ladder to the top of the hay stack or corn
rick that he was thatching.

Starting at the eaves he laid the wet straw
evenly on the stack in a layer four inches
thick and fastened this layer down by laying
a stick along it, midway up the layer, and
fastening this stick down by hammering in
broaches with a mallet. The horizontal stick
(often of hazel left "in the round") is called
a *sway*. The broaches, also of hazel, are
18 inches long, sharpened at both ends,
twisted in the middle and then bent over
like hairpins. The two sharpened ends
were driven into the stack or rick with the
wooden mallet.

Another layer of straw would be laid over
the first, slightly higher up but well covering
the sways and broaches, and so on, layer
overlapping layer. When the ridge was
reached bundles of straw would be laid
horizontally along it to form a roll and the
up-standing straw on one side bent down
over it, then the upstanding straw on the
other, and on each side of the ridge there
would be more sways and broaches to hold
these ends down.

Houses can also be thatched with long
straw. It is the cheapest method of thatching
used in England but even so it costs about
£90 a square yard to have it done.

LONG STRAW V. REED THATCH
In the days of cheap labour (or when people
had the time to do jobs for themselves)
thatching with long straw made sense. It
would last perhaps 20 or 25 years and then
you could simply put another coat on or
perhaps strip the roof and start afresh. If
you were a farmer the straw was free: if

you weren't you could buy it for practically nothing anyway. It was the cheapest kind of roof there was.

Nowadays it is hard to get long straw for nearly all straw has passed through a combine harvester which ruins it for thatching. Also, the price of labour being what it is, if a man pays for thatching a roof, he wants it to last a long time. Hence the growing popularity of reed thatching in spite of its high initial cost. And there is no doubt that reed makes the finest thatch in the world, lasting 70 years and maybe 100 years.

In spite of its name Norfolk reed (*Phragmites communis*) is not confined to Norfolk. It grows anywhere where there is enough water, as far as I know. The reeds among which the Marsh Arabs of the deltas of the Tigris and Euphrates live are, I imagine, the same plant. These Arabs build substantial houses, rafts and all kinds of day-to-day artifacts from reeds.

Much of the so-called Norfolk reed used to thatch houses in England now comes from Poland as the huge reed beds of the Biesbos in Holland, the traditional source of reeds, have been largely drained.

CUTTING REED
Plenty of reed is still cut in the Norfolk Broadland country of England. When I lived in Suffolk I knew Mr Russel Sewell for over 25 years, until he reached the ripe age of eighty-three. Although he no longer cut reeds for a living, he continued to do so until he was sixty-five.

I remember going out with him on a freezing winter's day into the reed beds next to Rockland Broad. The tide had flooded the bed that day and the ice crunched under our rubber thigh boots as we walked. He wore an ancient jacket and the sleeves and body of it were cut and worn by the sharp reeds. His hands must have been like iron for he wore no gloves. You can cut your hands badly on the sharp edge of reed leaves.

It was after Christmas and most of the leaves had frozen and been blown off the stems of the reeds. Russel would sieze a handful of stems in his left hand, cut through them at the bottom with a slice of the sharp hook he had in his other hand, clean the rubbish out of the base of the bundle with a few downward strokes of the hook, and lay the bundle to one side.

When he had a *fathom* of reeds (which is a super-bundle just big enough for a man to clasp his arms round – a fathom, or six feet, in circumference) he would bind it near the bottom with a piece of string. Before the days of cheap string, reed cutters would use twisted willow twigs and were in the habit of planting the odd willow in the reed beds to supply them. Nowadays you can often see a huge willow tree grown out of control in an old reed bed.

He carried the fathoms of reeds, slish-sloshing through the shallow freezing water, to the side of the *drain* (the name for a drainage ditch or dike in these parts), where lay a long flat-bottomed punt, called a reed-lighter, and into her he loaded his reeds. When fully loaded she had a stack of fathoms in her higher than Mr Sewell. The latter poled her up the drain to a *staithe*, as small quays or landing places are called in the Broadlands, and there unloaded, to await being taken away to the thatchers, sometimes by Norfolk wherry in those days.

It was Russel who explained to me that if a reed bed is not cut one year the reeds are not so good for thatching the next, and are termed *double wild*. Thatchers at one time would not buy this if they could help it, but when the combine harvester came into the wheat fields and the thatchers could no longer get long straw they were happy to buy double wild reeds and all.

THATCHING WITH REED
Although Norfolk reed is the best roofing material in the world you cannot make the ridge with it. The ridge is either made of long straw, sedge (*Carex spp.*), or sweet grass or rond grass (*Glyceria maxima*). The latter is called rond grass in Norfolk because it can be bent *round*, as over a ridge.

I found Mr Mindham thatching a house with reeds near Watton, in the country of Norfolk. Mr Mindham's father was one of seven sons and they were all thatchers. Their father was a thatcher too. Thatchers

DECORATION
Thatchers have always added decorative features to mark their work. The stack ornaments, above, are, like corn dollies, traditional and were once thought to encourage good harvests. The ship's wheel, left, is pure fancy.

At one time the corn harvest on a farm was carefully built into ricks and protected by long-straw thatch. Although this thatch was only destined to stay until the corn under it was threshed or the hay eaten, it had to look perfect for there was a fierce tradition of good craftsmanship among farm workers.

FOUR-POLE DUTCH-BARN
The permanence of thatch is exploited in the German Dutch-barn structure below. It has a pyramid-shaped thatched roof that can be adjusted in height or removed altogether as the store beneath is removed or replenished. This avoids the need for new thatching every year.

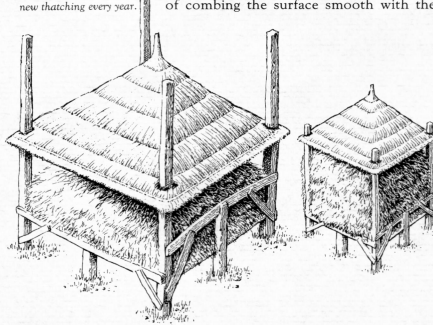

were plentiful in those days and they thought themselves a cut above farm workers and even brick layers. They would cease all thatching after the end of October and go into the woods to cut sways and broaches. After Christmas they would take to the reed beds, for by then frost and gales had defoliated the reeds. About April they would be back on the roofs again.

The technique for reed thatching is different from that for long straw. Instead of combing the surface smooth with the side rake the thatcher bangs the ends of the reeds up from below with the *leggat* – known as *dressing* the thatch. The leggat is a board with a handle on it and old horse-shoe nails driven into it. A reed roof has a severe appearance compared with the smooth, flowing lines of a long straw roof.

Mr Mindham hammered steel hooks down through the thatch into the rafters below to hold the horizontal hazel sways which held the reeds down – one sway to each course, or layer of reeds. Only at the ridge did he hold the sways down with broaches. He kept the broaches either in a bath of water or under damp sacks until he needed them – so that they could be twisted into shape more easily.

WHEAT "REED" THATCHING
There is a third kind of thatching in Northern Europe and that is what the thatchers of the West of England call wheat reed, or combed wheat reed, or Devon reed.

It is not reed at all but simply wheat straw – but wheat straw that has not been through a combine or a threshing machine. This means that the straws are unbroken, unbent and all lying the same way. In the West of England much wheat is grown especially for thatchers' use. The technique of thatching with it is almost the same as for reed and it will last for perhaps 45 years.

SLATE CUTTING

SLATE IS A METAMORPHIZED SEDI-mentary rock, such as shale, which has been deposited as mud or silt under water and compressed by subsequent deposits above it into rock. Because this process took place slowly over millions of years rather than violently, as with volcanic rocks, the slate was formed in flat sheets. It can therefore be split into thin slabs – or thick ones if required – with even, level faces, and is very strong. It is a magnificent roofing material and a hundred years ago half the great cities of the world were roofed with it. A great deal of the world's slate was quarried in north Wales, but only a few mines are still working.

Slate generally occurs in thick seams and often slants at an angle into the mountain-side. After the outcrops have been quarried, inclined shafts are driven along the dip of the vein following the walls and roof of *country rock*, the quarryman's term for rock that is not slate. Horizontal tunnels called *levels*, about 50 feet apart, and vertical shafts called *roofing shafts* are then hollowed out from the main shaft allowing access to the slate. The miners leave the hard country rock above their heads for a roof, and 40 foot thick pillars of slate every 45 feet or so to support the levels above. If they don't do this the mountain collapses on top of them.

Slate has a happy knack of splitting in two directions at right angles with each other. The rockmen utilize this habit to break slate out in rectangular blocks of about two tons each, generally blasting it with explosive. These are then taken out of the mine, split into smaller blocks of four to eight inches thick, and are then sawn, by special rock saws, into blocks a little larger than the size of the finished roofing slates.

The *splitter* then gets to work. Seated and wearing a leather apron, he balances a block of slate on his knee, places a chisel precisely in the middle of one edge, and gives the chisel a tap with a hammer. When the chisel has entered the stone he gives it a twist and the block splits in two. Then he splits each half block in two. And he goes on sub-dividing until he has split as many roofing slates as he can from the block, each slate being about one sixth of an inch thick. The splitter's job is highly skilled; one slip and a whole block of slate could be ruined.

FROM NARROW LADIES TO QUEENS
There are many different sizes of cut slate. In North Wales the splitters gave a certain dignity to their slates by ranking them with names of female nobility, from the smallest *Narrow Lady* up through *Princess* to the largest, dubbed *Queen*.

Finally the split slates are handed to the *dresser*, whose job it is to cut the roughly shaped slates to the required dimensions. This used to be done by hand, but for many years a water-powered dressing machine called a *Greaves* has been used.

SLATE DRESSING
Once the splitter *has finished his job, the* dresser *takes over, for while the slates are now the correct thickness, they still need to be cut to the final shape and size and given a chamfered edge. In days of old dressing was done by hand, the dresser laying each slate on a steel anvil and slicing right down the edge of it with a knife called a sax.*

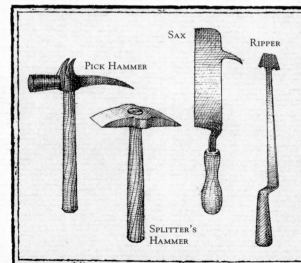

SAX

RIPPER

PICK HAMMER

SPLITTER'S HAMMER

SLATER'S TOOLS
A good slater could split slate accurately using the edge of a *splitter's hammer*, instead of the usual hammer and broad-headed chisel. The spikes on both the *pick hammer* and the *sax* are used to make the nail holes in roofing slates.

CRAFTS OF THE FIELD

Our rural landscapes were once tended by hand: not just the land itself, but also the boundaries that divide it, the ditches that drain it and the pathways that serve it. If it took days and days of hard labour to repair a dry-stone wall, or lay a hedge, that was accepted. Land owners could afford to pay wallers and hedgers for their skills. If such details as stiles were required, they were made with care. Now that the land is largely tended by machines, and labour costs are so high, there is neither time nor money for such things. Those that love the land are the losers as features of the landscape that have existed for centuries tumble into disrepair. In very few years modern factory-farming techniques which, among many other abuses, ignore such details of landscape as hedgerows, have spoiled our countryside.
Let us hope that crafts of the field that have been passed down the generations will never be completely forgotten.

HEDGE LAYING

HE PROPER WAY TO SERVE A HEDGE is to *lay* it, in the winter months. It keeps the hedge thick near its base and so stock proof, and stops gaps appearing. Once layed the hedge may grow unattended for many years.

The first job is to clear dead wood and weeds and to cut back any growth not needed in the final laying. If the hedge runs uphill you start at the uphill end and slash about half-way through each component stem of the hedge in turn. Then, wearing thick leather gloves if the hedge has thorns in it, and leather trousers too if you can get them, you bend each stem over until it is nearly, but not quite, horizontal. You work your way down the hedge laying the stems towards the sunlight and, if possible, away from the prevailing wind so that the part-cut stems have the most favourable conditions for regrowth.

Nearly all we hedge layers half-cut through the small tree stems of the hedge with a downward stroke of a sharp bill hook. Some purists maintain that it should be an upward stroke so as to stop rain water getting in the cut. I have never found this to be the slightest problem, for white and blackthorn, the commonest of hedges, are

tremendously resilient. And I am sure that the up-cutters would be left far behind in any race with we down-cutters, who can manage 60 yards of hedge on a good day.

STAKING AND ETHERING
For a fancy job you save any stems cut out of the hedge, clean off the side growth and use them as stakes to support the laid stems until they grow into place. You drive them in every yard or so, intertwining them with the laid stems. The stakes should be driven down into the hedge so cattle do not use them as rubbing posts and work them loose.

Lastly, for a very fancy job, you *pleach* the stakes with *ethers*. That is, you weave thin, whippy stems, such as hazel rods, into the tops of stakes so as to make a continuous strip of basketry along the hedge.

MAUL

BILL HOOK (KENTISH)

LONG-HANDLED SLASHER

HEDGING TOOLS
You first take a long-handled slasher, and clear the ground up to the hedge and trim back the side growth. The essential operation is to cut partly through the main stems almost to the ground with the bill hook, as in the inset picture above. The maul is the hedger's cudgel for driving in the supporting stakes, which can be seen neatly bound in the main picture.

DRY-STONE WALLING

HEN I WORKED AS A LEARNER farmer on a Cotswold farm more years ago than I like to think about, I was allocated as an assistant to an old gentleman who came to the farm to repair wall gaps. The two things I remember about this old gentleman are that he had a big white moustache and he was grumpy. Whenever I tried to lay a few stones he would throw them down and put others in. It seemed my duties were to hand him stones and to fill the centre of the wall with rubble. Maybe if I had served him in this capacity for seven years or so I would have graduated to laying a stone or two myself. In fact, there is no great mystery to dry-stone walling. Anyone can learn to do it with practice. It is the endurance of the skilled waller that is so impressive.

To walk over the Pennines, or other northern hills of England, is to be amazed at the distances of beautifully-made walls that stretch over the bare hills, up the steepest slopes, plunging down into deep valleys, clinging to desperate contours. The labour they represent makes the building of the Egyptian pyramids small beer indeed.

Dry-stone walling means building walls of stone without the use of cement or lime mortar. Strictly speaking, if mud or clay mortar is used the process is no longer dry-stone walling, but since building walls with certain kinds of stone required it, such walling can be included here.

TYPES OF STONE

There are as many kinds of stone wall as there are kinds of stone, and these vary enormously. There are, however, two main classifications of all building stone: *free-stone* and *non free-stone*. Free-stone is the quarryman's (and the waller's) word for stone that splits naturally into rectangular lumps. Non free-stone breaks up any-old-how. There is an intermediate kind of stone that breaks into layers so that the top and bottom of each piece of stone are parallel but the sides and edges can be any shape. True free-stone, such as that marvellous Jurassic limestone found on the Isle of Portland in Dorset, can be made into massive walls with vertical sides that will last for ever. Very few wallers have used or will use good quality free-stone, however. Layered stone, such as the Jurassic oolitic limestone found in the Cotswold Hills, is fine to build with but requires more walling skill and, once built, such walls will not last for ever without maintenance. Finally, there are the shapeless, random, uncooperative lumps, often of granite or other igneous rock, that have been dumped by some glacier of a past ice age, which wallers in places such as West Wales or parts of Ireland have the misfortune to use.

WALLS CALLED HEDGES

As a waller, you cannot build a true dry-stone wall at all with stone of the last mentioned kind. Instead you build what in Wales and the West Country is called a *hedge* and in the part of Ireland in which I now live, a *ditch*. It consists of two rough stone walls, leaning in towards each other quite steeply, mortared with earth and with an earth infill between them. Because of all

DIFFERENCES IN STONE
The next time that you are travelling in dry-stone wall country, take the time to look at the quality of stone used by local wallers. It will range from huge interlocked lumps of granite to exquisitely-jointed blocks of limestone.

WEST COUNTRY GRANITE

YORKSHIRE GRITS

the earth, grass and other plants quickly grow over the newly-built hedge and it is possible, indeed desirable, to plant a quick-thorn hedge along the top of it. In spite of the thorn hedge, I have never known such a construction that would keep a determined mountain sheep in for more than a few minutes. A tell-tale fence of rusting wire netting along the top of this type of wall gives the game away.

Walling with Cotswold stone, or the carboniferous limestone of the north of England, or the Millstone grits, is a very different matter, and walls constructed with

these layered rocks are very effective stock barriers. Indeed, properly maintained, a well-made dry-stone wall is about the most effective stock barrier there is.

Wall dimensions vary according to the type of stone used. With the sort of stone that breaks out of the quarry in layers, such as Cotswold or Pennine stone, it is better to *batter* the walls, that is starting the base of the wall wide and drawing in the thickness to a narrower top. Using Cotswold stone, for example, the batter is traditionally an inch in for every foot of height. A five-foot wall would be typically two feet

LONELY WORK
You need a walling frame to guide the direction, thickness, batter and height of a dry-stone wall. This waller is working in classic fashion, a hand either side of his guide string, plenty of stone led on to the site, but most characteristic of all, he is alone.

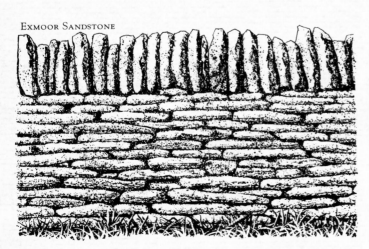

EXMOOR SANDSTONE

NORTHUMBERLAND LIMESTONE

CONSTRUCTING A WALL

In areas of good walling stone you can attempt the sort of ideal construction shown right. The two skins of the wall rise up from the large foundation stones with an even inward lean. The best stone is used for the facing while the middle is packed with small stone debris. Much of the wall's strength comes from the throughbands – flat stones large enough to reach through the full width of the wall about half-way up its height.

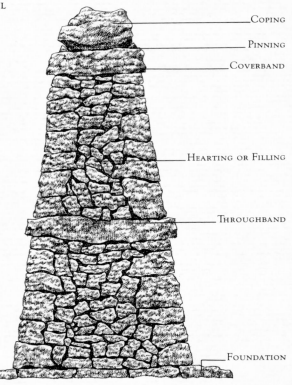

COPING

PINNING

COVERBAND

HEARTING OR FILLING

THROUGHBAND

FOUNDATION

FREE-STONE

INTERMEDIATE

NON FREE-STONE

STONE FOR WALLING

As soon as you start to build with stone rather than just look at it, the very different nature of stones from different regions becomes clear. Good walling stone breaks into lumps with flat faces that stack well. The best, free-stone, breaks cleanly in two dimensions. Intermediate stone gives good flat faces in one plane while non free-stone presents the waller with random-shaped lumps.

wide at the base and about 14 inches at the topmost horizontal course of stones. Such a wall would be considered pretty high and massive though; most field walls are smaller than this, especially where the stone is not so good.

HOW TO BE A WALLER

To build a new wall of this kind you need a template, sometimes called a *walling frame*. This is a simple timber frame and it should have a plumb bob with a lubber-line attached to one of the horizontal members so that the frame can be judged vertical. The template must match the dimensions of the section of the completed wall and is positioned along the line of work as a guide.

The professional waller knows what the dimensions of a wall should be: the amateur has only to look at the nearest professional wall.

The stone is, in farming parlance, *led on* to the site. In the old days this meant

the stone was dragged there by horse and cart or, on steep slopes, horse-drawn sled. It is quite daunting to discover just how much stone is needed to make only a short length of wall. A small mountain of loose stones seems to fit into nothing. It is conversely cheering to find what a lot of stone can be quarried from quite a small hole in the ground. Wallers obviously avoid hauling stone uphill so they always seek their little quarries above their place of work.

When building a new wall a trench is marked with pegs and line and taken out to the length of the section of wall to be built. On uplands only the top layer of turf need be removed to get down to firm subsoil or the rock itself so as to ensure that there will be no uneven subsidence as the living soil is compressed under the weight of the wall. On lowlands, the trench might have to be dug deeper. The trench is cut a little wider than the intended width of the wall.

With the stone on site, the waller lays the foundation first. This may seem an obvious statement but near my house in Ireland there is a small castle on which the authorities have fixed an information notice which tells us: "the top part of the castle was built in the fifteenth century – the bottom part was added in the sixteenth century". Flat stones of even thickness are chosen for this foundation and are laid carefully. If they subside the wall will come down.

The two facings of the wall are then built up, keeping pace with each other with good, big stones at the bottom and the space in between them carefully packed with smaller stones that form the *hearting*. The stones of the facings must break their bonds, as laid bricks must. In other words a waller must "lay two stones on one" or "one stone on two". Vertical joints running unbroken up the wall are anathema.

The smaller and rougher filling stones inside the wall must also be carefully fitted together and interlocked with the facing stones as far as possible. Ideally, the facing stones should be laid so that each one slopes very slightly from the inside of the wall down towards the outside. This construction will ensure that the wall sheds water from its interior in the same way that thatch does. It is water that will eventually bring down a wall, just as the same element will eventually erode Mount Everest.

The art of the waller lies in knowing which stone to lay his hand on next, and how to place it. The best face of a squarish

WALLS IN POOR STONE AREAS
Where the local stone occurs in large, unbreakable amorphous lumps, as it does on the land I farmed in Wales, walls tend to be low and devoid of strengthening details. They need regular maintenance.

stone is put to the outside of the wall. Guide strings on both sides of the growing wall are raised up, course by course, with one end of each string pegged to the last completed section of wall and the other ends fastened to the walling frame.

THROUGHBANDS AND COVERBANDS

About half way up the wall is made as level as possible in preparation for *throughbands*. These stones, each a little longer than the width of the wall at that height, are laid with their long axes across the line.

They are vital to the wall's strength. In some areas they are chosen to be considerably longer than the width of the wall so that they project several inches on either side. This can be seen in some of the noble walls of the Pennines. If such long stones are in good supply the whole course will be made of them; if they are scarce, then there will only be one throughband every yard or so with normal walling in between.

With the throughbands laid walling goes on as before with the middle of the wall becoming narrower and the facing stones generally smaller until the wall is once more levelled off in preparation for the *coverband*. This is a layer of flat stones that completely covers the width of the wall. Some wallers nowadays lay these stones in cement mortar. This may sound like cheating but it is a good idea, if the owner can afford the mortar, for it keeps the water out and so prolongs the life of the wall. Some wallers say that the use of mortar is detrimental to a very good dry-stone wall as it takes away the essential flexibility that the wall needs as it settles after construction.

CROWNING THE WALL

On top of the coverband comes the *coping*, the crown of the wall. This is a row of fine, big flags, or flat stones, set on edge and usually slightly leaning, which gives the wall a crest. Coping stones are chosen with a fairly level edge to sit on the coverband and they are about the same width as the top of the wall. They are jammed and wedged if necessary.

Dry-stone walls may well last centuries if well-maintained. Gaps always occur in old walls and must be built up again before more of the wall goes. Botching up with strands of barbed wire, or netting, always leads to more trouble in the end even if it saves time in the short term. Alas, the few remaining custodians of the hills can hardly manage essential day-to-day farming, and such jobs as wall repairs are neglected. However, with the increasing price of fencing materials, the care of existing dry-stone walls and the building of new ones, may well become a priority again.

MAKING GOOD STOCK BARRIERS WITH POOR STONE
Stock farmers need effective barriers and in areas where there is plenty of stone for walling it makes sense to use it. Poorer walling stones make less effective barriers so in different parts of the world various methods to improve them have been used. These include the Cornish hedge, with its real hedge planted in the hearting soil of a stone wall and the American wall with a rail construction on top.

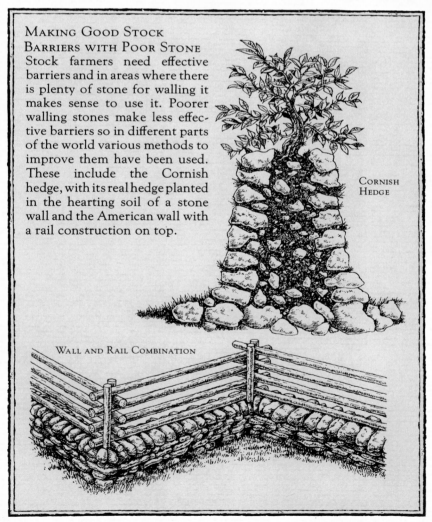

CORNISH HEDGE

WALL AND RAIL COMBINATION

MAKING STILES

T IS A REMARKABLE FACT THAT human beings, slow, cumbersome and stupid though they may be, can get their bodies through, over, or under obstacles that defy much livelier animals. In wooded areas, or districts with no suitable stone, estate carpenters in the past have devised various devices, some of them very cunning and some beautiful, to fulfil this purpose of letting *Homo sapiens* out, but keeping *Os domesticus* or *Ovis ovis* in. The commonest of these devices is the *two-step stile*, simple and fool-proof and long-lasting (provided the components are of chestnut or heart of oak), but climbing over it requires a modicum of agility and, in days of long skirts, was considered a little indelicate for ladies. It is conceivable that the escort of one of these delightful creatures might hope for just a glimpse of a trim ankle as his beloved climbed over.

I suppose that the *kissing gate* might lead to some other immorality as its name implies. It is a cunning device consisting of a small gate that swings between the arms of a V-shaped frame. If properly proportioned, and the local carpenter invariably makes sure that it is, the zig-zag gap produced will stop even a Welsh sheep.

FOR THE AMUSEMENT OF SQUIRES

The *collapsing fence stile* works surprisingly well and is a lot of fun. It makes a great clatter as it falls down and poachers are

WOODEN SQUEEZER
This V-shaped gap in a fence allows the passage of human legs, but bars the body of heavy lowland sheep.

CANTILEVERED STEP STILE
Found in the northern limestone regions of England, such monuments to the waller's art defeat the heavy sheep bred in the dales.

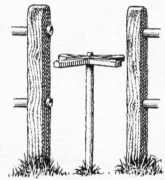

TURNSTILE
Turnstiles were once part of the country scene, simply but attractively made with two wooden crossbars pivoted on a central post.

STONE SQUEEZER OR PINCH STILE
This gap is similar to its wooden counterpart above, but the tighter pinch keeps out more agile mountain sheep and demands more agility of the user too.

CORNISH SLAB BARRIER
This is an unusual barrier consisting of parallel slabs of local stone set apart at distances that make it difficult for stock to traverse them.

wise to avoid it. It is commonly found in large estate parks, where it was built for the amusement of the squire and his guests, and tends to go together with such things as *ha-has*. The ha-ha is a fence built down in the bottom of a deep ditch. Standing only a few yards away from such a fence you do not know there is a fence there and the splendid view is saved.

Knowing the Two-legged Beast

The best stilemakers not only know the sort of livestock they are trying to keep in, but also the nature of the two-legged beasts likely to be roaming the countryside. A fine example of the sort of ingenuity required is seen in the *bastard stile*, which has a small gate above a stile. It owes its efficiency to the fact that the gate is set at such an angle that gravity always pulls it back into the closed position. There is no need for a

latch and the human going through it need not stop to close the gate.

Stiles in Stone Wall Country

Dry-stone wallers have been similarly clever in their making of stock-proof gaps, not all, I might add, for the use of humans. You will often see a *hare gate* – a hole left in the bottom of a wall big enough to let a hare through but not a sheep. This is no doubt a great convenience to hares, but it is also a convenience to poachers who can set their *purse nets* (see p.126) across the opening. Lest the landowners be given too much credit here for humanity to hares, let it be mentioned that these holes were made with the ancient sport of *coursing* in view. I have seen my own lurcher dog Esau (a deadly hare catcher) after a hare where there was such a gate; the hare shot through the gate and Esau took the wall at a flying leap.

Two-step Stile
Ask someone to describe a stile and they will invariably tell you about the two-step stile – a classically simple design.

Ladder Stile
Agile stock, such as the Welsh mountain sheep, would be up and over a cantilevered step stile (opposite) in the twinkling of an eye. To keep them in more drastic measures must be taken, such as this tall ladder stile with its very necessary hand rail.

Bastard Stile
This stile and gate combination is a clever product of both the carpenter and the blacksmith. No latch is required.

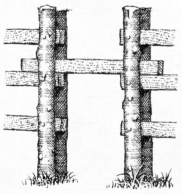

Rail-in-a-fence Stile
Where large, placid cattle are the animals to be contained, the human way through can be delightfully simple, such as this rail across a fence gap. You slide the rail aside to pass through.

Collapsing Fence Stile
The product of precise and beautiful carpentry, this collapsing stile masquerades as a normal section of fence.

WELL DIGGING

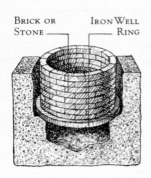

STEENING
This method of well digging only works in soft ground. The weight of the steen (meaning stone) helps push the iron well ring further into the ground as the spoil is removed from underneath.

WELL HOUSING
The superstructure of this well is very simple: a windlass for the rope and bucket and a little wooden roof. The fencing is to deter man or beast from blundering into the abyss.

 TODAY, IF WE WANT WATER, WE simply turn on the tap and out it flows. To extract water from below the land's water table now we use expensive machinery and power and drill for it, just like drilling for oil. But it was not so long ago that every community used to have its own specialist well-digger who not only knew where to find water, but how best to dig a well to get at it. There is nothing miraculous about digging wells: it is simply hard, back-breaking work, and very time consuming too. And I speak with all the authority of an experienced and proficient well-digger.

THE RISKY METHOD

After I left my job working in a copper mine in Zambia, I got employment with another ex-miner sinking a well at Chisamba, just north of the capital Lusaka, in the centre of the country. The well was to be sunk in hard limestone rock which luckily needed no supporting but did need to be drilled and blasted, rather than just dug out. Jack and I used to take turns to be lowered down the well very slowly,

squashed into a small bucket and hoping that the rope would not slip through the windlass at the top. I had to squat on the floor at the bottom and make shot holes with a hand-held *bit* (like a cold chisel) and a *lump hammer*. You pour a little water into the hole to act as a lubricant, wrap a rag around the drill bit so as to stop the water splashing you in the eye, then wallop the bit, turning it between each wallop to stop it getting stuck.

After drilling about 10 holes like this, each perhaps two feet long, I would ram a stick of gelignite, a detonator and a safety fuse into each hole, light the fuses, stand on the bucket and shout to Jack to winch me up. It used to occur to me at such moments that then was the perfect time for the chap on top to pay off any grudges he held against his partner!

After the blast, we would wait a little time to let the fumes get away – we used to hang a blanket down into the mouth of the well to help this. (The blanket, for some reason, caused a down-draught on one side and an up-draught on the other.) Then one of us would go down the well and shovel the broken rock into the bucket, clearing the well floor ready for the next round of blasting. We were paid 10 shillings a foot for sinking that well, and we earned every penny of that money.

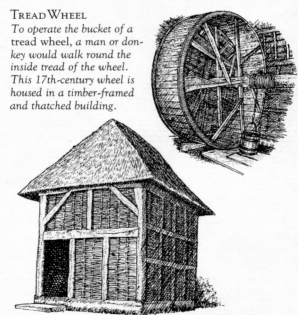

TREAD WHEEL
To operate the bucket of a tread wheel, a man or donkey would walk round the inside tread of the wheel. This 17th-century wheel is housed in a timber-framed and thatched building.

An Ancient Technique

Well sinking with the help of explosives might be messy and sometimes dangerous, but at least some of the back-breaking labour has been taken out of the job. But before gelignite and gunpowder, all wells were dug by hand. I once drank water from what are known as the Queen of Sheba's wells at Wajir in Kenya, near the Somalia border. These go down some two hundred feet into solid rock. The only way Her Majesty, or more likely some of her subjects, could possibly have sunk them would have been by the same technique the Romans used for mining. They would light a fire against the rock, and when the rock was hot enough, douse it with cold water, causing it to split. Then they broke up the rock, carted it away, and lit another fire.

Lining a Well

Not every well is dug in solid rock; some are dug in soft ground, which can just be excavated rather than blasted out. Digging these wells presents other problems though, particularly how to stop the walls of the well falling in once the well is dug and full of water or, worse still, while it is in the process of being dug.

When I was in India, in the Punjab, I saw an ingenious method of overcoming this problem. There they propped up the loose soil walls with timbering until, having reached the bottom, they would build up a lining of bricks, removing the timber as they went.

The method used in England for centuries was to build the brick lining from the top down, not the bottom up. This is not as stupid as it sounds. The way it was done was to first encircle the proposed well hole at ground level with a strong iron hoop and to build a low brick wall on top of it. Then the well would be dug directly beneath the hoop, causing the hoop and its circle of bricks to be undermined. As the well was dug deeper, the hoop would slowly sink to the bottom, and more bricks would be added to the wall at ground level. When the well reached the required depth, and the surrounding wall was complete, the well would be topped with a simple windlass and protected by a tile roof. Elaborate shelters were also constructed around the well head. This method of construction has not changed very much over the years, apart from brick being superseded by reinforced concrete hoops the diameter of

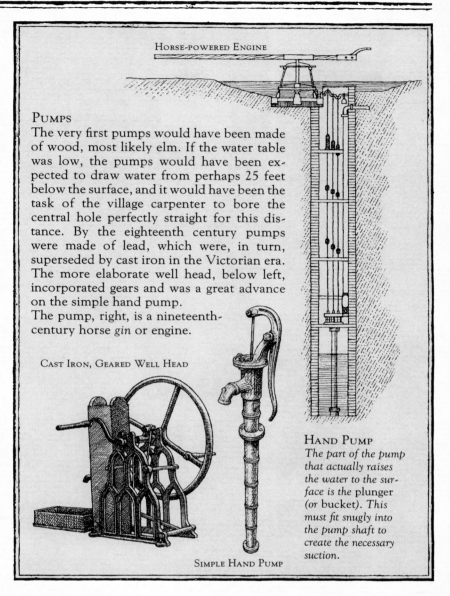

Pumps

The very first pumps would have been made of wood, most likely elm. If the water table was low, the pumps would have been expected to draw water from perhaps 25 feet below the surface, and it would have been the task of the village carpenter to bore the central hole perfectly straight for this distance. By the eighteenth century pumps were made of lead, which were, in turn, superseded by cast iron in the Victorian era. The more elaborate well head, below left, incorporated gears and was a great advance on the simple hand pump.

The pump, right, is a nineteenth-century horse *gin* or engine.

HORSE-POWERED ENGINE

CAST IRON, GEARED WELL HEAD

SIMPLE HAND PUMP

Hand Pump
The part of the pump that actually raises the water to the surface is the plunger (or bucket). This must fit snugly into the pump shaft to create the necessary suction.

the well and about five feet high. The hoops are piled on top of each other as the lowest one sinks down the newly built shaft.

Dew Ponds

Not all water has to be drawn up from the depths of the earth, however, and many a downland field has a dew pond nestling in it, providing water for the flocks of sheep and other livestock in need of a drink. These ponds are hollowed out by hand and lined with a layer of *puddled* or kneaded clay up to six inches thick, which serves as a waterproof lining. Over this is spread a layer of lime to set the clay hard, then a layer of straw, and then finally a lining of earth, about one foot of it, to protect the clay and lime from erosion. Such ponds are filled up by rainwater and kept topped up by fresh rainfall and dew.

PEAT CUTTING

THE EXISTENCE OF PEAT THAT CAN be cut for fuel has made it possible for people to inhabit the remoter areas of our countryside. Even today the distant peat beds of Scotland and Ireland are invaded by small armies of diggers, cutting and removing their fuel for the long winter months.

WHAT EXACTLY IS PEAT?

Peat, or turf as it is called in Ireland, is only formed in very damp climates. It is formed, so the scientists say, where wet anaerobic conditions (conditions that exclude oxygen) prevent putrefactive bacteria from decaying dead vegetable matter quickly enough. The slowly decaying vegetation forms a wet, acid mass which, if left to lie where it is, grows to a great thickness. The weight of the turf on top compresses the layers below making them hard and firm. Subsequent growth on top of the mass dies in its turn, adding to the turf below. These beds can be up to 20 feet deep, the bottom layers browner and lighter in consistency.

RAISED BED AND MOUNTAIN FORMS

In the western and northern parts of the British Isles, peat occurs in two forms, as *raised-bed peat* and *mountain peat*. The former, seen in vast deposits in the bog country of central Ireland, has built up since the Ice Ages into huge masses acting like giant sponges, retaining the rainwater that falls in the winter and releasing it into the atmosphere later in drier weather. The mountain peat is found in small irregular beds on mountain sides, wherever the configuration of the ground has allowed it to form. Luckily, the giant machines that are greedily eating up the raised bed peat cannot manage the more inaccessible and

HOT SUMMER WORK
It is only possible to cut and carry peat when it has lost some of its water, and therefore weight, in the heat of summer. A family can provide itself with winter heat for a week's toil in the sun.

Peat Cutting Tools
Diggers arm themselves with a marking iron, for making vertical cuts through the grass layer into the peat; the paring iron, to expose the peat; and the slane, for cutting out the peat bricks themselves.

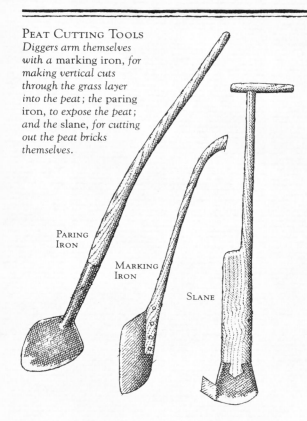

Paring
Iron

Marking
Iron

Slane

Transporting the Peat
The means of transporting the treasured fuel reflects the nature of peat country— wet and boggy. Wheeled vehicles would sink to their axles in an instant so their place is taken by the hand barrow and the sled (see pp.112–13). Most peat regions also have traditional wooden, peat-carrying boats ranging from the small vessel shown here, to larger sea-going varieties.

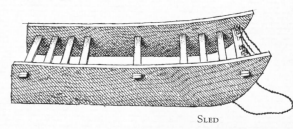

Sled

Irish Peat Boat

difficult mountainous areas, so there will still be enough mountain peat left for those adventurous enough to exploit it.

You can only dig by hand in summer when the peat has a chance to dry. Wet peat is far too heavy to transport, and too soft and boggy to travel over.

The Pattern of Work
Almost invariably the people work on the edge of an existing pit, a pit which has been worked for perhaps hundreds of years. Each family or worker has their own front line allotted and works up on the high peat near the edge of the pit, paring and then digging down strip after strip, each strip being nine inches or so wide. When it is too far to lean down with the *slane* (above) the digger simply marks out another strip and works that one.

Soon he can climb down into the second cut to go on working the first cut at a deeper level. Probably his wife and children back him up by picking up and carrying away the turfs he has cut. Each turf is about 10 inches long by four inches wide and deep, although in some parts of England the peat is cut into cakes, or *mumps* as they are called in Somerset. These are the length of the blade of the slane and then cut again into three blocks when drier. Depending on the depth of the turf and its condition, a man

can cut an area of turf about 10 by 40 yards a week if the weather stays fine.

Stacking the Peat
The turfs are piled up to dry in *windrows*, which look like low, loose walls, and then *ruckled*, or gathered into pyramid-shaped heaps. The shape of these piles of turf varies in different districts, some looking like giant beehives, others more like haystacks, but provided the air can get through them the shape does not matter very much. After drying, and this can be a long, slow process in a wet summer, the by now lighter peat can be transported.

Small sleds are sometimes used, as are wheelbarrows with special bodies and very large, wide wheels, hand barrows and, where there are water-courses, shallow-draught boats. Once home, the turf must be well stacked, and covered somehow to keep out the rain. Wet turf will not burn.

Peat cutting is a time consuming and laborious business, but the smell of a peat fire and the warmth it gives off makes all the effort worthwhile. But it leaves its mark on the countryside as vast swathes of land are cut up and taken away for burning. The Norfolk Broads in the east of England and many of the meres or lakes that surround Amsterdam and Delft in Holland are the flooded remains of ancient peat diggings.

Peat Ruckles
The sort of drying heap, or ruckle, shown here, is used in Somerset. It must be contructed to allow a good passage of drying air between each of the mumps, as the peat bricks are called in that part of the world.

WORKSHOP CRAFTS

W hile sitting in the town workshop of a local basket maker
recently, I learned much more than the intricacies of
basketry – impressive as these are. During the course of the day
several people dropped in, fellow townsmen and women who had
ordered, or were ordering, baskets, and other people, friends of
the basket maker, who just came in for the chat. In a rural
community with its share of local craftsmen, workshops can be
convening places where you go to discuss your needs, and where
the craftsman meets the customer. In this way the artifact you end
up with is not just any kitchen chair, any 20-foot boat, any saddle,
it is your chair, your boat, your saddle, made with only you in
mind and incorporating any subtlety you want. If the craftsman
is also your neighbour, the transaction is the beginning of a
relationship. Your payment helps to keep your
neighbour. If there is any hope for the
rural community, workshop
crafts must prosper.

CHAIR MAKING

 CLOSE FRIEND OF MINE, JOHN Brown, makes quite the most beautiful chairs I have ever seen. He draws his inspiration from very early Windsor chairs and from the colonial tradition of North America. Besides making chairs he runs a small farm and he is the only carpenter I know who works in Wellington boots.

John cuts all his wood from trees he has felled himself. He cross-cuts the trunks into suitable lengths and rives these into the pieces he needs. The seats are sawn from inch-and-a-half, well-seasoned elm planks and then beautifully shaped to fit the average posterior with an adze and draw-knife before being finished with a cabinet scraper, in a process known as *saddling*. He chamfers wood from lower edges of the seat to give an impression of lightness to the wood.

The legs of his chairs he makes from oak and shapes them perfectly round with his draw-knife. Unlike the *bodgers* of old (see p.41), John does not use a lathe for legs and spindles, preferring the appearance of hand-shaped wood. He does not fit *stretchers* (leg braces) either as he thinks the legs should be strong enough without them. The holes he drills in the seat for the legs must be angled just right so that the front legs end up at a small angle to the seat while the back legs splay out at a greater angle.

Once the legs are in place it is time to make the *spindles*. These are the rods that hold up the back and arms of the chair, and oak is his favourite for this. If he is making the Welsh traditional Cardiganshire chair, he will need eight 30-inch spindles for the back. Each has to be half-inch in diameter at the ends, increasing to five-eighths of an inch about 12 inches from the seat. And each spindle he shapes by hand, as he does for the 12 shorter arm spindles.

Two Arms in One

When the spindles have all been set in place John then turns his attention to the arms. He makes them from one piece of inch-by-inch ash, steamed in a *steam chest* to wrap around the back of the sitter. Each end

Carpenter's Tools
The chair maker's set of tools is common to that of most country carpenters. Chair makers still favour the spoon bit *for augering. The* trying plane *is the second longest of traditional planes, its length spanning bumps and hollows for a level finish. Decorative mouldings were once planed using concave and convex pairs of planes called* hollows *and* rounds.

Cutting a Comb
This is John Brown, country chair maker, cutting out a curved comb *for one of his chairs using a bow-saw. After hours of labour, the comb will form a silky-smooth shoulder support in a beautiful-looking chair.*

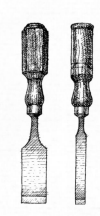

FIRMER CHISELS

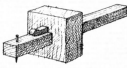

MARKING GAUGE

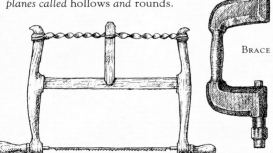

BOW-SAW

BRACE

SPOON AND CENTRE BITS

TRYING PLANE

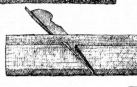

PAIR OF HOLLOW
AND ROUND PLANES

makes an arm. John's steam chest is a piece of iron pipe, closed at one end, tilted at an angle, with water in it and a small fire underneath. He puts the wood to be steamed inside the pipe, plugs the open end with rags and leaves it to steam for at least two hours. Over the years he has made all the *jigs* he needs. These are the shaping devices made of scrap wood around which he bends the steamed wood. When he thinks the wood has been steaming long enough he hauls it out and, working with gloves on because the wood is hot, bends the wood round the jig. An assistant then drives wedges in to hold the wood in place. The wood is left on the jig for at least a day, taken off and a piece of string tied across it to prevent it opening again.

He next drills the arms to take the spindles, shapes and surfaces them with a spoke shave (to remove staining caused by the steam) and finishes them carefully with a cabinet scraper. To get the arm to fit, there is considerable twisting of spindles. At this point you realise that every piece of wood in the chair is under some sort of tension and from this it gains its strength.

THE COMB

John cuts the ends of the arms to taste, and then makes and fits the *comb*. This is the curved piece of wood that goes along the top of the back spindles. Sometimes he cuts this on the curve from the solid wood – sometimes he steam-bends it. Sometimes he carves a design on it. Whatever the shape, it must please both himself and his customers. Glueing the spindle ends and malleting home the comb again slightly distorts the spindles, adding to the overall tension within the chair, and thus strengthening it.

In the early days, Windsor chairs were often painted red, green or black. Now they are usually stained and polished, revealing the different colours and grains of the wood. The wood can be oiled with linseed oil for a different effect.

THAT INDEFINABLE THING

Whatever country chair you want John will make: there is only one stipulation – the chair must please him. If it pleases him it will also please you. There is that indefinable thing *quality* about his work – perfect form and line and proportion. No computer could work out what this quality is nor could any mechanized production line ever hope to reproduce it.

FOUNDING

I NEEDED A TON OF BALLAST FOR MY new boat *Dreoilin*. I intended to have iron ballast as it can be shaped to grip the keel so that it stays put if the boat lies over in a breeze.

Luckily for me the little town near where I live happens to have a four-man foundry in it run by Sonny Power, known as "Slasher" to his friends, and his three sons. Reiner, the builder of my boat, had made me two wooden patterns of the ballast from which we were to make eight castings, each about 1½ hundredweight. These I took to the foundry where they were carefully laid in a square iron-framed *casting box*. Sand, and it has got to be just the right sort of sand, mixed with a little coal dust to give it cohesion, was tightly packed round the patterns to take an impression of one side of them. Another iron box was laid over the bottom box, two pins engaging in two sockets so as to position it correctly, and

more sand was rammed in to take an impression of the other side. The top box was then lifted off, ever so carefully so that the sand did not fall out, and runnels were cut in the sand of the top box through which the metal was to be poured. My wooden patterns were taken out, oh so gently, and the top box was then replaced on its partner.

The Powers spent a week *laying down*, as they call it, about 30 items in sand boxes, eight of which were my ballast pigs. Then the great day dawned when my ballast was to be cast. The *cuplo*, as the blast furnace is known, is as high as an average room and perhaps four feet in diameter, standing in its glory among piles of scrap iron, coke and broken limestone. This is needed as a flux and to purify the iron. A fire of sticks was lit in the bottom of the cuplo and a lot of old boards and firewood were then flung in the top. When a strong fire was going, in went most of the coke.

A centrifugal wind blower, driven by an electric motor and attached to the cuplo by an old rusty pipe increased the draught. Bits of rag were tied round to plug any holes in the pipe: the whole arrangement would have been thought worthy of Heath Robinson in his more ingenious days.

In a surprisingly short time the fire was hot enough and a hole was poked into the clay bunging up the flow hole. Out came a little trickle of red-hot molten iron. Now there were a number of buckets with long iron rods fastened to them, and these buckets, lined with clay, were placed under the spout to catch the molten iron. The first sample was not hot enough so was flung back into the cuplo, but after not very long the iron was judged fit to cast and Mr Power himself filled the first bucket. He carried it into the shed and carefully poured the molten iron into a sand box. Many little cones of clay lay at hand and each time a bucket was filled one of these was shoved into the flow hole to restrain the iron until the bucket was ready again.

Then, spectacularly, one of the boys flung buckets of water on the cuplo and vast clouds of hissing steam obscured the scene. The pouring was over, and all I had to do was to wait until the next day before opening up the moulds and inspecting the work. And that was how my ballast was made.

IRON CASTING
Pouring the red-hot molten metal into a mould is a dangerous business that requires great strength and precision if an accident is to be avoided. Speed is also essential for the iron cools and solidifies rapidly. The metal must be allowed to cool before the sand boxes can be opened up and the object inside inspected. Then the stem caused by the metal solidifying in the pouring hole can be removed and the finished piece is smoothed up on a grindstone and polished.

BLACKSMITHING

REMEMBER, IN THE VILLAGE NEAR the east coast of England where I was brought up, going often to the village blacksmith shop (no trace of it left now) and being entranced by the scene: whiskery old horsemen with their corduroy trousers tied beneath the knees with pieces of string, holding their huge gentle horses, or lounging about in the shop, their faces lit red by the glare of the forge fire, a boy about my age working the long wooden handle of the bellows. How I used to envy him. The music of the hammer on the anvil was beautiful to me. The fierce hissing as the blacksmith pressed a red-hot shoe into the horn of a horse's hoof and the smell of burning horn were magic. The old horses seemed to enjoy it all, as did their masters, and the place was like a club.

THE MAGIC OF THE ART

Later, when I went to agricultural college, the only useful thing I learned was blacksmithing. I didn't learn very much of that,

THE BLACKSMITH'S TOOLS

The blacksmith is in a unique position as far as tools are concerned. Understanding the strengths and weaknesses of metals, and how you *temper*, or regulate the hardness of steel, he can make his own. Working metal involves cutting, shaping and punching it, when it is cold or, more commonly, when it is hot. You need tools of different tempers for hot or cold work and you never mix the use of the two for risk of badly blunting the hot tools on cold metal, or changing the temper of cold tools on hot metal. Generally, hot tools are longer so the smith can keep his hand away from the hot metal. There are cold and hot chisels, grasped and struck, for cutting. Cold and hot *sets* are for heavier cutting, having handles and being struck by an assistant wielding the sledge hammer. Some shaping tools come in two halves: one fits into a hole in the anvil, the other has a handle and is positioned over the lower half with the work sandwiched between. The top half is struck to shape or flatten the work. These include *swages*, *fullers* and *flatters*. When the blacksmith was also the farrier, he would also require a set of tools for shoeing.

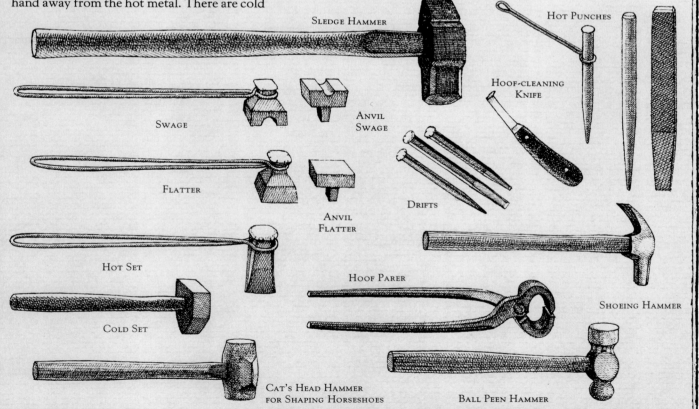

SLEDGE HAMMER

HOT PUNCHES

HOOF-CLEANING KNIFE

SWAGE

ANVIL SWAGE

FLATTER

DRIFTS

ANVIL FLATTER

HOT SET

HOOF PARER

SHOEING HAMMER

COLD SET

CAT'S HEAD HAMMER FOR SHAPING HORSESHOES

BALL PEEN HAMMER

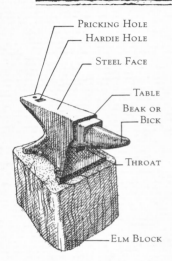

- PRICKING HOLE
- HARDIE HOLE
- STEEL FACE
- TABLE
- BEAK OR
- BICK
- THROAT
- ELM BLOCK

THE ANVIL
I learned some smithing on an anvil just like this one, with a step down, called the table, *just before the beak. It is not surfaced with blister steel like the main face, and here you cut iron without blunting the cold chisel. You punch over the* pricking hole *while the* hardie hole *accepts the square end of fullers and similar tools, especially the upside-down chisel, called a* hardie.

THE SMITHY
To this day I can't walk past a smithy without looking in, hoping for such a scene as this. Farriery tools, such as rasps and paring knives, are collected in a work tray on the floor in the foreground. Next to it is the tripod sometimes used to support a weighty horse hoof. Behind the tray, on an elm block, is a swage block, with its multitude of recesses and holes used to guide hot metal into shape. The array of tongs, skirting the forge, were all made by the smith himself for grasping every different size and shape of hot metal. The work in hand proceeds at the anvil, the smith shaping iron strip with one of the many different weights of ball peen hammer *he has always to hand.*

but I did learn how to make a chain out of a wrought iron bar, and this involves the business of *welding*, one of the blacksmith's basic skills. It depends on bringing the two ends of wrought iron to a white heat, so that sparks just begin to fly from the iron, then hammering the ends together fast and furiously. If you fail to raise the two ends to welding heat they will not unite; if you make them too hot they will simply burn away. No doubt there are scientific explanations as to why wrought iron will weld together when it reaches a certain heat, why cast iron will stand high temperatures and not melt or burn, why steel can be made hard by getting it very hot and then cooling it very quickly, or soft by heating it and cooling it very slowly, but I do not know them. I prefer that they remain part of the mystery of blacksmithing. My tiny bit of knowledge about working with iron or steel has been very helpful during my life, particularly in areas where blacksmiths were few and far between. And I can understand why the first metal workers were counted magicians among their stone age fellows and guarded the secrets of their craft.

REPAIRING AN ANCHOR
George Whelan is a blacksmith friend of mine. He claims he is retired, but I seldom go past his shop without hearing the sound of the hammer. His shop is a long, rough building with a forge in one corner of the biggest room, an anvil by it, a trip hammer which tends to go wrong so that he has to rake somebody in to wield the sledge hammer in the old-fashioned way, a power drill and what may look, to the ignorant, like an indescribable muddle everywhere. But out of this muddle he finds, in a miraculous way, every bit of iron, steel, chain or other oddment that he needs for whatever job he has in hand. He told me that, at one time, the then local priest used to come into the forge and fish out all the odd bits of iron from under his bench with his walking stick – just to try to guess what they were.

I met George, as I have met many other craftsmen, because of the need to fit out my wooden boat *Dreoilin* (see p.114). I needed anchors and, because *Dreoilin* is built in the traditional way and is to be fitted out traditionally, the anchors have to be traditional too. I had bought a fine big *fisherman* anchor from a gypsy friend in Wales, but it lacked a *stock* (the cross member that runs at ninety degrees to the shank). I took

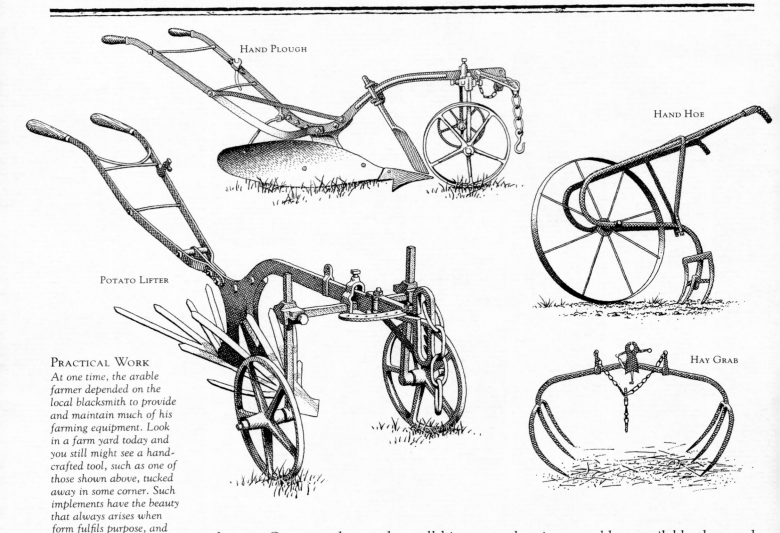

HAND PLOUGH

HAND HOE

POTATO LIFTER

HAY GRAB

PRACTICAL WORK

At one time, the arable farmer depended on the local blacksmith to provide and maintain much of his farming equipment. Look in a farm yard today and you still might see a hand-crafted tool, such as one of those shown above, tucked away in some corner. Such implements have the beauty that always arises when form fulfils purpose, and they last much longer than mass-produced equivalents.

it along to George and started to tell him exactly what I wanted. He cut me short very quickly, telling me that he had made plenty of stocks in his time.

He took my anchor, found a suitable bar of steel and, shaping the curving end of the stock in the forge fire, he quickly fitted a traditional stock. This lies flat along the shank when the anchor is not in use so that the anchor can rest flat on the deck. In use, the stock is held in position with a steel wedge or *cotter*, which hangs on a chain.

HOW THE BLACKSMITH'S CRAFT HAS CHANGED

George's history is typical of many black-smiths. He told me how he was the last in a long line of blacksmiths in his family, how throughout the Second World War there were horses to shoe by the thousand and how four men could hardly keep pace with the work. There were also wheels to *shoe*, or *tyre* (see p.92), and a hundred other blacksmith's jobs to keep the farms of the countryside running smoothly. There were

no electric arc-welders available then and so it was all forge work. After the war tractors came in, horses went out, and, worse still for the blacksmith's trade, every other farmer bought an electric arc-welding set. So many farmers can now do welding for themselves that blacksmiths, including George, are left with shaping work. Shaping steel or iron into intricate designs still has to be done with forge and anvil. The last time I went into George's shop he was forg-ing 130 ferocious-looking steel hooks, each about a yard long, with barbed points, look-ing exactly like giant fish-hooks. George was taking them out of the fire and holding them on the anvil, while his son – back for a few days from college where he is learning industrial chemistry – walloped the iron with a sledge hammer. George would indi-cate the position and direction of the sledge with a tap on the anvil from a hand hammer. If I had had to guess the purpose of these ferocious-looking instruments I would still be guessing now. They were for sticking into the bottom of a lake. If there is any

DECORATIVE WORK
Fine decorative shaping has always been an element of smiths' work, but as electric arc-welding has superseded fire-welding techniques for mundane metal-work, more smiths now specialize in decorative work, such as gates.

MAKING SCROLLS
Scrolls are an obvious feature of much decorative ironwork. Various stages in making three sorts of scroll are shown right, and some of the tools used by the smith appear below. You pull the hot metal around a template called a scroll iron, using scroll wrenches. Effects such as the leaf and the snub end require the crimp and the halfpenny scroll slotted into the anvil.

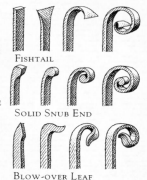

FISHTAIL

SOLID SNUB END

BLOW-OVER LEAF

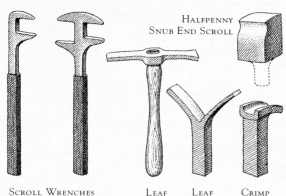

SCROLL WRENCHES

LEAF HAMMER

LEAF TOOL

CRIMP TOOL

HALFPENNY SNUB END SCROLL

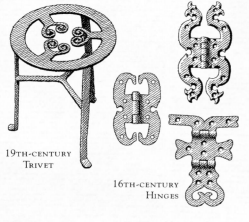

19TH-CENTURY TRIVET

16TH-CENTURY HINGES

18TH-CENTURY WEATHER VANE

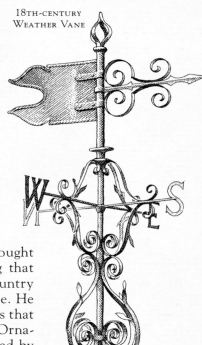

IRONWORK OF EXCELLENCE
Ironwork at its best is a lasting joy to me. The examples above are all English and I know that the decorated hinges in particular were made by Suffolk smiths.

body of water in Ireland with salmon in it there will be fishermen trying to get them out. I pity any fisherman who dips a net into those waters.

George is still called upon to make harrows, for the hand-forged job is far better than the machine-made article. He specializes in what he calls the Scotch harrow, or S harrow – a series of S-shaped pieces of steel with spikes bolted into them. The spikes are graded, with the longest ones at the back. This causes the harrow to dig in at the rear keeping the spikes to the ground.

THE DEMISE OF WROUGHT IRON
Wrought iron is the blacksmith's metal *par excellence* and all the really fine examples of the ornamental blacksmith's art are made of it, welded and shaped by the heat of the forge alone. But wrought iron has been wholly superseded by mild steel, and modern steel will not weld well using traditional forging techniques. Steel is stronger, but it rusts and does not last as long as wrought iron. George uses steel

mostly, but he still has a supply of wrought iron obtained from the iron fencing that once surrounded the many large country houses that pepper the Irish landscape. He uses this precious stuff for special jobs that need to last, such as boat fitments. Ornamental work made in mild steel welded by the electric arc method (and most is nowadays) is nothing like as beautiful as traditionally forged wrought iron.

TEMPERING BLADES
The official way to temper an edge, such as a chisel blade, is take the blade to blood red, quench it in water, then take back the heat by laying the blade on a special steel block which is hot. Various colours creep down the blade: light straw, dark straw, blue, brown and a bee's-wing colour. When that last colour comes you quench the edge in oil. However, no village blacksmith would do it that way. He would heat the blade, cool the edge, then let the colours grade down, quenching when the edge gets to the right bee's-wing colour.

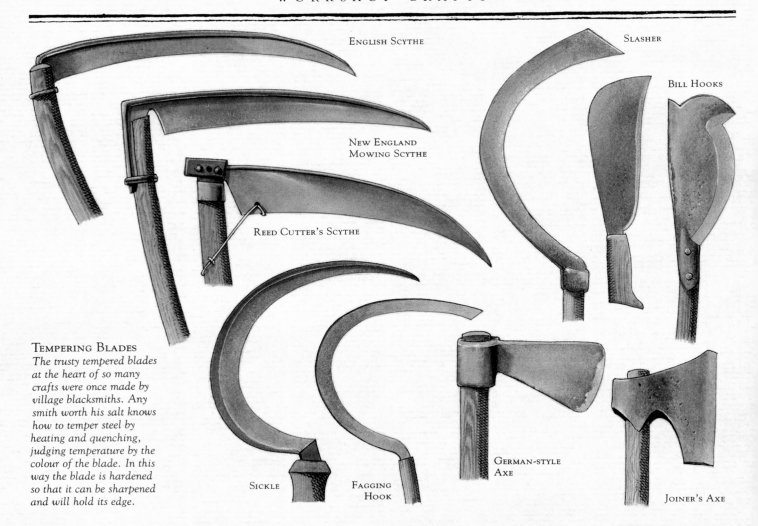

ENGLISH SCYTHE

SLASHER

BILL HOOKS

NEW ENGLAND
MOWING SCYTHE

REED CUTTER'S SCYTHE

GERMAN-STYLE
AXE

JOINER'S AXE

SICKLE

FAGGING
HOOK

TEMPERING BLADES
The trusty tempered blades at the heart of so many crafts were once made by village blacksmiths. Any smith worth his salt knows how to temper steel by heating and quenching, judging temperature by the colour of the blade. In this way the blade is hardened so that it can be sharpened and will hold its edge.

FORGING COW-BELLS
A smith in a cattle-farming area might well be called upon to cut out and forge cow-bells like the one shown below. The exact shape is dictated by local tradition and the whim of the smith himself.

In former times, particularly when good steel was in short supply, George Whelan used to forge all sorts of blades for farm implements from the spring steel of old car or lorry springs. I have a Gurkha *kukri* which is probably made of such steel and its edge is both hard and sharp, and it keeps its edge. George said that a blacksmith relation of his used to make up a mixture of white and yellow clays and water, and mould the block of clay into the shape of the blade he was to temper. Using this the whole length of the blade could be tempered at exactly the same time.

If you temper light sheet steel, such as is used for spades – particularly turf-cutting *slanes* (see p.70) – you have to keep the quenching water spinning to stop the blade from buckling as the water vapourizes.

FARRIERY
When the horse was part of everyday life, shoeing them was a major part of every blacksmith's work. As horses became fewer and more widely scattered, the farrier

THE TINKER

THE WORD TINKER WAS ONCE APPLIED TO AN honourable group of men and women who travelled the roads, in Scotland, Ireland and other parts of Europe, performing the most necessary task of making and supplying goods made of copper, tinned plate and, sometimes, sheet iron. Tinkers could also *tin* copper vessels by melting tin and coating the inside of the vessels with it.

Tinkers did what work there was to be done and then moved on. When they returned some years later, the tin or copper goods they originally supplied would have worn out and there was another spate of work for them.

Tinkers would most likely join two sheets of metal by lapping them, that is folding the edges of the sheets into a joint. This was done so

well that the folds in the metal met perfectly and objects like those at the bottom of this page are still perfectly watertight years after.

Another method of joining metal used by tinkers was riveting and I have watched them make rivets. You cut a little triangle of metal from an old tinned can, roll it into a cone, place it, point first, in a suitably sized hole in a bar of cast steel and hammer the cone to form a flat head. The piece of cast steel with the hole in it, which in fact had up to six different-sized holes in it, was called a *nail tool* and was one of three portable anvils forged in mild steel for tinkers by village blacksmiths. The other two were the *stake* and the *hatchet stake* (below). With these, a hammer, a pair of tin snips and soldering iron a tinker could make any useful artifacts.

SWISS TINKER
Although associated with Ireland and Scotland, here is a tinker at work in the Swiss Alps.

STAKE AND HATCHET STAKE
The tinker would carry two small, forged steel anvils, set on wooden blocks. They provided the different beating surfaces needed for round-work and bending sheet metal.

STAKE

HATCHET STAKE

OIL CAN

MILK JUG

COFFEE POT

WATERING CAN

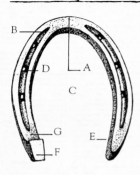

PARTS OF A HORSESHOE
A TOE CLIP
B FULLERING TO RECESS
  NAIL HEADS
C FROG OF HOOF
D NAIL HOLE
E HEEL
F CALKIN
G BRANCH

HORSESHOE TYPES
When you look at horseshoes closely, what strikes you is how far from "horseshoe-shape" most are. The farrier has to modify the shape of every shoe he makes to suit the unique shape of every hoof. Good farriers become skilled in making shoes that help a defect of gait, or an injury, and the more extreme of these shoes are referred to as veterinary shoes.

became a separate craftsman and he now travels to the horses with an anvil, a small forge, an electric air pump, his tools and blank shoes all in the back of a van.

The old-fashioned European farrier worked in his forge and horses had to be taken to him, but then there was a smithy in every hamlet and no horseman had far to walk. Jack Turner was such a farrier. His hands and wrists were scarred and discoloured by the red-hot scales that had landed on them at the forge. He could show you a big toe completely flattened by a heavy horse. The weight of "them horses", and the unremitting toil expected of a country blacksmith in his younger days had also ruined his heart. But at 76 his spirit was unbroken and when he talked of his life of toil he could still laugh out loud.

Jack worked with his two brothers and his father and they had two main classes of customer. There were the farmers."We looked after about seven hundred horses of farmers I suppose and shod them all every three months." And there were the lightermen. Travelling the labyrinthine waterways of the Fenlands, near the central eastern coast of England, was a strange race of men called the *Fen lightermen*. As the few locks they had to pass through were small they had small *lighters* (flat-bottomed barges), and to make a living they used to work these in pairs – the two vessels being pulled by a horse. When the wind was fair they would set a square sail on the leading lighter and the horse would jump aboard the following one and have a rest.

The lightermen would draw up at the pub that adjoined Jack's forge, leave their horses to be shod and stabled, fill themselves up with beer, and then stumble aboard their lighters to sleep. Jack remembers many a night of fun with these wild men.

Jack's forge was cut off from some of the local farmland by the wide River Ouse. Horses would be brought to the far bank and Jack and his family would row over, carrying ready-forged shoes and their hand tools, and shoe the horses cold – that is, without first applying the shoe hot to make a slight impression on the hoof to see if the fit is perfect. With hot shoeing, the smith can still alter the shoe slightly at this stage. With cold shoeing, the shoe has to fit exactly first time. Jack came to know all the horses he shod.

A man can shoe 10 heavy horses in a day and that is all. When you pick a horse's leg up it is inclined to lean a lot of its weight on you and a big cart horse weighs a ton. Not that I have ever shod a horse – I feel that to drive those nails in, knowing that you could ruin the animal for life by driving one at the wrong angle, is just too much responsibility for me, but I have removed many a shoe, and trimmed many a hoof, and know that to pick up a horse's hoof and work on it is back-breaking work. And horses can go mad while they are being shod. Jack told me of one which reared up and rolled down the river bank and into the river when he was trying to shoe it. They only saved the horse from drowning by getting a rope round it and hauling it out.

OTHER SHOES
Horses are not the only beasts that smiths might be called on to shoe. I have picked up little sickle moon-shaped ox shoes in the Namib Desert, made in pairs for cloven hooves. Mule and donkey shoes are shaped like magnets.

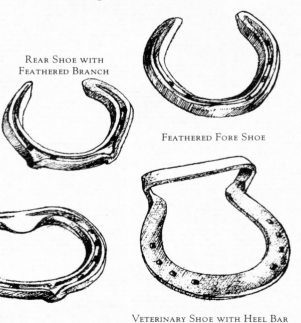

REAR SHOE WITH
FEATHERED BRANCH

FEATHERED FORE SHOE

FORE SHOE
WITH CALKIN

VETERINARY SHOE
WITH MERGED BRANCHES

VETERINARY SHOE WITH HEEL BAR

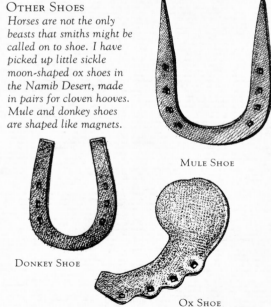

MULE SHOE

DONKEY SHOE

OX SHOE

KEEPING SATAN AT BAY

Such were the economics of the Great Depression in England that shoeing 10 horses a day was not enough to earn a living and nor was getting up at three in the morning to shrink on a dozen wheel tyres. Jack Turner's papa was a good man to have around at this time. Like every other master blacksmith in the days when people really had to work for a living, he subscribed to the belief that "Satan yet finds work for idle hands to do" and was determined that his sons, and others under him, should offer no chink for the Evil One to creep in. If there were no horses to shoe at any one moment, or tyres to shrink on, or chain harrows, or potato-lifters, or reapers, or other machines to repair, he set the family of forgers to making spike harrows, for there was always a sale for these. Nothing was wasted. Old Turner would buy stuffed horse collars and forge the iron fittings for them. Old iron cart tyres, too worn to be used again, would be cut into strips and these strips made into horse shoes. Scythe blades would be bought from Sheffield and handles from some place in Norfolk and the two married together by forging fittings to hold the blades in place. They forged most hand tools and mended all farm machinery. "My father could work with two of us striking – he could turn the iron over while we were striking and we'd never lose a stroke.

Such was the hard old life of a real blacksmith. His skill in shoeing horses was important, but it was his skill in the forge that he liked to demonstrate most.

HOT SHOEING

Horseshoes have to fit perfectly, there are no two ways about it. A farrier usually leaves the shoe he has shaped hot and uses it to burn a slight impression in the hoof horn, to make sure that the fit is correct, as below. Slight adjustments can be made before the final nailing.

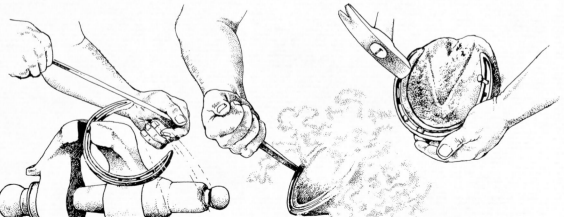

NAIL HOLES

Nowadays, the farrier will buy shoe blanks in various sizes, ready for fine shaping to the hoof. Once he had to bend the shoe for himself. The farrier above is punching nail holes in a part-bent shoe which is being made in the old way.

WHEELWRIGHTING

T WAS IN SOUTH WEST AFRICA (now Namibia) that I fell in love with wooden wheels. In that vast, empty, desert and semi-desert territory the classic vehicle was then the ox wagon. The early Dutch and English settlers had used it to drive their way north from the Cape deep into the hinterland of Africa. In my time there, I joined in an expedition with the wagon of an Afrikaaner to see what lay west of the settled country out toward the Namib Desert. His wagon was pulled by 10 oxen. If it had been loaded it would have needed 20, but all we carried was two huge drums of water and some food. The wagon was 18 feet long and could carry eight tons. Such was the standard South African wagon: a mighty ship of the veld.

Nothing would stop the great wooden, iron-shod wheels. They would smash small trees, crash and crunch over rocks and boulders and plough through the soft sand of river beds.

The front pair of wheels was smaller than the rear pair so that the turn-table on which they were fixed could turn under the front of the wagon. Even so, they were massive and of great weight. The rear wheels were huge, for the bigger a wheel is the easier it runs. The *nave*, or hub, spokes and *felloes* (the rim components of a wooden wheel and pronounced "fellies") were made of exotic hardwoods like stink-wood, or sneeze-wood.

The iron tyres were massive: perhaps four inches wide and three quarters of an inch thick. The weakness of these wheels was that their wood shrank in such a hot and dry climate. No matter how well-seasoned down near the coast, up in the desert under the tropical sun the wooden wheel parts had to shrink some more. The only prevention was to keep the wheels wet. Whenever we reached a waterhole, or a steel windmill over a well on some out-lying farm, or a river that actually contained pools of water, our first consideration (after quenching our thirsts and the cattles') was to soak the wheels. If we were able we would support the wagon on blocks, take the wheels off and lay them in the water. When we emptied the dregs of our coffee mugs it was over the wheels. If we had to relieve ourselves, we did so on the spokes.

THE WHEELWRIGHT'S SHOP
When you know how subtle a thing a wooden wheel is, it is natural to look for clever devices in the wheelwright's shop. The truth, as you see, is that he relies on beautifully simple woodworking tools and home-made measures, such as the spoke set gauge *bolted to the wheel hub in the foreground. You might note the* boxing engine, *with its T-shaped handle, leaning against a splendid old lathe behind the wright's bench, the neat stack of embryo rim parts* (felloes) *on the floor and the* spoke dog *that the wright is using.*

THE GEOMETRY OF A WOODEN WHEEL

I began to study the *rationale* of the wooden wheel. It looks so simple but is, in fact, subtle and complex. That this piece of engineering in wood and iron, without nail, bolt or glue to hold it together, could take the force of carrying two tons over the bare, hard rocks of the veld, was a wonder to me.

I noticed that the ends of the steel axles that carried the wheels were not straight but inclined downwards. This caused the wheels to be slanted out at the top and in at the bottom. Wheelwrights call this inclination of the wheel the *hollow*, or the *dip*.

Another most noticeable thing is that the wooden wheel is *dished* – shaped like a saucer with the hollow side away from the wagon. This dishing counteracts the hollow of the wheel to bring the working spoke (the spoke that is carrying the weight of the wagon at any particular time) more or less vertical but not quite. The working spoke only becomes absolutely vertical when the wagon is running along the contour of a slope when the wheel will come under the greatest sideways strain. The angle formed by the inclination of the spoke to the vertical on level ground is called the *strut*. The combined effect of the hollow and dish strengthens the wagon wheel against lateral movement, especially the normal side-to-side movement caused by the walking pattern of the draught beast. Flat, vertically-set wheels, such as those on an Asian ox cart, are not so strong.

Another subtlety of the wooden wheel is that the metal rim – the tyre of the wheel – does not run at right angles to the spokes. If it did the rim would only run on its inner edge. Nor does it run at right angles to an imaginary straight line between two opposite points on the rim of the wheel. If it did, the tyre would run on its outer edge. The rim of the wheel is in fact cut to a precise *bevel* so that the whole width of the rim runs in contact with level ground. Every angle of the wooden wheel has to be exact and they must match those of the other wheels in the set. If any angle is wrong, the wheel will neither run nor stand up to heavy treatment.

Wagon wheels are massive things and give an impression of brute strength despite their careful construction. It was only when I returned to Britain and saw light carriage wheels, and in fact owned some, that I realized the importance of the wheel's

A HOLLOW
B DISH
C STRUT
D BEVEL

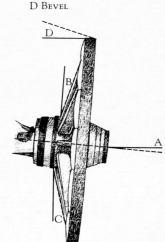

FITTING FELLOES TO SPOKES
If you think of the radiating nature of spokes you will realize that the ends of the spoke tenons are too far apart to engage the holes in the felloes. The wright has to wrench the spokes together temporarily and he uses a lever called a spoke dog *(see also p.90). He puts his weight on the lever as he drives each felloe home.*

ANATOMY OF A WAGON WHEEL

THE HEART OF A HEAVY WAGON WHEEL, THE hub or *nave*, is turned from well-seasoned elm to a barrel shape that will accept two iron *stock hoops*, shrunk on hot. The nave is set in a cradle and the spoke mortices marked, drilled and cut. You have to use an existing spoke to mark the mortices around the nave. The mortices allow for the tapered fit and angle of dish of each spoke. The spokes, always of oak that will take the heavy shocks from the weight of the load, have square *feet* (the tenons that fit into the hub) and round *tongues* (the tenons that fit into the felloes, or rim parts).

There are always two spokes to every felloe. These are of ash (preferably grown curved) and are sawn out with a bandsaw to match templates that are seen hanging in every wheelwright's shop. An adze and a curved plane might be used for the shaping. The felloes are joined with strong oak dowels. The tapering joints of the wheel only come together completely under the pressure of the iron tyre (dished to match the bevel of the rim) as it cools and shrinks in the tyring process.

The nave is precisely augered with the boxing engine (see overleaf) to receive a cast iron *box* or *metal*, which is driven in hard and is a bearing for the axle arm. The wright has to remove a piece of the nave so that you can get to the *linch*, or *cotter pin*, which holds the wheel to the axle, when you partly remove the wheel to grease the axle.

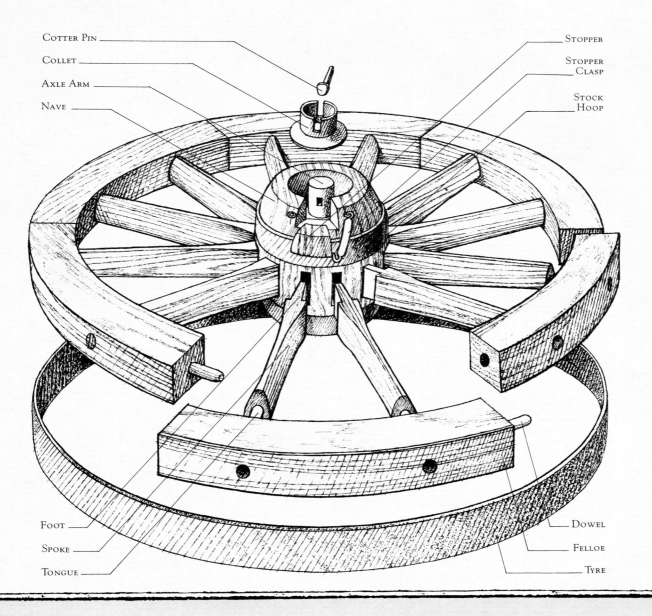

COTTER PIN
COLLET
AXLE ARM
NAVE

STOPPER
STOPPER CLASP
STOCK HOOP

FOOT
SPOKE
TONGUE

DOWEL
FELLOE
TYRE

subtle angles. Such delicate objects can only stand up to rough roads if every aspect of their construction is perfect.

Is it to be supposed that the people who made such artifacts were skilled geometricians? Strangely enough the answer is no. I would guess that until a hundred years ago most wheelwrights could neither read nor write: but they knew how to make a wheel. And wheelwrighting is certainly not a modern science. A dished wheel of the first century BC was dug up in Anglesey in 1947.

A Little History

The wooden wheel is a link with our most ancient rural history. Before spoked wheels there were solid wheels that were either hewn from a single piece of wood or made up of several planks joined and braced. Archaeological finds prove that the solid disc wheel was certainly used by 3500 BC and its use has been preserved in out-of-the-way places until quite recent times, especially for carrying heavy loads. An example that comes to mind is the Welsh truckle cart, which was particularly used on the Gower peninsula on the south coast of Wales. This is a very simple horse-drawn vehicle which is very like a simple sled on a pair of small, solid wooden wheels, each usually made up of three planks of wood and no more than two and a half feet across. The Irish have a similar traditional vehicle, but I have not seen it in use. I would not be surprised, however, to see a bullock cart with solid wheels today in parts of Asia. Even the spoked bullock cart of India seems to be half-way to the solid disc. When I look at it closely I can see little of the subtlety of construction that has so attracted me to the European-style wagonwheel and to the wrights who made them.

The Wheelwright

There are very few active wheelwrights left, certainly very few who have complete

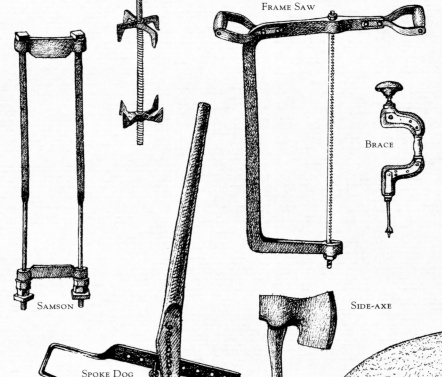

BOXING ENGINE

FRAME SAW

BRACE

SAMSON

SIDE-AXE

SPOKE DOG

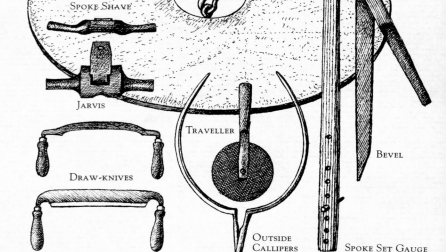

TYRING PLATFORM

SPOKE SHAVE

JARVIS

TRAVELLER

BEVEL

DRAW-KNIVES

OUTSIDE CALLIPERS

SPOKE SET GAUGE

The Wheelwright's Tools

I have not come across a wheelwright who has not inherited the majority of his tools – very beautiful examples at that. New versions would certainly have to be specially made, probably by the wright himself. This, however, is not the tall order it might seem as the specialized tools are quite simple, considering the subtle uses to which they are put. The tools for measurement, such as the traveller (used to measure the circumference of the rim), the spoke set and bevel gauges, are crude devices that require the wright's eye and experience for accuracy. The levers and cutting tools needed are similarly simple but effective in skilled hands.

knowledge of making a wooden wheel, from choosing wood while it is still growing to fitting the finished wheels to the wagon, cart or carriage and watching them roll out of the yard. Moreover, the wheelwright was often the village wainwright too (see p.106), providing the whole range of wooden-wheeled agricultural vehicles, from wheelbarrows to huge farm wagons. In the heyday of horse-drawn transport the cart or wagon was the work of a team of craftsmen – wainwrights concentrating on the body of the vehicle and blacksmiths forging the necessary ironwork. But the wheelwright's magic was always at the heart of the work and when business was not so good he could undertake most of the work in making wheeled vehicles himself. In fact, a good wright could turn his hand to most things. If your eye is good enough and you have spent perhaps 10 years perfecting the art of making a wheel that runs, there is little you cannot do with wood.

Before the First World War there was need of a wheelwright in every village. After it, the horseless carriage quickly started to remove the demand for wooden wheels and wrights became jacks-of-all-trades or went out of business. Those very few wheelwrights who have survived have recently experienced a surge in demand because, perversely, horse-drawn vehicles have become the rich man's interest.

KNOWING WOOD

True wheelwrights develop an uncanny feel for wood. The wheel's strength depends on the natural characteristics of different woods – elm for the nave because it will not split, even with twelve spoke mortices cut from it, oak for spokes because of its strength and ash for felloes because of its flexibility combined with toughness. Beyond this the wright would get to know the wood growing in his area and would buy it as it stood for future use. He would find that wych-elm was probably the elm least

ADJUSTING THE BOX
The final balancing of a wheel, so that it runs perfectly smoothly, involves hammering hard oak wedges into the nave to adjust the position of the box – the metal bearing. The wright runs the wheel on a fixed axle to test it and cuts the wedges flush.

SORTS OF WOODEN WHEEL
The bullock cart wheel with its heavy members contrasts with the light handcart wheel which shows the elegance and strength the wright can achieve. His skill is most severely tested by the accuracy demanded in making the smallest barrow wheels.

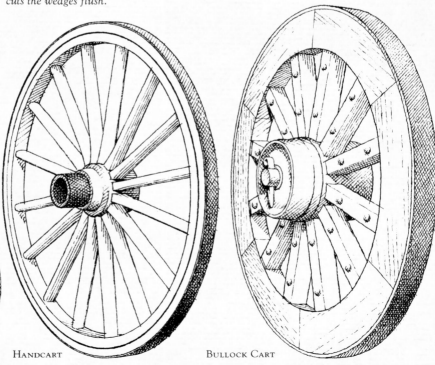

BARROW   HANDCART   BULLOCK CART

likely to split if he could find it and that ash from a hedgerow was probably the toughest and best for his use. I have heard that a good wright would spot the right ash on his travels, noting its natural curves, or *crooks*. He would buy the tree, then cut it and probably leave it lying at the roadside for anything up to two years before using the wood. Long but very necessary seasoning times apply to all wheel wood. Nave blanks need to stand stacked for five years or so, oak billets for spokes for at least four years.

CONSTANT CHECKING FOR ACCURACY

There is no room for error at any stage in the process of making a wheel. When a hub blank is turned at the lathe, for example, the wheelwright checks size and shape continuously with large, curved calipers. The slightest mistake and the precious hub blank is lost. Marking out and cutting the spoke mortices is particularly critical. With the nave gripped tightly in a cradle, he marks and then cuts, first drilling out much of the waste with a brace and bit. The final dish of the wheel is created by the slight angle of cut at the front and back of each mortice and the wright uses a very simple gauge – the *spoke set* gauge – to guide him.

This is a batten of wood temporarily bolted to the exact centre of the nave like the hour hand of a clock. A bone peg is set in the batten the length of the visible part of a spoke from the wheel's centre and projecting from the batten to describe the circumference to which the spokes should be angled. The wright turns the gauge to each spoke position as he cuts each mortice.

HOW THE WHEEL IS HELD TOGETHER

It is the fact that iron or steel expands when it is hot and contracts when it cools that holds the wheel together. The tyre is forged so that it is a little smaller in circumference than the circumference of the wooden rim of the wheel.

When this tyre is heated to a dull red it will expand an eighth of an inch for every foot. Traditionally the tyre is heated in a circular fire and then rushed to the wheel, which is clamped in position on a tyring plate. The hot tyre is fitted over the wooden rim of the wheel, banged home with sledge

HEATING THE TYRE
Some wrights have a purpose-built oven for heating tyres on edge, but most build an open, circular fire. The fire is stocked up with wood shavings to give a fierce heat and the tyre is set in the middle of it.

TYRING THE WHEEL
1 *With the wheel clamped firmly to the tyring platform and assistants ready, the red-hot tyre can be lifted from the heat, carried across and dropped on to the rim. Once the tyre touches the wood it will start to singe so the tyre has to be lowered carefully with the tongs.*

2 *As soon as the tyre touches the rim, there is a flurry of hammering and levering (with tyre dogs) to position the hot metal evenly around the rim. As soon as it is in place, water is poured on to start the quenching.*

hammers and immediately quenched with water before the wood begins to burn. The subsequent shrinking of the iron or steel compresses all the wooden components of the wheel, crunching it together. The hissing of singeing wood and water on red-hot metal, together with the speed of the operation, make tyring a dramatic part of the wheelwrighting process. Again, measurement and craftsmanship are critical. The wheelwright entrusts his precious wheel to the experience of the blacksmith. If the tyre is too big, it will fail to clamp the wheel and will soon run off the rim. If it is too small, it will distort the wheel, or even break it.

Iron tyres for working carts are commonly four inches wide and three-eighths of an inch thick. A tyre for a large wheel needs 15 feet of iron strip and weighs a hundredweight. For a century or so blacksmiths have had the use of tyre-bending machines – simple sets of rollers so placed that when you push a hot strip between them, and turn a handle, the strip emerges bent to a perfect circle. A few old blacksmiths can remember bending tyres without such a machine. They would heat the iron strip to cherry red and poke it through the fork of a tree and gently bend it into a curve.

The only other metal components of a wagon wheel, besides the tyre, are the two hoops which are similarly shrunk on to the nave to stop it from splitting.

LASTING QUALITIES

A well-made wooden wheel has an indefinite life, as it can be repaired and retyred if necessary. On my farm in Wales I had a *gambo* (a traditional two-wheeled cart of the locality) which was at least a hundred years old. Not only were the wheels wooden but so was the axle. Indeed, it was the wooden axle that dated the vehicle. Alas, a disaster befell it. One of the shafts broke when I was coming down a steep hill with a load up and an uncertain horse. The horse reared and plunged and the cart was badly smashed. The wheels, however, were still perfect and so was the axle.

If I could have found a good wheelwright at the time the gambo could have been rebuilt as good as new around those wheels. Much of the village wheelwright's work was repair work, especially through the agricultural ploughing, sowing and harvesting seasons when farmers would bring in repairs left over from the previous year.

It would be during the quieter times of winter that the wright would make most new wheels and fulfil special orders like making wheelbarrows. Not the unpleasant but efficient modern excuse for a wheelbarrow, but the traditional all-wood barrow that lasts a life-time or more.

The little wheelbarrow wheel with its four opposing spokes, one to each felloe, has the reputation of being the most difficult wheel to make. I have been told of one old wheelwright in his eighties who, although his eyesight is not so good now, has recently made two old-style wheelbarrows. Once you have spent years developing the skill of making a wheel that runs true, it must become engrained.

STRAKES
Sections of iron, called strakes, were sometimes fitted to wagon wheels as an alternative, or as well as, a continuous iron tyre. The wright could fit strakes on his own, beating them on hot using big, square-headed spikes and quenching each strake as he went. He would use the samson (see p.90) to pull adjacent felloes together before fitting each strake.

3 *As the tyre cools and contracts it crunches the joints of the wheel tight. The dish of the wheel can be made more pronounced at this stage, if need be, by loosening the tyring platform clamp and letting the nave rise up to it. This platform has a tank beneath it and the wheel can be plunged into it for final quenching.*

COOPERING

OOPERING BIDS, ALAS, TO BECOME a lost art unless circumstances change somewhat. This is very sad because the cooper's craft is truly an art, extremely difficult to learn and one requiring long experience and great skill. You can get a pilot's licence to fly an aeroplane in the United Kingdom after 40 hours' flying time. To learn to make anything like a good barrel will take you an apprenticeship of four years (not long ago it was five). And at this moment, as far as I can find out, there is not one apprentice cooper in the British Isles.

It is interesting to speculate how man first discovered that you can store liquids inside vessels made of slats of wood. My own feeling is that coopering is an offspring of boatbuilding: if you can keep liquids out of a vessel then, surely, keeping them in is a logical step.

The secret of a barrel's tightness is its shape. It allows iron binding hoops of fixed

IRON AND ASH-BOUND SLACK BARRELS

COMPONENTS OF A CASK
Over hundreds of years the parts of a cask acquired traditional names that are now part of the cooper's mysterious language. The names of the sections of the top or bottom of a cask – the heads *– and of the hoops, are shown right.*

MIDDLE
CANT
QUARTER

BULGE HOOP
QUARTER HOOP
CHIME HOOP

THE VARIETY OF USES
The wooden cask can be made in a great variety of sizes and of different resiliences from tiny portable carriers to the Great Tun of Heidelberg.

TRADITIONAL CAPACITIES
In cooper's language, a *barrel* is a cask that holds 36 gallons. Smaller casks are the *kilderkin,* the *firkin* and the *pin.* Larger casks are the *hogshead, puncheon* and *butt.*

| BUTT 108 GAL | PUNCHEON 72 GAL | HOGSHEAD 54 GAL | BARREL 36 GAL | KILDERKIN 18 GAL | FIRKIN 9 GAL | PIN 4½ GAL |

THE COOPERAGE
The fully fledged cooper takes great pride in his dexterity combined with strength and speed. With more than one cooper at work the cooperage becomes a hive of noisy and productive activity. Here a cooper drives on a permanent chime hoop.

sizes to be driven towards the widest part, squeezing the slats, or *staves* as they are known, together – impossible with a cylindrical shape, for example. Another advantage of the barrel's peculiar shape is that, if you know how, you can handle a very heavy barrel with great ease. A weight that would be impossible to carry, lift or drag if it were in the shape of, say, a box, can be rolled by a small child if it is a barrel. A barrel can be "trundled", that is tilted on to one of its rims and spun along; it can be rolled as it lies horizontally; and it can always be hoisted from the horizontal to the vertical by rocking it through its longest axis and then finally heaving it upright.

If you examine a barrel stave you will see why a barrel is a very difficult thing to make. The stave is hollowed out on the concave side, rounded somewhat on the convex side, tapered at each end and, finally, its two long edges are cut on a chamfer. Now if you consider the geometry of a barrel, it is obvious that all the staves in it must be exactly the right shape in order that, when the hoops are driven on, all the staves fit their neighbours exactly. If one stave is out of shape by the slightest degree the barrel will leak. I don't know if any mathematician has ever worked out the ideal shape of a barrel stave (I doubt it), but someone who has done his cooper's apprenticeship can

THE COOPER'S TOOLS

I N MODERN COOPERAGES the drive for maximum efficiency has led to the development of power tools to take some of the effort out of the cooper's craft – steel power grabs to force the iron hoops on to the barrel for instance. But such tools are newfangled and are no real substitute for the traditional set of cooper's tools, shown below. The cutting tools are particularly specialized, their curved blades and bodies betraying the curves of casks they fashion.

The short handles of the heavy-headed tools, such as the adze and side-axe, are characteristic.

They are made for accurate one-handed use so that the other hand is free to support the embryo cask. There is little room for swinging long-handled tools.

Hammer and driver are never far from the cooper's hand. Most coopers make their own driver with its grooved, wedge-shaped piece of iron that engages the edge of the iron hoop being hammered on to the barrel. You might see a cooper's driver without a groove, but this would be an ancient tool used when stout ash hoops were used to bind casks for liquids.

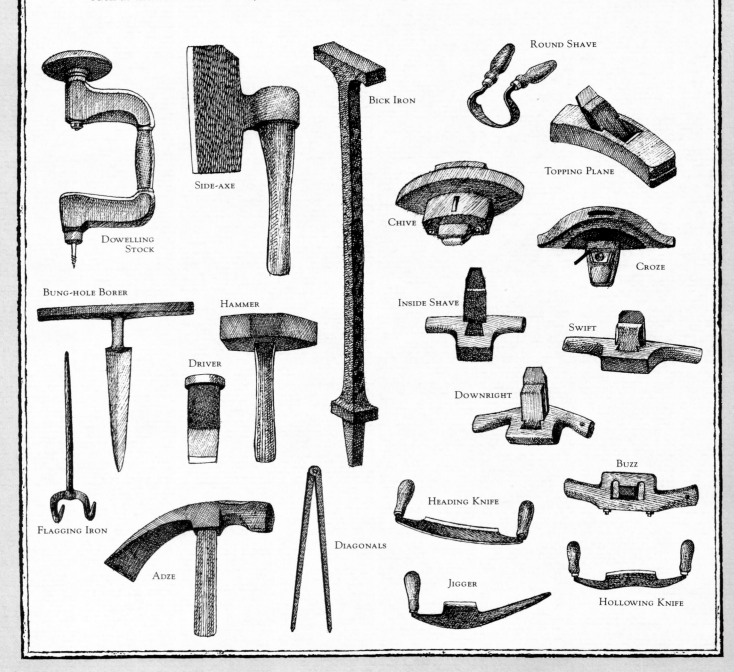

DOWELLING STOCK

SIDE-AXE

BICK IRON

ROUND SHAVE

TOPPING PLANE

CHIVE

CROZE

BUNG-HOLE BORER

HAMMER

INSIDE SHAVE

SWIFT

DRIVER

DOWNRIGHT

FLAGGING IRON

BUZZ

HEADING KNIFE

DIAGONALS

ADZE

JIGGER

HOLLOWING KNIFE

achieve it in a few minutes, just by eye, and get it right ninety-nine times out of a hundred. When the iron hoops are driven on the barrel the staves will come together like loving brothers.

THE RISE AND FALL OF THE CASK

Barrels are mentioned in the Old Testament, are supposed to have been used in Classical Greece (although the use of so many *amphorae* argues that there were not many), and were certainly used by the Romans. There were coopers' guilds in England in the early Middle Ages. A London Livery Company was formed in 1502 and the Coopers' Guild that still operates (or would do if there were any coopers left) was founded in 1662. The cooper's trade was organized in Dublin earlier still, the Dublin Guild being founded in 1501. The Dublin Guild was wound up in June 1983. The sad end of a long story.

The demise of British and Irish cooperage is due to a number of factors, some of which have been operating for a long time. One of the oldest is that British Isles oak does not seem so suitable for cooperage as the imported varieties, which have fewer knots. Staves have been imported from Russia and the other countries linked by the Hanseatic League since the Middle Ages, Eastern European oak being found most suitable. Then, as early as the seventeenth century, American white oak started to be imported for the making of barrels.

A severe blow was dealt to the native industry by the eighteenth-century propensity of the English gentry to drink foreign wines, in particular ports and sherries. These, of course, came in foreign barrels and it was not worthwhile returning the empties. So the spirits trade in these islands came to rely entirely on recycled barrels from the Continent.

A STRANGE THING ABOUT BOURBON

The next blow, similarly severe, came in the form of an American law. This originally stipulated that bourbon had to be matured in new oak casks only. True, this has since been modified to allow distillers of certain bourbons to use a cask twice, but nevertheless an enormous number of American whisky barrels have been made redundant and have since flooded the market.

It might be wondered why, if American distillers cannot use a maturing barrel more than twice, Scots and Irish distillers are able to mature what they (and I) would claim to be far superior whisky, in second or third-hand barrels? The answer is that bourbon must draw certain substances (mainly tannic acid one suspects) from the virgin oak in order to mature properly, whereas the Scots and Irish versions do not need these particular substances.

Used American barrels originally arrived in the form of *shooks* (barrels that have been knocked down and the staves packed in bundles), but now, more and more, distillers are importing complete barrels. This means no work for British and Irish coopers. In Scotland, some whiskies may still be matured in home-produced sherry casks, but even there distillers increasingly turn to the American 108-gallon butt.

WHAT ABOUT BEER BARREL MAKING?

There was always beer to be stored, however, and indeed brewery coopers held out much longer than the distillery ones, but then the *coup de grâce* fell on them in the shape of that horror of our age of mediocrity: the metal cask. Metal casks can be made by machines minded by unskilled

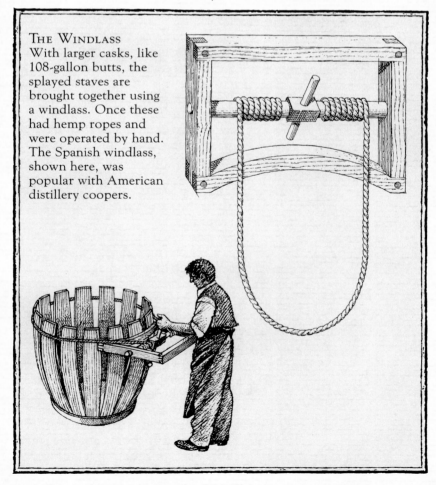

THE WINDLASS
With larger casks, like 108-gallon butts, the splayed staves are brought together using a windlass. Once these had hemp ropes and were operated by hand. The Spanish windlass, shown here, was popular with American distillery coopers.

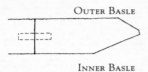

OUTER BASLE

INNER BASLE

THE HEADS

The top and bottom of a cask, the heads, are measured and marked on boards that have been dowelled together. The radius is exactly a sixth of the circumference of the groove in the cask waiting to accept the head. Each head is cut out with a bow saw then shaved smooth, allowing for the squeezing of the joints once the head is in the barrel. To ensure a tight fit, the edges of the heads are bevelled with a draw-knife, making the inner and outer basle.

labour, whereas wooden barrels have to be built by craftsmen. With the advent of the metal cask, filled with its characterless fizzy liquid, not only was the taste of a famous beer-drinking nation corrupted, but a great tradition of craftsmanship was finally knocked on the head. A faint glimmer of hope is held out by the gallant enthusiasts of various "real ale" societies in the British Isles. Unfortunately, there are still enough old casks in circulation.

WHY USE WOODEN CASKS?

Many attempts have been made by the men in white coats to find a way of maturing spirits without using oak casks. They have even put planks of wood or shavings into stainless steel containers. So far, thank Bacchus, to no avail. Distillers of whisky, brandy and gin still find that there is no substitute for a good oaken cask. The oak "breathes", allowing some exchange between the spirit and the air outside. A small percentage of the contents is lost by this exchange, but the remainder is far better for it. In Great Britain and Ireland whisky must be matured in the cask for three years by law. Much of it is matured for twelve years or even longer.

Beer barrels are smaller, but much stouter, than the casks used for maturing whisky because they have to withstand the pressure of gas given off by the fermenting liquid. A man who worked most of his life coopering for a brewery told me that in the old days beer was much stronger and, therefore, kept much better in the wood than the weaker stuff does now. In fact, the old beer coated the inside of the barrel with a crust, like that of old port. Weak ale eats this off, "the weak feeding from the strong" as they say in brewing circles.

TALKING TO A WORKING COOPER

In Cork, Irish distillers still make whisky barrels. Most of the work consists of remaking American barrels, but the coopers there can still make barrels from scratch if need be. Mr Joe Foley showed me how.

Joe had started work as an apprentice at 14 years of age, as had all the men working in the cooperage, including the manager. Joe has been in the coopering trade for 32 years. As he said, he is one of the "last of the Mohicans", for when his generation retires it will mark the end of coopering in Ireland. Joe was jolly and good-natured, and everything he did he did at astonishing speed

making it difficult to follow his movements. His speed of action did not prevent him from keeping up an unbroken stream of Irish raillery.

A WORD ON STAVES

I have seen staves cut in Spain. Firstly, a large, straight, clean-boled oak was felled and crosscut sawn into lengths a little longer than the staves were to be.

These sections were then riven in halves, quarters and then into smaller fractions, until the staves remained about an inch, or slightly more, thick. By riving them out along the radius of the oak (see diagram below) at least one medullary ray of the oak grain remained in each stave. Sawn-out staves might only have part of a medullary ray in them and these would make a barrel that would either break during its making or soon after. A very big oak will yield two rings of staves. The very heart of the tree and the outer sapwood are not used.

Joe started at the beginning by selecting blank staves for his cask. These were

STAVES

Tree trunks have ribs of strength running out from the heart to the bark. These are called medullary rays and, through trial and error, the cooper has learned to cleave oak trunks so that these rays remain unbroken and make liquid-proof staves.

Each oak plank is turned into the stave shape, shown right. One side is rounded, the other hollowed out. The edges are first tapered and then bevelled.

PATTERN FOR
CLEAVING STAVES
FROM A TRUNK

ordinary looking planks of oak a little longer than the height of the finished barrel. He examined the grain of each blank carefully before beginning to shape, or *dress* them, as the coopering expression goes. If you look at the diagram of a stave, left, you will see the subtle shaping required. Each stave is clamped into a device called a *horse*. This is made of steel, but works in the same way as the wooden shaving horse shown on page 33, although Joe worked at the horse standing up. He told me that coopers who make the smaller barrels for beer use a similar clamp, but it is worked at sitting down and is called a *mare*. Others simply clamp the stave under a hook on the chopping block, pressing it against their stomachs. Using a draw-knife with a convex blade called a *hollowing knife*, Joe hollowed what was to be the inner face of the stave, then turned the stave over and changed to a concave knife to *back* the outer face.

Taking the stave to an ordinary chopping block, he took a crude-looking axe, with a huge head and a short handle (the *side-axe*, so called because its blade is sharpened on one side only, like a chisel), and cut the edges of the stave so that each end tapered. In an operation that would have taken me an hour to spoil, Joe *listed* the stave (the cooper's expression) with a few deft strokes in perhaps a minute. To me this was the most

impressive exhibition of skill in the whole performance. He used no gauge, no measure, no template; merely his eye. The list of each stave will give the cask its belly.

The stave was then taken to a giant inverted plane. It was perhaps five feet long and set at a slant with one end on a stand and the other on the floor. This he called the *jointer* and instead of running the plane along the wood he ran the stave along the plane, bevelling its long edges. The bevel on each side of each stave will ensure the circular shape of the barrel. Given that each stave can be of different width, it is a wonder that Joe could judge the right bevel, but of course he did.

Raising-up the Cask

You can see how a master cooper constructs a cask on pages 100–1, but, like a novice apprentice, you need to know more than your first study of the process reveals to understand exactly what happens. Talking of novices, I have seen an amateur start to construct a cask and the result was hilarious with staves falling all over the place. To see an expert cooper make the same start, catching all the staves in an end hoop (the *raising-up hoop*) is like watching a piece of legerdemain. A slight pressure on the last stave in keeps enough pressure on all the others around the circle. Joe simply

DRESSING STAVES
The physical process of dressing a stave to the correct shape is wondrous, because no prior measurement is made. The cooper selects exactly the right number of stave blanks, considering variations in widths, and shapes them all to fit one another by eye only.

The picture, above left, shows the concave hollowing knife being used, while the picture above shows the final bevelling of a stave on the cooper's jointer.

pushed the iron hoop down with his hands to effect the first tightening of the staves. This, the *raising-up* stage, is completed by driving another hoop down over the staves, this time using a hammer and driver.

FIRING DIFFERENT SIZES OF CASK

You will have noticed that I started talking about "barrels", but now the barrel is a "cask". The reason is because a cooper is very particular about volumes. His skill is not so much that he can make a watertight wooden container, wonderful achievement though this be, but that he can ensure that any of his containers holds a specific, time-honoured quantity. These are in gallons and have marvellous old names, only one of which is "barrel" (see p.94).

There is another thing to know about types of cask; some are *slight* and some *stout*. Slight casks have staves of less than one and a half inches thickness, while a stout one has staves thicker than this. Both of these factors, size and thickness of stave, have given rise to different ways of bending the staves to the correct barrel shape. This part of coopering is called *firing* because the village cooper damped the staves well, then stood the cask over a cresset of burning shavings to soften the staves enough for bending. Stouter casks might be put in a steam chest or soaked in boiling water before bending. Whatever the preparation, the shaping is a dramatic affair with plenty of shouting and hammering and steam and smoke. The longer it takes the harder it is to bend the cooling wood. A thick truss hoop is hammered down towards the splayed end of the barrel, then a smaller one follows until the original falls away. Then over goes the barrel, splayed end up, and then wallop, the cooper hammers one side of the truss hoop back towards the belly of the barrel, pulling the staves together until a smaller truss hoop can be caught on to the splayed stave ends above.

FITTING THE HEADS AND FINISHING

It is in the fitting of the top and bottom (the *heads*) into grooves cut into the inside face at the ends of the cask and in the finishing of the cask that the cooper uses most of his specialized tools. Each process in the mystery has its name.

Joe showed me how the cask is *chimed* by cutting a bevel around the top and bottom of the staves with a small hand adze; how the *sun* or *topping* plane evens off the stave

CONSTRUCTING A CASK

The cooper divides the making of a barrel into distinct stages, of which preparing the staves is the first. This complete, the cooper then proceeds with the construction. To understand the process you first need to know that the hoops the cooper uses to shape a cask are not the hoops that will finally bind it. The shaping hoops are of standard sizes and are part of the cooper's tool kit. He has *raising-up hoops* that contain the required number of staves to start the various sizes of cask, and for every raising-up hoop, a *dingee hoop* that closes the cask at the opposite end. The bending of the staves is brought about using *truss hoops* which are thick and made to take a deal of beating. These were once made of ash, but those you see now in use are likely to be of iron. Similarly strong *chiming hoops* are needed to support the ends of the cask while they are being shaped.

After raising-up, the cask has to be *fired*, that is the staves softened by heat or steam, and then curved so that they come together into the dingee hoop and can cool and set to become a *gun*, as the cooper has it. Then there is *heading* – the fitting of the two cask lids and finishing the outside of the cask prior to the making and fitting of the permanent iron bands.

1 *With all the staves dressed, the cooper gathers them one by one in a raising-up hoop.*

5 *The cooper makes the permanent metal hoops using dished steel strip. The strip is offered to the cask and he holds his thumb at the point where he must rivet the ends of the hoop on the* bick iron.

6 *Each head is made by dowelling four or five planks of wood together and cutting a circle from the result. The cooper saws out the circle, then uses the adze and the* heading knife, *above, to cut the* basle *around the upper and lower edges.*

2 *He uses* truss hoops *to shape one end of the cask, then wets the staves and heats them over a burning cresset. Smaller truss hoops bring the now malleable staves together until the cask can be upturned and the splayed staves closed with truss hoops driven from the opposite direction.*

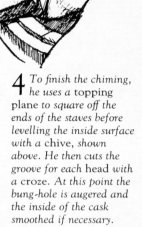

3 *When the cask has cooled and set (it is called a* gun *at this stage), the cooper cuts the chimes, or ends of the cask. He replaces the raising-up hoop with a* chiming hoop *and leans the cask against the block. He uses an adze to cut the bevel.*

4 *To finish the chiming, he uses a* topping plane *to square off the ends of the staves before levelling the inside surface with a chive, shown above. He then cuts the groove for each head with a* croze. *At this point the bung-hole is augered and the inside of the cask smoothed if necessary.*

7 *To fit the heads, the cooper releases the chiming hoops, slackening the staves. He taps home the back, or bottom, head first from inside the cask, forcing flagging into the groove. He pulls the top head into place using a* heading vice *(a metal handle) screwed into the hole made in the head for the tap.*

8 *With the permanent chime hoops in place, the cooper removes the remaining truss hoops and smooths the outside of the cask with a* downright plane, *followed by a* buzz *– the cooper's curved two-handled scraper.*

9 *The cask is finished by fitting the remaining permanent hoops using a hammer and driver.*

SLACK COOPERING

Slack coopering is the term given to the making of casks that do not have to hold liquid. These were made of much lighter wood and were bound with willow or hazel hoops, twisted and nailed (see p.35). I remember when many perishable items, such as fruit and shellfish, travelled in slack casks. They were non-returnable, on the whole, and provided the cooper with batches of less-exacting work.

ends; how the inner surfaces are prepared for the heads using a curving, 90-degree plane called a *chive*, then grooved with the similar looking *croze* with its two steel teeth, one called the *hawk* and the other the *lance*.

Joe revealed another secret when he showed me how the cooper checks the capacity of the cask he is making using a simple pair of dividers called the *diagonals* before cutting the second groove. He can adjust the capacity slightly by altering the exact position of the groove.

The heads are beautifully made from oak planks dowelled together with *flagging*, or rush, between the joints. Traditionally, they are rough-shaped with the side-axe or cut out with a bow saw before being worked at with a draw-knife.

The cask is complete when it has been smoothed down with a *downright* followed by a *buzz* (both concave-bladed planes), and the permanent dished iron hoops have been prepared and driven home.

WHITE COOPERY

White coopery is a branch of the craft concerned with the making of liquid-tight wooden vessels, either iron or brass-bound, other than casks for spirits, wines or beer.

When I was a boy on the Essex-Suffolk border, every cottager I knew, without exception, had a *back'us* as they called it: a back house. Every farm had one too and in it the *back'us boy* used to have his being. Hanging on the wall of the back'us there was always a *piggin*. This was for a multitude of uses – anything for which a water-holding vessel was needed but it could not, of course, be boiled. Wooden buckets, with *grommets* as the hemp handles were called, were still in common use and you would see one hanging down the well.

Dairying had already passed beyond memory in most parts of East Anglia, but when I moved to Wales I found that every small farmhouse still contained dairying implements. There was always one or more *slates*, which were slabs of slate, troughed out on top, about three feet by five feet, with a hole bored in them. You bunged up the hole with a stick and poured milk into them. It was allowed to settle, then the stick was withdrawn and the skimmed milk ran down into the *buck*, which was a wide shallow tray made by the white cooper, leaving the cream adhering to the slate to be scraped off.

The cream, when taken off, is allowed to sour a little before it is churned. The older type of churn is the one at the bottom right hand corner of this page – the *plunger churn*. The stick coming up from it has a plunger on the bottom of it and it is pumped up and down. By far the best kind of churn, however, is the end-over-end-churn. This is a very beautiful artifact and perhaps represents the peak of the cooper's craft.

The buck (see above) was also used in that most hallowed art, practised throughout the world, brewing beer. The boiling *spree*, which is what the beer is called before it is properly made, is allowed to run into the buck to cool quickly before the *balm* (yeast) is put in. The successful brew has often been quaffed from fine mugs – further examples of the white cooper's craft.

Let no one underestimate the wooden cask. It is a masterpiece of craftsmanship and an object of beauty. One of the Spanish stave makers I watched told me that there was many a barrel still holding Cognac after a hundred years' use.

END-OVER-END BUTTER CHURN

COAL SCUTTLE

SCANDINAVIAN ALE VESSELS

PIGGIN

BUCKET

DOMESTIC KEG

BUTTER CHURN

TURNING

HE FINANCIAL REWARDS FOR A woodturner today are not what they might be. Wood for turning is hard to come by and expensive. The attractiveness of turned objects lies very largely in the revealing of beautiful patterns of graining by the cutting and polishing of the wood. Elm, yew, apple, pear, cherry and walnut are all suitable. When you buy such wood it is almost certainly unseasoned, which you have to do yourself, thereby tying up your capital.

The woodturner's reliance on making objects of beauty to sell to people who appreciate them is a new thing. Traditionally, woodturners were fully engaged in making things of strictly utilitarian value, the beauty of which was of the type that attaches to all honest objects made well for a good purpose. Years ago I remember meeting Mr Ellis of Boston, Lincolnshire,

who earned his living as a woodturner there. He made things he called *working women's pianos*, which were also called *dolly-pegs*. These were for women to stir their washing with in the *dolly-tub*. He also made *wringer-rollers*, which were the rollers made of sycamore for fitting into mangles, and *yokes*, which are the things eighteenth-century dairymaids always carry in paintings, their wooden buckets full of frothing milk. Mr Ellis told me he didn't like making yokes because it was "not strictly a turner's job. They entail a lot of wood carving, too." They were very wasteful of wood because they had to be cut from a big chunk of it. Mr Ellis made them not for pretty dairymaids but for fishermen who, in the Wash (which is what the sea in that part is called), carry large baskets of cockles or mussels across the sand or mud at low tide.

CAREFUL SEASONING

Phil Leyton, my son-in-law and woodturner, fells his own trees whenever possible. He *rips* them (saws them along the grain) into inch, two inch or larger planks with a double chain-saw he has fitted to a frame. He stores the planks, held apart by slats of wood to let the air through, in a shed or in the open if he has to, for several years. Then, if making bowls, he cuts a plank into square sections and roughly cuts these round on a small circular saw. He then sticks a small square of waste wood on what is to be the bottom of the bowl and puts the roughed-out wood near the stove in his house to season even further. Many

BOWL TURNING
A bowl, like the one you can see being turned below, starts out as a large lump of wood, which accounts for the high price of the finished work. Here, the turner is using an inside knife *to remove the bulk of excess wood from what will be the inside of the bowl. An adjustable rest helps to support his left hand at the right height.*

TOOLS OF THE TRADE
The wood turner uses an assortment of differently shaped tools depending on whether he is working on the outside or inside face of the bowl. The cutting edges also differ. The long handle (up to two feet including blade) provides great leverage and allows you to hold the cutting edge of the blade firmly against the turning wood.

INSIDE AND OUTSIDE HOOKING KNIVES

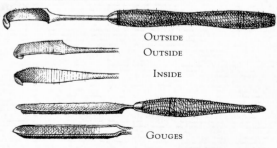

OUTSIDE

OUTSIDE

INSIDE

GOUGES

turned wooden objects today are not seasoned sufficiently, which is why they warp, crack or do other horrible things.

Phil owns an ancient treadle lathe, which is powered by the craftsman's foot. This is a technical advance on the old pole lathe (see p.42) where when the treadle was depressed the work was turned towards the gouge, but once released the work spun the wrong way for cutting and the turner had to wait for the next change of direction before cutting again – a very tricky operation to perfect. Phil's treadle lathe has a crank and heavy wooden flywheel and gearing to transmit the movement of the treadle up and down to turn the work continuously in the right direction.

I only once saw Phil use the treadle lathe, when he had an order from a wheelwright to turn some elm wagon-hubs that were too big for his electrically driven lathe. Because of the large diameter of the hubs it took three of us to work the treadle while Phil held the gouge – but it worked and the hubs were produced on time.

TURNING A BOWL

Now, to get back to our bowl. Phil, or his apprentice, screws the piece of waste wood previously glued to the roughed-out wood to the *head* of the lathe, which is the part that spins round. Older turners were apt to cut their bowl blank out of a thicker piece of wood than necessary and leave a *pillar* of wood to screw to the head. The pillar was later cut off. But this is too wasteful now that wood is at such a premium. Taking the appropriate gouges or chisels the turner then sets the lathe spinning and, holding the tool against a rest, starts to remove wood. Very quickly he has his bowl shape on the outside at least. Then, using a different-shaped gouge, he removes the wood from the inside. The actual turning takes very little time. Next, the turner applies sandpaper to the spinning bowl. When it is sufficiently smooth, he applies such things as beeswax to give it a deep, rich shine and to fill the pores of the wood. Any excess is taken off by holding clean shavings up against the spinning bowl.

WOODEN SPOON CARVING

In Wales, the traditional *cawl* spoon and bowl are still in demand. Cawl is a kind of broth that the Welsh people consume in large quantities and it is my belief that nobody but a Welsh lady can make it properly. The broth I feel sure would not taste the same out of an ordinary china soup-plate, and the traditional wooden bowl keeps it hot much longer. Also, the cawl should be eaten with a wooden spoon.

Both cawl spoons and bowls should be made of sycamore wood felled in winter time. For the 10-inch long spoons, sycamore logs are sawn into 12-inch lengths and split in half with an axe, and split again to blanks about the right size for a spoon. Then, with a small, very sharp axe, the blank is roughed out to the outward shape of the spoon. The bowl of the spoon is then cut out with what the Welsh call a *twca cam*, or bent knife. Spoonmakers I know use ordinary kitchen knives that they have bent over themselves.

The Welsh *love spoon*, now sometimes produced in terribly debased form to sell to the tourists, is properly only made by young men as tokens of their affection for their sweethearts. These articles are very beautiful, most inventive and elaborate, and quite useless. Some have balls carved inside wooden cages and others have wooden chains hanging from them, or hearts and other motifs.

TRIMMING KNIFE

HOOKED KNIFE

ADZE

SPOON CARVING
Undecorated spoons are easy to make, but to do so quickly enough to earn a living is something else. To hold the work steady during the final stages, the craftsman braces the spoon handle with his body. The small trimming knife can be adapted from an ordinary kitchen knife.

CARVER'S TOOLS
For a ladle, a little adze is used to shape the bowl. This is refined using a long-handled hooked knife and finished with a trimming knife.

WAINS & COACHES

IF YOU HAVE EVER HEARD AN IRON-tyred wagon or carriage being drawn along a modern metalled road surface, the din might make you think that there will never be need of such vehicles again, and that they must have been a terrible trial when they were the only means of carrying a load. But then if you had ever seen the same wagon or carriage being driven along a cart track across country you would realise just how marvellous a means of transport they can be. Big iron-shod wheels were made for coping with rough ground and tracks with ruts worn in them perhaps two feet deep. I have

talked elsewhere (see p.86) about the giant ox wagons I travelled in across the African plains and how their wheels made light of the roughest countryside. Before that time, in England, I remember the farm wagon as part of daily life. Up until the Second World War there was an unbroken tradition of making mostly wooden horse-drawn vehicles that stretched back to the invention of the wheel. It was a tradition that became highly developed in England.

Every county of England had its own style of wagon that had been slowly developed among its wainwrights and was handed down from master craftsman to apprentice over hundreds of years. The wainwright was probably the village wheelwright. Making the wheels was the most difficult part of the process and it was the wheelwright who held the key to the successful geometry of the wagon, so he was at the centre of operations. If need be he could make the whole wagon himself, otherwise he was foreman to a smith and wrights who specialized in making the undercarriage frameworks and the bodies of the wagons. Working on his own, it would take a wainwright several months to

BARGE WAGON
The barge wagon comes at the end of the long tradition of wainwrighting, this example from Oxfordshire being made at the turn of the century. Its details in wood and iron are far simpler than the box and bow wagons.

THE ENGLISH BOW WAGON
The peak of the English wainwright's craft was the bow wagon, a wagon designed for hilly areas. It was called a bow wagon because the raves or sideboards were hooped so as to clear the back wheels, and the body of the wagon was waisted, that is it narrowed behind the front wheels to allow them a greater lock.

CONSTRUCTION OF A SUFFOLK WAGON c1880

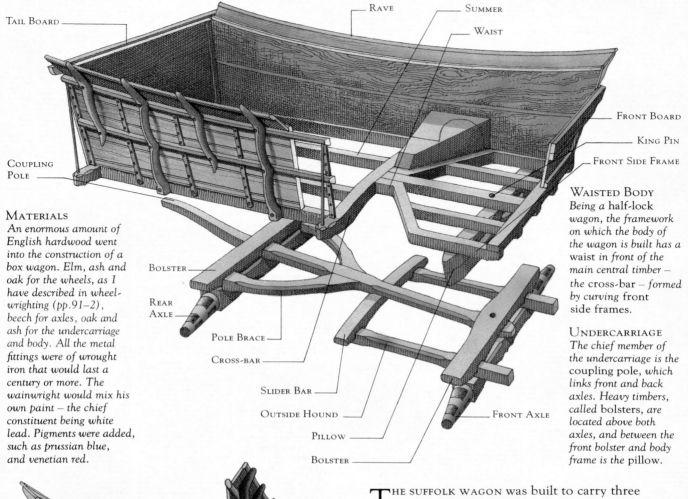

TAIL BOARD

RAVE — SUMMER

WAIST

FRONT BOARD

KING PIN

FRONT SIDE FRAME

COUPLING POLE

BOLSTER

REAR AXLE

POLE BRACE

CROSS-BAR

SLIDER BAR

OUTSIDE HOUND

PILLOW

BOLSTER

FRONT AXLE

MATERIALS

An enormous amount of English hardwood went into the construction of a box wagon. Elm, ash and oak for the wheels, as I have described in wheelwrighting (pp.91–2), beech for axles, oak and ash for the undercarriage and body. All the metal fittings were of wrought iron that would last a century or more. The wainwright would mix his own paint – the chief constituent being white lead. Pigments were added, such as prussian blue, and venetian red.

WAISTED BODY

Being a half-lock wagon, the framework on which the body of the wagon is built has a waist in front of the main central timber – the cross-bar – formed by curving front side frames.

UNDERCARRIAGE

The chief member of the undercarriage is the coupling pole, which links front and back axles. Heavy timbers, called bolsters, are located above both axles, and between the front bolster and body frame is the pillow.

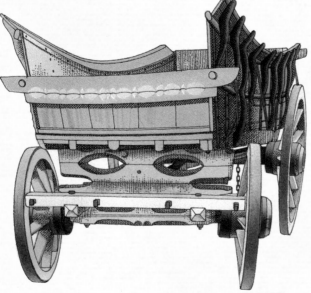

THE SUFFOLK WAGON was built to carry three or four tons of cereal across flat country. Huge wheels (six feet in diameter at the rear) made traction easy despite the weight of the wagon itself. It is a fine example of the *box wagon* – the square, high-sided vehicles favoured in the east of England. This example has planked sides and panelled ends, or *front board* and *tail board* as they are known. The high-sided body adds to the massive quality of the wagon but as you study the nature of construction through the body framework and undercarriage you will see that all of the timbers are weighty. The *cross-bar*, for example, the main timber of the body framework, is about 10 inches deep! Smaller and lighter wagons, particularly the *bow wagons* of the Western counties (see the Oxfordshire wagon overleaf), would have lighter timbers and more of them, in a more complicated arrangement. The red colour of the undercarriage and wheels is common to all wagons that you might see. The blue of the body is traditional to most East Anglian wagons.

OXFORDSHIRE BOW WAGON

BOW AND HAY WAGONS AND MUCK CART
The English bow wagon was generally smaller and shallower in the body than the box wagon, with sideboards shaped over the rear wheels. Ladder-sided wagons are still a common sight in much of rural Europe, while the tip cart or Scotch cart was the last horse-drawn farm vehicle seen regularly in England.

TIPPING MUCK CART

FRENCH LADDER-SIDED WAGON

build a wagon and in the 1930s he would have charged about £30 for his finished work, painted and standing in all its glory.

WAINS

Such a wagon was for load carrying – as much as four tons of corn. It would have massive wooden axles sawn out and hewn to a hair's breadth accuracy to complement the complexities of the wheel geometry. The axle arms would be made with a deliberate forward cant (*forehung*) so that the wheels ran very slightly together. This counteracted the tendency for the *dished* and *dipped* wheel to run off its axle.

The front axle was made to turn in a framework about the *king pin* – a central iron post. How much it turned is one of the features that points out the origins of a wagon. There are *quarter-lock* wagons, in which the front wheels can only turn as far as the straight sides of the wagon. Then there are *half-lock* wagons, where the body of the wagon has been given a *waist*, a recess on each side into which the front wheels can turn. With *three-quarter lock* wagons, the front wheels can be turned underneath the body of the wagon as far as the *coupling pole* (the main member that joins the front and rear axles). Finally, the *full-lock* wagon has front wheels small enough to turn right under the wagon floor. Generally, the wagons with more lock were made in

hillier areas where the wagon was likely to encounter restricted and twisty routes.

There was also a great variety in the sorts of wagon body that sat on the undercarriage. Some were square and business-like, such as the Suffolk wagon, others had curves like Rubenesque women, such as the wagons from Devon and Somerset. The plainer sorts were broadly termed *box wagons*, whereas curved ones were called *bow wagons*. You could fit *ladders* or *gates* front and rear, which were frameworks that overhung the ends of the wagon to give it more carrying capacity. Side rails, called *raves*, *lades*, *raths*, *shelvings* or *surboards* (there are almost as many local words for the same part of a wagon as there are types of wagon) similarly increased the capacity widthways.

The finished wagon would have chamfers cut from most of its edges, not just for decoration (and some were very elaborate) but to lighten the construction. Paint was a protection that it paid farmers to preserve. Every part from undercarriage to raves was painted in colours traditional to the area. Blue above with red for the wheels and undercarriage was fairly common. And painting, fine craftsmanship with plenty of *stringing and lining* (the painting of fine lines along the body of the wagon) brings to mind the skills of Colm Breen, a wheelwright and coachbuilding friend of mine who is a master with the brush.

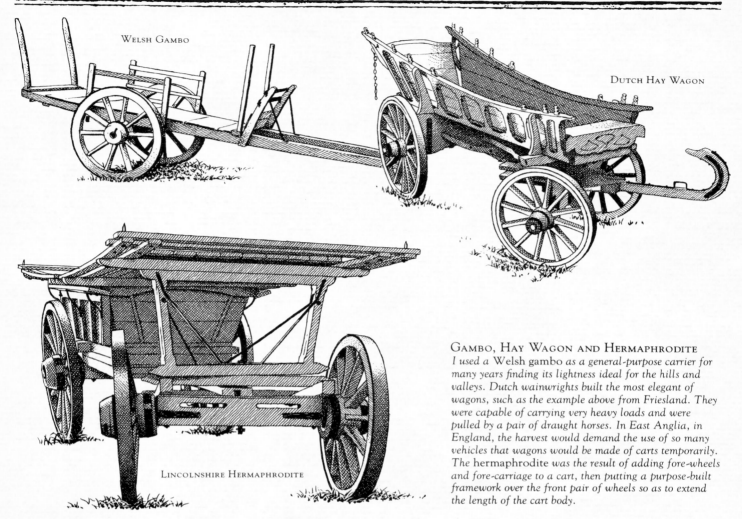

WELSH GAMBO

DUTCH HAY WAGON

LINCOLNSHIRE HERMAPHRODITE

GAMBO, HAY WAGON AND HERMAPHRODITE
I used a Welsh gambo as a general-purpose carrier for many years finding its lightness ideal for the hills and valleys. Dutch wainwrights built the most elegant of wagons, such as the example above from Friesland. They were capable of carrying very heavy loads and were pulled by a pair of draught horses. In East Anglia, in England, the harvest would demand the use of so many vehicles that wagons would be made of carts temporarily. The hermaphrodite was the result of adding fore-wheels and fore-carriage to a cart, then putting a purpose-built framework over the front pair of wheels so as to extend the length of the cart body.

I have talked so far of the truly forgotten art of wainwrighting, but Colm's craft is making the most exquisite of sprung vehicles, made for those who want the real joy of being pulled by horse today (and their numbers are swelling).

Colm Breen is a dapper man, smallish but obviously physically very tough, generally smiling or laughing, taking his trade so lightly that it is difficult to extract information from him: he prefers to tell funny stories of which he has a limitless fund.

ALADDIN'S CAVE
Wandering around Colm Breen's large workshop is like wandering in some strange Aladdin's cave. The bodies of the carts and carriages are so varied that it is impossible to describe them. There is a very pretty little *dog cart* there that has just been built. In days of old there was a box under the driver's seat for the carrying of terriers to the hunt. This box had louvres, or ventilation slits, in its side. Colm now paints

WAGON ACCESSORIES
You would find a *rope roller* at the rear of a wagon. When loading you would pass the binding ropes through the roller and tighten it with levers. Both the *drop chain* and *dog stick* stopped a wagon rolling.

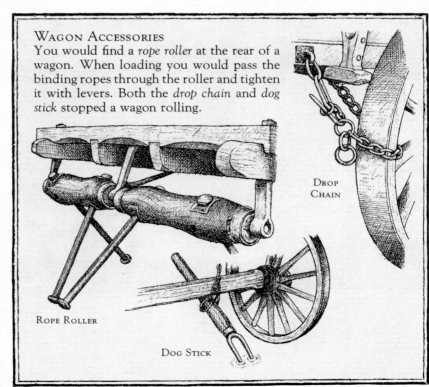

DROP CHAIN

ROPE ROLLER

DOG STICK

WAGONS FOR EVERYDAY USE

It is very easy to forget just how complete and how recent was the demise of horse-drawn transport. I can remember when elegant sprung wagons were the most common of everyday sights. These two examples are from the United States. You can tell this from the style of springing. Single elliptical springs set transversely, along the line of the axles, are an American practice which was never popular in the United Kingdom.

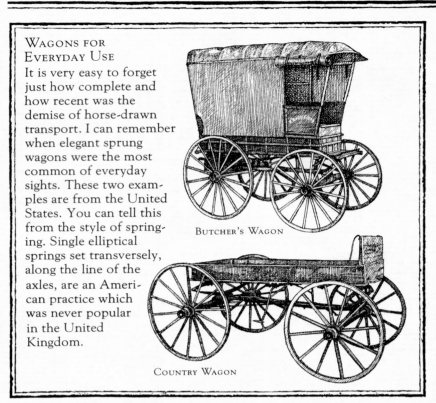

BUTCHER'S WAGON

COUNTRY WAGON

louvres on the sides of the seat box, although no dogs are ever kept there any more.

The curved panels, of which so many small cars and larger vehicles too are made, were moulded in steamed ash. This was a very specialized calling and there were large factories which did nothing else. The curved sheets had to be seasoned, after bending while quite green, for several years and so these big bending factories had piles and piles of them, of all shapes and sizes, stuck away to season. No ordinary coach-builder made his own. Colm still uses existing ones of which there are plenty, but when the crunch comes, he will have to start making his own again.

The *shafts*, which are linked to the horse's harness, often used to be of lance wood (which was a wood of Asian derivation from which the weapons of – for example – the Bengal Lancers were made) but now, with this unobtainable, they are of ash. They can be steamed to shape, but often a composite construction is used: sections of wood glued together, for

CONESTOGA WAGON
The Conestoga wagon was a mighty cargo carrier that once plied the freight routes of the Eastern seaboard of the United States. It was named after the Conestoga Valley in Lancaster County, Pennsylvania. The deep sides are reminiscent of the English box wagon, but this was a giant, to be pulled by a whole team of horses, oxen or mules.

FEED BOX

IRON HASP

CONSTRUCTION
The Conestoga wagon combines very high ground clearance with simple, strong running gear.

FINE FINISH
Despite the size of the Conestogas, the craftsmen who built them paid great attention to detail and the finish of their wagons. There would be a feed box at the rear of the wagon and a tool box with finely wrought iron fittings.

TOOL BOX LID

WAGONETTE

BROUGHAM

COACH BUILDING

I came across the two carriages shown here in the workshops of an Irish master coachbuilder. His business encompasses fine carpentry, elegant ironwork, patent wheel hubs, opulent upholstery and paintwork with a finish like glass. Some of his customers want him to refurbish carriages like the enclosed brougham, *which was once one of the most common vehicles about town, while others want him to build new vehicles like the* wagonette *for the now-popular sport of driving teams of horses. A few, like myself, want him to build vehicles for the sheer joy of using them.*

strength. Lance wood was fine and springy when it was new but Colm showed me some old broken lance wood shafts: they splinter into needle-sharp points which can go right through the side of a horse.

The *perch* (the main longitudinal member that underlies a carriage), *bolsters* (transverse members) and all such timbers are made of straight-grained heart-of-oak. Colm finds all the timber he needs of any sort within a few miles of Enniscorthy in Ireland.

Colm still trades with tinkers sometimes (see p.83). He still occasionally paints their traditional barrel-topped living wagons. He told me that a tinker in a remote part of Ireland would hand his wagon over to another man who would pay him the price of the wagon and drive it as far as, say, Dublin. At Dublin he might hand it over to a third party who would have to pay him for it. This man would bring it to Colm who would paint it. The man would then collect it, drive it back to the man in Dublin who would pay him for it (plus a commission for doing the job). That man would in turn get his money back, plus a commission. Nobody had to trust anybody that way!

In coachbuilding you could never be bored, because there is such a great variety of jobs to be done. As Colm himself told me, a coachbuilder has to be master of several trades: wood turner, wheelwright,

blacksmith, carpenter, upholsterer and painter. And the last of these trades is the peak of the art of the brush, for the delicate *lining-out* performed by coach painters is a miracle of skill which involves putting thin, razor-sharp lines of paint along parts of the carriage and the spokes of the wheels.

He told me that some Germans came over to take delivery of some carriages that he had built and he entertained them – and they entertained him – exceedingly convivially. The vehicles had to be loaded on lorries at six o'clock the next morning. At half past two in the morning, after they had certainly each consumed a bottle of whiskey, Colm told them that he had got to leave them – he still had two hours work to do on the carriages. He went down to the factory and finished lining-out. The paint he used was quick drying and when the lorry came, an hour and a half after he had finished this careful and skilful operation, they could be loaded straight into the lorry and they caught the boat for the continent. If that is not professionalism I don't know what is!

I first went to see Colm Breen because I am thinking seriously of going in for horse transport again. I have travelled across southern England in a *governess car* and know the joys of driving horses for pleasure. I want Colm to build me a fine *gig* one day, although he does not know it yet.

111

SLED MAKING

I N TIMES BEFORE WHEELED VEHICLES became the universal form of transport, sleds, sleighs or sledges (the names are interchangeable) provided the best method of moving heavy loads. To the present day there are a number of terrains in which the wheel is almost useless, and the sled comes into its own, whether there is snow on the ground or not.

In very hilly areas, for example, sleds are ideal. The reason for this is that a horse, or any other draught animal, does not enjoy being pushed from behind and it is only a very steady horse that will hold back the weight of a laden cart, with no brake to its wheels, down a steep hill.

SIMPLE SLEDS

On my own farm in Wales I used my *gambo* – a fine cart of local design with no brake – wherever I could, but on the steepest fields I preferred to use a sled that I knocked up, quite simply, from oak and ash I cut on the farm. This sort of sled will not slide downhill without a little pulling and, therefore, the horse is not worried by having to hold it back. I did not even use shafts with it: it was simply pulled by *trace chains* attached to the horse's collar.

A sled very like mine is shown opposite – its basis is a forked branch stripped of its bark and protruding branches, and fitted with a platform of planks. Such sleds are common throughout northern Europe and parts of Africa.

HARVEST SLED CONSTRUCTION

Throughout mid and north Wales sleds, like the one shown opposite top, are built for use at harvest time. They consist of two long side pieces of solid timber, measuring up to a couple of yards in length, morticed together with eight or more cross members. Front and back are tail ladders to hold the bails in place, each ladder up to a yard high with horizontal rails. Side rails run the

TYPES OF RUNNER
Sled runners can be effective on mud and grass as well as on snow and ice, the basic requirement being a curved-up front achieved by steaming in the case of wooden runners. A broad section is best over soft mud or snow, but thinner iron-faced runners are much better for ice.

SAPLING

HALF-ROUND RIVEN POLE

BEECH SAPLING RUNNER ON HICKORY

IRON RUNNER ON ASH

MUDFLAT TRANSPORT
On the vast mudflats off the coasts of South Wales and Cumbria, a rare breed of fisherman exists. He follows the tide out on to the wet mud using a strange sled to support himself and the cockles he rakes. He half lays over the sled and propels himself with his feet.

length of the sled and are pegged at each end to the tail ladders and supported with vertical spindles. These sleds are tilted forward on their runners, making the sled a deadweight which will not slide down a slope unless pulled. But in some places the steep mountainsides defy even the best built of sleds to remain still, so two horses are used – one to pull from the front, and the other to act as a brake at the back.

WHEELED SLED COMBINATIONS

Welsh farmers have always made use of wheels as well as runners, ingeniously combining the two to produce a vehicle with wheels behind and sled runners in front. This gives a fairly easy pull uphill or on level ground but, with the weight thrown forward when coming downhill, the runners slow the wagon and spare the horse.

Sleds are particularly suitable when loads have to be brought downhill but no load taken up again. It is a very common sight in the Alps to see a farmer or his wife coming downhill with a small, hand-pulled sled, called in the French-speaking part of Switzerland a *luge*, with one or two churns of milk on it. The churns will be empty on the way back so that the sled will not be too heavy to pull. Such sleds work very well on snow as well as on the bare grass in summer.

UNUSUAL MUD SHOES

A specialized use of runners, as shoes, is on tidal mud. When I was a boy I used to shoot duck among the tidal backwaters of estuaries on the east coast of England. Some of the mud was so soft that it was dangerous to go out on it in our usual waders. We used to construct mud shoes called *plashers*, which we laced to our boots. Some people made them out of old barrel staves. You could, if you were used to it, walk about on the softest mud with these; if you were not you could go sprawling.

THE DRAG

Drags or drogues are slip-on runners that were carried chained to the back of wagons and were slid under the rear wheels for going downhill. They converted the rear wheels into a pair of runners and saved the horse.

TYPES OF SLED

Sleds are constructed in many ways because of the very different uses to which they are put, and the different craft traditions they come from. The "working" sleds, used on the land for carrying of all sorts, would either come from the wainwright's shop or be constructed by the farmer himself. The elegant ice sleds that glide across the snow scenes painted by the Dutch masters of the seventeenth and eighteenth centuries are beautiful examples of the blacksmith's art.

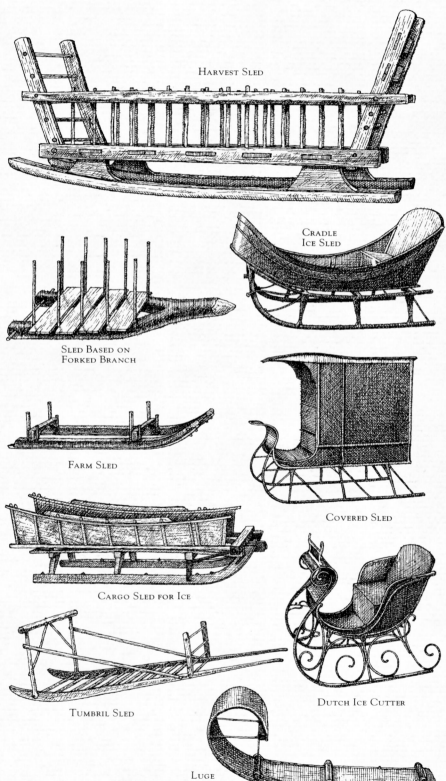

HARVEST SLED

CRADLE ICE SLED

SLED BASED ON FORKED BRANCH

FARM SLED

COVERED SLED

CARGO SLED FOR ICE

TUMBRIL SLED

DUTCH ICE CUTTER

LUGE

BOATBUILDING

HE FIRST BOAT I COMMISSIONED TO be built in England was a 14-foot sailing dinghy. Mr Harry King was a magnificent-looking old gentleman and was known to be by far the best boat builder on the east coast of England and I had to woo him like the suitor of a particularly wealthy princess. At first he would not even speak to me, but I managed to get him round in the end and he built me a beautiful boat in which I sailed all over the Thames estuary, up to Lowestoft and I would have sailed to Holland if I had had the time.

The boat was *clinker* built, meaning the planks (or *strakes* as they are called) of her hull overlapped each other, as did the planks of Viking boats. The method of construction was to lay the strakes first, fixing them together with copper rivets, then to add the *frames* (what landlubbers call ribs) later. The shape of the strakes determined the final shape of the vessel and these were softened in a steam-chest until they could be bent to the shape that Harry King knew instinctively. The thin rock-elm frames were also steamed and then bent into place within the hull and riveted.

CARVEL-BUILT BOATS

There is another ancient wooden boat building technique which is the opposite of clinker building. With *carvel*-built boats the frames are built first and the strakes fastened to them. The strakes do not overlap, as in clinker construction, but are butted together edge-to-edge.

If you are at all interested in boats (and here I must admit to one of my life's passions) you will notice that every type of waterway or coastline has produced its own ideal vessels, whether for fishing or cargo. Most of the larger boats are carvel built.

On coming to live by a river in Ireland I found a small local, carvel-built boat called a *prong* (see p.117) very useful. She has an exactly semi-circular section and curves up to both stem and stern. Thick strakes of pine are simply nailed edge-to-edge on to heavy semi-circular frames made by bolting several pieces of curved wood together. Now the river by which I live is very tidal and has sloping mud banks at low water. When my prong is left by the high tide at

THE BOATBUILDER'S YARD

To wander into a boatyard where wooden boats are still made is a rare experience today. Most boatbuilding is now a matter of fibreglass and ferro-concrete. But you might still find a workshop, or the corner of a bigger yard, where traditional vessels are being made in wood – and these are likely to be small and clinker-built. The boat in the foreground of this scene is such an example and shows the overlapping strakes, or planks, all copper-riveted together. The wooden boatbuilder is both the master of the wood he cuts and bends to the subtlest of lines, and a man of the sea, who knows how to make an efficient and sea-worthy vessel that will last.

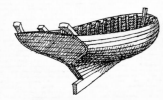

BUILDING DREOILIN
My boat Dreoilin is half-decked, 25 feet long, with a wide beam (extreme breadth) at the water level and a steeply raking stern. In the method of building employed – carvel construction – the frames, or ribs, are built first and the strakes, or planks, are fitted on to them, butting together.

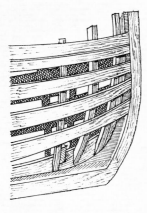

PLANKING THE HULL
The builder of Dreoilin employed the French method of planking the hull, fitting each alternate strake to the frames and then filling in the gaps. Each strake must be individually sawn to the correct curve and flare, and must fit its neighbouring strakes exactly.

the top of this mud I can board her, let the *painter* (mooring rope) go, and she will toboggan down the mud at high speed and hit the water with a splash! It is possible, when coming in at low tide, to haul her up the mud using a capstan. You could not do these things with a flat bottomed boat – nor with a keel boat: both would stick.

Useful as this little boat has proved, my love of boats has since been directed towards the Galway hooker family of boats. The Galway hooker is quite a large carvel-built vessel, up to 40 feet long. It is half-decked (with a decked-over fore-deck but open aft) and cutter-rigged (with one mast with fore and aft sails). These boats were used, and some still are, to carry cargo between the mainland of Ireland and the islands off the west coast, notably the three Aran Islands. They also double as fishing boats. There are two smaller versions of the hooker. The smaller is the *puchan*, a mere sliver of a boat of 16 to 18 feet, but still capable of sailing the Atlantic billows. Between the puchan and the hooker is the *gleoiteog*, which is between 23 and 28 feet.

THE GLEOITEOG

Like the other two, the *gleoiteog* is half-decked. There is room under the fore-deck for two bunks in which her crew can sleep. The open aft of the *gleoiteog* is traditionally for the easy loading of turf (peat) to be carried to the turfless islands, and cattle to be carried back.

One day while I was thinking on these matters and wishing that I had the money to buy a *gleoiteog*, I saw a young man with a

pack on his back approaching my home. His introduction, believe it or not, consisted of:

"I have read your book about sailing the north German coast and I am going to build you a boat."

"What sort of a boat?"

"A *gleoiteog*."

"I have no money, no money at all," I said.

"I still build you a boat" he insisted.

And he did. When I first saw his work I realized that this determined stranger was a superb boat builder in the traditional style – one of the few remaining who are schooled in the art of building in wood.

Reiner Schlimmer bound himself apprentice for three and a half years to a boat yard in northern Germany and learned how to build traditional wooden fishing boats. Having served his time, he built himself a yacht on Norwegian fishing boat lines, and sailed off to Ireland.

DESIGNING THE BOAT

Building a new boat on traditional lines is a matter of copying the lines of the best examples of the type. Reiner had to draw the lines of the boat and then to make *patterns*, or templates, of each of the frames. He knew of an existing *gleoiteog*, noted for speed and seaworthiness, and took the lines of my boat from this.

Reiner then made the patterns from his drawings, cutting them out of hardboard. The 25-foot hull would have 13 frames and each would be of a completely different shape.

PRIMITIVE BOATS

MY INTEREST IN TRADITIONAL BOATS HAS been fuelled throughout the world. When I went to Africa I soon became acquainted with dugout canoes. The finest ones that I came across were those made on the Upper Zambezi by the Balozi people. Called *makoros*, they are slender and graceful, square in section, rising slightly to both stern and bow, and propelled by standing up in the stern and using a very long paddle. I owned one and believe I was one of the few Europeans to master the rather delicate balancing act involved. When mastering it I had the strong incentive of knowing that the Upper Zambezi is full of crocodiles.

The makoro is made with an adze, hollowing out a suitable tree and setting light to it to help the process along. The builders are adept at getting the hull very thin without breaking through to the outside.

On the Zambezi I was introduced to another kind of craft, known locally as *barges*. These craft are completely flat-bottomed, with no keel, the sides and bottom made of thick regular planks hammered over a simple framework. The ends come up at a slight angle and it is on these ends that the paddlers stand.

When in India, I voyaged in the beautiful *wallam* (below), the workhorse of the Malabar coast. Built in much the same way as the Zambezi barges, they have curved *chines* (the angles where the bottom meets the sides of a boat) and beautiful stern-post and stem-heads.

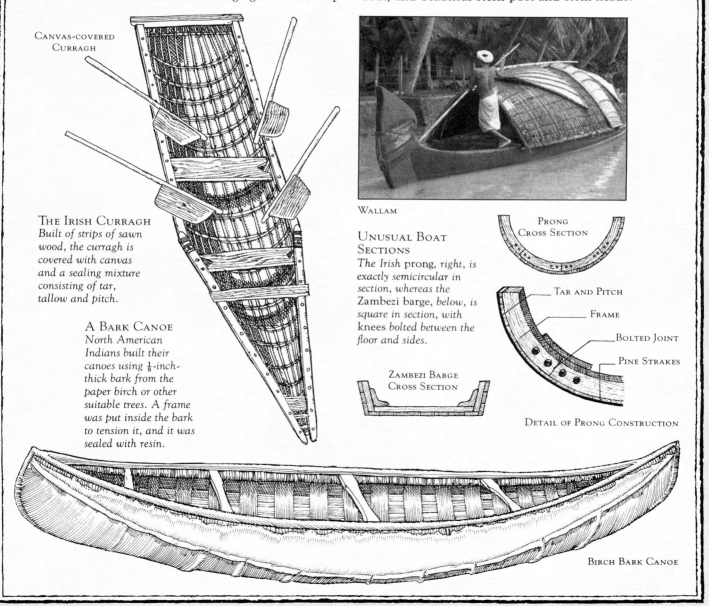

CANVAS-COVERED CURRAGH

THE IRISH CURRAGH
Built of strips of sawn wood, the curragh is covered with canvas and a sealing mixture consisting of tar, tallow and pitch.

A BARK CANOE
North American Indians built their canoes using $\frac{1}{8}$-inch-thick bark from the paper birch or other suitable trees. A frame was put inside the bark to tension it, and it was sealed with resin.

WALLAM

UNUSUAL BOAT SECTIONS
The Irish prong, right, is exactly semicircular in section, whereas the Zambezi barge, below, is square in section, with knees bolted between the floor and sides.

ZAMBEZI BARGE CROSS SECTION

PRONG CROSS SECTION

TAR AND PITCH
FRAME
BOLTED JOINT
PINE STRAKES

DETAIL OF PRONG CONSTRUCTION

BIRCH BARK CANOE

DEADWOOD   DEEPLY-MORTICED FLOOR TIMBER

STERN POST

CONSTRUCTING THE FRAME

Once the keel of Dreoilin was laid down, work started on constructing the frames of the boat. Each frame consisted of five pieces of wood, the middle piece, or floor timber, lying directly on top of the keel and jointed to it with a deep mortice. To hold each frame firm until the planking was applied, a donkey, made from a rough larch pole, was rigged up in the rafters of the shed, parallel to the keel. Slats of rough deal were attached to the donkey and each of the frames in turn.

CHOOSING TIMBER

Ordering timber is a very important step in wooden boatbuilding and in itself a forgotten art. Reiner's first requirement was for oak and very special oak at that. Most of the wood in a boat is curved and, while you can bend oak after steaming, it is impossible to bend very heavy pieces and over-bending weakens lighter pieces. So ship builders have always valued *grown crooks* – oak that has grown crooked. One of the reasons why so many park trees were planted in England and Ireland in days gone by is because an oak growing crowded in a forest will grow up straight and clean with few of the treasured crooks. An oak growing free in a park sends out huge branches and these twist about and have plenty of crooks in them. There are very few boat builders left who can select such crooked pieces of timber that can be sawn out into the required shape with the grain running along the curve of the wood.

Larch for the planking had to be straight-grained but it also had to be in long pieces and at least one and a half inches thick.

In addition to the frame members, there was timber to find for the stem post, the false stem, which is peculiar to hooker-type vessels, the apron, or dead wood, and the massive stern post (see the diagram above right). Most boats of this size have a stern post made of several pieces of wood scarfed together. Reiner insisted on one piece with the grain running true through it. Nor was the keel easy to find. Again, the general practice is to scarf two or more pieces of wood together, but Reiner looked until he found one piece that was straight-grained,

three inches wide, 10 inches deep and 20 feet long. It had a very slight bend in it but Reiner corrected this by hauling it straight by tackles and driving posts each side of it to hold it as it was *laid*, or set in position.

JOINING THE FRAMES TO THE KEEL

Reiner lashed a rough larch pole in the rafters of the boat shed above and parallel to the keel and called it the *donkey*. As each frame was built up of its five curved timbers, it was connected to the donkey by two slats of rough deal.

He made the floor timber (the bottommost member of the five pieces forming each frame) very deep, so that he was able to cut a deep notch, or mortice, in it to engage the keel. This is by no means common practice: many builders merely lay the timber on top of the keel and bolt it.

SETTING THE SHEER OF THE BOAT

The keel had been purposely laid on a slight slope, raking downwards aft, while

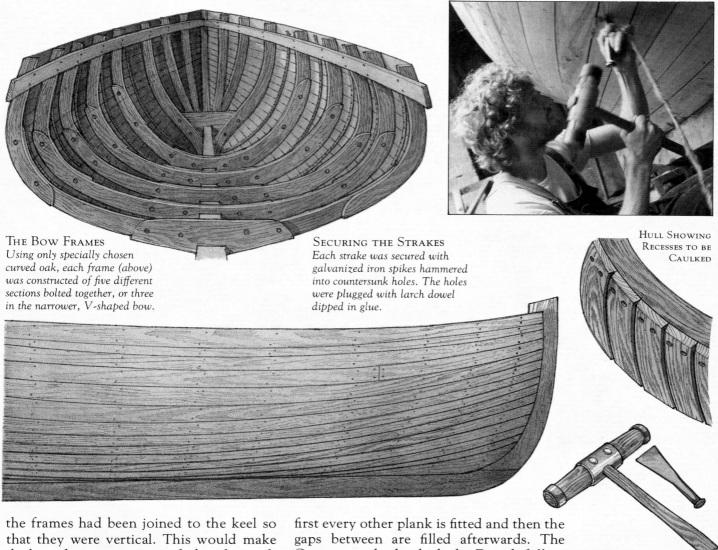

THE BOW FRAMES
Using only specially chosen curved oak, each frame (above) was constructed of five different sections bolted together, or three in the narrower, V-shaped bow.

SECURING THE STRAKES
Each strake was secured with galvanized iron spikes hammered into countersunk holes. The holes were plugged with larch dowel dipped in glue.

HULL SHOWING RECESSES TO BE CAULKED

CAULKING IRON AND MALLET

the frames had been joined to the keel so that they were vertical. This would make the boat draw more water aft than forward. He made a spline of very thin deal, perhaps slightly longer than the length of the boat. This he tacked along the outside top edge of all the frames. The master boat builder can stand back and look at this spline and adjust it by eye until he has created the sweet, sheer line of the boat – the line that the planking of the side of the hull will follow. This is one of the operations that demands that the builder be not only a craftsman but an artist. By measuring from the correctly positioned spline, he marked how much should be cut from each frame top to make it the right height to initiate that beautiful sheer, and then the outside edge of each frame to give the necessary bevels for a snug fit to the curving planks.

PLANKING UP

Reiner, being German, planked up according to the French method. In this method,

first every other plank is fitted and then the gaps between are filled afterwards. The German method, which the French follow of course, is to start at the bottom and work upwards leaving no gaps to be filled. Why it is that the Germans use the French method and the French the German, I have no idea.

Planking up is not just a matter of banging straight planks on to the waiting frames. Each plank has a flare – it has to be sawn into a curve and the curve must be exactly right. Each plank is quite different from its neighbours and before being fitted it is put in the steam-chest. The nails used to hold the plank initially are temporary. The permanent fastenings are galvanized iron spikes, heavily countersunk into holes drilled deep into the planking so that the outside of the hull can be planed.

Reiner turned a thousand little plugs from offcuts of larch planks. These were dipped in glue and driven into the holes to protect the iron spikes from corrosion.

CAULKING THE HULL
Since the hull of Dreoilin is curved, only the inner edges of each plank butt together, leaving V-shaped recesses between the planks on the outside of the hull. These gaps had to be caulked with oakum – a teased out hemp rope – banged in hard with a caulking iron and mallet. When the vessel was put in the water, all the planking swelled, making the caulked joints even tighter. My painstaking boat builder had to do this laborious job by hand – and often in the most uncomfortable of positions.

Some boats and ships are copper fastened. Copper practically never corrodes but it is very expensive and nothing like as strong as iron. A boat builder never mixes copper and iron as the two metals set up an electrolytic reaction and corrode each other. Most working ships are iron fastened and, if the iron is galvanized and protected, it should last for at least a century. I know a sailing barge from the east coast of England that is 180 years old and her iron fastenings are still sound. The fittings are, however, of wrought iron, which is very long lasting.

With alternate planks fitted, Reiner was left with the small task of fitting, and fitting absolutely exactly, the remaining planks to fill the gaps. He made more thin, flexible splines of wood and pinned them between the planks already attached. He then worked along each spline from stem to stern, attaching little pieces of wood to the

spline at right angles and exactly fitting the gap. They were templates for the cutting of the intermediary planks.

LAST CONSIDERATIONS

When the planking up was completed, Reiner had the laborious job of *caulking* to do, filling up the U-shaped recesses between the planks with hemp. He then went to the additional trouble of fitting steam-bent oak frames between the grown-oak frames for extra strength.

Two very heavy, horizontal *knees*, or supports, fitted on each side of the boat between midships and the stern (the quarter) further strengthen the aft section.

Finishing of such boats includes giving the inside of the hull a few coats of paint above the bottom boards and a thick coat of tar below them. The outside of the hull is heavily tarred, except for the rubbing strake which will be painted white.

When I first visited the shed where Reiner was starting work, a wren was nesting in the rafters. My *gleoiteog* is now called *Dreoilin*, which is Irish for wren.

THE COBLE

Dreoilin is not the first of my boat-building dreams come true. Some years ago now, when I lived near the east coast of England, I went to Filey, in Yorkshire, and saw a fleet of open boats running in with a strong wind behind them and a big sea. There is no harbour there and just before they hit the beach they swung round and faced the curling breakers and came in stern-first! It was a most stirring and spectacular sight. Tractors were waiting for them on the beach and as soon as the boats had backed in far enough two-wheeled axles were pushed underneath them and these towed up the beach. I decided, willynilly, I had to have one. So I went to Amble, in Northumberland, and ordered one to be built. I named her *Willynilly*. She was 20 feet long.

There being few harbours along the coble coast, cobles are designed so that they can fish straight off the beach. So they are launched bow first into the waves – their high sharp bows cutting the waves and their flat sterns sliding easily off the sand – and they are brought to land stern-first (if there is a big sea running at least) so that their deep fore keel cuts the sand and keeps them head-on to the breakers and their flat stern comes up easily on the sand. They are far and away the best beach boats in the world.

THE COBLE
The coble of the north-east coast of England is specially designed so that it can be launched and recovered from a beach. It is remarkable in being a keel boat forward and a flat-bottomed boat aft, the deep, pointed keel in the bow section of the boat giving way to a flat, shallow aft section. Steerage is maintained with a deep rudder that is hung from the transom, dropped into place once the boat is underway and removed just before the stern hits the beach. The peculiar shape of the boat makes it an ideal fishing boat for an area without many natural harbours. The scene below, at Whitby, in Yorkshire, shows two cobles, the one on the right being a 17-foot sailing version.

CORACLE MAKING

THE FIRST TIME I ENCOUNTERED those ancient, canvas-covered boats called coracles, I was cruising down the River Severn in a pleasure craft, and had reached Ironbridge. There I met Mr Harry Rodgers, who was the last working coracle builder and fisherman left on the Severn. He found time to show me how his coracle was made and when I later lived in Wales I learned about the *curachs*, as coracles are known in Welsh, in use on the River Teifi, and even rowed one.

A Teifi coracle is made with a framework of nine riven ash rods 6 feet 8 inches long, crossed by nine other rods 5 feet 3 inches long. Each rod is about an inch wide and a quarter of an inch thick. Once the rods have been soaked in the river for about a week to make them pliable, they are woven into a framework. This is done in two ways, either by sticking the rods into the ground and as the frame is built up bending them over with heavy weights to achieve the flat bottom of the craft, or by weaving the flat bottom first and then bending the rod ends up to make the sides. Either way the framework is then strengthened by weaving withies or hazel rods, basket-fashion, through the tops of the timbers, two of which are inserted through holes in a wooden cross piece that tensions the vessel and forms a seat. The framework is left to dry for a few days before being covered with calico or canvas which is then tarred. In days of old it would have been of ox or horse hide. The final touch is to fix a loop of hide, cord or canvas webbing so that the coracle can be carried on its owner's back.

The coracle is propelled by a small paddle worked over the bow of the vessel with a twisting motion that draws the boat forward. This only takes one hand, leaving the other free to work a fishing net. Coraclemen generally fish with the current, and get out and walk rather than row upstream.

In 1977 I helped organize an expedition by the coracle fishermen of the River Teifi to Westminster to lobby MPs about a bill proposing to outlaw coracle fishing. A fleet of four coracles paddled up the Thames and in our muddy Wellington boots we all fetched up in due course in the bar of the House of Lords where we were entertained in a most lordly manner. Nothing, unfortunately, came of our expedition, and I suspect that I will never again be invited to enter that noble establishment.

TYPES OF CORACLE
The size and design of the sturdy Ironbridge *or* Severn *coracle was governed by the ox or cow hide used to cover it. Welsh coracles like the* Llangollen *and* Teifi *coracles were more primitive in construction, their sides pulled in over the seat to allow clearance for a paddle. Wicker boats were made like baskets, a central seat strengthening the framework.*

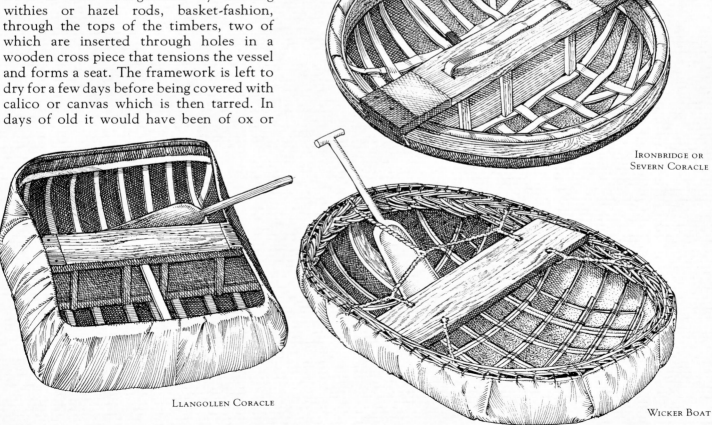

IRONBRIDGE OR
SEVERN CORACLE

LLANGOLLEN CORACLE

WICKER BOAT

SAIL MAKING

Y BOAT DREOILIN SETS A BASIC *gaff* rig, that is one small sail in front of the mast and a larger one behind, hung from an angled spar called the gaff. To equip her wardrobe properly, I required a basic suit of sails consisting of a *mainsail* (the larger sail), *foresail* or *staysail* (the smaller), a *working jib* and a *storm jib* (varieties of foresail).

Searching for a sail maker near to where I live in Ireland, I discovered Mr Gerard Downer of Dunlaoire. I soon decided that he must know something about sail making because his great-grandfather was a sail maker on the Isle of Wight, his grandfather had migrated to King's Town (as Dunlaoire was then called) and set up his business there, his father carried it on, he took over from his father, and his son now works with him. He is the sort of sail maker who sails aboard the vessels which set his sails so that he can watch and evaluate their performance in action.

Mr Downer showed great patience and considerable wisdom in the somewhat protracted talks about what sort of sails he was going to make for me. I tried hard to persuade him to make my sails of linen, which modern sailors now damn, even though their forebears, including Nelson, managed perfectly well with it for hundreds of years. But linen does stretch a little when it's new, and unless stowed away completely dry it will rot. Synthetics, on the other hand, all eventually degrade in sunlight, which flax does not.

Anyway, after some correspondence, linen proved too hard to get, so we had to compromise with a cloth that mixes flax with some synthetic substance, but woven in such a way that it looks like and feels like genuine linen. Sailcloth rolls are called *bolts*.

Mr Downer kindly let me watch him during the more crucial operations of making the mainsail. The time-honoured names for parts of a sail are shown in the daigram of Dreoilin's sails, right. The mainsail was to have an 11-foot *head*, a 21-foot *leech*, a 10-foot *luff* and a 14-foot *foot*, a total of 168 square feet. First, he chalked out the shape of the sail on the lovely polished wooden floor of his sail loft. This was a job requiring not only experience but considerable mathematical skill, for it is vital that the mainsail has an efficient aerodynamic shape when it is full of wind.

He then unrolled the cloth so as to cover the shape chalked on the floor. The sail was to be vertically cut, the panels of cloth running parallel to the leech. Starting from the leech itself, he rolled out his bolt of cloth, cut the length off quickly with a sharp knife, then rolled out the next strip, and so on until he came to the *tack* of the sail. All these strips overlapped the pattern at both ends and each other by a few inches.

Then came the job of *scribing* the sail, making chalk marks on it, much as a tailor might on a suit, as a guide to the two busy women who sat behind industrial sewing machines at the end of the loft. Now, working very quickly and entirely by eye, he chalked in *swellings*, or dart lines, up to two feet long at both head and foot of the sail. The object of these darts is to provide a slight belly to the sail, for a flat sail obtains less power from the wind.

The strips of sail were then machine-sewn together. The machinist overlapped the cloths by an inch or two and sewed both edges of the overlaps, and then put in a

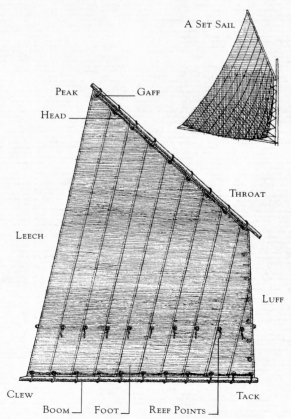

A SET SAIL

PEAK — GAFF

HEAD

THROAT

LEECH

LUFF

CLEW
TACK
BOOM FOOT REEF POINTS

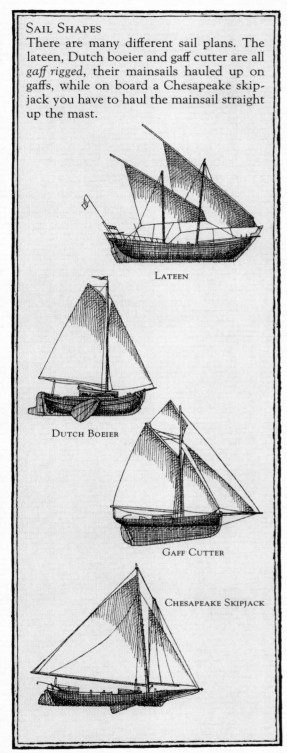

third row of stitching right down the middle. The sail was then laid out again on the floor, and Mr Downer began the task of scribing the edges of the sail. Starting with the leech, he measured each of the four sides of the sail in turn, pulling the cloth tight as he did so by driving a *pricker*, a steel pin set in a handle, through each corner, spread-eagling the sail on the floor. Then he ran a thin line of string around all four prickers and chalked along the line. He then cut the surplus cloth off, leaving about six inches all round. The final shape of the sail was now apparent.

Next he marked out and fitted the *reef points*. *Reefing*, for those who may not know, is reducing the area of a sail which you do in a strong wind or a gale. The reef points, small pieces of cord hanging down from each side of the sail, are sewn across the sail in rows, and are used to tie the sail securely along the boom. Some sails have up to three rows of reefing points, and if you ever need to use the highest row, you shouldn't be out sailing in a wind that strong!

Next, by eye, he marked out on the *clew*, *tack*, *throat* and *peak* – the points and corners of the sail (see the diagram opposite again), where the layers of sail cloth reinforcings were to be sewn and where holes should be pierced in them. He stamped a *delring*, or metal eyelet, into the four holes and reinforced them further still with leather patches, for these important places take an enormous amount of strain. Lastly, he marked out where the lacing eyes were to be fitted along the foot, luff and head, through which passes the rope that attaches the sail to the spars, and turned his attention to the *bolt ropes* around the sail. A bolt rope is sewn along the foot and luff of the sail, giving it strength and protection from chaffing. The leech and head of the sail have doubled webbing tape sewn into them for additional reinforcement.

And that was how my mainsail was made. Made to last, by the look of it, for my lifetime and for many winter gales to come.

TOOLS OF THE TRADE
Once sails were stitched and finished entirely by hand, the sail maker using a needle and sealing palm wrapped around his hand. The serrated metal pad of the palm helped him push the needle through the tough sail cloth. Today all the sewing is done by machine, and almost the only work done by hand is the fitting of the eyelets, or thimbles. A spike is used to pierce the cloth, which is then shaped to size with a cutting knife. The two parts of the eyelet are placed either side of the sail on top of an eyelet block and jammed hard together using a fid and mallet.

ROPE MAKING

ROPE FROM STRAW
Ropes are made by twisting fibres together and the principle of this is no better shown than by watching a straw rope being made. This rope maker is twisting straw into the rope by hand as he walks away from a fixing point, which in this case is an improvised device using an old bicycle wheel.

WHEN I WAS A BOY I WORKED ON A farm in Essex for a summer. Old Bill Keeble, the foreman, called me to help him one day. He had with him a small instrument rather like a carpenter's brace that turned a hook – I later learned it was a *whimbel* (see p.54). Bill led the way to a straw stack, caught up a hank of straw in the hook and told me to start cranking and walking backwards. As I turned he kept catching more straw into the straw that was already twisted. In not many seconds we had quite a long rope; not very durable, but as long as it was not allowed to untwist, it was quite strong. Bill used it for tying down the thatch on corn ricks. The simple twisting of fibres in this way is the basis of all rope making. For a useful, long-lasting rope, however, you need to use a stronger fibre than straw.

The best rope-making material in the world is hemp. The rigging for Nelson's ships, and those of almost every other navy in the world, was made of hemp. It is very strong, long-lasting and does not chafe that easily. However, most governments forbid us from growing hemp in case we smoke it.

HOW TO SPIN YARNS
Ropes are made by twisting hemp *yarns* together. Hemp has to be *retted*, or rotted in water, and then *shived*, that is stripped of all its short fibres. A *spinster* (not necessarily an unmarried lady) then ties great bunches of the fibre to his waist, catches the ends on a turning hook, and walks backwards, paying out the fibre as he goes. The yarn produced is then hardened by twisting, *sized* by rubbing with a horsehair rubber, and then *laid*, or doubled back on itself.

OTHER ROPE-MAKING MATERIALS
Cotton is not as strong as hemp, nor as long-lasting or water resistant, but since it is far nicer to handle it is often used for sheets in dinghies and small boats. Other materials used for making rope include sisal, which was used for binder and bailer

twine until artificial fibres came in; jute, a hemp-like plant grown in Bengal, but much inferior to hemp; and manilla, which is grown in the Philippines and makes a fine rope. But unfortunately all of these are being superseded by artificial fibres, which, incidentally, do not last for ever either.

FROM YARN TO ROPE

Many English seaports once had their rope-walks – long areas of open ground used for laying out the individual yarns of a rope prior to twisting them together. Such walks would be at least 80 yards long and some up to 240 yards. Every 20 yards or so there would be a T-shaped post called a *beaver* or *skirder*, which had a row of upward-pointing pegs that kept the yarns from tangling.

At one end of the walk was the *jack* (below), with at least three revolving hooks all turned independently by one handle. At the other end was a swivelling hook fixed to a post on a trolley or a sled – the *traveller*. The yarn was looped from end to end of the walk round the single hook and each of the three hooks in turn, the maker walking miles in his effort to make a thick rope.

When the yarns were all in place, the rope maker's assistant cranked the hooks on the jack while he kept the groups of yarn separate using the *top* held close to the traveller. As the yarns twisted into *strands* they pulled the traveller towards the jack.

When the yarns were twisted so they were almost kinking, the rope maker fixed the traveller in place and the real magic started. He pushed the top towards the jack and the tension in the strands twisted them together behind the top in the opposite direction to the twist of the yarns. That is why rope does not unravel itself. A good maker knows how much tension to use.

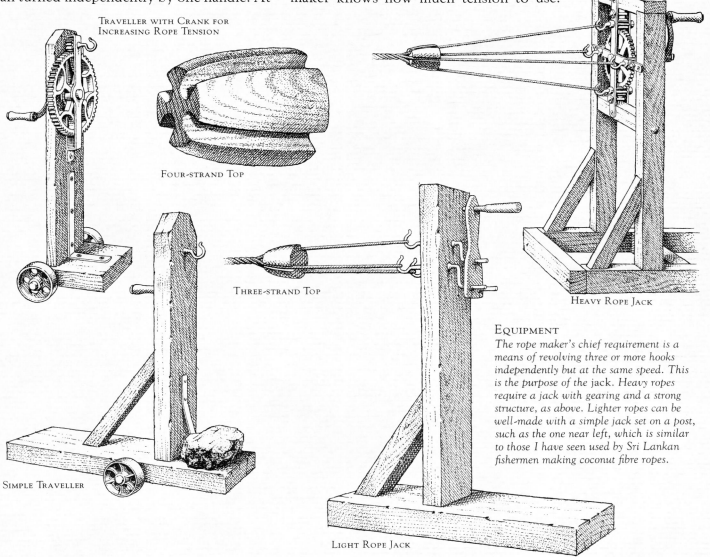

TRAVELLER WITH CRANK FOR INCREASING ROPE TENSION

FOUR-STRAND TOP

THREE-STRAND TOP

SIMPLE TRAVELLER

HEAVY ROPE JACK

LIGHT ROPE JACK

EQUIPMENT

The rope maker's chief requirement is a means of revolving three or more hooks independently but at the same speed. This is the purpose of the jack. Heavy ropes require a jack with gearing and a strong structure, as above. Lighter ropes can be well-made with a simple jack set on a post, such as the one near left, which is similar to those I have seen used by Sri Lankan fishermen making coconut fibre ropes.

NET MAKING

NETS ARE MADE FOR A THOUSAND different purposes to a thousand different designs. Yet all hand-made nets are made in much the same way, and the process itself, although very time consuming, is very simple. All you need is a head rope, tied up at a convenient working height and running the intended width of the net, plenty of twine and mastery of two knots – the *clove-hitch* and the *sheet bend*. Of course, there are refinements to learn, such as using a piece of wood to space the mesh consistently and making sure that every knot is tied to a similar tension, but the principle is easy.

The Netting Needle

To haul the whole length of twine through each loop of the mesh would be very cumbersome and would, I should imagine, drive the net maker mad. So the netting needle was invented. It is a small piece of wood or bone with a groove at one end and a tongue carved out in the middle of it. The needle is loaded by winding the twine around the groove and the tongue, and is quite easily passed through the mesh, making the knots as it goes, without tangling.

Nets for Trapping

Most common of the countryside trapping nets are ferreting or *purse nets*, which are small bags of netting placed over the mouths of rabbit holes before a ferret is sent down the burrow. The rabbit bolts and finds itself caught in the net. *Long nets* are set up on small stakes and then dropped on the rabbits as they move between their feeding ground and their burrows.

Fishing Nets

Most of the nets made in the world are made for catching fish. Needless to say, the variety of designs and uses are legion.

Nimble Fingers

I suspect that large nets are now made on sophisticated machines but it is comforting to recall that very large fishing nets can be made by hand. And where there is any need for subtle shaping or mending, the practised fingers of ladies, such as those below, are best.

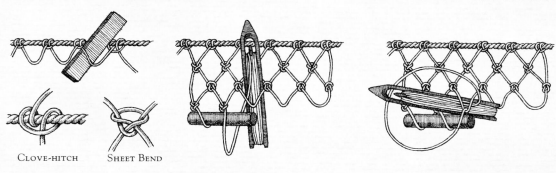

The twine is clove-hitched to the head rope using a spacer that gives half-size mesh. For the second and subsequent rows, you use a spacer twice the size and use sheet bends to join each loop of mesh. Once the net is underway, each sheet bend is made with swift loops of the needle.

CLOVE-HITCH   SHEET BEND

Gill or *tangle nets* are either fixed to a drifter, or float free in the sea, in which case they are better known as *drift nets*. They have been used for thousands of years to catch pelagic fish, those such as mackerel, herring and sea trout that swim close to the surface, ensnaring them by the gills as they try to swim through the mesh.

The salmon fishermen who fish the river in front of my house in Ireland, completely illegally I might add, use what they call *stake nets*. These are gill nets that have an anchor off-shore to hold them against the current, and a stake driven into the shore to hold them firm. Very light, almost invisible, synthetic twine, has revolutionized this sort of fishing, for the fish cannot see the net and can thus be caught in the day as well as at night.

A variation of this long, floating type of net is the *set net*, which is weighted at the bottom causing it to sink to the sea bed, and catch the deeper-swimming fish. Many small fishing boats work up to 10 miles of these nets, and the destruction to fishing grounds can be easily imagined.

TRAWL NETS

The next big group of nets are the *trawl nets*, which are bags of netting dragged through the sea, their mouths kept open by devices called *trawl heads* or *otter boards*, which act like kites in the water.

A variation on the trawl net is the ancient fine mesh *stow net*. It is fastened to a stationary boat in a tideway, and the fish are driven in by the incoming tide. Smaller versions are used in creeks and small rivers where they are fastened to each bank to catch whatever the tide can offer.

SEINE NETS

Seine nets are particularly effective if used in the right conditions. One end is fixed to the bank, the other is attached to a boat. The boat pulls the net in a semi-circle from the fixed end and then both ends are hauled in up the beach with the fish enclosed. Recently, the seine net has been adapted for use by trawlers at sea, one end being *shot* (that is, thrown into the sea) and marked with a buoy, or even the ship's boy, who is left bobbing in a small boat attached to the end of the net. The trawler sails in a large circle and returns to the buoyed, or boyed, end, ringing the water and its fish with net. Then the foot rope, which runs freely through rings in the bottom of the net, is hauled in and the whole package is slowly hauled aboard the boat.

FISHING ENGINES

A fascinating kind of net is the *dip net*, or fishing engine, which is a square net hung from its corners on lines which connect it to a pole above. The net is lowered to the bottom of the water, where it lies flat on the bed, and is then raised after an appropriate interval. Any fish swimming around as the net is raised thus get scooped up. I have seen such nets in use in Cochin, in India, and am told that they are commonplace in China. Recently I saw one in action in the Venice lagoon so big that it covered nearly a quarter of an acre.

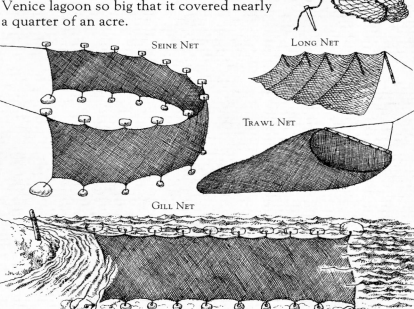

PURSE NET

SEINE NET

LONG NET

TRAWL NET

GILL NET

TANNING & CURING

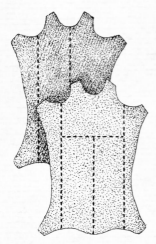

F YOU SKIN AN ANIMAL AND JUST leave the skin alone it will become as hard as a board and you will be unable to bend it or use it for any purpose at all. If you keep it wet it will simply rot. There are two ways to avoid these results: one is to steep the hide in a chemical which will convert the proteins in the hide to a stable non-putrefying material and will prevent the crystallization which causes the skin to harden. The other method, used by Eskimos, American Indians and Kalahari bushmen, is to *work* the skin. Eskimo ladies, we are told, chew their husbands' boots. Whether this is so I have no means of knowing, but I have seen Kalahari people working rawhide rope.

KALAHARI CORKSCREW
A cowhide, or the hide of a large antelope such as a *kudu* or a *gemsbok*, would be laid out on the ground and cut in a spiral to make a long continuous strip, about as wide as it was thick – in each case perhaps an inch. This strip, many yards long, was then threaded over and over the branch of a tree and through a loop of heavy wire which had been twisted round a rock. A pole was thrust through the wire loop and the coils of hide were twisted up into knots by a tribesman pushing the pole round and round, turning the rock. When the man could twist no further he would withdraw the pole with a jerk and the rock would spin violently as it straightened out the tortured hide and headed towards the

ground again. When this momentum-spinning stopped the tribesman thrust his pole into the wire loop again and started turning again, but in the opposite direction.

At the end of not just a day, but a week of repeating this process, interspersed with daily applications of ostrich fat to the hide and re-arrangement of the loops, the tribesman would be left with a long rope which would remain permanently supple. It would defy the weather, and would easily pull an eight-ton ox wagon out of rough ground.

MINERAL AND VEGETABLE TANNING
Nowadays tanning is almost invariably done by soaking the hide in *chrome alum* (chromium potassium sulphate), preceded by a pickling process in an acid solution. This is termed mineral tanning and it is the way I prepare the odd sheep skin to lay on the floor. Only in cases where very high-quality leather is required (as in surgical uses) is vegetable tanning still employed.

Oak bark was used for this and it was once gathered for the purpose in large quantities and sent to local tanneries. My dear old friend, Mr Penpraise of Morwelham in Devon, still owns his oak bark *stripper* which was made from the leg bone of an ox. With this he used to strip the bark off oak trees in the spring time, first taking a cylinder of bark off the standing tree as high as he could reach, then felling the tree to strip the rest.

The chemical process of vegetable tanning is understood now, how the *tannin*

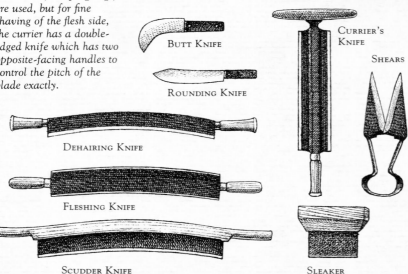

DEHAIRING KNIFE

FLESHING KNIFE

SCUDDER KNIFE

BUTT KNIFE

ROUNDING KNIFE

CURRIER'S KNIFE

SHEARS

SLEAKER

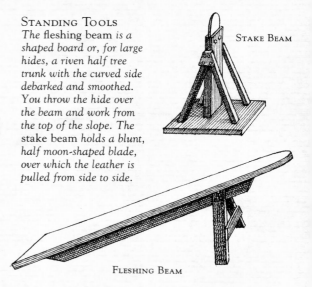

STAKE BEAM

FLESHING BEAM

TANNING
The tanning process involves messy, hard work. The soaked hide of a large animal is very heavy to haul in and out of the tanning pit, while fleshing, above, means removing waste flesh with the sharp convex blade of the fleshing knife – not a job for the squeamish.

(tannic acid) from oak bark seeps, very slowly, through the pores of the hide and drives out the water, coating each fibre with preservative, but it amazes me that early man discovered that such a thing as oak bark could achieve this.

THE TANNER AND THE CURRIER
At one time the crafts of tanning and curing, or currying, were separate (by law in the United Kingdom). The tanner produced hide that was stiff and of poor colour; the currier then turned it into supple, highly polished leather fit for the saddler, and other leather workers, by further soaking and then working and scraping and cutting or splitting the hide. More recently, the two crafts have been brought together under one roof and this was the case when I visited the tannery at Llangollen in Wales just before it closed down.

The manager told me that the first job had been to soak the hides in a lime pit for two weeks (to loosen the hair), then in *bait* for a week. The latter rather unsavoury stuff was made from the excreta of dogs. In other tanneries hen manure was used, and pigeon droppings too were considered efficacious. The Llangollen Tannery got its dog manure from hunt kennels.

After this the hides were washed (thoroughly one hopes) and *fleshed* in the beam house. Each hide was laid over a *fleshing beam*, and all fat, flesh and membrane removed by careful scraping.

The *tan* was made by steeping finely ground oak bark for a few days. The liquor was then pumped, several times, on to fresh bark and allowed to stand. The hides were then soaked in this liquor in pits. At first the hides were said to be *hungry* and *thirsty* for the tan, so for the first three months the hides were continually moved from the solution they were in into freshly steeped solution.

The hides were then *laid away* in strong tan for six months, before being hung up to drip, and then dried, or *sammied*, by heavy rolling.

Currying involved cutting the hides into sections, and scraping them with *sleakers* before soaking them in a solution made from the dried and chopped leaves and shoots of the sumach tree. When half dry after this the sections were *flatted*, which means shaved on the flesh side using the double-sided currier's knife (see opposite), which is sharpened and then the edges turned, as a cabinet-maker turns the edges of his scrapers. The hides were then stretched over a table and *glassed* (with steel blades), rubbed with cod-liver oil and tallow on the flesh side, dried, the grease cleaned off, and were then ready for sale.

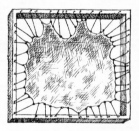

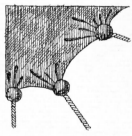

STRETCHING HIDES
An Australian who came to my farm cured sheep skins with the wool on. After soaking and scouring, he stretched the skins, wool side downwards, over a wooden frame. He folded pebbles into the edges of the skin and tied binding lanyards to them, so as to avoid cutting slots into the precious leather. He could then easily work at the skin and apply the mineral tan, chrome alum, as a paste.

HARNESS MAKING

E ARE TOLD, BY PEOPLE WHO I should imagine know very little about it, that the first men to drive horses did so by tying their plough or some other device on to the horse's tail. No horse that I ever met would put up with this for more than five seconds. It is obvious to me that the first person who had the idea of making some creature, other than his wife, pull a cart, would have devised something very like our modern *breast plate* harness. The animal pulls with his chest (sorry mares) against a broad, padded band of leather and, provided the breast plate is not too high and not too low, pulls quite well. But when it came to heavy loads, or heavy ploughs in heavy ground, it was found that the breast plate hampered the animal's breathing and the *collar* came into use (see p.136).

Now a horse cannot control a wheeled vehicle which is just dragging behind him, even if it has brakes. There must be rigid *shafts* to hold the vehicle at a decent distance from the horse.

HARNESS FOR COLLAR AND SHAFTS
You need a wide, padded saddle to take the weight of shafts (and maybe part of the load if the vehicle is a cart, which has only two

wheels, and it is front heavy) and you also need a *girth*, or strap round the belly, to hold the shafts down if the vehicle is back heavy. Then again, to prevent the vehicle from overrunning the horse, you have to have a *breechin* (generally pronounced "britchin"), which is a wide strap that goes round the horse's buttocks. There are *tugs* (small chains or straps) on all of these that connect with fittings on the shaft. And further, to hold the whole system of harness from slipping forward on the horse's back, you have a *crupper*. This is a strap with an eye in it which is put over the horse's tail. It is most important that all harness should be adjusted perfectly, otherwise you have an unhappy and inefficient horse.

PRINCIPLES OF THE CRAFT
I have made breast plate harness from old car tyre inner tubes before now but, although effective, it was a far cry from the beautiful leather harness produced by a skilled harness maker.

For the real thing, leather is cut into strap widths with an instrument called the *plough*. This is like a carpenter's depth gauge, but instead of scribing a line, it cuts. To make strips thinner, the harness maker uses a *splitter*, which is a very sharp blade, screwed to the bench horizontally. Edge tools are used to remove any sharp edges from the strips and most edges are *creased* with little sharp-edged tools that are heated over a flame (but not made so hot as to scorch the leather). Creasing is a decorative line impressed close to the edge of the strap.

The crux of the art of harness making is stitching the leather. Flax thread is used because it is extremely strong and long-lasting, but is flexible and does not cut the leather. You need eight times as much thread as the length to be stitched and all thread must be waxed by dragging it across beeswax. All stitching holes are marked out with *pricking irons* before they are finally pierced with an awl. If you want to join two ends of a strap, the ends are *skived*. This is done with the *half-moon* or *round knife*, and the idea is to remove some of the flesh side of the leather until both ends are wedge-shaped and can be joined without a bulge in the thickness of the harness, so creating a much neater finish.

HEAVY HARNESS
The harness below is suitable for pulling a heavy, wheeled vehicle, such as a farm wagon. You have to imagine the shafts of the vehicle running up along the side of the horse and joined to the tug chains on the breechin, saddle, belly band and the collar.

SADDLE

RIDGE CHAIN

CRUPPER

HIP STRAP

LOIN STRAP

BREECHIN

COLLAR

GIRTH

BELLY BAND

SADDLERY TOOLS AND THEIR USE

Tools for leatherwork have a very individual feel. Those shown here are a selection from tools used for harness making, saddle making and collar making – the three crafts collectively referred to as saddlery. The *clam* is placed butt end on the floor, with the opening jaws between the knees. By squeezing with the knees, you can grip the work for sewing while leaving both hands free to pierce the leather with the awl and stitch with the needles. I have used laundryman's pincers as a clam but they are very makeshift. With the work clamped, stitching proceeds, usually with two needles at once. You pull the entire length of thread through the first hole of the run of stitching, then, with a needle threaded on to both ends of thread, you take thread through each hole from opposite sides, tying a half-hitch or half reef-knot in each hole. The stitching must not come undone even if cut or broken.

Most of the other tools can be divided into those used for cutting the leather (the *punches* and knives) and those for marking it (the *creases* and *prickers*). The creases are usually heated before use – the large *shoulder crease* being used on heavy leather with the weight of your shoulder behind it. The *palm iron* is a species of thimble. It sits in the palm of the hand, its indented surface stopping the needle slipping.

The *masher* is gripped with the fist and used to compress the stuffing in the padded parts of the saddle. The *bulldogs* are special pliers used for pulling materials tight over an edge. You use the side projection, near the jaws, as a fulcrum to lever against as you pull webbing and the like tight for tacking to the saddle tree.

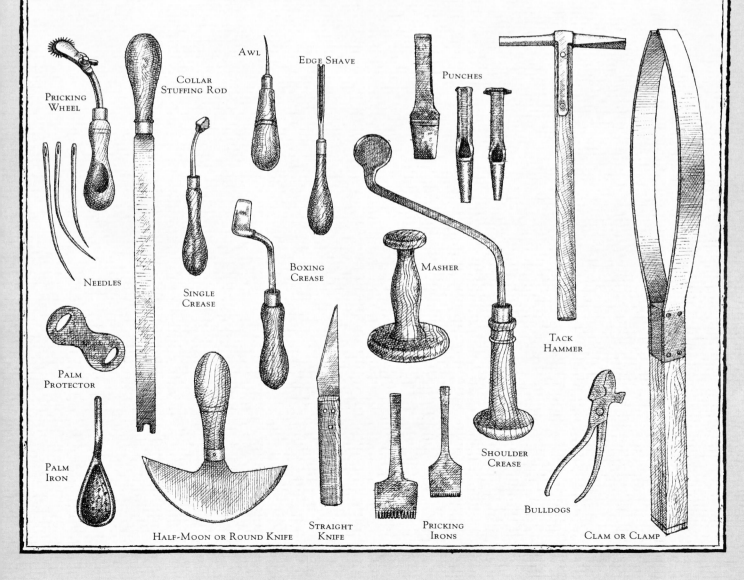

PRICKING WHEEL

COLLAR STUFFING ROD

AWL

EDGE SHAVE

PUNCHES

NEEDLES

SINGLE CREASE

BOXING CREASE

MASHER

TACK HAMMER

PALM PROTECTOR

PALM IRON

SHOULDER CREASE

BULLDOGS

HALF-MOON OR ROUND KNIFE

STRAIGHT KNIFE

PRICKING IRONS

CLAM OR CLAMP

SADDLE MAKING

I ONCE CAME INTO VERY INTIMATE contact with a saddle while working on a sheep farm in the Karoo area of South Africa way back in the 1930s. For six months I sat on a saddle for 10 or 12 hours every day, except Sundays, and after a few weeks of this, a boil grew up on a certain part of my anatomy. This boil seemed to me, though I was unable to inspect it visually owing to its peculiar location, to be as big as an ostrich egg. The memory is painful indeed, but not so painful as it would have been if I had had a poor saddle, or worse still, no saddle at all. And not just painful to me but painful to my horse too, for a good saddle is a necessity for an efficient horse/rider combination. I believe that the horse should be an important means of transport and power in the future and I rate the noble craft of saddle making highly.

The saddles I used to ride in Africa were known as *semi-military*, and were made in far-away Walsall, in the West Midlands of England. They had fairly high *pommels* (the front part of the saddle), fairly high *cantles* (the hind part), and large knee-rolls on the flaps in front of the knees. They also had several D-shaped buckles of brass in various places to hang things on, like a waterbottle or a pair of *hobbles*, which were like handcuffs to chain the horse's fetlocks together so he could graze but not run away. A pair of leather saddlebags held rusks and *biltong* (strips of sun-dried lean meat) and, if I was to be away for a few nights, I strapped down a tightly rolled blanket over the pommel. This reinforced the knee-rolls to give a feeling of security.

What all we young back-velders really wanted was an *Australian stock saddle*. This was enormously heavy, with a very high cantle and a deep seat, and it looked pretty flashy. It was also very expensive – far out of the range of most of us, certainly of me.

HISTORY OF THE SADDLE

There were two major technical discoveries connected with saddles. The first was probably adopted by the Romans from the Mongolian nomads. It was found that a horse would go further, faster, and certainly more happily if there was no direct weight pressing down on its backbone. Therefore raised pads on each side of the backbone were introduced.

The second great innovation which really made the horse an effective vehicle and certainly an effective war machine, was stirrups. With stirrups a man can really stay on a horse, manoeuvre, use a lance or a sword, or jump fences. Quite who did invent this simple yet effective device is not known, but it is certain that stirrups were in use in Asia by AD500, spreading across to Europe during the next few centuries.

In the little museum in the cloisters of Westminster Abbey is what is claimed to be the oldest complete saddle in the world. It was used by Henry V, and was carried in his funeral procession in 1422. What interests me about it is that it is almost exactly the same as the saddles I have seen Ethiopians riding about on, mounted on mules. Henry's saddle was made chiefly of wood, with high vertical pommel and cantle without much dip or shape to the seat. It looks the sort of saddle you would not be knocked out of easily by a lance.

STRUCTURE OF A SADDLE
The cutaway diagram, below, shows how the tree – the rigid frame of laminated beech (here with additional steel springing) – is sandwiched between an upper saddle and a well-padded lower saddle called the panel. The points of the tree slip into the point pockets (sewn on to the panel) when the panel is finally laced to the upper saddle.

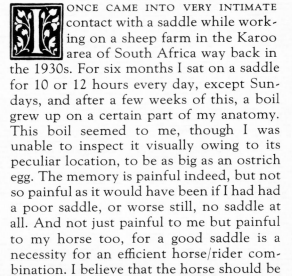

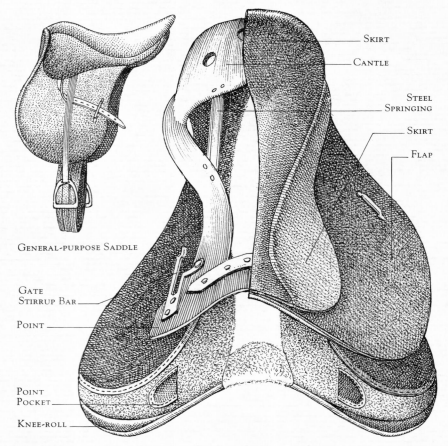

GENERAL-PURPOSE SADDLE

GATE STIRRUP BAR

POINT

POINT POCKET

KNEE-ROLL

SKIRT

CANTLE

STEEL SPRINGING

SKIRT

FLAP

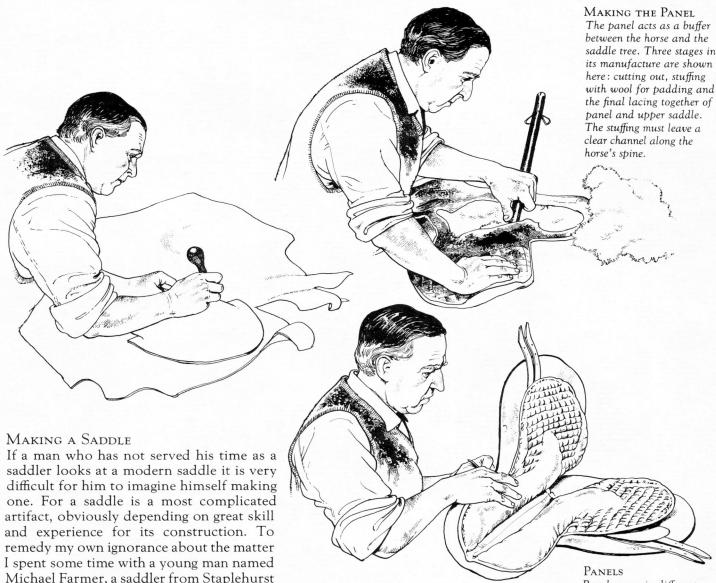

MAKING THE PANEL
The panel acts as a buffer between the horse and the saddle tree. Three stages in its manufacture are shown here: cutting out, stuffing with wool for padding and the final lacing together of panel and upper saddle. The stuffing must leave a clear channel along the horse's spine.

PANELS
Panels come in different sizes and shapes for more or less contact with the horse. The ample proportions of a well-made full panel, shown here, with its beautiful quilting, makes you feel as safe as houses.

MAKING A SADDLE

If a man who has not served his time as a saddler looks at a modern saddle it is very difficult for him to imagine himself making one. For a saddle is a most complicated artifact, obviously depending on great skill and experience for its construction. To remedy my own ignorance about the matter I spent some time with a young man named Michael Farmer, a saddler from Staplehurst in Kent, England.

If Mr Farmer is to make a bespoke saddle, which is to fit a particular horse, he goes and visits the horse with a piece of equipment which I am certain the Romans did not have, nor the Mongols, and that is a piece of lead-covered electric cable. He lays this over the horse's back and bends it (and it bends quite easily) to the shape of the horse. Then, being careful to preserve its shape, he draws the outline of the lead cable on a piece of paper.

THE TREE

Back at the workshop he chooses a *tree*, a U-shaped framework, mostly of wood, which fits exactly the shape of the horse. English saddlers get their trees from specialist manufacturers in Staffordshire. There is no reason why a good carpenter should not

make trees but, so far as I know, all saddlers actually buy them from specialist producers. Nowadays they tend to be made from laminated beechwood, reinforced by steel straps.

There are two edges to the piece of laminated wood that forms the *head*, or front end of the saddle tree, and these must be extended by rivetting flaps of leather to them. These flaps will ultimately be pushed down into two leather pockets in the *panel*, which is the under section of the saddle.

WEBBING AND BELLIES

The next operation is to fit the *webbing*, a system of very strong canvas bands, some longitudinal and some lateral. The longitudinal pieces are tacked to both head and cantle, the lateral pieces tacked over the

SADDLER'S CLAMP
The traditional harness maker's clamp (see p.131) is a free-standing affair grasped between the knees while you sit on a suitable stool. Some saddle makers have a heavier duty clamp combined with a stool and operated by foot pressure on a treadle.

front part of the tree only. These lateral pieces are enormously important, for the *girth straps* (the straps that hold the saddle on the horse) will be stitched to them. Before putting on the webbing all the steel parts of the tree must be covered with leather. The edges of the lateral webbings are stitched together and then the whole of the rear part of the saddle covered with a tightly-stretched piece of waxed canvas.

Now the *bellies* have to be fastened to each side of the rear part of the saddle. These are leather pockets of shoulder hide (the saddler has to select exactly the right leather for every part of the saddle, see tanning and curing, p.128) and in days of old they used to be stuffed with wool to make soft pads under the rider's buttocks.

ADDING THE SEAT
The *seat* now has to be added. These days this tends to be of rubber rather than canvas stuffed with wool as it used to be. Probably rubber is better because it cannot lose its shape. The seat is glued to the webbing and the bellies, and is stuck down by rolling it with a rolling-pin.

A piece of serge cloth is stretched tightly over the seat and tacked down very tautly where it overlaps underneath the wood of the tree. This I might say, after watching the process, is much easier said than done. It must be dead tight and have no creases.

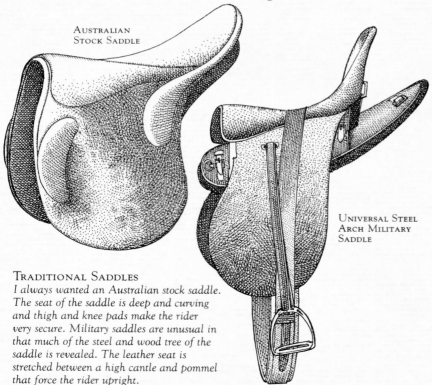

AUSTRALIAN STOCK SADDLE

UNIVERSAL STEEL ARCH MILITARY SADDLE

TRADITIONAL SADDLES
I always wanted an Australian stock saddle. The seat of the saddle is deep and curving and thigh and knee pads make the rider very secure. Military saddles are unusual in that much of the steel and wood tree of the saddle is revealed. The leather seat is stretched between a high cantle and pommel that force the rider upright.

Next comes the *blocking* of the seat, which means shaping the piece of leather that we actually sit on. This should be of pigskin and it is a sign of the poverty of our times that there are actually machines for impressing a pattern on cowhide to make it look like pigskin. It is sad that the Western manner of dealing with a pig causes the skin – one of the finest materials that there is – to be turned into pork crackling, to break people's teeth, or to bacon rind which is mostly thrown away. The Chinese fortunately are no such fools and carefully skin their pigs, and it is from China that our pigskin comes.

The pigskin is soaked and then tacked into position, but not too tightly for the tacks will have to be withdrawn. The pigskin is then boned out to smooth it and left to dry. But we have not finished with the seat just yet.

SKIRTS, GIRTHS AND FLAPS
Next come the *skirts*. These are the two stiff and thick components that extend the seat laterally up near the pommel of the saddle. They are built up with pigskin, other pieces of leather, and canvas, and are stitched to the seat with a *welt* between the two components. The welt is a piece of cord with very thin (*skived*) leather sewn round it like a piece of sausage skin. The seat is removed from the saddle while this operation is done and it is an operation demanding great skill, for the correct marrying of these two skirts with the seat can make or mar the whole saddle. The seat is then wetted again and *set*, that is pulled on to the tree, very tightly, and this time tacked for good.

The girth straps are stitched on next. This process is very important because if the stitching goes the rider goes too and may break his or her neck. Saddlers, incidentally, roll up their own threads, twisting and waxing several strands of best hemp twine together.

Then the *flaps* have to be prepared. These are the very big pieces of leather that hang down each side of the saddle and take the pressure from the rider's knees. The leading edges of both flaps have to be blocked, wetted and tacked down on a board on which is nailed a block shaped exactly like the knee-roll, the raised ridge that restrains the rider's knee. When in position the flap must be allowed to dry naturally. A folded strip of panel hide is stitched round the front of the flap to reinforce it and the flap is

GREEK PACK SADDLE

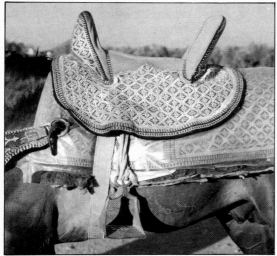

MOROCCAN SADDLE

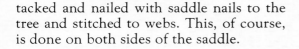

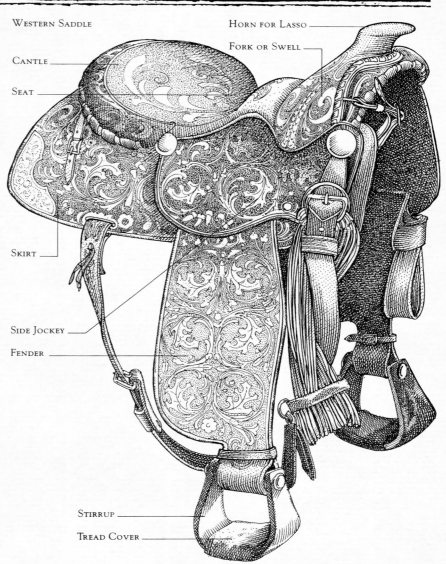

WESTERN SADDLE — HORN FOR LASSO — FORK OR SWELL — CANTLE — SEAT — SKIRT — SIDE JOCKEY — FENDER — STIRRUP — TREAD COVER

tacked and nailed with saddle nails to the tree and stitched to webs. This, of course, is done on both sides of the saddle.

MAKING THE PANEL

Now the saddler has completed what I would call the top saddle, he has to make the *panel*, or under saddle, which comes in contact with the horse. The panel is, if anything, more complicated than the top part of the saddle, with 11 leather and canvas components of strange shapes and various sizes. Basically it is two sheets of leather sewn together and stuffed with wool, which fits underneath the tree, to act as a cushion between the tree and the horse, just as the top part of the saddle acts as a cushion between the tree and the rider. When the panel is made, the *points* (the ends of the head or pommel, extended by flaps of leather) are pushed into little leather

pockets which have been stitched on to the panel, and the panel laced to the seat.

It is inconceivable that anyone could design the modern saddle from scratch without the thousands of years of experience that has moulded it. And then there are so many different sorts of saddle, from donkey pack saddles, which are still a part of day-to-day life in the less industrialized parts of the world, to ornately tooled Western saddles made for sitting in all day that remind me of the long hours I have spent on horseback. If anyone is interested in what happened to the ostrich-egg-sized boil that I introduced at the start of this article, well, I had to stand in the stirrups until, suddenly, my horse put his hoof in a meercat hole and – bang – down I went, experiencing a feeling that seemed like sitting on a red-hot poker. But it did the trick for, blessed relief, the boil was burst.

EXOTIC SADDLES
The saddle maker's art has developed along sharply contrasting lines in different parts of the world. In northern Africa and southern Europe, saddles are still made using a heavy wooden frame which remains evident even when the saddle is padded and decorated. The heavy Western saddle is often highly decorated with tooling of the leather parts (gouging and cutting the leather surface). The maker also adds a deal of ornamental metal work that increases the weight of the saddle further. It amazes me how comfortable Western trail horses appear – I am sure the length and width of such saddles help to spread the load.

MAKING HORSE COLLARS

ATCH A HEAVY HORSE PULLING A plough, if you are lucky enough to find a farm that still uses horses, or a dray horse delivering beer barrels, and the first thing you notice is how well suited the horse is to pull a heavy load. But look closely, and you will notice that it is the rigid collar that is taking the strain, putting the load evenly across the horse's shoulders rather than on its neck and windpipe. It all looks so simple, yet the horse collar is a comparatively recent invention.

CAMELS, OXEN AND HORSES

It was not until around AD500 that a camel-driver in China first harnessed his beast of burden with a fixed, rigid collar, and the invention, adapted by the Mongols for the horse, did not arrive in Europe for quite some centuries. Previously, horses had been put in *breast plate* harness (see p.130), or had been yoked to their loads, rather like oxen, the throat-straps of the yoke cutting into their windpipes, or had been harnessed with a soft collar around the neck that tightened with use. Such arrangements severely restricted the work the horse could do, and prevented it replacing the ox as the main draught animal used in farming. The Romans even had a law to protect their horses, which prevented a pair from pulling a load in excess of about half a ton, which a modern dray horse can do by itself with ease. But once equipped with a rigid collar, the horse came into its own, and it was this that allowed the agricultural revolution of the Middle Ages to take place, and encouraged the industrial one of the eighteenth and nineteenth centuries by releasing manpower from the land to run the ever-expanding factories.

MAKING THE FOREWALE

Horse collars are made by saddlers, usually those who specialize in making *black saddlery*, the saddler's term for harnesses and the like. The collar is made of the *forewale* and the *body*, which are then joined together.

The forewale is simply a long strip of leather sewn into a tube, with one edge of the seam extending well beyond the other to make a flap, known as the *barge*. This tube is then stuffed tight with rye straw, wool flock or even horsehair. Whatever the material, the stuffing is rammed hard into the wale with an iron rod, and when tightly packed in, the wale is placed over a wooden model of the horse's withers, on which the collar is eventually to sit. There it is beaten into shape with a mallet. If the collar is closed at its ends, as is usual, the two ends of the wale are sewn together, otherwise they are left apart. Open collars are only used for those horses, like heavy horses or donkeys, that have exceptionally large heads and do not take kindly to having collars put on. These collars are simply prised apart, slipped over the head of the horse, and then clamped shut with straps and buckles. Closed collars are put on upside down, so that the widest part of the collar passes over the broadest part of the head, and are then turned the right way up and pushed down the neck into position.

PARTS OF THE COLLAR

A horse collar is in three parts, the leather wale *and the* body, *both stuffed tight with either rye straw or wool flock, and the metal* hames, *fitting snugly into a groove on either side of the collar. The largest collars have a raised leather shield behind the tops of the hames called the* housen. *Folded back, it stops rain trickling down a horse's withers.*

HOUSEN

HOUSING STRAP

COLLAR PAD OR AFTERWALE

HAMES

REIN RING

BODY

TUG

WALE

MAKING THE BODY

The next stage is to make the body. For this the saddler cuts out a broad strip of leather and stitches it to the barge, together with one edge of a strip of heavy woollen cloth. Then taking straw or whatever padding is being used, he encloses it in the leather and cloth at the throat of the collar, stitching around from the throat to the neck, stuffing and shaping as he goes. After all the stuffing, stitching and shaping necessary to produce exactly the right collar for the breed of horse in hand, the maker sews on a piece of soft leather called the *afterwale* to stop the collar rubbing on the neck of the horse.

THE HAMES

The final job is to attach the *hames*. These are the tubular arms that fit either side of the collar in the groove between wale and body to which the traces and reins are attached. Once the hames were made of hardwood, but now they are of brass-plated steel. At their top is a pair of rings which takes the housing strap that clamps the collar together. Below them are the rein rings through which the reins pass on their way from the harness to the driver's hands, and below them are the two *tugs*, one each side. These are rings that take the chains that lead to the *traces*, the leather straps by which the horse pulls its load.

Much of this work is detailed and precise, for the collar must fit its intended horse perfectly. There should be just enough room to place a hand between the bottom of the collar and the horse's wind-pipe. If it is too tight, the horse cannot breathe, too loose, and it will rub its neck raw. Yet few measurements are made by the saddler – he prefers to work by eye.

THE RUSH COLLAR

One unusual collar I have come across is the rush collar. These are rarely made today, and I have never yet met a man who can make one. They are made of plaited rush weave, the ends of rush bound together and the centres frayed with a metal comb so that further lengths of rush can be worked into the fibres to pad the collar out. The whole length is then bound tight with a three-inch wide plait, and the ends joined together. A rough cover made of hessian, or some such material, is sewn round the whole structure, and the collar is then ready for use – as a strong but light collar used for young colts unwilling to accept the heavier affair.

SHAPING THE WALE

STUFFING THE COLLAR
Long straw fillers were harness makers who specialized in nothing else but putting the stuffing in horse collars. They preferred to use long rye straw, although wheat straw would do, wetting the straw and leather to make them supple enough to work with. A filler would complete three collars a day.

THE WALE AND THE BODY
Once the wale has been sewn and stuffed, it is beaten into shape over a wooden mould. The saddler then stitches on the body, sewing the leather to the barge, the loose flap of leather that forms part of the wale. All this is done by hand and eye, and few measurements are taken.

BOOT & SHOEMAKING

I N AFRICA IN THE 1930s, I HAD TO make my own shoes, because if I didn't, I didn't have any. The shoes were called *veldschoenen*, which is Afrikaans for field shoes. They were fashioned out of the leather made by soaking hides in copper sulphate solution.

They were the simplest things in the world to make. You got a fairly tough piece of leather, placed your foot on it and drew the outline. You then drew another line half an inch outside the first one, cut the shape out with a knife, and you had your sole. A more flexible leather was used for the uppers, which were sewn to the sole.

North American Indians have a far more sensible way of making shoes or *moccasins*. They simply bend a piece of rawhide into the complete shape of a foot, sides and all, stitch it through to one or more sole pieces,

and then add a top piece that encloses the toes and outstep. I have worn Indian moccasins. They are marvellously comfortable and, as the piece of hide that goes round your foot is all one piece, watertight.

SACRED BOOTS

To meet a real boot maker I went to Crete. Boots are almost sacred objects to a Cretan man, like the dagger he wears on festive occasions. These boots are of black leather, made carefully to measure, and come nearly to the knee. They last 20 years and are worn every day.

High up on a Cretan mountain is the village of Angia and here at least two boot makers ply their craft. One of these, Mihalis Roditis, a boot maker for 40 years, told me that he fails to make a sufficient living these days, not because of competition from factory-made boots but because of better roads. The mountain men are now more apt to travel in cars and their boots last longer!

It would take Mihalis two days to make a pair of boots if he did nothing else. He went to endless trouble to show me how to make a pair. When a customer came he would draw the outline of his feet on a piece of leather. He measured the height the boot should be, the circumference of the ankle and leg in various places – six measurements in all. He then made paper patterns and cut out the different pieces of leather. There are five patterns for the

THE SHOEMAKER'S TOOLS
Shoemakers require a considerable number of hand tools for their trade, for a shoe is a very complicated item to make. The only nails are in the heel, the rest of the shoe being stitched together through holes already prepared by an awl. The leather is cut to shape with a variety of different knives depending on its quality and use, and is glazed and burnished with special irons. The pieces of leather that make up the heel are finally trimmed with a heel shave. Seat and fudge wheels are used to score the leather, which is moulded to the sole with a waist iron.

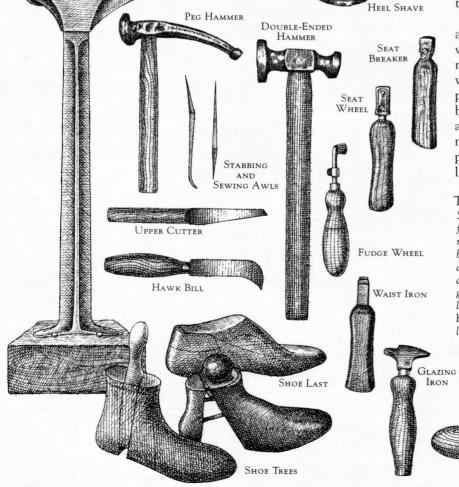

uppers of the boot: *psidi* (toe-cap), *kalami* (vamp or front), *fittet* (the two lacing panels) and *fterna* (quarters or heel).

The uppers were sewn together, three times by sewing machine then once more by hand, then a canvas lining was made to match. Mihalis had dozens of *lasts* and he chose the right pair to suit his customers' patterns. Now the last is a wooden foot to which the maker tacks the *insole* (leather cut to the shape of the outline of the foot). Last and insole are then pushed down into the embryo boot, the boot turned upside down, and the sole of the last becoming the maker's working platform as he makes the boot. Both the lining and the leather of the uppers have to be pulled hard to overlap the insole – "as tight as glass" were Mihalis's words. When satisfied he tacked the uppers and lining to the last through the insole – all the steel tacks used were removed once they were replaced by stitching.

The thing about stitching the sole of a boot to the uppers is that you cannot get your hand inside the boot to sew, and stitches inside the boot would be very uncomfortable anyway. The solution, as Mihalis showed me, is to use a curved needle, to stitch the uppers only part way into the insole, then to join a strip of leather to the insole and uppers that can be stitched to the sole proper from the outsides of the boot only. This strip is called *vardoulo* in Greek, *welt* in English. Mihalis attached the welt and indeed the sole itself with wooden tacks called *sites*. These were permanent and were first hammered home then rasped flush. Before stitching sole to welt, Mihalis cut a slanting groove around the sole that he could stitch into and so protect the stitches. After stitching, he stuck back the leather cut from the groove to protect the stitches even more. The only place where steel tacks were used for permanent fixing was in the heel which was made with thick pieces of hard leather, called *lifts* in English.

WEST END BESPOKE TRADE

There is a street in London's Soho called Meard Street. It is not the sort of place you would let your unaccompanied daughter wander down. When I first went there I was introduced to the bespoke shoe trade by Mr Bill Bird of the firm of H. Peen, tree and last makers. At that time you could have a pair of boots made to your exact measurements for just £600. This included the wooden lasts on which the boots are

made. These are stored by the shoemakers so that in 30 years' time when your boots wear out (they should last this long) the maker can build another pair. The price also included a pair of *trees*, which you put inside your boots every time you take them off. These are exactly the same size and shape as the lasts and prevent your boots from wrinkling. It is the wrinkles that form in neglected shoes which collect injurious dampness and acids that rot the leather. Bill Bird told me, "they are born on the last and they are reborn on the tree."

As well as the tree and last makers, there are *clickers*, the foremen shoemakers who cut out the leather (the noise of cutting gives them their name), and distribute the work; *closers*, who trim and sew the uppers; and *makers*, who add the soles and heels. It is highly skilled work and there are few people left now who can do it.

THE VILLAGE COBBLER
Sitting on his specially made low stool while he worked, the cobbler was once a familiar sight in every village. When I was a boy there were still boot makers in East Anglia, and they would make a pair of boots for two weeks' wages of a farm labourer. At that time a labourer received 30 shillings a week, so a pair of boots would cost him £3.

CLOG MAKING

S FAR AS I KNOW, CLOGS SUCH AS the Dutch, Belgians and northern French still wear, which are made out of one piece of wood, were never popular in the British Isles. If you go to a Dutch cattle market you will generally see a clog seller with some hundreds of new wooden clogs (known as *klompen* in Dutch) and a pile of worn-out clogs beside him. Farmers come up, shuffle off their worn-out clogs, which are added to the pile, buy a new pair and depart newly shod and well pleased. The clog maker presumably doesn't have to buy any firewood.

Dutch clogs are usually cut from willow, roughly to size with a cross-cut saw, froe and bench-knife, then hollowed out with a special machine that drills out the interior wood (see opposite) and hand-finished with specially shaped chisels. I wore a pair for years while working round the garden. Once your feet get used to them they are very comfortable – but you cannot run in them. Or at least I could not.

The British clog, found chiefly in the north of England and in Wales, is another kettle of fish. I have a pair that I have worn for 10 years and which still could be refurbished to extend their life even further. They have wooden soles but leather uppers. They are excellent if you are on your feet a lot, as the well-shaped wooden sole gives great support. Furthermore, they are ideal for working in such places as dairies, mills, slaughterhouses or similar locations, where the floors are apt to be stone, hard, cold and often damp. They are warm to wear and healthy – in the past, I would have sought out Mr Luther Edwards in Carmarthen Cattle Mart for a new pair, but his shop has gone, and with it one of the few Welsh clog makers left.

Mr Edwards hailed from Cynwyl Elfed, just north of Carmarthen town. When I met him

PROTECTOR OF FEET
At one time the clog maker shod the working feet of most fellow villagers. He would keep paper patterns of his customers' foot sizes and provide long-lasting and comfortable footwear. Attaching an iron ferrule, as below, protected the edge of the wooden sole from wear and preserved the sole thickness almost indefinitely.

ATTACHING THE UPPERS
After the uppers have been cut out and stitched, the clog maker grips the leather with lasting pincers and pulls it over the last (1). When shaping is complete, the uppers are placed over the sole (2) and secured in the rebate with tacks. A welt (leather strip) is then tacked around the rebate (3) and a brass toe plate added (4).

he was getting on in years but still very active and productive, and he supplied clogs to quite a large clientele of discriminating farmers. He had no apprentice and said that boys did not want to work hard any more.

THEN AND NOW

Mr Edwards served a four-and-a-half year apprenticeship to an orthodox boot maker and another year and a half to a clog maker before he felt ready to start making clogs on his own. He cut all his own wood, preferring sycamore, although many of the old clog makers used the less expensive alder – about the only thing alder was good for. In times of old, *cloggers* were men who made a living by going into the wild wet alder woods of west Wales, felling trees, cross-cutting them into clog lengths, riving the logs with the froe, and then rough-shaping the pieces right there in the woods. Each man had his own portable bench with a *stock* or *bench-knife* hooked to it. You can obtain great leverage with the bench-knife and it will cut through any piece of wood you can get under it. The step of the heel would be sawn with a hand saw then cut out to the sawmark with a drawknife. The steeply bent shape of the bottom of the sole would be cut with the bench-knife. The rebate that runs right round the sole to take the upper would next be cut by hand using a *gripping knife*, which works like the bench-knife but has a gouge-like blade. The soles would then be stacked in neat piles to season. *Clogging*, however, is a distinctly different craft from clog making (see p.40).

In his day, Mr Edwards felled trees on his neighbours' lands, cross-cut the trunks on the spot and took them back to his work-shop to shape. He did the job in exactly the same way as the cloggers of old. The next stage of clog making is attaching the leather uppers to the shaped wooden sole.

Depending on the design of the clog, the upper can be made from either one, two or three pieces of leather. Clogs for women or children often have a one-piece upper fastened with a single button. A more usual arrangement consists of two pieces of leather and a clasp fastener. One piece of leather is used to form the front and tongue while the second piece is for the back and sides. The first step is to mark out on the leather the size and design for the particular clog. A village clog maker would once have had paper patterns for most of his custo-mers' feet. The leather is then cut out with a *clicking knife* (see p.138) and, for extra comfort, the inside edge round the ankle area may be thinned before the pieces are stitched together. Next the uppers are fitted over a wooden last, a wooden replica of the human foot, pulled into position with *lasting pincers* and tacked securely to the last itself. A hot *burnishing iron* may be rubbed over the leather to help perma-nently shape it. Shaping complete, the uppers are removed from the last and placed on the clog, with the leather fitting into the sole rebate. The maker then tacks the uppers to the sole before adding a *welt* or strip of leather right round the rebate secured with brass and steel tacks.

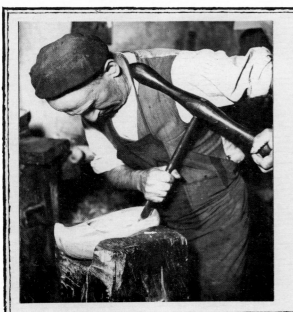

WOODEN CLOGS

The clogs worn for centuries in countries like Holland, where they are called *klompen*, and France, where they are known as *sabots*, differ from the common British clog in that they are made entirely from one piece of wood, without leather uppers. The French *sabot* is, in fact, where our English word "sabotage" comes from. The connection isn't really that obscure when you realize that the French workers, during the late nineteenth century, used their *sabots* to damage machinery as a form of indus-trial protest. Modern clogs are shaped using traditional tools, such as the special gouge you can see being used on the left. The finished clogs are then stacked and left to season, right. In Holland you might easily see wonderfully colourful, hand-painted and decorated clogs used on special occasions.

FINISHED CLOGS
STACKED AND SEASONING

KNIFE MAKING

T IS HARD TO SEE HOW MEN COULD survive without knives, and when I was a boy I was always told by countrymen older and wiser than I was that I should never be without "a shilling, a shut-knife and a piece of string". But when it came to finding a knife maker, outside the huge factories of, for example, Sheffield, I had to go to some strange places. I went, for instance, to the slopes of Mount Idi, in Crete. To a little village very high up, called Zoniana. Zoniana means "the god of the gods' village". Zeus was born in a cave nearby you see.

The true Cretan man must have his dagger, which he sticks into the front of his cummerbund on all festive occasions and carries in its scabbard at his side while working or up in the mountains. He is not content with a factory-made product.

When I visited Anastasios Parasiris over 10 years ago he was the last knife maker in Zoniana, and he was over 80 then. He told me, quite simply, that he would not be making knives for much longer because soon he would die – something he did not seem at all worried by. He still made me a knife and I learned that all is not lost for the knife-users of Crete, however, for his 12-year-old grandson is already learning the craft from him.

THE FRENCH TECHNIQUE
The knife makers of Thiers in France, lie on wide planks over their water-powered and water-lubricated grindstones. In this way they can get more purchase against the wheel, and the planks protect them from the heavy spray of water that shoots off the spinning wheels.

KNIFE MAKERS NEED SMITHS

Besides being a knife maker, Anastasios had always been a shepherd and still owned a flock of sheep. He took to knife making to augment his income. His workshop was a small dark dusty room, with an electric grinder in it, an electric pillar drill, and a bench with some simple tools. He worked in league with the village blacksmith who roughly forged and tempered the blade.

I watched the blacksmith forging a knife blank from an old truck spring. He heated it red hot, cut it roughly to shape on the *hardie*, a chisel head fixed in the anvil (see p.78), took a heat again, then rough-shaped the blade on the anvil with the hammer. He did not take much trouble with tempering the blade at this stage, putting in the final temper after Anastasios had fashioned it.

Anastasios did most of the blade shaping on the electric grinder. As he ground he continually dipped the blade in water to stop it getting too hot. He made the blade with a *tang*, or handle, and he shaped the metal in the manner preferred by Cretan villagers. After this he drilled three holes in the tang with the electric drill. I asked him what he had done before he had got electricity and he showed me a hand-turned grinder and said his son used to turn the handle, before he grew into the village schoolmaster. He also showed me a drill which you pushed against the work with your chest and caused to rotate by means of a bow, the string of which made several turns round the rotating part of the drill.

FINAL TEMPERING

The blade went back to the blacksmith for its final tempering. He moulded a pad of clay into exactly the same profile as the curved edge of the blade, took a heat with the latter, then plunged the edge only into the damp clay. Thus the cutting edge only was tempered hard while the spine of the knife was left with a softer temper. With this treatment the blade would take a good edge and keep it, while the knife itself was flexible enough not to snap with heavy use.

Anastasios then took the blade back and buffed it well with cloth discs spinning on the grinder, the edges of the discs dressed with emery powder, and then what looked to me like knife polish, and then he fitted

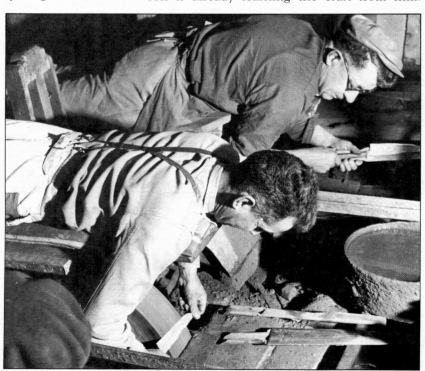

the handle. This, in the case of my knife, is two pieces of olive wood, carefully and elegantly shaped, and riveted through the tang of the blade with three rivets. He then put a final edge on the blade, gave it a final buffing and the knife was complete.

THE SCABBARD

The scabbard couldn't be simpler. It is made of two pieces of willow cut into such shapes that, if put together, enclosed the knife blade comfortably. He then glued them together, wrapped a strip of thin steel around the open end and soldered the two ends together. He banged three small nail-holes in each side of the strip so that the resulting burrs in the metal penetrated the wood a fraction to prevent the strip sliding off, cut a groove round the scabbard at the pointed end and twisted a piece of copper wire round this. It is by far the best knife I have ever had, and when I took it to a black-smith friend of mine in Ireland, he tested it and pronounced it an excellent blade.

Anastasios showed me a whole collection of antique knives he has, all of them made in the time when the Turks occupied the island. Many had flamboyant handles made from ivory, or bone, or rams' horn. These knives, he said, belonged to Crete.

FRENCH KNIFE MAKING

To see a more organised, but still small-scale knife-making industry, you can go, as

I did, to Thiers, in France. The blades are forged first from strip steel with a trip-hammer, which is driven by a waterwheel, and then by hand. The blades are tempered simply by plunging the blade into hot oil.

Grinding is done on water-driven sand-stone wheels. The grinder lies on a cushion on a plank set above the wheel, lying on his stomach and looking down over the spin-ning wheel below him. I noticed in old photographs that the workman's dog would often appear lying on the grinder's back. And lo and behold, on my visit, there was the grinder on his belly, and the dog on his back: a matey arrangement!

KNIFE FROM ZONIANA
This is a drawing of the knife and scabbard made for me on Crete, by a knife maker from the village of Zoniana. The blade is nearly seven inches long and holds a good edge. The handle, fitted either side of the same steel as the blade (the tang), is of beautiful dark olive wood, while the scabbard is made of willow.

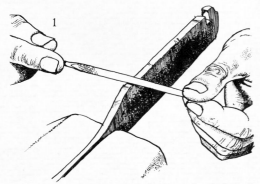

FITTING THE HANDLE TO A HUNTING KNIFE
Knives like my Cretan knife and those from Thiers, like the one made here, are particularly strong because blade and handle are fashioned from the same piece of steel. Once the blade has been roughly tempered and ground to shape, the knife maker shapes the tang (1), the section of steel that forms the core of the handle. He then drills the tang (with an ancient hand drill if he is a knife maker from Thiers, 2) so that the hand pieces can be riveted in place (3).

MILLSTONE DRESSING

ILLSTONES, WHETHER TURNED BY water or by wind, wear as they grind and their grinding surfaces have to be *dressed* periodically, that is recut so that they grind efficiently again. A pair of stones working full time (10 hours a day) grinding corn probably have to be dressed about once every 10 days, if made of Derbyshire Millstone Grit, but at longer intervals, perhaps three weeks or a month, if of the quartz-like stone that French millstones, or *burrs*, were hewn from. British stones tend to be monolithic, cut from a single piece of material, while the French stones were more usually constructed from shaped and faced segments bound with iron. Towards the end of the nineteenth century *composition stones* came into use, which were harder still and made from a bond of cement and stone chips. Obviously, for a working miller dependent on the turning of his stones to make a living, the less he had to dress his stones the better. For while they were being dressed they were out of action and – unless he employed a man to do his dressing for him – so was he. A big mill with four pairs of stones would seldom have had more than three of them working at any time.

KNOWING THE STONE

The late Mr Sid Ashdown, who lived at Cross-in-Hand in the Weald of Sussex, was a windmiller all his working life. Even in retirement (or semi-retirement) he was still called on frequently to go and dress the stones of the few stone mills that are still working. The number of working mills is growing in the British Isles, as it happens, as more and more people are rebelling against the wrapped-sliced-pap that modern milling and bread factory techniques turn out and are insisting, again, on bread. The real bread campaign is marching now alongside the real ale campaign and God bless them!

The dressing of millstones is a very difficult art. It is not simply a matter of picking out the grooves so as to deepen them. For one thing, the wear on a pair of stones is not even – it is greater near the circumference than at the centre. This problem is corrected by marking the stone with *staff, jack-stick* and red ochre. The jack-stick is a wooden gauge, part of which fits through the hole in the *bed stone* (the lower one), while the other part sweeps the face of the stone and shows the dresser how much he has to remove from the stone nearer the centre to make up for the greater wear nearer the outer edge. Most millstone dressers would lay a penny coin on the stone near the centre after they had worked on the stone. They would run the jack-stick around again and make sure that it cleared

DRESSING PATTERNS

The science of grinding corn is as old as the hills. Through its history millers have altered the patterns of furrows and lands (the channels and raised grinding edges respectively) for more efficient grinding. But it is marvellous to think that the pattern of dressing that you are likely to see now is almost identical to the dressing found on Roman millstones. The breast, or milling surface of the stone is divided into sectors of furrows called quarters *or* harps, *because they are shaped like harps.*

ROMAN DRESSING
4TH CENTURY AD

19TH-CENTURY
STRAIGHT DRESSING

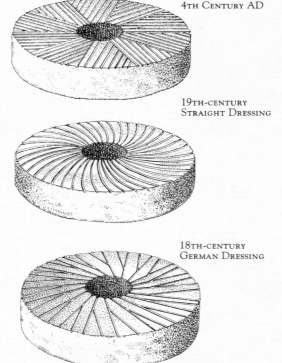

18TH-CENTURY
GERMAN DRESSING

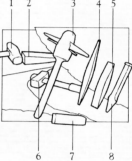

DRESSING TOOLS
1 Sledge hammer 2 Wedge for supporting upturned runner stone 3 Thrifts – wooden handle that holds interchangeable mill bills and picks 4 Mill pick 5 Mill bill 6 Hand hammer 7 Sharpening file 8 Chisel.

the penny, showing that their dressing compensated for the extra wear that would occur towards the outer edge.

The staff is merely a straight-edge. It is smeared with red ochre and then passed over the stone. Any areas of the stone that are standing proud show up as red and can then be taken down level. This process is called *proving the stone.*

Next comes *knocking it down.* This is achieved either with the *flat bill* or *mill bill*, which looks very similar to a miniature adze or, if only a little stone has to be taken off, by rubbing it with a *rub stone*, which is an old piece of French burr stone. The tools used by the millstone dresser may look clumsy and crude, but in the hands of a skilled craftsman they are capable of producing very delicate work.

Then, if necessary, the furrows in the stone have to be deepened with a tool called the *pick*. In the case of Peak Stone (with the apt geological name of Millstone Grit), which is softer than French burr, you would probably have to do this every time the stone was dressed. The depth of these furrows is important as it is the device by which the meal is expelled around the circumference of the stone.

DRESSING THE LANDS

Now the *lands* have to be dressed. These are the pieces of high ground between the furrows or grooves. In the case of French burrs this operation is called *cracking,* and consists of cutting out tiny furrows in the face of the stone as close together as you can get them without actually breaking in to each other. In the case of Peak stone the operation is known as *stitching* and in this, tiny peck-marks are made all over the face of the stone. If this cracking or stitching is not done, the stones do not cut the *bran* away cleanly from the wheat. The outer skin of the grain kernel is called the bran and it is the roughest, most fibrous part. It makes extremely good and healthy food for all stock, from guinea pigs to horses, if you can obtain it nowadays. It is sieved out of the *meal* – the term for what comes out from the millstones.

Recently, of course, the importance of bran in our own diet has been rediscovered, after years of eating over processed, fibre-free foods, and lots of people are experimenting with bran-full diets. A finer sieve removes the next coarsest extraction, called *middlings* or *sharps*. If the flour that is left is 80 per cent of the original weight of the

AMERICAN
POST MILL

ENGLISH
TOWER MILL

GERMAN
STOCK MILL

wheat it is called *standard flour. White flour* is only 75 per cent of the total original weight. But this is by the way.

THE WORKING LIFE OF A STONE

A Peak stone, working full time, would last anywhere from 20 to 25 years. When new, the *runner stone* (the top stone that revolves) would be perhaps a foot thick. The stationary bed stone would be 15 inches thick. The bed stones would wear out first, and these would be replaced by the runner stones, so the miller only had the expense of replacing the runner stones each time. Sixty years ago one stone, unbound and undressed, would cost about £8 delivered to the mill. Bound, that is with an iron hoop right round it, and also with *the work put in* (meaning with the initial furrows of the milling surface cut), a pair of stones would cost about £20. Normally the stones would come in the raw state from the quarry (just cut into the round) to a firm like the Silex Works, on the Isle of Dogs in London, where they would dress them or *set them out*.

The hole in the middle of a stone, where the grain enters, is called the *eye*. A heavy hooped iron bar goes across the eye of the runner stone and this is engaged by the *driver* or *mace*, which is the piece of the mechanism that turns it. A new runner stone alone probably weighs the best part of a ton so you can imagine that the supporting structure has to be massive. It is also important that the stones do not *run dry*, that is turn without grain between them.

WORKING ON A BEDSTONE

Millstones are pretty uncomfortable things to work on. The classic working pose involves kneeling over a softening sack with one hand controlling the fall of the bill very precisely. The projection in the middle of the stone is called the mace *(see diagram below).*

Damage is done to the stone faces if the supply of grain stops while the runner stone is in motion, for the grain acts as a lubricant to the stone.

It takes an experienced dresser two days to dress a pair of stones, so in a mill with four pairs of stones, dressing was pretty much a full time occupation, and many dressers were needed in the heyday of traditional milling. Harder modern composition stones need less regular dressing but even so, the increasing popularity of traditional milling must swell the numbers of dressers again, many of whom will have to learn the craft from scratch.

POWER SOURCES

Milling on a local scale could be totally self-sufficient again, the mills being powered by wind or water. Examples of windmills are shown above and the beautifully simple mechanism of a watermill is shown right. Although the stones weigh several tons, they are a small part of the workings of a mill. More than one pair of stones is necessary, each with its own gearing that can be engaged or disengaged into the great spur wheel.

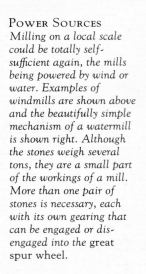

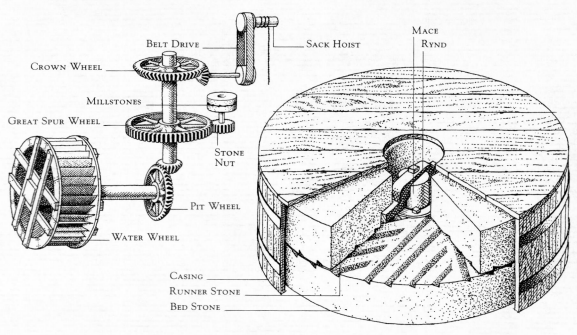

BELT DRIVE
SACK HOIST
MACE
RYND
CROWN WHEEL
MILLSTONES
GREAT SPUR WHEEL
STONE NUT
PIT WHEEL
WATER WHEEL
CASING
RUNNER STONE
BED STONE

STICKS & CROOKS

 DIFFERENCE BETWEEN YOUNG MEN of today and those of the time when I was one, is that we used to carry walking sticks. We didn't use them to help us to walk: we could walk quite well in those days. We carried them jauntily and, if they were the type with crooked handles, spun them round like the sail of a windmill.

I used to scorn sticks bought in shops and cut my own. I would search the hedges for ash plants, which had to be dead straight, the right thickness (they were never peeled), and have a nice knob on the end. The knob was nice to grasp and I had a belief that I could use it on the head of a transgressor if necessary. But although I used to effect a distain for the shop-bought stick with that bent-over handle, I used to wonder how they were made.

I found out one day in a strange wood in Sussex. It contained thousands of young ash saplings all twisted in an extraordinary manner into the shape of walking sticks. Many had templates of iron strapped to them to ensure that they grew straight and that the crooks were in the right place. I had come across a walking stick farm.

SHEPHERDS' CROOKS

I was introduced to shepherds' crooks on the Romney Marsh when I worked as an assistant to a *looker*, the local word for a shepherd. My looker had a fine white beard, a gentle and faithful dog, and a large *crozier* or crook. The crook had a long pole and was wide enough in the *bite* for it to go round a sheep's chest. The crook itself was made of wrought iron. My looker told me that Marsh crooks were made big like this so that you caught a sheep by the chest and not its hind leg because small wounds caused by nicking the leg would fester.

In Wales, where I next saw crooks, I found they were small things made to fit the hind leg of a sheep. The best of them are carved out of a single piece of wood – again an ash or thorn plant with a good stool to its base. In Wales, too, there are fancy crooks, highly decorated, with running dogs carved in the handle or very often leaping salmon. The one-piece models can be used for sheep, but those with stuck-on handles are ceremonial or for the tourists.

TYPES OF CROOKS AND STICKS
Most country folk use walking sticks more as ornamentation than as an aid to mobility. The group of four below gives some idea of the variety available. Crooks, on the other hand, are working tools, invaluable to the shepherd. The two on the right are made of ram's horn and their wide mouths are designed to catch sheep round the chest. The metal crook, far right, is known as a leg crook.

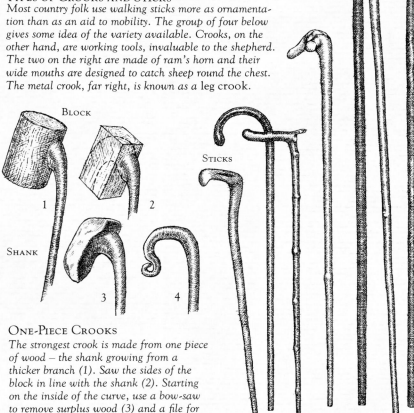

ONE-PIECE CROOKS
The strongest crook is made from one piece of wood – the shank growing from a thicker branch (1). Saw the sides of the block in line with the shank (2). Starting on the inside of the curve, use a bow-saw to remove surplus wood (3) and a file for the final shaping (4).

SHAPING THE HANDLE
Simple, elegant walking sticks can be fashioned from wood taken from well-established hedges. A variety of different woods can be used, including oak, sycamore, ash or hazel. In the photograph, left, you can see one method of shaping the handle – over a source of heat. This is a tricky process, because too much heat will scorch the wood.

MAKING FIELD GATES

NCE, THE VILLAGE CARPENTER was often hard at work making a wooden field gate for a local farmer. The carpenter's job was a skilled one, for sawn timber field gates were made to traditional local designs individual to various parts of the country. A good carpenter would add one or two details of construction that made the gate his own – an extra brace or decorative chamfers. Such gates were built to last, to withstand constant use as well as wind and weather.

Nowadays few gates are made in this way, for not only are there not many village carpenters left in business, but the coming of wide farm machinery such as combine harvesters has meant that many a beautiful wooden gate has been replaced by a wider, cheaper metal one. True, there are many machine-cut softwood gates made nowadays, pressure-treated with creosote to stop them rotting quite so quickly, but they are merely another sign of the deteriorating quality of our times.

HEREFORDSHIRE GATE
A few gate makers prefer to use cleft oak for parts of their gates. The craftsman, below, from Herefordshire, is such a one, and is seen here joining a slat, *or upright strap, to the top rail of a gate. The strong uprights at either end of the gate, the* heel *and the* head, *are of sawn wood so that the hinges and catch will align accurately.*

How Gates are Made

Good field gates should be constructed of heart of oak, or a wood which is similarly strong, such as chestnut. They measure up to 10 feet long and four feet high. The most important parts of a gate are the two uprights, one at the hinged end, called the *heel* or *harr*, to use its Scandinavian name, the other, thinner one, at the opening end, known as the *head*. Between these uprights are the top and bottom *rails*, with a number of *bars* in between. The total number of crossbars varies, according to the local design, from four to seven (a six-barred gate is the most common), but the lower bars are placed closer together to stop lambs slipping through. These crossbars are morticed into the uprights and made to fit tightly up and down, but not too tightly across for the carpenter might split the uprights at their most vulnerable point. Dowels are driven through the joints to ensure the bars stay firmly in place and there is a trick to this. The good carpenter deliberately drills the holes for the dowels so that the holes through the tenons are slightly off-line with the holes through the walls of the mortices. The effect is to draw the tenon even tighter into the mortice. When the crossbars are rammed home and the dowels driven in, considerable tension

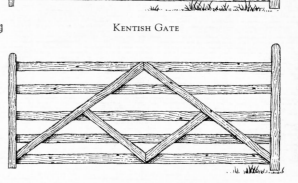

KENTISH GATE

DEVONSHIRE GATE

SOUTH EASTERN GATE

is created as the dowels have to find their way through the staggered holes.

Braces, or diagonal pieces, are used to prevent the gate sagging. Again, local custom determines the number and position of the diagonals, although the main brace always reaches from the bottom of the heel up to the top rail to counter the weight of the hanging gate. Upright straps can be fixed between the top and bottom rails of the gate in order to keep the crossbars firm and taut.

A very important part of the gate is the post it hangs from. Yew is the best wood for posts because it is the strongest, and if the post is tapered at the top it prevents water settling and rotting the wood. They are squared up by hewing with an axe, but only the visible part of the post above ground is so treated; that part below ground is left naturally rough. This makes for the securest possible fixing in the earth.

RIVEN ASH GATES

I have often made gates by nailing pieces of riven ash together, with no morticing and tenoning at all. The more important joints were bolted together. Of course, it was necessary to drill holes for the nails and bolts as otherwise the wood split. Ash gates made like this are very strong, but will only last for 20 years or so in the British climate and, obviously, they are primitive compared with the sawn oak gates made by the village carpenter of old.

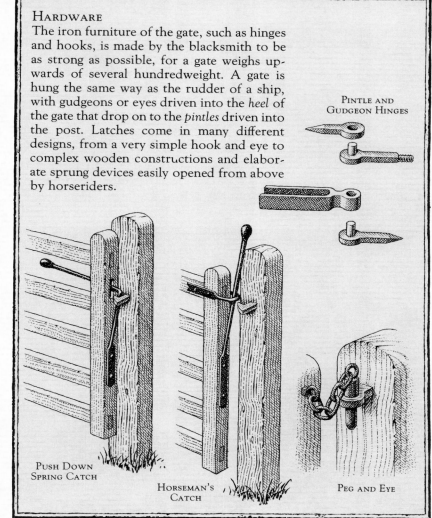

HARDWARE

The iron furniture of the gate, such as hinges and hooks, is made by the blacksmith to be as strong as possible, for a gate weighs upwards of several hundredweight. A gate is hung the same way as the rudder of a ship, with gudgeons or eyes driven into the *heel* of the gate that drop on to the *pintles* driven into the post. Latches come in many different designs, from a very simple hook and eye to complex wooden constructions and elaborate sprung devices easily opened from above by horseriders.

PINTLE AND GUDGEON HINGES

PUSH DOWN SPRING CATCH

HORSEMAN'S CATCH

PEG AND EYE

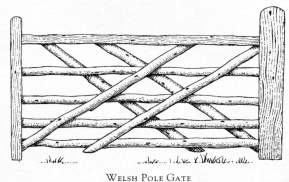

WELSH POLE GATE

HINGELESS GATE FROM SUSSEX (HEAVED INTO PLACE)

CAMBRIDGESHIRE GATE

CAMBRIDGESHIRE GATE

POTTING

UST AFTER THE SECOND WORLD War I was cruising up the Yorkshire Ouse in my home, which happened to be a Dutch sailing barge at the time, when, near a village called Littlethorpe, I saw a sign by the riverside which read: "The Pottery". Following the sign I came to what I took to be one of the last surviving traditional potteries in England. Mr Curtis, I am told, throws pots to this day in the traditional way and still fires them in two large old brick bottle kilns which, when I was there, he heated with coal. He dug his own clay from a pit behind his long brick shed.

Mr Curtis tried to show me how to *throw* a pot – to turn a lump of clay into a vessel of sorts while it turned on a wheel. He took a big handful of clay and flung it hard down on his steel potter's wheel as near the centre as he could. Splashing water over the clay he then cupped his hands over it and, exerting great pressure from both sides, let the clay spin between his palms until its eccentric motion ceased. This is *centring* the clay and is the most difficult thing about potting. If you cannot manage it you will never pot; if you can you have no problem. I might as well come out with it now: I cannot.

After the centring you can do any number of things with the clay. You can draw it up into a high cone; you can push it back down again; you can hollow it out with your fingers; in fact, you can turn it into any round shape that you like. After you stop spinning the wheel you can even pull it out of the round if you like. A good potter is

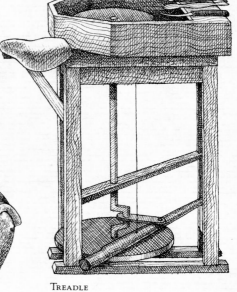

TREADLE KICK WHEEL

SIZE GAUGES

SHAPING TOOLS

TREADLE

POTS FOR EVERYDAY USE
Potting used to be a vital craft that provided earthenware vessels for everyday use. Many of the products, such as chimney- and flowerpots, were fired once only (biscuit ware). They were turned out in their thousands (above) to fixed sizes and shapes. Big, part-glazed storage crocks were similarly thrown on the potter's simple treadle wheel, as well as jugs and bowls of all sizes.

STORAGE CROCKS

marvellous to watch, for potting is surely one of the most beautiful of the human skills still practised.

Nowadays there is hardly a village in Northern Europe that does not have its *studio potter*. This person works inside a house or cottage, generally using an electric wheel (Mr Curtis used an electric wheel too I recall), and firing (the vital hardening process of potting) in a small electric or gas-fired kiln. These kilns are so small (perhaps two or three cubic feet) that the pots studio potters fire must be small and worth a lot for their size. Both electricity and gas are expensive and to fire flower pots in such kilns (Mr Curtis made most of his living from flower pots) would be quite un-economical. These potters, if they make a living at all, do it by the quality of their decoration. Nearly all of them buy their clay from centres like Stoke-on-Trent.

Traditional Potters Today

To find working potters nowadays who follow the old ways of one of the first and most basic of man's crafts, you must travel further afield. I found Mr Yanis Atsonios at work in a very basic pottery in Marousi, a suburb of Athens. Yanis's father came from an island in the Cyclades (where *his* father had been a potter before him) in 1924

and set up in Marousi because the clay there was good and Athens was a ready market. Mr Atsonios's work place is in a yard off a backstreet in what is now the ugly chaos of a modern suburb, but which was, only a couple of decades ago, an ancient and beautiful town on its own. There is a large open space in which stand huge piles of big unglazed pots – like most Greek potters Mr Atsonios seldom uses glaze. The pots are of a beautiful light brick-red colour and are of a dozen basic patterns and uses.

Mixing the Clay

In the middle of the yard is a *pug mill*, which in this case is a circular well, about six feet deep and five feet in diameter, with a steel paddle in it which is made to revolve by a small petrol engine. The paddle could easily have been powered by the once universal means of transport and power in the Mediterranean – the donkey – or indeed any draught beast. The clay, dug from a pit round the back, is thrown into the well, together with a lot of water, and worked with the paddle non-stop for about 24 hours. The local clay is red and Mr Atsonios puts five wheelbarrow loads of this in his

Finishing a Jug
After throwing, the jug is sliced off the wheel with a wire, and the rim pulled to make the pouring lip. A roll of clay is pulled to the correct length for a handle and attached to the body opposite the lip with plenty of slip (clay and water slurry). You then bend the other end round to join with the body.

Throwing a Jug
Once a lump of clay is centred on the wheel (that is, forced to spin symmetrically in the middle of the wheel), the skilled potter pushes down with the palm of his hand to open out the clay and create the thickness of the base (1). With the fingers of one hand controlling the outside face, the fingers of the other hand start to form the rising wall of the embryo jug (2). It is magical to watch a potter using his knuckles and fingertips to pull the clay upwards and into the shape required (3 and 4).

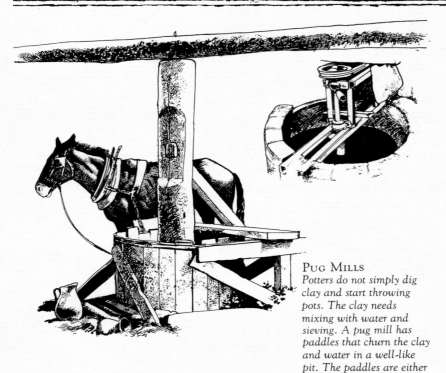

PUG MILLS
Potters do not simply dig clay and start throwing pots. The clay needs mixing with water and sieving. A pug mill has paddles that churn the clay and water in a well-like pit. The paddles are either driven by a draught beast, left, or they are powered through belts and pulleys.

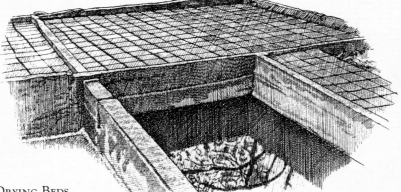

DRYING BEDS
When the clay has been mixed thoroughly, it is pumped through sieves and into drying beds (outdoors in warm climates) to allow the water to drain. Then the clay can be divided up ready for wedging, shown opposite.

ATHENIAN POTS
The Athenian potter I visited made the big, unglazed pots, shown right. They were decorated by scratching into the clay before the pots were dried and fired.

pug mill together with five barrow loads of a white clay that he has to buy in to give the right consistency and colour.

After the stirring is completed he pumps the liquid (for there is much more water than clay) through a screen, which removes any stones, and it runs into big open pans, some 20 feet square. These are just shallow depressions in the ground lined with brick. The water gradually drains away, leaving a layer of clay deposited about 10 inches thick. This is cut into cubes with a blade on a long handle. Mr Atsonios says it is like cutting spinach pie.

WEDGING THE CLAY
The cubes are taken, when they're needed, into the long brick shed that serves as the wedging and throwing room. Here Mr Atsonios and his assistant *wedge* the clay. This is a process known to all potters, traditional or otherwise, where the object is to expel any minute air bubbles which might be trapped in the clay. The smallest bubble will cause a damaging explosion in the kiln during firing. The potter simply takes the lump of clay to suit the work in hand, throws it down on to a firm, smooth surface and then repeatedly cuts through the clay with a wire to remove a section before banging it back into the main piece.

POTS FOR SMASHING
I saw Mr Atsonios's assistant throwing pots about two feet high on an electric wheel. He worked with deftness and great speed, drawing the pot up until it was shaped rather like a huge egg with its rounded side down. To my surprise he closed the top

completely, leaving no way into the pot nor any way out. "What," I asked, "is such a pot good for?" For answer the man took a knife and cut a tiny slot high up in the side of the pot, just large enough to take a coin.

"These are given to children," he explained. "Kind uncles put in money. When the child grows up he gets the money out."

"How?" I asked.

"By smashing the pot."

The newly thrown pots are dried indoors, for two days in the summer and 10 in the winter, and then put outside in the sun. After a few days they are put in the kiln.

A Strange Use of Nut Shells

The kiln is a brick, tunnel-shaped structure, four yards long, four yards wide and four yards high. The potters fire it twice a week and they were taking fired pots out when I was there. The kiln is never allowed to go cold and it was still enormously hot inside.

In one end of the kiln is the mouth for loading and unloading it and beneath the opposite end is a grate. Both ends open into brick sheds and the shed at the grate end is full of almond shells. Mr Atsonios buys the

Wedging the Clay

Wedging is the business of kneading and dividing the clay to check its consistency and for the presence of air-bubbles. The technique is to slam the clay down, knead, slice or pull it in two, then slam the divided sections together and knead again.

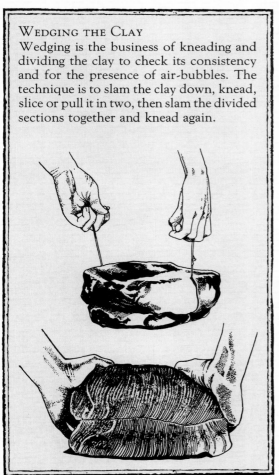

almond shells for one and a half drachmas a kilo from a nut factory in Pireus. The shells burn hot and clear and, as he said: "put a gleam into the pots." When he is firing he starts with gentle heat, warming the pots gradually, but then he goes on stoking hard for 12 hours to reach the required 1000 degrees centigrade.

Stepping Further into the Past

To find an even more basic potter I went to the village of Margerites in Crete. This is high up on the flank of a mountain and is a village of potters, for in that mountain, close by, good clay is found. There is an inexhaustible supply of it but, as the potter I found there said, somebody has to go and dig it out and return with it to the village using donkeys, which is very hard work.

Mr Kalfakis Pantelis is a shortish man, with a moustache, like nearly all Cretans, and he wears the fine leather top boots that all real Cretan men wear. His pottery is a rough flat-roofed building with fine mountain views on both sides.

The potters of Crete found the way to make good pots back in Minoan times, and they have not found it necessary to change their methods or designs very much since.

Kick Wheels

Some traditional village potters still make beautiful pots working at primitive kick wheels. This French potter is seated at such a wheel, which has a large fly-wheel beneath the throwing wheel that is pushed around by foot. The throwing wheel is chocked while she attends to a finished vessel.

TRADITIONAL DESIGN
Cretan pottery has a four-thousand-year history. Some of the traditional storage crocks are shown below. After drying in the warm Mediterranean air, simple coloured designs are painted on using a piece of sheep's wool twirled around a stick. The paint is really slip (clay and water) with a coloured mineral added, which, like the clay, is dug locally.

CRETAN POTTER

When I travelled to Crete I found a potter working at a simple kick wheel. He sat on a ledge in his workshop, driving the heavy wooden underwheel around with one foot while he braced himself with the other foot. He was constantly dipping into a bowl for water to lubricate the spinning clay.

Preparation of the clay is as basic as the clay itself. The method is to mix two portions of the local red clay with one portion of a grey powder, which Mr Pantelis calls *aluminium* (but in Greek) and is also dug on the mountain. The mixing entails first bashing the dry red clay on a brick floor with a large wooden mallet and then screening it to get any stones out. This reduces the clay to a coarse powder which is then put into a huge 10-gallon-or-so pot (made on the premises, of course), together with water. Mr Pantelis then roughly mixes this with a plunger, and slops the mixture from one big pot to another, screening it between each transfer and finally dumping it on the floor. At this stage he mixes in the dry grey powder and then makes a heap from which he takes clay as needed for wedging and throwing.

SIMPLE TECHNIQUES IN AN ANCIENT TRADITION

The Cretan potter throws on a kick wheel, which looks very home-made, or ethnic as we must call it now. The small wooden throwing wheel is driven round when you push a heavy wooden underwheel with your foot. He throws with great dexterity and cuts the finished pot off with a piece of wire.

He makes designs on the pot with a small piece of metal curved at both ends which he calls a *xystri* and he also uses a wedge-shaped knife. The designs have not changed since Minoan times and you can see pots decorated just as he decorates them in the museum at Iraklion. Mr Pantelis does not copy Minoan pots (he has never bothered to look at any), he is simply working in an unbroken tradition that goes back at least four thousand years.

Mr Pantelis dries his pots on shelves in his shed, amongst bunches of onions and his farming gear – for like all true Cretan craftsmen, he is a farmer too. The pots are left there for a day or two. Then they are put out in the sun, upside down on planks without touching one another.

The kiln is a round, well-like structure of fire bricks, open at the top with a hole in the side at the bottom. It is packed very carefully, to cram as many pots as possible into its five foot height and four foot diameter, and then the pots are covered with old broken shards of pottery and then a layer of mud to seal off the kiln. Faggots of whatever light wood are available fuel the kiln, mostly prunings of olive trees. Firing starts slowly, then Mr Pantelis speeds up the process and achieves the right temperature in 12 hours or so. He knows when he is up to temperature when the broken pots on top go black and then go white with the heat. Such mountain potteries serve the practical needs of local people. The produce is, technically speaking, *biscuit ware*, since it is only fired once, and includes bread-mixing bowls, little aladdin lamps for burning olive oil with wicks, pitchers for various liquids, often designed for tying round the necks of donkeys, pots for storing beans, olive and olive-oil crocks, bread crocks and crocks for storing some of the dough from the last baking. The yeast in the dough will stay alive for three months if kept in one of these vessels, with a little oil.

ELEFTHERNA AND VESSELS TO ENCOURAGE MODERATION

If you go to Knossos or any other of the many excavated palaces of the ancient Minoan civilization in Crete you will see plenty of enormous pots called *eleftherna*, rather like amphorae. They are enormous: two fat men could hide in one. Because one or two have been found with bones inside archaeologists have been led to think that they were burial urns. I am perfectly sure that most of them were used just as their direct descendants are used today – for storing wine and oil. They are still made and are to be seen all over the island: there is hardly a peasant family without at least two of them.

Mr Pantelis makes them but only in the summer, for they must be made out of doors. He makes them on the wheel but with the coiled pot technique. He first throws the base, up to about 18 inches high, allows this to dry, and then builds up a coil of clay on it. He stops building after about two feet and then turns the pot and smooths the inside and outside. He allows that stage to dry and then builds up another stage. He goes on like this until he has finished. After drying in the warm atmosphere, the pot is carried to the kiln, very carefully, by four men and fired.

Although their enormous size makes the coil pot technique the only way of making *eleftherna*, it is possible to throw pots of a size that would surprise most studio potters. I remember how Mr Curtis of Yorkshire, whom I introduced at the beginning of this article, used to throw chimney pots four feet or more high. He had to stand over the spinning wheel rather than sit at it, and the operation was a wonderful demonstration of skill combined with great strength. He was keen to pass on the techniques but I fear they will die with Mr Curtis.

Mr Pantelis sometimes makes little pots he calls *mugs of justice*. These are so devised that if you pour wine into them to a moderate level you can drink out of them and very good luck to you. If, however, you are greedy, as I am, and fill them too high, the wine runs out on to the floor – or into your lap as luck may deal with you. These have also been found among the ruins of the ancient cities so they are no new thing.

GIANT COIL POTS
Potters of the old school had to throw some very large pots using lumps of clay that you or I would have difficulty carrying. But it is impossible to make the giant Cretan pots, called eleftherna, *on a wheel. Only the base and the beginnings of the sides are thrown; the rest is gradually built up by adding coils of clay.*

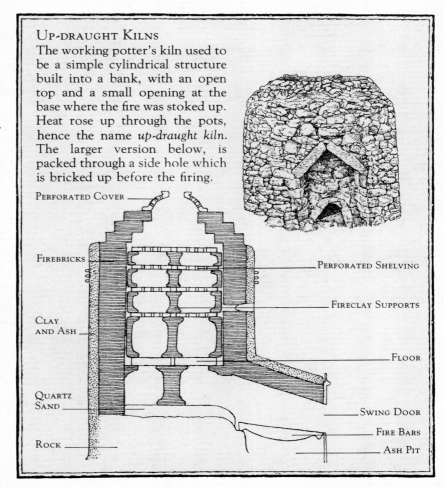

UP-DRAUGHT KILNS
The working potter's kiln used to be a simple cylindrical structure built into a bank, with an open top and a small opening at the base where the fire was stoked up. Heat rose up through the pots, hence the name *up-draught kiln*. The larger version below, is packed through a side hole which is bricked up before the firing.

PERFORATED COVER

FIREBRICKS

CLAY AND ASH

QUARTZ SAND

ROCK

PERFORATED SHELVING

FIRECLAY SUPPORTS

FLOOR

SWING DOOR

FIRE BARS

ASH PIT

BRICKMAKING

Y EXPERIENCE OF MAKING BRICKS was gained in Africa, many years ago, when the only way of obtaining most building materials was to make them yourself. Bricks were made, quite simply, by finding a suitable brick earth, moulding this into brick shapes and then air- and sun-drying them. Finally the bricks had to be fired, using either dry wood or charcoal.

Finding the right brick earth is not as simple as it sounds. Bricks are not made of pure clay but of a judicious mixture of clay and sand, and other grades of earth. The only way you can test a sample of earth is to mould it and fire it. Even a test in a very hot oven is better than nothing. Pure clay will crack in the firing, whereas a too sandy mixture will not hold together at all. Choosing the right earth is a matter of experience.

First, the earth has to be thoroughly *puddled*, which, in Africa, was an easy and even musical matter. I watched half a dozen Africans trample it with their bare feet singing heartily as they did so and took a

leaf from their book. Once mixed to a smooth consistency the clay would then be forced into brick-sized moulds (slightly more than brick-sized actually because earth shrinks as it dries), placed on planks in the sun for a week or two (you can be sure there will be no rain in the dry season), and then built into a kiln and fired. In northern Europe the drying process is carried out under cover and takes a month.

ALTERNATIVE METHODS OF FIRING

There were two methods of firing the bricks. Both involved building a *clamp* of bricks, but in the first the brick piles crisscrossed so as to leave spaces in between them. Cavities (*fireplaces*) were also left at ground level along the windward side of the clamp. The whole thing then had to be plastered with mud, except for the fireplaces (which were no more than a yard apart) and some small vents on the leeward side where the smoke could escape during the burning. Next, the fireplaces were filled with well-dried wood and set alight. It was

ORNAMENTAL BRICKS
The main demand for ornamental and decorative bricks is from restorers of old buildings requiring replicas to replace damaged originals and from individuals and builders wishing to add a touch of originality to a new brick wall. The bricks are made individually in wooden moulds scaled up in size to allow for shrinkage as the bricks dry out. The design is raised in reverse in the base of the mould.

necessary to keep these fires burning for a week, which required a lot of firewood.

I gave this method up (although it produced perfectly good bricks) in favour of the charcoal method. In this layer after layer of bricks were built, with wide spaces between them, and the spaces filled with small pieces of charcoal. When the clamp was at least seven feet high – and as long and wide as you had bricks for – it was plastered all over with mud. As with the dry wood method, small holes were left high up on the leeward side to let the smoke out, and slightly larger holes at ground level on the windward side to act as fireplaces. We then lit the charcoal and just let it burn inwards, consuming all the small pieces of charcoal within the clamp. It would burn away quite happily for several days, and after about a week it would be cool enough to break open.

BRITISH BRICKS
Brickmaking in Britain goes back to Roman times. I have seen the hard and level sites they selected with an eye to drying their thin, wooden-moulded bricks.

The usual method of making bricks by hand today is *pallet moulding*. The brick

CLAY WINNING
While most clay for bricks today is extracted with excavators and dumper trucks, there are still a few individuals left making their own bricks who win, or dig, their clay by hand. This is a laborious and backbreaking job but it does allow the brickmaker to choose the best clay and reject the sub-standard.

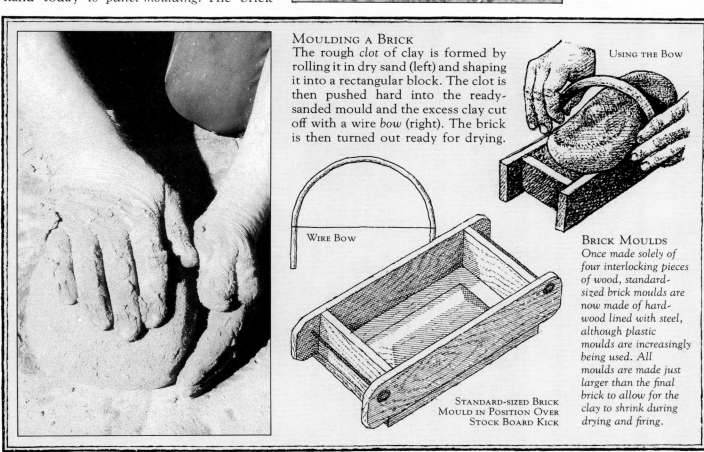

MOULDING A BRICK
The rough *clot* of clay is formed by rolling it in dry sand (left) and shaping it into a rectangular block. The clot is then pushed hard into the ready-sanded mould and the excess clay cut off with a wire *bow* (right). The brick is then turned out ready for drying.

USING THE BOW

WIRE BOW

STANDARD-SIZED BRICK MOULD IN POSITION OVER STOCK BOARD KICK

BRICK MOULDS
Once made solely of four interlocking pieces of wood, standard-sized brick moulds are now made of hardwood lined with steel, although plastic moulds are increasingly being used. All moulds are made just larger than the final brick to allow for the clay to shrink during drying and firing.

maker prepares his work bench by nailing to it a *stock board* on which there is a raised *kick* which forms the *frog* or recess in the brick and over which the mould is placed. Dusting the board, and the mould, with sand, he rolls out a lump of clay to form a rectangular *clot* or *warp* of clay which is then pressed into the mould, ensuring that every crevice is filled. The surface of the clay is then levelled with a wire *bow* or a *strike*, which is just a damp stick and the mould is then turned out on to a *pallet board*. When

sufficient bricks are made, a *bearer-off* transports them to a drying platform called a *hack*. Drying can take as long as six weeks, depending on the weather, although such refinements as underfloor heating do help.

The other process for making bricks, *slop moulding*, is not used so much now. In this process, the brickmaker wets the mould rather than sanding it, and the mould is placed directly on the bench without a stock. Since a slop-moulded brick is wetter, it requires more drying time before firing.

A Brick Kiln

The major requirement of a brick kiln is constant heat, produced by wood, charcoal, or I suspect anthracite would work. The bricks are piled up in a clamp, the fuel installed and whole edifice plastered with mud and topped with fire bricks to seal it, with only a vent left to fuel the fire and some smaller vents on the leeward side to allow the smoke to escape. Once alight, the fire slowly burns itself out and after about a week the kiln can be dismantled and the fired bricks taken out.

The Hack Barrow

The traditional brickmaker's hack barrow is sideless, for easy loading, and carries as many bricks as the brickmaker himself can comfortably lift. It is much in use as the bricks have to be carried from the pallet board where they have been placed after moulding to the hack or drying platform, and from there to to the ovens when dry.

TILE MAKING

RADITIONAL CLAY TILES ARE MADE from the same materials as hand-made bricks and made in much the same way. Tiles, though, are made in many different sizes and shapes, and different parts of the world have different patterns. Those beautiful pantile roofs of Italy and the South of France are curved to exactly the shape of the thigh of some Roman tile maker centuries ago. The tiles were made flat and to the right size, then folded over the thigh to form a curve.

Nowadays, tile clay is shaped and pressed in moulds and the tiles, after air-drying, are fired in the same way as bricks. Tiles can also be salt-glazed – with the kiln at a very high temperature salt is thrown in and the resulting gas hardens the surface of the tiles. Flooring tiles are often glazed on one side, as is pottery – *true glaze* as tile makers have it. Tiles are one of the artifacts though which, so easily made by machine, are practically never made by hand now.

ROOFING

There are many ways to fix tiles to form a roof. The Italian tile, thigh-formed or otherwise, is attached in tiers. The individual tiles are laid alternately convex and concave. In this way, rain water runs from the tile with its convex side uppermost into the troughs formed by its neighbours with their concave sides uppermost. This arrangement forms a series of troughs, kept watertight by successively overlapping tile edges, running right down the roof. The design makes it possible to have the comparatively flat roofs one sees in Mediterranean countries without fear of leaks.

Most northern European roofs are covered with small rectangular tiles, measuring $10\frac{1}{2}$ by $6\frac{1}{2}$ inches – time-honoured dimensions. They are punched, for two roofing nails, and are moulded with two *nibs* (little projections) along one of the short sides. On the roof, the nibs hook over the tiling battens that are fixed parallel to the eaves and ridge. Plain tile roofs have a much steeper angle, or *pitch*, to help the overlapping tiles shed rain water.

PLAIN TILES
Plain tiles require peg, or nail holes and protruding nibs to hold them secure on steeply pitched roofs.

MAKING A TILE
You can make tiles by hand in a mould, the back of which must be hinged to a square iron frame with the two prongs that punch out the nail holes in the tile. You shape the clay in the mould with a bow, using the flat wooden surface for smoothing the surface of the tile (1), and cutting away the superfluous clay with the wired end (2). The tile can then be removed for firing (3).

PAPER MAKING

 HE FIRST PAPER MAKERS WERE wasps. They chew wood up, mix it with their saliva, and make those beautiful papery nests. Anyone can make paper. I know a lady who lives in Herefordshire and makes paper of the weirdest things – from nettles to Swedish turnips. She sent me once a little clip of samples of paper made from linen, bracken, rush, rush and linen, cotton straw, chamomile, spent hops, artichoke, cabbage and nettles. Some of these I had never considered suitable.

To see paper made by hand on anything like a sensible scale (small is beautiful but minute can be ridiculous) I had to go up the charming valley of the little River Dore, which flows into the Allier in the Auvergne, in central France. There I inspected the paper mill of the late Richard-de-Bas. The mill has been producing paper, with only one small interruption, since the seventeenth century with its present machinery, and before that there had been a paper mill on the site since the fourteenth century. The mill survives partly because visitors are allowed to inspect it (and pay for the privilege) and partly because it turns out fine paper used in limited edition books. Thankfully, there is still a demand for this type of product, albeit on a limited scale.

There is a fine overshot waterwheel, which has been turning continuously (except for halts for occasional repairs) for 300 years. The wheel turns an enormous horizontal beam, called the *chapabre*. This beam has pegs of apple wood sticking up from it in a pattern that resembles the workings of a musical box. As the beam revolves, the pegs catch the ends of huge wooden hammers, which cause the hammers to lift a few inches. As the pegs turn, the hammers drop. They drop into large stone mortars (called *creux de pile*), thus hammering whatever happens to be in the bottom of the mortars.

As the waterwheel revolves, these hammers thunder up and down in a strange

1 *At the Richard-de-Bas* paper mill cotton rags are pounded for 36 hours by huge water-powered hammers.

2 *The rag and water pulp is transferred to a vat. The* ouvreur *scoops out just the right thickness of pulp from the vat using a wire mesh tray.*

3 *The* coucheur *takes the tray and turns out now-consolidated pulp on to a sheet of felt. He builds up a pile – a layer of felt, a layer of pulp.*

rhythm of their own (determined in fact by the arrangement of the pegs on the great shaft). The material from which the paper is to be made is mixed with water (diverted by ancient wooden channels from the stream that drives the mill) and poured into the mortars under the hammers. The material used now in the mill is cotton rags, which make the best-quality paper. Wooden chips or shavings would do – practically anything, in fact, of vegetable origin. And for 36 hours these rags are mercilessly hammered to a fine pulp.

The pulp is then run off into the *cuve*, a simple vat. Here the liquid is heated by means of a charcoal fire and kept constantly stirred. Now for some team work: a man called the *ouvreur* takes up a shallow tray with a fine gauze bottom and with a deft motion he inserts this into the liquid, lifts it, to allow the surplus water to run through the gauze, and hands the tray to another man standing beside him who calls himself the *coucheur* – the "putter to bed". The *coucheur* has already laid a square of woollen felt beside him, and he turns the tray over and allows the sheet of pulp to fall on to the felt. He then immediately places another piece of felt on top of this. Thus he builds up a pile of alternating pieces of felt and layers of paper pulp.

Next he removes the pile to the *press*. This is a massive wooden press almost

exactly as can be found pressing apple pulp for cider or grape pulp for wine. Great pressure is applied to the pile and most of the moisture is squeezed out. The sheets – and now I suppose one can call it paper – are taken out and hung up from racks in a huge loft, which is warmed in winter, to dry. Now they are really paper.

Various Origins of Good Paper

I saw a paper mill in central India many years ago. The pulp was made by a heavy round stone being dragged around in a circular stone trough by a cow. The sheets were scooped from the pulp, then pressed

Mould and Deckle
The paper maker's most important implements are the mould and deckle. The mould is a rigid framework covered in the fine wire mesh that strains the pulp and gives handmade paper its characteristic pattern of laid lines. If you scooped out pulp using the mould only, the paper would end up thicker in the middle of the sheet than at the edges. The deckle is a detachable raised frame the maker uses to contain the pulp evenly across the sheet.

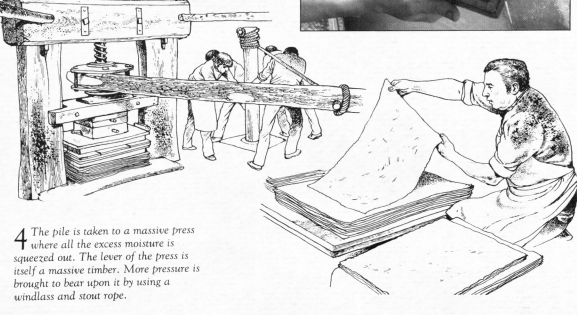

4 *The pile is taken to a massive press where all the excess moisture is squeezed out. The lever of the press is itself a massive timber. More pressure is brought to bear upon it by using a windlass and stout rope.*

5 *After pressing, the pile is dismantled, each sheet of paper being unpeeled and hung to dry.*

WEIGHING MINERAL
PIGMENT FOR
COLOURING PULP

THE COCK BAG
The cock bag, as paper makers have it, is simply a piece of felt or heavy linen, set in a handled frame. You put any pigment you want to add to the pulp in the bag, then dunk it into the pulp, giving the soggy bag a good squeeze to filter out the colour.

and simply stuck to the wall of a shed where they dried quickly in the warm atmosphere of that region.

Less far afield, I found Mr John Sweetman supervising the paper factory at Wookey Hole in Somerset. Here anybody can be shown the old mill where paper is made by ancient and traditional methods. Old rags are first boiled under pressure in caustic soda. In days of old, the rags were thumped by hand in a large pestle and mortar. Nowadays, a machine called a Hollander is used, which consists of a serrated roller turning in a tank. The serrations just touch the bottom of the tank and thus pummel the *half-stuff*, as the mixture of pulp and water is known in England. The operator of the Hollander is called the *beater* and, as probably every batch of raw material he is given is different, he must exercise good judgment. The severity with which he beats the half-stuff is all important to the quality of the final paper, as is the amount of water he allows to mix with the paper pulp.

Just before the end of the *beating* some alum (aluminium sulphate) and sometimes soap are added to *size* the paper. The *stuff*, as it is now called, passes to the *stuff-chest*,

where it is mixed with enough water to make it from one to two per cent by weight of dry matter to water. It is then passed, as required, to the *vat*.

The vat has an agitator in the bottom and a warming device to keep the stuff at a pleasant temperature. The *vatman* (the English equivalent of the French *ouvreur*) takes a *mould*, which is a shallow tray of fine wire mesh. Around this he fits a *deckle*. This is a frame that is laid over the mould to give it more depth. He holds mould and deckle together, dips them into the stuff, gives them a shake to remove excess and even the stuff out, lifts off the deckle and hands the mould to the *croucher*. The croucher turns it over on a piece of felt and the future paper falls out. The two of them can make 10 sheets of paper a minute. The resulting pile of felt and paper is called a *post*. This is then pressed in a hydraulic press. After excess water has been removed, the paper is sorted out from the felts and put in a pile, which is called a *pack*. This is, sometimes, pressed again and the sheets laid out on hessian trays in an airy room. The sheets may then be sized by being dipped in a solution of gelatine or starch, pressed again and dried. If a very smooth finish is required, the sheets are interleaved with shiny steel plates and then rolled. High-quality paper made in this way comes at a premium, and this reflects the time and skill of craftsmen using centuries-old techniques.

FOOLISH LAWS
In the eighteenth century, hemp (*Cannabis sativa*) was the most favoured material for the making of paper. In fact, the hemp plants were grown on a large scale for this purpose alone. Old worn-out ropes made of hemp were eminently suitable for this purpose, too. The British navy of the time must have been a plentiful supplier of old ropes. Now, however, owing to foolish laws in many countries, the cultivation of this magnificent and useful plant is outlawed, and so we continue to use up the world's forests, destroying the ecological balance through vast areas.

It can be argued that, no matter how good hand-made paper might be, it would be impracticable to provide the paper for, say, one of the mass-circulation daily newspapers. This may well be so, but perhaps the world would be a better and finer place if there were more emphasis on quality and less on quantity.

BASKETRY

CAN REMEMBER A TIME, not all that long ago, when most things that are now packed in cardboard or plastic came in a basket. All sorts of farm produce and seafoods were harvested and then travelled in baskets which now you would have to pay a deal of money for in their own right, supposing you could find someone who knew how to make them. Basketwork protected your bottles from breaking, your hats from squashing and your picnics from ants. Nor was packing and storage the end of the matter – basketwork was so much a part of everyday life that you might very well catch sparrows in a basket trap when you were young, and end up being pushed in a wicker bath-chair when you were old.

THE SUPREMACY OF WILLOW
When I lived in Wales I had a very good friend named John Jones, who was a Gypsy man and proud of it. He used to sit at my fireside many a night and, among the things he taught me, was basket making. He would often say that a man can walk out into the country with nothing on him but a knife and make any kind of a basket. He opened my eyes to using split hazel, blackberry briars with the thorns scraped off, dog rose briars and even honeysuckle and other creepers for basket making. (Elsewhere you can read about making baskets with oak, see p.47, and rush, see p.172). But he always insisted on the supremacy of the thin pliable wands of various kinds of willow tree as basket-making material.

Willow basket making is what we refer to when speaking of *wickerwork*. It is the flexibility of willow that allows the most ingenious work and it is the ease with which willow can be grown and harvested that allows basket making on a large scale. What you call the young willow fronds used for

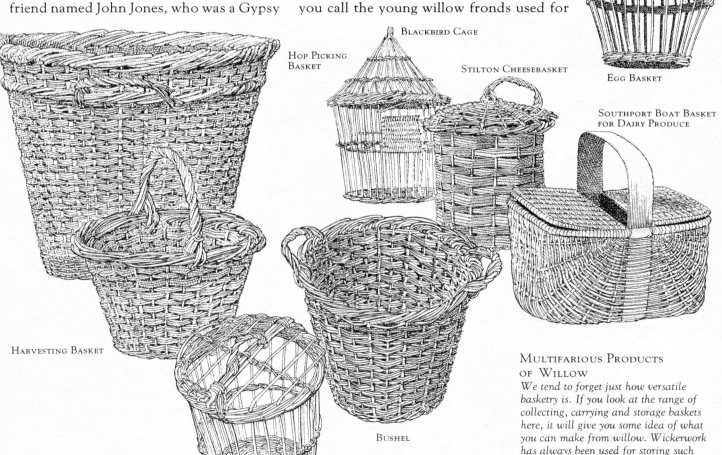

HOP PICKING BASKET

BLACKBIRD CAGE

STILTON CHEESEBASKET

EGG BASKET

SOUTHPORT BOAT BASKET FOR DAIRY PRODUCE

HARVESTING BASKET

BUSHEL

POULTRY BASKET

MULTIFARIOUS PRODUCTS OF WILLOW
We tend to forget just how versatile basketry is. If you look at the range of collecting, carrying and storage baskets here, it will give you some idea of what you can make from willow. Wickerwork has always been used for storing such perishables as dairy produce, because it breathes. Another attribute of weave is that you can make it tight or open. Make it open enough and you have a cage.

CUTTING THE WITHIES

Withy beds are established by pushing willow branches into damp ground in rows – they grow with no trouble at all. They are left to grow for the first three years and then cut down to the *stools* (cut down to ground level) every year thereafter. The cutting itself is back-breaking work and, like the harvesting of reed and rush, is a wintertime activity. You need a trusty curved blade, such as the sickle used by the venerable gentleman above, and you have to bend double to cut the withy branches off flush.

The withy cutters that used to work near my home in Ireland were salmon fishermen making the most of the winter when they could not fish. The withies were poled down the river in barges with the tide and off-loaded near the basket works. Here the withies were seized on by an army of workers ready to strip them. Each worker would have a post, driven into the ground with a brake bolted to the top of it. The withies were pulled through the V of the brake, to bruise the bark. When the children were let out of school they would all come running down to the basket works and strip the loosened bark off with their fingers.

THE BRAKE

The brake consists of two pieces of round iron bar welded to each other at the bottom to form a narrow V shape. You simply pull the withy down into the V to split the bark ready for stripping.

basket making depends on where you come from. *Withy* is the term I use although it has West Country origins, whereas *osier*, or simply *rod*, are more widespread. In Ireland, from where my most recent experience of basket making has come, they talk of *sallies*, from *sallow*, the old word for a willow.

THE WORLD'S BEST BASKET MAKER

Thinking of the old time baskets that were once so common set me to finding a basket maker of the old breed. I began to enquire around. Simple, said everyone. The best basket maker in Ireland – nay in the British Isles – probably in the world – lives in the next town, 40 miles from you. This sort of advice is difficult to ignore. So is the fact that the first person I happened to meet when I went to the next town had worked at Shanahan Willow Craft for 26 years. He went on to say that Joe Shanahan, the great man himself, was the most famous man with baskets in the whole world and that I was the luckiest man alive to have found him so easily.

It was, however, some days later that I followed Joe Shanahan through the door of his workshop. Inside was a large room absolutely littered with basketry of various sorts, and basket materials. A very pretty girl sat on a low stool at one side of the room making, very deftly, a small rectangular basket with a lid. On the other side of the room sat a young man, similarly engaged.

THE BASKET MAKER'S PLANK

Both workers had a big old door flung on the floor near the wall – the basket maker's *plank*. On top of this was a board like a table-top, about five feet by three feet, on the slant. This is the *lap-board* and the bottom end of it was caught against a piece of wood nailed to the bottom of the plank so that it would not slip. The top of it was propped up on wooden blocks. The basket maker sat with his back against the wall, on a low stool, facing the raised end of the lap-board. If he wanted the lap-board higher he simply put another block or two under it. If he wanted it lower he took a block or more out.

SOAKING THE WILLOW

An open door led into a yard in which willow bundles were soaking. Beyond this again was an enclosed garden. In it stood a shaving horse (see p.33). Like many old town gardens, surrounded by ancient stone

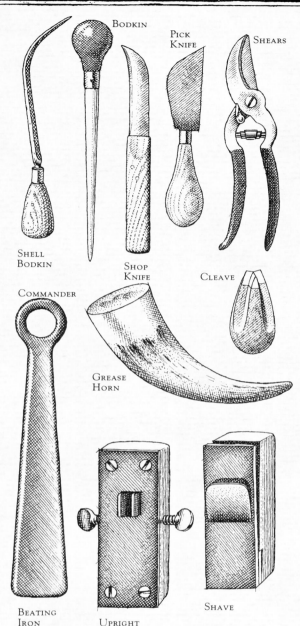

SHELL BODKIN · BODKIN · PICK KNIFE · SHEARS · SHOP KNIFE · CLEAVE · COMMANDER · GREASE HORN · BEATING IRON · UPRIGHT · SHAVE

THE TOOLS
The basket maker's toolkit is small, comprising of clever little instruments for shaving and cleaving the willow rods, knives and shears for cutting and trimming and devices for arranging the weave. The cleave, in skilled hands, will split a rod three ways while the two planes, the upright and shave, are used to reduce thickness or width. Split and shaved rods are used for binding. The shop knife is used for slyping rods (pointing one end) while shears and pick knife are the tools for trimming ends when the work is finished. Bodkins are greased from the grease horn and used to divide the weave so you can drive in other rods. You beat the weave down tight with the beating iron, using the ring end (the commander) to straighten the framework of square work.

walls, it seemed a delightful place to be. I asked Joe if he was not tempted to sit there sometimes and make his baskets. He told me no – the willow would dry out too quickly in the sunshine.

The essence of willow basket making is the flexibility of the withies. The willow is stored dry, however, and must be soaked well before it is used to restore its flexibility for the time when the basket is being worked. Most basket makers soak the willow for the next day the evening before. The willow bundles I saw soaking would be taken from the stone trough after an hour or so, depending on the sort of willow, and left to *mellow* overnight, that is to allow the surface water to penetrate to the pith of each withy, making it ready for use.

MORE ABOUT WILLOW

There are *brown withies, buff withies* and *white withies*. Brown withies simply have the bark left on them. They are used for large and rough baskets. Buff withies are boiled, in their jackets, for at least three hours (nearer five as a rule) and then skinned or stripped. The boiling causes the tannin and other dyes in the bark to stain the wood a pleasant tan colour. White withies are simply stripped without boiling. In order to make the stripping easier the bundles of withies for white withies are stood in muddy pools from the time they are cut, in winter, until they are transported in Spring when they actually begin to sprout.

All this work had been done by the Shanahan firm, but now, alas, most of the material is imported. When people can make a fair living otherwise they are not going down the river in a boat to cut withies

it seems. A few are still cut by salmon fishermen in winter, but the bulk come from Somerset where farm workers and smallholders still make osier bed cultivation part of their livelihood.

THE YEAST BASKET

There is square basketwork and there is round basketwork. They are different mostly in the way you start the work and Joe was kind enough to show me the intricacies of both, while conveying great enthusiasm for his ancient craft. To demonstrate square basketwork he chose to make a yeast basket. Now this is a basket with a history that says much about the basket trade and its produce.

In days of old distillers used to produce as a by-product many tons of yeast, and this was sent out to bakers. The small bags of yeast were packed in baskets which were non-returnable. Shanahan's had once turned out as many as 1200 of these baskets a week, each man producing up to 40

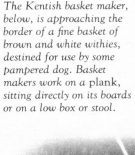

KENT CRAFTSMAN
The Kentish basket maker, below, is approaching the border of a fine basket of brown and white withies, destined for use by some pampered dog. Basket makers work on a plank, sitting directly on its boards or on a low box or stool.

baskets every long working day.

"What used to happen to them after they had been delivered to the baker?" I asked.

"Into the fire with them! Under the oven."

It seemed to me to be a measure of the extreme cheapness of basketry, provided labour was cheap, that baskets could be made for such a transient use. True the basket was a rough creation knocked up, lid and all, in a quarter of an hour. But my belief is that that basket could have stood up to dozens of trips between distillery and baker before it would have come undone.

In 1957, the cardboard box came in and killed the industry because it was just a little cheaper than the yeast basket. The cost of human misery involved in the sacking of most of the hundred men working in the basketworks could not, of course, be taken into account. Nor could the fact that the cardboard boxes entailed the cutting down of forests, while baskets rely on the annual harvest from self-perpetuating willow beds.

USING THE CLAMP

The base is the start of any basket and to make a square base you need a *block*. This is two strips of wood with two bolts through them to form a clamp. In this Joe clamped 13 resilient withies so that they stood up vertically, and settled at his work station. He quickly wove two withies together along the bottom of this little fence. "We call that the *passover*," he said. He then started what he called *slewing*. This was ordinary plain weaving, but with five or six withies all together and parallel. It was obviously a very quick method of filling in space. He then finished off the little wall in front of him with two intertwined withies again, and this he called the *pass-off*.

HIGH SPEED BASKETRY

Now he took the piece of basketry he had woven out of the block and laid it on the slanting table before him. He dumped a large stone on it to keep it steady. The withies Joe had used projected way beyond the woven section of base, and now he *kinked* each withy where it projected and bent them up at right angles to make the *stakes*, or uprights of the basket body. Kinking is a matter of sticking a knife-blade in along the grain of the willow and giving it a slight twist. This opens the grain enough for the withy to be bent without breaking.

BASKETRY TECHNIQUES

The principles of basketry are similar to those of weaving. You need a row of parallel rods (stakes) through which you weave another rod at 90 degrees. You can use more than one weaving rod at once and you can weave in patterns if you like. To make a square of basketwork, you clamp the first set of stakes temporarily and when you reach the end of the row you can simply twist the weaving rod back on itself and continue the weave. For round basketry you must have an odd number of uprights so that the weaving rods weave alternatively in front and behind the same uprights every other circuit.

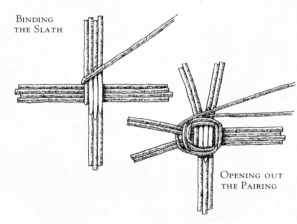

BINDING THE SLATH

OPENING OUT THE PAIRING

TYING THE SLATH
If you look in the middle of the bottom of a round basket, you will see the slath where the basket maker starts to work by laying three short rods over three others. He then binds the cross with a weaver and opens them out into a star shape, either weaving with two rods (pairing) or with one around an odd number of star points.

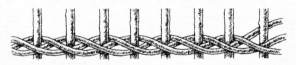

THREE-ROD WALING
You start three weavers and take each behind two, in front of one.

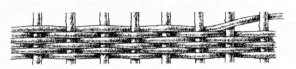

RANDING
This is basic weaving, behind and in front, using one rod.

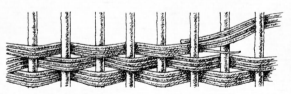

SLEWING
Slewing is randing with three or more weavers. It is quick to do and looks good.

FIVE-ROD BORDER
There are many decorative borders. This one involves five uprights at once.

OPENWORK
A basket maker will sometimes leave a section of a basket open, for decoration or for some practical purpose. The upright stakes have to be bound in tightly above it.

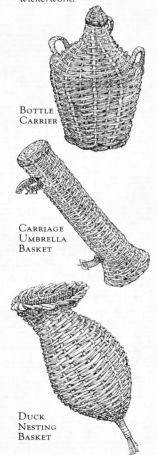

BOTTLE CARRIER

CARRIAGE UMBRELLA BASKET

DUCK NESTING BASKET

As each stake was bent up it was held there in a light loop. When all the stakes were in place he quickly slewed the two ends and the two sides of the basket. One side he continued slewing much further than the others, finishing off with a pass-off. The extension was bent down and became the lid. All loose ends were trimmed off with a pair of shears, like garden secateurs but purpose-made.

Joe worked like lightning. It was hard to follow what he was doing.

"Anyone can make a basket, but if you want to make a living at it you've got to be fast!" he said.

THE TURF BASKET

The yeast basket was cast aside and at this point Joe held me to his assertion that I should make a basket. The basket I made, rather the basket that Joe made with a very little help from me, was a turf basket and it illustrates round basketwork nicely.

Turf is the name Irish people give to what we call peat, which is dug and dried for the fire (see p.70). I have the basket still and it is a perfect general purpose basket. At the moment it is full of potatoes.

The *slath*, or beginning of the base of this basket, is made by cutting six short lengths of withy and laying them, three across three, at right angles. Now John

Jones (my Gypsy friend, you will remember) had taught me to split one lot of these and stick the other lot through the slit. Joe abhorred this method and said he preferred the traditional way, which is just to lay one set on top of the other. He set his lap-board flat, put the crossed withies on top and steadied them with his foot. Stooping over, he bound them together with a very thin and whippy withy, which he twisted to make more flexible. Then, pulling the 13 rod points he had bound together into a star (the end of the binding withy forms one extra point of the star), he began to weave other withies in and out of them. The thirteenth point is vital as the number of withies that form the *warp* (to use a cloth weaving term) must be an odd number, for if this were not so, after one round of weaving the pattern would begin to repeat and all the weaving withies (the *weavers*) would be lying the same way and the basket would just not hold together.

As we got further from the middle of the base, the *warp* withies began to get too far apart, so extra withies were driven into the weave to augment them. The ends of these new withies were *slyped*, that is cut to a point with the knife. After about half of the bottom of the intended basket had been thus woven, we started slewing to fill out space more quickly before the edge of the circular base was completed by *pairing*, a sort of plait using two withies. Look at the underside of a circular basket and you will notice it is concave so that only the strong edge of the base contacts the ground. My turf basket is similarly dished.

THE SIDES AND BORDERING OFF

With round baskets the stakes for the side weaving have to be driven into the weave of the base. Twenty-nine strong rods are selected and slyped at their bottom ends. The slyped ends are driven hard into the edges of the circular base, then they are *kinked* and bent up sharply. This is called *upsetting*. Strong weaving holds the base of the stakes tight. Then a bit of slewing with four withies at once increased the pace. Next Joe showed me a new trick – a kind of plait he called *French weave*, which involved driving newly-slyped withies into the weave and plaiting them with alternate reverse turns of the basket.

When the top was near, Joe produced a complicated border, plaiting with five rods at once. The tops of the stakes were themselves woven into the border, their ends being bent down at right angles and driven into the weave below with a heavy iron tool, called the *hand iron*. Strong handles were made at each side from a simple hoop of withy pushed through the weave (a spike, known as a *bodkin*, was used to enlarge the holes for this). Slender withies were then selected, twisted hard to make them pliable, and wrapped round and round the hoop and woven into the basket below.

A WEALTH OF EXPERIENCE

After witnessing these displays of basketry I realised that Joe Shanahan could build any kind of basket there is or could be. I learned that he had even built balloon baskets. When he first started there were a hundred people employed full time in basketwork. They made a virtually endless variety of objects. A few of them were cane chairs, laundry baskets and heavy strong baskets for the railways (you used to see baskets standing about on all railway platforms). They made potato baskets, log baskets and shopping baskets, and plenty of industrial baskets in large quantities (mostly for protecting bottles and flasks), bread baskets, and even far-out things like wicker-work goal posts for polo fields (the ponies do not hurt themselves if they bang into them), calf muzzles (to stop calves from

sucking their mothers), bicycle baskets and even ducks' nests.

BASKETRY FOR THE SEA

I wanted some special basketry made for use on board my wooden boat *Dreoilin* (see p.114). In the first place, I was going to go fishing in the estuary here where my home is and this body of water is famous for eels. You may not like the idea of eels, but I consider them one of the most delicious of seafoods, and smoked they are worth many times their weight in smoked salmon. I needed East Anglian eel *hives*.

The best hives are designed and made by the eel catchers themselves to suit the rivers they fish. A typical hive is up to five feet long and consists of two chambers connected by a funnel. The hive is flat bottomed to allow it to lie on the bed of the river where the eels swim. One end is wide open, the other narrow and enclosed. The hive is baited by placing a piece of dead fish in the chamber in the enclosed end, for the eel is a carnivore, and likes the dead flesh of fish as well as the occasional live newt, frog or small fish. Attracted by the smell, the eel swims in, and since it cannot find the small entrance, gets stuck in the hive. The English have a reputation for jellying eels but people of most other nations smoke them or simply fry or stew them.

I also wanted to set lobster and whelk pots. Of course, I know all about the advantages of lobster traps made of expanded metal, and wire mesh, and all the rest of it, but I am not a professional fisherman and derive more pleasure from using

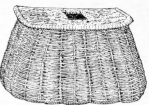

FISHERMAN'S CREEL
The traditional fisherman's basket for tackle and catch is called a creel and is best made of fine wickerwork. It has a shoulder strap and is subtly shaped to hang snuggly by the user's hip, next to his free hand.

SHRIMPER'S CATCH
The harvesting basket, below, belongs to a shrimp fisherman from the northwest coast of England. The fish are an incidental bonus to the shrimp catch they lie on.

traditional methods, and so I wanted traditional pots. I thought that if I could watch a professional basket maker weave these items I would be able to copy him and make any extra that I needed myself. Joe was confident of producing any *exotica* I could mention and he made time to make me a whelk pot that day.

FISH TRAPS
Wicker fish traps come either in the form of pots that you bait to trap creatures that crawl across the sea-bed, such as lobsters, or funnels that allow swimming fish in but not out. Most famous of the funnel kind is the salmon putcher. Serried ranks of these devices have been built into the mud of the Severn estuary, near South Wales, for 500 years, waiting to trap the fish as the tide carries them to sea. Of course they need a little maintenance from time to time, as the picture below shows.

LOBSTER POT

FISH TRAP

EEL HIVE

SALMON PUTCHER

WHELK POTS
Now I have been to sea, many times, with the whelkers of Wells, in the east of England. I have a lovely little painting of a typical whelker (a very specialized open boat) in front of me as I write this. The east-coast fishermen use pots made of iron woven with tarred twine in between the iron bars. They shoot these pots 20 or 30 miles from land in shanks of 40 pots on a rope, each pot baited with fish. The whelks crawl in and, owing to the shape of the pots, cannot crawl out again. They are taken back, over the dangerous sand bar, and boiled in whelk sheds.

Joe made a shape exactly the same as the shape of the Wells pot. It took him about half an hour. The framework is established on a circular template with 17 small holes drilled in it. The funnel is made first, using a simple randing weave for a few inches. Then the stakes are bent over and the body of the pot is woven. The flat bottom is made separately and then woven into the pot. A lobster pot is made in the same way, with a broader base to accommodate the bigger lobster. I have the finished whelk pot hanging on a wall and I shall try it here down in Waterford harbour one day. If I am to have any catch at all I will need a few more pots to go with the one Joe made. Looking at it again, perhaps I was being optimistic to think I could copy them!

THE SOMERSET CHAIR

GOOD BASKET MAKER CAN MAKE A CHAIR entirely out of wickerwork, and it will be strong and light, but it will not last forever; certainly not as long as the Windsor chair on page 73, for example. It is asking rather a lot of thin whippy withies, even when strongly woven, to stand up to the wear and stresses that a chair is put to. For a piece of furniture which has to be reasonably light but is destined to carry the weight of a large human being (who is quite likely to sway back and forth like a pendulum) has to be a piece of rigid engineering.

The Somerset chair manages to combine basketwork with the more rigid construction necessary for a good chair. The solid elm seat which forms the foundation of a wooden country chair is expensive and difficult to obtain and so using their native skills of basket working, the country chair makers of Somerset have evolved a chair in which basketwork forms the seat and back-rest, and hazel or heavier willow forms the framework and gives the chair its strength. Compared with the Windsor chair these chairs are very rustic, but no elaborate tools are required, and they are strong and light. What is so unique about the Somerset chair is that it is the only country chair made in the British Isles without using any hardwood. Even the most basic of rural chairs have at least the legs and back of wood, and the seat of rush or cane. It is a tribute to the basket workers of Somerset that they have developed a chair over the centuries that breaks all the rules of chair making, but doesn't break when sat on.

MAKING THE CHAIR
Once the basic framework of sturdy willow or hazel rods has been cut to length and tacked together, the basket worker starts to give the chair real strength by weaving the seat and back (left). Using a basic randing weave for the flat surfaces, the chair maker has to use a more complex weave to bend the willow rods over the sides and front of the seat to act as a cushion against the hard edges. He is tacking on the rounded batten that forms the mould for the roll of weave at the front of the seat, above.

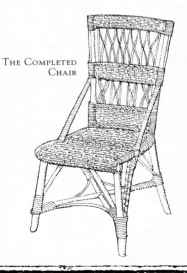

THE COMPLETED CHAIR

RUSH & STRAW WORK

CONSTRUCTION MATERIALS
All you need for making a wide variety of basketwork is wheat straw, formed into a loose rope by being pushed through a cow's horn, and brambles, tied at regular intervals and used to hold the straw together. Straw bee skeps are made from rye straw as this material is longer and tougher than the wheat straw variety.

F YOU PUSH STRAW OR RUSHES through a conical tube (into the larger end is recommended) it will emerge from the smaller end in the form of a rough, loose rope, but with no twist in it. If you tie straw or some other fibre or string around the rope at short intervals as it emerges from the cone, you will have a stable, although not very strong, untwisted rope. If you then coil this rope round and round in the shape you want, and tie each coil to the next at fairly frequent intervals, you can make a basket or other similar container. You might be wondering at this point how you can thrust your tie between two already tied coils of rope in order to tie a third one on. Well, traditionally, you have a goose's leg bone, cut off at an acute angle so that it makes a shape rather like the end of a giant hypodermic needle. You push this between the coils and feed the tie through the hollow centre of the bone. The conical tube used for moulding the fibre rope in the first

place is, traditionally, a hollowed cow's horn. Objects like dog or cat baskets and other artifacts that do not take much stress and strain are made like this, as were old-fashioned straw beehives.

LIP WORK
Before the days of extruded plastic and aluminium, many domestic as well as farm objects were made of straw or rush, formed into coils as I have described and built up to make anything from a cradle to a chair. This process was called *lip work* and is probably a corruption of the Scandinavian *lob*, meaning coiled basketry. Rush work was popular and widespread throughout Europe and Scandinavia because the raw materials were readily available and the techniques employed needed no machinery, just a few simple tools. In Britain you can find examples of lip work anywhere from the Orkneys to Cornwall, and in Wales, where it was particularly popular, there are still some traditional craftsmen plying their trade, especially in Dyfed.

To make a straw object you need wheat and bramble. And winter wheat, which is the strongest variety, is considered the best to work with. After the wheat is thoroughly dry, the heads are removed and the stalks piled up. Bramble was commonly used as the binding material to keep the newly formed rope together. It is important that there is no sap between the bark and the core of the bramble, so winter, when there is no sap rising, is the the best time to go collecting. Before the bramble can be used, however, it has to be split in four using a sharp knife and the pith removed.

The base of a basket can be of three basic designs. In one, all the coils run from a single central point, making a shape a little like that of a snail. In another common design the coils form the shape of a cross and, finally, the coils can all radiate outwards somewhat like a rosette.

BEEHIVES
Straw beehives, or *skeps*, were usually made out of rye straw because it is longer and tougher, although wheat straw was sometimes used. These one-chamber beehives, however, went out of fashion for three main reasons. First, it was not possible for

BASKET UNDER CONSTRUCTION

BEE SKEP

PEAT BASKET

LOG BASKET

TRADITIONAL BASKETRY
There are a number of baskets which have always been made from coiled straw. The log basket, right, has heavy-duty plaited handles, while the peat basket has simple, integral handles.

your local friendly bee inspector to check your swarm for disease such as *foul brood* (he could not see the bees). Second, you cannot (or I should say could not) extract the honey without killing the bees. In the past, a little piece of sulphur was burned under the skep to achieve this. The third reason for the decline in popularity of the straw beehive is that you cannot put the comb in a centrifugal extractor and spin the honey out, free of the comb.

Fortunately, all these objections can now be overcome owing to a simple discovery, although unfortunately you cannot prevent the death of the larvae, or grubs, still in the cells – they have to go. The discovery is simply that you do not put a coiled straw bottom in the skep (in the past very few people probably ever did). When you want to extract the honey you carefully turn the skep upside down and place an empty, bottomless skep the right way up on top of it. The bees, which always tend to go upwards, crawl into the empty skep. You then remove the new skep, bees and all, and carry the old skep, full of honey and comb, away to some bee-proof place. I have never done this, but I have been assured that it works. And as a modern wooden, compartmental hive is a pretty expensive item, it is worth a try.

STRAW PLAITING

Straw plaiting was an important cottage-type industry in Britain even as late as the 1920s. Records indicate that this craft was introduced sometime in the sixteenth century. The popularity of straw plaiting is linked directly to that of the hat-making industry, which absorbed most of the plaiters' output. By the mid-nineteenth century the plaiting of straw was concentrated around the Dunstable and Luton area, and within this area there were plait markets every day of the week, with the exception of Sunday, of course.

Many simple but ingenious tools were introduced either to split or sort the wheat stalks. A series of sieves fitted into a wooden frame was sufficient to sort the straw into its different thicknesses. Bundles of stalks were placed, end on, over the sieves, starting first with the finest mesh sieve. As the stalks fell through, they were collected and bundled. Intricate work was not possible with complete, round stalks of plaited straw. Originally, the straw was split using a sharp knife, but by about 1820 a device containing up to 13 blades was being used. Each straw stalk was pushed into a hole at the centre of the blades and emerged from the other side in as many strips as there were blades.

TEXTILES

The making of textiles involves crafts that were once commonplace in most ordinary families – the history of words like spinster and distaff are witness to this. In Crete every decent mother weaves cloth for her daughters. Not only does she weave the cloth but she often weaves skilful patterns into it, or embroiders designs on it once it is woven. When I visited Crete I was shown chests full of beautiful woven articles, which had been set aside for the day the daughters of the family got married. For every daughter, on marrying, is supplied with an heirloom. This is her right. If there is no heirloom that has been handed down in the family, then one is made for her by one of the loom makers on the island. We met such a man in the village of Margherites. His looms were so beautiful that we simply had to buy one to bring home. I am not saying that we should all weave our own cloth, far from it. I am saying that it is wasteful of our limited resources to use oil to transport textiles, for example, half way round the globe when there is an excellent local tradition of cloth making to use and encourage.

WEAVING

T IS INTERESTING TO SPECULATE how such a difficult concept as turning raw, natural fibres into cloth by spinning and weaving was first discovered. Certainly people would quickly have discovered how to make *felt*. If you clobber wet wool fibres with a mallet, the minute scales which cover the individual fibres of the wool will knit together and you end up with felt. The Mongols make their *yurts*, or tents, of this material, and considering the climate they live in, if there was a more protective covering than felt they would surely be using it.

THE ORIGINS OF WEAVING
But how was weaving developed? My own belief is that weaving must have followed basket making. Early people hit upon the idea of weaving reeds or grasses together to make baskets to carry things in. It was only a short step from this for some modest cave lady to discover that if she twisted sheep's wool between her hands she could make coarse thread, and then if she lay some of these threads parallel on the ground, and wove another set of threads across them, basket fashion, she had a piece of cloth to make a garment out of. She was the first cloth weaver and she invented the *warp* and the *weft* (or *woof*) too, for the first lot of parallel threads formed a warp, and the second lot at right angles to the first formed what is known as the weft.

THE FIRST LOOMS AND SHUTTLES
Human ingenuity has taken us a long way since those early days. All modern *looms* look fiendishly complex, but every working part is the produce of many centuries' development, and once you have got to grips with what bit does what, and why, operating a loom becomes second nature.

The first loom was probably a simple square frame made by lashing four sticks together. The warp was wound round and round the frame, and the weft or wool

NORTH AMERICAN
INDIAN FRAME LOOM

thread passed alternately under and over the warp threads from one side to the other, round the end and back again, just with the fingers or a makeshift shuttle.

The first shuttle was simply a stick with a notch in both ends around which the yarn was wound. To load any such shuttle involved the tedious business of first unwinding the yarn from the spindle and rewinding the thread around the shuttle. Thus came the development of the

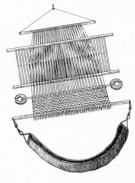

BACKSTRAP LOOM

EARLY LOOMS
The most basic looms are simply frameworks that hold the warp threads steady while the weaver laboriously weaves weft threads in front of one, behind the next. This is how the Navaho Indian who used the loom, left, would have woven a blanket. The backstrap loom, above, is also very primitive but it has a heddle – the rigid frame running across the warp. You hook the loom to the wall, clip the strap around your back and operate the heddle with one hand while you pass the shuttle with the other.

BOAT SHUTTLES
Good, even weaving depends on the smooth passage of the shuttle through the warp. Boat shuttles are shaped like little canoes and they carry the weft yarn on a bobbin. With some shuttles the bobbin is the same spindle on which the spinning wheel winds the yarn, saving the time of winding bobbins separately.

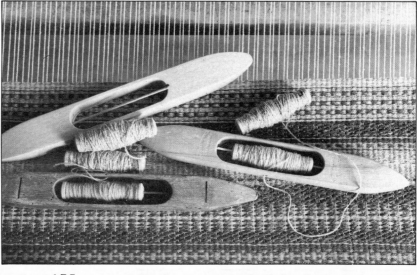

LOOMS

THE SIMPLEST LOOMS CONSISTED OF A BASIC wooden framework that held the warp threads steady while the weaver laboriously wove the weft threads in and out. Free-standing floor looms were fitted with up to ten heddles, making the weaving process easier and quicker. To operate the loom, the warp thread was first rolled round the warp beam and secured with a weight. Then the warp was stretched to another roller called the cloth beam, so called because the cloth was wound around it when completed. Every warp thread passed through the holes and sections of the heddle, which was connected to the pedals via lams or marches. When the weaver pressed the pedals, the heddle raised and lowered each warp thread alternately, thus creating a gap for the weft to pass through. The weft was driven from one side of the warp to the other by means of a shuttle, and then packed up close to the last weft thread by the batten.

FAMILY TRADITION
The Dougherty family of Russellville, Tennessee, have been spinning and weaving excellent cloth "since the first settlers came westward across the Blue Ridge". Their cloth is characterized by fine workmanship and thoughtful designs.

FLOOR LOOM

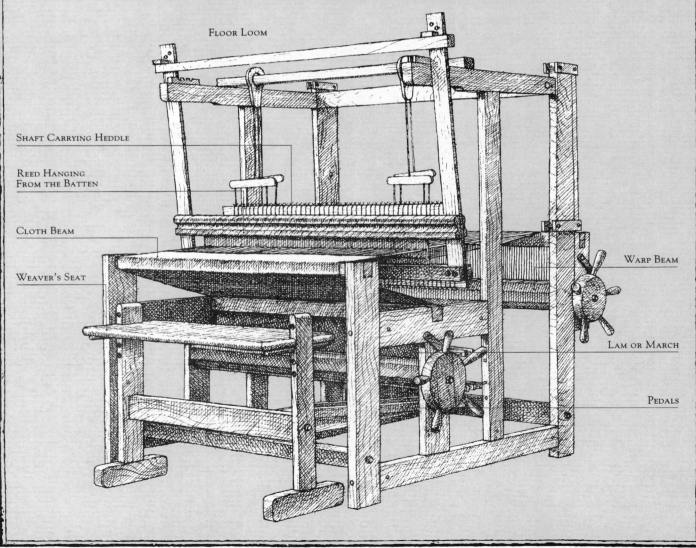

SHAFT CARRYING HEDDLE

REED HANGING FROM THE BATTEN

CLOTH BEAM

WEAVER'S SEAT

WARP BEAM

LAM OR MARCH

PEDALS

boat shuttle, which incorporates the already-loaded spindle inside it. A basic loom will have only one shuttle, but this means that a weft of only one colour can be woven into the warp. For colourful cloth, you need lots of shuttles each loaded with a different colour.

TENSION AND LONGER WARPS

When making cloth, it is very important that the weft is pulled together to produce a tight cloth. This is the task of the *reed*, originally a hand-held stick poked through the warp, but on a modern loom, a frame with many vertical divisions, looking rather like a large comb, between which the warp passes. One sharp pull towards the weft every so often will ensure that the cloth remains tightly packed.

Warp tensioning is important too, and this was originally done by hanging weights on to the loose ends of the warp. But since the other end was fixed, this meant that the length of the loom determined the length of the finished cloth. Whoever thought of putting both ends of the warp on to a roller solved the problem, allowing the warp tension to be maintained and making continuous cloth possible. It was a simple but brilliant idea.

THE HEDDLE

If all these developments were merely common sense, it must have been an inventor of real genius who developed the *heddle*. If I had to choose the half-dozen most significant inventions of mankind, the heddle would be one of them. And like most inventions, it is stunningly simple.

Pushing the shuttle through every alternate thread of the warp to make the weft was a slow process when all the warps lay at the same level. But if they could be separated, allowing the shuttle to pass straight through in between them, rather

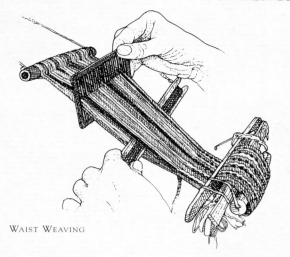

WAIST WEAVING

DECORATED SCANDINAVIAN HEDGE

than having to weave over and under them, then the shuttle could move with greater ease. Hence the invention of the heddle, which, like the reed, is a comb-like frame with holes in the uprights through which are passed alternate warps. When the heddle is raised, up go those warps which pass through the holes, leaving the other warps which pass through the gaps between the uprights where they were. The space thus created, through which the shuttle can now be passed with ease, is known as the *shed*.

With the floor loom the weaver operated the heddle or heddles by pressing down a foot pedal, leaving his or her hands free to catch the shuttle. The width of weave was determined by the distance the weaver could throw and catch the shuttle. Consequently, until the development of the flying shuttle, cloth widths were always narrow – certainly no more than twenty-six inches.

From here it was only a short stage to developing a flying shuttle, which is caught automatically before returning back through the shed at great speed. Equipped with a loom like this, any home weaver is really in business.

THE HEDDLE
The wonderfully simple device that separates alternate warp threads is called a heddle. Simple heddles are a series of alternate slots and holes. You can see below how threads that pass through the holes are lifted while those passing through the slots stay where they are.

FAST WEAVING
Mankind owes a great debt to the person who first thought of how much easier weaving would be if you could lift every other warp thread in turn and then simply pass the shuttle through the weft. The gap you pass the shuttle through is called the shed.

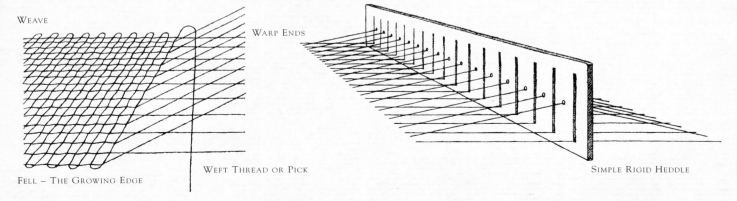

WEAVE

WARP ENDS

FELL – THE GROWING EDGE

WEFT THREAD OR PICK

SIMPLE RIGID HEDDLE

WARPING AND DRESSING

A WEAVER HAS TO PREPARE THE WARP THREADS so that they don't tangle and are easy to thread on to the loom; this is called *warping*. Most hand weavers use the technique called *chain warping*. You position two sets of three pegs apart by the length of the intended piece of cloth, plus about three feet extra *for the loom*, as weavers say. You do not cut every warp thread to length but instead wind the yarn around the pegs until you have the right number of threads. You leave cutting through the end loops until you have arranged the warp on the loom. The threads remain separate because you loop the ends in a figure-of-eight pattern around the three sets of pegs and then tie the group of threads before taking the warp off the pegs. It is at this stage that you gently pull the warp into a chain for safe-keeping until you come to thread it through the reed and heddles of your loom – known as *dressing* the loom. There are various ways of dressing the loom, but it is usual to work back from the warp beam to the cloth beam.

DRESSING ON SKYE
Weavers will tell you that they far prefer to work on big hand looms rather than small ones. One of the reasons it that it is easier to get inside a big loom in order to dress it – the threading of the warp yarns through reed and heddles. This weaver is dressing his loom on the Isle of Skye, Scotland. Notice the twine heddles in front of him.

WARPING FRAMES AND MILLS
To avoid running up and down the 30 or 40 yards of a long warp, warping frames and mills allow you to fold the warp on to a zig-zag of pegs, or wind it on to a framework, between the sets of three pegs where the figure-of-eight looping takes place. A warping mill is shown below, together with the business ends of a frame with its sets of three pegs. How you arrange pegs to take the warp between is up to you.

FIGURE-OF-EIGHT LOOPING AND TIED WARP THREADS

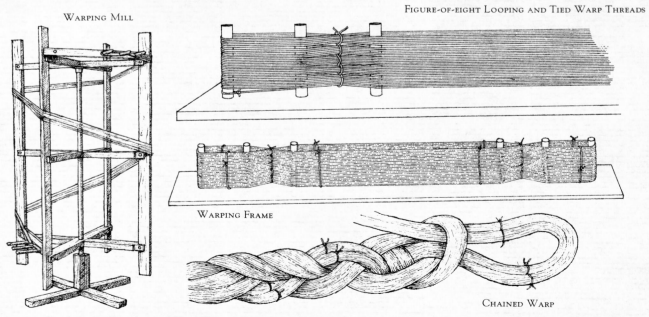

WARPING MILL

WARPING FRAME

CHAINED WARP

Not that operating a loom is an easy task. To co-ordinate the shuttle, heddle and reed requires great concentration, especially since many patterns of cloth require different colours on both warp and weft, using a number of heddles and shuttles.

PROFESSIONAL WEAVERS

Weaving in England, and also in the United States, long ago became the work of men. Women spun, men wove. There were sedentary weavers in towns and villages to which housewives would bring the yarn that they had spun during the year.

There were also travelling weavers. If we are to believe early nineteenth-century novelists, such as George Eliot, many large farm houses and country houses had looms that were used by itinerant weavers, who would come and stay for the time it took them to weave up the yarn that the spinsters of the household had spun. For before the widespread introduction of the mule and the jenny – the first mechanical spinning machines – spinning was the activity that took up most of a woman's time. Weaving was a comparatively quick and productive activity: it did not take a weaver long to weave up all the yarn spun in a household

during the entire year. As a result, hand weaving was able to compete much better with the big mills than spinning. It survives quite competitively even today in such places as County Donegal in Ireland and the Western Isles of Scotland, although hand weavers have to use yarn that has been spun in the factories: they would be unable to compete with industry if they had to rely on home-spun yarn.

COOPERATIVES

It was the invention of the flying shuttle loom that saved Irish and Scottish hand weavers. This enabled them to step up their production enormously with only a very small investment of capital. A sling caught the flying shuttle as it emerged from the shed and flung it back again through the next shed; the motive power being provided by the weaver's arm.

Today, Scottish and Irish hand weavers work in cooperatives. They weave at home, or in small sheds next door to their homes, usually using warps that have already been made up for them in a warping shed owned by the cooperative. For the making of the long warps that they need requires special equipment for which

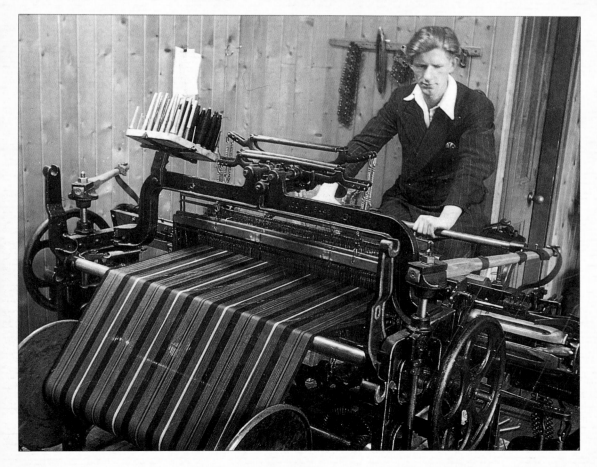

HOME WEAVER
A weaver working from home during the 1960s on the Isle of Lewis in the Hebrides. Here the loom is a fairly advanced mechanized unit, capable of a large output but losing the human touch which makes home-made cloth so individual.

most of them don't have the space. Many of the weavers are crofters, who weave only part of the time, and generally run their small farms and go fishing as well. If you compare the quiet and peaceful atmosphere of the cottage weaving shed with the dust and deafening din of the mechanical weaving factory you cannot but mourn the coming of the power loom.

Power looms are, of course, part of another world, making a pleasurable activity into an uncomfortable, noisy job people are forced to do for little money. The shuttle is flung around at 60 miles an hour, and the resulting noise is terrifying. Go into any pub in the weaving towns of the north country, and talk to a weaver. You will have to shout, for the noise in the factories has deafened them. And factory work has reduced them to mere extensions of their machines, for their tasks are merely to

repair broken threads and refill shuttles. Once again the machine has become the master of the man and the only ones to benefit are those who take the profits. It is a pattern repeated again and again.

But, thank God, hand weaving is coming back as a pastime and at the moment the demand for looms is not being fully met. So far, the new generation of hand weavers has not discovered the flying shuttle. Maybe the new weavers won't take to it: weaving is quieter and more pleasant without the jerky movement associated with it. Perhaps, when the huge clattering weaving mills grind to a halt, there will be enough skilled hand weavers to meet moderate demands of the people of the world for cloth. I hope so, for there is no comparison between the lovely living feel of hand-woven cloth and the lifeless monotony of that made on a machine.

TAPESTRY WEAVING IN AUBUSSON
Tapestries are generally woven on upright looms so that you can see the design you are making clearly. Aubusson, in central France, has an ancient tradition of tapestry weaving and this is one of its practitioners, weaving against a guiding pattern that shows through the warp threads.

LINEN CRAFT

INEN COMES FROM THE FLAX PLANT, and flax was probably the first vegetable fibre ever made use of by man. The Egyptians were growing and weaving flax four thousand years ago, and it is known that the Phoenicians were trading fine quality linen throughout the Mediterranean by 1250 BC. The Romans cultivated flax and introduced it to northern Europe, and it was being grown extensively in Ireland and Wales by the fifth century AD. In Ireland, as in ancient Egypt, the bodies of chiefs and kings were wrapped in linen for burial, and Irish linen is still considered to be the finest in the world. It is a superb fabric, infinitely superior to any of the man-made materials we have today. Consider the finest table cloths, sheets, napkins, shirts and other garments made of linen. Cloth from the flax plant, *Linum usitatissimum*, has qualities all of its own. And the plant has a second and a third use for man – it is *usitatissimum* indeed – for it provides linseed, the source of the best of all non-edible oils, and the residue of the crushed seeds makes linseed cake.

I have grown flax, experimentally, on my farm in Wales, and processed it through to linen thread ready for weaving. But few people grow flax any more. Two hundred years ago nearly every village in Europe was self-sufficient in linen, and the poorest peasant used freely what only rich people can afford today. Which causes one to question the whole idea of "progress". Progress from the widespread use of the very finest of materials to the use of third-rate synthetic rubbish seems to me to be progress in the wrong direction.

GROWING FLAX

Flax will grow in most soils, but it prefers a good loam and to make fine linen it should have fairly cool and damp weather throughout the summer months. If it be dry for harvesting, so much the better, but you can't have everything.

The little shiny black seeds which, when crushed, provide such magnificent oil, must be planted in a very fine tilth, in late March or early April, at a rate of about 90 lbs an acre. The seed can be drilled, or sown by hand by a skilled man, and then harrowed and rolled in.

The flax plant grows three or four feet high and produces beautiful pale blue

MARVEL OF FLAX
Linum usitatissimum, *flax, is a most versatile plant. I have sailed in a trading barge under a linen mainsail which had been used for 40 years, winter and summer, night and day, with only a dressing of fish oil, linseed oil and cutch (a product of the Burmese betel tree) once every five years. On the other hand, linen can be made into the finest of handkerchiefs.*

FROM STEM TO FIBRE
The bundles, or beets, far left, are of harvested flax stems. In some small flax mills these are left to rot (ret) submerged in trays until they begin to split and reveal the linen fibre, as shown middle left. The true linen fibres, near left, have been hackled and are displayed hanging from the iron comb used for rippling, or removing the flax seed heads.

FRENCH HACKLING
This French flax worker is hackling the retted flax stems. Pulling the fibrous stems through a bed of nails separates out any non-fibrous material that may still remain among the line, or linen fibres, and also pulls out any short fibres. These go to make tow, used for caulking and stuffing.

flowers. A flax field in bloom is a delightful sight, and when the flowers die down the seed begins to form. If a crop is grown for linseed oil production only, this seed should be allowed to ripen completely, but if the flax fibres of the stem are the main object, the crop should be harvested as soon as the first of the seed begins to ripen in late July. Harvesting is done by hand. The plants are then tied together in *beets* (like wheat sheaves but smaller) and stooked up in order to dry.

RIPPLING AND RETTING

Once harvested, the next operation is *rippling*, which is the pulling of the seed heads through a fixed upright steel comb. This removes the seed bolls, which are then crushed for oil or fed to cattle.

The beets, minus their seed heads, now have to be *retted*. This means, encouraging

bacteria to attack and decompose the gum which holds the flax fibres together, and to rot the unwanted inner core of the stem. Retting can be done either by laying the beets out on the ground to let the dew and the sun work on them for from two to five weeks, turning them over from time to time, or by dunking the crop into a stagnant pond for from eight to 14 days. When the stems begin to crack and open, the retting is done. The warmer the weather the shorter the time the flax should spend in the pond, and it is important that the retting time should be correct for the quality of the finished linen depends largely on this factor. I am told that only experience can help the operator here. When I tried retting, I sunk the beets in the duck pond for a week and a half, and it worked perfectly well. But I may have just been lucky.

After retting, the stalks must be washed clean in water and then dried. This is sometimes done by opening the beets up and spreading the stalks out evenly on a cut grass field if the weather is fine, or by stooking the beets (standing them up in tiny stacks). In some places in England, where the weather is so unpredictable, the flax was laid up to dry on a platform under which a small fire was lit. This was risky, however, because it took just one stray spark and the crop was lost.

SCUTCHING AND HACKLING

Scutching is the process of removing the *line*, or true linen fibres, from the flax stems. On a small scale you use a *brake* – a very simple device consisting of two fixed parallel battens of wood with a hinged batten that falls between them. You drag a

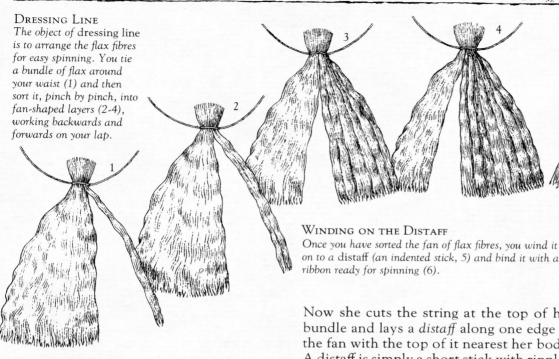

Dressing Line

The object of dressing line is to arrange the flax fibres for easy spinning. You tie a bundle of flax around your waist (1) and then sort it, pinch by pinch, into fan-shaped layers (2-4), working backwards and forwards on your lap.

DISTAFF

Winding on the Distaff

Once you have sorted the fan of flax fibres, you wind it on to a distaff (an indented stick, 5) and bind it with a ribbon ready for spinning (6).

READY FOR SPINNING

handful of flax over the fixed battens while beating it with the hinged one. This breaks and crushes the woody pith in the fibres so that it can be removed.

Hackling is the next process. This consists of drawing the line through a large comb, once a bed of nails, to get rid of any fibres too short for spinning. The short fibres are known as *tow* and can be used for caulking decks, stuffing mattresses, making cord and hundreds of other uses.

Dressing and Spinning

Before spinning, the line must be *dressed*. This can be a beautiful process if accomplished by a pretty woman wearing a long apron. Taking as much fibre as she can clasp into one hand, the dresser ties a piece of string around one end of this bundle, lays it on her lap and ties the two long ends of the string around her waist to secure it. She now lays the whole bundle on her left knee (assuming she is right handed), takes as much fibre as she can easily take between her finger and thumb and lays this on her right knee. She then takes a pinch more of the fibres and lays them next to the first pinch, but further to the left. She continues doing this until she has laid out a fan of fibres. Then she lays another fan of fibres on top of the first, working left to right, then another right to left, until the whole bundle is laid out in fan-shaped layers.

Now she cuts the string at the top of her bundle and lays a *distaff* along one edge of the fan with the top of it nearest her body. A distaff is simply a short stick with rippled edges. Winding the fan up on the stick, she keeps the top of the fan (which had the string around it) pretty tight, but the wide bottom of the fan looser. Then she sticks the distaff in the hole provided for it on her spinning wheel, takes a ribbon and ties this round the top and criss-crosses the two ends down to the bottom, tying the two ends in a bow.

Taking a bit of yarn that has already been spun, she winds this on to the bobbin of her wheel. The loose end of this is twisted into some of the loose ends of line at the bottom of her distaff and then she begins to spin, wetting her fingers in a bowl of water so as to moisten the flax to make it more supple. With her left finger and thumb she stops the spin from travelling up into the fibre on the distaff; with her right hand she draws the fibres out and clears any knots. Occasionally she turns the distaff as required and when necessary unties the bow in the ribbon and ties it again further up. In this way she spins the whole hank.

Once spun, the linen thread is ready to be woven on a loom like any other kind of thread. In days of old every farm which could grow it grew flax, every spinster spun it – and many a good wife too – and the distaff side of the family concerned itself for much of the year with its preparation. And, once a year, a travelling weaver would visit the farm, carrying his loom, and weave it all up for the family. And thus was real wealth created.

WOOL CRAFT

I AM THE HAPPY OWNER OF SEVERAL garments made from the wool of my own sheep, which had grazed on my own land. Now both land and sheep are gone but the cloth remains, a pleasant grey colour produced without adding any other dye since some of my sheep were black.

I would like to be able to claim that I, or others on my farm, carded, spun and wove the wool too, but this was not the case. We had spinning wheels, we had looms, but, as I mention on page 332, if you are to spin and weave your own cloth you will spend 12 times as much time spinning as weaving. Now nothing is more soothing than to listen to the whirr of the flyers and the soft rumble of the spinning wheel itself as one sits by a warm fire. I have listened to this sound for many hours but, I have to admit, somebody else was turning the wheel. The pressure on our time nowadays sometimes makes spinning enough wool to weave with an impossible barrier, a luxury that cannot now be afforded.

Although my family did, over the course of the years, both spin and weave much wool (my daughter, Anne, spent three years at a college learning how to do it) on the whole, while my sheep provided my wool, it was spun and woven in a big mill.

CHOOSING THE WOOL

The hand spinner has to select the type of wool carefully. There are countless breeds of sheep, and each one has a distinctive type of wool. The so-called *Persian*, for example, found throughout Africa and Asia, has no wool at all, only straight hair like a dog that is quite useless for spinning. The best wool in the world, on the other hand, is *Merino* wool, which is from a sheep not hardy enough to keep in Britain, but it has to be said that it has rather a short *staple*, and is therefore difficult for hand spinners to use, though I have seen it spun. The staple, by the way, is the length of the individual fibres and is an important consideration when assessing the suitability of a wool for spinning and weaving.

In Britain there are three main classes of sheep: *Down Sheep*, *Mountain Sheep* and the long-woolled descendants of the *Leicester*. Down Sheep have a very short staple, the wool is fine, and non-lustrous. The Mountain breeds have medium length staple, and half-lustrous wool. The Leicester-founded breeds have very long staple (the Leicester itself produces a staple of up to 10 inches), very lustrous and silky, and very strong. Of the Leicester breeds, the *Lincoln* has superb wool, the staple as long as 18 inches and you can shear as much as 14 pounds, sometimes more, off one sheep.

There are two breeds considered intermediate between Mountain and Down: the

SUFFOLK-WELSH SHEEP
The sheep contentedly munching below are Suffolk-Welsh crosses on my farmland in Wales. One of their uses was to provide fleeces for spinning and weaving. Both the black and the white fleeces I sheared were combined in the process and the result was a good grey-coloured cloth that needed no dye to colour it.

A SPINNER'S VIEW OF SHEEP
If I lived in a mountain area and was a hand spinner I should choose the Cheviot as my breed of sheep. If I lived on lowland plains, I would choose between the South-down (despite its very short staple, or fibre length), the Oxford Down or the Romney Marsh, although the Shropshire gives a splendid wool, too.

LINCOLN

ROMNEY MARSH

KERRY

Kerry Hill and the *Ryeland*. The Kerry Hill has a soft, white, dense fleece, while the Ryeland has very fine, good quality wool with a staple length of three and a half to four and a half inches. I have kept Ryelands and while I admire their wool I don't think much of the sheep: I found them not very hardy. They probably do well enough in their own area though, which is the English-Welsh Marches.

Another sheep I must mention is the *Welsh Black*. This provides a rather coarse wool, but it is a rich brown-black colour, makes an attractive cloth by itself and is fine mixed in with white wool – that is if you wish to keep the natural colour of the wool and not dye it.

Considering Crimp

As you work with wool you find all sorts of qualities about it. *Crimp* is important – it gives elasticity to the wool. It is the wavy pattern that each minute strand of a fleece has, and some breeds have far crimpier wool than others. It is desirable for knitting wools to be crimpy: the *Southdown*, which is a sweet little sheep (the smallest of our breeds) has very crimpy, fine wool, good for lightweight tweeds and hosiery. For heavier tweeds, the *Oxford Down* is good, being much longer in staple than the Southdown but coarser, and the *Cheviot* is famous for the best tweed wool in the world. The *Welsh Mountain* also makes tweed, although flannel is its main use – a much softer cloth than tweed. The long-woolled breeds are fine for carpets and hard-wearing, tough cloths. The *Romney Marsh*, which is a long-woolled breed, is fine for hand spinners: I know a lady at Chepstow whose husband keeps a flock and who spins the finest yarn from the wool. The *Shetland* is kept by some hand spinners: it has an inner layer and an outer layer to its fleece. The outer layer is fine for tweed, the inner for knitwear. A

new phenomenon which is hitting the spinning world is the *Friesian Milk Sheep*. This huge sheep, which is as tame as a dog, gives half a gallon of milk a day besides fine long wool. And I knew a lady in Suffolk who kept, and swore by (and sometimes at) Angora goats. Their hair spins into a yarn of delightful softness that knits or weaves into a soft and fluffy cloth which is much sought after.

Preparing the Fleece

Now farmers sell wool either *washed* or *in-the-dirt*. To produce washed wool you simply throw your sheep in a pond or a

Shearing in Cumbria
Shearing with hand shears is something of a forgotten art in itself. It is very hard work but very satisfying when you become proficient. Good shearing is not a traumatic affair for the sheep and without the noise of electric shears and a frantic shearing shed the operation can be as relaxed as the Cumbrian scene above appears.

Friesian

Southdown

Cheviot

Welsh Mountain

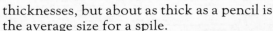

WOOLLEN-SPUN

WORSTED-SPUN

WAYS OF SPINNING
There are two distinct ways of allowing the twist of woollen yarn to form. If you let the fibres spiral together naturally you get a slightly shaggy yarn for soft warm cloth. Comb the fibres straight before spinning, you get a smooth yarn for finer cloth.

CARDING
Carding sorts and aligns the fibres of wool prior to spinning for woollen-spun yarn. The picture shows stripping off fibres from one carder to the other.

stream a few days before you shear them. The many villages in England called Washbrook, or Sheep Wash, derive their names from this practice. You get more for washed wool but it has less weight, and the differential does not make up for the loss of weight and extra trouble, so practically no commercial farmers wash their sheep now. Hand spinners sometimes do though, for washed wool is easier and pleasanter to work with. Having got the fleece off the back of the sheep, either with hand or electric shears (it doesn't matter much which type you use), the spinner is now faced with spinning it.

ALTERNATIVE ROUTES TO YARN
If you go to a spinning factory, a mill where they turn fleece into yarn, you may be daunted by the complexity of the machinery needed to do it. The raw fleece is scoured clean in a large machine, dried, and then torn into pieces in what in a Greek mill I heard called *likos*, or wolf (and it had a very wolf-like biting action), before it goes into the *carding* machine. This consists of a large number of big drums all covered with fine wire brushes (called *cards*) which revolve at differential speeds so that the tiny wires tear the fibres of the fleece apart. The finely teased-out and fluffed up fibres are then put into the spiling machine which, very skilfully, collects and unites them in long continuous *spiles*. These can be various

thicknesses, but about as thick as a pencil is the average size for a spile.

The slowly moving spiles then travel straight to the spinning machine, which takes the place of the spinning wheel of old and which in modern mills has many spinning heads, not just one. This then spins the wool into yarn ready for weaving. If all this sounds very complicated, bear in mind that even in a very small mill, the whole series of machines can be 20 to 30 yards long and every inch of that length is used in the processing of the wool. All this may seem strange when you have seen your wife, as I have seen mine, take a fleece which has come straight off a sheep, lay it on the floor beside her and, leading a pinch of the wool from it to the spinning wheel, spin a perfect yarn straight off the fleece! But to do this needs considerable skill and it can be a very slow job.

HAND CARDING
The average hand spinner first *cards* the fleece. Hand carders are small tools with handles, covered on one side with that weird stuff called *card clothing*, a flexible fabric densely packed with tiny wire hooks. I don't know how to make it nor how it is made and all I can say is, that if I couldn't buy it I would have to use a *teasel*. The teasel, or *Dipsacus sativus* to give it its botanical name, is a thistle with a prickly head that grows almost everywhere in Europe, North Africa and North America. The teasel head, was the first carder, and is still used industrially today for *teasing* cloth, that is scratching it so as to *raise a nap* on it to make it fluffy. For this the thistle heads are set on a frame. In days of old spinsters set a few heads on a handle like a modern carder and carded the wool with that.

The carding of wool is a subtle process. A lump of raw wool is pulled apart by hand a little, and then placed between two hand carders. With the carders pulled in opposite directions, the wool is then combed or *scarified*, until the tiny wire hooks tease it apart. Then, with both the carders facing the same direction, the wool is collected on one carder only. Then one carder is turned around again, so that its hooks again oppose the hooks of the other, and with some more hard combing, the wool is scarified again. This process is repeated about five times until the wool is properly carded, that is when all the tiny fibres are separate from each other.

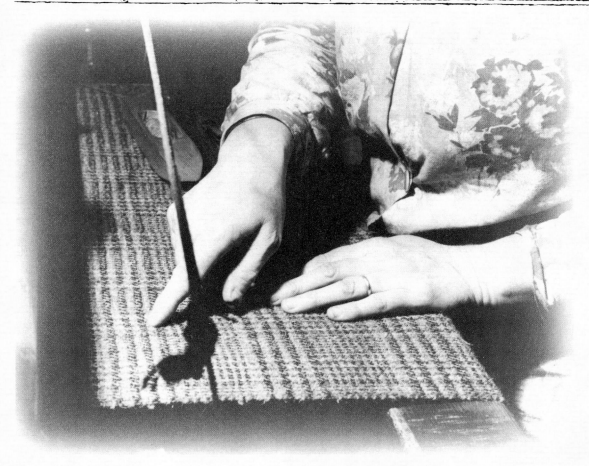

HARRIS TWEED
Tweed is a magnificent, slightly-rough woollen cloth which is still made on hand looms in the Western Isles of Scotland, particularly on Harris where traditional designs, such as Glen Urquhart (shown here) or Prince of Wales check, have ancient origins. The Harris island weaver is here using five shuttles to carry the weft back and forth.

When the combing is done, the wool is taken off by hand, and is rolled gently to form a *rolag*, which is the equivalent of the long, continuous, never-ending spile of the big mills. Your rolag, however, will only be the size of a long sausage, made of fluffy wool. Now it is easy to spin the wool, and subsequently knit or weave it into what is an incomparable material.

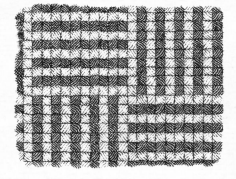

A Fibre for all Seasons

I cannot finish without saying something about the qualities of wool, for I do not think it possible to sing the praises of woollen material too highly. Marvellously warm, extremely long lasting, water-shedding, weatherproof, with a pleasant feel about it, it is the perfect fibre for cold countries. No textile that man has invented comes anywhere near it for versatility. If you follow the process of preparing the wool fibres as I have outlined above, and then proceed to spin the wool you will end up with a springy yarn with the fibres spiralling around each other. It is termed *woollen-spun* and is light but bulky, and therefore warm. This is the sort of woollen fibre that is ideal for knitting.

But this method is not the one and only way of preparing and spinning wool. If you look at a piece of fine woollen cloth the individual fibres look very different from those knitted into a pullover. It will have been *worsted-spun*. Instead of carding the wool into a rolag, you pull locks of it through the teeth of a steel comb to sort out the long fibres (called *top*) from the short ones (*noil*) that occur in a fleece. You keep the long fibres parallel and twist them together a little to form a *roving* from which you spin. The yarn you end up with is very fine and smooth and is ideal to be woven into dense, flat cloth suitable for all the products of tailoring and dressmaking.

COLOUR PATTERNS
Colour patterns can be created by having different coloured yarns in the warp, or by having more than one shuttle, each loaded with a coloured yarn.

SILK CRAFT

*Silkworms spin their
cocoons in an elevated
position away from the
mulberry leaves on which
they feed. Straw or twigs of
heather and bushy herbs
are ideal for this task, and
are placed in the trays. The
worms crawl up the twigs
and spin without ceasing
for three days, emitting
from their bodies a thick,
viscous liquid that hardens
in the air and forms a
thread that they wrap
around themselves. In total,
each worm produces an
astonishing mile and a
half of continuous thread.*

N 1900 A MILLION PEOPLE IN southern France were employed in the production or processing of native silk. By the 1960s this number had fallen to zero. Except for a few faithful souls who just kept a few silkworms and a few mulberry trees for fun or sentiment, the industry had died out. The great silk mills of Lyons were and are still operating, and so are those of Milan, another silk city, but they are operating on raw silk imported from China and elsewhere in the Far East.

THE FRENCH SILK INDUSTRY
The silkworm was introduced into France in the fifteenth century from Spain and Italy, and by the late seventeenth century

sericulture, the culture of the silkworm, flourished, supported by the government of Louis XIV. It was nearly wiped out by disease in 1853, but Louis Pasteur found a cure for the worms and the industry took off again and became the mainstay for many of the peasants living in the rural South of France. Alas, with the opening of the Suez Canal things took a turn for the worse, for the canal made it possible to import cheaper silk from the East. Now the production of native silk in France is almost but a memory.

Wherever you go in the Cévennes, in the South of France, look out for long buildings on the side of farmhouses, with very small windows and many chimneys. Look inside one and you will find the building empty, or merely being used for storage, and the walls blackened by ancient fires. You may still find the remains of the woven cane trays on which millions of silkworms once lived and munched their way through tons and tons of mulberry leaves. These buildings are called *magnaneries*, which is an Occitan word derived from the ancient *langue d'oc* word for silkworm, *magnans*. It was in these buildings that the silkworms were fed. Other, even larger, buildings, often special in that they have large pointed-arch windows, are the *filatures*. There is about one to a village. Into these the farmers brought their silk cocoons and sold them to the owner. He, or at least the young women he employed, performed the delicate task of winding the silk off the cocoons. The silk was then bought by travelling buyers who transported it to Lyons to sell to the big spinning and weaving mills there.

AN INDUSTRIAL RENAISSANCE
Although the French silk production industry all but died during this century, like many other so-called "Forgotten Arts", it did not quite die, and is now experiencing marked re-birth.

In search of this I took myself to the village of Monoblet, where the young village schoolmaster is acting as midwife to this renaissance. Monsieur Wolgram Mollison has aroused enough interest in his locality to have raised the cash to build a small factory which takes silk from the cocoon stage to the finished, dyed, garment. He has delicate machines, invented by the clever Japanese, which wind the silk off the cocoons, spinning machines, automatic looms and sewing machines. When I visited him, in 1983, the mill was still using some oriental silk, but it is hoped to phase this out as time goes on, for Monsieur Mollison has persuaded many landowners to let him plant mulberry trees on their disused land (of which there is an enormous amount) and he has already planted thousands. He is managing to persuade more and more peasant people, chiefly women, to start cocoon production again, though he admits that at the moment silk farming is something of a labour of love. Imported silk is still too cheap for it to be possible to compete against it economically, but he points out that wages in South Korea, where most imported silk comes from, are rising and the time will come when it will not pay them to produce it there and then transport it half way round the world. One day, he feels sure, the Cévennes silk producers will be in business again and, due to his efforts, off to a flying start. So, thanks largely to the enthusiasm of a small group of local people, inspired by the hard work and dedication of this one man, the skills of silk craft are being relearned and preserved for future generations.

LEAVES AND WORMS

To produce a decent amount of silk you need a prodigious quantity of leaves from the mulberry tree. *Morus alba*, the Chinese white mulberry, is hardy and most suitable, but M. *nigra*, the black mulberry, has a fruit which is nicer for *us* to eat than that of the white mulberry, and seems just fine for silkworms too. A young girl named Marie, whom I met on a farm near St Hippolyte du Fort in the Cévennes, raises 10,000 worms, and they eat the leaves of 25 mulberry trees in a month – about three bushels of leaves a day. Marie has to pick the leaves fresh every day, which she does simply by holding each branch in a big sack and stripping the leaves off with her hand. To miss a day is fatal: it puts the worms off their routine and could kill them.

The worms occupy a corner of Marie's father's old *magnanerie*. From hatching eggs until starting to spin silk takes the worms about 27 days, and the larger they get the more they want to eat. Marie told me she has to be scrupulously careful about removing the droppings, which are abundant, and any leaves not eaten. When the worms are first hatched out she has to chop the leaves up small for them; after a few days this is not necessary. She uses racks of

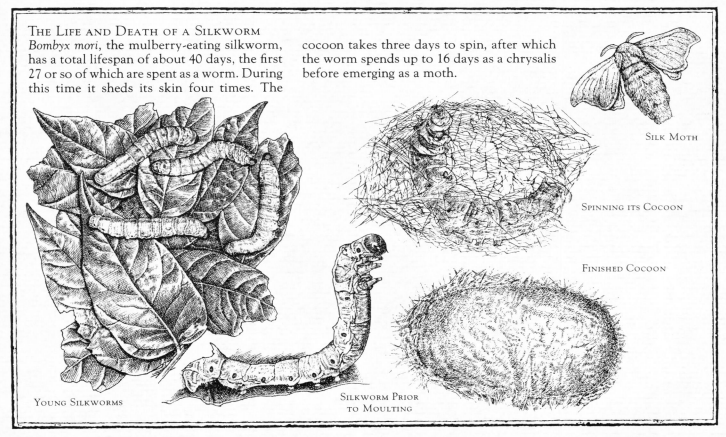

THE LIFE AND DEATH OF A SILKWORM

Bombyx mori, the mulberry-eating silkworm, has a total lifespan of about 40 days, the first 27 or so of which are spent as a worm. During this time it sheds its skin four times. The cocoon takes three days to spin, after which the worm spends up to 16 days as a chrysalis before emerging as a moth.

SILK MOTH

SPINNING ITS COCOON

FINISHED COCOON

YOUNG SILKWORMS

SILKWORM PRIOR TO MOULTING

A HOME-MADE SPOOL
Marie made her own simple spool out of two interlocking pieces of cardboard, each about 10 inches square, and a twig handle, around which she can wind the threads of silk off the cocoons.

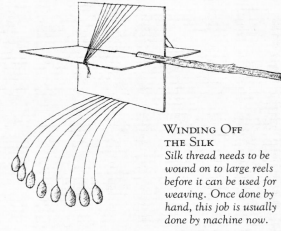

WINDING OFF THE SILK
Silk thread needs to be wound on to large reels before it can be used for weaving. Once done by hand, this job is usually done by machine now.

trays woven from osiers and, as the worms get larger, she lays branches of heather and bushy herbs on the worm-laden trays. Feeling the urge to make their cocoons, the worms climb up into the twigs of these plants and spin their cocoons there.

When the worms have finished spinning, after three days' solid work, they must be killed, for if left alive they will secrete an alkali which will eat its way through the cocoon and ruin the silk. Marie kills them by putting them in a paper bag and the bag into an oven at 200°F for 20 minutes, but she told me that if you lay them in hot sun for a day it would do the same thing.

SPINNING THE SILK THREAD
After killing the worms, the silk must be wound off fairly smartly because if it isn't the worms will start to stink and taint the silk. Marie showed me how she does this.

Although most of her cocoons go to the new factory, she is producing thread herself in a small way and does it with the simplest possible method, using a homemade spool made of two interlocking squares of cardboard with a twig handle.

Taking eight cocoons she flings them into a bowl of water which is nearly – but not quite – boiling. (The inside of the bowl is black, making it easier to see the silk threads.) Very soon the threads on each cocoon begin to come loose and float in the water. With a pair of tweezers she gathers the eight loose ends up, twists them together, and fastens the end of the thread thus formed to a notch in the "wheel". Very carefully she then begins to turn the spool and wind the silk thread. After the silk is completely unwound from the cocoon, a little wizened grub falls into the water: quite unlike the three-inch-long fat caterpillar that started to build the cocoon.

Marie told me she likes making silk, but there is no way she can make a fortune at it. It takes 500 silkworms or 80 kilos of cocoons to create one kilo of raw silk. So Marie's total production, from 10,000 worms and 25 mulberry trees, is 20 kilos a year. Not a good return.

SILK AND STEEL
Silk production may seem a slightly frivolous pursuit to be included in a book such as this, but consider this: silk is by far the strongest material we have, and thickness for thickness, it is said to be stronger than steel. It makes a superb fabric, warm when it's cold and cool when it's hot. Why should we Westerners deny ourselves such a luxury, which we can produce quite well by ourselves, even if it does require much labour. It is a labour of love.

COTTON CRAFT

SINCE PREHISTORIC TIMES, COTTON has been spun, woven and then dyed, and the ancient civilizations of India, China and Egypt produced fine quality cloth worked with ingenious and beautiful designs. The use of cotton slowly spread to Europe from India, and by the ninth century AD the Moors were growing cotton in Spain. But it is the New World that has been the biggest producer of cotton, first cultivated in the Jamestown colony in 1607. Vast numbers of slaves were employed on the plantations that turned the southern states of America into one big cotton field, laboriously harvesting the crop by hand. The raw cotton was then shipped off to England, where thousands of workers toiled in the mills of Lancashire and the mill owners made their fortunes in the production of cotton cloth.

The cotton plant belongs to the mallow family and is a shrubby plant that only grows in hot climates. The raw cotton *lint*, or fibre, surrounds the seeds in the *boll*, or seedhead. The seeds must first be removed, work which used to be done by the nimble fingers of the slave women. Nowadays this is done mechanically in a gin mill by a cotton-gin, which separates fibre from bol and then bails the raw cotton.

Cotton has a short *staple*, or fibre length, but is easily turned into thread. As the harvested cotton dries the fibres flatten and twist naturally, and must be *willowed*, whipped with willow rods to fluff out the cotton and clean it. Next it is *carded*, just like wool but easier to do because of its short staple, and then *combed*, its fibres laid parallel ready for spinning. When spinning cotton, you must keep your hands close together and treadle quickly, making sure that you do not hold back too much cotton from the bobbin or else it will kink. Once spun, it is strong enough for weaving.

When I was in India I came across workers whom I dubbed *cotton twangers*. These men sit, in darkened sheds, cross-legged on the floor and operate objects like bows, as in bows and arrows. In one hand the twanger holds the bow, in the other a wooden club with a sharp ridge cut round it. He keeps twanging the string with the wooden club and dips the vibrating string into the tangled mass of fibres. This fluffs it up for rolling into *rovings* – long, slightly twisted sausages of cotton for spinning.

THE COTTON BOLL
The seeds of the cotton plant are contained in a seedhead called a boll*, well protected by a white or creamy coloured fibre. It is this fibre that is the raw material for cotton, the seeds producing an oil used in cooking and some cosmetics.*

THE COTTON TWANGER
Cotton production is mostly mechanized but in India I have seen cotton twangers like this man, whose job it is to prepare the cotton for spinning by carding it, or fluffing it up with his bow.

PART TWO

FORGOTTEN HOUSEHOLD CRAFTS

THE OLD-FASHIONED KITCHEN
*A large, solid table and all manner of implements and cooking vessels
mark the domain of the traditional cook (see Kitchen Crafts, p.205).*

INTRODUCTION

"I'm only a housewife, I'm afraid." How often do we hear this shocking admission. I'm afraid when I hear it I feel very angry indeed. Only a housewife: only a practitioner of one of the two most noble professions (the other one is that of a farmer); only the mistress of a huge battery of high and varied skills and custodian of civilization itself. Only a typist, perhaps! Only a company director, or a nuclear physicist; only a barrister; only Prime Minister! When a woman says she is a housewife she should say it with the utmost pride, for there is nothing higher on this planet to which she could aspire.

INTERIOR DECORATING
Whitewash was ritually applied to ceilings every spring as part of the spring cleaning. Wall stencilling and papering was not carried out as frequently. However, when a room was repapered the new paper was pasted directly on top of the old, as such strong paste was used that it was virtually impossible to scrape off the last layer! (See Painting & Papering, p.362.)

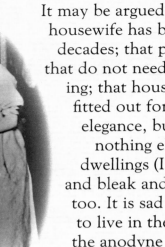

It may be argued that the profession of the housewife has been downgraded in recent decades; that people nowadays eat meals that do not need any preparation or cooking; that houses today are not built and fitted out for comfort, beauty, or even elegance, but for "easy working" and nothing else. There are indeed such dwellings (I will not call them homes) and bleak and cheerless places they are, too. It is sad that so many people have to live in them, but then they do have the anodyne of the telly. Glued to that flickering screen they can ignore their own dull surroundings: we can all live in Dallas. But real homes and real housewives do still exist and this book has been written in praise of them both. It describes the art of housewifery through the ages, but it is not just a museum-on-paper. Many of the activities may be seldom practised nowadays—some of them are sadly dead and gone—but many of them are living activities and several of the skills that seemed to be dying are now being revived, for many people have passed right through the pimply-adolescent stage of post-industrial civilization. They have tired of the take-away way of living and the machine-for-living way of living. They have found that art galleries, theatres, public libraries, shopping precincts, public houses and even bingo halls, though good facilities in themselves, are no substitute for a real home. They have tried living in the dwelling in which the television is the most important feature of any room and rejected it, turning anew to the true altar of the hearth.

And therefore I believe that this book, the work of many hands, both male and female, will be of great use. It records the past, and that in itself can be quite a useful thing, but it has been written also to inspire and instruct us for the future. For, I am convinced that the future does not lie in the direction of fish fingers, and telly snacks, and Formica and other plastic rubbish. It lies in the recreation of real homes.

Why should a man write about such a very feminine subject? Of course, if a woman had written it, the book would have been very different—it would have been a look from the inside rather than from the outside, but, by looking from the outside, I have been able to see both the broad principles and the familiar detail, and, possibly, I have been able to praise more abundantly the housewife's art than a practitioner might have done. For this writer stands in awe of the real housewife: an accomplished housewife must be far more knowledgeable than the average so-called professional man or woman and much of the knowledge, as she will tell you, is difficult to achieve.

When we think of civilization we tend to think of people like Michelangelo, Shakespeare, Beethoven and Einstein. Well, all praise to such people, their works have enriched our homes, but of what use would their endeavours have been without the basis of a civilized home; of what comfort would their works be to us if our homes were brutish and boring, if we lived, like Nebuchadnezzar, like the beasts but without the beasts' natural grace and dignity? Everything that people do outside the home—on the farm, in the forest, in the factory and counting-house, down the mine or out at sea—is done to provide the essentials of a seemly and comely human existence: to sustain and embellish the home. If the home itself is allowed to go to pot then what is the use of it all? Whatever an honest man is doing, always somewhere in the back of his mind is the thought of his home.

Our age has produced more rubbishy substitutes for home than any other: the beastly burger bars and fried-chicken mess-ups, and fast-food this and take-away that (the places where both plastic chairs and tables are fastened to the floor so that the customers have to perch like parrots to eat their food). What kind of domestic culture do we call this? These things save work? I was talking to an old lady in the Golden Valley of Herefordshire many years ago and she gave me an account of a week's work when she was a child: washing on Monday, selling eggs and butter at the market on Tuesday, baking on Wednesday, and so on. "Wasn't it all a lot of work?" I asked her. "Yes," she said. "But nobody had ever told us there was anything wrong with work." She was one of the happiest old ladies I have ever met and as fit as a trout at eighty.

WASH DAY

Before the advent of the washing machine, the weekly wash was an awesome task, which took up the whole day, usually Monday. Most of the linen had to be pounded with a peg dolly in the wash tub, then rinsed and passed through the mangle, before hanging out to dry; more delicate pieces had to be rubbed gently by hand with soap; and many articles had to be starched. (See Washing Linen, p.278.)

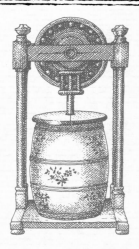

And what do people do with all the time they "save" by not having to look after their homes properly? Do they spend all that time improving themselves or their environment? They do not, for life without the firm base of a good home is unsatisfactory and unpleasing. So such people seize on any cheap thrill that comes along to allay the boredom. They besot themselves with the telly; they fly to the Costa Brava, where they find the same sorts of fast-food bar that they left behind. They lead lives which, in any other age since the Palaeolithic, would have been looked upon as barbarous.

So it is fitting that we should look at the homes of former ages, which were not barbarous, to see if we can learn from what we find. We will find, of course, that some labour-saving devices have come along which have freed men and women to do rewarding things. The vacuum cleaner has eliminated fleas, God bless it. Electricity, properly and moderately used, enables us to run and embellish our homes better. But we must not delude ourselves; labour-saving devices can never of themselves create a home. This is the work of human hands. And working to create a home is only drudgery if we think of it as such. It saddens me to see mothers carrying far too heavy a load of housework while thousands of young girls fritter their lives away. But it delights me, as it must delight everyone, to enter a home that is a real home, where the children are joyful and secure and show every sign of growing up to be proper home makers themselves.

In the great ages of the world the home was held sacred and so it must be again or we have no future on this earth. I feel sure that Beecher and Stowe, the authors of *The American Woman's Home*, published in 1867, would have agreed with me. They declared in the introduction to their excellent volume that they wished "to elevate both the honor and the remuneration of all the employments that sustain the many difficult and sacred duties of the family state, and thus to render each department of woman's true profession as much desired and respected as are the most honored professions of men." *Homo sapiens*? What a ludicrous and arrogant title we men have given ourselves and those that we evidently feel are our appendages! "Woman the home maker" would be a better title. And, not to leave him out altogether, "man the husbandman". These are the people we must become or, I am convinced, there is no future for either of us.

Why do I assume that it is only women who can really understand the mysteries of the home? There is a strong move in the Western world today to pretend that there is no difference between women and men at all. I once lived in a farm community in which this view was the prevailing one. The women were out in the fields ill treating the tractor, with which they had absolutely no affinity, while the men struggled on in the kitchen and living quarters, making a mess. Our pet pig, Esmeralda, reared on the bottle and accustomed to grunting about under the dining-room table at meal times, eventually stopped coming inside the door. I had no doubt whatever that the pig, like myself, was simply disgusted with the state of the place: she had higher standards. Without the firm base of a comfortable and well-ordered household the whole farm suffered: soil, crops, animals and people alike. The community collapsed.

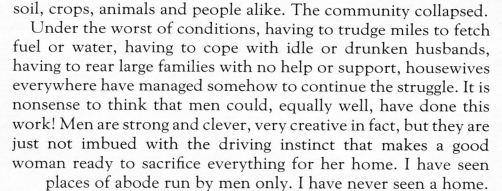

Under the worst of conditions, having to trudge miles to fetch fuel or water, having to cope with idle or drunken husbands, having to rear large families with no help or support, housewives everywhere have managed somehow to continue the struggle. It is nonsense to think that men could, equally well, have done this work! Men are strong and clever, very creative in fact, but they are just not imbued with the driving instinct that makes a good woman ready to sacrifice everything for her home. I have seen places of abode run by men only. I have never seen a home.

I can even now hear the howls of rage at what I have written. Most will start with the words: "This male chauvinist wants to chain women to the kitchen sink!" Of course, everybody in the house, if tall enough to reach it, should take a turn at the kitchen sink. Going, we hope, are the houses in which the man, on his arrival from work, gobbles up a meal, belches, and slumps in front of the telly with a six-pack of lager beside him. Such a man does not deserve a happy home, and certainly he won't be getting one.

QUILTING BEES
*In the nineteenth century
quilts were often given as
presents to women about to
be married. This custom
was practised mostly in
America, where groups of
women would gather
together enthusiastically to
make beautiful decorative
friendship quilts: their
quilting parties came to be
known as quilting bees.
(See Quilting &
Patchwork, p.356.)*

Vive la difference! What was wrong with the Victorian age was not that it did not recognize the difference between men and women but that people of both sexes believed that one sex was superior to the other. Men are different from women just as apples are different from oranges and the qualities of both put together make the greatest human power for good there is; not the power to "conquer the earth" as the brutish, male-dominated thinking of the Victorian age had it, but the power to nurture and husband the earth peacefully, so as to turn it into something very akin to our conception of paradise.

This book celebrates the home makers and the home. It recognizes and records some of the diligence, high skills, and love that has gone, over the ages, into creating and nurturing the true basis of all civilization. This book is the creation of a team of people, at least half of them women, but I would like to dedicate my small part of it, most gratefully and humbly, to the priestesses who serve the high altar of the hearth.

KITCHEN CRAFTS

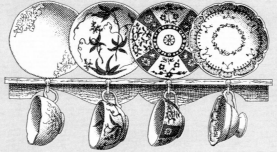

Fifty years ago George Orwell was struck by the "physical degeneracy" of the people about him. "Where are the monstrous men with chests like barrels and moustaches like the wings of eagles, who strode across my childhood gaze?" he demanded. Where are they indeed? I remember them, too, but it does not surprise me that they are not much in evidence today. For such men were not fed on fish fingers, ready-to-eat this and packeted that. They were reared on good beef, pork and mutton, fine fresh vegetables, fresh fruit, good bread and beer, and their food was properly prepared and cooked for them by skilled women. Undoubtedly there is much labour in the preparation of meals from fresh ingredients. To shell a bushel of peas, for example, takes a long while and you can do nothing else at the same time. But those of us who are privileged to live in a home where the ancient skills of preparing and cooking food are still carried out often wonder, as we contemplate another culinary delight, if the time saved by the "modern" housewife is really worth it. For, my God, what a world of difference there is in taste between the heated-up instant meal and the meal that is carefully prepared and cooked from fresh ingredients.

PREPARING FOOD

HE GREAT, IMMOVABLE, WELL-scrubbed table of the old-fashioned kitchen, built of heavy slabs of beech or other white wood and supported by extremely solid legs, aptly symbolizes the stability of country-house life before the unsettling days of the Second World War.

I remember huge joints of beef being prepared on that table. You never saw the boned, rolled-up pieces of meat so common today—the joint was always on the bone—and there was such a thing as mutton (as opposed to lamb) in those days, and mutton joints could be noble things.

SAVOURY PUDDINGS

The country people of the east of England, in Essex and Suffolk, always had pudding with their roast beef. Similar to Yorkshire pudding, it was eaten as a dish on its own before the meat in some cottages and always with plenty of "dish gravy" poured over it. Serving the meat last ensured that there was enough for all as everyone was too full by then to eat much. Preparing such a pudding meant there would be a big, glazed, earthenware mixing bowl on that great white table, scoops of flour from the bin, and tins of baking powder. There would be plenty of scrubbing and clearing up afterwards, too.

Another common activity that took place on the kitchen table was the grating of suet. Beef suet is the hard fat that lines the abdominal cavity of the ox. It was often used in pastry, which was far more prevalent in those days—there was nearly always a pastry-encased game pie in the larder to be eaten cold by anybody who came into the house hungry. It was also used to make that marvellous stuff, suet pudding. The grated suet was rubbed into the flour and a little water added to make the dough. The dough was then pressed inside a white china pudding basin, lining it completely. A mixture of meat and onions was placed in the middle and a cap of dough on top. Finally, the whole lot, bowl and all, was wrapped in a pudding cloth and lowered into a big saucepan of boiling water. The resulting meat "pudden" was the staple food of those who performed hard, manual work out of doors, whatever the weather. Sailors, fishermen, wildfowlers and farm labourers, who all

THE VICTORIAN KITCHEN
The kitchen was always a hive of activity—the very heart of the home. If the family was a large one there was an enormous amount of work involved in preparing the main meal of the day, and all offers of help were gratefully accepted.

SUGAR NIPPERS
After refining and clarifying, sugar was poured into conical moulds to set. Metal sugar cutters or "nippers"— small, hand ones, or larger ones mounted on wood— were used to break up the sugar loaves. Grippers could be used to hold the sugar while cutting it.

SCALES

For centuries the most common type of scale has been made on the even-arm balance principle. A pin is inserted through the centre of the beam and a dish is hung from it on one side for the ingredients to be weighed and a plate on the other for the weights to be piled. Steelyards worked on the uneven-arm balance principle and allowed heavy goods to be weighed. Hanging spring-balance machines with a dial to indicate the weight have been in use since Leonardo da Vinci invented them, although the free-standing type was not in common use until this century.

expended great amounts of energy in the winter time, relied on it to keep them going. I have often had the pleasure of sharing a beautiful suet pudding in the fo'c'sle (the forward cabin) of an Essex fishing boat.

DESSERTS

Honey was used by many as a sweetener until the supply of sugar increased and the price dropped towards the end of the eighteenth century. The sugar was still black with molasses when bought and the housewife had to embark on the long process of refining and clarifying it before she could cut it up into lumps for table use or pound it for cooking. This involved adding beaten egg white and water to the sugar and boiling and reboiling it, continually skimming the scum off the surface. When the sugar seemed clear she would strain and then boil it once more. Four pounds of unrefined sugar usually

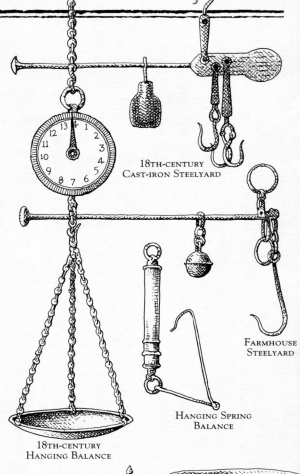

18TH-CENTURY
CAST-IRON STEELYARD

FARMHOUSE
STEELYARD

HANGING SPRING
BALANCE

18TH-CENTURY
HANGING BALANCE

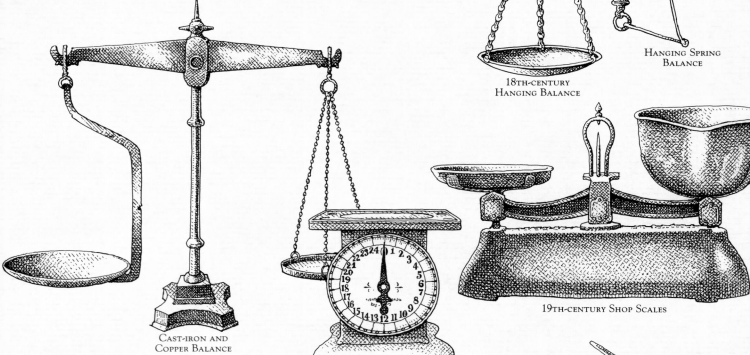

CAST-IRON AND
COPPER BALANCE

TABLE SPRING BALANCE

19TH-CENTURY SHOP SCALES

WEIGHTS AND MEASURES

Iron weights were fitted with iron lifting rings to slide on to steelyards, while bell and stacking weights were made for the beam and shop scales. Measuring cups were used to measure more than just liquids—potatoes were often measured by the gallon, nuts by the quart and butter by the pint.

BRASS BELL
AND STACKING
WEIGHTS

EXTENDED
ENGLISH MEASURE

IRISH BALUSTER
MEASURES

18TH-CENTURY
BALUSTER MEASURE

18TH-CENTURY
WOODEN MEASURE

made about a pound of clarified sugar. Fine sugar was added to breadcrumbs, flour, minced dates, currants, pepper, shredded suet, eggs and warm milk to make the delicious "Cambridge" or "college" pudding. A slab of butter was placed in the centre and the pudding wrapped in a pudding cloth and thrown into a pot of boiling water.

Cream was the main ingredient of many desserts: whitepot was a mixture of cream thickened with eggs; cabbage cream was simply a mixture of cream, sugar and rosewater; trifle was the same with the addition of ginger; and fool was a rich, creamy custard. Meringues arrived from France in the middle of the eighteenth century. They were shaped with a cool, wet spoon until that ingeniously simple tool, the piping bag, arrived in the nineteenth century.

CHOPPING, POUNDING AND PULPING

The cook had to do all cutting and chopping by hand until the end of the nineteenth century and by the middle of the eighteenth century there was a large number of implements made specially for use in the kitchen, from simple knives, choppers and scissors to mechanical cutting devices, such as marmalade cutters and hand-operated food choppers and mixers. She could choose from a large array of tinplate graters, from the tiny, flat, portable graters with a lid, suitable for grating nutmeg into the hot evening drink, to the large, rounded graters for grating breadcrumbs.

Dried herbs and spices were pounded in metal mortars, for, as every housewife knew, they penetrated wooden mortars, spoiling the individual flavours. Alabaster and marble mortars were used for pounding sugar, and traditionally the potato masher and the sugar crusher were shaped like a club.

She would crush and press fruit and vegetables to extract the juice for cooking. Probably, she would have had a lemon squeezer made of hard wood and containing a dip in which to place the fruit. By the nineteenth century they were more sophisticated: a pottery cone was inset into the dip of one piece of wood and a perforated dish into the other; the two pieces of wood were hinged together, so they needed only to be closed to squeeze the juice out of the fruit inside, making the job that much less messy! Sieves, colanders, strainers and funnels were in common use from early times, but potato peelers and raisin stoners were not widely available until the late nineteenth century.

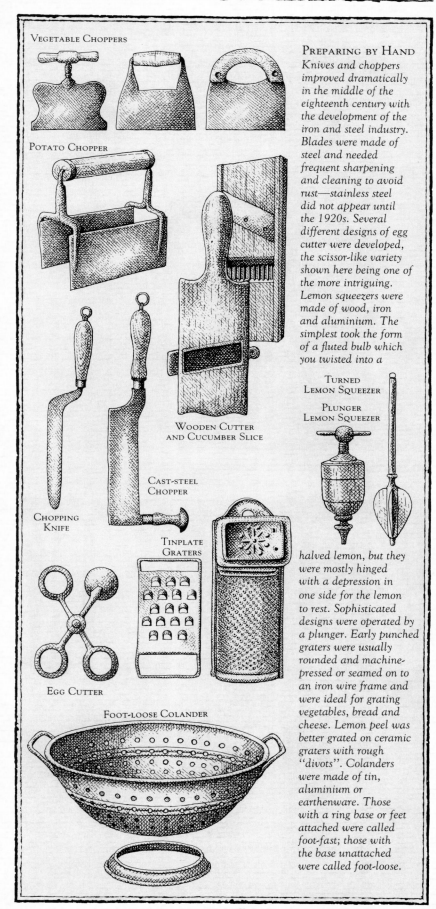

VEGETABLE CHOPPERS

POTATO CHOPPER

WOODEN CUTTER AND CUCUMBER SLICE

CHOPPING KNIFE

CAST-STEEL CHOPPER

TINPLATE GRATERS

EGG CUTTER

FOOT-LOOSE COLANDER

TURNED LEMON SQUEEZER

PLUNGER LEMON SQUEEZER

PREPARING BY HAND
Knives and choppers improved dramatically in the middle of the eighteenth century with the development of the iron and steel industry. Blades were made of steel and needed frequent sharpening and cleaning to avoid rust—stainless steel did not appear until the 1920s. Several different designs of egg cutter were developed, the scissor-like variety shown here being one of the more intriguing. Lemon squeezers were made of wood, iron and aluminium. The simplest took the form of a fluted bulb which you twisted into a halved lemon, but they were mostly hinged with a depression in one side for the lemon to rest. Sophisticated designs were operated by a plunger. Early punched graters were usually rounded and machine-pressed or seamed on to an iron wire frame and were ideal for grating vegetables, bread and cheese. Lemon peel was better grated on ceramic graters with rough "divots". Colanders were made of tin, aluminium or earthenware. Those with a ring base or feet attached were called foot-fast; those with the base unattached were called foot-loose.

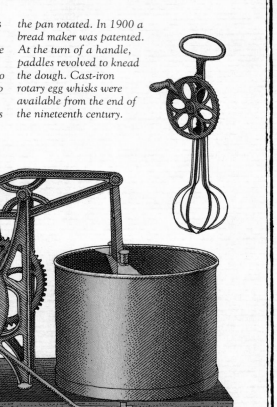

MECHANICAL DEVICES
Hand-operated chopping and mixing machines were available after 1850. As you turned the handle, two chopping blades moved up and down within a cylindrical tinplate pan as *the pan rotated. In 1900 a bread maker was patented. At the turn of a handle, paddles revolved to knead the dough. Cast-iron rotary egg whisks were available from the end of the nineteenth century.*

Mincemeat was never bought ready-made from the butcher's when I was a child and every kitchen I ever saw then had a mincing machine in it. Spinach was forced through a horsehair sieve with a wooden "mushroom" to emerge a kind of green porridge, which I, personally, found revolting. There were no electric food mixers; in fact, in the house in which I was brought up, there was no electricity at all.

BEATING
Until the late seventeenth century the only way of whisking eggs was in a bowl with a bunch of birch or willow twigs bound into a small brush. At this time copper bowls began to be made in quantity and housewives discovered that if the bowl was held over the heat a much thicker stiffness was obtained with eggs beaten in a copper bowl than those beaten in an earthenware bowl. Because copper conducts heat so well copper pans became popular despite their cost.

I don't remember the days before the American egg whisk—a cunning steel device with two interlocking beaters that rotate in opposite directions when the handle is turned—that, apparently, crossed the Atlantic in 1873. I remember my mother's fury at finding the cook making mayonnaise with one. Barbarous! Mayonnaise, she said, should be made by beating the oil and vinegar into the egg with a fork, stirring clockwise all the time (to reverse the turning would, everyone was assured, be fatal) and slowly dribbling in the oil. That matriarch of the English Edwardian kitchen, Mrs Beeton, however, recommends a wooden spoon for the beating. But it was done with a fork in Maryland, where my mother was born, and therefore, to her way of thinking, it *must* be the right way.

CAKE MIXES
As a small boy I nipped into the kitchen many a time to beg to be allowed to scrape the recently prepared raw cake mix from the sides of the mixing bowl. Sometimes this privilege was granted unconditionally; sometimes the granting was preceded by a lecture on how indigestible the stuff was (I never seemed to have any trouble digesting it); sometimes, if the cook was a grumpy one, a blank refusal might be encountered, in which case speed and cunning had to be employed. It always seemed to me that the finished cake was not a patch on the lovely uncooked batter.

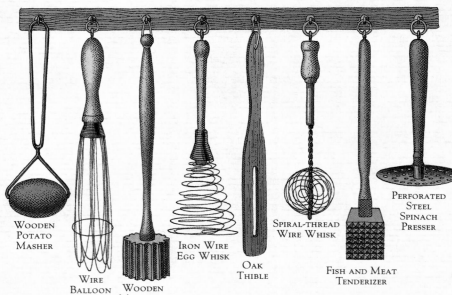

WOODEN POTATO MASHER

WIRE BALLOON WHISK

WOODEN MOLIQUET

IRON WIRE EGG WHISK

OAK THIBLE

SPIRAL-THREAD WIRE WHISK

FISH AND MEAT TENDERIZER

PERFORATED STEEL SPINACH PRESSER

HANGING TOOLS
Milk and eggs were beaten with cocoa using a moliquet to make a frothing chocolate drink. It was also used to beat egg whites for puddings and cakes until a variety of iron wire *whisks were marketed in the mid-eighteenth century. Preserved fish and meat had to be soaked and pounded with a wooden hammer-like utensil called a meat tenderizer before cooking. Vegetables were* *mashed or pressed with either a wooden, pestle-like implement or a perforated metal disc. The metal type gave a finer mash but the wooden presser could also be used for pounding meat.*

Pastry Making

A crude, indigestible oil-and-flour paste mixed in earthenware, stoneware or wooden bowls and rolled with a straight-sided stoneware flagon made the first pie shells or "coffins". Butter and lard gradually replaced oil in the paste, and the most buttery "short" pastry was eaten by itself.

The cook was making delicate flaky, or puff, pastry by the middle of the seventeenth century. Butter and eggs were mixed with fine flour and the resulting paste divided into pieces. The rolling pin now came into its own. Each piece was buttered, refolded and rolled five or six times to make decent puff pastry. By the eighteenth century wooden pie moulds were available in a large range of sizes, and "hoops" or "traps" (wooden or metal bands) supported the tarts and pies in the oven while they baked. Rowel-wheeled jiggers of various sizes and thicknesses were used for cutting rolled-out pastry for tarts, or the edge of an unbaked pie crust, making an attractive, wavy edge. Tinplate pastry cutters and jiggers and flat baking sheets were in use by the end of the eighteenth century.

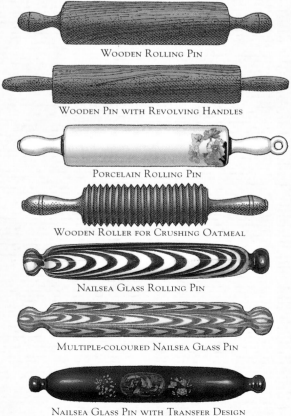

WOODEN ROLLING PIN

WOODEN PIN WITH REVOLVING HANDLES

PORCELAIN ROLLING PIN

WOODEN ROLLER FOR CRUSHING OATMEAL

NAILSEA GLASS ROLLING PIN

MULTIPLE-COLOURED NAILSEA GLASS PIN

NAILSEA GLASS PIN WITH TRANSFER DESIGN

Rolling and Crushing

The young woman above is using one of the flat wooden rolling pins found in many nineteenth-century households. They were usually made of sycamore, which does not colour or flavour food. Some were ridged to crush oatmeal and salt. Although more expensive, porcelain rolling pins were also common. They could be filled with water to provide extra weight and keep the pastry cool whilst rolling. Nailsea glass rolling pins were very popular. Hot, molten glass was rolled in coloured enamel chips, reheated and then reblown to create marvellous coloured patterns. Made near English ports, they were often given as "love tokens" by departing mariners. Many held salt and were hung by the fire so that the salt kept dry.

OPEN-HEARTH COOKING

DURING SEVERAL YEARS OF LIVING IN the bush of southern and central Africa I ate very little food that was not cooked on an open fire, outside on the ground. Meat (usually antelope) was thrown on the fire, turned once or twice in the hot flames with a stick to seal it and then pulled to rest in the glowing embers, turning it once so that both sides were cooked. Meat cooked in this way, with the addition of a little salt, was delicious beyond any telling of it: the most elaborate preparations of the finest chef in the world couldn't come near it. Sweet potatoes and cobs of maize were also cooked like this, and corms and bulbs dug up in the veld with a sharpened stick or oryx horn were also simply thrown into the hot ashes to cook.

The only cooking utensil in common use in those parts was the three-legged iron pot; it had to be three-legged because any object with four legs will not sit comfortably on uneven ground. The metal trivets or pot stands used in the eighteenth and nineteenth centuries for open-hearth cooking had only three legs for the same reason. In the pot was cooked the ubiquitous mealie-pap or ugali—a stiff porridge made by boiling ground maize in water. Porridge is perhaps a misnomer, for it was nearly as solid as bread and was eaten, usually after dipping it in gravy, with the fingers, and sometimes in alternate bites with grilled meat.

INDOOR FIRES

I mention these practices to give an idea of the very simplest cookery of all. In dry weather the cooking was always done out of doors, but during heavy rain it was transferred to an open fire on the beaten earth

RAISED BRICK HEARTH
The development of the raised, brick-topped hearth in the seventeenth century reduced the danger of cooking in long, spreading dresses, as the fire was made in the centre of the wide brick top. The wood was stored underneath.

SCOTTISH COTTAGE HEARTH *(right)*
Coal took a long while to reach the Scottish Highlands but peat was widely available as fuel. An iron fender contains this peat fire over which an iron cauldron is suspended by a pot-chain and hook.

IRON CAULDRON
An entire meal for the whole family could be cooked in one large iron pot or cauldron, and the hot water supplied for washing at the same time. For example, bacon was wrapped in linen and placed at the bottom of the cauldron beneath a pierced wooden board. Earthenware jars filled with fowls and meat stood on the board, while puddings and beans wrapped in linen were suspended in the water.

AMERICAN FIREPLACE *(right)*
The cauldron is suspended above the fire from an adjustable chimney crane, while the kettle, complete with lazy-back (see p.217), hangs from a ratchet-hanger or trammel.

inside a grass and mud hut. There was no chimney, of course, and when you walked into the hut the smoke would appear intolerable. However, if you sat down immediately, as politeness required that you should, most of the smoke passed above your head, where it did an excellent job of keeping all the flies and mosquitoes away.

In an Anglo-Saxon farmhouse a wood or peat fire was built in the middle of the floor. Sometimes a small hole was cut in the thatch especially to allow the smoke out, but more usually the smoke had to find its own way out. You could still find chimneyless houses in remote parts of the British Isles as late as the nineteenth century; one is preserved at the Folk Museum at Saint Fagan's in Wales.

THE CHIMNEY

The widespread introduction of the chimney in the fourteenth century made cooking a much more pleasurable business, for it was then possible to keep an eye on the cooking without being choked by the smoke. The

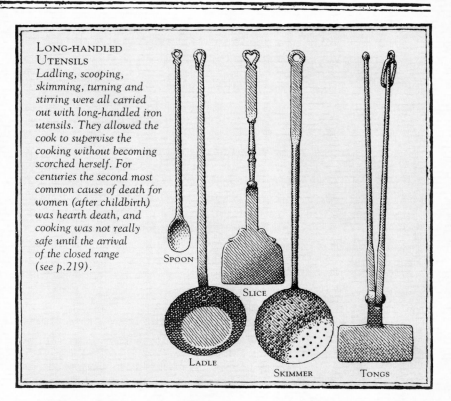

LONG-HANDLED UTENSILS

Ladling, scooping, skimming, turning and stirring were all carried out with long-handled iron utensils. They allowed the cook to supervise the cooking without becoming scorched herself. For centuries the second most common cause of death for women (after childbirth) was hearth death, and cooking was not really safe until the arrival of the closed range (see p.219).

SPOON

SLICE

LADLE

SKIMMER

TONGS

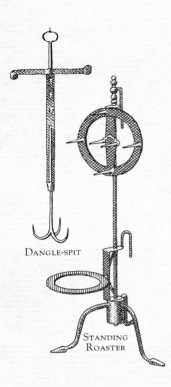

DANGLE-SPIT

STANDING
ROASTER

hearth was gradually moved from the centre of the room to the side, where the fire was built on the ground or on a slab of stone. Wood was the most commonly used fuel until the nineteenth century, although peat, or turf, was also used in some areas, and in Ireland it was more often used than wood.

The more prosperous country houses in turf-burning parts of Ireland had (and some still have) a machine called a "fanner" to encourage the fire. This is a centrifugal wind pump, operated by a handle and mounted to one side of the open hearth. A pipe leads from it, passing under the floorboards to emerge through a hole in the hearth floor. The housewife has merely to give a few turns of the handle to transform the smouldering turf fire into a hot blaze. Most of these little machines were made in Pierce's famous foundry in Wexford. By the seventeenth century firewood was in short supply and coal gradually began to take its place. Now coal needs a draught from underneath to burn well, so by the late seventeenth century the iron fire-basket was in use, raising the coal well above the hearth.

ROASTING METHODS
Instead of roasting your meat on a horizontal spit, as shown in the main illustration, you could use a standing roaster. You simply fixed the joint of meat to the spikes of the iron or steel roaster and positioned it before the flames. A circular stand lower on the main shaft of the implement held the dripping bowl. Dangle-spits were commonly used in open-hearth cooking over small fires and, like standing roasters, became more common as the coal-fire grate took over from the open wood fires. You hung the meat to be roasted over the fire or in front of the narrow grate opening and caused the spit to rotate. Weights were added to the arms of the dangle-spit to add impetus to the turning and the more sophisticated versions were turned by means of a clockwork device called a bottle jack. Whatever the type of spit used, meat roasted before an open fire always tasted wonderful!

BOILING
Boiling was always the most common method of cooking and large pots or cauldrons stood in the fire or were suspended over it first by means of a wooden stick or rope, or later an iron chain or rod, fixed to a wooden or iron crossbar. From the middle of the eighteenth century the housewife could raise or lower the pot by adding or removing pot hooks. A more sophisticated device called a chimney or kettle crane was invented in the eighteenth century, enabling the cook to alter the angle and position of the pot. I lived in a house with an open hearth for many years and we had a beautiful and most elaborate crane. You could swing it out into the room, so that you could stir the contents of the pot out of the smoke.

A whole meal could be boiled in the one iron pot if the ingredients were put in at different stages and kept separate while cooking. Our Welsh neighbours tended to boil all their meat. Their main dish was cawl—a mutton, bacon and leek soup. For some reason nobody but a Welsh lady can cook this to perfection. We had a large iron boiler with a lid and a tap, which we kept either suspended from the crane or perched on a shelf by the side of the fire. Provided that you remembered to top it up from time to time it gave constant hot water.

CHIMNEY CRANES
The first chimney crane to be invented was the single-movement crane. A horizontal bar extended from a vertical iron post, hinged to the side of the fireplace. The pot was hung on this bar, which could swing through an angle of ninety degrees, allowing easy access by the cook to the cooking vessel and making it possible to vary the amount of heat allowed to reach the pot. From this simple crane were developed the two-movement and the three-movement crane with which it was also possible to raise and lower the level of the pots and move them along the bar.

ROASTING

Spit roasting was a common method of cooking meat on the open hearth. Usually the meat was skewered by a spit, which was then placed horizontally before the fire, supported by wrought-iron fire-dogs, or, if the fire was a coal one, the grate bars. Meat was also roasted by suspending it over the fire by means of a hook hanging from a crossbar in the chimney. In our house we roasted chickens, ducks, geese and, occasionally, for a great feast, a small pig or sheep on a spit. You had to turn the spit by hand and I used to look upon this as my job. It was also necessary to baste the meat frequently with dripping and a dish was placed under the spit to catch it. I used to judge the length of time that a fowl or joint would take to roast by the number of bottles of wine I could consume during the operation; thus, a goose was a four-bottle bird.

Until the eighteenth century spits were often turned by animals, especially small dogs. The poor dog would be made to tread a small wooden wheel attached to the spit until the joint was done "to a turn". However, this arrangement was not found to be terribly practical as the dog was never anywhere to be seen if it suspected there was to be roast for dinner.

By the eighteenth century two sorts of mechanical device were available to turn the spit: the wind-up jack and the smoke jack. The first was powered by a weight on a rope or chain. You operated it by winding up the weight and letting it descend, pulling against gear wheels that turned the spit. The smoke jack consisted of a fan situated above the fire inside the chimney. The rising hot air and smoke caused the fan to rotate, activating the rods and gearing that turned the spit below. By the nineteenth century there were many new designs to suit the smaller coal fire-baskets. Many were operated by clockwork: the bottle jack was one such. The joint was suspended vertically underneath it and was turned first one way and then the other, giving an even roasting.

The first roasting screens appeared in the eighteenth century. They were placed in front of the roasting joint to reflect the radiant heat on to the meat and shield it from the draughts that blew across the floor and up the chimney. The Victorians manufactured beautiful tinplate screens raised on legs and arched across the top, so that they enclosed the front of the fire-box and chimney. They had doors in the back so that you could baste the meat. Hasteners or Dutch ovens (see p.220) were developed from these.

GRILLING AND TOASTING

Meat and fish could also be grilled on a gridiron—a long-handled framework of iron bars—and there was a wide variety of toasters for bread, cheese and slices of meat. Standing toasters with prongs set at different levels were commonly used and there were the traditional hand-held toasting forks.

Flat loaves of bread and oatcakes were baked on a suspended circular baking sheet known as a griddle or girdle or sometimes a bakestone (see p.223). Bread was usually baked in a dome-shaped oven built into the wall to one side of the hearth, but could also be baked by placing it in a portable lidded container and burying the lot in the hot ashes of the open fire. This was especially common in peat-burning areas (see p.223).

THREE-MOVEMENT CHIMNEY CRANE

SINGLE-MOVEMENT CHIMNEY CRANE

STANDING THREE-MOVEMENT CHIMNEY CRANE

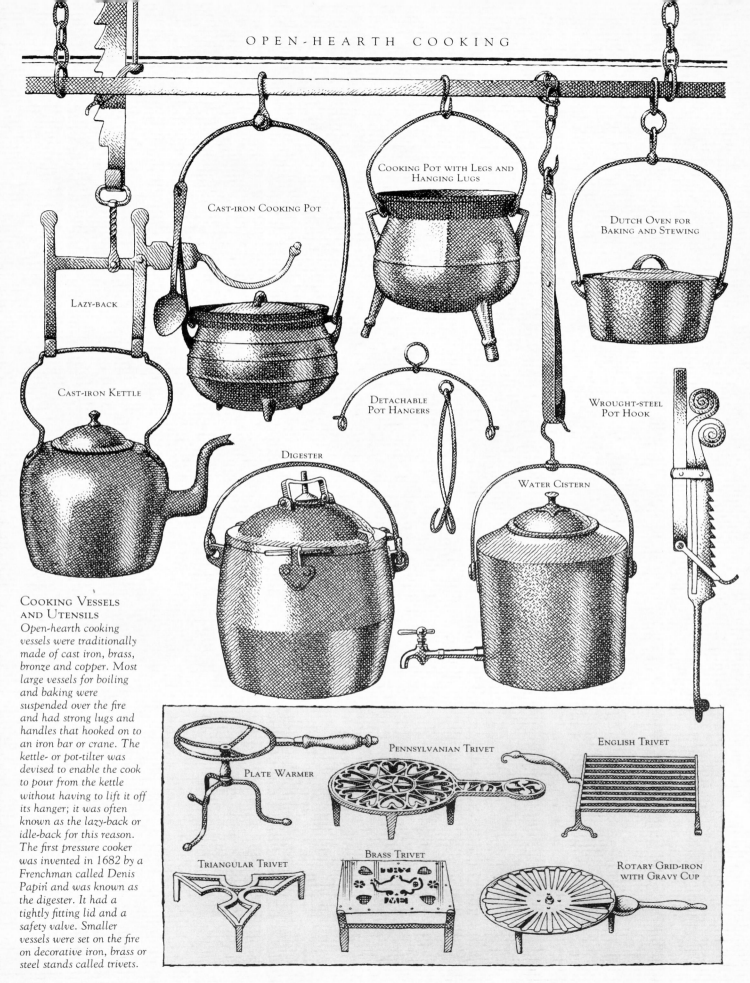

CAST-IRON COOKING POT

COOKING POT WITH LEGS AND HANGING LUGS

DUTCH OVEN FOR BAKING AND STEWING

LAZY-BACK

CAST-IRON KETTLE

DETACHABLE POT HANGERS

WROUGHT-STEEL POT HOOK

DIGESTER

WATER CISTERN

COOKING VESSELS AND UTENSILS

Open-hearth cooking vessels were traditionally made of cast iron, brass, bronze and copper. Most large vessels for boiling and baking were suspended over the fire and had strong lugs and handles that hooked on to an iron bar or crane. The kettle- or pot-tilter was devised to enable the cook to pour from the kettle without having to lift it off its hanger; it was often known as the lazy-back or idle-back for this reason. The first pressure cooker was invented in 1682 by a Frenchman called Denis Papin and was known as the digester. It had a tightly fitting lid and a safety valve. Smaller vessels were set on the fire on decorative iron, brass or steel stands called trivets.

PLATE WARMER

PENNSYLVANIAN TRIVET

ENGLISH TRIVET

TRIANGULAR TRIVET

BRASS TRIVET

ROTARY GRID-IRON WITH GRAVY CUP

COOKING AT A RANGE

OPEN-RANGE COOKING
The first open ranges consisted simply of a cast-iron "perpetual" oven (one with its own grate and flues) built into the fireplace to one side of the open grate. By 1815 ranges were available not only with an oven but also a boiler, both heated by a central grate. In many designs the boiler was L-shaped, extending along the back of the grate.

T HE GREAT KITCHEN RANGE WAS A product of the coal and iron age of the eighteenth and nineteenth centuries. In the middle of the eighteenth century a way of making good quality iron using charred coal (coke) was discovered, and ironmasters no longer had to use dwindling supplies of charcoal to make poor quality, brittle cast iron. Immediately, iron became abundant and good enough for large castings to be made and sold cheaply throughout the British Isles. At the same time, a cheap, plentiful supply of coal meant that coal gradually took over from wood as the most popular domestic fuel, and lead to the development of grates.

Free-standing iron grates were being made in the eighteenth century (see p.214) and these were soon developed to fit into the fireplace, where they were flanked by iron plates or hobs on which pans and kettles could stand. The open range was born.

THE OPEN RANGE
In 1780 Thomas Robinson designed the first open kitchen range. At the centre of the range was a hob grate. To one side of the metal hob was an iron oven with a hinged door and on the other an iron tank for hot water. Fitted to the top bar of the fire grate was a hinged trivet which would swing forward for a pan or kettle to stand on.

One of the main disadvantages of this range was that food cooked in the oven tended to be burnt on one side (the side nearest the fire) and undercooked on the other. Fortunately, modifications were soon made to the design, and passages for the circulation of warm air round the oven were introduced, improving the evenness of the cooking dramatically. Other disadvantages of the open range were that it made the kitchen unbearably hot and burned vast amounts of coal. Dampers were introduced to control oven and fire heat but these ranges were never efficient and the fire-box could still become hot enough to melt the fire-bars!

THE CLOSED RANGE
By the 1840s the enclosed kitchen range or kitchener became widely available. A metal hot-plate covered the fire-box and was fitted with rings for pans and kettles to rest on. Movable panels covered the front of the grate so that you could still roast meat in front of the fire if you wished, or warm the kitchen after cooking. Later versions featured a metal door and eventually the fire was completely encased in iron. Ovens were placed on both sides of the fire-box in some designs or a boiler might stand on one side and an oven on the other. An arrangement of flues and dampers controlled the temperature of the oven and boiler to some degree and the systems were gradually improved.

The arrival of the closed range spelt the end of the soot-blackened pots. No longer hung over the open fire from pot hooks and kettle cranes, pots were placed on the iron plate that formed the top of the stove, where

OPEN PEAT-BURNING RANGE

OPEN COAL-BURNING RANGE WITH OVEN AND BOILER

THE CLOSED RANGE

GEORGE BODLEY PATENTED THE CLOSED RANGE in 1802. Similar to Robinson's open range (see p.218), he reduced the size of the open-range grate and covered it with a cast-iron hot-plate. A fire brick was inserted between the grate and the oven to reduce the heat on that side and flues were incorporated on the other side, so that the heat could circulate round the oven. In the 1820s William Flavel began making closed ranges, which he called "patent kitcheners". The name stuck and closed ranges became generally known as kitcheners. The closed range was much more economical than the open range, as the heat was contained within the (smaller) grate instead of being allowed to disappear up the chimney. Pots and kettles stood on the clean hot-plates, so they were not blackened and trivets and chimney cranes were no longer needed. Roasting in front of the fire, using a hastener (see p.220), was only possible with those kitcheners where the fire was open at the front and the grate adjustable at the bottom, so that the size of the fire could be increased. With the completely enclosed ranges special ovens were provided that allowed sufficient air to circulate for roasting.

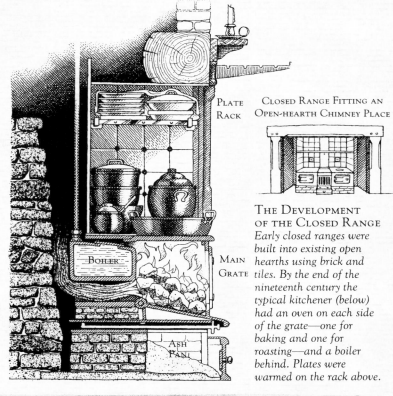

PLATE RACK

BOILER

MAIN GRATE

ASH PAN

CLOSED RANGE FITTING AN OPEN-HEARTH CHIMNEY PLACE

THE DEVELOPMENT OF THE CLOSED RANGE
Early closed ranges were built into existing open hearths using brick and tiles. By the end of the nineteenth century the typical kitchener (below) had an oven on each side of the grate—one for baking and one for roasting—and a boiler behind. Plates were warmed on the rack above.

ROASTING IN
A HASTENER
*After the dangle-spit, the
standing roaster (see p.214)
and the roasting screen
came the hastener,
sometimes known as the
Dutch oven (not to be
confused with the true
Dutch oven, see p.222).
Designed to stand in front
of the coal-grate fire,
hasteners were crafted out
of sheet tin and shaped to
increase the heat in which
the joint cooked. The meat
was hooked on a dangle-
spit, which was turned by
means of a bottle jack.
Dutch ovens had doors in
the back so the cook could
baste the meat while it
was roasting.*

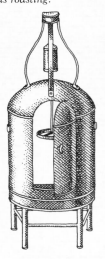

they could become red hot if the cook
wanted. Later, circular holes were cut in the
hot-plate. These were usually plugged by
iron plates, but, for a quick boil, one of
these plates could be removed and a pot or
kettle placed directly over the flames.

MAINTAINING THE CLOSED RANGE

The kitchener made the kitchen a cleaner
place. No longer did great dollops of soot
flop down the chimney and burst into the
room; no longer could the pot or the kettle
call the other black. But the soot was still
there all right, up the chimney, and the
chimney had to be swept even more than
before. The complicated system of flues and
dampers that channelled the heat around the
range also had to be kept clean. This was the
poor cook's job, unless she had a kitchen
maid to do it for her. I well remember the
cooks we had in my childhood home—
large, motherly women, with strong, usually
bare, arms, sometimes a trifle short-
tempered but kindly underneath. Cooks
were always called *Mrs* something even
though they were never married. The other
maids, who were always smaller in bulk,
were called by their Christian names, *tout
simple*, no matter how old they were.

The open fire could be kept in, often for
weeks at a time, by throwing on huge logs
last thing at night, but the kitchener went
out at night. So, before the cook could so
much as make an early morning cup of tea,
she had to clean the thing, black-lead it,
polish it, and then re-light it. Once the range
was lit the kitchen was soon transformed
from a cold, cheerless place to the cosiest
room in the house.

THE GAS COOKER

Three factors contributed to the end of the
great kitchen range within 150 years, at
most, of its inception. The first was the
widespread introduction of gas. To begin
with the gas was coal gas, produced by a
diversity of private companies and distributed throughout the towns and cities in the
1880s. The gas stove had a number of
advantages over the coal range. The temperature could be regulated to a much finer
degree simply by adjusting a tap, and the
temperature could be maintained for as long
as was required. It was smaller than a range,
for it was designed simply to cook food, not
boil water and heat rooms, too, and could
therefore be installed in smaller kitchens at
much less expense. Gas cookers were far

INTO THE TWENTIETH CENTURY
*The gas cooker became
more common in the
1850s when cast-iron
black boxes with four
legs, containing an
oven, a grill and a hot-
plate with burners were
marketed. Gas cooking
didn't become popular,
however, until the
introduction of the
prepayment slot
machine in the 1890s,
which for the first time
made gas affordable for
those on lower incomes.
The more expensive com-
bination gas and coal
ranges were available
by the end of the
nineteenth century.*

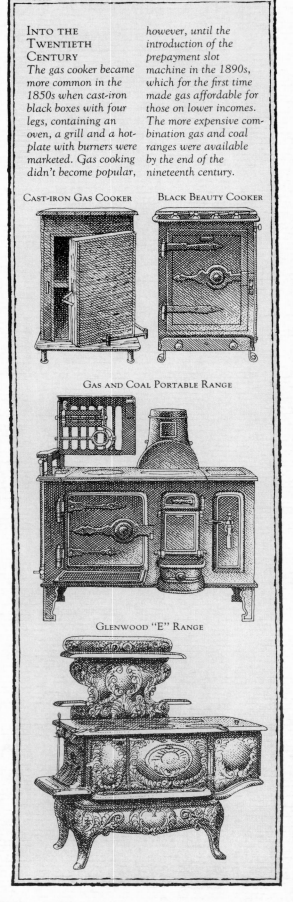

CAST-IRON GAS COOKER

BLACK BEAUTY COOKER

GAS AND COAL PORTABLE RANGE

GLENWOOD "E" RANGE

cleaner than the guzzling coal monsters that preceded them and the cook could lie in for a bit since there was no early morning lighting up to do—the gas cooker could be lit in a moment. However, it was still made of cast iron, and still required black-leading and polishing.

Efficient, properly ventilated gas ovens were available by 1900. The ovens were well insulated with shelf runners, grills and removable enamelled fittings. Thermostats were not included until 1923 when, for the first time ever, food could be cooked at a specific temperature, making cooking a much more precise art.

THE ELECTRIC COOKER

The second factor was the advent of electricity. Electric cookers were first designed in the 1890s but they took some time to catch on because of the slow spread of electricity supplies throughout the country and the high initial cost of both electricity and electric cookers. By the late 1920s electric cookers were cheaper, featured longer-lasting, more efficient heating elements, enamel finishes and automatic temperature controls, and electric cooking finally began to compete with gas.

AGA COOKERS

The third factor was the arrival from Sweden during the late 1920s of the highly efficient, fully enclosed Aga stove still in use today. The Esse arrived later and worked on exactly the same principle.

The original Aga oven operated on solid fuel but was clean and economical to run. The coal was held inside a cast-iron fuel-box enclosed in an insulated jacket. The fire was strictly regulated by restricting the amount of air allowed to it. The heat was stored in a mass of cast steel—the Aga weighs nearly a ton—and conducted to the hot-plates and ovens at precisely the right temperatures.

These stoves were, and still are, extremely efficient. You can carry out different types of cooking at once, the hot-plates are always ready for instant boiling, the hot oven and cool oven (or ovens) always at their working temperatures, and the fuel consumption is a small fraction of that of the ranges.

The great kitchen ranges—those magnificent shiny monsters—have now nearly all gone for scrap. They were too hungry and they belched forth too much heat, which went where it was not wanted and spoilt the temper of the cook.

CAST-IRON SAUCEPAN

CAST-IRON FISH OR HAM KETTLE

COPPER SAUCEPAN

BRASS KETTLE

COPPER TEA-KETTLE

METAL FOOD WARMER

COOKING VESSELS
Now that cooking vessels stood on hot-plates they needed to be flat-bottomed and equipped with handles that could be held. Saucepans or stewpans appeared in the first half of the eighteenth century when they were made in sets of varying sizes. Fish was boiled in a pan called a kettle with an inside container or strainer. Tea-kettles proliferated as tea drinking became increasingly popular (see p.241). By the beginning of the twentieth century pans of food could be reheated in tin containers filled with hot water.

BAKING

IT IS EASY TO SEE HOW LEAVENED bread was invented. The people who first ground wheat or barley between two stones, wet the meal and roasted it near a fire must soon have discovered that if they left the moistened dough overnight in warm weather, it would rise. Although they would not have realized it at the time, this was due to the action of wild yeast. The yeast organism—a microscopic fungus—eats sugar and excretes carbon dioxide, and it is the carbon dioxide that as it expands causes myriad holes to form in the dough, making it rise.

I have used wild yeast many times in Africa, where the tame stuff was not for sale. You make a sweet, sloppy dough and leave it exposed to the air for a day or two. When it begins to froth you add it to the main dough and knead and bake it. Making yeast bread is a time-consuming and skilful business. You must first knead the dough thoroughly with

your hands, then allow it to prove, or rest for a few hours until it has risen. You then knock it down, kneading it thoroughly once again, before placing it in baking tins and allowing it to rise once more. Finally, you must transport it to the oven without bumping it if it is to bake well.

OVENS IMPROVISED AND PURPOSE-BUILT

We made ovens in termites' nests, which might have been designed for the purpose. We dug a cavity in the side of the nest, ran an air vent from it to the top of the nest and lit a big fire in the chamber, keeping it roaring for about three hours. We then let the fire go out and popped the dough in the hot ashes, which retained sufficient heat to bake the bread perfectly.

The early brick and stone ovens worked on exactly the same principle. They were usually let into the wall to one side of the fireplace and had a wooden door. Small

BAKING IN A POT OVEN

In peat-burning areas bread and pies were often baked in a pot oven. The dough was placed directly on the heated and cleared hearth and covered with an iron pot, which was then surrounded by burning peat. Oval or round cast-iron portable ovens, often known as Dutch ovens, worked on the same principle. These were stood among the hot ashes of the open fire and burning peat or hot embers placed on the lid to speed up the cooking.

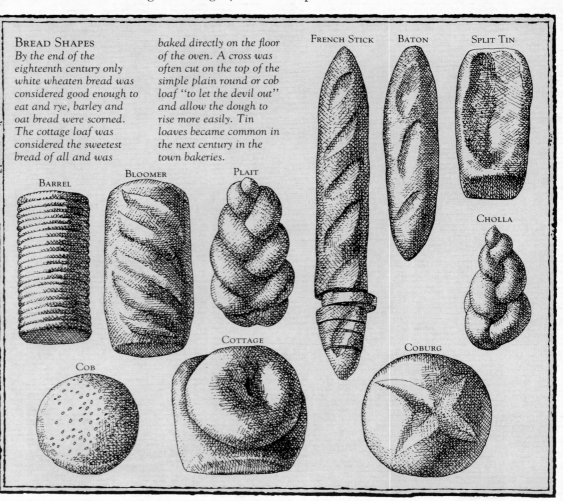

BREAD SHAPES
By the end of the eighteenth century only white wheaten bread was considered good enough to eat and rye, barley and oat bread were scorned. The cottage loaf was considered the sweetest bread of all and was baked directly on the floor of the oven. A cross was often cut on the top of the simple plain round or cob loaf "to let the devil out" and allow the dough to rise more easily. Tin loaves became common in the next century in the town bakeries.

BARREL
BLOOMER
PLAIT
FRENCH STICK
BATON
SPLIT TIN
CHOLLA
COB
COTTAGE
COBURG

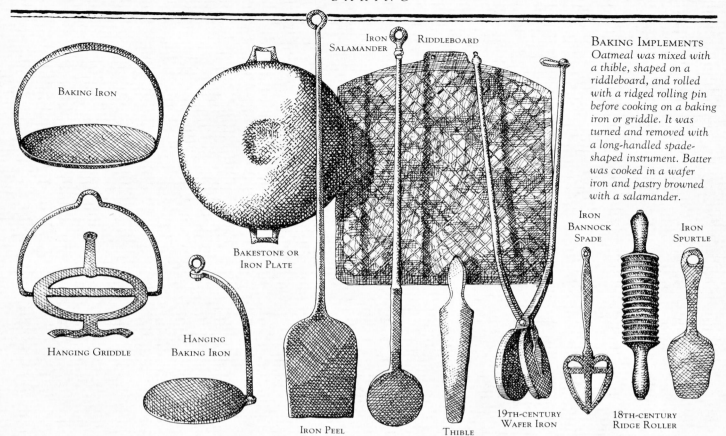

BAKING IRON

HANGING GRIDDLE

HANGING BAKING IRON

IRON SALAMANDER

RIDDLEBOARD

BAKESTONE OR IRON PLATE

IRON PEEL

THIBLE

19TH-CENTURY WAFER IRON

IRON BANNOCK SPADE

IRON SPURTLE

18TH-CENTURY RIDGE ROLLER

pieces of wood, such as hedge trimmings, were generally used for fuel, together with a few faggots (compressed sticks). The ash was brushed out and the floor of the oven wiped clean before placing the bread inside. By the middle of the nineteenth century, ovens with cast-iron doors and two chambers were common. The fire was kept burning during baking in a chamber beneath the baking chamber. Solid-fuel ovens also worked on this principle but were usually part of the kitchen range and had damper-controlled flues to help distribute the heat evenly.

BAKING ON THE FIRE

You could also bake bread (as the Irish, Scottish Highlanders and Welsh country people very often still do) by placing the dough in a lidded iron or pottery container and burying it in the hot ashes of the open fire. Peat-burning areas commonly baked bread in this way. Of course, it takes good judgement and experience to know how hot the ashes should be and when to take the bread out of the pot.

Oatcakes, flat bread and pies were all cooked over the fire on a bakestone, griddle or baking iron. In Wales they baked bara planc, the Welsh version of griddle cake, on a circular iron baking sheet and cooked and crisped batter in a waffle iron.

COMMUNAL OVENS
Communal ovens were often built into the thickness of an outside wall and bakehouses were still popular when I was young. I remember staying at a fisherman's cottage in the summer holidays, where the small kitchen contained a simple coal range with no oven. It was my delight once a week on baking day to run down to the bakehouse, carrying an array of uncooked bread, pies and cakes. There I would hand over our creations, together with a few pennies, and the baker would open the great cast-iron door of the oven, revealing a glowing chamber, and place them inside beside those of half the village. When they were perfectly done, he would pull them out again for me with a long-handled wooden paddle called a peel.

STORING FOOD

EFORE YOU COULD BUY ASPARAGUS grown in Mexico in Soho in December, and strawberries flown from Spain in March, and before the advent of freezers, storing and preserving food was a matter of supreme importance.

Storing Meat and Fish

At school we were told that in former times most of the cattle had to be killed in the autumn and salted down because there wasn't enough winter fodder to feed them on. We were not told that the reason there was not enough winter fodder was that it was customary to remove all the fences after the harvest so that everybody's cattle could graze on everybody's land. As it paid no individual farmer to grow winter fodder crops, none were grown, and the cattle had to be slaughtered in the autumn.

It was certainly not a good idea to slaughter a bullock during the summer months as the meat would deteriorate rapidly in the heat, and fly-proof, well-ventilated buildings were not very often available. A city butcher could do it only because he was able to sell the meat within a day or two of slaughtering. The practice of corning beef—lightly salting it in brine—extended the period that he could store the meat by a week or two.

There was no refrigerator, of course, but by the nineteenth century nearly all houses had a spacious, walk-in larder or pantry. Fish and vegetables were laid directly on its cool stone or marble shelves and covered with muslin, while meat and game were hung in the larder or in a meat safe.

Storing Dry and Dairy Foods

Grain—the edible dried seed of plants—was the foodstuff that made civilization possible. Small grain—wheat, barley, oats and rye— would keep perfectly well stored in the rick or stack, provided that you kept the rat and mouse population in reasonable check and covered the rick with a good coat of thatch. Held securely in the straw, the grain would gradually dry out naturally and would keep quite well for years. When the farmer wanted to sell or use some he simply threshed out a rick, or part of a rick. The housewife stored grains in wooden bins, which she stood above floor level to keep them out of the reach of greedy mice.

When I was a boy, every cottager I knew had a bin in his outhouse. This was a large wooden box (big enough for a man to hide in) with a sloping roof, lined with sheet zinc. It was used to store the barley meal for the cottager's pig. There might be another to hold bran, which would also be food for the pig or for the rabbits. In the larder there would be a flour bin of some sort—often a four- or five-gallon earthenware crock, which was sometimes glazed on the inside only, and often not glazed at all. This crock would have a wooden plug that fitted the hole in the top exactly. There might be another, smaller, crock for dried peas and another for broad beans. Peas pudding was a common dish among country people and broad beans, or fava beans as they are known in America, were a good, high-protein standby.

Eggs, cheese and butter all need to be kept in a cool place and so were all stored in the larder. Between them, the larder and the kitchen housed a great variety of wooden, earthenware, glass, and stoneware containers for the dry goods that the good wife needed, or thought she needed. These included salt, sugar, pepper and a few spices such as cloves, cinnamon and ginger (country food was not heavily spiced). Herbs were stored in paper bags, while sugar and flour kept best in wooden tubs. There would also always be some earthenware or glass jars containing pickled onions or shallots and other pickles. Fruit was often kept in nets and apples were usually dried, cored and strung to the ceiling, or laid on shelves in a cool, dry loft.

Carrying Food

Always somewhere in the kitchen, usually at the end of a shelf, you would find a little pile of calico bags. These were used for collecting the shopping. They were taken to the grocer's or the village shop and filled with the goods the housewife needed—flour, sugar, lentils, rice, or whatever. This marvellous system eliminated all need for the messy and environmentally damaging "packaging" that litters our countryside today. There were no horrible plastic bags and there was no "rubbish mountain". In fact, there was practically no rubbish. Tinned food was only just creeping in and most country

MEAT SAFES
Meat was generally hung before cooking to ripen its flavour. In wealthier households it was stored in a large meat safe which was suspended from the ceiling. In this way it was kept out of reach of vermin and its muslin covering prevented the flies from landing on it.

people never saw it. You might find the odd tin of Tate and Lyle's golden syrup (with that fascinating picture of the apparently dead lion with bees buzzing round it), the very occasional tin of sardines from Portugal, and sometimes a bottle of Bovril.

STORING LIQUIDS

The flood of tasteless fizzy water (known today as "mineral water") had not yet started: most country women brewed their own wines and farm workers took a bottle of home-made wine with them to the fields to drink with their morning "snap". I've been given many a swig from such a bottle, the proffering of which was always preceded by a ritual wipe over the top of the neck with

an earthy hand. Before glass bottles were widely available at the end of the seventeenth century, housewives would fill wooden, barrel-like containers with hot or cold drink, depending on the time of year. Wood was ideal because it did not conduct heat but bottles and jugs made of tough ox hide were also widely used. When I was young small stoneware ginger beer bottles might appear at fêtes or special occasions (see p.228); they had screw tops with threaded stoneware "corks" in rubber washers. Lemonade was sometimes sold in glass bottles with glass marbles inside the neck, held firmly against a rubber ring at the top by the pressure within the bottle. I remember smashing the bottles to get at the marbles.

(see p.228)

THE LARDER
Many different types of container were used in the larder for storing all sorts of food. Stoneware or earthenware jars were used for storing vinegar and pickled foods, while jams, jellies and salted food were stored in salt-glazed earthenware jars. Bread was kept in large crocks or bins, and tin jars were used for storing tea and biscuits.

OVAL-SHAPED WALL SALT

19TH-CENTURY PINE WALL SALT

WALL SALTS
Salt was often stored in a container known as a wall salt. It was hung on the kitchen wall in a position convenient for the cook to take spoonfuls to add to the cooking pot.

SALTING & PICKLING

WHEN I WAS YOUNG THE SALTING trough was found in every country household of any standard. In the east of England it was likely to be made of wood, although I have also seen lead and stoneware troughs. I once had a stoneware ham bath the size and shape of a large ham. This was used for sweet pickling: curing a ham in a brine that included salt, sugar and various spices. Every country lady had her own favourite recipe.

In Wales, and every other slate country, salting troughs were hewn out of slate. Twenty years ago every Welsh farmhouse, large or small, had slate troughs set up on stone buttresses in the dairy and larder. In the dairy the trough was used for skimming the cream off the milk (see p.261), and in the larder it was used for salting pig meat. In some houses the same trough was used for both purposes: skimming milk in the summer, salting pig meat in the winter.

Dry pickling took three weeks to three months to complete, depending on whether you were salting thin joints or massive hams. In either case the meat had to be frequently turned and rubbed in the salt.

Meat from larger animals was cured in wet pickle. Before I had a deep freeze I pickled the greater part of many a sheep in brine. The meat was completely immersed in a brine with enough salt in it to float a potato or an egg, and placed in a cool larder. After curing, the meat was generally soaked for twelve to twenty-four hours to extract some of the salt and then boiled. Such meat, generally beef or mutton, was used to victual ships until very recently.

Hand-salted meat tastes better and is more reliable: the meat is cut into pieces and rubbed carefully with dry salt a couple of days before being put into the brine. The initial dry salting extracts some of the moisture so that the brine is not diluted.

A sensible precaution, if you are going to keep the meat many months, is to draw away the brine from time to time. Either add water to it and augment its salinity by boiling in some more salt, then let it cool and return it to the meat or, if you can afford to waste the salt, throw it away and pour in some freshly made brine. A handful of peppercorns, or even a few chillies, thrown into the cask can do only good.

PICKLE JARS
Pickles were preserved in vinegar in sealed pickle jars. Glass pickle jars were preferred as glass is not porous and does not admit air, which would spoil the pickles.

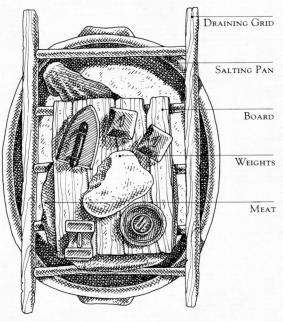

DRAINING GRID

SALTING PAN

BOARD

WEIGHTS

MEAT

DRY PICKLING *(above)*
The meat was compressed by placing a board laden with weights on top. In this way the juice was forced out and the salt could penetrate the meat more quickly.

PICKLING FISH *(left)*
Fish was baked in good vinegar and then rolled up and preserved in a vinegar-and-onion pickle in a sealed jar.

SALTING A WET PICKLE
Before pickling, meat was rubbed with dry salt and left to drain over a trough of brine for several days, more salt being rubbed into it each day. It was then immersed in the brine and left to soak in a cool place for a few weeks. As the pickle became diluted with the meat juices more salt was added to the solution.

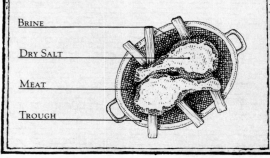

BRINE

DRY SALT

MEAT

TROUGH

DRYING & SMOKING

 NYONE WHO HAS VISITED THE COAST of Belgium will have seen dabs or flounders nailed to the walls of fishermen's sheds to dry. After placing them for an hour or two in brine they are left in the sun and cool sea breeze to dehydrate and are then eaten raw.

DRYING IN THE WIND
We caught an occasional skate or ray when fishing in the South Atlantic. We would head and gut them so that just the "wings" remained joined together, and hang them in the rigging without further ado. They would keep like that for weeks and improved with age. We also caught some sea birds on baited fish hooks, which we skinned and gutted and hung in the same manner.

DRYING AND PRESERVING IN THE SMOKE
Smoke helps keep away the flies and preserve meat, and I have sat over many a fire in central Africa, watching strips of buck or buffalo meat drying in the smoke.

If you peer up a great chimney in a farmhouse or mansion kitchen in Europe you will probably see the remains of horizontal rods or perches fixed across the width of it. Bacon and ham were hung from these, or in a separate smoke-house.

Two methods of smoking have evolved: cold smoking and cook smoking. With cold smoking the fire is damped down and built so that no heat but a lot of smoke encircles the meat, allowing the pyroligneous acid in the smoke to preserve it, but leaving the meat uncooked. Bacon, kippers, bloaters and haddock should be cold smoked. Salmon, eels, buckling, and mackerel are generally cook smoked, that is they are subjected to enough heat to cook them as well as smoke them and are ready to eat immediately. I have also cook smoked both ducks and geese and they are quite delicious.

HICKORY SMOKE
Traditionally the North Americans are great smokers and my Maryland cousins are always talking to me about the supremacy of hickory smoke. Certainly they smoked fish of many kinds and some American housewives still have plenty of recipes for bacon and ham, generally smoked in some kind of outdoor smoking house.

SMOKING
Meat was most commonly smoked by hanging it in the chimney but some people used a smoke-house or an inverted barrel in which the bung hole served as a smoke vent. Inside, the meat was hung from hooks and smoked over a sawdust fire. The home-smoker was similar but used smoke from a wood-burning stove.

CHIMNEY SMOKING

SMOKE-HOUSE

HOME-SMOKER

COMMUNITY DRYING
Fruit was dried to last families throughout the winter. Sometimes, after a bumper harvest, the whole community was involved in the work of preparing the fruit for drying.

FRUIT DRIER

DRYING IN THE HOME
The fruit to be dried was stacked on the wire-mesh racks of the drier. This was then positioned over the kitchen stove and the heat that rose from it would dry the fruit most effectively and speedily.

BOTTLING & CANNING

IF YOU HEAT ANY KIND OF FOOD stuff sufficiently to destroy the bacteria and mould organisms and then, while it is in this sterile state, seal it completely, it will keep indefinitely. When the tins of "bully-beef" left by Scott of the Antarctic's party back in 1912 were opened when rediscovered years later, the beef was found to be in perfect condition.

POTTING MEAT

From the days of Elizabeth I in England, and no doubt before then in Spain, extensive sea voyaging stimulated the search for effective methods of preserving foodstuffs. Salt meat was considered good enough for the poor sailors who had to do the gruelling work of sailing the ships but when gentlemen began to go to sea, and even more so, gentlewomen, then salt tack was not considered good enough and the art of potting meat and poultry was perfected. The meat was cooked and the fat used to cover it. The bladder of a pig or sheep or ox was wetted and then stretched over the top of the pot and tied down. As it dried it shrunk, making a very tight seal and preserving the meat.

THE FIRST BOTTLED FOOD

A Frenchman named Nicholas Appert pioneered the art of bottling. He was making a bid for the prize of 12,000 francs offered by Napoleon to the person who could find a way of preserving food for his army which, as every schoolboy knows, marched on its stomach. Appert placed the food in glass jars and cooked it by immersing the loosely

CANS AND JARS
After tin cans had proved their value in war time, they became part of daily life and revolutionized the storage and preservation of food. Apart from their improved design, cans have changed very little since then. The tradition of preserving fruit in jars continued and several types of sealer were used to seal the jar tightly.

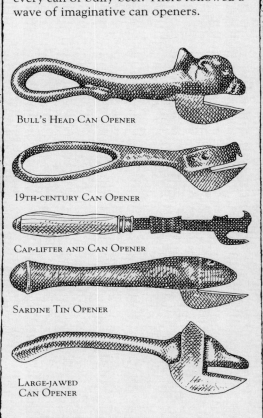

THE CAN OPENER
The first canned foods carried the helpful instruction that a chisel and hammer were the best tools for opening them! Sixty years later, in 1875, the first can opener was invented. It was made of cast iron and steel and at one end was a carved bull's head, especially apt as it was sold with every can of bully-beef. There followed a wave of imaginative can openers.

BULL'S HEAD CAN OPENER

19TH-CENTURY CAN OPENER

CAP-LIFTER AND CAN OPENER

SARDINE TIN OPENER

LARGE-JAWED CAN OPENER

CAN OF PROCESSED PEAS

CAN OF OYSTER SOUP

EMERGENCY WAR RATIONS

CAN OF ROASTED VEAL

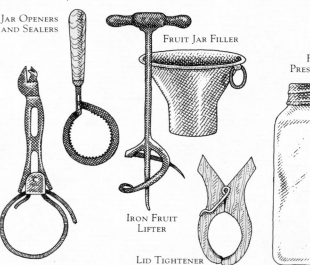

JAR OPENERS AND SEALERS

FRUIT JAR FILLER

FRUIT PRESERVE JAR

IRON FRUIT LIFTER

LID TIGHTENER

corked jars in boiling water. He then pressed home the corks and sealed the jars.

The famous Kilner jar was long used in England for preserving fruit and is still manufactured. All good country house-wives "put up" tomatoes, plums, goose-berries and other soft fruit in Kilner jars in times of surplus and a few shelf loads of such produce is a great standby: we use Kilner jars to this day. The ubiquity of the deep freeze, however, has meant that the art of bottling is now practically lost. This is sad, as tomatoes, plums, strawberries and other soft and mushy fruit taste infinitely better bottled than frozen.

THE FIRST TIN CANISTERS
An Englishman named Peter Durand took out a patent in 1810 for tinned iron or steel cans and by 1814 a firm named Donkin and Hall was supplying tinned meat to the Royal Navy. At first the process was improperly understood. Sometimes temperatures were not high enough to destroy all the bacteria and sometimes the tins were too large and the heat was not able to penetrate to the centre of the contents. Tins would blow up and sometimes people would be poisoned.

It was not until Louis Pasteur discovered the facts about bacteria, and how to kill them, in the 1860s that canning, as it was called in America, or tinning, as it was known in England, became a safe and re-liable process. By 1840, the Australians were sending tinned meat to England and, soon after, the United States and the Argen-tine went into the production of canned beef in a big way. Upton Sinclair's novel *The Jungle* contains a vivid and pretty horrifying description of large-scale beef canning in Chicago in the early twentieth century.

In the late nineteenth century cheap tin-ned cans became available. Made of tinned steel plate, the cans were boiled with their contents already inside them. Then the tops were clamped on to make an airtight seal and they were boiled again. Using this method, the contents were sterilized completely and would remain sterile until the tin was opened, however many years later.

The famous wedge-shaped can of bully-beef kept the Allied armies fed during the First World War and the British armies in the Second. I lived on it for months at a time in the Second and can honestly say that I never got *really* tired of it. You soon learned the rationale behind the wedge-shaped can. You opened it by unwinding a special strip near the middle of it with a little key that came with it. You ate *half* the contents (no man was ever known to eat more) for lunch, then fitted the top half of the can to the bottom half and put it away until supper time when you ate the second half. Occa-sionally, misguided people would make attempts to cook the stuff. The result was disgusting in the extreme.

HOME CANNING
During both wars the Homcan was a com-monly used device. I managed to get hold of one in Suffolk after the Second World War and canned many a sheep with it. You bought the Homcan tins from the Women's Institute (they got them from the Metal Box Company) and sealed them with the Homcan machine. Meat and fruit could be canned at home simply and safely using this method. However, green vegetables were not sufficiently acid for safe home canning and would, likely as not, be "off" by the time you opened the tin.

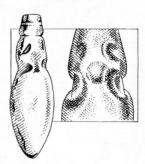

THE MARBLE STOPPER
Corking was but one way of sealing bottles. An alternative method was to seal the bottle with a glass or marble stopper. These were used most frequently in fizzy drink bottles. The pressure inside the bottle wedged the marble stopper tightly against the rubber ring in the bottle neck, thus sealing it.

VICTORIAN
THREE-SIDED
GLASS BOTTLE

BROWN
GLASS
BOTTLE

STONEWARE
GIN BOTTLE

CHAMPAGNE-TOP
STONEWARE BOTTLE

MOULDED GLASS
MEDICINE BOTTLE

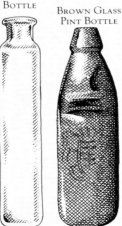

MEDICINE
BOTTLE

BROWN GLASS
PINT BOTTLE

BOTTLES IN THE HOME
A wide assortment of bottles was produced. A lot were specifically used for storing drinks, from gin to ginger beer, while other bottles, usually narrower and ridged so you could tell them straight away, were used for keeping medicines and poisons.

PRESERVES & CONFECTIONERY

OST FRUITS AND VEGETABLES CAN be preserved using one of the following five methods: salting, immersing in alcohol, pickling in vinegar, drying or sugaring.

Salting is inappropriate for fruit, although absolutely the perfect way to preserve runner beans. If you cover any fruit in brandy, or any other strong spirit for that matter, you will preserve it indefinitely. By soaking fruit or vegetables in vinegar you make pickle; by boiling them in vinegar you make chutney. Small fruits, such as grapes and blackcurrants, will keep for a long time if they are dried quickly enough. Plums dried in this manner become prunes. Drying fruit is common in hot, dry areas, such as the lands bordering the Mediterranean and southern California. Figs and dates can be preserved by drying and pressing.

SUGARING
The art of preserving fruit in sugar or syrup is a very old tradition in northern Europe. No doubt before cane sugar arrived from the Near East, honey was used. Before preserving in syrup, fruit must be boiled or blanched in water. In this way the skin of the fruit is softened sufficiently for the syrup to permeate it. Two parts of white sugar should be dissolved in one part of water to make the syrup. The old cooks always knew the exact strength of the sugar solution needed for any purpose. Today few householders bother to

PREPARING FRUIT
Before fruit could be dried or preserved in syrup it usually had to be peeled and stoned. There was a large number of paring devices available, ranging from a simple hand-held parer to the extremely complicated "Bonanza" fruit parer, which was not, in fact, very effective as it only worked with fruit that was "standard-sized".

MARMALADE CUTTER

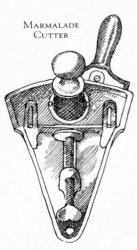

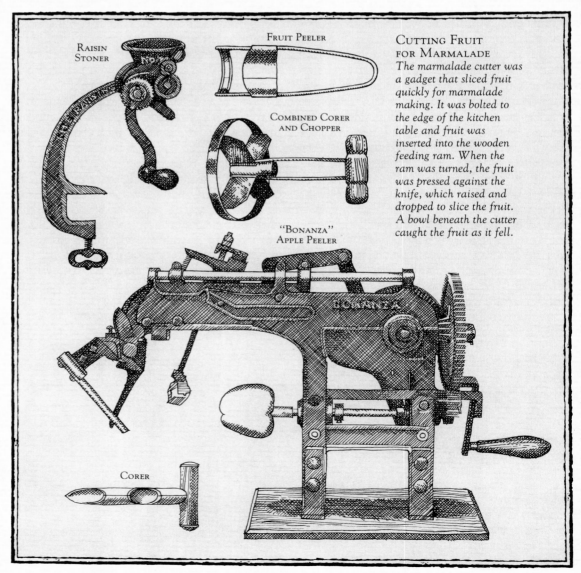

RAISIN STONER

FRUIT PEELER

COMBINED CORER AND CHOPPER

"BONANZA" APPLE PEELER

CORER

CUTTING FRUIT FOR MARMALADE
The marmalade cutter was a gadget that sliced fruit quickly for marmalade making. It was bolted to the edge of the kitchen table and fruit was inserted into the wooden feeding ram. When the ram was turned, the fruit was pressed against the knife, which raised and dropped to slice the fruit. A bowl beneath the cutter caught the fruit as it fell.

make syrup: they buy candied or crystallized fruit, or fruit in syrup directly from the confectioners. In any case, nowadays we can buy fresh fruit at any time of the year, rendering fruit preservation less important.

MAKING MARMALADE

Marmalade is said to have been invented especially for Catherine of Aragon. When that unfortunate lady married Henry VIII, and had to leave her glorious sunny land and come to live in gloomy England, she found that she craved oranges. These could not be shipped to England in their natural form without deteriorating so much that they were inedible on arrival. So it was necessary to discover a method of preserving them on their long journey. It was not long before marmalade was born.

MAKING JAM AND JELLY

Jamming and jellying are both methods of preserving fruit. To make jam you simply boil the fruit with plenty of sugar until much of the moisture has boiled away. Until comparatively recently most households consumed a colossal amount of jam: they ate jam tarts and jam-filled roly-poly puddings, and bread and butter spread with copious amounts of jam made up a considerable part of the diet of both rich and poor. After all, after the settlement of the West Indies sugar became extremely cheap and, in the country-side at least, fruit was there for the picking and usually was.

To make jelly you simply boil the fruit, strain it through a fine strainer, preferably one made of muslin, mix the solution with sugar, and boil it again until it jellies. The mixture jellies because of the action of pectin, usually present in the fruit. If pectin is not present in sufficient quantity the fruit will not jelly, no matter how much you boil it or how often you spoon some of it out, taste it, and pour a dribble on to a cold plate. If your fruit will not jelly you must either add pectin, bought at a shop (surely a base expedient), or give up and brew the stuff into wine, perhaps not a bad idea in itself.

Nowadays, with the realization that sugar is really quite bad for you, jam and fruit jellies are not made or consumed in such vast amounts, which is probably just as well. Of course, jelly does not have to be sweet or contain fruit. Jelly made with a type of gelatin known as isinglass was being used as a basis for sweet and savoury dishes from the sixteenth century.

CHOCOLATE AND CANDY MOULDS

METAL CHOCOLATE MOULD

COPPER JELLY MOULD

VICTORIAN COPPER JELLY MOULD

PRINCE OF WALES FEATHERS JELLY MOULD

GLAZED EARTHENWARE JELLY MOULD

POTTERY JELLY MOULD

METAL EASTER EGG MOULD

COPPER "TIMBALE" MOULD

CONFECTIONERY MOULD

CLASSIC COPPER JELLY MOULD

JELLY AND CANDY MOULDS
The housewife took great pride in presenting attractive desserts at the table, and there was a wide choice of decorative moulds to use for jellies, puddings and sweets. Jelly moulds were often made into elaborate castle shapes, while candy and confectionery moulds popularly came in the shapes of birds, animals and flowers. Moulds were also made in two halves, which were held together with straps while the confectionery set inside— the chocolate Easter egg is an obvious example.

CHILLING FOOD

Hoisting tongs were used to haul ice blocks on board ship and up steep slopes. They gripped the blocks securely as they were dragged or lifted.

HOISTING TONGS

I WENT TO SCHOOL IN SWITZERLAND and every winter we used to move up into the mountains to a ski resort called Villar sur Bex. The Palace Hotel, even at that late date, which must have been about 1927 or 1928, had its own natural ice plant. They had a large wooden frame at the back of the hotel on to which a man would play water from a hose every morning. The water would freeze almost instantly into the most wonderful shapes and, as the winter went on, the whole thing began to look like the creation of one of the architects of Kubla Khan's stately pleasure dome at Xanadu. In the spring men would wade in with sledge hammers and smash it all up (an operation in which I longed to assist) and then sled it all to the great cellar under the hotel, which doubled as an ice house. This store of ice would always last the hotel until the freezing cold winter came round again.

STORING AND TRANSPORTING ICE

From Tudor times on, the ice house was a common adjunct to most big country houses. The climate of northern Europe was colder then and only in Dickens' time was the snow-bound winter becoming more of a nostalgic memory than an actuality. In any event the ice houses that were built up and down the country could be stocked each winter with ice cut from the nearest pond, canal or river. As the nineteenth century wore on, and the British winter was no longer severe enough to provide enough ice to stock the ice houses, sailing ships, which had sailed to the Baltic with freights of coal, would return loaded with ice.

It was not as easy as one might suppose to obtain the ice needed to load the ships. Special ice picks were used to cut holes through the ice and saws were inserted into these holes and the ice sawn out in huge chunks. Irons designed for the purpose were

ICE HOUSES

There were conflicting views over the siting of an ice house. Some held that it should be constructed above ground in the shade of trees, and perhaps made into a garden feature. Others believed that an underground pit made the coolest ice house, but an important requirement for this type of ice house was that there should be good drainage. In either case, the ice house was lined with straw to keep the ice cold and to keep out the heat. Ice was inserted in the underground pit through an opening at the top and was accessible through an underground passage. Water was allowed to drain off whilst the ice was kept in the pit by the siting of a cartwheel directly over the drain.

GARDEN ICE HOUSE

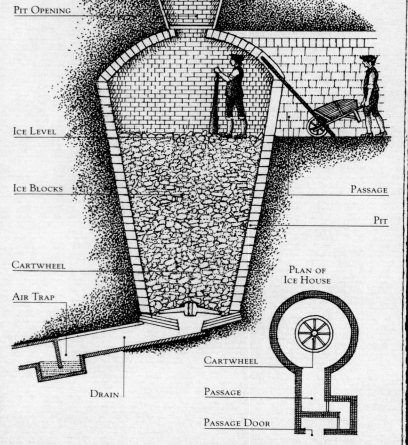

PIT OPENING

ICE LEVEL

ICE BLOCKS

PASSAGE

PIT

CARTWHEEL

AIR TRAP

DRAIN

PLAN OF ICE HOUSE

CARTWHEEL

PASSAGE

PASSAGE DOOR

inserted under a chunk and the whole thing—weighing perhaps tons—was levered up on to the uncut ice and dragged by horse to the waiting ship. Once there it would be slung up by tackles and dumped into the hold. In the United States ice was cut on various lakes in the north and transported to the warmer parts of the country and abroad. Ports in Britain housed great insulated ice warehouses by the 1830s to store the imported ice before it was distributed.

THE ICE BOX

Before the coming of refrigerators and, eventually, deep freezes, the ice box was in common use in households throughout the United States and, eventually, England. To begin with these were simply wooden boxes lined with zinc or slate and insulated most commonly with charcoal, ash or felt. Ice was delivered daily and the housewife placed it in the inner casing. She then put the fish or other food to be preserved on top of the ice. By the second half of the nineteenth century ice boxes were built into the top half of a chest or cupboard and the food placed in the

bottom half. The cooler air from the ice box descended on to the food as the air warmed by the food rose to melt the ice. It was a very effective cooling system.

In Africa, we wild colonial boys used to build makeshift ice boxes called "charcoal coolers". We built the boxes out of galvanized steel sheet and constructed a wire-netting covering over them. We stuffed charcoal between the two and contrived a shallow water tray on top with small holes in the bottom of it. The water dripped from the tray down on to the charcoal and evaporated, taking the heat out of the box. Provided the air was dry enough the thing worked marvellously.

The ancient Greeks also understood this principle and kept drinking water in porous pottery containers. As the water nearest the edge of the vessel evaporated, the water remaining inside gradually cooled. Everyone who has soldiered in the desert will know the chargal, or canvas water-bag. You hung it on the mirror bracket of a lorry and the water always kept cool—much cooler than the desert air.

THE FIRST "FRIDGES"
The first refrigerators were wooden cabinets insulated with zinc and porcelain. Blocks of ice were kept in the top compartment, and the cold air from this cooled the food stored below, while the warm air from the food rose, gradually melting the ice.

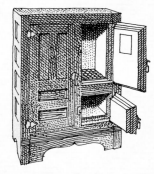

MAKING ICE IN THE HOME
Before refrigerators were common, ice-making machines could be found in many homes. The Raplin ice-maker was one of the many machines available. It froze water at the turn of a handle, making a block of ice in about twenty minutes. Once made, the ice block was put in the ice box where it kept perishable foods fresh.

THE RAPLIN ICE-MAKER

DOMESTIC PICKS AND SCOOPS
Ice picks were used to chip demarcation lines in a large block of ice so that smaller blocks could be sawn off. Ice scoops were used for shovelling up crushed ice.

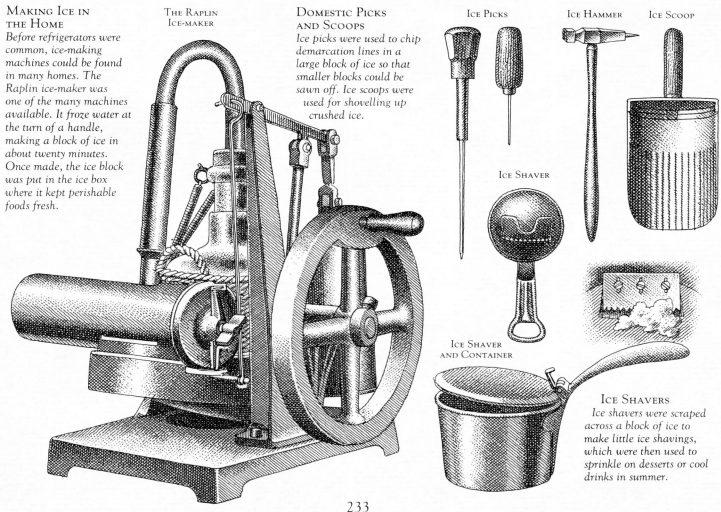

ICE PICKS

ICE HAMMER

ICE SCOOP

ICE SHAVER

ICE SHAVER AND CONTAINER

ICE SHAVERS
Ice shavers were scraped across a block of ice to make little ice shavings, which were then used to sprinkle on desserts or cool drinks in summer.

CLEANING & MAINTENANCE

I N SMALL FARMS AND COTTAGES *everything* was done in the kitchen, which very often doubled as the living room, too. Sometimes, in fact, it was the only downstairs room and keeping it clean was a major task. Slightly larger houses would also have a parlour—a freezing cold, often damp room, used only for formal occasions, such as funeral parties.

In large farmhouses and the country houses of even moderately prosperous families the kitchen was reserved for cooking only. Washing up and cleaning were done in a small adjoining room called the scullery and food was stored in the larder. Even crockery and cutlery were very often not kept in the kitchen itself, as any room with a fire in it tends to be rather dusty.

It was the fire that created the most cleaning problems. With an open fire soot is apt to fall down the chimney and all over the floor, and the wind is almost certain to blow smoke into the room. It was extremely difficult to maintain a high standard of cleanliness in these circumstances but, with the introduction of the enclosed stove in the early nineteenth century, smoke ceased to be such a problem.

SWEEPING THE FLOOR

Up until the nineteenth century most kitchen floors were made of beaten earth. Such a floor was usually swept with a besom broom until it became as hard and as smooth as concrete, but it could not be scrubbed with water in the way that a tiled

THE RANGE
The kitchen range involved a great deal of work for the housewife: each morning the fire-box had to be cleaned, the ashes removed, the flues swept, and the oven scraped, washed and dried. Then the whole iron case had to be black-leaded and the brass fittings polished vigorously till they shone.

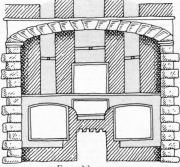

FLUE NETWORK

CLEANING THE FLUES
Warm air from the range fire was directed along a network of flues, or passages, to heat the ovens of the range. Soot was continually deposited in the flues and, to prevent them from becoming clogged, they had to be cleaned daily. Special long-handled flue brushes were used for this dirty but essential job.

FLUE BRUSH

floor, for example, can be scrubbed. Although those with stone floors were not spared the weekly scrub, the sort of aseptic cleanliness that has become almost an obsession today was not possible.

I am not old enough to remember the regular visits of the sand man, although my mother used to tell me that the sand man visited me every night and sprinkled sand in my eyes to make me go to sleep. In earlier days most kitchen and dairy floors were sanded and so, often, were halls and stairs. Once a week perhaps the sand would be swept out, together with any dirt that had collected, and clean sand sprinkled on.

LEAVING THE KETTLE BLACK
For most of the history of civilization cooking was performed over an open fire (see pp.212–17), and it was this practice that gave rise to the saying about the pot calling the kettle black. For, anything that is hung over

an open fire becomes black very quickly, just as the hands of anyone supervising the cooking over an open fire tend to become black. It was pointless trying to remove the black from the pots and kettles as, within minutes of putting them back into use, they would be black again. However, many women would still scour them regularly with handfuls of sand.

The changeover to coal-burning grates in most of Britain during the eighteenth and nineteenth centuries increased rather than decreased the amount of kitchen cleaning, as coal is a far dirtier fuel than wood and carting coal about the house resulted in a constant stream of dirt and dust, which had to be removed immediately it fell or it would be trodden everywhere. Pots continued to be suspended above the fire or placed on hobs or trivets directly on top of the fire (see p.218), so they were still black.

MOPPING AND SCRUBBING
Stone and tile floors were mopped frequently using long-handled string or rag mops. Mopping was quite a skill—the floor had to be left clean yet almost dry! Wooden floors were always scrubbed on hands and knees, using flat scrubbing brushes, soapy water and lots of elbow grease. Strapped on knee-pads, or kneelers, were often worn for this gruelling task.

WEARING PATTENS
Pattens are wooden clogs or sandals with a raised wooden platform. Housewives wore them, with or without shoes, to keep their feet dry when they were mopping and swilling the floor.

LIFTS FOR SWILLING
Lifts were solid squares of pottery or stone that were set underneath the legs of dressers and chests to raise them off the floor. Then, when the floor was swilled and mopped, the furniture was kept dry.

"BASKET" SLOP PAIL

SLOP PAIL AND LID

TIN PAIL

DOUBLE WING STOVE BRUSH

BASS SINK BRUSH

SCRUBBING BRUSH

BENT OVAL STOVE BRUSH

IPPER HEARTH BRUSH

KNEELER

REEDED HEARTH BRUSH

STRING MOP

RAG MOP

KEEPING THE RANGE CLEAN

The introduction of the enclosed, coal-burning range or kitchener (see p.219) meant that pots, frying pans, and kettles were no longer blackened by the smoke and could therefore be kept burnished and polished.

The smoke was led into the chimney by stove pipes, so it was impossible for soot to fall down and burst out into the room. Chimneys ceased to smoke very much, if at all, and the ashes were confined. But, if anything, there was even more cleaning to be done, for the great iron ranges sooted up very quickly and their numerous flues had to be swept out frequently. Wide-angled stove brushes were made especially for this purpose. I well remember the servants in the houses in which I spent my childhood spending much time black-leading the kitchen range with special little black-lead brushes with turned handles. This prevented it from rusting and made it shine; cooks took great pride in their gleaming ranges.

SHORTAGE OF WATER

The difficulty of obtaining water (see p.274) made cleaning a problem for both city and country people. My old friend Mrs Light of Brockweir in Gloucestershire, a smallholder's wife, told me she used to bath the children every night and then wash the kitchen floor with the dirty water. Washing-up water was often used for the same purpose. In spite of such difficulties the great kitchen table was always kept scrubbed (as white as snow, the cook would boast) and, with the advent of tiles, the floor, too, was frequently scrubbed. In addition, stone hearths were whitened at least once a week with hearth stone.

BUTLERS AND FOOTMEN

Before the advent of stainless steel at the beginning of the twentieth century, cutlery had to be scrupulously cleaned and especially scrupulously dried or it would quickly corrode. Many larger households had knife cleaners which were operated by turning a handle. In great houses cleaning the silver generally fell to the butler or footman.

But most of the work was done by the cook and, as a reward for all her labour, she reigned over a glorious queendom. The gleaming black iron stove, with its hot coal fire visible behind its bars, was the focus of the house and, as a child, I far preferred the kitchen to any other room. The company there was better, too.

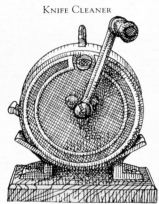

KNIFE CLEANER

CLEANING KNIVES
Knives were cleaned by rubbing them to and fro on a long, flat board called a knife board, sprinkled with brick dust. They were then wiped clean. A knife-cleaning machine could clean up to ten knives at once. Knives were slotted into the holes around the rim and cleaned, at the turn of the handle, by a rotating brush covered with emery powder.

THE KITCHEN DRESSER

THE BEAUTIFUL OAK DRESSERS THAT FETCH such a high price in antique shops nowadays, only made their appearance in any great number in the eighteenth century with the advent of cheap china. Before that a few small shelves fixed on brackets to the walls and generally covered with American oil cloth, or paper with scalloped edges, sufficed for the few plates and utensils people owned. Saucepans and other pots were hung on nails fixed to the wall and cups, jugs and tumblers were placed in one small cupboard, sometimes glass-fronted, let into the thick stone wall. I know many old people, both in Ireland and Wales, who continue to manage perfectly happily with similar simple arrangements.

The first dresser consisted of a flat board fixed to the kitchen wall at waist height. Food was prepared or "dressed" on this hanging table. Soon shelves were fixed above the board and by the end of the seventeenth century cupboards were also constructed underneath. It was but a small step to joining the three elements together in one piece of furniture. The back of the dresser, which was often as tall as the room, was boarded and the shelves were set apart at different widths to suit different-sized crockery.

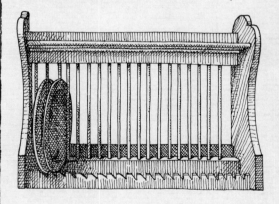

RACKS FOR STORAGE
Before drawers and cupboards were commonly used, kitchen utensils were stored in open wooden racks. Plates and cutlery had separate racks, which stood on table tops or were hung on a convenient wall for easy access.

WASHING UP

THE HOUSEWIFE WOULD OFTEN clean her greasy dishes by rubbing ashes on them, for if you rub wood ash on greasy plates you make soap. To shift more stubborn dirt she would use sand or brick dust, which was once transported round the towns and villages by old men driving donkeys, and sold to housewives for cleaning dishes.

SINKS WITHOUT TAPS

In the days before the closed range, water was heated in the big black boilers that were either hung over the open fire or sat on hobs by the side of the fire. Provided that the housewife remembered to top them up, she had as constant a supply of hot water as any modern housewife. The only inconvenience was that she had to carry the hot water to the sink; she could not simply turn on a tap.

Kitchen or scullery sinks tended to be made of wood, or slate, if you lived in slate country. When the big commercial potteries started up, glazed stoneware sinks became commonplace. I remember many a cottage in which the sink drained into a bucket and the housewife had to empty the slops by flinging them outside the door whenever the bucket was full. Sometimes lead piping carried the dirty water through the wall and simply dumped it in the yard.

NOT SO LABOUR-INTENSIVE

Although there was a large amount of labour involved in washing up, it should be remembered that in days of old there was very little to wash up! I saw houses in the west of Ireland in the early 1950s that contained practically no crockery at all. There would be a huge black kettle hanging over the fire, an equally big and black pot, chiefly for cooking potatoes, and a few wooden bowls. When cooked, the potatoes were placed in a shallow basket and perched on top of the cooking pot; the family would sit about it on three-legged stools and eat with their fingers from the common stock. And the food, I imagine, tasted none the worse for that.

In Europe cheap china and earthenware infiltrated all classes of society from the late eighteenth century onwards and by Victorian times eating utensils had proliferated to absurd lengths in wealthier households and washing up had become a considerable chore. Happily the tendency now is towards greater simplicity.

WATER AVAILABILITY
Apart from the rain that ran off the cottage roof into the butt below, all water had to be fetched from the nearest well, spring, stream or village pump. By using a wooden yoke supported across the shoulders, the woman of the house could carry two buckets of water at a time.

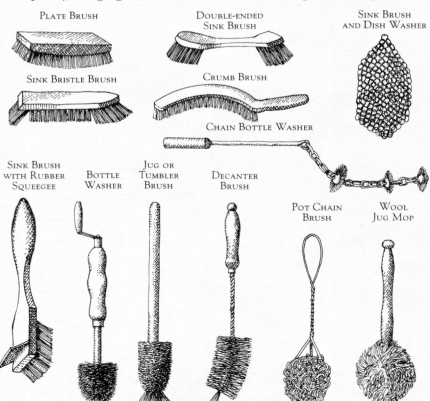

PLATE BRUSH

DOUBLE-ENDED SINK BRUSH

SINK BRUSH AND DISH WASHER

SINK BRISTLE BRUSH

CRUMB BRUSH

CHAIN BOTTLE WASHER

SINK BRUSH WITH RUBBER SQUEEGEE

BOTTLE WASHER

JUG OR TUMBLER BRUSH

DECANTER BRUSH

POT CHAIN BRUSH

WOOL JUG MOP

BRUSHES AND MOPS
There was a huge number of washing-up brushes and mops to choose from. The fan-shaped, stiff-fibred sink brush was very common and was used for scrubbing pots and pans as well as the sink. Short-handled bristle brushes were used for cleaning plates and, occasionally, sinks, while wire brushes called pot chains were used exclusively for cleaning pots. Long-handled wool mops or brushes were used for china and glass. Long, thin bottles were scoured with chain bottle washers: wooden, lead-weighted beads surrounded by bristles were set at intervals down the chain, which was connected to a wooden "stay" or handle, so that it could not drop to the bottom of the bottle, never to be seen again!

THE SINK

The arrival of piped water in the kitchen itself, either through a tap in the wall or a pump, changed the lives—and the kitchens— of people who had been used to carrying it long distances in all weathers. A wide, flat-bottomed stone sink, or "slop stone", was built against the wall under the tap: this was shallow enough to be used as a work-table for boning or chopping meat and poultry, gutting fish and preparing vegetables. The sink was set at a slight angle, taking the water down to a drain hole and into a bucket beneath or, better still, away through a waste pipe. More sophisticated glazed white stone sinks had a built-in overflow. Washing up was never done in the sink itself, but in a bowl or wooden tub standing in the sink. A separate, smaller, basin was kept for the more delicate jobs.

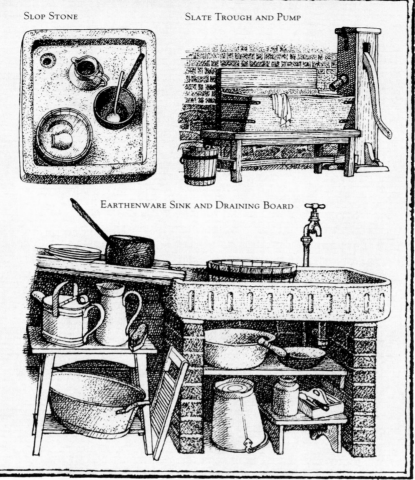

SLOP STONE

SLATE TROUGH AND PUMP

EARTHENWARE SINK AND DRAINING BOARD

SINK BASKET

Manufacturers began to produce special equipment for the sink at the turn of the last century, and an early twentieth-century kitchen might have boasted a perforated iron sink basket like the one below. This stood in the corner of the sink and any waste matter was drained through to catch solid material that might otherwise block the pipes.

ENAMELLED IRON
SINK BASKET

THE DEVELOPMENT OF PLATES

The earliest plate was made of bread. The dough (1) was cooked until it had risen (2), when it was turned over (3) until it had finished baking (4). The bread then had only to be cut in half (5) to make two "plates". Even when the trencher came to be made of solid wood, washing up was no chore: it would simply be wiped clean. The first real plates were made of pewter, which did not stand up well to frequent scouring. The growth of the Staffordshire potteries made cheap china and earthenware available and washing up began in earnest. The Victorian kitchen maid scoured endless dishes, whilst the more delicate china was washed at the dining table.

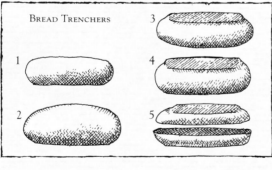

BREAD TRENCHERS

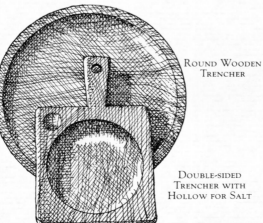

ROUND WOODEN
TRENCHER

DOUBLE-SIDED
TRENCHER WITH
HOLLOW FOR SALT

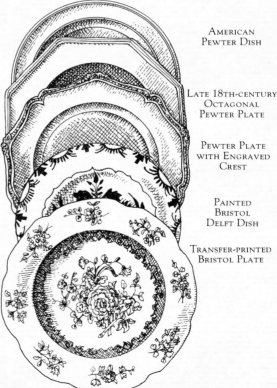

AMERICAN
PEWTER DISH

LATE 18TH-CENTURY
OCTAGONAL
PEWTER PLATE

PEWTER PLATE
WITH ENGRAVED
CREST

PAINTED
BRISTOL
DELFT DISH

TRANSFER-PRINTED
BRISTOL PLATE

PROVIDING WATER

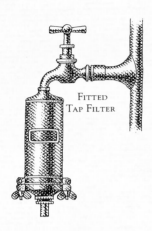

FITTED
TAP FILTER

DRINKING WATER
Unless you happened to live near a spring or fresh water stream, table water had to be boiled or filtered before it was fit to drink. As a result domestic water filters, whether fitted directly to the tap or cistern, or free-standing, became extremely common household items from the middle of the nineteenth century. Filtered water tended to taste flat and servants in well-to-do houses would pour the water from the filter into the table jug from a great height, or throw it back and forth between two jugs to aerate it.

APS WERE UNKNOWN TO MOST country people during my childhood, sixty years ago. Every farmhouse and cottage had a rain butt to store the rain water so prized for washing because it was soft—I seem to remember that cats were always drowning in them. However, the rain butt never provided enough water for the whole household and more had to be fetched, as a routine chore, from a pond or well. Many houses actually contained a well under the floor in the scullery or kitchen and sometimes the inhabitants benefited from the luxury of a pump, in which case the water supply was no problem at all! Generally, though, the well was situated at the bottom of the garden and the water had to be carried into the house. Lucky was the family that lived near a spring, for their water would be clean and fresh to drink.

Occasionally streams and rivers were polluted by untreated sewage and industrial waste, and water from a shallow well could be contaminated by drainage from the scullery or privy. In such cases, drinking water had to be boiled and some country dwellers constructed their own filters. They filled a wooden bucket or barrel with Fuller's earth or sand and poured the doubtful water into it, drawing it from the bottom by means of a small tap as it was needed.

Piped water is still not universal in the countryside and plenty of people still carry water some distance. Many country people declined piped water when it was offered to them because they didn't like the taste of it, most of it being heavily chlorinated. You got used to the bugs in your own horse pond and they did you no harm, they claimed.

WATER IN THE TOWNS
By the mid-nineteenth century water was piped to many towns in England from outlying districts. This did not mean that every house in the town had its own water taps: one tap at the end of the street for communal use was much more usual. Indeed, it was only after the Second World War that indoor water taps became common in the poorer houses in towns—generally one brass tap in the scullery and nothing more.

Although water was supplied by conduits in many towns and cities, mains and household drainage was still appalling and water supply to the poorer districts almost non-existent until the town corporations began to take over responsibility from the private, profit-making water companies in the second half of the nineteenth century. Even then progress was slow and piecemeal, and drawing unpolluted water for drinking in urban areas continued to be a problem. This unhealthy situation gave rise to the development of the domestic filter.

19TH-CENTURY WATER JUG

LATE 19TH-CENTURY
TIN WATER PITCHERS

DECORATED
STONEWARE
FILTER

LATE 19TH-CENTURY
POTTERY JUG

LATE 19TH-CENTURY
GLAZED JUG

TEA MAKING

Just as Americans could not really continue to function without coffee, so the inhabitants of the British Isles could scarcely support life without tea. It is also a fact that Americans seem totally unable to master the art of tea making but have no trouble making coffee, while the British fail shamefully at making coffee but produce excellent cups of tea—perhaps it has something to do with the Boston Tea Party.

Tea found its way to Britain in the seventeenth century, when it was probably imported by the Dutch. The British were used to "infusing" herb drinks and soon adopted tea despite its being expensive. By the end of the eighteenth century tea drinking was widespread and all watery hot drinks had become known as tea. Moralists condemned it, saying that it led to idleness and gossip. William Cobbett held the view that "the rattle of the tea tackle" was "the short road to the gaolhouse and the brothel". Today, however, many a charlady manages to get through twenty or thirty cups of the stuff a day and still avoid both institutions.

The Art of Making Perfect Tea

The secret of making really good tea lies essentially in the amount of time the water remains on the leaves, although, of course, the water should be freshly drawn and the pot warmed first. According to priests returning from China in the seventeenth century, the tea should stand for "as long as it takes to say three Pater Nosters slowly".

EARLY 19TH-CENTURY
DUTCH TEA URN

Making and Taking Tea

Many of the first teapots were of a shallow, rounded design, to allow room for the leaves to expand. However, the globular-shaped teapot copied from the Chinese design soon became more fashionable. Elegant silver, brass and copper tea-kettles, which could be heated by a spirit stove, became popular for drawing-room use, together with the tea urn. The first china teacups and saucers were made in the mid-eighteenth century and the popularity of tea drinking helped the enormous growth of the ceramic industry.

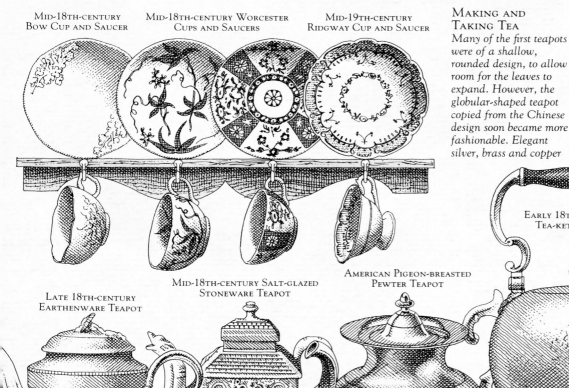

MID-18TH-CENTURY
BOW CUP AND SAUCER

MID-18TH-CENTURY WORCESTER
CUPS AND SAUCERS

MID-19TH-CENTURY
RIDGWAY CUP AND SAUCER

LATE 18TH-CENTURY
EARTHENWARE TEAPOT

MID-18TH-CENTURY SALT-GLAZED
STONEWARE TEAPOT

AMERICAN PIGEON-BREASTED
PEWTER TEAPOT

EARLY 19TH-CENTURY
STAFFORDSHIRE
EARTHENWARE
TEAPOT

EARLY 18TH-CENTURY SILVER
TEA-KETTLE AND STAND

WIRE STRAINER

TEA PARTY
*Tea parties were genteel,
restrained affairs from
which children were
normally excluded. These
three girls show that it was
by no means just the
grown ups who took tea
drinking seriously.*

STORING TEA

To protect its delicate flavour, tea should be kept in an airtight tin, where moisture and strong odours cannot get to it. When it first arrived in Britain tea was very expensive and the first tea caddies came equipped with locks, so that the mistress of the house could dole out only as much as was required daily to the servants. Caddies were made of silver, earthenware and wood and some had compartments for different teas.

LUDWIGSBURG
TEA CADDY

ENGRAVED
TEA CADDY

In the tea-producing areas of Sri Lanka and India a method of brewing tea has been developed that would appal any English tea guzzler. The tea is brewed, mixed with lots of milk and plenty of sugar and then poured from glass to glass (it is drunk from glass or metal tumblers) until it foams like beer. Strangely, in those climates, it tastes rather good drunk like this.

As for the British soldier, he would be a miserable fellow without his tea and would certainly be defeated in every war. In Africa and Burma during the Second World War, tea was commonly made in four-gallon petrol tins heated over a fire built of twigs. A double handful of tea leaves would be dumped into the boiling water, together with a couple of tins of condensed milk and a double handful of sugar. We would then each dip our mess tins into it—drinking tea out of the corner of a rectangular mess tin was an experience all its own. This tea was very refreshing and there was no way that we could have carried on the war without it. Both Nelson and the Duke of Wellington, we are told, would not go to war without their tea and the duke took his famous silver teapot with him everywhere.

The Russians and Persians are also addicted to tea. They make it in graceful samovars, pouring water into a jacket around a cylinder full of burning charcoal. Drinking tea is gradually becoming more popular throughout the rest of Europe, too, but Continental Europeans still do not really know how to make it. Furthermore, they drink it out of glass tumblers and commit other barbarous practices—unfortunately, use of the pernicious tea-bag is widespread in those countries.

THE RITUAL OF TEA DRINKING

The making and drinking of tea bears a ritual quality in some countries—a ritual usually presided over by the female of the species. You will often hear one of a group of tough and macho navvies say to another on requesting that he pour out the tea, "You be mother!" In Japan the tea ritual has been elevated to the status of a religious ceremony and even in Britain it can be quite an art. Anyone who has had the privilege of taking a delicate cup of China tea, together with cucumber sandwiches and toasted tea-cakes, with an English country vicar's wife out on the lawn will know how different from the brutish swilling of "char" out of chipped enamelled mugs tea drinking can be.

COFFEE MAKING

BYSSINIAN GOATHERDS, WE ARE told, noticed that their charges leapt about in a happy and abandoned manner after eating the berries of a certain small tree and, wishing to share in their felicity, they ate some of the berries themselves. They didn't have to eat many before they became addicted to them. No doubt they tried to soften them by boiling them, and on doing so they found that the flavoured water that remained was what they were after, and the noble art of coffee making was born.

Coffee drinking spread rapidly throughout the east African and Arab world, where it holds first place in the league of beverages to this day. If you make a social or business call in any Arab country, the coffee is inevitably brought out. The Arab coffee pot is an elegant vessel, often with Koranic scripts incised on it, and the cups are very small. The coffee is drunk black and very sweet, and there is always a sediment of finely ground coffee at the bottom of each cupful. On being proffered a second cup it is polite to accept it. However, on the offer of a third, good manners require that you refuse it.

ROASTING AND GRINDING THE BEANS
When I was in southern Africa before the Second World War coffee was very cheap and we used to buy it by the hundredweight

sack. We roasted the berries in a frying pan over the open fire, ground them in a small hand mill, and then threw a handful of the ground coffee in a saucepan of boiling water. After the mixture had boiled for a few minutes we would take up a burning stick from the fire and plunge it into the brew. This was supposed to cause the grounds to sink. We would then pour it out to drink. I have never tasted better coffee and would prefer it to filter coffee today.

COFFEE DRINKING
In 1650 the first coffee house was opened in Britain. Coffee houses abounded in the eighteenth century but coffee drinking was gradually superseded by tea drinking as the nation's favourite drink.

It is interesting to note that in England today, where tea is the hot beverage of the masses, there is a certain snobbery about drinking coffee, and in America, where coffee is the universal drink, the opposite is true. Moreover the British are as inept at making coffee as the Americans are at making tea. So difficult and mysterious does this simple process seem to them that they resort to those horrible ersatz mixtures, either in powder or liquid form, which have no right to be called by the name of coffee. Perhaps there should be an exchange of missionaries between the two countries.

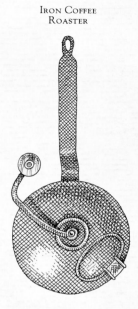

IRON COFFEE ROASTER

COFFEE ROASTERS AND MILLS
As coffee became more popular, a wide variety of hand-operated roasters and mills was produced. Pan-like iron roasters were developed for roasting beans over the kitchen range. The roasted beans were then ground in a mill and the ground coffee stored in a drawer.

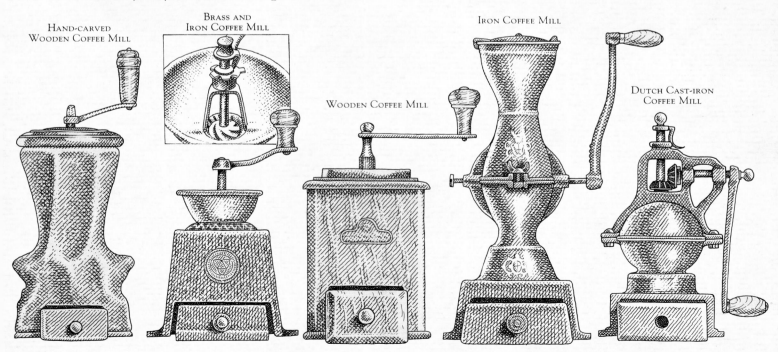

HAND-CARVED WOODEN COFFEE MILL

BRASS AND IRON COFFEE MILL

WOODEN COFFEE MILL

IRON COFFEE MILL

DUTCH CAST-IRON COFFEE MILL

POTS, URNS AND BOILERS

The business of coffee making soon developed its own special rules of etiquette. After the coffee was made, it was kept hot in a coffee pot, from which it was served at table. There was a vast array of pots, urns and boilers for the housewife to choose from. They ranged from plain earthenware or tin pots to the more ornate silver urns mounted on splayed legs over a spirit heater and fitted with brass taps.

GROUND COFFEE

FILTER

HOT WATER

THE REVOLUTIONARY PERCOLATOR

At the beginning of the nineteenth century Count Rumford invented the percolator. Ground coffee was compressed in a container inside the coffee pot, which had a filter at the bottom. Heated water passed through the coffee and the filter and into the space beneath.

TIN COFFEE BOILER

COFFEE URN WITH BRASS TAP

SILVER COFFEE URN

EARTHENWARE COFFEE POT

SPOUT STRAINER

COFFEE INFUSER

TINPLATE COFFEE PERCOLATOR

TIN COFFEE POT

ALE & BEER MAKING

EFORE THE CONTINENTAL HABIT OF hopping ale was introduced in about 1520, the English drank ale not beer. "Turkeys, Heresies, Hops and Beer All came to England in the One Year." Beer is simply ale that has had some of the dried flowers of the hop plant boiled in it. The hop, *Humulus lupulus*, is closely related to the nettle and, incidentally, to the cannabis plant. It has a bitter-tasting flower and once people began to flavour their ale with it they never returned to the old ways. Henry VIII passed laws to prevent hops from entering the country but nobody took any notice of them. I have made ale without hops and it is insipid stuff.

MAKING THE MALT

The main constituent of beer is not hops but barley. The grain of barley is mostly starch, which, though rich in stored energy, is not soluble, and before the beer can be brewed the grain of the barley must be chitted, or caused to germinate. After germinating, the starch can be turned into sugar, which is soluble. It is the sugar that is turned into alcohol by that marvellous living organism, yeast. Traditionally, the maltster germinates the barley grain by wetting it and keeping it warm for about ten days until it spears, chits or shoots, as countrymen say. He then kilns it, turning it on a perforated plate with a fire underneath. It is then cracked in a mill after which it is ready for brewing.

The process of malting takes place today in huge maltings, where the maltose, which is the sugar produced inside the grain, is extracted and sent to the brewery. Beer made from maltose is nothing like as good as that made by the old method of steeping the whole malt. I have made many gallons of both sorts and I know.

Once, many small country mills combined the malting of barley with the grinding of grain. An old neighbour of mine in Wales used to malt the local farmer's barley for them in a little water-driven mill.

BREWING THE BEER

Whenever the malt was made, the beer tended to be made by the individual householder, in the countryside at least. However, the unholy alliance between the big commercial brewers and the nonconformist

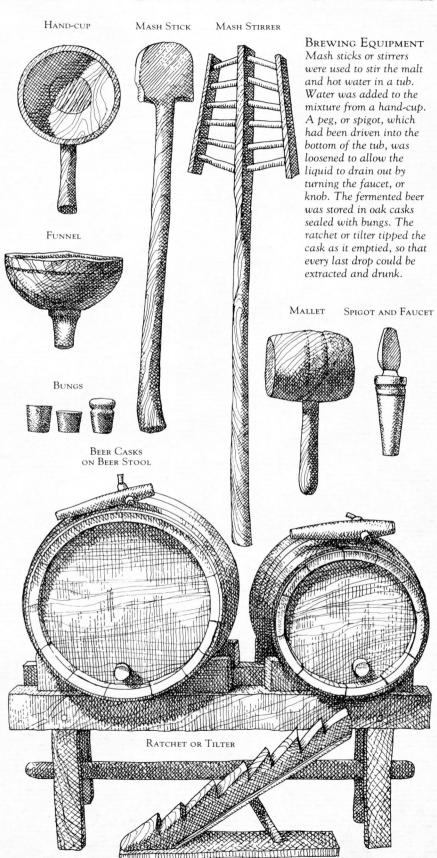

HAND-CUP MASH STICK MASH STIRRER

FUNNEL

BUNGS

BEER CASKS
ON BEER STOOL

RATCHET OR TILTER

BREWING EQUIPMENT
Mash sticks or stirrers were used to stir the malt and hot water in a tub. Water was added to the mixture from a hand-cup. A peg, or spigot, which had been driven into the bottom of the tub, was loosened to allow the liquid to drain out by turning the faucet, or knob. The fermented beer was stored in oak casks sealed with bungs. The ratchet or tilter tipped the cask as it emptied, so that every last drop could be extracted and drunk.

MALLET SPIGOT AND FAUCET

churches that grew up in Victorian times caused laws to be passed that restricted home brewing. Despite the laws, it lingered in some places and in the part of west Wales that I farmed for twenty years it continued in unbroken tradition.

The process is simple. The malt—the crushed, sprouted grain—is put into a container, together with water heated to a temperature of 150°F—if it is any hotter, the water will destroy the enzymes that make the beer. The resulting sloppy porridge is called the mash. The mash is left, well wrapped up to keep the heat in, for twelve hours or so and then the liquid in it (the spree or wort) is strained off, put into another container and boiled. A small quantity of hops, generally wrapped in a muslin bag for ease of removal, is added to the boiling spree.

After boiling for say an hour the spree is poured into a container and cooled rapidly. Speed in cooling is important, for if too many wild yeast organisms become established in it they may spoil the flavour of the beer. As soon as it is cool enough for yeast to survive, the yeast is added. The stuff is then left to ferment for several days.

STORING THE BEER
Traditionally all beer-making vessels and storage containers were made of oak and it is not imagination that leads one to think that beer stored in oaken casks has a superior flavour to that stored, say, in stainless steel. However, it is necessary to point out that the oaken casks must be scrupulously clean before the beer is poured into them and the reason brewers and innkeepers tend to favour metal casks is that oaken ones, carelessly cleaned, can cause beer to be undrinkable. But the good farmer's or cottager's wife who brews beer will ensure that the oaken casks are perfectly clean and her beer will be like the nectar of the gods.

REAL ALE
The Real Ale Campaign in Britain saved British beer in the nick of time. The big commercial brewers had gone over to pasteurized, highly chemicalized, top-pressure beer in aluminium or stainless steel casks. This stuff would keep nearly indefinitely and was quite consistent in taste but it took all the *pleasure* out of beer drinking. But now, thank God and the Real Ale enthusiasts, real beer is coming back and gradually the corrupted taste of the English beer drinker is being re-educated.

The pernicious law that prevented home brewing has now been lifted, in the British Isles at least, and brewing is enjoying a strong revival. Hopefully home brewers will gradually be weaned from kit beer, or beer made from malt extract, and graduate to the harder discipline of brewing with true malt.

BARREL SIZES
Strictly speaking a barrel should only be called a barrel if it holds thirty-six gallons. Each of the seven sizes of "barrel" is given a specific name by the cooper, according to its capacity (see below).

BUTT
108 GAL

PUNCHEON
72 GAL

HOGSHEAD
54 GAL

BARREL
36 GAL

KILDERKIN
18 GAL

FIRKIN
9 GAL

PIN
4½ GAL

BREWING AT HOME
Large households often had their own private brewhouses. These took a lot of the physical effort out of home brewing. The equipment was arranged on varying levels to make the brewing process run more efficiently. The copper supplied water along a pipe to the mash tun, which contained malt. The liquid produced from the water and malt (the wort) was in turn pumped back to the copper, where it was boiled with the hops, and then piped to the cooler to cool before the yeast was added and the beer was left to ferment.

BEER TANKARDS

Tankards were popular drinking vessels for beer and cider up to the eighteenth century. They were usually made of pewter or silver and came in varying shapes and styles. The thumb-piece, the knob attached to the hinged lid of the tankard, was often decoratively fashioned.

CYLINDRICAL
ENGRAVED TANKARD

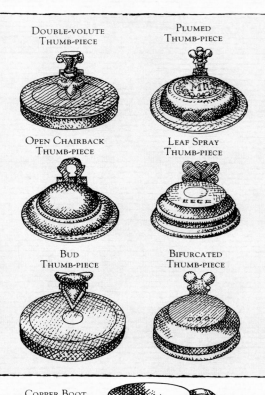

DOUBLE-VOLUTE
THUMB-PIECE

PLUMED
THUMB-PIECE

OPEN CHAIRBACK
THUMB-PIECE

LEAF SPRAY
THUMB-PIECE

BUD
THUMB-PIECE

BIFURCATED
THUMB-PIECE

QUART
TANKARD

BRASS PINT
TANKARD

BRISTOL TULIP-SHAPED
TANKARD

PEWTER-MOUNTED
TANKARD

ALE MULLERS

Ale was heated with spices over hot coals in a muller, or warmer, to make mulled ale. Mullers were sometimes slipper-shaped so that they would not fall over when full.

BEER MULLER
ON HOT COALS

COPPER BOOT
ALE WARMER

TIN BOOT
ALE WARMER

COPPER ALE WARMER

COPPER ALE MULLER
WITH SPIRIT HEATER

BEER MEASURES

In an ale-house, beer was often served in containers known as measures which, as their name suggests, held an exact measure of beer. A popular Irish measure was known as the "harvester" or, sometimes, the "haystack", which came in sizes ranging from half a gill to a gallon capacity. Bottled measures were also available. These were stoppered with bungs and had handles to make them easy to carry.

EARTHENWARE
"HARVESTER" BOTTLE

COPPER ALE MEASURE

IRISH "HAYSTACK"
MEASURE

WINE & CIDER MAKING

RAPES AND APPLES, THOUGH VERY different in most ways, have one thing in common: they both have on their skins the benevolent yeasts that are capable of turning their juice into superb fermented drinks. If you squeeze the juice out of grapes and leave it alone completely you will end up with wine. If you do the same thing with apples you will end up with cider.

WINE MADE FROM GRAPES

Wine is made by peasants and farmers in every country in Europe where the sugar content of the grape is sufficiently high. The process is so simple and the product so delightful and beneficial that it would be amazing if they did not make it.

First the grapes must be crushed or broken. Traditionally this is done with the feet: in this way the grapes are crushed but the pips are left whole. If the pips are broken they might spoil the flavour of the wine. The crushed grapes are then pressed to extract the juice, which is then simply left in a vat and allowed to ferment in its own yeasts. If red wine is being made the skins of the red grapes are left in the must, or grape juice, during the fermentation process. If white wine is required the skins are removed before fermentation.

OTHER SORTS OF WINE

Grapes are not the only fruit from which you can make excellent wine—blackberries and elderberries also make good wine, but for these, as for most of the flower and vegetable wines, you need to add boiling water and yeast. The yeast is thrown into the liquid or placed on slices of dry bread called "toasts", which are then floated on top. The liquid is then left to ferment. Parsnip and

CIDER CHEESE PRESSES
Once the apples had been crushed to a pulp, the juice was extracted using a cheese press. The pulp was wrapped in cloths to make cheeses and then stacked in the press. This had either one central screw or two side screws which supported a heavy block of wood. When the screws were turned by means of a long pole the block of wood was forced down on the stacked cheeses. This pressure squeezed out the juice, which was collected in a vat below.

HAND-OPERATED CIDER PRESS

TREADING THE GRAPES

CRUSHING THE GRAPES
This is the first stage of wine making. Crushing the grapes enables the fermentation process to begin, as the yeast present on the skin of the grapes reacts with the sugar in the fruit. Traditionally it was done by treading the grapes in a barrel with bare feet. In this way the fruit was crushed but the pips were left whole. Broken pips added an unpleasant taste to the wine.

potato wines are old favourites in England and recipes for dandelion wine go back a good few years. Ginger is usually added to dandelion wine to give it extra flavour and lemon and orange rind are often included.

MAKING CIDER

Cider making is still performed on many a Somerset and Devon farm in England. The apples are first crushed—traditionally in a circular granite trough, or chace, around which a huge circular stone is trundled by a blindfolded horse. The crushed apples are then wrapped in strips of coarse hessian cloth to make what are called cheeses, which are laid, separated by square planks, under a press and great pressure exerted upon them. After the juice has been forced out, the cheeses are overhauled by stirring the mush about in the cloths, and then subjected to more pressure to extract even more juice. Finally the spent mush is given to those great waste-disposal units, the pigs.

The juice is then pumped into great tuns, or casks, often as tall as a house, and left there to ferment. Many farmers add sugar or syrup, which is cheating in a way, but modern tastes cannot always cope with the extreme dryness of pure rough cider, called scrumpy by aficionados. When fermentation is in progress the cider is said to be hungry. There are many stories, most one suspects apocryphal, of cider makers throwing legs of beef or other meat into the cider vats to give strength to the brew, and it is said that if a rat, or a cat, or indeed the farmer himself, happens to fall into the vat of fermenting liquor nothing will be left of him (except, one supposes, in the case of the farmer, his buttons).

ADDING SPIRITS

In Normandy the tradition of cider making is well developed but I would not put my neck out and make any comparisons between the virtues of French and English or Welsh cider. The Normans also make calvados by distilling cider (the roughest cider, produced by swilling the crushed mass with water) into a spirit. The west countrymen in England are prevented from practising this beneficial skill for their own use by stupid laws. In apple-growing country in America people make applejack by distilling cider. Some allow the cider to freeze: the water turns to ice before the alcohol and is thrown away to leave an extremely potent brew. Owners of deep freezes please note.

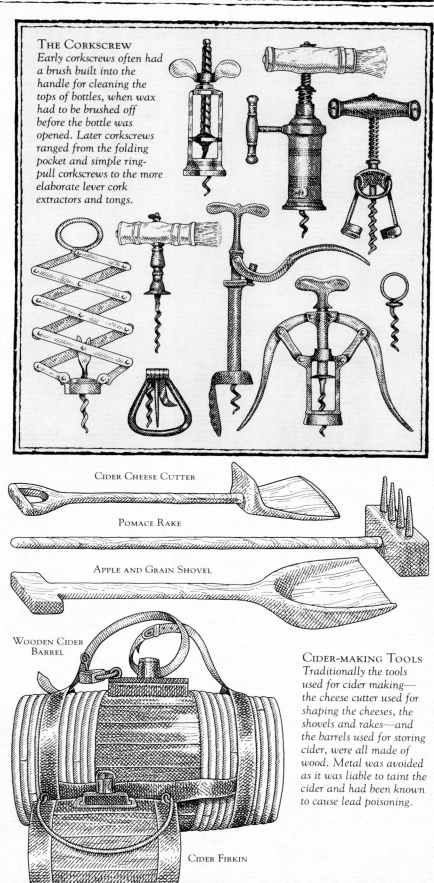

THE CORKSCREW
Early corkscrews often had a brush built into the handle for cleaning the tops of bottles, when wax had to be brushed off before the bottle was opened. Later corkscrews ranged from the folding pocket and simple ring-pull corkscrews to the more elaborate lever cork extractors and tongs.

CIDER CHEESE CUTTER

POMACE RAKE

APPLE AND GRAIN SHOVEL

WOODEN CIDER BARREL

CIDER FIRKIN

CIDER-MAKING TOOLS
Traditionally the tools used for cider making— the cheese cutter used for shaping the cheeses, the shovels and rakes—and the barrels used for storing cider, were all made of wood. Metal was avoided as it was liable to taint the cider and had been known to cause lead poisoning.

HERBS & SPICES

BELL GLASSES
Bell glasses were, in effect, miniature greenhouses. About eight inches wide and made from clear glass in the shape of a bell, they were placed over young cuttings and tender plants in the ground in winter to protect them from the cold and frost.

ESSENTIAL TOOLS
Gardening tools have hardly changed. The hoe and fork were used for loosening the soil and removing weeds, and the trowel and onion hoe for digging holes and making planting channels.

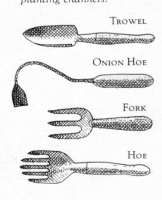

TROWEL

ONION HOE

FORK

HOE

NGLISH COOKING WASN'T ALWAYS dull and flavourless as is often the case today. In addition to a few spices that were imported at great expense from the East, plenty of native herbs were grown and used liberally in cooking and many herbs that seem pretty exotic to us today—Mediterranean plants like oregano and angelica—were well known to English gardeners in Elizabethan times.

THE VALUE OF HERBS
Herbs have long been valued for their medicinal qualities and in the Middle Ages monks began obtaining those herbs known to have physic properties by the ancient Greeks from orders on the Continent. They planted them in their gardens and acted as physicians to the neighbourhood until the dissolution of the monasteries.

Herbs were grown in the manor house gardens, too, from the Middle Ages. The lady of the manor treated the minor ailments of her family and servants, and sometimes the neighbours, too. She prepared, dried and distilled the herbs for medicinal, culinary and scenting purposes in the still room (see Home Doctoring p.301).

HERB GARDENS
Culinary and medicinal herbs were generally to be found in separate parts of the garden. In the monastery garden, culinary herbs were planted in a series of rectangular beds with paths between them for easy access. They were usually planted near the kitchen along with some vegetables. The physic herb garden was planted near the infirmary.

The herb garden at the manor house was often elaborate and formal arrangements such as chequerboard patterns and wheels were favoured. Patterns of knots based on lacework designs were very fashionable among the rich during the sixteenth and seventeenth centuries: herbs such as thyme, marjoram and lavender outlined the basic pattern and if open knots were created, they were filled with flowers.

Even the poorest cottager had a kitchen herb garden. This was not a formal knot garden but a simple "patch" in which the housewife grew her favourite culinary herbs, together with herbs for making perfumes, ointments and pot-pourris.

KNOT GARDENS
The knot garden was created in the sixteenth century. Different herbs—scented, culinary and medicinal—were planted in such a way that the textures and colours of the foliage overlapped to produce the impression of cords looping over and under one another.

COOKING WITH HERBS AND SPICES
Sage, parsley, fennel, thyme, mint, savory and garlic were popularly grown in the Middle Ages to flavour the main meal of the poor—vegetable broth or pottage—and to make green sauces to accompany fish. The rich required strongly flavoured and scented sauces to disguise the often tainted meat and game that they feasted on. It was fashionable to perfume food during the sixteenth and seventeenth centuries, when sweet herbs, or the bouquet garni, were introduced.

With the opening of trade with the East through the East India Company, spices began to be incorporated into cooking and even to replace herbs. Spices are aromatic berries, buds, bark, fruit, roots or flower stigmas taken from various plants grown in hot countries. Soon spice dealers and grocers were selling a wide range of spices and herbs, both fresh and dried, to housewives in the towns and sadly the herb garden began to disappear until today it can be found in only the most remote rural home. However, there is nothing to prevent you from planting your own herb garden or border. What could be more delightful and useful than a simple herb "patch" with your own favourite culinary and tried and tested medicinal herbs? You might even like to plant a camomile lawn.

STORAGE AND PREPARATION

Herbs and spices were dried before being stored in one of a variety of containers. The chest-of-drawers spice box had a drawer for every spice. There were also pie-shaped and stacked column boxes. In the latter, spices were kept in separate sections which screwed together to form a column. Some tin boxes were divided into cake sections, leaving the centre space for nutmeg. When the spices were needed, they were pounded in a pestle and mortar. Dried herbs were finely chopped with iron choppers before being used.

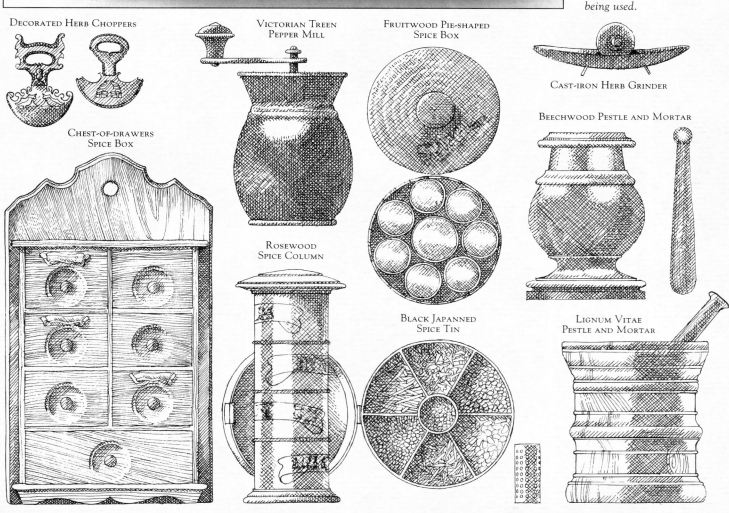

DECORATED HERB CHOPPERS

VICTORIAN TREEN
PEPPER MILL

FRUITWOOD PIE-SHAPED
SPICE BOX

CAST-IRON HERB GRINDER

CHEST-OF-DRAWERS
SPICE BOX

ROSEWOOD
SPICE COLUMN

BLACK JAPANNED
SPICE TIN

BEECHWOOD PESTLE AND MORTAR

LIGNUM VITAE
PESTLE AND MORTAR

KEEPING LIVESTOCK

HE IRISH PEASANTS USED TO CALL the pig "the man who pays the rent", and "a pig in the sty and a pig in the pot!" was an oft-used phrase of my rural neighbours in Wales. Of course, there should have been no rent to pay and the Irishman should have had the pig himself for the sustenance of his family, but that's another story.

Only fifty years ago it would have been considered odd if a country house or cottage did not have a pigsty attached to it. Sties were strongly built of brick or stone because something that all pigs have in common is a predilection for pulling down and totally destroying their housing. Even so, if your pig could get his snout into it somehow, he would, and before you knew where you were the whole thing was in ruins and your pig was roaming free. For pigs do not like to be cooped up and, indeed, always used to be kept out of doors, when they were commonly ringed, like the pig that featured in *The Owl and the Pussycat*, to lessen the amount of havoc that they could create.

In his book, *Cottage Economy*, William Cobbett advised every countryman to keep a cow. In his day many did, but the practice was dying as the "big bull frogs", as he termed the grasping larger farmers, were grabbing all the land, including the old commons, for their own private use.

THE FAMILY HOLDING

A family that could fatten a pig or two a year and also milk a cow was a family that would never know real poverty, for these animals fitted marvellously into the natural ecology of a family holding. The pig consumed all the vegetable and animal wastes that are nowadays carted away at great expense and dumped. It also provided plenty of good manure for the garden, in which cabbages and kale were grown for the cow as well as the humans. The cow provided milk, butter, cheese and buttermilk for the family and whey (full of protein and minerals) for the pig. It also conferred fertility on the land.

Such a family might also have had a few dozen hens, which lived partly on the undigested grain that the cow voided. They helped to keep down the baleful insect population *and* provided chicken meat and eggs. During my childhood, goats were common in country areas, as people with insufficient land to keep a cow could tether goats along the roadside. They were even known as the poor man's cow! If there was a pond or a stream nearby, ducks were an obvious component and, if there was enough grass on the holding, or access to the grassy common, geese were, too. A householder who had all, or even some, of these animals and a good garden didn't need any dole money, even if there had been any!

DOMESTIC LIVESTOCK

Other commonly owned domestic livestock were tame rabbits, which were bred for meat, and ferrets. Traditionally the children looked after the rabbits, coming home with huge armfuls of sheep's parsley, clover, hog weed and other vegetation garnered from the road verges on the way from school. The ferrets were kept for poaching rabbits. A lad with a ferret and a few purse nets could go out at night and return with a rabbit or two for the family. Rabbit pie or stew made a magnificent meal for the whole family, particularly if it had a lump of fat bacon thrown in it. The rabbit hutches and ferret houses were usually made out of old packing cases: doors were hinged on them with strips of leather and a piece of the wood was cut out and replaced by wire netting. I remember many a cottage with these appurtenances sitting at the bottom of the garden.

Keeping pigeons was much more widespread fifty years ago than it is now. Men in the grimmest of industrial conurbations would keep a shed full of racing pigeons, which they railed off to far destinations on weekends, their hearts with them as they winged through the sky on their way home. Country people, too, would keep pigeons, sometimes to eat, sometimes just to look at: pouting pigeons, tumblers, fan-tails and many other ornamental breeds gave delight.

Country people always had a dog and a cat or two as well. The unluckier dogs would spend much of their time chained outside the back door to a kennel or an old wooden barrel turned on its side. Most of them were luckier, though; they were friends of the family and lolled in front of the fire upon a dirty old rag rug, which they saw as theirs by right. As for the cats, they were a law unto themselves, of course.

THE MEAT HOOK
This was an iron hook used for suspending joints of ham in the chimney, where they would be smoked from the fire and thus preserved.

PIGSTIES

In medieval times, pigs roamed in herds, under the charge of a swineherd. During the eighteenth century, they were moved back to the farmyard and changed, through selective breeding, from being hairy and hardy, to being pink and bristly, and vulnerable to cold weather and draughts. Pigs needed some form of housing and shelter, so pigsties were developed.

The first pigsty was a low, loose box, about four feet high, with a ventilation slit or window opening, and a door leading to a small exercise yard. The exercise yard was surrounded by a tall, stout wall and a chute led from the outside of the wall to the trough to prevent the hungry pigs stampeding the person feeding them.

Some pigsties doubled up as hen houses, thus saving space and buildings. The hens were kept above the pigsty in the loft which was accessible for egg collection and feeding, via outdoor stone steps. The Welsh pig pen differed in shape, being round with a conical roof, and built entirely of stone. Large-scale pigsties were known as piggeries and consisted of a series of walled boxes, which looked like a single-storey cow barn. There was a feeding passage and sometimes a manure passage, both under cover.

PIGSTY AND POULTRY LOFT
Pigsties sometimes doubled up as hen houses. The pigs had the run of the ground floor, while the hens lived in the loft. There was direct access to the poultry loft via outdoor steps.

WELSH PIG PEN
This was a circular pigsty with a conical roof, and looked similar to an igloo. Built entirely of stone, the walls curved gently inwards to meet at the top of the roof. A small, walled exercise yard was attached to the pig pen.

THE STANDARD STY
The standard pigsty consisted of a low, single-storey box, large enough for one or two pigs, with a ventilation slit or a window opening, and a door leading to a small exercise yard. The yard, which was larger than the box, contained a feeding trough and was surrounded by a tall, stout wall. There was often a chute leading from the outside wall to the trough, for the pig swill to be poured down.

TYPES OF LIVESTOCK

THE COUNTRY PERSON'S LOVE OF ANIMALS was not purely utilitarian. She or he loved a good-looking bird or beast and chose a breed for its looks as much, sometimes, as its usefulness. This explains the popularity of the bantam. These miniature hens and cocks were not really as useful as the full-sized breeds but some of them were as colourful as living jewels. The game breeds, too, were beautiful to look at; the fighting cockerels the epitome of macho virility. Game breeds made fine table birds but were slow to lay eggs. The pigs tended to be rotund fellows—the older breeds like Wessex or Essex Saddlebacks, Tamworth or the delightful Gloucester Old Spots were favourites. Most cottagers bought their pig for fattening as a "weaner", perhaps eight weeks old, straight off the mother, but a few cottagers would keep a sow and provide weaners for other people. Such a pig would be fed for perhaps six months and then fattened on barley meal or boiled potatoes for another three. Most of the meat would be home-cured for bacon and ham, but joints of fresh pork would be liberally distributed round the neighbourhood, as gifts or tokens of appreciation for favours received.

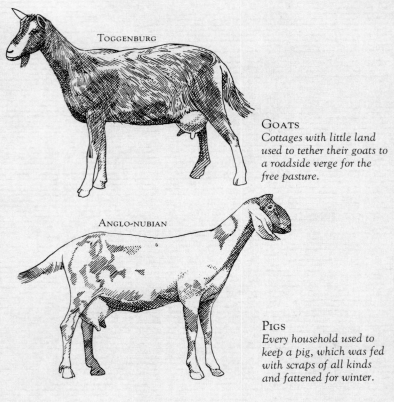

TOGGENBURG

GOATS
Cottages with little land used to tether their goats to a roadside verge for the free pasture.

ANGLO-NUBIAN

PIGS
Every household used to keep a pig, which was fed with scraps of all kinds and fattened for winter.

BERKSHIRE

GLOUCESTER OLD SPOT

TAMWORTH

OLD ENGLISH

BUFF ORPINGTON

WHITE LEGHORN

BRONZE TURKEY

TURKEYS
There was usually one turkey per farmyard, which was fattened up to be eaten on a special occasion, usually of course, Christmas.

RHODE ISLAND RED

LIGHT SUSSEX

ROMAN GOOSE

HENS
Hens were cheap to keep, required less space than other livestock, and provided a regular supply of fresh eggs.

GEESE
Geese were fattened up for roasting, and their soft, downy feathers were often used to stuff eiderdowns and pillows.

KEEPING BEES

O NON-BEE-KEEPERS THERE IS SOME-thing mysterious about the dedicated keepers of bees. In every decent village there is at least one of them. He is "sent for" whenever a swarm has been found and is expected to be ever ready to remove a wild swarm from somebody's roof. People stand not unnaturally in awe of a person who can work coolly and calmly amid a raging swarm of flying insects which are, after all, quite dangerous. I remember when I was a pupil on a South African farm school seeing one of my fellow students being wheeled away in a wheelbarrow because he had fainted after being heavily attacked by bees. I kept bees later in England and Wales for nearly three decades but left them severely alone unless I was heavily protected. No slap-happy nonchalance for me. If I could have laid my hands on an astronaut's space suit I would not have scorned to wear it.

Hiving a Swarm

If you are an apiarist, the day will come in the summertime when a neighbour will knock on your door and announce that there is a swarm in his garden. What can you do about it? So, you grab an empty bee skep, or a basket, or even an old cardboard box, and follow him to his garden, where a seething bunch of bees as big as a rugger ball hangs in a tree. Your neighbour is terrified of them. You, on the other hand, are not, for you possess the knowledge that they are almost certainly not going to sting you, as they have filled themselves with honey before flying from their old hive to seek a new home. You go up to the swarm, hold the container under it, and give the branch a good shake. The swarm drops with a plomp into the container and you walk away with it nonchalantly. Your neighbour is amazed at your intrepidity. You don't tell him that swarming bees are almost always completely harmless. "Oh, I suppose I just have a way with them," you murmur.

Making and Using Skeps

Before 1851 bees were kept in straw or rush skeps. Any countryman could make a skep. All he needed was some long wheat or rye straw and some split bramble, together with a cow's horn with the point cut off and a

Bee Smoking
When the bee-keeper needed to open the hive, either to inspect the bees or to extract the honeycombs, smoke was puffed into the hive from a smoker to make the bees sluggish and less aggressive. The smoke was produced by the slow-burning fuel contained in the fire-box of the smoker.

Bee Smoker

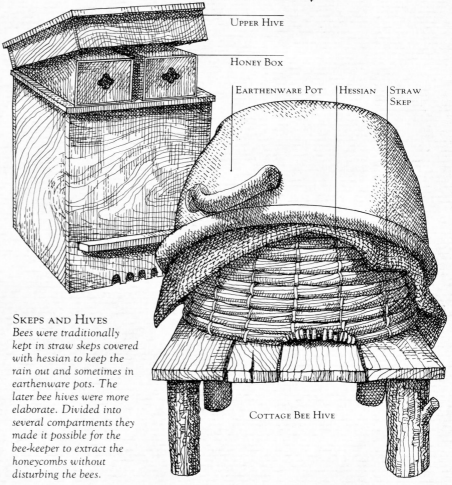

Upper Hive

Honey Box

Earthenware Pot | Hessian | Straw Skep

Cottage Bee Hive

Skeps and Hives
Bees were traditionally kept in straw skeps covered with hessian to keep the rain out and sometimes in earthenware pots. The later bee hives were more elaborate. Divided into several compartments they made it possible for the bee-keeper to extract the honeycombs without disturbing the bees.

EXTRACTING
THE HONEY
*The decapped honeycombs
were put into a cage in the
centrifugal machine. The
bee-keeper would turn the
handle and the cage
would spin very fast first
in one direction and then
in the other. This process
drained all the honey out
of the honeycombs but left
them fully intact.*

DECAPPING A COMB
*When a honeycomb was
brought out of the hive it
was covered with wax. To
extract the honey, the bee-
keeper had to remove the
wax, which was best done
with a sharp, hot knife.*

CENTRIFUGAL
MACHINE

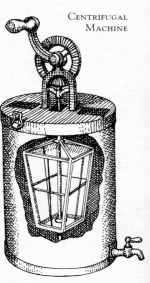

A BEE STINGER
*The bee stinger was not,
as might be supposed, an
instrument of torture but a
device said to help relieve
rheumatism. A bee was
put inside the glass tube
and the stinger was placed
over the patient's skin.
The base was then slid
open and the plunger
depressed so that the bee
touched the skin and stung
the patient!*

goose or turkey bone. He would feed the straw into the larger, open, end of the horn, pushing it through so that it fitted tightly, and bind it with the bramble as it emerged. In this way he made a straw rope, which he then coiled and sewed together, using the piece of bone as a needle.

The bees hived in a skep built their comb according to their own sweet will. The queen laid an egg in every cell and when the bee-keeper wanted to extract the honey he placed an empty skep on top of the full skep and forced the bees up into it (a whiff of smoke would help them on their way). He then removed the first skep and whipped out the comb, baby bees and all, and squeezed out and strained the honey. The colony thus ousted, and bereft of both brood and honey, might or might not survive. However, in those days there were thousands of skeps about the countryside, huge reserves of nectar for bees, no poison sprays, and new swarms were to be had for the taking all through the summer. There was no shortage of bees then as there is now.

The skeps, not being waterproof, had to be kept out of the rain. This was done by placing hessian or sometimes conical straw hats called hackles on top to protect them. Sometimes the skeps were placed in specially built wooden buildings called bee boles.

HIVES

Modern hives are based on the invention of a Philadelphian named Langstroth, who, in 1851, established the optimum width of the bee space. The bee space is the distance between two vertical surfaces in which bees will build their comb in an orderly manner on both surfaces, and also have enough room to crawl about. The Langstroth hive, and all its imitators, makes it possible to exclude the queen from the area where most of the honey is situated, making it impossible for her to lay eggs in it and easy for the bee-keeper to avoid killing the baby bees when he extracts the honey.

I saw a wonderful bee house in Switzerland. It was essentially a timber shed with Langstroth hives built around the inside. The hives were connected with the outside world through the walls of the shed, but the bees could be inspected and attended to inside the shed by taking off their roofs. This struck me as an eminently sensible arrangement, for the bee-keeper and the bees.

DAIRY CRAFTS

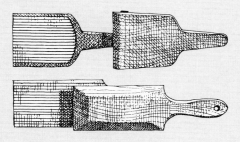

I don't know if you have heard the saying, "Man to the Plough, Wife to the Cow", but on small farms and holdings that was the way it used to be. Not only did the wife milk the cow but she churned some of the milk to make cream and butter and, in times of surplus, she used some to make cheese. Many wives also sold some of the butter and cheese they produced at the local market. So, the possession of a cow meant the possession of a fountain of health for the whole family, something of which Cobbett was well aware. In his marvellous book, *Cottage Economy*, he recommends strongly that the farm worker keep a cow if he possibly can. If he has as little as forty roods of garden, plus access to some common land, he could, in Cobbett's opinion, feed a cow. He might be able to keep little else on the forty roods — and certainly he will not "suffer his ground to be encumbered with apple trees that give only the means of treating his children to fits of the belly ache" — and he might have to farm the land intensively, but, in Cobbett's view, he is bound to consider such disadvantages more than offset by the huge advantage of owning a cow. And I agree with him wholeheartedly.

MILK & MILK TREATMENTS

MILKING A COW
Cows have been milked by hand for centuries. The dairymaid sat on a three-legged stool, enabling her to keep her balance while leaning forward, and the milk collected in a wooden skeel. Milking by hand continued after milking machines were introduced because of their expense.

 WAS LUCKY ENOUGH TO BE brought up in a large country house in north Essex, where we kept two cows and employed a cowman. If any one factor has contributed more than any other to a lifetime of good health, I should say it was those cows.

KEEPING DAIRY COWS
The house cow was commonplace among country people in both Europe and North America until the First World War. City people had to be content with milk delivered daily from the town dairies, in which large herds of cows were kept permanently indoors and fed on hay and corn brought in from the countryside. These cows were kept in what were called "flying herds". After one lactation, as soon as their milk yield fell off significantly, they were either sold to the butcher or sent back to the country. It is thought that this intensive method of keeping milk cows encouraged tuberculosis.

This system was already on the way out when I was a child and there were milk churns on every railway station. The milk train imposed a new discipline on the farmer: he had to catch it with a horse-float full of overflowing milk churns every morning, which meant that he had to be up and milking his cows probably by four or five o'clock. Pasteurization had not yet been developed and so the milk had to be absolutely fresh. Milking utensils were sterilized and the milk cooled as soon as it left the cow to combat attack by micro-organisms.

THE MILK ROUND
I remember working on a mixed farm in the Cotswold Hills in 1934. I had to be up at five every morning to milk the cows, run the milk through a cooler and then put it into the clean churns. After breakfast the farmer drove round the nearby town of Northleach delivering the milk. Whenever he went away this job fell to me. A billycan stood outside the doors of our many customers and I would stop the pony at each and ladle two or three pints into the billycan, plus, at the command of my employer, a splash over: he followed the biblical injunction to give "full measure running over".

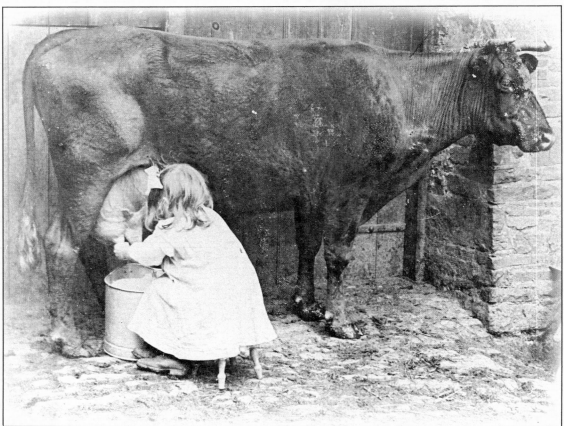

MILKING ITEMS
When cows were being milked, their legs were often tied with a cowband to stop them from kicking. If they were milked in the fields, the milk was carried back to the farm in a back can. A wooden yoke, carved to fit comfortably around the shoulders, was used to carry pairs of milk pails around the farm. It had adjustable chains that hooked on to the pail handles, which you had to hold firmly to prevent the milk from slopping out. When the milk arrived at the dairy, it was left to cool in wooden tubs before being strained through a strainer set on a wooden brig. It was then emptied into tin churns for delivery by rail and road. Many of the churns bore the name of the farm. The delivery man used a tinplate ladle to pour a precise measure of milk into the housewife's jug.

DAIRYMAID'S YOKE

PLAITED COTTON
COWBAND

OAK BRIG

OAK SKEEL

VACUUM MILKING MACHINE

OAK
MILKING
STOOL

BACK CAN

TINPLATE MEASURE

DAIRYMAN'S
DELIVERY CAN

SMALL MILK
CARRIER

MILK
STRAINER

TIN MILK CAN

TWO-HANDLED MILK CHURNS

ONE-HANDLED MILK CHURN

THE DAIRY COW

Not so long ago, many smallholders kept a dual-purpose or dairy cow and a goat. If the cow was kept purely for her milk, she might come from the local farmer to whom she was returned when dry before calving, at which point the goat took over as chief milk provider. Victorian nurses considered goat milk to be good for babies and certainly it was bound to be free of tuberculosis. The Jersey made, and still makes, an excellent house cow. Hardy and affectionate, she is easy to rear and produces the richest milk there is.

Few cows are milked out of doors nowadays, but at one time, in the summer at least, the dairymaids would trip out with their stools and buckets and wooden yokes, milk the tame cows where they stood no doubt knee-deep in grass and buttercups and return to the farm, swinging the heavy buckets full of foaming milk from the yoke chains and trying (or not trying?) to give the slip to the swains who, the poets tell us, were ever trying to waylay them.

RED POLL

This dual-purpose cow produces reliably good milk and beef.

DAIRY SHORTHORN

This dairy shorthorn makes poorish beef, but produces really excellent milk.

AYRSHIRE

This hardy dairy breed from south-west Scotland provides milk rich in butterfat.

BRITISH CANADIAN HOLSTEIN

Primarily a dairy cow, this large, heavy breed, derived from the Dutch Friesian, produces fine beef calves—given the right bull!

JERSEY

GUERNSEY

Jersey and Guernsey cows are exclusively dairy cows and are the only breeds permitted on the Channel Islands from which they originated. Both are small, lean, and easy to rear, and both produce very rich, creamy milk.

MAKING & USING CREAM

REMEMBER THE MAIDS "SETTING" the milk at my childhood home in Essex by putting it, straight from the cow, into wide, shallow white china bowls, covering these with muslin to keep the flies out, and leaving it until the next day. Overnight the cream would rise to the top. And who was to stop a small boy creeping into the dairy when nobody was looking to dip a grubby finger into the thick, yellow cream and lick it off?

SEPARATING THE CREAM FROM THE MILK

The cream was removed from the milk with what was called a fleeter in East Anglia and a skimmer in other parts of England. This was a round, almost flat but slightly dished, perforated disc made of white enamelled metal. It had a handle and the whole thing was perhaps eight inches across. You simply skimmed the thick cream off the set milk with it: the dead white skimmed milk escaped through the holes. I well remember the beautiful way the cream wrinkled as you pushed it to one side: it looked almost solid. But our cows were Jerseys, which yield the richest milk of all.

In the western and northern parts of Britain cream was often separated from the milk by placing the milk in a shallow slate trough (often the same one was used for salting–see p.226), waiting for it to set, and then pulling the plug out. The milk ran away into the under-bucket below, leaving the cream clinging to the slate. The cream was then simply scraped off.

People with more than a couple of cows invested in centrifugal separators in those days. These had the advantage that they extracted more cream from the milk, while the milk was still fresh. Indeed the milk was put through the separator straight from the cow; it was not even cooled first.

USING THE CREAM

We didn't have any nonsensical ideas in those days about cream being bad for you. We poured it over fruit and puddings and even made some richer by scalding it. We heated it with spice, sugar and perhaps some orange-flower water, then, when it was cool, stirred in some soft fruit and more sugar, and ate it! We fed the skimmed milk to the calves or pigs.

CREAMY RECIPES

As well as being an accompaniment to fruit pies and puddings, cream was the principal ingredient of a variety of delicious custards, blancmanges and creamy desserts. Chocolate cream was a rich dessert made with thick cream, eggs and melted chocolate, whipped together until light and frothy. Blancmange flavoured with almonds was another favourite. This was made by heating the cream with lemon rind, sugar and crushed almonds and then leaving it to set in an oiled mould. A simple but pleasant custard was made with boiled cream mixed with egg yolks, sugar and rosewater. This mixture was poured over breadcrumbs, sprinkled with sugar and left to set.

DELIVERIES

Cream was delivered together with the milk in what was known as a "dairy pram", a handcart with three wheels. The fresh milk was carried in the large churn, whilst the cream was carried in separate cans, hanging on the side of the pram.

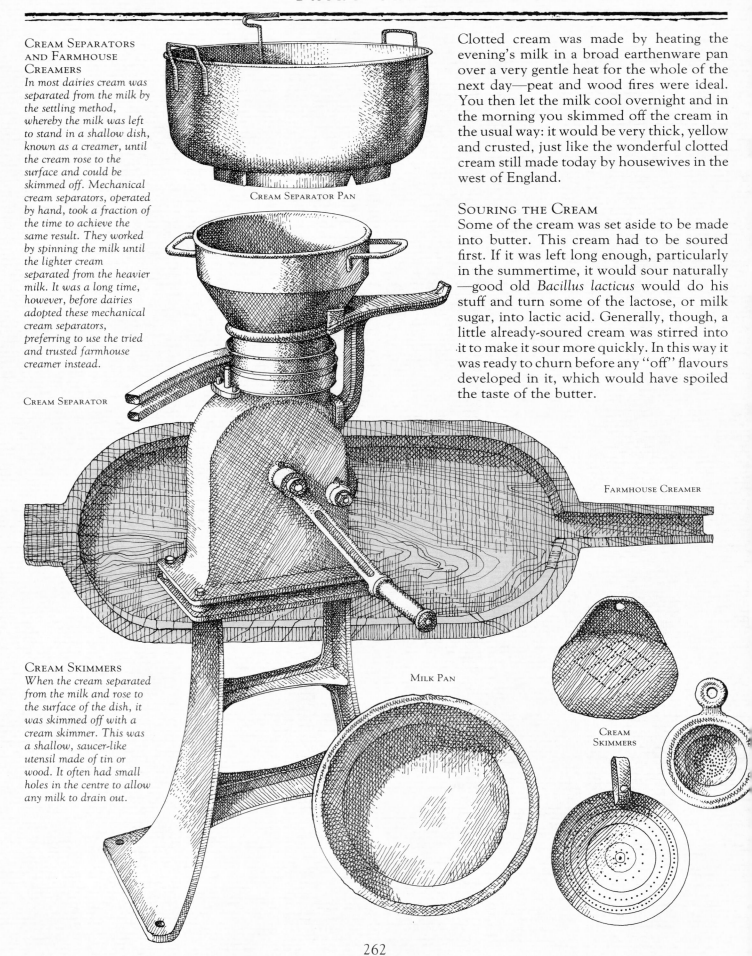

CREAM SEPARATORS AND FARMHOUSE CREAMERS

In most dairies cream was separated from the milk by the settling method, whereby the milk was left to stand in a shallow dish, known as a creamer, until the cream rose to the surface and could be skimmed off. Mechanical cream separators, operated by hand, took a fraction of the time to achieve the same result. They worked by spinning the milk until the lighter cream separated from the heavier milk. It was a long time, however, before dairies adopted these mechanical cream separators, preferring to use the tried and trusted farmhouse creamer instead.

CREAM SEPARATOR

CREAM SKIMMERS

When the cream separated from the milk and rose to the surface of the dish, it was skimmed off with a cream skimmer. This was a shallow, saucer-like utensil made of tin or wood. It often had small holes in the centre to allow any milk to drain out.

CREAM SEPARATOR PAN

FARMHOUSE CREAMER

MILK PAN

CREAM SKIMMERS

Clotted cream was made by heating the evening's milk in a broad earthenware pan over a very gentle heat for the whole of the next day—peat and wood fires were ideal. You then let the milk cool overnight and in the morning you skimmed off the cream in the usual way: it would be very thick, yellow and crusted, just like the wonderful clotted cream still made today by housewives in the west of England.

SOURING THE CREAM

Some of the cream was set aside to be made into butter. This cream had to be soured first. If it was left long enough, particularly in the summertime, it would sour naturally —good old *Bacillus lacticus* would do his stuff and turn some of the lactose, or milk sugar, into lactic acid. Generally, though, a little already-soured cream was stirred into it to make it sour more quickly. In this way it was ready to churn before any "off" flavours developed in it, which would have spoiled the taste of the butter.

BUTTER MAKING

AKING BUTTER IS SIMPLE. SOURED cream (see p.262) is put in a container and shaken until it turns into butter. In Essex we had an over-and-over churn, which I was sometimes allowed to turn. One heard of all kinds of devices for turning churns: water-wheels, horse-engines, even dogs running round in a treadmill, but I never could understand the necessity of these, for if the cream is sour enough and at the right temperature (about 68° Fahrenheit), the butter will "come", as the term is, within a few minutes. So, little exertion is required.

BUTTER CHURNS

The over-and-over churn was undoubtedly the most efficient butter churn and churn-works making them sprang up in small towns throughout the country. Alas, there are no churn-works now and the only churns one can buy are ageing ones, which, no matter how well they have been looked after, will not last for ever.

The plunger churn was an older device used quite recently in Wales, Scotland and Ireland. The operator simply plunged a plunger up and down, thus agitating the cream. It was just as effective as the over-and-over churn but possibly the latter was better for the actual washing of the butter. People with just a cow or two often had a blow churn, which was a glass jar with a small wooden paddle in it turned by gearing and operated by a small handle. I have often seen butter made in very small quantities by beating the soured cream with a fork, whipping it with an egg whisk, or shaking it in a jar or bottle.

WATCHING THE BUTTER "COME"

The over-and-over churn had a small glass window in it, which you peered through to see how the cream was doing. When little grains of butter manifested themselves ("as big as Number Six shot," we were always told), the butter had come. You then opened the end of the churn, flung some cold water in it, and went on churning for a few minutes. The liquid was then carefully poured out: this was the precious buttermilk; what remained was the butter. The generations of mankind that do not know this marvellous drink are deprived indeed.

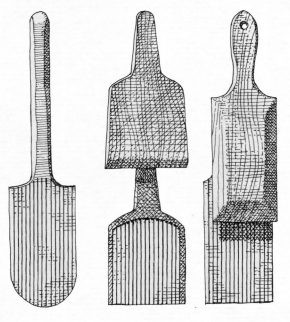

BUTTER HANDS

Butter hands or pats were small wooden bats with deeply grooved blades. They were held one in each hand and were used to divide and shape the butter into square or rectangular blocks. The pat and slap of the butter hands against the butter was a commonly heard sound in the dairy.

EQUIPMENT

THE MOST ESSENTIAL ITEM OF EQUIPMENT needed to make butter was the butter churn. An early sort of churn was the plunger churn, a cylindrical, upright churn fitted with an agitator—a broom handle with a perforated wooden disc fixed to the bottom. The operator plunged the agitator up and down until the cream turned into butter. Hanging churns that worked on a rocking principle were also popular in the eighteenth century. Smaller box churns were developed made of wood to begin with and later of glass and earthenware. These were fitted with slatted paddles connected to a central spindle: the paddles were moved up and down by turning a handle outside the box or jar. Barrel churns were mounted on sturdy stands and turned end over end by means of a handle. After the butter had "come" the excess water had to be squeezed out. The butter worker was excellent for this part of the operation. Wooden scoops were needed to dig out the butter from the butter worker, after which it was formed into blocks, rolls or rounds, or pressed into storage dishes. If it was for sale it was weighed on wooden butter scales.

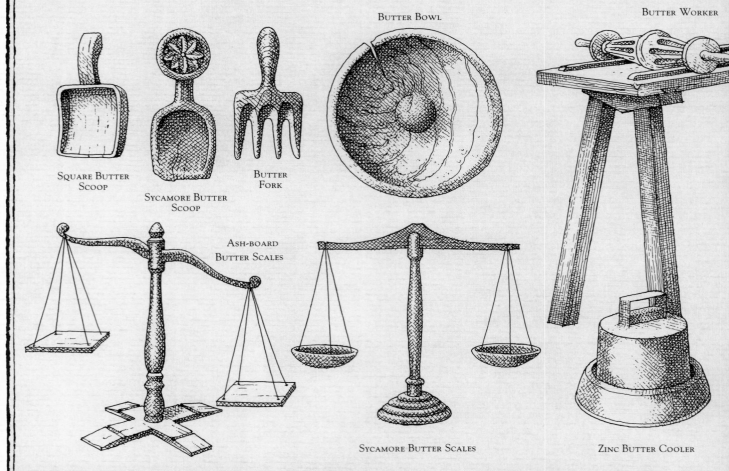

SQUARE BUTTER SCOOP

SYCAMORE BUTTER SCOOP

BUTTER FORK

BUTTER BOWL

BUTTER WORKER

ASH-BOARD BUTTER SCALES

SYCAMORE BUTTER SCALES

ZINC BUTTER COOLER

Swinging Churn

Glass Butter Churn

Mechanical Churn

Dasher Head for Plunge Churn

Butter Churn on Stand

Pump Action Churn

Earthenware Plunge Churn

How people can talk of "progress", in any but a perjorative sense, in a world where fizzy coloured sugar-waters have come in and buttermilk has gone out I cannot for the life of me understand.

WASHING THE BUTTER
After the rescuing of the buttermilk came the washing of the butter. Clean, cold water was poured into the churn in large quantities, the churn turned and the water tipped out.

Now the butter worker came into play. Ours was a shallow wooden trough, kept scrubbed clean, with a wooden fluted roller that rolled up and down the trough when you turned the handle. Copious water was played on the butter while the butter was squeezed by the roller, for it was essential to wash the butter absolutely clean, or it would not keep and "off" flavours would develop in it.

STORING THE BUTTER
Once you were sure there was no buttermilk left in the butter, the butter was salted and worked some more. Afterwards it could be stored in an earthenware crock. The butter was flung into the crock in handfuls to drive out the air and water. When it was full, the butter was rammed hard with a mushroom-shaped wooden tool. All the water and air had to be expelled, otherwise the butter would go rancid. The butter had to be very salty for storing but you could always wash the salt out again before eating it. Well salted butter properly stored would keep indefinitely and taste just as good as fresh.

BUTTER PRINTS
Butter was stamped with decorative designs to make it look more attractive at the table or at the market if it was to be sold. Three types of butter print were used for this purpose: roller markers, flat prints and two-piece moulds.

PRINT MOTIFS
The charming motifs carved on the butter prints were often of flowers, birds or animals. They were usually decorated with a simple repeating pattern around the edge.

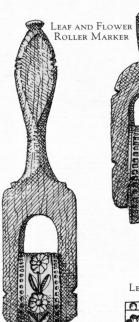

LEAF AND FLOWER
ROLLER MARKER

LEAF ROLLER
MARKERS

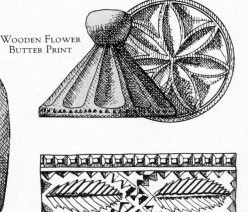

WOODEN FLOWER
BUTTER PRINT

LEAF PRINTS

LEAVES AND FLOWERS PRINT

OVAL BUTTER PRINT

TWO-PIECE SWAN MOULD

COW BUTTER PRINT

Sensible people milked their cows in the summer, when grass was plentiful, and stored the milk in the form of butter and cheese for the winter, when one cow might be kept in milk but not fed too highly, just enough to provide milk for the tea and any small children. The present practice of steaming cows up to high winter yields with imported protein was not done.

DECORATING THE BUTTER

Before the sad triumph of industrial agriculture, farmers' wives used to market their own butter, many of them driving into the nearest town market once a week. They would also sell eggs and, in some cases, cheese. Often, too, they would sell fruit and vegetables, such as field mushrooms and blackberries, and any other produce they had available. The money raised from such produce was the farm wife's perk and she could spend it in any way she liked.

It was therefore desirable for the farmer's wife to mark her butter with her own trademark, and there were many rollers and stamps made by village craftsmen for this purpose. The night before market she would pat the butter into brick shapes with butter pats or scotch hands. Then she would add the finishing touches with a ribbed roller or perhaps a specially crafted butter stamp.

Direct selling of butter has now been outlawed and instead of being able to buy fresh butter, prettily decorated and prepared with loving care by a housewife with her reputation at stake, we now have to be content with factory-made grease wrapped in nasty plastic paper. I remember the maids in my mother's house taking great pride in "patting-up" the butter in different pretty shapes with scotch hands to send it up to the table, generally with a sprig of fresh parsley on it. It is a shame that this tradition has almost disappeared.

BUTTER BY THE YARD

It was not uncommon for butter to be sold by the pint in some areas of Britain and in one or two places in East Anglia it was the practice to sell butter by the yard. In fact, in Cambridge the butter sellers, generally men, were once famous. They took the long tube of butter, which looked rather like a long, narrow French loaf of bread, and measured it with a ring gauge. Why they sold the butter in this way is not really known. Perhaps it was easier for the housemaids, or wives, or college butlers, to cut it up into the butter pats which used to be served.

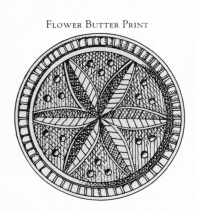

FLOWER BUTTER PRINT

EAGLE BUTTER PRINT

THISTLE BUTTER PRINT

SHEEP BUTTER PRINT

PRIMROSE BUTTER PRINT

CHEESE MAKING

I F YOU LEAVE MILK ALONE IN THE summer it will curdle. That is, it will separate into curds and whey, which will taste slightly sour. No doubt this was the stuff that Miss Muffet was consuming before she had that disturbing encounter with the spider. You can also cause fresh milk to curdle by adding rennet, which is present in a calf's belly to help it digest its mother's milk.

If you take curds and whey, however curdled, and put them in a muslin bag and hang the bag up, the whey will drain out, and the curds will turn into soft cheese. If you then press the soft cheese, expelling more liquid, it will become hard cheese. The value of cheese making is enormous. It enables us to preserve milk, a high protein, very nutritious food, obtained from the cow in summer when the grass is plentiful, until the winter, when we need the energy more and grass is rather thin on the ground. This process is known in all the countries of Christendom and cheese has been made in them for centuries.

Cheese making is not practised in eastern countries, nor in Africa or other parts of the tropical world, as the temperatures are too

CHEESE-MAKING TOOLS *To encourage the milk to curdle with the rennet, the liquid was stirred with a curd agitator. When the curds formed, they were chopped with one of a variety of knives, whippers and cutters, before being wrapped in muslin. The wrapped curds were then placed on a strainer, or in a cheese vat, mould or press with holes in the bottom, so that the whey could drain out. The finished cheese was cut with a fine wire slicer and served on a cheese board.*

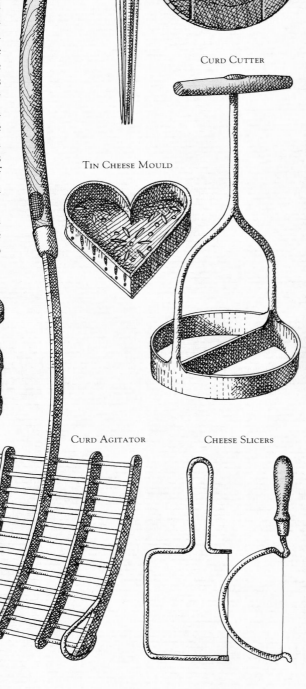

CURD WHIPPER

CHEESE BOARD

CURD CUTTER

TIN CHEESE MOULD

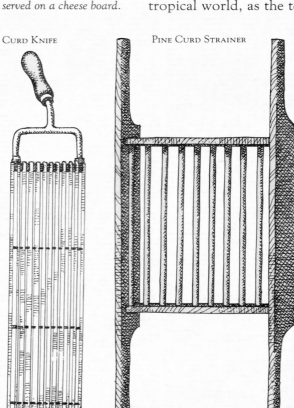

CURD KNIFE

PINE CURD STRAINER

CHEESE VAT

CURD AGITATOR

CHEESE SLICERS

high. The peoples in those countries do not preserve milk except in so far as the Indians turn butter into ghee, which is storable even in their hot climate.

A Disciplined Approach

Cheese making requires a severely disciplined approach. It is easy enough to turn milk into cheese, but not very easy to turn it into *eatable* cheese. For cheese making is a biological process and the living organisms that accomplish it for us must be very carefully controlled. Otherwise you will have to throw the result to the pigs and even *they* have been defeated by some efforts. In the nineteenth century Suffolk cheese had a terrible reputation and would, we are told, defy the teeth of a starving swine. The stuff was made from skimmed milk, though, as all the whole milk went to London to be sold at a high price on the liquid market. The cheese was just a by-product of the butter.

Cheese is now mostly made out of pasteurized milk in huge factories. The whole process is industrial and there is no individual skill required by the workers: temperatures, acidity, the type of bacteria present: every factor is controlled precisely. The result is that the cheese is completely consistent but consistently dull. Thank God farm-made cheese is coming back on the market. This is (or should be) made of unpasteurized milk; either subjected to the naturally occurring micro-organisms of the dairy in which it is made, or inoculated with strains of bacteria carefully bred, and allowed to ripen properly. All the best cheese in the world is made like this.

Hard Cheeses

To make hard cheese the farmer and his wife would pour the evening milk into a vat and then the next day mix in an equal amount of the morning's milk. By then the cream of the night before's milk would have risen and this was sometimes skimmed off and used for making butter. Half evening and half morning milk was the traditional recipe for Cheddar and most hard cheese. Sometimes a ripener (a culture of bacteria) was also added. Then, when the milk reached exactly the right temperature, rennet was added. After this came the skilful process of stroking the top of the milk as it curdled to "keep the cream down".

The milk was left to curdle, after which the curds were cut into cubes. Those making cheese on a small scale would use a kitchen knife but larger producers would use a pair of curd knives (one with blades laid horizontally, the other with blades laid vertically), or later what was called in England an "American curd knife", which was simply two curd knives joined together. The cutting had to be done very gently so as not to destroy the very delicate curd.

The curd was then left to pitch, as the expression was, in the whey; that is, it was just left. The longer it was left, the more acidic it became and the timing of the pitching was extremely important. In larger farms an instrument known as an acidimeter was used to measure the acidity. Many a farm wife, however, measured the acidity using the hot iron test. They touched a piece of curd with a hot iron and drew it away. If the curd broke away from the iron when the string of cheese drawn out from it was under half an inch long it was not acid enough and needed to be left a little longer. If the string was longer than half an inch the curd had been left too long and was too acid: it would have to be given to the pigs as it would never make good cheese.

When exactly the right level of acidity was reached the whey was drained off. It had many uses besides feeding the pigs. Paint was made from it and it was used for washing floors. Thirsty farmers drank it if they had nothing better.

STRAINING THE CURDS
After the milk had curdled, separating into curds and whey, it was poured into a trough lined with muslin. The muslin strained the curds to be used for making cheese, allowing the unwanted whey to pass through.

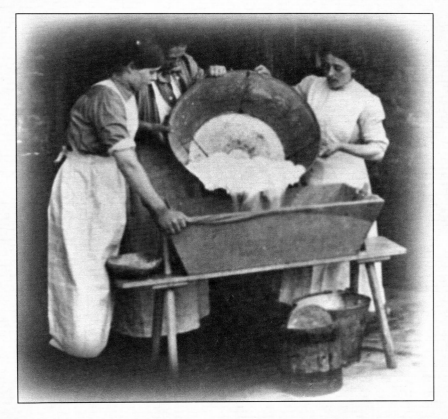

A cool, well-ventilated, spotlessly clean room is essential for cheese making, as indeed it is for all dairy crafts, and dairies were usually sited on the north side of the house, often under the shade of overhanging trees. Stone working surfaces were common as stone is both cool and easy to keep clean.

WOODEN-SCREW PRESS

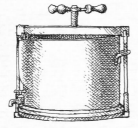

SPRING-LOADED
TINPLATE PRESS

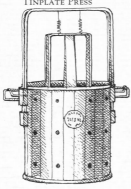

CHEESE PRESSES
There were many gadgets invented for pressing cheese. The curds were packed in a metal or wooden container with holes in the side or bottom, called a chessit. Weights were used to exert pressure on the cheese inside and these were operated by a lever. The cheese was pressed for at least a day until the whey had drained out through the holes and the cheese had become solid. Spring and screw thread presses replaced lever presses late in the nineteenth century.

As for the curd, this was subjected to a variety of treatments, according to the kind of cheese that was to be made. It would be milled (broken up into pieces the size of a walnut), either by hand or by inserting it into a curd mill, a simple instrument with two spiked rollers. Then, if true hard cheese was required, it would be wrapped in a cheese-cloth and placed in a chessit, or vat, made of wood or metal with holes pierced in the base to allow the cheese to drain. Finally it was put in the cheese press, where it was turned after about an hour. There were many kinds of cheese press and some could exert a pressure of a couple of tons.

After pressing, the cheese was taken out of the press and put away for ripening. Choice of storage room was most important: the temperature had to be an even 65 to 70° Fahrenheit, the ventilation good, the humidity just right and the deleterious cheese-mite non-existent. The cheese had to be turned every day for many weeks and scrupulous hygiene had to be observed.

The bigger the cheese, especially with true hard cheese such as Cheddar, the longer it would keep and the better tasting it would become. The Dutch make a great distinction between "niewe kaas", or new cheese, and "oud kaas", or old cheese. The latter is much more expensive and has a fine bite to it, delightful to the taste of your true cheese lover. It is noteworthy that all the best Dutch farm-made cheese is sold to France, whereas all the Dutch cheese sold to England (or very nearly all) is factory made. This tells us a lot about the gastronomic tastes of the French and English.

OTHER CHEESES

Cheeses such as Roquefort (which is made from sheep's milk) and Stilton (which is made from cow's milk) are not true hard cheeses, for they are not pressed. They are inoculated with a mould to turn them blue or green and cannot be stored indefinitely but must be eaten when they are ripe.

Then, of course, there is the great tribe of soft cheeses, or semi-soft cheeses: Brie, Camembert and, in France, at least 100 others, all made locally by farmer cheese makers, all quite distinctive from one another, and nearly all delicious.

General de Gaulle once asked how he could be expected to govern a country with so many different kinds of cheese. Fortunately, you can't, and that is why the French are such a happy race.

MAKING ICE CREAM

CE CREAM IS SAID TO HAVE BEEN invented by Catherine de Medici. It was made by placing a tin or pewter container inside another container, which was filled with a mixture of ice and salt. Cream was then poured into the inner container and sugar and flavouring, such as fruit juice, liqueur, or even jam, added. The mixture was then stirred continuously with a spaddle or revolving paddle, generally made of copper, and, at the same time, the inner pot was turned by a handle. By keeping the mixture constantly on the move, the ingredients would not separate before congealing and no lumps would form. As the cream was churned it also froze slowly to make ice cream.

ICED PUDDING
To make iced pudding, the housewife stirred together milk, sugar, eggs and sometimes almond paste over a medium heat until it thickened. She took the mixture off the heat and allowed it to cool naturally before placing it in the ice-cream freezer to freeze in the usual way. Iced pudding was delicious with fruit compote.

SORBETS
Sorbets were invented in Persia. Snow was brought down into the roasting hot streets of Tehran from the Elburz Mountains, where the eternal snows sit. In Tehran it was flavoured and coloured with fruit juice before being presented to the Shah and his court: they ate it to cool their throats.

ICE-CREAM MOULDS
Once the ice cream or iced pudding was frozen, the housewife would usually place it in a pewter or lead mould. The filled moulds would be kept on ice until the family was ready for dessert. Moulds came in a huge range of designs and many were hinged to make it easier to extract the ice cream without spoiling the pattern.

ICE-CREAM APPLIANCES
Ice-cream makers came in different styles and sizes, but they all worked by turning a handle which turned an inner metal drum in the ice-filled pail. When the ice cream was made it was left to set in decorative moulds and was served using a scoop, or disher. Most scoops had a blade that released the ice cream cleanly from the sides of the scoop.

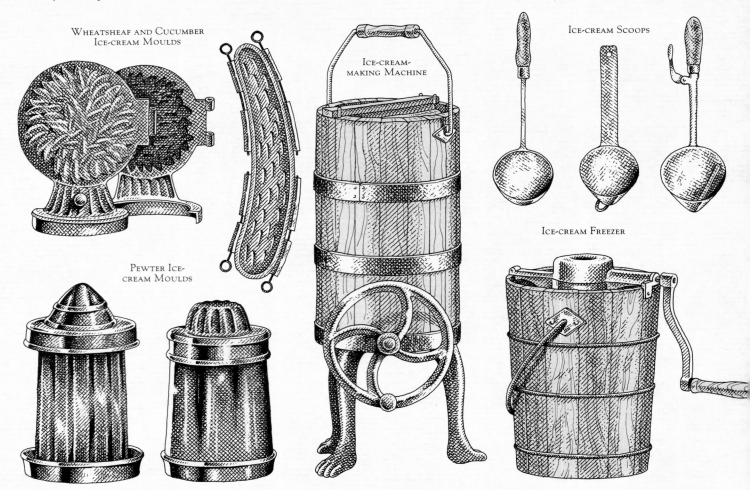

WHEATSHEAF AND CUCUMBER ICE-CREAM MOULDS

ICE-CREAM-MAKING MACHINE

ICE-CREAM SCOOPS

PEWTER ICE-CREAM MOULDS

ICE-CREAM FREEZER

LAUNDRY CRAFTS

In these days of turbo-boost washing machines and
tumble driers, it is difficult to appreciate just how
arduous doing the laundry was in the last century.
Washing machines were not generally available until
the 1880s and even then much energy was required to operate
them, as they were hand cranked. In most households one
day a week, usually Monday, was set aside for doing the
washing and the housewife devoted the whole day to
soaking, pounding, rubbing, boiling, starching, rinsing and
drying the family's linen. She was lucky if she could fit in
the ironing, as well. And as for "dashing away with the
smoothing iron", such an action was very much easier said
than done in the days of heavy flat irons. The rich, who
owned many clothes and could afford to buy their
underwear in sets of twelve, employed washer women to
come and do their washing once every six weeks in a
mammoth session that usually lasted four days. On the
other hand, the poor, who had only the clothes they stood
up in, had to wash their clothes at night, just before
retiring to bed. With any luck the garments would dry overnight
and be ready to wear again the next morning.

DRAWING WATER

HE ODD THING ABOUT THE adventure of Jack and Jill is that they went *up* the hill "to fetch a pail of water" instead of *down* it. Country water supplies tended to be in lower ground. Few people would try sinking a well at the top of a hill, as they would have to sink it that much further to reach the water table. So most people had to carry their water uphill, if their country was hilly, making the operation even more laborious.

CARRYING WATER

People who have never had to fetch their water imagine that carrying it would be quite unacceptably onerous, but, in fact, it is not a horrific task at all. For the first two years of living in our present house, we carried every drop of water we used up a very rough track from a spring 300 yards away and seventy feet below us on the hill. On ordinary days we required ten gallons of water for household purposes. We could each carry five gallons at a time, in two-and-a-half-gallon containers, so this meant one trip each. On wash days, which occurred twice a week, the amount was nearer forty gallons or four trips each. If we had owned a yoke we could easily have carried eight gallons at a time but we never got round to obtaining one. Bath night was once a week and meant fetching a further ten gallons, or two more trips. Each trip took perhaps twenty minutes (for we had to bail the water up from the spring and fill the containers) and few country people, I should imagine, ever had to carry their water much further.

When I was a boy, water was often carried in two buckets suspended from a yoke. Using a yoke meant that the carrier's shoulders bore the weight of the water and the buckets did not bang against her or his knees. Simple hoops made of split hazel were sometimes used, too. The carrier attached the containers to the hoop at either side, got inside the hoop and carried the

containers by hand. The hoop served to keep the buckets from bumping into the legs. In some countries—Wales was one—women carried large containers of water on their heads. Buckets were often made of wood and crafted by the village cooper. Galvanized iron sheet gradually displaced wood and the wandering gypsies or tinkers would knock up such buckets and repair them in a trice.

PUMPING WATER

I remember as a child in Essex that nearly every cottage had a well near it, generally in the garden. Often a well was actually dug in the kitchen, in which case there would be a pump over it so that you could pump the water directly into the sink. If the well was in the garden it would generally have a windlass over it and the water would be wound up in the big heavy well bucket.

Most villages had at least one village well with a pump or windlass. The task of fetching water from the village well was welcomed by the village girls because it always led to their hearing some gossip, for the well acted as a sort of women's club.

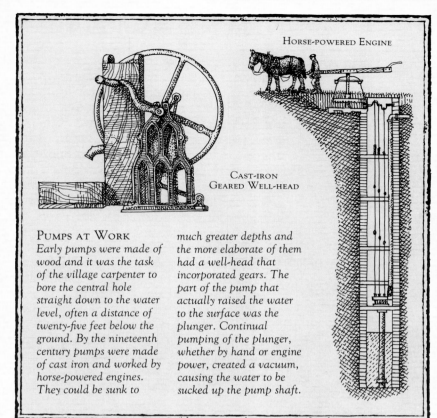

HORSE-POWERED ENGINE

CAST-IRON GEARED WELL-HEAD

PUMPS AT WORK
Early pumps were made of wood and it was the task of the village carpenter to bore the central hole straight down to the water level, often a distance of twenty-five feet below the ground. By the nineteenth century pumps were made of cast iron and worked by horse-powered engines. They could be sunk to much greater depths and the more elaborate of them had a well-head that incorporated gears. The part of the pump that actually raised the water to the surface was the plunger. Continual pumping of the plunger, whether by hand or engine power, created a vacuum, causing the water to be sucked up the pump shaft.

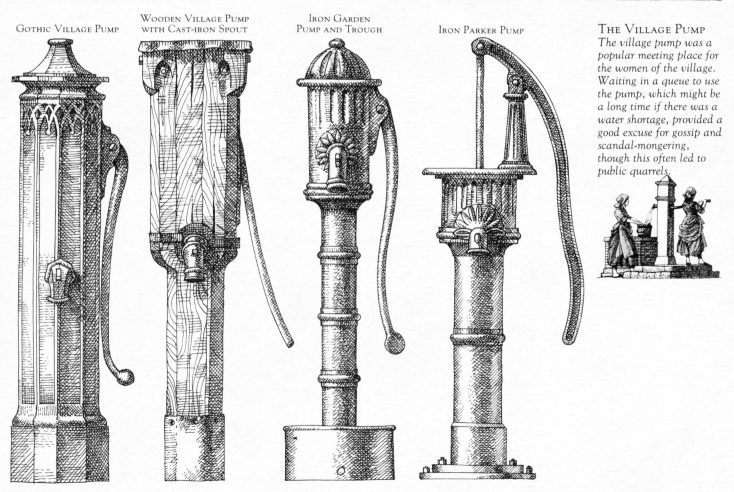

GOTHIC VILLAGE PUMP

WOODEN VILLAGE PUMP WITH CAST-IRON SPOUT

IRON GARDEN PUMP AND TROUGH

IRON PARKER PUMP

THE VILLAGE PUMP
The village pump was a popular meeting place for the women of the village. Waiting in a queue to use the pump, which might be a long time if there was a water shortage, provided a good excuse for gossip and scandal-mongering, though this often led to public quarrels.

MAKING LYE & SOAP

MY MOTHER, WHO WAS BROUGHT UP in Maryland, used to complain that her English servants drank tea "as strong as lye". When I asked her what lye was, she explained that it was an alkaline liquid made in her childhood days before caustic soda was widely available and used to wash clothes. Grease and dirt in the linen were loosened by the alkaline solution and were therefore easier to remove. Lye was made by allowing water to seep through wood ash, placed on top of a cloth on a lye dropper, into a tub. Lye could be used by itself for washing clothes in the "buck wash" or added to fat to make soap.

MAKING LYE

I made lye years later and partly experimentally. I drilled holes in the bottom of a barrel, put a layer of gravel in on top to help drainage, then filled the rest of the barrel with wood ash: hardwood ash worked best. I then trickled rain water through the ashes very slowly. After quite a long wait, the filtered water, or lye, dribbled out of the holes in the bottom of the barrel to be caught in the under-bucket. I then took the liquid and "boiled it down" until it was concentrated enough to float an egg.

You could also make lye out of ferns. These were collected (free) from the countryside, half dried in the sun and burned in pots to make reddish-grey potash. In many parts of the country the ashes were not only used by the makers but also turned into balls and sold in the towns and cities.

Weeds were sometimes mixed in with the fern, burned together and formed into loaves, which would keep for up to twenty years if completely dried. This was the usual practice in Ireland.

TESTING THE LYE

To make soap with lye the housewife had to make sure the lye was the correct strength. To do this, she would make an absolutely saturated solution of brine. Then she would take a stick, weight it at one end, and float it in the salt and water mixture. Because of the weight, the stick would bob upright and she would make a notch in it at the point at which it emerged from the brine: she now had her lyeometer.

Next she dropped the lyeometer in the lye. If the stick floated so that the notch aligned with the surface of the liquid, then the lye was the correct strength for making soap. If the notch was visible above the liquid she simply added rain water until it did align. The solution was never too weak. The lye could then be used for making soap.

MAKING SOAP WITH LYE

To make soap with lye the housewife mixed one pint of lye with two pounds of clean, melted fat or oil, and simmered it gently for three hours, stirring frequently: cow, pig or sheep fat all made excellent soap, and vegetable oils could also be used. As the mixture cooled, she would stir in one pound of salt. This would fall to the bottom but still hardened the soap. Once the salt had settled she poured the molten soap into wooden moulds lined with damp cloths, leaving the brine behind. Finally she added colouring and scenting ingredients: traditionally a mixture of herbs was used. She then left the soap to set. Soap made with lye improved with keeping, but only if it was kept in a cool, but not freezing, airy place.

MAKING SOAP WITH SODA

I first saw soap made in south-west Africa, where if you didn't make it you didn't have it. I saw it made from the fat of the ox, the fat of the ostrich and, rather surrealistically, the

SOAPWORT
Soapwort is a wild plant often found growing near streams. Its leaves were boiled in water to make a lathery liquid, which was then used for washing woollen clothes.

USING A LYE DROPPER
A lye dropper was a wooden box or trough with holes in its base. It was balanced on top of a tub with a layer of drainage— twigs or gravel—arranged in the bottom of the dropper. The drainage material was then covered with a cloth, and topped up with wood ash. Water was slowly poured over the ash and, as it trickled through to the tub beneath, it took with it the alkaline salts from the ash. The resulting liquid was lye, used for washing clothes.

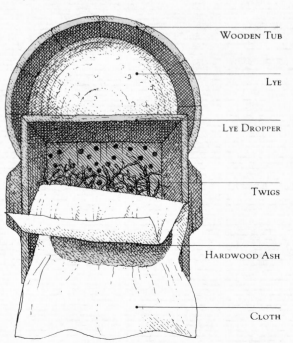

WOODEN TUB

LYE

LYE DROPPER

TWIGS

HARDWOOD ASH

CLOTH

fat of a young lioness that was shot in the act of killing a donkey. Ostriches were much hunted in the days before the Second World War for that very purpose.

The fat (acid) was boiled with caustic soda (alkaline), which neutralized it and so formed soap. There was, I was told, a bush that grew in the veld called the *seep-bosch*, which was so strongly alkaline that it would take the place of the caustic soda. However, we early settlers in that desert country, although too poor to buy soap were rich enough to lash out on a tin of soda, which cost very little and lasted a long time.

In Europe, soda was not cheaply available until the end of the eighteenth century when a Frenchman named Nicholas Leblanc found a way of producing it from salt. Before that, households that really wanted to keep clean were in the habit of using sand and brick dust, or various stone dusts, for scouring and washing clothes, which they would bash against a rock in the stream with a wooden bat called a beetle. Some people made lye and boiled the linen in that in the "buck wash".

Soap was heavily taxed in England until 1833 and ordinary households made do without it until about 1880, when cheap factory-made soap began to flood the market. This soap was used in two ways: it was rubbed on particularly dirty areas of the fabric; and it was dissolved in boiling water to form soap jelly, which mixed easily with the hot water and created a strong, soapy solution for the clothes. The American colonists certainly made it and so, as I said, did the South Africans. Soap was certainly known in England in the sixteenth century but as it was made of fat, and fat was needed for making candles and rushlights, it was always a prerogative of the rich. Many housewives economized by using soap for only some of their linen: their favourite things, perhaps, or the more delicate garments. The rest would go in the buck wash. When soda began to be mass produced, cost-conscious housewives replaced lye with it. Wealthier households used soap for all their linen and boiled it all in lye afterwards, maintaining that the lye softened the water and whitened the linen.

MAKING SOAP CAKES
The liquid soap mixture was poured into a wet wooden mould lined with a damp cloth and left to set. After twenty-four hours, the cloth containing the soap was lifted out and the soap cut into cakes with a thin wire cutter.

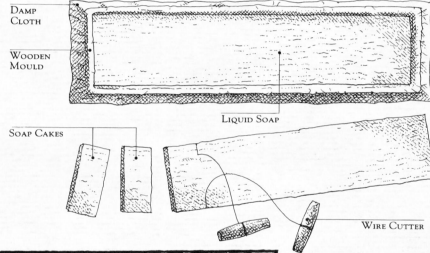

DAMP CLOTH
WOODEN MOULD
LIQUID SOAP
SOAP CAKES
WIRE CUTTER

COLOURING AND PERFUMING

Before the liquid soap set hard in the mould, colourings were added to enhance the soap's appearance, and perfumes were mixed in for a pleasant scent. Any number of ingredients could be used, provided they did not contain alcohol, which would ruin the soap. Vegetables such as carrots, spinach and beetroot coloured the soap yellow-orange, green and pink, while herbs and plants such as lavender, rosemary and lemon balm gave á natural perfume to the soap.

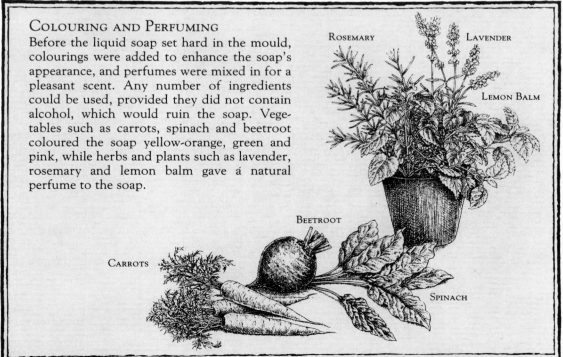

ROSEMARY
LAVENDER
LEMON BALM
BEETROOT
CARROTS
SPINACH

WASHING LINEN

NYONE WHO HAS BEEN TO INDIA will have seen the *dhoby wallah* standing in a stream, or by a well, bashing clothes against a rock. Taking one garment at a time, he dips it in the water and slams it down hard a few times on the rock, dips it again, slams it, and so on. Off fly all the buttons if there are any but the *dhoby* man cares not a straw and bashes away regardless. In this way, without using a scrap of soap or any other chemical, he gets the clothes perfectly clean before laying them in the hot sun to dry and bleach.

Eighteenth-century artists in Europe delighted in making paintings or drawings of buxom country girls with their skirts tucked up to expose their pretty plump legs, either tramping their washing clean with their feet in washing tubs, or bashing it on the rocks of a stream with flat-headed clubs called beetles. They washed their clothes without soap or lye or anything else, bleached them in the sun, and went away rejoicing.

THE WASHING TUB

In the most engaging of autobiographies, *The Book of Boswell*, Gordon Boswell relates tales from his childhood when the family travelled around England in a horse-drawn home. His sisters each had their own washing tub, which was made of oak and had brass hoops, and the little girls used to vie with each other to see who could keep her brass hoops the most brightly polished. Whenever the "vardo", as the caravan was called, was halted for a few days in some green lane to allow the "grais", as the horses were called, to "poov", or graze, the little girls washed the family clothes, draping them on the nearby bushes to dry. Old Gordon's lyrical description brings this delicious pastoral scene to life. It is a scene unlikely to be seen again in our present world of tarmac, hooting motor cars and "authorized municipal sites for itinerants".

Some twenty years ago, when walking from one end to the other of the largest of the Irish Aran Islands (Irishmore), the most delightful singing I ever heard in my life reached my ears. Immediately I sat down and listened. It was a young girl's voice and she was singing in Irish Gaelic. She sang in that haunting melodic style that gives credence to the view held by some people that the early Irish people came from north Africa via Iberia. When finally I could restrain my curiosity no longer I got up and walked round the corner to see a little thatched cabin and before it a beautiful teenaged girl washing clothes in just such a brass-bound tub as Gordon describes, singing as she worked. She was not a bit abashed at the sight of me and willingly sang me another song at my request. Now Irishmore has an airstrip and tourists, and such an experience will never be repeated there.

WASH DAY

Before the twentieth century, washing was a job requiring strength and stamina. In large households it took a whole day to do, and that day was nearly always Monday. The

FAMILY WASH DAY
Whilst the dirtier clothes were left to soak, the more delicate clothes were washed by hand in one tub, and then rinsed in clean water in another tub. Wash day was very tiring for the housewife and she never looked forward to it.

reason for choosing Monday as the day to do the washing was not simply to honour the nursery rhyme, which designates it for that purpose, but because on Sunday the great Sunday joint was cooked and there was always plenty of cold meat left over for dinner on Monday. Consequently the housewife was saved the chore of cooking a proper dinner on Monday and could devote the whole day to washing. I remember a fine dish that was concocted on Mondays from left-over meat, cabbage and potatoes. It was called "bubble-and-squeak".

Washing wasn't merely a matter of shoving everything into a washing machine as it is now. Garments and other articles were carefully sorted, the heavier and dirtier things put to soak for a long time in lye or soda (see p.277) and then well boiled in the copper, and the lighter and more delicate articles put aside to be washed in a tub of cold or luke-warm water by hand.

Stubborn dirt was rubbed away on the fluted washboard or, more often perhaps, by agitating the material in the dolly tub. This was, in the days I remember at least, a fat-bellied tub made of fluted galvanized steel. The housewife "spun" the clothes with a peg dolly, which was a device made by a local wood turner usually out of sycamore. A wooden disc was fixed to the bottom of a rounded shaft and four pegs secured to the underside of the disc. I once heard the peg dolly called a "working woman's piano" by Mr Ellis, who was a wood turner at Boston in the county of Lincolnshire.

There was a range of remedies, some of them pretty strange ones, for getting out stains. Fuller's earth was very useful for removing grease and oil, and chalk and pipe clay were also supposed to work. Lemon juice, onion juice or even urine would all lift ink successfully and if the housewife applied a hot coal

TUBS AND DOLLIES
An effective though laborious method of washing was to spin the clothes in a wooden tub of water using a peg dolly or washing paddle. This loosened the dirt from the linen, which then collected at the bottom of the tub. The spinning action used by the housewife—first turning in one direction and then in the other—is the same as that used by today's washing machines.

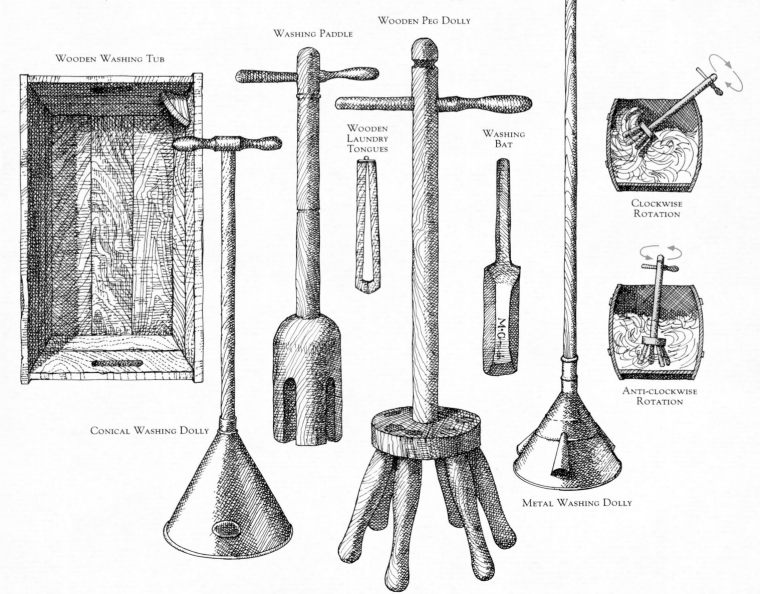

WOODEN WASHING TUB

WASHING PADDLE

WOODEN PEG DOLLY

WOODEN LAUNDRY TONGUES

WASHING BAT

CLOCKWISE ROTATION

ANTI-CLOCKWISE ROTATION

CONICAL WASHING DOLLY

METAL WASHING DOLLY

WOOD AND IRON WASHBOARD

Using a Washboard
The washboard was made of ridged wood, corrugated zinc or ridged glass. The washing was rubbed up and down against it in the wash tub to loosen the dirt. It was often used in conjunction with the dolly and tub, for cleaning the less dirty washing.

LAUNDRY BRUSH

GLASS CORRUGATED PLATE WASHBOARD

The American Washer
This mechanical gadget was a substitute for the washboard. The machine was simply rolled up and down against the linen in the wash tub. It was less hard work and kinder to the hands and knuckles than the washboard.

The Wash Tub
Wash tubs were made of wood and were often rectangular and trough-like in shape to make them easy to use with a washboard. Barrel-shaped tubs were also frequently used with peg dollies.

wrapped in linen to a wax stain, the wax would be removed. Milk was used to combat urine, vinegar and fruit stains. Finally there were some rather complicated recipes for multi-purpose, stain-removing liquids, which called for enormous pounding energy before the housewife had even made a start on the stain!

The Copper
I remember as a child in rural Essex that every farmhouse or cottage had at least one copper. The copper, which was often not made of copper at all but of thin cast iron, was a hemispherical vessel that would hold from twenty to forty gallons of water. It might be found in an outhouse (known as the "backus", or backhouse, in East Anglia, and the blue house in the Midlands), or in the kitchen. Great houses, like Tendring Manor House, where I was brought up, would have them, too.

The copper was built into a brick surround and had a fire grate under it. In the best installations the bricks were laid in such a way that the heat and smoke spiralled around the copper before reaching the chimney. Such built-in coppers were very effective. I inherited such a copper when I moved into a gamekeeper's cottage near Orford in Suffolk in the early 1950s, and was amazed by its efficiency: a fire fuelled by a few dry twigs would boil a good twenty gallons of water in no time at all.

The copper was an absolute boon. It served to wash the clothes, boil the pig food, boil the pig, provide scalding water for scalding the pig; boil the water for making beer or home-made wine, heat the water for baths, and even, in big families, boil the stew or soup. In days when bachelor farm workers lived in the house—as they commonly did in the west and north of England until fairly recent times—the farmer's wife, or her maid, would put a huge joint of beef in the copper and boil it up. This would last the extended family for several days.

Bleaching
Linen was bleached well into the nineteenth century by the disgusting practice of soaking it in urine, which contains ammonia. Human urine was, after all, free and was collected assiduously for bleaching purposes. Hog manure was also used, mixed with a little cold water. In both cases the clothes were washed thoroughly in fresh water afterwards, of course!

The sun, too, was a great bleacher. Linen was laid out on the village "bleaching green" to be whitened by the sun. The bleach that we use today—a compound of lime, salt and oxygen—was not freely available until the late nineteenth century.

The "blue" bag was something that I remember vividly from my childhood days because, whenever I got stung by a wasp, which was not infrequently, a wet blue bag would be pressed on the sting. The "blue" was a powder containing a blue pigment made from the indigo plant or ultramarine. A squeeze of the blue bag went into the rinsing water of every white wash to make the white clothing even whiter.

STARCHING

Wheat, potato gratings, rice or another substance rich in carbohydrate was boiled in water to make starch to stiffen clothes. Starch was made commercially in England on a massive scale in the 1840s, when Reckitt and Sons Ltd was going strong.

It seems to me that our ancestors made life unnecessarily difficult and uncomfortable for themselves. The social conventions that made it necessary for a "gentleman" (or indeed a poor counting-house clerk) to wear starched shirts and collars so that he could hardly bend over or turn round, also put an intolerable burden on the wretched laundry maids. Thank God those days are over.

A SOCIAL OCCASION
As there was so much heavy work to do on wash day, from sorting and soaking the washing to pounding it in tubs and hanging it out to dry, everyone (except the men) had to help out. This often became quite a social occasion for the women of the household.

WASHING BY MACHINE

IN THE NINETEENTH CENTURY THERE WERE MANY attempts to design an effective washing machine. Most were based on the traditional method of washing—that of pounding the washing in water to loosen the dirt—and only got as far as mechanizing the pounding by the peg dolly. A lot of manual labour was still required: the washing machine had to be filled with water and then emptied afterwards, and a wheel had to be turned or a lever pushed backwards and forwards continually to operate the peg dolly. Nevertheless, washing machines were coveted by many housewives.

The Vowel Y washing machine tumbled the washing about using wooden slats, instead of the traditional peg dolly. The Faithful machine set the washing in motion by a manually operated side-to-side rocking action.

Gradually, wooden washing machines were replaced by steel or copper ones, which were smaller and neater in appearance. At the end of the nineteenth century the first steam washing machine was invented. Water was heated in the washing tank by gas jets, and dirty washing was cleaned by the combined forces of water and steam, which proved much more effective.

TOP OF HAND-CRANKED PEG DOLLY

THE WOODEN TUB
After the dolly tub (see p.279) came the hand-cranked wooden tub. Water was added to the tub and emptied by hand. A five-legged peg and dolly was attached to the lid of the machine and this was agitated back and forth in the tub by turning the large wheel at the side. A small mangle was incorporated at the other side of the tub.

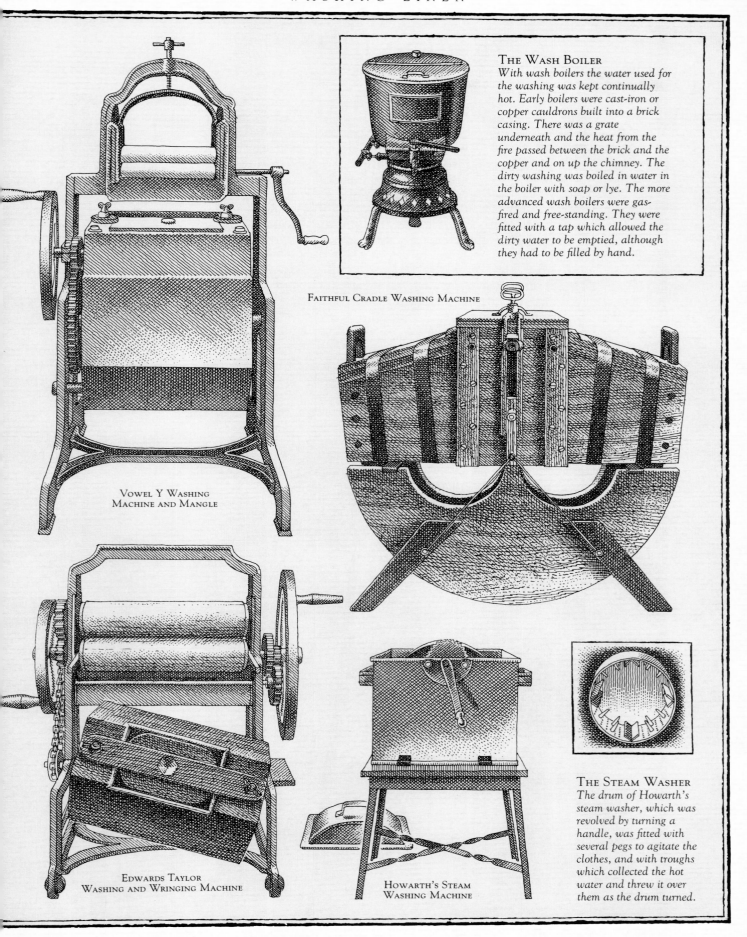

VOWEL Y WASHING
MACHINE AND MANGLE

THE WASH BOILER
With wash boilers the water used for the washing was kept continually hot. Early boilers were cast-iron or copper cauldrons built into a brick casing. There was a grate underneath and the heat from the fire passed between the brick and the copper and on up the chimney. The dirty washing was boiled in water in the boiler with soap or lye. The more advanced wash boilers were gas-fired and free-standing. They were fitted with a tap which allowed the dirty water to be emptied, although they had to be filled by hand.

FAITHFUL CRADLE WASHING MACHINE

EDWARDS TAYLOR
WASHING AND WRINGING MACHINE

HOWARTH'S STEAM
WASHING MACHINE

THE STEAM WASHER
The drum of Howarth's steam washer, which was revolved by turning a handle, was fitted with several pegs to agitate the clothes, and with troughs which collected the hot water and threw it over them as the drum turned.

DRYING LINEN

RYING LINEN WAS A TIRESOME business. The laundress was always at the mercy of the weather, for it was difficult to dry clothes indoors in the cramped space before the fire, especially before the coming of the closed range, when the atmosphere could be smoky. In the towns, housewives had to contend with the soot outside, too, and the carters that drove along the back streets where the linen was hung from one side to the other were a great hindrance, as they would often tear down any washing in their way. As a result, the laundress would try to get her washing as dry as possible before hanging it out, by wringing it.

WRINGING AND MANGLING THE LINEN
The first wringing machine emulated the traditional hand method. The sheet was fixed to two posts and one post was turned tighter and tighter to squeeze out all the water. The box mangle was a much larger and more sophisticated machine, which evolved in the eighteenth century and was used for extracting water from linen and pressing the sheets.

A heavy, stone-filled box was trundled back and forth over loose wooden rollers which rolled over the linen beneath. Only those households with a separate laundry building had the money and space for a mangle, however, and it was not until the nineteenth century, with the invention of the upright mangle, that it could be said that every cottage had something to wring out the washing. Passing clothes through the wringer or mangle got most of the water out of them so they did not take long to dry on the line (or on the hedge).

Straightforward linen, such as sheets, towels, tablecloths and pillowcases, were flattened in the mangle after they had been drying for some time and did not need ironing afterwards. Often such articles were dipped in starch water before passing them through the mangle to stiffen them slightly.

MAKING PEGS
It was a gypsy man, not Gordon Boswell but a Welsh gypsy named John Jones (alas, like Gordon, gone to the great camping ground in the sky), who taught me how to make clothes pegs, sitting before my fire in Wales

HANGING OUT THE WASHING
If there was enough space the washing was pegged on a washing line outside and left to dry in the wind. Sagging lines were propped up with wooden clothes props, fashioned rather like large pegs. This method of drying clothes was much preferred to having wet washing draped indoors.

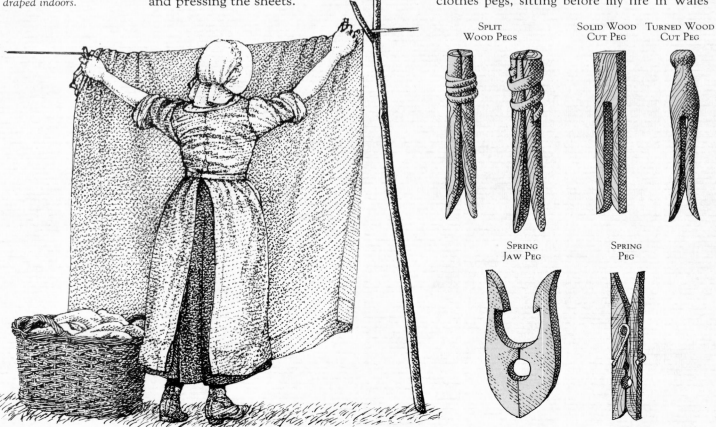

WRINGING MACHINES

The earliest wringing machines twisted the washing into a corkscrew shape to squeeze out the water. The large box mangle replaced these. This worked by a weighted box being wound backwards and forwards across rollers, which pressed the washing laid beneath. The upright mangle superseded the box mangle. The washing was fed between two rollers by turning the side wheel. Weights which were hung from the top roller applied the pressure needed.

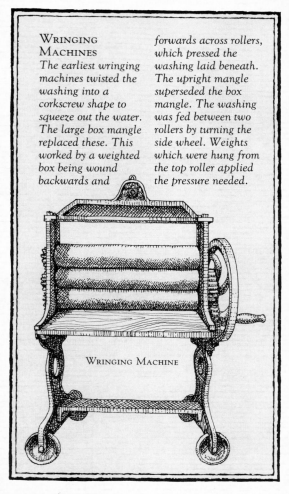

WRINGING MACHINE

(see p.39). Any gypsy man could make hundreds of these a day. He would clip them on to pieces of cardboard in what were called "hands" and the womenfolk would take them round when they went "calling" on householders and sell them.

HANGING OUT THE WASHING

In certain bourgeois circles it has always been considered undesirable to see other people's washing hanging out to dry. Personally, I can think of few more delightful sights. A line of brightly coloured washing flapping gallantly in the sun speaks to me of cleanliness, self-respect, and the habits of true industry. I am honoured when a member of the gentler but more competent sex entrusts me with the task of hanging out the washing. The scent of wind-and-sun-dried laundry is delightful: nothing like it ever comes out of a tumble drier.

SOCK DRIERS

So that they retained their shape when drying, socks and stockings were placed on wooden boards which were attached with string to the washing line. They were also dried on pottery sock driers. These were filled with hot water to heat the socks and dry them quickly.

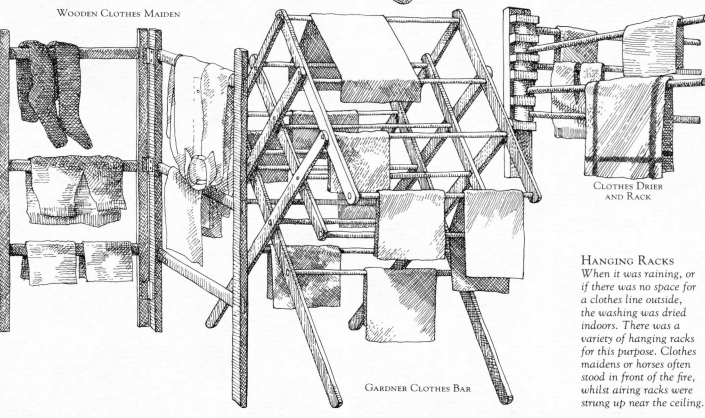

WOODEN CLOTHES MAIDEN

CLOTHES DRIER AND RACK

GARDNER CLOTHES BAR

HANGING RACKS

When it was raining, or if there was no space for a clothes line outside, the washing was dried indoors. There was a variety of hanging racks for this purpose. Clothes maidens or horses often stood in front of the fire, whilst airing racks were strung up near the ceiling.

PRESSING LINEN

THE LINEN PRESS
To ensure that sheets and
table linen had precise
creases and folds, they
were pressed in the linen
press after being ironed.
The linen press worked by
turning the central screw,
which lowered a heavy
board on to the folded
linen below. Pressed linen
was stored in the drawer.

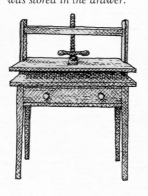

IRTUALLY ALL GARMENTS HAD TO BE
ironed. Flat irons were ubiquitous. They were heated on the iron
hob of the kitchen range and used
in turn. Generally when the ironing was
being done you would see a couple standing
on the hob taking the heat while a third was
being used. When the ironer needed to put
the iron down for a moment, she would rest
it on an iron trivet. Trivets of many shapes
and designs were made (see pp.288–9).

Where kitchen ranges did not exist, in
such places as Africa and British India, the
box iron was universally used. This was an
iron-shaped box into which was placed a
heated iron slug. These irons were num-
bered: the smaller the number the lighter
and smaller the iron.

CHARCOAL IRONS

Charcoal irons were based on the same box
idea. They had ventilation holes in the sides
and the *dhoby wallah* in India, or the laundry
boy in Africa, spent much time swinging
them vigorously through the air to encourage the charcoal to burn.

I knew a man who made a fortune out of
selling charcoal irons. I met him in Barotse-
land, in what was then called Northern
Rhodesia but is now known as Zambia. He
turned up at the village of Mulobesi with a
Chevrolet pick-up truck full of charcoal
irons. He then went to the only store in the
place—the only store, in fact, for several
hundred miles—and unloaded an impressive number of charcoal irons.

Later, over a bottle of whisky, he confided
to me that he owed his success to a team of
ladies whom he employed to go into the
local store a week before he arrived and ask
for a charcoal iron. They staggered their
visits so that the store-keeper found himself
besieged for several days by ladies demanding these, then comparatively unknown,
objects. So when—providentially—a van
drew up several days later with a load of the
requested articles he bought up a good
quantity. So my friend made his way
through Africa obtaining very good sales
and a great deal of money. Thus are industry
and foresight rewarded.

SPECIAL-PURPOSE IRONS

In addition to the basic flat and box irons a
multitude of special-purpose irons were
available to the laundress. To provide a
glazed or polished finish to starched garments a polishing iron was used. Similar to a
flat iron, it had a convex, rounded base and
the ironer would rock the iron forward with
one hand while sponging an additional thin
starch glaze to the material to be polished
with the other: it was a highly skilled job.

The Italian, or tally, iron (see p.288) was
used to iron made-up bows and bonnet
strings, and to "get up" ruffs and frills. It
consisted of one or more barrels of different
diameter, into which were placed iron pok-
ing sticks, which the housewife heated over
the fire. She would hold the tied ribbon or
the top of the frilled material around the
heated barrel until it was smooth and dry.

PRESSING BYGONES
Ironing boards were
usually wooden and had a
shelf underneath on which
the pressed clothes were
stacked. Very dry clothes
were first sprinkled with
lavender water from a
clothes sprinkler before
being ironed, generally
with a flat iron, which
came in a huge range of
sizes. The fluting iron was
used to crimp material.
Charcoal or self-heating
irons had to be fanned
with bellows or swung
vigorously through the air
to keep the fire going
inside them.

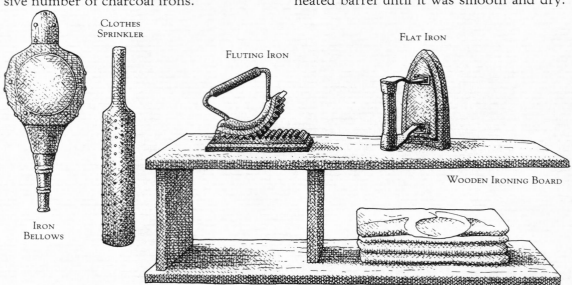

CLOTHES
SPRINKLER

FLUTING IRON

FLAT IRON

WOODEN IRONING BOARD

IRON
BELLOWS

The French or mushroom iron much resembled the Italian iron but had a more rounded top and was used chiefly for rounding out puffed sleeves.

Various goffering devices were developed from the late eighteenth century especially to make flutes in material. Scissor-like metal tongs called fluting or goffering tongs were popular, as were the fluting board—a corrugated wood or metal board—and ridged roller. The starched material was placed on the board when still damp and the roller run back and forth over it. The goffering stack was in use for many years: it consisted of twenty or thirty wooden or metal spills slotted into two posts. The damp material was threaded through the stack and the whole thing placed in front of the fire. The wheel goffer or crimping machine was developed from this in the second half of the nineteenth century. It operated in the same way as the upright mangle (see p.285), only the rollers were hollow, so that heated cylindrical irons could be inserted as in the tally iron, and, of course, they were corrugated on the outside.

Gas Irons and Beyond
As a child I saw gas irons in use and once owned a Tilley iron. This contained a reservoir for paraffin (kerosene) and a small pump to maintain the pressure.

I remember the maids at the Manor in Essex, where I spent most of my childhood, keeping a small sprig of lavender in a bowl of water next to the ironing board. They would frequently dip their fingers in the water and sprinkle it over the material they were in the process of ironing to keep it moist and achieve a crisper finish. After it was ironed, they would fold the linen and put it away in piles, inserting lavender faggots at regular intervals to keep it smelling freshly laundered. The coming of the electric iron, and especially the thermostatically controlled electric iron with a steaming device, made ironing less of a chore and rendered the bowl of lavender-scented water unnecessary.

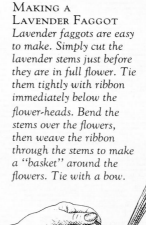

MAKING A
LAVENDER FAGGOT
Lavender faggots are easy to make. Simply cut the lavender stems just before they are in full flower. Tie them tightly with ribbon immediately below the flower-heads. Bend the stems over the flowers, then weave the ribbon through the stems to make a "basket" around the flowers. Tie with a bow.

CRIMPING AND
GOFFERING
When dresses had lots of ruffles and frills, crimping boards were used for pressing material into neat ridges, whilst goffering machines pressed pleats into a frill.

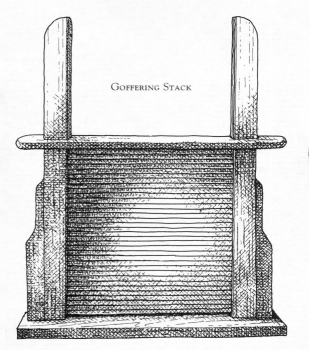

GOFFERING STACK

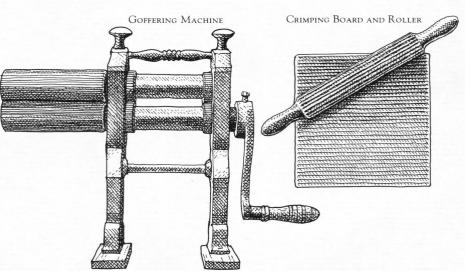

GOFFERING MACHINE

CRIMPING BOARD AND ROLLER

THE IRON AGE

TWO BASIC TYPES OF IRON EVOLVED IN THE seventeenth century: the flat iron and the box iron. Flat irons were of various weights—heavy for thick material, light for muslin. They were either heated in front of the open fire or on the kitchen range, although some large houses had a purpose-built heating stove. Box irons were much deeper in the belly, designed to contain a cast-iron slug, which was heated until red hot and then placed inside the iron with tongs. Later box irons burned charcoal or coal and featured a row of holes in each side for ventilation. Several special-purpose irons were also made: the Italian or tally iron was indispensable for ironing bows and penetrating gathers. Spirit and petrol irons became common in the second half of the nineteenth century but were gradually superseded by the electric iron, first patented in the United States in 1883.

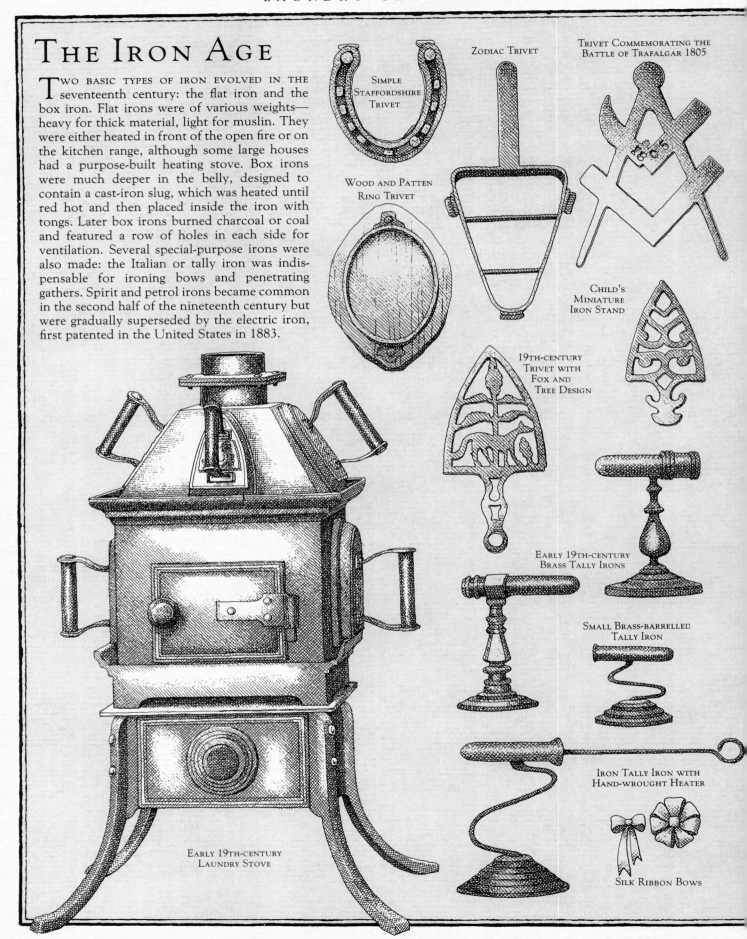

SIMPLE STAFFORDSHIRE TRIVET

WOOD AND PATTEN RING TRIVET

ZODIAC TRIVET

TRIVET COMMEMORATING THE BATTLE OF TRAFALGAR 1805

CHILD'S MINIATURE IRON STAND

19TH-CENTURY TRIVET WITH FOX AND TREE DESIGN

EARLY 19TH-CENTURY BRASS TALLY IRONS

SMALL BRASS-BARRELLED TALLY IRON

IRON TALLY IRON WITH HAND-WROUGHT HEATER

SILK RIBBON BOWS

EARLY 19TH-CENTURY LAUNDRY STOVE

288

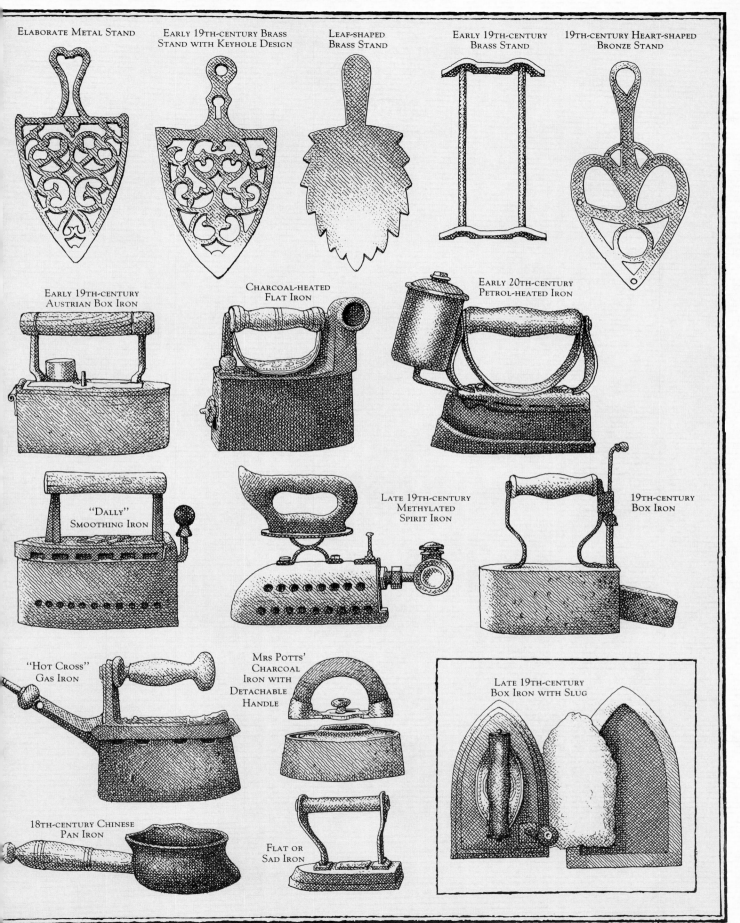

ELABORATE METAL STAND

EARLY 19TH-CENTURY BRASS STAND WITH KEYHOLE DESIGN

LEAF-SHAPED BRASS STAND

EARLY 19TH-CENTURY BRASS STAND

19TH-CENTURY HEART-SHAPED BRONZE STAND

EARLY 19TH-CENTURY AUSTRIAN BOX IRON

CHARCOAL-HEATED FLAT IRON

EARLY 20TH-CENTURY PETROL-HEATED IRON

"DALLY" SMOOTHING IRON

LATE 19TH-CENTURY METHYLATED SPIRIT IRON

19TH-CENTURY BOX IRON

"HOT CROSS" GAS IRON

MRS POTTS' CHARCOAL IRON WITH DETACHABLE HANDLE

LATE 19TH-CENTURY BOX IRON WITH SLUG

18TH-CENTURY CHINESE PAN IRON

FLAT OR SAD IRON

DYEING

NE CANNOT CLAIM THAT THE ART OF dyeing was practised in many households in the last two centuries, but it is certainly enjoying a brisk revival now. Since the seventeenth century the story of textiles has been one of increasing specialization and industrialization. However, little by little, the modern craft weavers and dyers have unearthed the ancient lore, and begun using the many natural vegetable dyes that people used before the invention of aniline dyes during the nineteenth century.

VEGETABLE DYES

There is absolutely no doubt that the colours obtained from natural dyes are infinitely kinder than the brighter, more garish colours provided by artificial dyes. We may have to go to the tropics for brilliant natural dyes, such as indigo and cochineal, but many subtle colours can be obtained from plants of temperate countries.

DYEING WOOL
The ingredients for the dye were placed in an iron pot and the pot covered with a weighted board pierced with holes. Water was then added and the dye was boiled up. The wool was boiled in the dye for several hours.

DYEING OUTDOORS
Very early dyeing of wool and yarn took place outside. The cloth was boiled in the dye in an iron pot suspended over an open fire. This was hot and tiring work as the cloth had to be continually stirred with a wooden stick for several hours until the dye was absorbed to the strength of colour that was required. Then there was the rinsing and drying to do.

Most vegetable dyes require mordanting. In other words, a chemical must be added to the dye to cause the dye to "bite" into the yarn so that it will remain permanently that colour. Chromic acid, stannous chloride (tin crystals), iron and copper sulphates, alum, and bichromate of potash can all be used as mordants. One cannot but wonder how the actions of these chemicals were discovered, nor how someone found out that the leaves of the tansy (*Tanacetum vulgare*), the birch (*Betula alba*), lady's mantle (*Alchemilla vulgaris*), cow parsley (*Anthriscus silvestris*), a kind of heather called ling (*Calluna vulgaris*) and barberry (*Berberis vulgaris*) all make beautiful yellow dyes. Red can be obtained from crottle (*Parmelia saxatilis*), and the roots of bedstraw (*Galium boreale*), while zinnia and some dahlia flowers provide a yellowish-red. The list is enormous.

DYEING FLAX AND COTTON

In the days when many cottagers spun and wove their own linen, and grew flax in their gardens, the yarn was generally bleached white by simmering it in a weak solution of caustic soda and then laying it in the hot sun. A delightful cloth was made by weaving bleached and unbleached yarn in a pattern. Unfortunately, with the passing of time, the unbleached yarn, which was a pleasant shade of fawny-grey, would become bleached and the pattern would disappear. To prevent this from happening, it was usual to soak the unbleached yarn in a strong solution of juniper juice and water.

Flax and cotton are both cellulose materials and they share a reluctance to take most vegetable dyes, although a dye made from oak-apples is effective, as is one made from several kinds of bark and twig. In any case, cotton arrived from the hot parts of the world where it is grown, too late ever to have been woven and dyed in the home on any big scale: it went straight into the factories.

DYEING WOOL

Wool is a protein fibre and takes all dyes well. There have always been black sheep as well as white sheep and spinsters and weavers have produced attractive fabrics by intermixing black and white wool. Such black and white mixtures vat-dyed in indigo result in a very pleasant-looking cloth.

Around The Home

If you stray into one of the many ruined cottages that dot the countryside you'll probably stand on the brick or tiled floor, through the cracks of which grasses and even small trees are beginning to peep. Look up at the sky through the holes in the roof and you should feel a sense of reverence and awe. For, even though the upper floors are rotten and the smoke-blackened fireplace has long lain idle, you are standing in what was for many years a *real* home. There is far more to a home than stone and mortar, slate or thatch. The true home is a temple that has been tended and served faithfully by generations of devoted men and women. The men went out into the field, or even over the sea to provide the necessities, while the women looked after the home, cleaning and polishing, making up fires, topping up lamps. They nurtured the children, too, and saw to it that they learned the skills they would need in the future to tend homes of their own. This may not often be the way it is now but it is the way it was when that crumbling ruin was lived in, before cruel economic forces led to its abandonment.

GATHERING & MAKING FUELS

LTHOUGH MEDIEVAL LORDS OF THE manor jealously guarded their trees, almost everywhere in Medieval Europe the right of "hook and crook" belonged to the local peasants. In addition to being allowed to take any small, wind-blown timber for firewood, they could take any dead wood that could be dragged from the trees. To obtain such wood they would use either a hook tied to a piece of rope, which they flung up, so that the hook hooked over the branch, or a crook fastened to a long, wooden handle. Woodland was extensive then, especially in proportion to the human population, and there was no shortage of firewood for diligent people, however poor, and no need to cut down growing trees.

HARDWOOD AND SOFTWOOD

Not all wood makes good firewood, however. Hardwoods—oak, ash, holly, birch, beech, hornbeam, elm, maple, sycamore and lime—burn well and throw out a lot of heat. However, all except ash and holly must be well seasoned. If you are cutting down living trees for firewood you should cut down next year's supply this year. Burning green wood, unless it is ash or holly, will not warm your back or your belly. Softwoods don't throw out as much heat as hardwoods and they must be very well seasoned in the dry to give out any heat at all.

The great overhanging roofs of alpine chalets were not built just to look pretty, they serve to shelter the winter supply of firewood, which is absolutely crucial to the

FELLING TREES
The felling of trees for firewood required special tools. First a V-shaped notch was made in the tree with an axe. The trunk was then sawn from the opposite side with a two-handed cross-cut saw; more leverage was provided by driving a wedge in behind the saw with a sledgehammer. The felled tree was then split, or rived, into smaller, more manageable, logs by driving wedges into the wood until the trunk split down its length. To split smaller wood, a froe was driven into the wood, using a club, and worked from side to side to ease open the grain.

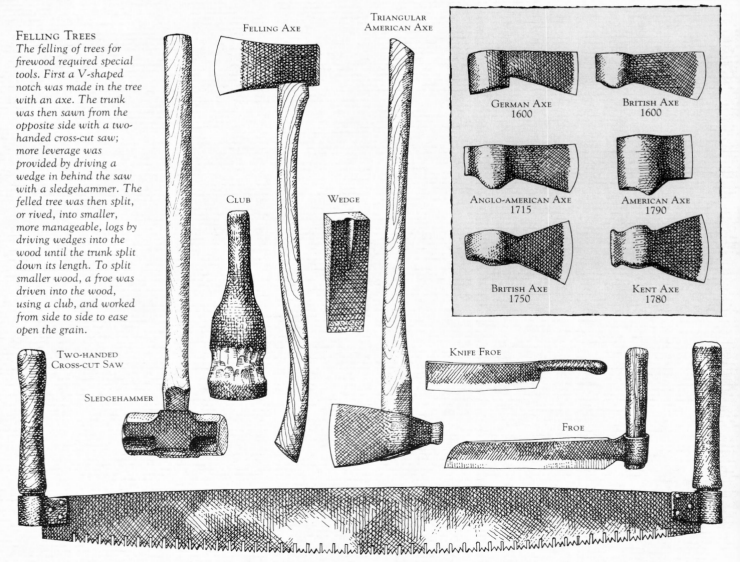

FELLING AXE

TRIANGULAR AMERICAN AXE

CLUB

WEDGE

TWO-HANDED CROSS-CUT SAW

SLEDGEHAMMER

KNIFE FROE

FROE

GERMAN AXE 1600

BRITISH AXE 1600

ANGLO-AMERICAN AXE 1715

AMERICAN AXE 1790

BRITISH AXE 1750

KENT AXE 1780

survival of the people who live in the chalet. Softwood is the only wood that grows high in the Alps and, as it spits when it burns, and as the houses are also made of wood, it cannot be burned in open fires. Instead they burn it in magnificent tiled stoves, often in every room. These stoves are massive, although the fire-box is quite small, and they store heat extremely well, so that the room remains warm after the fire has gone out.

Peat or Turf

It is providential that in many countries where firewood is hard to come by, peat, or what the Irish call turf, is there for the digging. Peat forms naturally in wet climates, where the drainage is poor. When the vegetation dies in such places it does not rot away aerobically but sinks into the wet bog and is preserved in its own acidity. After many centuries, deposits of peat many yards deep accumulate. Broadly there are two kinds of peat beds: mountain beds, which have formed in poorly drained hanging valleys in the uplands; and flatland beds found in the plains. Much of the centre of Ireland is composed of a huge peat bog.

Peat digging and burning has been going on for thousands of years. As mentioned on pages 70–1, in spring and early summer you will see peat diggers in the wetter parts of the Scottish Highlands and Islands, and anywhere in the west of Ireland (indeed there is turf digging in every Irish county). They use a special type of spade to dig out the peat or turf bricks, which is called a slane in Ireland (see p.71).

As they are dug, the brick-shaped lumps of peat are laid in windrows to dry. If the weather is wet they have to be turned frequently. When partly sun- and wind-dried they are stacked in stooks and often thereafter in high stacks. The peat is positioned in such a way that the topmost and outermost bricks are set at an angle so that they shed most of the rain.

Culm or Boms

A fuel now obsolete but once used widely in Wales and Ireland is what the Welsh called culm and the Irish called boms. To make the fuel clay was mixed with coal or anthracite dust (about four parts clay to one part dust). With the addition of a little water the mixture was moulded into balls. Culm had to be burnt on a raised grate to let the air get to it. It was a long-lasting and very satisfactory fuel, but rather a palaver to make!

Cutting Peat

A marking iron was used to make vertical cuts in the peat, which was then exposed with a paring iron. The slane cut the peat into rectangular turfs, which were transported in a hand barrow, as heavier wheeled vehicles sank in the wet and boggy ground. The peat was then stacked in loose piles to dry, before it could be used as fuel.

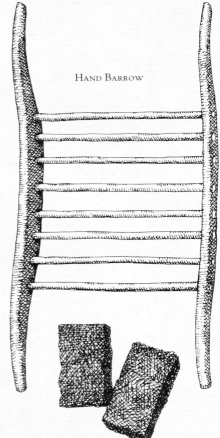

HAND BARROW

PEAT TURFS

HEATING

T IS UNDOUBTEDLY CONVENIENT TO live in a house that has some form of central heating but, unless you have lived with one, it is hard to imagine the *magic* of spending a winter's evening in front of a great, open wood fire. True, it took a strong will on a freezing winter's night to get up, light a candle, and go up the draughty stairway to an icy bedroom, but it didn't do one any *harm* and colds were no more prevalent in pre-central-heating days than they are now. In fact, I've heard it said that central heating has caused more colds to be caught because it lowers the body's natural resistance.

Before the Fire

Living in a house with only a single open fire resulted in a way of life that few people can imagine nowadays. I lived for many years in such a house. Every member of the family *had* to cluster close to the great fire and, in the absence of very good light, it was hard even to follow that solitary activity, reading. Consequently story telling, talking, singing and even reciting verse was the order of the long winter evenings.

My good friend Vernon Jones, who now lives in quite a modern house in Pembrokeshire (although he still has an open fire), told me how he, his parents and his grandfather used to sit around the big "simnai fawr" (large chimney) in their farmhouse in Carmarthenshire, generally with a neighbour or two, simply talking and telling stories. Late at night his great grandfather would come stalking in, having walked five miles from a pub in Carmarthen, and, without saying a word, would pull out his knife and cut a huge slice of salt bacon from a flitch hanging from the ceiling, stick it on the point of his knife and roast it in front of the fire. Four generations—and the neighbours—were united by that fire.

Nowadays great grandpop would be in a "home", grandpop would be living alone in his own bungalow, mum and dad would be silently watching the television and little boy Vernon would be in his own centrally heated room reading comics. As for the neighbours—they would not bother to visit because if they did they would only be subjected to the same TV programmes they could watch on their own telly.

Keeping the Fire Going

The secret of maintaining an open wood fire is to put really enormous logs on it that will smoulder for a week. My predecessor used to drag logs into the house with a horse. One day, when dragging a huge oak log in by this method, the log stuck between the front door posts. They tried to force it through but could get it neither in nor out and had to send a child up to the neighbouring farm to borrow a stronger horse. This animal was able to haul the log out again but meanwhile their own horse had evacuated itself liberally on the kitchen floor!

Bellows were very important for keeping the open fire going—although in parts of Ireland, where boms of anthracite dust and clay (see p.293) were burned, the fire wheel (a hand-turned centrifugal wind pump) was more common (see p.214).

Wood-burning Stoves

Open fires, particularly those fuelled by spitting spruce and fir wood, are hazardous in houses built entirely of wood, and it is therefore not surprising to find that it was in the coniferous regions of Scandinavia and the Alps, that enclosed stoves were first made and developed into things of great beauty: many of them were ornamented with beautiful tiles.

In Russia and Siberia, where the largest continuous forest in the world can be found, the same conditions prevailed and it was there that the bed stove was developed. Anyone who has puzzled over references in Russian books to peasants "going to sleep on the stove" will be interested to know that the author was referring to the bed stove. Made of brick, the bed stove took the form of a massive platform with a fireplace in it, which retained its heat right through the coldest night even if the fire went out.

The American pioneers made their own enclosed stoves out of sheet metal, which no doubt burnt through rapidly. Later they were able to obtain cast-iron stoves made in foundries, which would last for several lifetimes. They tended to make great play with long iron chimneys, which radiated the heat. In severe winters in not very well insulated houses a huge supply of firewood must have been necessary to survive at all. I am told that in the north-eastern woods they would

Storing Firewood
The drier the wood, the easier it was to burn. When the wood was collected it was chopped into manageable logs and stacked in a woodrick. The woodrick roof kept out the rain, allowing the logs to dry out before they were used as fuel.

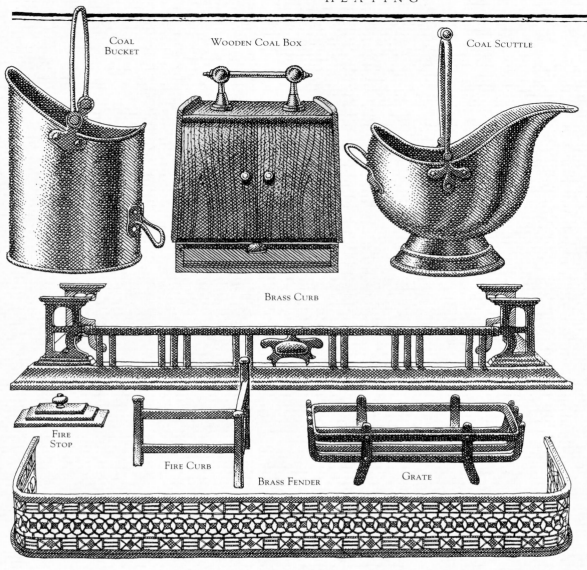

COAL
BUCKET

WOODEN COAL BOX

COAL SCUTTLE

BRASS CURB

FIRE
STOP

FIRE CURB

BRASS FENDER

GRATE

FIRESIDE APPLIANCES
Coal was kept at the side of the fireplace in a coal box or scuttle, which was made of wood, brass or copper. A fender was placed in front of the fire, and a curb at either side of the grate, to confine logs and fallen coals to the hearth. Fire kindlers were dipped in paraffin and used for lighting the fire, and bellows were used to fan the flames. Fire irons were kept within easy reach: tongs and a shovel for lifting the coal, a poker for livening the fire, and a brush for sweeping up the ash.

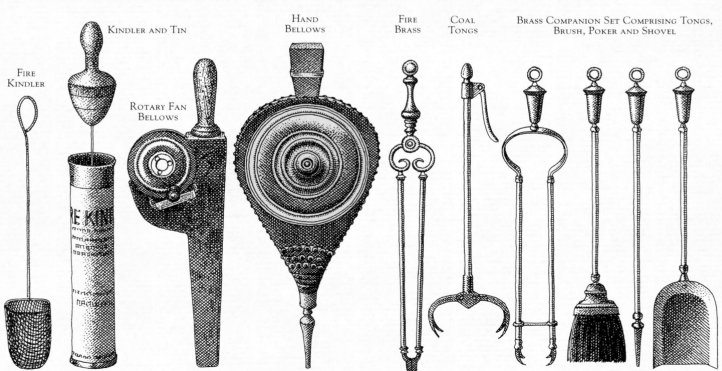

FIRE
KINDLER

KINDLER AND TIN

ROTARY FAN
BELLOWS

HAND
BELLOWS

FIRE
BRASS

COAL
TONGS

BRASS COMPANION SET COMPRISING TONGS, BRUSH, POKER AND SHOVEL

fell trees in the summer and autumn and then wait for the snow before sledding them to the homestead. Storing enough firewood could be a matter of life or death.

CHARCOAL- AND COAL-BURNING STOVES

In Spain, Portugal and parts of Italy charcoal was much used for both cooking and keeping warm. Winters are very cold in Spain and I have often been amazed at the poor heating arrangements there. But the charcoal brazier under the table was not a bad device and one often used.

Anyone who was ever in the British army during the Second World War or before will remember (perhaps with mixed feelings) the "tortoise" stove. This was a pot-bellied, cylindrical monster made of heavy cast iron, which burned coal. It had a hole in the top enclosed by an iron ring and could be made (and frequently was) red hot. A kettle generally stood on top of it, bubbling away. It would keep at least the lucky end of a long wooden army hut very warm.

OIL-BURNING STOVES

A short-lived phenomenon of the early twentieth century was the oil cooking stove. This could be bought singly—a vertical cylinder of thin steel plate with a window, so that you could see the flame—or as part of a range, with as many as four burners and often an oven as well. The design varied: sometimes the burners contained their own oil reservoirs, filled with what the English call paraffin and the Americans, kerosene, and sometimes there was one large reservoir that supplied the lot.

The early burners had one or two simple wicks, which burned yellow and smoked and stank pretty disgustingly. Later burners had circular wicks that allowed the air to pass through the middle of them. Provided that you kept the wicks perfectly trimmed and the whole thing clean, the flames burned blue and were much hotter and less smelly than the early burners. However, they were still smelly enough. If the housewife was not on constant watch the blue flames would overheat, turn red and yellow and before you knew where you were, clouds of choking black smoke would emerge and everything in the room would be covered in minute greasy black smuts. Nevertheless, these stoves were popular in country districts of the United States and in what the English used to call the colonies, until the arrival of bottled gas.

The Primus stove, and its cousins, still lingers in odd corners of the world. It also burns on paraffin but with the Primus compressed air is pumped into the fuel container and the fuel is circulated around its own flame to pre-heat and vaporize it before it emerges from a jet. You must pre-heat the stove itself by burning methylated spirits under the coil and the jet has to

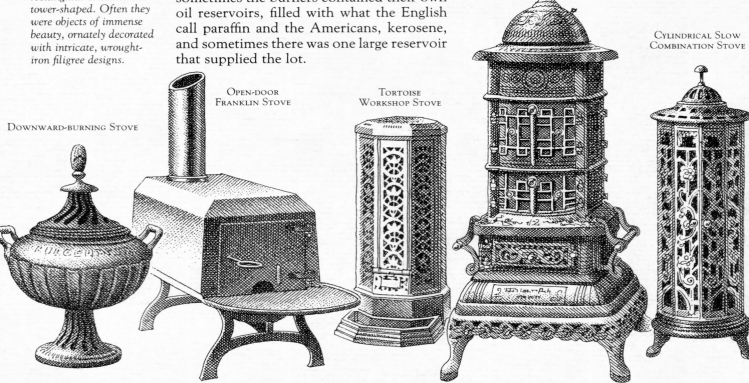

DOWNWARD-BURNING STOVE

OPEN-DOOR
FRANKLIN STOVE

TORTOISE
WORKSHOP STOVE

FREE-STANDING COKE
AND COAL STOVE

CYLINDRICAL SLOW
COMBINATION STOVE

be pricked with a fine wire from time to time to clear it or the flame will go out and the thing will hiss and spit raw paraffin all over you. The Primus is somehow rather an endearing thing to be with in the small cabin or fo'c'sle of a boat. A turn at the wheel or tiller in a freezing wind is made all the more bearable by the friendly hiss and cheering heat of this machine as hot soup bubbles on the jet. The Primus makes up for a lot of struggling with the wheel in my opinion. Sadly, bottled gas has almost completely wiped out the Primus stove and you would be hard put to buy one today.

PORTABLE TABLE
HEATING STOVE

OIL, GAS AND ELECTRIC HEATERS

Oil-burning stoves contained a reservoir of paraffin, which was burned to keep the wick alight. The flame was visible through a window in the side of the stove. Gas heaters operated by the gas being drawn through an open chamber at the base of the heater. This was then mixed with air, which resulted in combustion. In electric heaters, electricity flowed through spirals of wire, or heating elements, to provide heat.

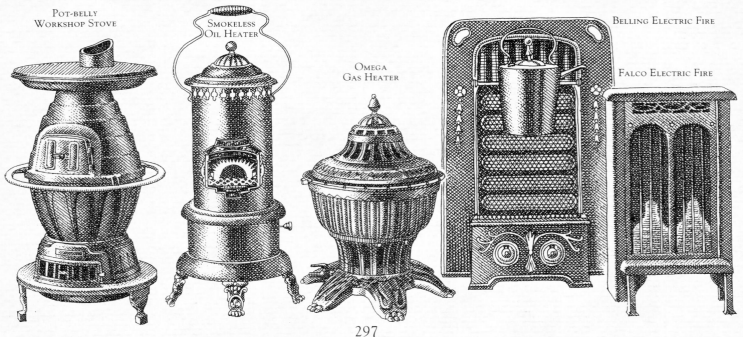

POT-BELLY
WORKSHOP STOVE

SMOKELESS
OIL HEATER

OMEGA
GAS HEATER

BELLING ELECTRIC FIRE

FALCO ELECTRIC FIRE

BEDS & BEDROOMS

THE BED IS PROBABLY THE MOST important piece of furniture in our lives. Most of us were conceived there (although some of us may happen to have been originated on the chaise longue), most of us were born there, and most of us will die there. And, if we know what is good for us, we will spend a third of our lives there.

THE SETTLE-BED
The settle-bed was the forerunner of today's sofa bed. During the day it was used as a sideboard, and at night its seat folded forwards to create a wide trough in which the bed was then made.

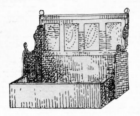

THE VARIETY OF BEDS
Odysseus built the bed that he shared with Penelope with his own hands. He laid out the bedroom around an old olive tree. Then he lopped off the silvery leaves and branches and hewed and shaped the stump into a bedpost. It was the memory of this marriage bed that kept him steadfast when the goddess Calypso offered to make him immortal if he stayed and married her.

In India, the string-bed, or charpoy, is ubiquitous but strangely most people in that country sleep on the floor. The charpoy is often kept on the back porch, or under the shade of a tree, for sitting cross-legged on during the heat of the day. It was an Indian maharajah who owned that strange and

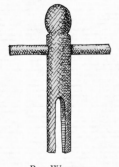

BED WRENCH

BED BASES
Bed bases were either made of ropes, which were stretched between the sides of the bed frame, and tightened with a bed wrench, or laced canvas, which was strung between the head and foot of the bed. The tension could be adjusted by turning a handle at the bed head.

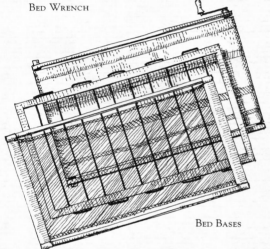

BED BASES

PERSONAL HEATING
Upon arriving at a country inn in England during winter, a warming pan filled with hot ashes was placed between the sheets of your bed to allay *some* of the damp, cold clamminess of an unslept-in bed. If the inn was a good one the landlady would also light a coal fire in the little bedroom fireplace. If not, you suffered the full rigours of the untempered climate.

The stationmasters of many country railway stations used to supply delicate passengers with hot bricks wrapped in flannels to warm their feet when travelling. With a hot brick under your feet, and a rug around your knees, you would be as warm as toast. Hot stone foot warmers and foot stoves were also common.

In Kashmir, high in the mountains, you see women walking about with their hands under their dresses. They look as though they are pregnant, but they are, in fact, clutching small charcoal braziers in front of their tummies.

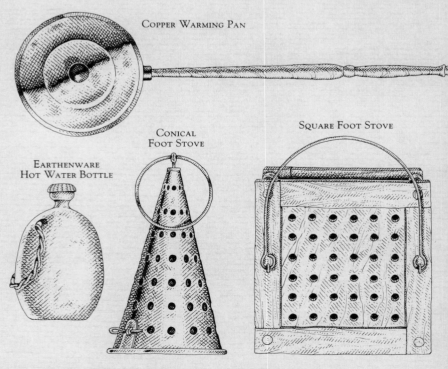

COPPER WARMING PAN

CONICAL FOOT STOVE

SQUARE FOOT STOVE

EARTHENWARE HOT WATER BOTTLE

extravagant bed made of solid silver. It had four life-sized nude female figures painted in realistic colour and detail, fitted with wigs of real hair, and equipped with feathered fans and fly-whisks. The maharajah had merely to lie down and the fanning would automatically commence.

The bed of Louis XIV was held to be so sacred that visitors to the room that contained it had to salute it even if His Majesty was elsewhere. This reminds me of a particularly demanding officer in command of a training camp I was in during the Second World War. So punctilious was he about those of the lesser ranks saluting those of the more important ones that he insisted that we salute the jakes as we passed by if we knew that an officer of higher rank was inside. So we all saluted it anyway just in case.

The stately four-poster bed provided privacy as well as freedom from draughts. Small cottages often had cupboard beds, which folded into the wall after use to look just like the door of a cupboard. I knew an old man in North Pembrokeshire who made cupboard beds to order until recently. In the Highlands of Scotland beds were built into recesses in the wall and shut off by sliding doors. They provided complete privacy as long as you did not mind being half suffocated. There was a disease well known in the Highlands and recognized by doctors and clients alike, which only afflicted husbands. Only ever obliquely referred to by the words, "He's ta'en to his bed", the disease struck only in the dark days of the winter, when the good man, stricken with it, would retire into his box bed together with a bottle of whisky and, despite all the tonics passed to him, remain there until the days grew longer again. It was never fatal.

MATTRESSES

Sailors used to sleep, like countrymen, on feather-bed mattresses if they were lucky or on "donkey's breakfasts" if they were not. These were no more than hessian sacks containing straw or hay. I knew an old "flat" man—a mate on a Mersey flat (the equivalent of the east coast barge, the Humber keel, or the Severn trow)—who saved his vessel from sinking after she had been holed due to a collision with a steamer by stuffing his donkey's breakfast in the hole.

Feather beds, incidentally, were very difficult things to clean. By far the best way was to take the feathers out and dry them, very carefully, in a slow oven or even, if one was available, in a malt kiln (a perforated iron plate) over a slow fire. Feather beds *could* be washed whole but drying them was a hideous business, necessitating endless shaking and fluffing and hanging in the wind. If you didn't dry them thoroughly you would invariably end up with a putrifying mess.

MOVABLE BEDROOMS

Gypsies, who came from India, lived for a couple of centuries in vardos or horse-drawn living wagons—the "gypsy caravans" of the story books. The vardo was simply a movable bedroom, for almost all the cooking was done on the open fire outside. You entered the vardo by climbing gaily decorated steps, placed between the shafts after the horse was taken out. To your left, just through the door, you would see a "Queen" or "Princess" stove—a small, highly ornamented, cast-iron enclosed stove. Such stoves threw out an enormous amount of heat and one would keep the vardo very cosy. In front of you, taking up the whole width of the living space and much of its length, too, would be a great bed, enclosed by shuttering and extremely colourful curtains. Below this bed you would find another bed in which all the children slept, regardless of age or sex: it held an enormous number of children.

STONE FOOT WARMER

HAND WARMER
WITH CHARCOAL
REFILL

HOT WATER
BELLY WARMER

THE BED-WAGON
The bed-wagon was a device for warming damp and cold beds. Like the warming pan, it was inserted into the bedding shortly before the bed was to be used. It consisted of a small brazier which was enclosed in a metal cage.

ADVERSE CONDITIONS
Damp beds were a frequent hazard for early travellers. To overcome the problem they measured the humidity of a bed with a damp bed detector before agreeing to stay at the inn!

CHAMBER POTS

Before houses had indoor bathrooms, a chamber pot was always kept under the bed in case of "emergencies". Its presence must have saved many a long and cold walk to the privy at the bottom of the garden! Far from being plain and inconspicuous, many chamber pots were often very prettily decorated.

DECORATED CHINA POT

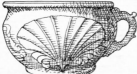

PLAIN MARBLE POT

LEAD-GLAZED EARTHENWARE POT

BOW DESIGN POT

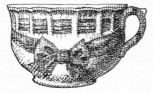

STATIC BEDROOMS

The cottager's bedroom tended to be virtually just that. In addition to the bed there would be a chamber pot, placed underneath it or concealed in a cheaply made piece of wooden furniture with a door, a wash stand with ewer and basin and slop bucket, a few pictures and possibly some poker-work, religious texts or sentimental messages hung on the papered walls.

People who were born in this central-heating age can have no idea of the rigours of an unheated English bedroom in the middle of an old-fashioned English winter! You would often have to break the ice on the washing water in the jug on the wash stand—that is, if you were foolhardy enough to want to wash! You were lucky if you had a feather bed, with a big feather-filled eiderdown, and luckier still if you managed to get your hands on at least one of the brown glazed porcelain hot water bottles that were common in my childhood days.

In wealthier households the bedroom was far more than just a place to sleep. In a lady's bedroom there was always an elaborate and beautiful dressing table, which supported and contained a mass of material most mysterious to a man. There were hairpins, ribands, bows, make-up and face powder, a selection of combs and hair brushes, bottles of scent and other lotions; there might also be mementoes and photographs of members of the family; and there would be mirrors set at angles, so that my lady could view herself from every direction, and, in addition, at least one silver-backed or tortoise-shell-backed hand mirror, too.

In this bedroom you would also probably find an elegant escritoire, or small writing desk, on which my lady would write her diary, compose poetry, and write secret notes to her lovers. She may also have had a couple of chairs set in front of the fireplace, and maybe a small occasional table, in case she wanted to have a little tête-à-tête with a close acquaintance. In larger houses, too, there were often dressing rooms attached to the main bedrooms: perhaps two, one for him and one for her. There would also be a bell pull, which would probably take the form of a tasselled rope hanging down from the ceiling. It was connected by a secret Heath Robinson-like system of ropes and pulleys to the great kitchen or the butler's pantry, or the hall between the two, where there was an array of small bells upon the wall, each struck by little hammers on springs. When the servants heard a bell they would rush to the place to see which little hammer was still swaying about to discover the room in which they were required.

WAKING UP

In 1902 one of the first automatic tea makers was advertised as "the clock that makes tea". It was a fascinating and complicated contraption, consisting of an alarm clock, a copper kettle, a spirit lamp and various springs and levers. However, it functioned efficiently and was very popular. All you had to do was fill the kettle with water the night before and put a couple of spoonfuls of tea leaves in the teapot. The action of the alarm clock ringing in the morning caused a match to be drawn across sandpaper and the spirit lamp to be lit. The spirit lamp heated the water in the copper kettle, which stood on a stand over the lamp. When the water reached boiling point, the kettle was tilted by a spring, and the water was poured into the teapot. The tilting of the kettle triggered the alarm, which rang again to announce that the tea was made.

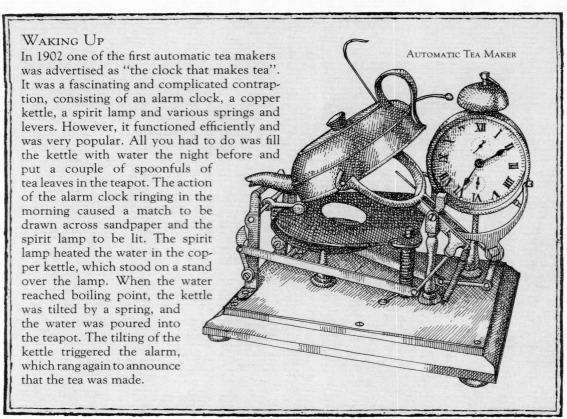

AUTOMATIC TEA MAKER

HOME DOCTORING

P UNTIL THE EARLY NINETEENTH century the still room was a part of every country mansion. In it the lady of the house presided at the distilling of, not only perfumes, spirits and cordials, but also essences of many plants used as remedies for a vast range of ailments. The body of knowledge that the well-bred countrywoman was expected to have in this respect was immense.

HERBALISM

It is remarkable how many of the medicines in the modern pharmacopoeia owe their origins to the old herbalists. Many old country people still use herbs or, more frequently, talk of using herbs. I know an old wind-miller in Suffolk who swears that every part of an elderberry tree is good to cure some disease, and I knew an old gypsy man, God rest his soul, who used to dig up mandrake roots for a living. Some mandrake roots, he assured me, were male and others female, and if you found a specimen of the one there was sure to be a specimen of the other nearby. According to him, when you hauled a root out of the ground it would "shriek like a man in torment, frightening a man's heart to hear it". Mandrakes, he believed, and so did many another old countryman, only grew on the ground over which a man had been hanged.

BEFORE ANTIBIOTICS

The Victorians were usually equipped with all kinds of medical knick-knacks, for they took sickness very seriously. Much of it was self-inflicted: the frequent fainting fits, the "vapours" and the wastings-away that young ladies were prone to then were largely due to the frightfully restrictive clothing fashion forced them to wear. Consumption, or pulmonary tuberculosis, was extremely common among both rich and poor, largely because of an absolute phobia about opening windows to let in fresh air.

I am old enough to remember the thick mat of straw laid on the public highway in front of a house containing a sick person. The straw deadened the noise of the wheels of passing horse-drawn traffic and I remember the sense of foreboding and awe when being driven over such a straw mat. Sickness —a very grave thing indeed!

MEDICAL PARAPHERNALIA
In Victorian times sickness was taken very seriously and houses were equipped with much medical paraphernalia. There were bed pans, throat sprays and brushes, inhalers, eye baths and smelling salts, plus, of course, a well stocked medicine chest.

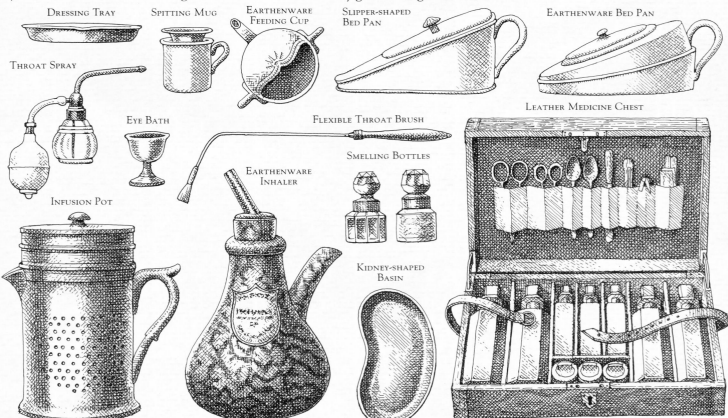

DRESSING TRAY
SPITTING MUG
EARTHENWARE FEEDING CUP
SLIPPER-SHAPED BED PAN
EARTHENWARE BED PAN
THROAT SPRAY
LEATHER MEDICINE CHEST
EYE BATH
FLEXIBLE THROAT BRUSH
SMELLING BOTTLES
INFUSION POT
EARTHENWARE INHALER
KIDNEY-SHAPED BASIN

BATHING & THE JAKES

WHEN I WAS A BOY, IF YOU WERE A guest in any decently appointed household you would always be woken in the morning by a housemaid tripping into the room and opening the curtains to let the sun come streaming in. A cup of tea and a plate of white bread and butter would be placed on the side table, with the bread cut thinner than the butter. A copper jug with a lid hinged to the main part of it and another tiny lid hinged to the spout was set next to the plate. Full of hot water for washing, the jug would have a clean towel draped over it to keep the water warm in case you were reluctant to get out of bed.

BEFORE PLUMBING

Such a house would probably have a perfectly good bathroom, and it was *de rigueur* for the trendy set to take a hot bath every morning. I think this strange idea emanated from the United States, where personal cleanliness was an obsession. Young American ladies were coming to England in increasing numbers in those days and their influence was making itself felt.

The bathroom tended to be a splendid affair. The bath would be long and encased in mahogany, and there would be a network of massive pipes made of galvanized iron or copper that made the place look like the

THE BATH

A popular bath for horsemen was the hip bath, as it eased any saddle-soreness! It was a very comfortable bath to sit in, with its rounded base and armchair shape, and you could dangle your legs over the side and lean back and soak in the steam. A jug of extra hot water was kept alongside the bath for topping up the water as it cooled.

The tin bath was a larger version of the hip bath. Long enough to allow you to immerse your whole body in the water, it required more hot water than the hip bath and was therefore more work for the chambermaid. This oval-shaped bath has remained the standard shape for baths ever since, though styles have altered: some early baths were decorated with engraved bows and clawed feet.

Bath heaters saved the constant tramping up and down stairs with pails of hot water. The gas heater could heat a bathful of cold water in about twenty-five minutes.

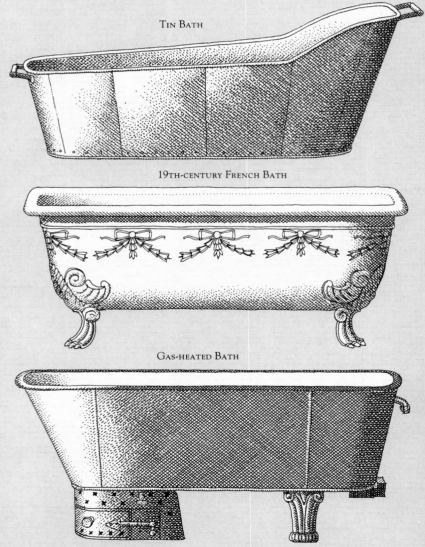

TIN BATH

19TH-CENTURY FRENCH BATH

GAS-HEATED BATH

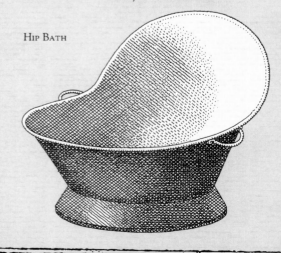

HIP BATH

engine room of a submarine. This was the age of the early gas geysers that would roar and hiss in a terrifying manner and spurt steam like a trans-Canadian locomotive.

Plumbed baths didn't make an appearance until the 1880s, but even after plumbing became fairly common, every big country house was sure to have a hip bath stored away in some box room. Hip baths posed a problem for the guest. For if you availed yourself of a hip bath it meant that some overworked housemaid had to lug several buckets of boiling water up several flights of stairs.

Plumbing took longer to creep into the bedrooms, which were equipped with a hideous wash stand. At least, I thought they were hideous but perhaps my general aversion to washing at all at that age accounted

THE FOLDING BATH
This was ideal for those with a cramped bathing area. When not in use, it looked like a bedroom cabinet.

The front opened outwards to the floor, revealing a zinc-lined bath, water tank, heater and waste water outlet.

for this aesthetic judgement. Most wash stands were simply tables with marble tops to them, the latter sometimes with holes cut out of them to hold a porcelain basin. In the basin would be a big jug, generally also made of porcelain but sometimes of white enamelled steel. This would be filled with cold water and a towel tastefully draped over it. Somewhere on the wash stand there would be a glass flask of drinking water, alas generally stale, with a glass tumbler inverted over it, and under the whole arrangement would be a slop bucket, usually of white enamelled steel. A concave disc with a hole in it covered the top of the slop bucket. You poured your dirty water into the hole, together with any urine from the chamber pot.

Commodes were fairly common in those days, for many a grand house would have only one jakes and that at a great distance from where you were likely to be. The commode was a large and stately mahogany chair. You lifted up the seat to reveal the top of a large pot; you were supposed to sit over this and relieve your nature. I am glad to say that I never availed myself of this device. I never used the potty either if I could possibly reach, and open, the window.

WOODEN SHEDS
Perhaps the most reprinted book in the world next to the Bible is a little book called *The Specialist*. The specialist of the title is an American country carpenter who specialized in building little wooden sheds at the bottom of people's gardens. They had little ventilation holes cut in a variety of shapes, according to the genius of the specialist; these often doubled as spy holes.

These sheds contained a seat with a bucket underneath and a box of earth or ashes next to it. You sprinkled some of this on top of the slowly mounting contents to protect the seat from the flies. Hopefully, before the bucket was full to running over the man of the house would carry it into the garden and tip the contents into a trench, where it would be buried to await the planting of next year's potatoes. It was such bucketfuls that contributed to the burgeoning fertility of country gardens.

There were even simpler methods of disposing of the wastes of the human body. One was used up to a very few years ago in a certain Shropshire farmhouse. The wooden shed was there, together with the seat with a hole in it, but there was no bucket. Spring water oozed out of the ground underneath

THE SHOWER RING
A novel way of taking a shower was to use a shower ring. You stood in the bath, attached the shower nozzles to the bath taps, and slipped the pierced ring over your head. This method of showering prevented any splashing over the walls and floor, and also stopped your hair from getting wet.

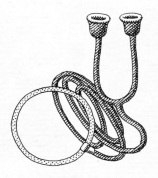

FOOT BATHS

If you got your feet wet while out in the rain, use of a hot foot bath was considered essential to ward off colds and fevers. Foot baths were generally oval-shaped and made of tin. Some had a ledge to rest your feet on while you dried them.

WASH STANDS

Early wash stands were simple wooden frames containing a basin, jug and soap dish. As their design improved, shelves, drawers and mirrors were added, and some wash stands were enclosed in elegant cabinets.

the seat and gently washed whatever was dropped into the hole down the adjoining hillside, where it fertilized the grass. The owners, not without a perverse sense of humour, had installed the snarling head of a stuffed fox hard by the hole and I remember my initial shock as, gingerly lowering my latter end past the head, my eyes slowly becoming used to the darkness, I suddenly became aware of those needle teeth.

FLUSH TOILETS

Sir John Harrington invented a flush toilet as early as 1596, and one was installed for the use of Queen Elizabeth I. Except for the one that disposed of the royal bodily wastes we do not hear of any others until, in 1775, a watchmaker named Alexander Cummings patented a water closet with a "U" bend in the outlet pipe. Because the water always remained in the "U", noisome odours were prevented from rising from below. Joseph Brahmah, a cabinet maker, further improved the design as did another installer of these useful devices, who had the almost unbelievably apt name of Crapper. Many of the very early water closets, with their accompanying overhead cistern, are still in use—some nearly two centuries old—whereas the latest plastic objects are apt to be broken or out of order within weeks of being installed. Certainly not one of them will still be in use in a hundred years' time.

EUPHEMISMS

Euphemism after euphemism has been invented to convey the meaning of the harmless jakes. The one I like most is the "thunder-box", which I believe is a British India expression. "W.C." is simply a shortened form of the words "water closet", which is what the thing was called when water-borne sewage was common in the nineteenth century. Water closets were born much earlier, however.

The monks of the Middle Ages had water closets: they cunningly sited their necessaria over a running stream, downstream, of course, from where they extracted their drinking water. The Cistercians used the water from their stream to drive their corn mill, and sometimes also a sawmill; provide their drinking water; fill their stewpond (in which they reared carp); provide their lavatorium (the place where they washed, *not* what we now call a lavatory); supply their tannery, their laundry and their brewery; and finally act as their sewer. Whether this depressed riparian property values downstream, we are not told.

Another euphemism born in Medieval times was the word "garderobe". This term originated because of the practice of hanging costly furs in the necessaria of castles and palaces: the ammonia gases did a great job of keeping away the moths!

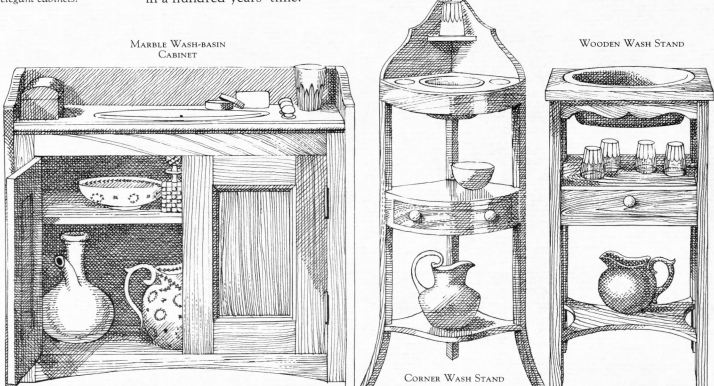

MARBLE WASH-BASIN CABINET

CORNER WASH STAND

WOODEN WASH STAND

THE PRIVY

THE EARTH CLOSET PRECEDED THE WATER closet as a household privy, yet they both followed the same principles of operation, one using dry earth, and the other water. The earth closet consisted of a wide wooden seat with a hole in the middle, under which stood a large pan. Dry earth was stored in a hopper-like container above the seat; a chute led from the hopper to the pan. After using the earth closet, the side lever was pulled, which released a measured amount of earth from the hopper into the pan. The pan was emptied manually. The earth in the pan absorbed and retained any offensive odours, so that the pan could remain unemptied for a week or more!

Water closets were developed from these early privies and are still used today, albeit with some refinements of design. They were usually built against a wall, with boxed-in sides, and often had highly decorated seats and china pans. The more ornate water closets had a sunken, pull-up handle on one side and a sunken box to hold paper on the other. The large cistern was mounted on the wall above the closet; the two were attached by a pipe. A long chain hung from the cistern and was pulled to release a measured amount of water down the pipe to flush the closet pan. The cistern then slowly refilled. Early water closets were often extremely noisy. It was said that if a burglar broke into the house, all he had to do was flush the water and no one would suspect he was there!

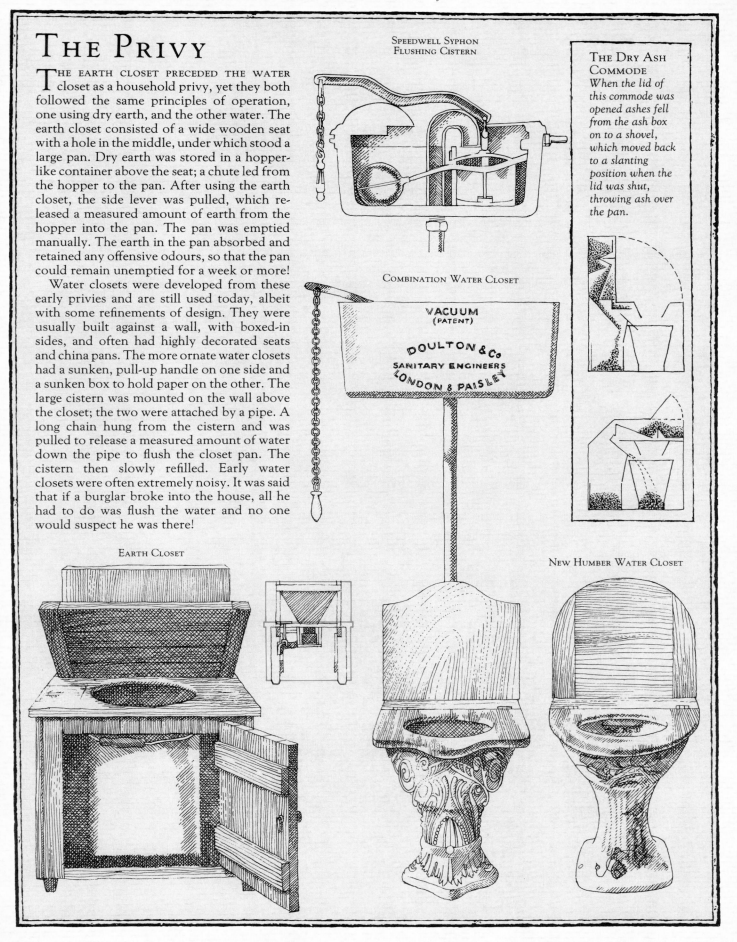

SPEEDWELL SYPHON
FLUSHING CISTERN

COMBINATION WATER CLOSET

VACUUM
(PATENT)

DOULTON & Co
SANITARY ENGINEERS
LONDON & PAISLEY

THE DRY ASH COMMODE

When the lid of this commode was opened ashes fell from the ash box on to a shovel, which moved back to a slanting position when the lid was shut, throwing ash over the pan.

EARTH CLOSET

NEW HUMBER WATER CLOSET

DINING & ENTERTAINING

ONLY TWENTY YEARS AGO I KNEW A wealthy sheep farmer in Wales who used to dine, together with his wife and many children, sitting round one huge bowl of cawl (mutton soup). Everybody was armed with a spoon and they all dipped into the same bowl. Washing up was a speedy business: everyone would swish his spoon in a bowl of water and the washing up was done. It seemed to me an eminently sensible arrangement, much more so than the ludicrous elaborations of the rich in Victorian times, when far more dishes of food were put on the table than anybody would possibly eat and spoons, knives and forks lay in serried ranks beside the plates, upon the snow white table cloth. Reading Victorian menus leads one to suspect that the wealthier people of that era dug their own graves with their knives and forks. They cannot have eaten that much food!

The meals of the working class in Victorian times were a stark contrast to those of the rich. Instead of the lush family breakfast of the rich, in which there was a choice of ham in jelly, chicken, potted shrimp, potted

GOBLETS AND TUMBLERS
Drinking water was always provided at the table, together with vessels such as goblets and tumblers. Goblets were made of thick glass and were heavy to hold. Crystal glass tumblers were made of a finer glass and were easily broken.

CUTLERY CANTEENS
Traditionally, a canteen, or chest, of cutlery was given as a wedding present. As the newly married couple usually had very little in the way of cutlery, the canteen included a set of everything, from knives and forks to mustard spoons and sugar tongs.

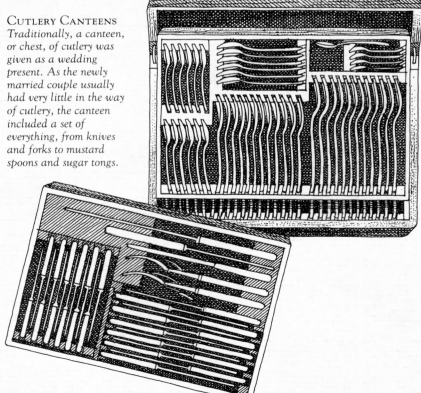

THE DEVELOPMENT OF CUTLERY

In the fifteenth and sixteenth centuries knives were long, narrow and rather skewer-like. Handles were made from amber, ivory, agate or bone, and were elegantly decorated with silver filigree. Forks were introduced in the seventeenth century and, as a result, knife blades became less pointed. The handles also became thicker and stouter. From the eighteenth century onwards, cutlery started to become more utilitarian and much less exquisitely fashioned.

SILVER HANDLES WITH COLOURED ENAMEL 1670

IVORY HANDLES WITH TORTOISE-SHELL PANELS 1710

POTTERY AGATE-WARE HANDLES 1740

RESIN-FILLED SILVER HANDLES 1770

SILVER HANDLES 1805

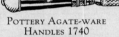

PRESSED-HORN HANDLES WITH BRASS RIVETS 1835

DECORATED IVORY HANDLES 1880

salmon, boiled eggs, hot rolls, toast, muffins, butter, preserves, caramel custard, sponge cake, tea and coffee, the poor ate only bread and butter and always drank tea (see p.241). They ate their main meal of the day at lunch time and called it dinner. However, it bore no relation to the evening dinners of the rich, with their four or five sumptuous courses. Instead, they ate mostly roast mutton, broth and pease pudding. Their supper nearly always consisted of bread and cheese or bread and jam, although occasionally the man might have fish for tea, and at Sunday tea time, as a special treat, there might be enough cake for everyone.

THE CEREMONY OF DINING

In Medieval times in the noble households of Europe the dining table consisted of a simple board on trestles. If the household was very grand they might have several such tables in the Great Hall. The older Oxford and Cambridge colleges feature some magnificent Great Halls. Two long tables run down the length of the hall for the hoi-polloi to sit at and a smaller table is set at right angles to these on a higher level at one end: this is the high table, where the dons and fellows sit. The hall is separated from the kitchen by a passage called the screens across which the food is carried.

The tables were not "laid" with cutlery as we lay tables today, as each diner owned his own nef, or eating utensils, which consisted of a knife, a spoon and a drinking cup. Forks had not yet come into use. The only permanent embellishment on the trestle table was a huge and ornamental salt cellar. You sat below it or above it according to your social status—at least everybody knew where they were. There were no plates as we know them today. Instead, trenchers of bread (see p.223) were used. These were brought in with the first course and given to those at the top of the table or at the high table if there were several. The diners with

bread would cut their trenchers to make as many plates as there were to be courses and lay their own knives and spoons ready to eat. Once they had finished the first course, which at an elaborate feast might consist of a choice of boar head and pudding, game and fish, they would pass their trenchers, now soaked with gravy, to the lesser orders sat further down the table or at the lower tables, who could then start eating.

As each course was brought in—held aloft by servants—it was heralded by a fanfare of trumpets. In the church of St Margaret in King's Lynn, Norfolk, there is a splendid depiction of a magnificent feast on the funereal brass of Robert Braunche, erstwhile Mayor of King's Lynn, who died in 1364. The brass depicts a long board, with eleven guests sitting along one side, and a twelfth guest in such a hurry to get at the victuals that he is leaping over the table! The main course of the meal is a splendid peacock, complete with feathers. Of course, the peacock had been skinned and roasted first, and then the skin placed over the bird again just before it was brought to the table: a glorious sight. At the flank of the board stands a group of musicians.

The scene highlights the difference between the Medieval attitude to the gifts of the good Lord and the attitude shown by many today, who sit down in front of the telly to eat some processed rubbish from the supermarket. Maybe we cannot all have a group of musicians playing to us as we eat our sausages and mash but we could at least approach the whole business of eating with some degree of respect.

HOUSEHOLD DEMOCRACY

It was not until late Tudor times that the fine old tradition of dining in hall—everybody together from the highest to the lowliest in rank—began to be replaced by the lord and lady eating separately from the workers in a "solar"—a private apartment upstairs. This

WARMING PLATES
To warm the plates before a meal, they were stacked on a plate warmer, which was then set in front of an open fire. The four corner rods prevented the plates from falling off the stand and breaking.

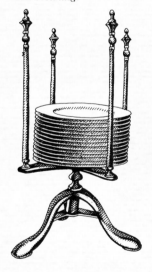

NAPKIN FOLDING
Napkins provided the finishing touch to the set table and if they were untidily or badly folded, the meal could well be ruined! All competent housewives were expected to master the art of napkin folding and produce designs like these with the minimum of fuss.

THE VASE

THE BISHOP

THE ROSE AND STAR

THE MITRE

THE COCKSCOMB

began the end of the tradition of the Great Hall. Cobbett bitterly regretted the tendency in his time (the early nineteenth century) of yeoman farmers to eat with their families in the dining room instead of at the great scrubbed kitchen table with the maids and farm workers, many of whom "lived in". He realized that this practice would mean that the servants would no longer eat the same quality or quantity of food as the master and mistress. He knew that it signalled the end of the true democracy that made English farming so splendid and gave the farmer's boy the chance that befell the hero of the song of the same name:

> They left the lad
> The farm they had
> And their daughter for his bride!

His fears were well-founded: the farm men and lasses have all gone to the cities, the boy who would have been "the farmer's boy" is on the dole, and the master and mistress sit alone in a tiny "modern" kitchen. The big mahogany table in the dining room now gathers dust and the great old farm kitchen is used as a store room.

THE ARRIVAL OF SIDEBOARDS
By Georgian times the master and mistress sat at opposite ends of a wide, heavy table and the other members of the family along each side. The sideboard became common then and often, like the dining table, was made of mahogany. Magnificent silver vessels and dishes, made along classical lines, adorned the table: it was not until the Victorian age that silverware became over-ornamented and vulgar.

Even in my childhood the sideboard was an important feature of the dining room. Breakfast was placed on it every morning, each dish set over a spirit stove to keep it warm for late arrivals. There would be bacon, eggs, sometimes mushrooms, and often kedgeree: a mash-up of fish and rice, which was excellent. Finally there would be a coffee percolator, which would be kept bubbling away throughout breakfast.

As my mother was American she made waffles for Sunday breakfast at the table, using an electric waffle iron. We ate them with maple syrup sent to her from America by her relatives and I remember never being able to eat enough of them. We boys could have gone on eating them all day or, I suppose, until physical illness intervened to save us from bursting.

VICTORIAN DINING ROOM
In a middle-class establishment, while the guests drank sherry and the master and mistress entertained them, the children, dressed in their Sunday best, were expected to help the maid lay the table for dinner; at least, that was what my mother used to tell me.

SERVING AIDS
A dinner carrier kept food hot until it was needed, proving an ideal serving aid for dinner parties and picnics. It was made of china in separate sections which fitted on top of each other, and was specially designed to carry four separate courses.

CANDLE & OIL LIGHTING

I N THE TROPICS THE SUN RISES AT six in the morning and sets at six in the evening and that's that. There is very little twilight. As you go further north or south of the equator, the differential between winter and summer daylight hours increases until you reach those unfortunate latitudes where the sun never sets all summer or rises all winter. To spend a winter in such a place without artificial light would surely drive you mad.

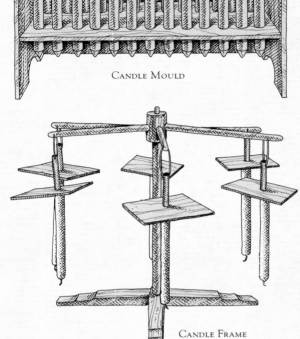

CANDLE MOULD

THE WICK MEASURE
The wick measure was used to cut the candle wicks to an exact length— usually eighteen inches. It was a flat piece of board with an upright rod at one end and a piece of bent wire at the other. The wick was doubled round the rod, held to the wire, and then cut with scissors.

THE LIGHT OF THE OPEN FIRE
You can see to cook and eat, and to perform simple or straightforward tasks by the light of an open fire and you can always pick up a burning stick from the fire and use it as a torch: I have done so many times in the African bush. Until the introduction of oil lamps most African people would use and enjoy the twelve hours of daylight, gather around the fire for three or four hours and then sleep for the rest of the night. At the time of the full moon they would sometimes dance all night. Even without a full moon, a leaping fire of dried sticks sends out enough light for plenty of dancing.

CANDLE FRAME

PRODUCTION LINE
An economical method of candle making was to dip several wicks at a time, setting up a kind of production line. As some were being dipped, others were hardening on a makeshift drying rack. The consistency of the tallow was important to the final result: too hard and the candles would crack as they dried; too soft and they would splutter as they burned. The method of making the wick was also crucial. If the wicks were plaited and then flattened out they tended to burn to one side of the candle. In this way, as the wick burned and collapsed, the charred portion did not smother the flame.

DIPPING AND MOULDING CANDLES
The most common type of candle was the dipped candle, made by dipping and redipping a wick in hot fat until the candle was the right size. These candles were hung on a candle frame to dry. Moulded candles were less laborious to make. A wick was simply inserted in the mould, hot wax added and the candle left to set.

THE DEVELOPMENT OF RUSHLIGHTS

Further north sustained indoor lighting was essential, particularly if people wanted to read (or paint pictures on cave walls). The first lamps were probably made from stones or rocks with natural depressions in them. The dips would be filled with animal fat, and a rush or a chewed twig laid in the fat and lighted. People learned to press oil out of plants, render fat from animals and, eventually, extract it from fish, whales and even sea birds. Early crafted lamps, found by archeologists in nearly every dig, were made of pottery, soap stone and other soft, natural stones. Sometimes they found lamps made of such beautiful hard stones as quartz, serpentine and lapis lazuli. They all had a small reservoir for the oil or fat and a lip on which the wick could be laid.

A natural progression from these simple lamps was the traditional rushlight. Rushes can be found in abundance. Peeled of their hard outer skin the inside pith makes a fine absorbent wick. If you peel a rush nearly all the way round, leaving a strip of skin the length of it to give it sufficient strength, and dip it in hot animal fat, once it is cooled you have a primitive candle. If you then devise a grip to hold it—perhaps a paperclip mounted on an upright stick—you have illumination. You can even read by the light of several of them. A rushlight fifteen inches long will burn for half an hour. They smoke and smell of burning fat but in 1700 they probably didn't mind, especially as it was the one light that was absolutely free: everyone who killed a pig or a fat sheep occasionally, or who could scrounge some rancid dripping, could have rushlights for nothing. Mutton fat made the best rushlights; pig fat was awful.

THE ARRIVAL OF CANDLELIGHT

Candles were certainly used in Elizabethan times and noblemen attending a banquet at the French court of Louis XIV used to carry a candle in order to appear subservient to the king. The first candles were often made by dipping a rush wick into fat, drawing it out for the fat to cool, then dipping it in again, and so on until the required thickness was reached. Alternatively the wicks were hung and hot fat was repeatedly poured over them. Occasionally they were moulded in a long rounded mould with a small hole in the closed end. You poked the wick into this hole and then simply poured in the fat from the other end and allowed it to cool.

When cotton began to be imported from hot countries it replaced rush wicks and linen was sometimes used, too. At first, bleached, twisted yarn was used but this had the disadvantage that it stuck above the candle fat as the fat burnt and had to be constantly clipped with scissors or candle snuffers. Eventually it was discovered that if the cotton wick was braided it curled over and was consumed in its own fire. Modern candles have braided wicks.

Beeswax makes the finest candles and candles burnt in churches have long been made of beeswax. This partly explains why monks obtained a reputation for being jolly. For to get beeswax they had to keep bees,

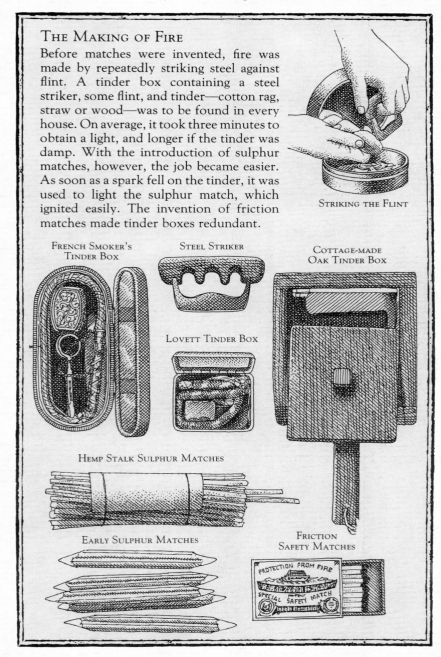

THE MAKING OF FIRE

Before matches were invented, fire was made by repeatedly striking steel against flint. A tinder box containing a steel striker, some flint, and tinder—cotton rag, straw or wood—was to be found in every house. On average, it took three minutes to obtain a light, and longer if the tinder was damp. With the introduction of sulphur matches, however, the job became easier. As soon as a spark fell on the tinder, it was used to light the sulphur match, which ignited easily. The invention of friction matches made tinder boxes redundant.

STRIKING THE FLINT

FRENCH SMOKER'S TINDER BOX

STEEL STRIKER

COTTAGE-MADE OAK TINDER BOX

LOVETT TINDER BOX

HEMP STALK SULPHUR MATCHES

EARLY SULPHUR MATCHES

FRICTION SAFETY MATCHES

CANDLESTICKS AND RUSHLIGHT HOLDERS

Candle and rushlight holders were invaluable. Rushlight holders were made of wrought iron, and held the taper of rushes firmly in the middle by spring jaws mounted on a stand. Candlesticks had small sockets in which the candles were inserted. Rushlight holders often had fittings for candles as well. As light was needed principally for getting up before dawn and going to bed after dark, many candle holders were designed specifically for bedroom use. Known as chamber-candlesticks, they had handles and extinguishers. For the kitchen, there were broad-based candlesticks, as these could not be knocked over very easily. The upright, columnar candlesticks, made of pewter or brass, were mainly used at the table. Wealthier families possessed silver candlesticks bearing one or two branches; these were known as candelabra.

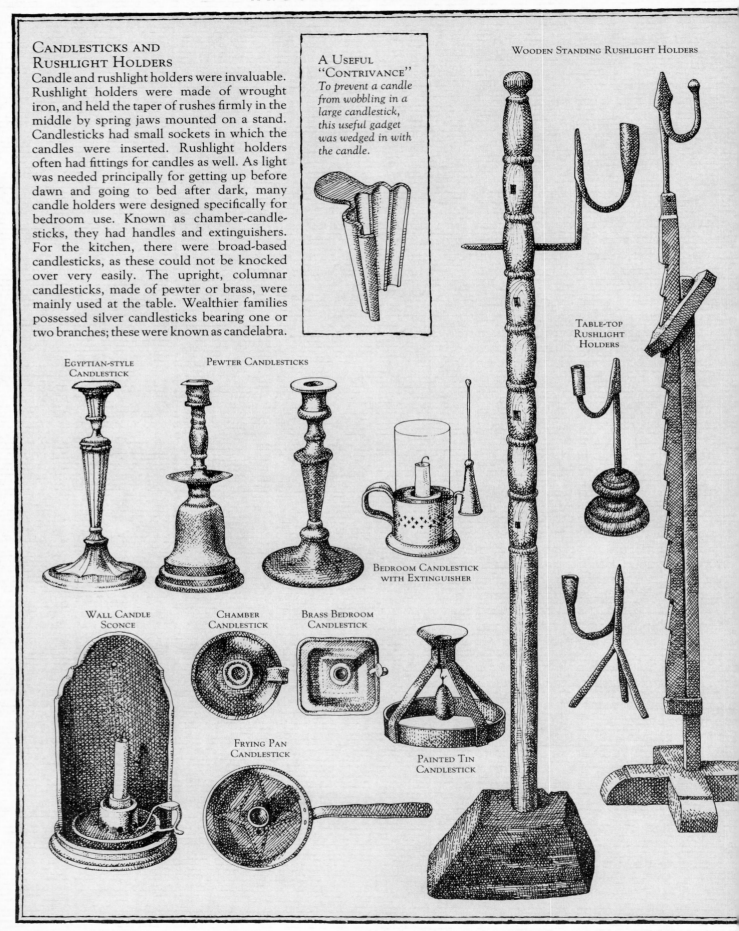

A USEFUL "CONTRIVANCE"
To prevent a candle from wobbling in a large candlestick, this useful gadget was wedged in with the candle.

WOODEN STANDING RUSHLIGHT HOLDERS

TABLE-TOP RUSHLIGHT HOLDERS

EGYPTIAN-STYLE CANDLESTICK

PEWTER CANDLESTICKS

BEDROOM CANDLESTICK WITH EXTINGUISHER

WALL CANDLE SCONCE

CHAMBER CANDLESTICK

BRASS BEDROOM CANDLESTICK

FRYING PAN CANDLESTICK

PAINTED TIN CANDLESTICK

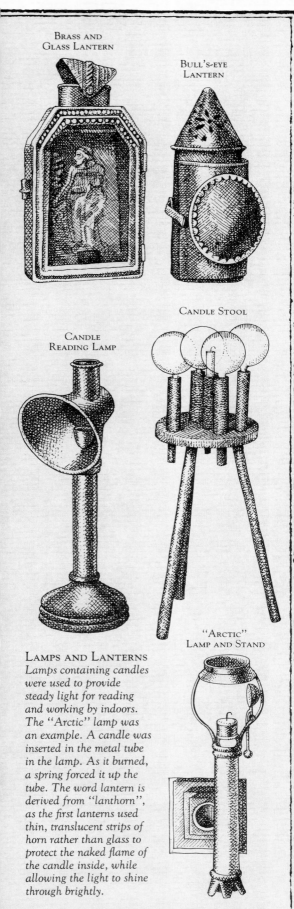

BRASS AND
GLASS LANTERN

BULL'S-EYE
LANTERN

CANDLE STOOL

CANDLE
READING LAMP

"ARCTIC"
LAMP AND STAND

LAMPS AND LANTERNS
Lamps containing candles were used to provide steady light for reading and working by indoors. The "Arctic" lamp was an example. A candle was inserted in the metal tube in the lamp. As it burned, a spring forced it up the tube. The word lantern is derived from "lanthorn", as the first lanterns used thin, translucent strips of horn rather than glass to protect the naked flame of the candle inside, while allowing the light to shine through brightly.

and to use the surplus honey they had to make mead: the rest follows. Paraffin wax, distilled from coal and oil shales, was first made in the United States by Abraham Gesner in 1846. The use of this made the candle a much cheaper and therefore much more common article.

A candle becomes shorter as it burns, of course, and lamps were soon made with a spring set below the candle to push the candle gradually upwards, so that its flame was always at the same height. The hole through which the candle was pushed was slightly smaller than the candle itself, so it was only as the top of the candle was consumed that it could be pushed through. I once had a pair of trap lamps that worked on this principle. I drove many miles of roads on dark nights with them, although the amount of light they shone on the road in front of the horse was—well—minimal.

THE DEVELOPMENT OF OIL LAMPS

The mighty Greenland whale of the Arctic and north Atlantic was nearly made extinct by the demand for lamp oil in northern Europe almost two centuries ago. Between 1753 and 1850 an estimated 2,761 whales were brought into one little whaling port alone and boiled down for lamp oil. Even the street lamps of some Dutch and English cities were lit by the oil of the whale. Oil from rape seed filled many a lamp as whales became scarcer, and vegetable oils were used before the widespread use of mineral petroleum in 1859.

The original oil lamp had a closed reservoir for the oil with a wick sticking out of the top. The wick hardly burned at all, as the oil, constantly rising by capillary action, cooled it. As the oil burnt, and smoked and stank, some light was emitted. The wick gradually wore away and you had to "turn it up" by operating a handle.

In the early 1780s, a Frenchman named Ami Argand invented a circular wick which allowed air to pass up the middle of it and resulted in a brighter flame. But the major improvement of oil lamps came with the invention of the glass chimney by Count Rumford. A draught was forced up the wick, causing the flame to burn bright yellow instead of smoky red. This invention was more beneficial to human civilization than the motor car or the aeroplane as, for the first time, ordinary people, who could not afford to buy batteries of candles, could read in the winter time.

CANDLE STORAGE
Candles were kept in tin or wooden candle boxes which hung horizontally on the wall. They were usually cylindrical in shape and had a hinged lid for easy access.

The final breakthrough in oil lighting came with the invention in 1884, by a German named Dr Karl Auer, of the incandescent mantle. The mainspring of this cunning device was a little balloon of fabric impregnated with asbestos. The fabric was quite flexible to begin with—like silky cloth. You simply put it in the lamp, lit it and, behold, the fabric burnt away, leaving a balloon of brittle white asbestos. A moth could destroy this delicate stem (in which case you would have to buy another one) but if nothing touched it and nothing shook it, the asbestos would become white hot and give out a brilliant white light as strong as that emitted by a 100-watt electric light.

ALADDIN AND TILLEY LAMPS

The Aladdin lamp was the primary illuminating lamp of the nineteenth century. Hanging Aladdins swung in gimbles from the cabin tops of sailing ships and barges; resplendent table ones stood on every Victorian table (whose owner could afford one). Overheating was a problem with these. When this happened flames shot out of the top of the chimney and tiny black smuts covered the whole room.

I don't have to delve back very far in my memory to recall the business of lamp filling, mopping up the inevitable spillages, wick trimming (if the wick was not perfectly trimmed it smoked and stank to high heaven), washing glass chimneys, smashing them and buying new ones, because our house was wired for electricity only the year before last. Cleaning oil lamps was a time-consuming business. You had to take apart the lamp and wash inside with soda dissolved in water and the chimney had to be wiped at least once a day, as you could lose a considerable part of the light through having a dirty chimney window.

I still have a brace of Tilley lamps, those fine pressure lamps that you pumped up, and which hissed as they gave light. Occasionally, too, the oil inside would fail to vaporize and great red flames would arise within, belching vast amounts of smoke, so that their glasses became sooted up. However, when in good order and using good paraffin, your Tilley would emit a brilliant light and would never go out even outdoors in a gale. I have gutted fish by their light on the deck of a small fishing boat in a gale in the south Atlantic. I'll tell you a secret, though. It's very nice to be able simply to switch on an electric light!

WIRE COIL NIGHT LAMP

LAMP WITHOUT A FLAME
This night light produced a small glow of light, not from a flame, but from a red-hot wire coil, wrapped around its wick. The wick was lit for a few minutes to heat the wire coil, and then the flame was extinguished. The wire stayed red and glowing due to the heated vapours of spirits of wine that rose from the base of the lamp.

LIGHTING WITH OIL
The earliest oil lamps were shallow earthenware dishes containing oil and a wick of twisted flax, which rested in a pointed lip at one end of the dish. Crusies, or betty lamps, were similar except that they were usually made of iron and had a tray underneath to catch the dripping oil. Crusies burned fish oil and were hung on the wall. When whale oil became too expensive to use, lard was discovered to be a good substitute and many lamps were designed specifically for burning this fuel. Half a pound of lard burned for sixteen hours! As oil lamps became more sophisticated and varied in design, so they became more popular. There were ornate hanging lamps, small portable lamps, free-standing and table-top lamps, made of tin, iron, copper, pottery and brass.

BETTY LAMP AND TRAMMEL

ADJUSTABLE MOUNTED BETTY LAMP

HANGING BETTY LAMP

CRUSIE FOR BURNING FISH OIL

Brass Sliding
Balance Ball

Hanging Lard
Oil Solar Lamp

Bronzed Suspension Lamp

Lard-burning
Tin Lamp

Oil Lantern
with Shoe

Twin Colza
Oil Lamp

Whale Oil
Lantern

Brass
Suspension Lamp

Bull's-eye Pewter Lamp

Brass
Spirit Lamp

Pewter Oil Lamp
with Drip Tray

Glass and Silver
Spirit Lamp

GAS & ELECTRIC LIGHTING

THE INCANDESCENT GAS BURNER
The first domestic gas burner was the flat-flame burner, which produced flames of from one to three candle power per cubic foot of gas consumed. Baron von Welsbach's incandescent gas burner increased the amount of candle power, while at the same time retaining the soot.

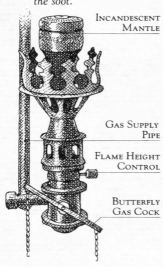

INCANDESCENT MANTLE

GAS SUPPLY PIPE

FLAME HEIGHT CONTROL

BUTTERFLY GAS COCK

THE ELECTRIC SOCKET
Domestic electric lighting was much safer than gas, as there was no naked flame, and it was much cleaner, as there was no smoke; the flex made it possible to put lamps wherever they were needed.

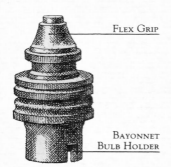

FLEX GRIP

BAYONNET BULB HOLDER

 ELIA FIENNES, THE DIARIST, RODE from Wigan to Warrington in 1698, and her guide "set ye water in ye well on fire and it burned just like spirits and continued a good while..." Thirty years before that a man named Thomas Shirley described how a well near Wigan took fire when approached by a candle. These were the very first references to natural gas.

COAL GAS LIGHTS
Apparently, as early as 1782, curious noblemen discovered that you could obtain an inflammable gas by heating coal. For a long time they put this discovery to no practical use, but in 1792 we hear that one William Murdoch lit his own house at Redruth in Cornwall with gas made from coal. By 1807 a German called Winsor lit up part of Pall Mall with coal gas: the first mention of gas street lighting. It was not until 1812 that the first Gaslight and Coke Company received a charter in London; after that gas lighting spread quite quickly throughout the towns and cities of the land. Piped gas never penetrated the countryside, and the large country house in which I was brought up had an acetylene gas plant: a noisome room tacked on to the house, containing large steel cylinders encrusted with carbide. Water dripped into the carbide, causing it to release the gas, which was then distributed throughout the house by iron pipes.

PORTABLE GAS LAMPS
Carbide and water provided the gas for the lamps of bicycles, motor cycles, and motor cars for several decades. Our great ambition when boys was to be challenged by a policeman (he on foot of course) as we careered past him on our bicycles in the darkness without any lights. He was to shout after us: "Where are your lights?" To which our triumphant reply was to be: "Next to our livers!" ("Lights" is the term for animal lungs.) Although I cycled many a mile through country lanes without lights this final felicity never befell me.

My old Triumph motor bike had an acetylene headlight. On a smooth road the light would shine only dimly but when you hit bumps and potholes it would brighten considerably. The agitation would shake

down more water into the carbide. I came upon carbide lamps again when I worked down a copper mine in northern Rhodesia just before the Second World War: each of we "whiteys" carried one. A little naked flame spurted out of the middle of a silvered concave mirror: it was a touch better than the candles that the black miners had to put up with. The famous Davy lamp used in British coal mines worked on the same principle, but the flame in this was protected by a piece of wire gauze because of the presence of fire damp—the inflammable gas found in coal mines.

PIPED GAS
Gas lighting, although used in mills and factories for many decades, and in street lights widely, did not really penetrate the homes of many people until around the 1880s. The fact was that it wasn't really much good until Dr Auer invented his incandescent mantle (see p.314). Until then gas lights gave out as much smoke and stink as they did light.

Widespread gas lighting for homes was short-lived. From the beginning of the twentieth century electricity made great strides and finally eclipsed its chief rival. Nowadays you might find some bottled gas lighting in some yachts and caravans, and perhaps in a few remote country houses.

THE SLOW SPREAD OF ELECTRICITY
Although electric arc lamps were available from the middle of the nineteenth century, it was not until the invention of the first practical incandescent light bulb in 1879 by Sir Joseph Swan and Thomas Edison that electric lighting was taken seriously. By the 1890s, many streets and large buildings were being lit by electricity but few people could afford to have electric lighting installed in their homes. The perfection of metal filament lamps in 1911 made it cheaper but cable laying and installation was still a costly business and electricity was still confined to the rich. Not until the standardization of the generation of electricity did electric lighting become cheap enough for everyone to have it installed. However, once it took off, electric lighting soon outstripped gas in popularity, for it was clean, silent and emitted no nasty smells.

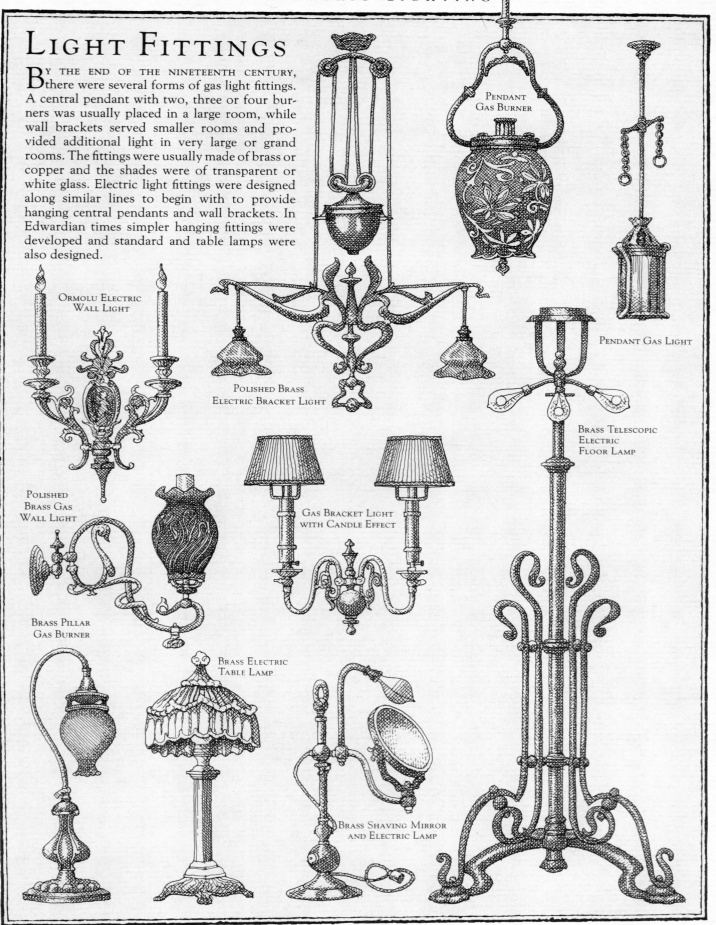

LIGHT FITTINGS

By the end of the nineteenth century, there were several forms of gas light fittings. A central pendant with two, three or four burners was usually placed in a large room, while wall brackets served smaller rooms and provided additional light in very large or grand rooms. The fittings were usually made of brass or copper and the shades were of transparent or white glass. Electric light fittings were designed along similar lines to begin with to provide hanging central pendants and wall brackets. In Edwardian times simpler hanging fittings were developed and standard and table lamps were also designed.

PENDANT GAS BURNER

PENDANT GAS LIGHT

ORMOLU ELECTRIC WALL LIGHT

POLISHED BRASS ELECTRIC BRACKET LIGHT

BRASS TELESCOPIC ELECTRIC FLOOR LAMP

POLISHED BRASS GAS WALL LIGHT

GAS BRACKET LIGHT WITH CANDLE EFFECT

BRASS PILLAR GAS BURNER

BRASS ELECTRIC TABLE LAMP

BRASS SHAVING MIRROR AND ELECTRIC LAMP

CLEANING

BRUSHES AND BROOMS
Cleaning was considered by many to be a moral duty. Indeed, there was a different brush available for every cleaning task in the house. Stiff-bristled brushes were used for scrubbing floors and carpets, while a range of soft-haired brushes was used on furniture, hearths and banisters, and for light dusting. There were also different types of broom that could be used, depending on how dirty the floor was!

HERE ARE STILL CABINS IN Ireland with earth floors. These are generally swept clean every day with a birch broom and become as hard (nearly) as concrete. They cannot be wetted or they turn to mud, so the only way of cleaning them is to sweep them. In India even better floors are made by laying a mixture of cow dung and mud. These, too, are fine if kept swept.

SWEEPING THE FLOORS
The birch broom, or brooms of heather, ling or other vegetation, has held sway to the present day. In England there still exist "broom squires"—people whose sole source of livelihood is derived from making besom brooms. Besoms are marvellous for sweeping the rough floors in most barns, out buildings, or yards, and for spreading the worm casts on lawns (instead of resorting to the dastardly use of worm poisons to destroy what is really the gardener's best ally; to say nothing of murdering the birds which eat the poisoned worms).

As artificial floors began to take the place of earth floors, brooms became more sophisticated. The harder and smoother the floor the softer the broom you need to clean it with. Hogs' bristle brooms became popular (the coat of arms of the Brush-makers' Guild had wild boars as supporters): most of the hogs' bristles were imported from Russia and eastern Europe.

The widely held opinion that people in former ages kept their houses in a filthy condition is, like so many other popular beliefs, mostly nonsense. True, different

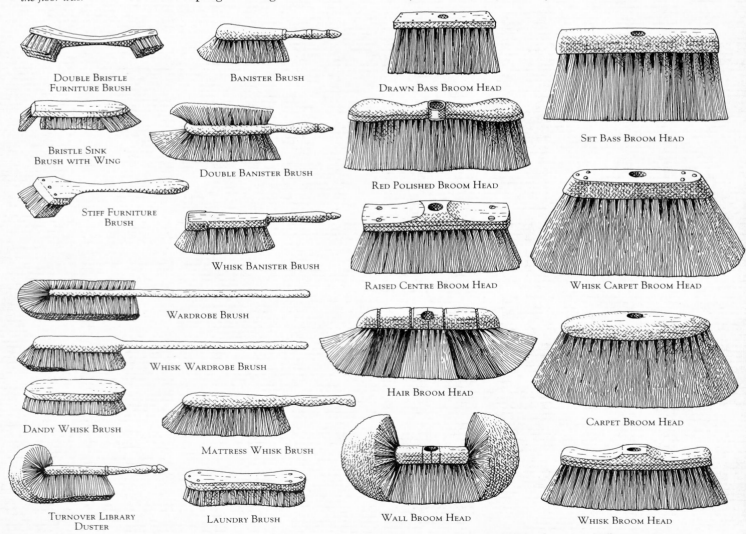

DOUBLE BRISTLE FURNITURE BRUSH

BRISTLE SINK BRUSH WITH WING

STIFF FURNITURE BRUSH

WARDROBE BRUSH

WHISK WARDROBE BRUSH

DANDY WHISK BRUSH

TURNOVER LIBRARY DUSTER

BANISTER BRUSH

DOUBLE BANISTER BRUSH

WHISK BANISTER BRUSH

MATTRESS WHISK BRUSH

LAUNDRY BRUSH

DRAWN BASS BROOM HEAD

RED POLISHED BROOM HEAD

RAISED CENTRE BROOM HEAD

HAIR BROOM HEAD

WALL BROOM HEAD

SET BASS BROOM HEAD

WHISK CARPET BROOM HEAD

CARPET BROOM HEAD

WHISK BROOM HEAD

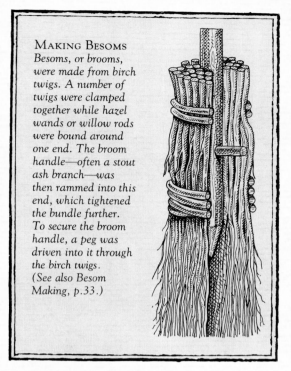

MAKING BESOMS
Besoms, or brooms, were made from birch twigs. A number of twigs were clamped together while hazel wands or willow rods were bound around one end. The broom handle—often a stout ash branch—was then rammed into this end, which tightened the bundle further. To secure the broom handle, a peg was driven into it through the birch twigs. (See also Besom Making, p.33.)

standards of cleanliness befit different types of house. I lived for eight years in a cottage in Suffolk that had brick floors. Brick is porous and if the floors were scrubbed too often with water they would remain wet for ages. A dry sweep every day with a broom was sufficient to keep the place perfectly habitable. Glazed tile floors can be washed as often as you like, of course, as they do not absorb water, and wooden floors such as parquet can easily be given a high polish.

In Medieval times the sensible practice of strewing the floor with rushes, or sweet-smelling herbs and grasses, was a very clean habit, and far less wasteful of resources than at first appears, for cow byres or pig-sties were inevitably attached to the Medieval country house and these needed to be heavily littered with dry vegetable matter. So the house rushes were raked up fairly frequently and simply thrown to the animals. They turned them into good farm-yard manure, which fertilized the land.

A DAILY CHORE
Every morning housewives swept their backyards clean and whitened their doorsteps with hearth-stone. Those housewives who were especially diligent also scrubbed their windowsills, as well as the pavement immediately in front of their houses.

HAND WHISK BRUSH

DUSTING BRUSH

POLISHED BRASS OVAL BRUSH

TOY SLIPPER BRUSH

TELESCOPIC HEARTH BRUSH

TOY HEARTH BRUSH

LARGE BRASS HEARTH BRUSH

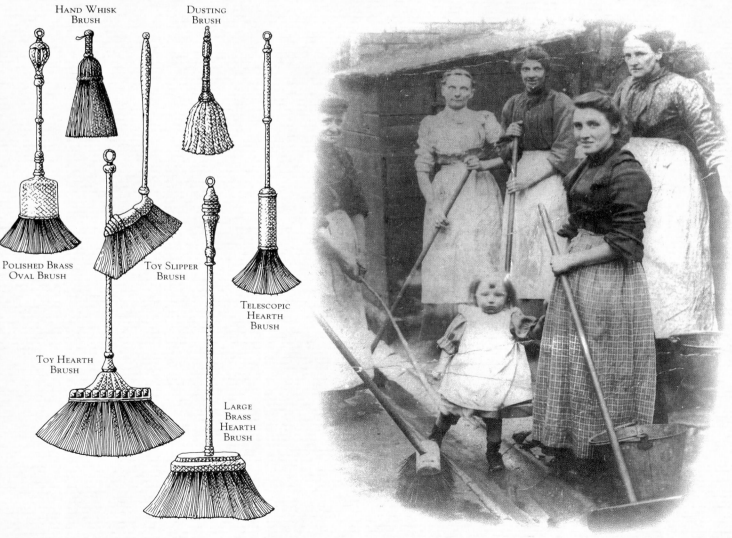

Sawdust, too, is a very hygenic floor covering. Even now all the best butchers use it on their floors and so do many of the best pubs. In times of old, kitchen floors and the like were often sanded (see p.235), and there were such people as sand men. They travelled round the towns with their donkeys loaded, and cooks and housewives bought sand off them to sprinkle on the floor. Traditionally the sand was renewed once a week and the old swept out with the dirt.

The Coming of the Vacuum Cleaner

The electric carpet sweeper or vacuum cleaner was predated by the mechanical carpet sweeper. In 1876 Melville Bissell of Grand Rapids, Michigan, invented the first carpet sweeper; he called it the Grand Rapids and it swept, in both senses of the word, America. The English equivalent was manufactured by Thomas Ewbank in 1889.

The first practical private household vacuum cleaner was invented by J. Murray Spangler in Ohio in 1907. The prototype comprised a tin can, a broomstick, a flour sack and an electric motor. He sold the rights to William Hoover shortly afterwards and Hoover brought it to England in 1912, where by 1927 a thousand a week were being sold and the verb "to hoover" was born.

I well remember, as a small boy, living in a rented house in London for a few months. While we were there a man knocked on the door and came in carrying a strange device. My mother immediately summoned the housemaid, who looked on with wonder, as no doubt I did, too.

With horror I watched as the man took a bag off the back of the device and shook a whole load of filthy dust on the carpet! Then, before anybody had time to summon the police, he put the bag back on again and plugged the device into a socket in the wall. Straight away it started humming and the pile of dust was gone in an instant! Not content with this he lifted a corner of the carpet and dumped some dirt underneath it. Behold! His device sucked the dirt up right through the carpet. My mother did not need any further demonstrations. She bought the device straight away and there and then we entered the Hoover age.

This happened in the early 1920s at the very same time that we bought our first wireless set, another magical machine. It had a crystal that you had to "tickle" with a cat's whisker (a fine wire). You had to listen to it through ear-phones and when, if you were

(see p.235)

Spring Cleaning
In the nineteenth century spring (and autumn) cleaning really did mean cleaning the whole house. Carpets were taken outside and beaten and shampooed, curtains and covers were washed, paintwork was scoured and washed, ceilings were rewhitened, glass, furniture and ornaments were polished: all in all, a monumental task.

The Perfect Carpet-beater
Before the invention of vacuum cleaners, carpets and rugs were taken outside and beaten to get rid of the dust. This carpet-beater, made from woven cane, was so effective that its design was left unchanged for over a hundred years!

THE EFFECT OF COAL
The use of coal as a fuel increased the amount of cleaning housewives had to do. As well as the smoke and smuts produced when coal was burning in the grate, everything was covered in coal dust when the coal was delivered.

CARPET SWEEPERS
The mechanical carpet sweeper consisted of a brush, fitted inside a box, which rotated as the sweeper was rolled backwards and forwards over the carpet, sweeping dirt into the box. Some sweepers also had "side whiskers" for cleaning skirting boards.

lucky, you had "tickled" it correctly, you would hear a very faint voice saying "2LO calling!" Then if you were even luckier you might hear some ghostly music: it was superb.

SCRUBBING AND SCOURING

In addition to the sand men there were men who hawked whitening stone, brownstone, holy stone (so-called because it was supposed to be stone taken from the walls of old churches), and donkey stone (a proprietary reconstituted stone with the figure of an ass impressed on top of it). All these substances were used for scrubbing, scouring and colouring the indoor environment. Stone doorsteps in towns had to be rigorously scrubbed very early every morning, and then often whitened with chalk or white stone. This practice served as a sign to the outside world that the housewife (or her

servants) was a hard-working moral woman without a spot on her character. This almost excessive scouring and scrubbing was all, no doubt, part of the Protestant work ethic, although there was a practical reason for all this cleanliness, too. In pre-vacuum cleaner days fleas were ubiquitous; lice, too, were common and so was the disgusting bed bug. They all thrive in dust and dirt. So keeping the place reasonably clean was essential.

MAKING POLISHES AND POLISHING

Before the age of proprietary polishes people used to make their own. For example, you could make a metal polish with two ounces of rottenstone, one ounce of emery powder, half a pound of soft soap, one teaspoon of vinegar, one teaspoon of olive oil and half a pint of water. The mixture had to be boiled for three hours.

One cannot imagine that there was much polishing to do in the Medieval household, except perhaps in connection with arms and armour. The simple trestle table did not need much polishing, the floor was probably strewn with rushes, and there was not a great deal of other furniture. When polishing did come into vogue, beeswax was the thing. Even today there is nothing to beat it and it is sad that it is almost unobtainable. Beeswax has always been a most desirable commodity and its present dearth is due to the invention of the modern bee hive, which conserves the wax that the bees make so that they can use it again next year. In the old days of the straw or rush bee skeps (see p.255) the honey cells of the bees, which are made of wax, were destroyed in the annual extraction of the honey, and could not be used again by the bees. Instead, the bee-keeper used it for making candles and polish. It is a magical substance and has a nice smell. Mrs Beeton recommends mixing three ounces of common beeswax with one ounce of white wax, one ounce of curd soap, one pint of turpentine and one pint of boiled water to make a furniture paste. For polish she recommends mixing equal portions of turpentine, vinegar, spirits of wine and linseed oil. She doesn't mention the elbow grease!

All English schoolboys of the cricket-playing classes come in contact with linseed oil early in life when they are exhorted to put it on their cricket bats. Many of we prep-school boys thought it had magical powers. I was always swamping my cricket bat with it, although it didn't improve my performance at the wicket in the least. Linseed oil is a product of the flax plant (*Linum usitatissimum*). To make the best linen, flax should be pulled before the seed is ripe, but you can wait until the seed is ripe and harvest the flax for both its seed and stem. In fact, much flax was, in better times than these, grown especially for seed. The oil was crushed out of the seed to be used in polishes, varnishes and substances for preserving wood, while the residue was made into that marvellous stuff, linseed cake, the best foodstuff there is for putting a bloom on beef cattle.

As for turpentine, another common ingredient of polishes, it is obtained from the sap of coniferous trees. Originally it came from the terebinth tree (*Pistacia terebinthus*).

Shellac was also much used in polishes and in varnishes, too. It is a dark, transparent resin produced by the action of an insect on the twigs of certain trees that grow in India. The word "lac" comes from the Hindi "lakh", which means 100,000. These little coccid insects swarm in lakhs, so there is never a shortage of shellac in India. It is perhaps a measure of the wide-ranging scouring of the planet for anything of use that the exudations of twigs irritated by insects in far-away India should have played a part in Victorian housekeeping.

French polishing was the rage in Victorian times and was made by dissolving shellac in methylated spirits. It was very laborious to do and required great skill. Furthermore, although a table that had been French polished looked very posh, the finish was destroyed if you put hot things on top.

POLISHING
A useful tool for cleaning windows and wooden furniture was this chamois leather brush. It combined the easy grip of a regular scrubbing brush with the softness of leather.

HOUSEMAIDS' BOXES
The most essential item of equipment required by the housemaid was the housemaids' box—it contained all the cleaning tools she needed, from leathers and black lead to brushes and emery paper. When cleaning the fire grate, the housemaid put the ashes in a cinder pail, which was sometimes built into the housemaids' box. The pail contained a wire sifter for separating the cinders from the ash, so they could be re-used.

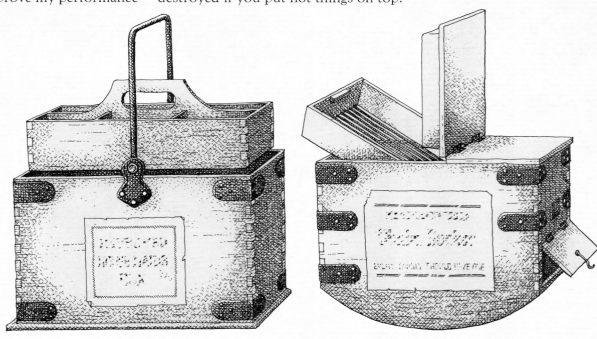

DUSTLESS CLEANING

THE FIRST STEP TOWARDS DUSTLESS CLEANING came with the invention of the carpet sweeper in 1876 by Melville Bissell. In addition to the main brush, Bissell's early designs also featured small rotary brushes to clean along the edges of skirting boards and furniture. There was also a knob that enabled the operator to adjust the main brush to various floor levels, and the dust box could be opened for emptying by pressing a lever. It worked very well and soon became very popular.

However, the cleaning power of the vacuum cleaner, when it arrived, greatly exceeded the efforts of the carpet sweeper. Hubert Booth devised the first suction cleaner in 1901 and coined the term vacuum cleaner. His machine was huge and powered by a petrol-driven engine. As it was too large to enter the house, it was parked outside and yards of flexible hose fed through the windows to reach every room (see below). King Edward VII and Queen Alexandra were greatly impressed with the machine and bought two, but clearly for ordinary household use a much smaller and cheaper machine was needed. Booth produced the Trolley Vac in 1906, which was driven by a

(rather large) electric motor and featured a glass section so that you could see the dust as it was sucked up. It came with a vast array of hoses and attachments and was an excellent vacuum cleaner, but it was still far too heavy—nearly a hundredweight.

Many bellows-operated vacuum cleaners were produced, such as the Harvey cleaner, patented in the 1890s. These were smaller and lighter but required two people to operate them: one to push the lever up and down that worked the bellows, and one to position the hose over the areas to be cleaned. The foot-operated cleaner, such as the Griffith, marketed in 1905, also required two people to work it, and even the plunge suction pump vacuum was difficult to work by yourself. It was not until J. Murray Spangler successfully fitted a light, compact vacuum cleaner with a small electric motor in 1907 and sold the rights to William Hoover that the upright domestic vacuum cleaner was truly born. In 1920 a revolving brush was added to agitate the carpet so that dirt was loosened deep in the pile. In 1926 revolving bars were added to help the brush by beating the carpet on a cushion of air.

PORTABLE VACUUM CLEANERS
In the race to design a portable vacuum cleaner, several machines were developed. The Trolley vacuum cleaner worked by an electric motor; the Griffith was operated by a foot pedal; while the "Baby Daisy" used a lever and bellows. The last two both required two people to operate them.

THE FIRST VACUUM CLEANER
Hubert Cecil Booth invented the vacuum cleaner in 1901. Powered by a petrol-driven piston engine, it was a massive and cumbersome machine, measuring four-and-a-half-feet wide, four-and-a-half-feet long and three-and-a-half-feet tall. It had to be transported on a horse-drawn cart and worked by a team of men.

THE CLEANER AT WORK
Painted bright red, the horse-drawn machine was parked outside the house to be cleaned and a team of liveried operatives entered the building dragging long pipes behind them. A crowd often gathered in the street to watch the extraordinary sight of several hundred feet of pipe being slung from the windows. Then the dust from the carpets, curtains and furniture was sucked down the pipes into the vacuum cleaner outside. The suction was so powerful that the weight of some carpets was reduced by fifty per cent after their first vacuum cleaning!

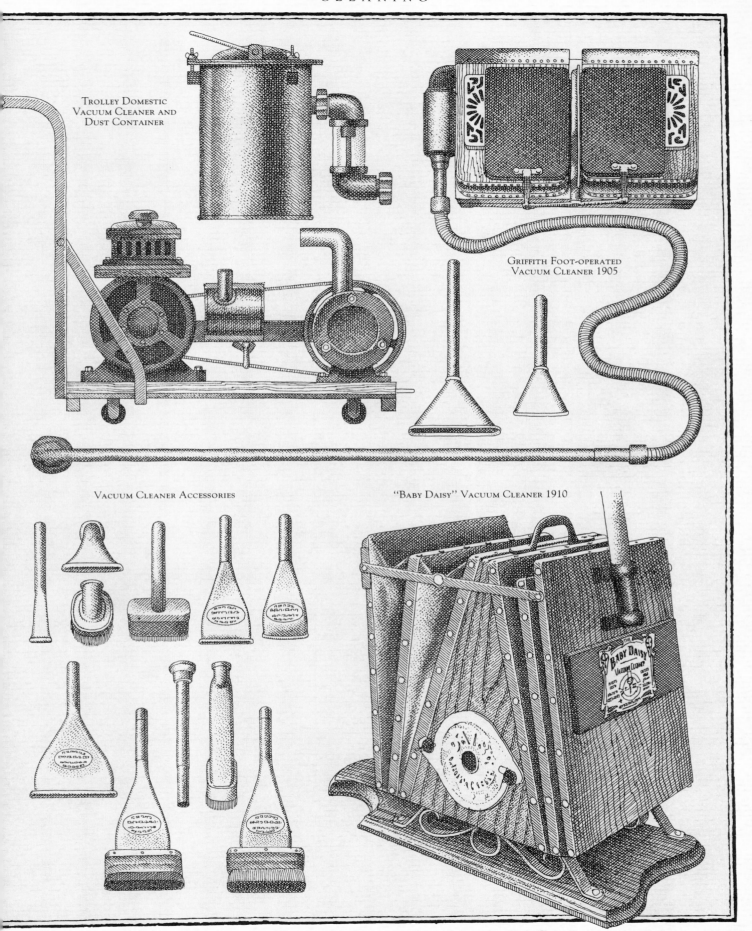

TROLLEY DOMESTIC
VACUUM CLEANER AND
DUST CONTAINER

GRIFFITH FOOT-OPERATED
VACUUM CLEANER 1905

VACUUM CLEANER ACCESSORIES

"BABY DAISY" VACUUM CLEANER 1910

CHIMNEY SWEEPING

ROFESSIONAL CHIMNEY SWEEPS have always been objects of, if not awe, certainly superstition: seeing one is supposed to bring good luck. In some countries, particularly Germanic ones, the sweep used to be an extremely dignified figure. He wore a black frock coat and a top hat and, of course, his face tended to be black, too. Riding solemnly along on his sit-up-and-beg bicycle, with his rods and brushes strapped to the crossbar, he was a noble sight.

All those who have grown up with smokeless fuel cannot imagine just how extremely dirty a fuel coal is and the huge amount of soot coal fires used to produce. The chimneys in prosperous houses, where many fires were burned, had to be swept at least once every three months, otherwise some of the soot was bound to fall down of its own accord, making a huge mess on the probably just whitened hearth below. Even most of the poor had their chimneys swept twice a year. For all that, even when the chimney was being cleaned regularly by a professional sweep, and the housewife was prepared for the descent of the soot, it was impossible to contain it all in the fireplace. Soot particles wafted out into the room and settled on every surface, creating an enormous cleaning task for the housewife after the sweep had left.

Chimney sweeping was a dreadful experience for the small boys who used to clean them in the early nineteenth century. They were often forced to climb up chimneys against their will and many got stuck and died as a result. Fortunately, this barbarous practice was outlawed in the middle of the last century.

PECULIAR CUSTOMS

A strange custom was observed in remote areas of Wales many years ago. In such areas it was supposed to be bad luck for a corpse

A DEJECTED SWEEP
The chimney sweep's lot was not a happy one. He performed a dirty and dangerous job in dreadful conditions, and often sustained burns, falls and chronic chest disease, caused by the dust.

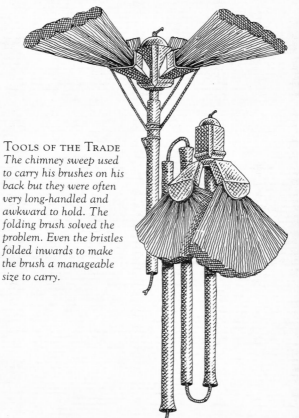

TOOLS OF THE TRADE
The chimney sweep used to carry his brushes on his back but they were often very long-handled and awkward to hold. The folding brush solved the problem. Even the bristles folded inwards to make the brush a manageable size to carry.

to pass through the door. As the windows were generally too small, the coffin—and its occupant— used to be hauled up the chimney! If anyone has seen the typical "simnai fawr" (large chimney) of a Welsh farmhouse they will know that it would provide passage for a very large coffin. I had such a chimney in my own house in Wales (fortunately, I did not have to avail myself of its right of passage) together with a smaller, ordinary-sized chimney, which served an Aga cooker.

The highlight of our calendar in that part of the world was "Hen Nos Galan"—the Old New Year. New Year's Eve, according to the old calendar, falls on 12th January. One 13th January found me very much the worse for wear (libations always went on all night) and, to add to my miseries, the Aga began to smoke: the chimney was blocked.

I clambered on to the roof and fired several rounds from a twelve-bore shot gun down the chimney. This filled the room below with soot but had absolutely no effect on the blockage. A neighbour came in and, on seeing my plight, fetched a holly bush. I lowered a cord down the chinmey and he tied the holly bush on the end. However, as he was in a similar state to me, he did not tie it on very well. Consequently, when I had pulled it half-way up the chimney the bush fell away from the cord. My friend went away again and this time returned with "the rods". Fixing a brush to the end of them he poked the rods up the chimney. "Keep turning the rods!" I shouted down the chimney, meaning that he should turn them clockwise to keep the threads engaged. Dutifully he turned them but, alas, he turned them in an anti-clockwise direction. Needless to say the brush joined the holly bush half-way up the chimney.

Desperate situations call for desperate remedies. After refreshing ourselves with home brew we both climbed on to the roof armed this time with four gallons of petrol, so that we could burn a hole through the blockage. Not realizing that the chimney was still very hot and the Aga, in fact, still just alight, we poured down the petrol without further ado. As we peered down the chimney to see if anything was happening before chucking down some lighted paper, we were thrown back by an immense explosion. The house shook, our eyebrows were blown off and we never found out what happened to the holly bush and the brush. Perhaps they were atomized. At all events the chimney worked perfectly well after that.

HOME-MADE METHODS
Those households that did not or could not employ chimney sweeps devised other, somewhat unorthodox, methods of cleaning their chimneys. One way was to throw a live hen or goose down the chimney: its flapping wings dislodged all the soot! People with more respect for their poultry lowered a cord down the chimney and tied a bundle of holly twigs half-way along it. Then, man and wife, one at the top, the other at the bottom of the chimney, worked the cord up and down, so that the twigs scraped the sides of the chimney. Eventually it was clear of soot.

KEEPING HOLD OF THE CORD

BUNDLE OF HOLLY TWIGS

PULLING THE CORD

WASTE DISPOSAL

ORROR IS EXPRESSED BY MOST people, used to the regular visit of the dust cart or garbage truck, that even now in many parts of the countryside in even the most "developed" countries there is no rubbish collection. I live in such an area and truly I do not find this deprivation very serious at all. I do what all good country people have always done: classify my rubbish and dispose of it.

I have a bin with a lid on it for organic waste that will rot down into a compost. When it is full I empty it on the compost heap. If I had a pig I would give it to him but just at present I have not. I have a box for inflammable rubbish. I empty this into a perforated steel drum at the bottom of the garden and put a match to it. Lastly I have a box for non-inflammable, non-organic rubbish. When full, I empty this into plastic bags and once a month drive a load of these in the back of a car to the local land-fill dump.

Nowadays great rubbish trucks come along and seemingly eat the rubbish as complicated machinery forces it into their reeking interior. Not so long ago, before the age of the black plastic bag, men had to carry the full galvanized dustbins to the lorries

ORGANIC WASTE
Organic household waste, such as vegetable parings, dish scrapings and tea leaves, was collected throughout the day in a domestic refuse holder. This was a metal pail containing a sieve. At the end of the day, the waste was either thrown on the compost heap or fed to the pig to fatten it up.

and empty them. I remember the dustmen of my childhood as jolly men, banging and rattling and shouting and laughing, and even singing. They wore special hats with leather flaps hanging down the back. I remember thinking that if I was a city person and had to have a job, I would rather be a member of their merry company than sit in a stuffy office, and I still would now.

BEFORE THE WASTE AGE

What happened before people had cars and plastic bags? Well, the fact of the matter is that they had hardly any rubbish! They lived before the age of waste: they possessed no tinned cans, no plastic, hardly any glass jars, and any metal utensils that they owned they made last as long as they could. They didn't throw things away just because they were broken either. Travelling tinkers would repair leaking pots and pans and even staple together broken china objects.

It must also be remembered that up until roughly the Second World War, tatters—rag-and-bone men, or any-old-iron men—penetrated everywhere in town and country. Everything salvageable was salvaged. An old gypsy man once told me that the thing he liked to discover most was an old feather bed. This could be sold to the tatter's yard for five shillings, which was a fortune to him in those days. Bones went to the super-phosphate factory (to be dissolved in sulphuric acid and turned into phosphatic fertilizer). Rags went to make paper. Iron found its way back to the foundry to be melted down again and recast. And then there was what the gypsy folk called "jewellery" by which was meant any metal that was not iron. This could be sold for much more than iron and went to whatever smelting works dealt with that particular kind of metal: brass, copper, bronze and gun metal all came into this category.

THE DUMP AND THE PIG

Any non-rottable, non-edible rubbish people did have they quite simply dumped, maybe in the edge of a piece of woodland near the house or even in a ditch. I have twice had the task of excavating such an ancient rubbish tip in order to create a garden on its site. It was interesting to note the frugal contents: old hand tools like bill-hook

blades worn down by use and sharpening until there was hardly anything left; an occasional rusty kettle or saucepan; the heel-irons off old boots, worn down nearly to extinction; and, nearer the top, the occasional Bovril bottle, bottles that had once contained somebody's famous cure-all elixir, Tate and Lyle's golden syrup tins, baking powder tins and the odd Camp coffee bottle. Coffee bottles were the first portent of the throw-away age to come not many years later.

In days of old, in the country at least, the pig was your great consumer of rubbish! Any rubbish that was remotely edible was given to him, and thus was rubbish turned into good bacon and ham. The pig was your compost heap, too. Any food that he ate that he couldn't turn into meat, and any organic material that he could not eat, he turned into the finest manure with which to fertilize the garden.

Sewers and Night Carts

Before this century and the advent of the night cart, sewage disposal was a terrible problem and many people, especially in the cities, lived in extremely unsanitary conditions. In London, cholera mortality was very high in the middle of the last century as a direct result of women obtaining cooking, washing and drinking water for their families from disgusting foetid ditches. They knew that sewage was dumped into these streams, indeed they were guilty of the same crime themselves, for they had nowhere else to dump it, but they had to use it, as piped water was not provided to the poor districts in the towns and cities. The profit-making water companies only laid on piped water to rich households and even

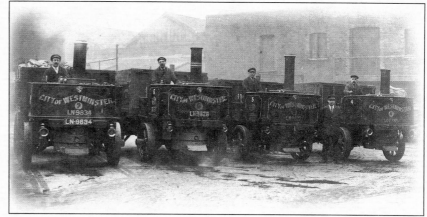

then it was not usually adequately filtered (see p.240). Piped water and mains drainage didn't begin to come to the poor until the second half of the nineteenth century. They arrived in the country even later but at least country people had access to springs and plenty of earth in which to bury their sewage (see p.303). From the beginning of the twentieth century they also had night carts.

The night cart was an institution in many a village and small town up to the Second World War and I even knew of one that worked a Suffolk village after the war. The cart was pulled by an old horse and driven generally by an elderly man. Sometimes it had a big tank on top but more generally there was a collection of steel drums. Late at night you would hear the friendly rattle of the iron-shod wheels of the night cart, as its driver stopped and started through the village lanes, emptying sewage buckets into the tank or drums. He was known as the "muck snatcher" in many a village and was, quite rightly, much respected. I, for one, mourn his passing.

REFUSE COLLECTION
Sewage was collected every evening in the night cart. This was a horse-drawn cart carrying a large steel drum (top). Early dust carts were much smaller than they are today and were operated by only one man (above).

CONTROLLING PESTS & VERMIN

N THE DAYS OF THE RAT CATCHER, before "rodent officers" came on the scene, there was a multitude of ways of catching mice and rats. Keeping cats was one of the ways of keeping the rat population down, although there was no guarantee that they would catch the wretched things. I knew a miller in Suffolk who kept forty cats, which seemed to do a good job. To see them all lapping milk out of saucers in the mill yard at the same time was truly hypnotic. I pointed out to him once that the cats must have cost far more to feed than the rats would have done. His abstruse reply was that he couldn't stop them making love and his wife wouldn't allow him to drown the subsequent kittens.

As for traps—they were many and various. By far the commonest trap was the ubiquitous "gin" trap, no longer allowed in England, thank heaven, which caught any wretched animal that walked over it by the leg. It was used extensively in farm buildings for catching rats and was usually set in a drain pipe, where the cats and dogs couldn't fall foul of it but the rats certainly would.

MOUSE TRAPS

Mice were generally caught in the little spring mouse traps that you can still buy from any village store. The base used to be made of wood: nowadays the whole thing is stamped out of steel. These little traps gave currency to the term "mouse-trap cheese", which describes British factory cheese so eloquently. Although it might be a cause of wonder why any self-respecting mouse would be drawn to the stuff; certainly no French mouse would.

I once had a simple and most effective wooden mouse trap that I bought from an old Danish man. It was an ingeniously simple device—the mouse ran up a little wooden ramp to get to the bait and its weight caused the ramp to pivot. When the mouse stepped off, the ramp, relieved of its weight, returned to its normal position, so trapping the mouse, which could not reach the end of the ramp to return by it. It was highly effective but to me completely useless. It caught mice by the dozen but I had not the heart to kill them and simply let them out again—on somebody else's land.

RATS AND MICE
Rats and mice were a constant hazard in the days of poor sanitation, and many ways were devised to get rid of them. Most of the traps contained bait to lure the animals, and then either a cage to entrap them, or, more harshly, a wooden block to crush them.

OTHER HOUSEHOLD PESTS
Wasps, flies and cockroaches were common pests, and there were numerous ways of dealing with them. Cast-iron fans were supposed to drive flies and wasps away, while cockroaches were lured into traps with sloping sides, which prevented any escape.

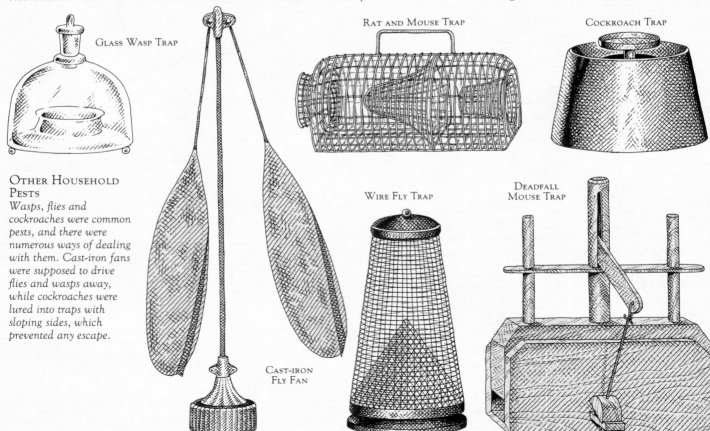

GLASS WASP TRAP

RAT AND MOUSE TRAP

COCKROACH TRAP

WIRE FLY TRAP

DEADFALL MOUSE TRAP

CAST-IRON FLY FAN

TEXTILE CRAFTS

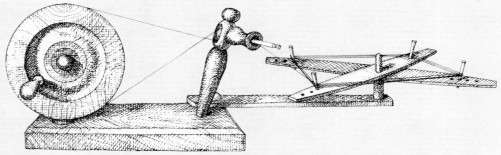

The arts of spinning and weaving are so old that I will not
even try to guess exactly when they were invented.
I imagine, however, that it was very early indeed in the
history of man- and womankind that people learned
to twist vegetable fibres together to make string or rope, and,
probably enough, not long after that, someone (my guess is
a woman) learned to weave such yarn into cloth.
Unfortunately, few early examples of textiles are left for us
to see, but I knew a man, alas now gone from this life, a
great writer and philosopher named Lanza del Vasta, who
never wore anything that he did not make himself out of
pieces of wool that he pulled off bushes and fences. He
turned this wool into excellent cloth, using, as he used to
boast, only six sticks. One stick formed his spindle, four
others, a simple weaving frame, and the sixth, his shuttle. It
was a very effective method of making cloth that could
have been taught to a child in a very short lesson.
However, it was rather slow: he should have used those
excellent inventions, the spinning wheel and the loom, and
saved himself some time.

SPINNING

 HAVE TO TRAVEL BACK IN TIME well before I was born to find the age, in industrialized countries at least, when spinning was a common household activity. It has lingered on in the more remote and peasant parts of Europe and in Greece and the Balkans you can still see women spinning with the spindle as they walk. They tuck the distaff that carries the wool under their left arm, and spin the spindle against their thigh with their right hand: a tricky operation.

COTTAGE INDUSTRY
There is nothing more soothing, at the end of a hard day's work, than the sight and sound of a treadle spinning wheel whirring away in front of the fire. And for the spinner, too, how much more enjoyable is spinning in the comfort of one's own quiet home than spinning in the dark satanic mill with the constant roar of machinery! At a time when the pressures of commercial and family life seem to drive us all towards

nervous breakdowns, the good news is that home spinning is enjoying a vigorous revival in every country in Europe and in North America, too.

It is easy to see why home spinning died out so speedily and so absolutely when industrial spinning was introduced. For non-industrial spinning is a very slow job. It takes twelve spinsters to keep one weaver going and, in my opinion, they would be hard put to do even that if the weaver was any good. Also, the preparation of the fibre, whether wool or flax, is a skilled and extremely time-consuming job.

Gandhi realized all this when he wanted to free India from industrialism. Village weavers wove quickly enough for India to do be able to do without the weaving mills, but spinning was a problem. So Gandhi exhorted every Indian to spin and even invented a small portable spinning machine which people could take into railway trains or to the office. I have seen members of the Indian Parliament in New Delhi spinning away as they listen to debates. Perhaps our Western assemblies would be wiser and more thoughtful in their deliberations if they did the same. Can you imagine the President of the United States or our own beloved Prime Minister spinning as they worked? It could have a calming effect on their counsels. Maybe they could start with the contents of the woolsack.

PREPARING WOOL FOR SPINNING
Wool can be spun "straight from the grease" and I have seen good yarn spun without first being carded. However, for fine thread you must break up the fleece, mix it together to make it more uniform, wash the grease and dirt out of it, and then grease it artificially with anything from goose grease (the best) to butter, vegetable oil or even paraffin (the worst).

After all this, the wool has to be carded (see page 186). This is an extremely time-consuming process. Made from small planks of wood, hand carders have handles attached to them and each is set with hundreds of fine, hooked wires. The wool is thoroughly scarified between two hand carders to produce rolags—little cylinders of very fluffy wool. The yarn is spun from these.

SPINNING BY HAND
The basic method of spinning is to use a drop, or hand, spindle. Raw wool is hooked on to the end of the spindle and, as the spindle is turned, the wool fibres are twisted together to form a continuous length. The weighted end of the spindle gives momentum to the spinning.

DROP SPINDLES

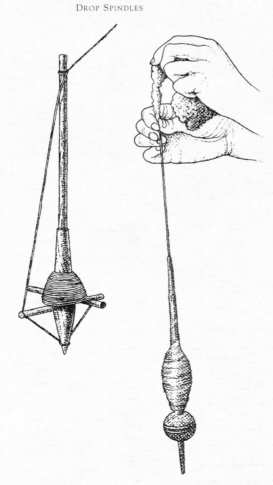

SPINNING WHEEL WITH SINGLE
BAND AND FRICTION BRAKE

FLYER

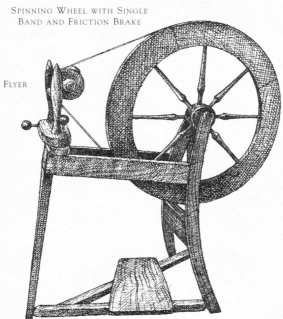

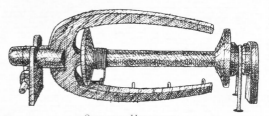

SPINNING HEDGEHOG –
ALTERNATIVE TO A SPINNING WHEEL

SPINDLES

Today you can take your pick amongst the many fine yarns that are on offer in craft shops. But it was not always so. All early attempts at weaving must have been considerably hindered by the inadequacy of the thread or yarn with which the cloth was made. Yarn doesn't occur naturally on the sheep's back or on the cotton plant in long, ready-made lengths. It has to be twisted into lengths from the original fibres.

SPINNING MACHINES
The spinning wheel is a sophisticated mechanization of the hand spindle, and produces spun wool of a much more even thickness. Textile fibres are pulled through the flyer and its turning twists them into thread. The flyer also winds the thread on to the bobbin, which it surrounds, as the bobbin spins slower than the flyer, either because of a friction brake, as with the spinning wheel, far left, or because of a separate drive from the wheel.

THE SPINNING WHEEL

THE SPINNING WHEEL WAS A NATURAL progression from the hand spindle. At some stage it was realized that the hand spindle could be held horizontally in a frame and turned, not by twisting with the fingers, but by a wheel-driven belt.

One of the first spinning wheels was the great, or walking, wheel. This consisted of a low table above which were mounted a drive wheel at one end and a spindle mechanism at the other. The wheel was turned by hand and drove the spindle mechanism by means of a drive belt. Many spinning wheels were fitted with a distaff, which held the wool fibres ready for spinning.

The invention of the U-flyer spindle enabled the yarn to be twisted and wound in one combined operation. As both the bobbin and the flyer spindle rotated at different speeds, the spun yarn was wound on to the bobbin. As the bobbin became full of yarn, its speed of rotation altered, so to spin a consistent thread, either the tension of the drive belt was adjusted, or friction was applied to slow the bobbin or flyer.

Early spinning wheels were operated by hand and it was not until the seventeenth century that foot treadles were invented. The foot treadle was condemned by some because the spinner could pedal a rhythm with the foot irrespective of the requirements of the yarn. However, the spinner welcomed the treadle as it freed both hands to guide the yarn.

AMERICAN WHEELS

American spinning wheels were similar to the European counterparts on which they were based, but with a few differences. The wheels were often mounted on three legs instead of four, a design that proved to be more stable on uneven floors. In addition, the spindle mechanism was removable, so there was a great variety of spinning wheels with similar types of spindle head.

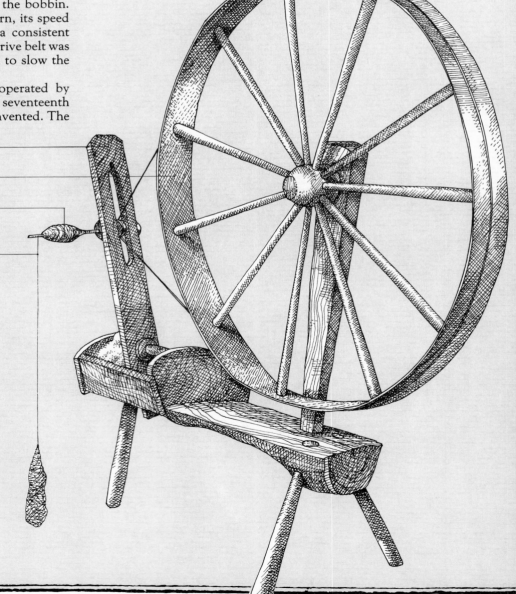

SPINDLE POST

DRIVE WHEEL

SPINDLE

UNSPUN YARN

THE GREAT WHEEL

This was sometimes known as the wool or walking wheel. It consisted of a wooden drive wheel which had a flat rim. This drove the spinning mechanism by means of a drive belt or cord of tightly twisted linen or cotton. The wheel was mounted on a post which rose from a low table. At the other end of the table a spindle post supported the spindle. The spindle post had a slot cut into it to allow room for movement of the pulley. Some types of great wheel also had a storage tray mounted on the table to hold the unspun yarn.

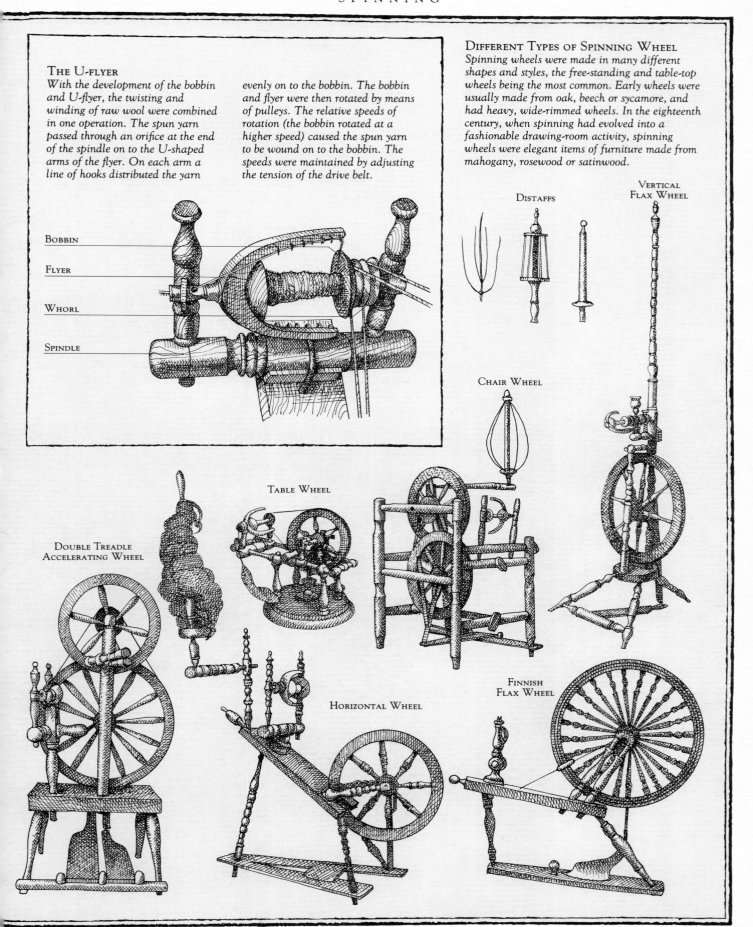

THE U-FLYER

With the development of the bobbin and U-flyer, the twisting and winding of raw wool were combined in one operation. The spun yarn passed through an orifice at the end of the spindle on to the U-shaped arms of the flyer. On each arm a line of hooks distributed the yarn evenly on to the bobbin. The bobbin and flyer were then rotated by means of pulleys. The relative speeds of rotation (the bobbin rotated at a higher speed) caused the spun yarn to be wound on to the bobbin. The speeds were maintained by adjusting the tension of the drive belt.

BOBBIN

FLYER

WHORL

SPINDLE

DIFFERENT TYPES OF SPINNING WHEEL

Spinning wheels were made in many different shapes and styles, the free-standing and table-top wheels being the most common. Early wheels were usually made from oak, beech or sycamore, and had heavy, wide-rimmed wheels. In the eighteenth century, when spinning had evolved into a fashionable drawing-room activity, spinning wheels were elegant items of furniture made from mahogany, rosewood or satinwood.

DISTAFFS

VERTICAL FLAX WHEEL

CHAIR WHEEL

TABLE WHEEL

DOUBLE TREADLE ACCELERATING WHEEL

HORIZONTAL WHEEL

FINNISH FLAX WHEEL

The invention of the drop spindle to make the yarn, therefore, represents a very considerable advance in weaving technology.

The drop spindle is a simple device consisting of a small stick with a hook or notch at the top and a weight at the bottom. Many Neolithic archaeological sites yield examples of such weights made of clay, two or three inches across with a hole in the middle through which the stick passes. To work a spindle like this is simple. Hook the notch on the top into the fluffy ball of raw wool or cotton, and give the stick a turn. The weighted end gives the spindle momentum, and as it spins the tangled threads are drawn out of the ball of fibres and twisted together to form a lengthening yarn. Pay out more loose fibre and the spindle will soon hit the floor below you, at which point you coil the thread round the spindle stem, and then start the process again. Soon you will have a spindle full of thread ready for weaving.

THE SPINNING WHEEL

Drop spindles are laborious to work but need little concentration and are preferable to twisting yarn by hand. But at some stage or other, someone discovered that the drop spindle could be held horizontally in a frame and and turned not by twisting with the fingers but by a wheel-driven belt. The spinning wheel had arrived, and with it a good supply of well-made, continuous yarn. As with so many effective inventions, it was a beautiful yet simple tool. Most wheels are operated by a crank connected to a foot treadle, which leaves the hands free to feed the loose tangled fibres on to the spindle. More complex spinners include a flyer, also driven by the wheel but at a different speed to that of the spindle, which ensures that the thread is always kept tensioned correctly. When the spindle is filled, the thread is wound on to a reel and removed in a skein. Wool winders take the skeins and wind two or three together to make a single thread.

SPINNING IN THE SUN
Here we see the beautiful hand-made wooden spinning wheel being used by a crofter on the Isle of Skye. What better way to pass the time of day in creative work.

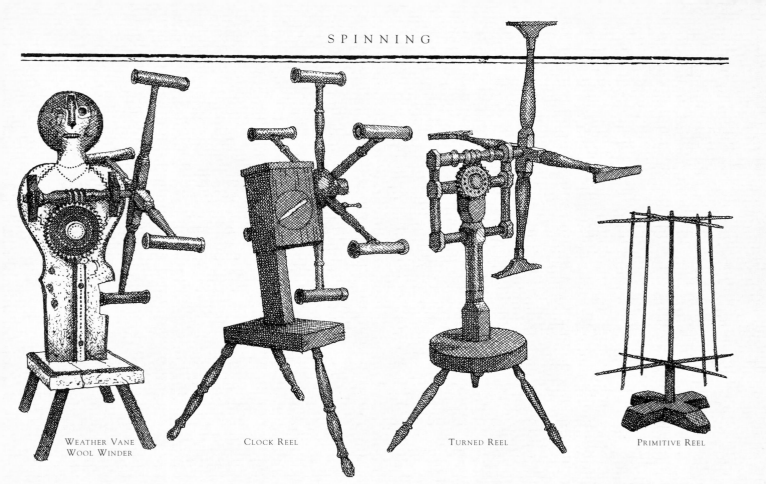

WEATHER VANE
WOOL WINDER

CLOCK REEL

TURNED REEL

PRIMITIVE REEL

SPINNING FLAX

The simplest method of spinning flax is by using the distaff and spindle. The flax is lapped around the stick or distaff and the spinner draws off a few fibres at a time with her thumb and forefinger to form a thread. She attaches these fibres to the spindle, which is round and pointed at one end, and twirls the spindle in her hand, twisting the thread together as she goes. The very able Flemish spinners used this method to great effect. They wound the thread on to the spindle by rolling it against their knee or against a leather strap, specially made for the purpose, hanging from a belt on their waist. Although a surprisingly fine thread can be wound by this very simple method, it does take a very long time to spin sufficient yarn to weave into, say, a sheet or an article of clothing such as a shirt.

The flax wheel speeded things up considerably and increased the evenness of the twisted thread. It is a simple machine to use: the spindle on which the thread is wound is turned by the motion of the wheel, which in turn is rotated by a treadle moved by the foot. A flyer makes sure that the flax is wound on to the spindle pole or bobbin regularly. When the spindle or bobbin is full of wound thread, or yarn, it

is taken off, thrown into the basket for the weaver and replaced by an empty one.

Linen yarn, when woven, makes the finest, strongest, longest-lasting cloth, whether for the mainsail of a sailing ship or the finest shirt. Linen cloth has been recovered from Egyptian pyramids still in good condition.

It is very sad that the cultivation of the flax plant, whether used for producing cloth or for making linseed oil, has almost entirely died out in the British Isles. Even the famous Ulster linen industry is entirely dependent now on foreign flax. In *Irish Traditional Crafts*, David Shaw-Smith describes how a group of young girls in County Donegal used to carry their spinning wheels to the house of one of them every evening and sit and spin flax together. They would also spin stories and sing the night away. Then every evening, when the spinning session ended, in stormed the young men with violins and bagpipes and dancing would take over.

Unmarried girls, by the way, were called spinsters because they were always spinning. They had to spin enough yarn to fit out their households with cloth when they got married: it was more than a full-time job, but one which they were mostly happy to do. The weaving tended to be done either by travelling weavers or professional male weavers resident in the town.

WINDERS AND REELS
Once spun, the yarn was removed from the bobbin to be measured and skeined. This was a tedious task which involved winding the yarn round and round the wooden arms of a reel or winder. Some reels had a geared cog that clicked every ten rounds; others had a clock face that indicated the number of rounds wound on the reel. The circumference of the skein varied according to the locality.

MAT & RUG MAKING

 UGS HAVE BEEN WOVEN SINCE 2000 BC. The first woven rugs were made by tying short lengths of yarn to the warp threads of a loom. A piled fabric was created, using the "Ghiordes" knot, which was later developed into the rya knot by the Scandinavians, who also developed a special canvas backing for it. Today these shaggy rugs can be worked on the Scandinavian backing with a continuous length of yarn and a blunt-ended rug needle. Bed rugs were developed from rya rugs and became very popular in America, where they always provided the top cover of the bed in the nineteenth century. Needletuft rugs are also made with a blunt-ended rug needle and a continuous length of yarn. It is a good idea to stretch the even-weave canvas backing on a frame when working this type of rug to make sure that the pattern comes out as expected!

RUSH AND STRAW MATTING
Floors were usually covered with rush or straw matting up to the eighteenth century. Such mats and mats made of other natural fibres, such as sedge, flags, jute and coir, were woven. Later, the housewife covered floors with straw matting in the summer, while the wool carpets were being cleaned, and sometimes used them to cover the "best" carpets to protect them.

STRAIGHT- AND PUNCH-HOOK RUGS
Although the technique for making simple hooked rugs was known for centuries in Scandinavia, it was the Americans and especially the New Englanders in the nineteenth century, who raised hooked rug making to such a high art. A hooked rug is made by holding a long strip of fabric under a backing of canvas or hessian and plunging a straight hook through the backing and pulling a loop of fabric strip to the top.

PLAITED RUSH MATS
Plaited rushes made very good mats. The rushes were first dried. Then three rushes were folded over a hook and plaited together to form a long, thick plait. Several of these plaits were shaped into a coil and stitched together with strong thread or twine. A variety of patterns could be worked into the design of the mat.

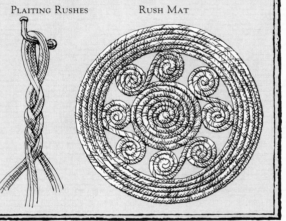
PLAITING RUSHES   RUSH MAT

TYPES OF RUG
The straight-hook rug is the most common type of rug. It is made by pushing up yarn through the backing fabric to form loops on the surface. The traditional rag rugs were made in this way. The punch-hook rug looks similar but is easier to make. The backing fabric is stretched on a frame and the loops of yarn are then pushed through, using a punch hook. The latch-hook rug, which is a dense pile rug, is made by knotting lengths of yarn on to open-mesh canvas. Needletuft rugs have a very thick pile. They are worked on even-weave canvas using a long, blunt-ended rug needle and continuous lengths of strong yarn.

STRAIGHT-HOOK RUG
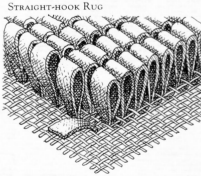

LATCH-HOOK RUG

PUNCH-HOOK RUG
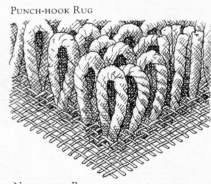

NEEDLETUFT RUG
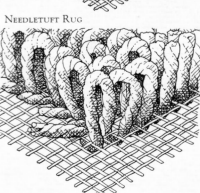

HEMMING BIRDS
These were used to keep material taut while it was being sewn. The bird was clamped to a table, and the material inserted into its beak, which was opened simply by pressing the tail.

Punch-hook rugs look similar but can be worked more quickly. You simply thread the yarn through the punch hook and punch the hook through the back of the canvas to the front: this special hook regulates the size of the loops on the top. For straight-hook rugs and punch-hook rugs a frame is used to ensure even hooking.

These were the most common sorts of hooked rug and an American housewife might well make two each winter using a simple, repetitive design. More elaborate floral patterns might grace the living room but simple geometric designs were more commonplace. You could make simple patterns with a latch-hook or rag rug.

LATCH-HOOK OR RAG RUGS

There was a time when you would find a rag mat in front of the fireplace of every English country cottage. Generally, a cat or dog would be lying on it.

I first came into intimate contact with a rag mat as a child when my mother let me live in the cottage of the father of one of our maids. The family lived near Landemeer in Essex, and Annie's father was head horseman on a farm. I remember the couple of stays I made with them with the most intense pleasure. The kitchen-cum-living room was a small room with religious oleographs and texts around the walls. The fireplace was set in a recess and contained a substantial iron range on which all the cooking was done. Winter or summer, there was always a glowing coal fire on this range and I used to be bathed (I was only seven or eight years old) in a galvanized iron tub in front of it. After bathing, I would stand, dripping, upon the rag mat and dry myself. This did not take long because the heat of the fire dried me as well as the rough towel.

MAKING A RAG MAT

I once watched Annie's mother making a rag mat. She used a jute sack for a base: the sort of sack that you found in their hundreds on every farm in those days, before horrible plastic bags had been invented. I didn't know it then but the jute was grown in faraway Bengal, and years later I saw a huge stand of it as I went up the Brahmaputra in a troop-carrying paddle steamer.

The sack was opened out and then pieces of rag, all cut to the same length, were woven through the "fabric". This was done with a rugging or latch hook, which was a small steel hook with a wooden handle. The hook

had a latch across its mouth to enable the hook to be pulled out of the sacking without catching in it. Knotting was extremely simple and quick, and you were left with the two ends of the bit of rag sticking up.

The rug would be kept clean by bashing it against the outside wall of the house every day, and when it had gone beyond remedy, as you might say, it would be thrown on the compost heap and another one made. The sacks were free—no farmer ever missed a sack and rags cost nothing.

For all that my recollection of the Fisher household is one of contentment and happiness. In the autumn, all the children were sent blackberrying and searching for mushrooms. For a treat I used to be taken down to the tidal creek at Landemeer to fish for little crabs by dangling a length of string with pieces of meat on the end of it into the water. These were simple joys and contented people and whenever I think of the word "home" I think of that place.

THE HOOK

The hook is an essential tool in rug making. The straight hook has an end shaped like a crochet hook to pull the yarn into loops. The punch hook is first threaded with yarn and then pushed through the backing fabric of the rug to form loops.

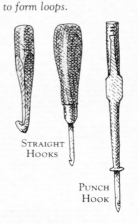

STRAIGHT HOOKS

PUNCH HOOK

LACE MAKING

HORTLY AFTER THE SECOND WORLD War, when walking along the shore in south Devon, I came across the little village of Beer, which is where the last chalk cliffs can be found as you wander westward. Going up into the village in search of a pub I found two ladies sitting outside a cottage door busily making lace.

They sat with lace-making cushions, or pillows, on their laps and worked complicated stitches with large pins and small wooden bobbins: they were making Honiton lace. Beer, they told me, was one of the last refuges of the true lace makers of England: the lace for Queen Victoria's wedding dress was made there as was that of Queen Alexandra and Princess Alice.

FROM NEEDLEPOINT TO BOBBIN LACE

Needlepoint lace was developed from the pulled linen decoration found in the wrappings of Egyptian mummies. The designs gradually became more complicated and needlepoint lace reached its zenith at the time of the Renaissance with Venetian gros point. This sophisticated needlepoint was mostly used to decorate heavy ecclesiastical cloths at that time but was gradually adapted to be used on finer personal materials.

As the Renaissance spread across Europe, so did needlepoint lace making. By the time it reached the Netherlands finer threads were being spun and the bridges, or brides—the bars between the flower shapes—were replaced by thread twisted into net, using bobbins. Soon after this the needlepoint patterns were dropped and the flowers and foliage created with bobbins, too. It was but a small step from assembling the shapes to weaving the whole pattern as one piece.

TYPES OF BOBBIN OR PILLOW LACE

Lace-making techniques developed differently in different countries and the various forms of lace came to be named after their original place of manufacture.

In that best of all books on needlework, *The Encyclopedia of Needlework*, Thérèse de Dillmont provides descriptions in easy-to-

PRICKER

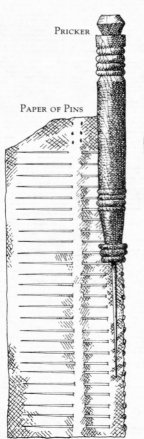

PAPER OF PINS

PARCHMENT PRICKED FOR MALTESE LACE

CLUNY-TYPE BUCKS LACE

CLUNY LACE

TORCHON LACE

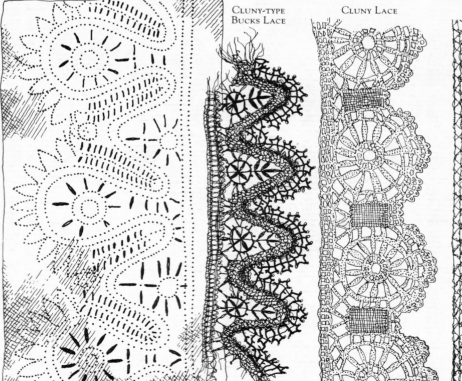

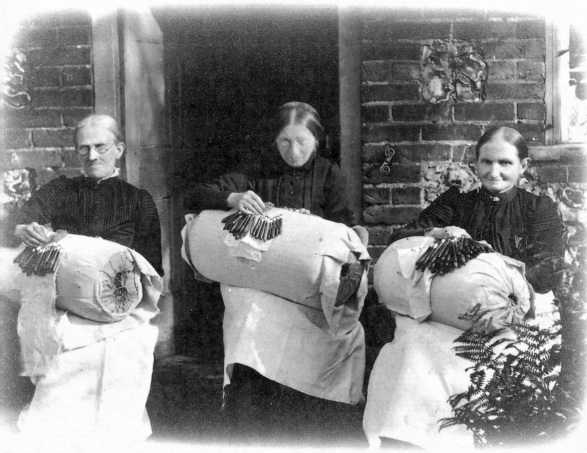

A SOCIAL OCCASION
Before machine-made lace took over in the second half of the nineteenth century, it was a common sight to see lace makers, both men and women, sitting together so that they could talk at the same time as they worked. In this photograph, the lace makers are using bolster pillows. These were stuffed hard with straw so that they held the pins firmly. When the central strip grew soft with use, they were "new-middled".

follow steps of how to make lace of every degree of delicacy and elaboration, including Venetian, Netherlands, French, English, Irish, Chantilly, Brussels and Sedan point lace: "names", as she says confidently, "familiar to everyone".

Brussels lace found its way from the Low Countries in the sixteenth century to Devon, in the south-west of Britain. From Devon it came to London, inevitably on the Honiton coach, and has been called Honiton lace in Great Britain ever since. With their sprigs and leaves joined with bobbin net, Brussels and Honiton lace are identical to this day.

French lace from Lille, Chantilly and Mechlin was brought to Britain by fleeing Huguenots and took root in Buckinghamshire. Bucks lace differs from Honiton lace in that each piece is surrounded by a thicker thread called a gimp or trolly, which is woven into the main piece.

Demand for a coarser, cheaper lace in the last century was met by lace made in Bedfordshire and known as Beds lace, based on Maltese, Torchon and Cluny lace patterns.

All these different laces were derived from the same basic lace-making techniques, using a pillow and bobbins.

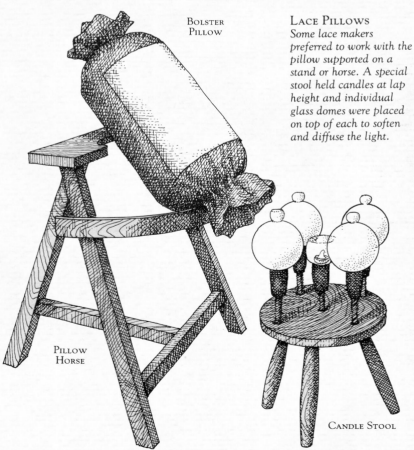

BOLSTER PILLOW

PILLOW HORSE

CANDLE STOOL

LACE PILLOWS
Some lace makers preferred to work with the pillow supported on a stand or horse. A special stool held candles at lap height and individual glass domes were placed on top of each to soften and diffuse the light.

BOBBINS AND SPANGLES

Most bobbins were made of hardwood or bone. Wooden ones were more common as they were cheaper but bone bobbins lasted longer. Occasionally you might come across a thin brass, iron or pewter bobbin and glass and silver bobbins were given as presents. To provide extra weight a "spangle" or "jingle" was fitted on the end of most bobbins. The spangle was simply a ring of attractively coloured beads wired on to the end of the bobbin to give it extra weight and hold it steady against the lace pillow. Some of the beads on the spangle were spherical and some were square-cut, and there was usually a larger spherical bead at the bottom. Sometimes the lace maker would detach the beads from the wire and thread her own charms and mementoes on to it instead. Bobbins used for making Honiton lace were pointed and light so that they could be passed easily through a loop of very fine thread to connect different parts of the motif.

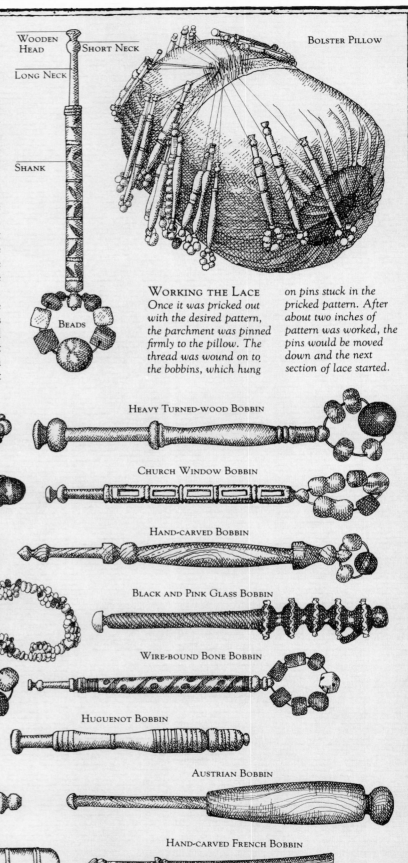

WORKING THE LACE
Once it was pricked out with the desired pattern, the parchment was pinned firmly to the pillow. The thread was wound on to the bobbins, which hung on pins stuck in the pricked pattern. After about two inches of pattern was worked, the pins would be moved down and the next section of lace started.

WOODEN HEAD — SHORT NECK

LONG NECK

SHANK

BOLSTER PILLOW

BEADS

"OLD MAID" BOBBIN

HEAVY TURNED-WOOD BOBBIN

TURNED WOODEN BOBBIN

CHURCH WINDOW BOBBIN

COLOURED BONE BOBBIM

HAND-CARVED BOBBIN

BITTED WOODEN BOBBIN

BLACK AND PINK GLASS BOBBIN

INSCRIBED BOBBIN

WIRE-BOUND BONE BOBBIN

HONITON "LACE STICK"

HUGUENOT BOBBIN

MALTESE BOBBIN

AUSTRIAN BOBBIN

NORMANDY BOBBIN

HAND-CARVED FRENCH BOBBIN

MAKING BOBBIN OR PILLOW LACE

The art of making lace with a pillow and bobbins was invented by a German lady—one Barbara Uttman—in the middle of the sixteenth century.

To make pillow lace—sometimes called bone lace because the bobbins were often made of bone—cotton or silk thread was first wound around little bone or ivory bobbins. A pattern was then drawn up and the design pricked on to a piece of paper or parchment. This was placed over the pillow, or cushion, which sat firmly on the lap of the lace maker or was supported by a pillow horse. She would then fasten the ends of the thread together, stick pins into the holes of the first part of the pattern and twist the threads over and under one another and around the pins, according to the design.

As soon as the first part was finished, the lace maker would move the pins down to the next section of the pattern and begin winding the threads around those. So she would continue until the whole piece of pillow lace was completed.

THE VALUE OF LACE MAKING

Lace making requires greater concentration than knitting and is an extremely rewarding occupation. During the last century there were lace schools to which children would be sent from the age of four to learn the rudiments of lace making in addition to the three Rs. A heart-shaped pincushion hung at the side of each pillow and the children had to stick ten pins a minute. They chanted "lace tells" as they worked to keep up the momentum. If they could not work fast and accurately enough by the age of seven, they were apprenticed to another trade.

Lace making was a skill that provided women of very poor countries with profitable employment. I remember seeing groups

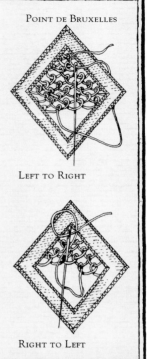

IMITATION LACE

Point lace experienced a revival in the Victorian age. Many Victorian ladies decorated cushions, bonnets, handkerchiefs, parasol covers and dresses with this attractive imitation lace. They traced out the pattern on glazed calico, which they then sewed to a piece of card. Pink calico was recommended so that the worker could see the traced pattern more easily by gaslight. With a large needle and some fine linen thread they sewed the point lace braid firmly along the lines of the pattern. When the braiding was completed, an open overcast stitch was worked into the outside edge. Finally, the open parts of the design were filled with fancy stitches. Of course, it was only with the braiding stitches that the needle passed through the calico and paper: the fancy stitches were done on the surface. Here, point de Bruxelles is shown being worked first from left to right and then from right to left—row upon row of buttonhole stitches are worked to fill the braided area.

POINT DE BRUXELLES

LEFT TO RIGHT

RIGHT TO LEFT

of Sinhalese women in remote Ceylon villages sitting making splendid lace—the craft having been taught to them by a helpful English lady several years before.

MACHINE-MADE LACE

Unfortunately men learnt how to make something resembling lace with a loom and this, aided by the general decline in taste, has led to the elimination of most delicate hand-made pillow lace.

The "lace" hawked around by gypsy women, when they are "calling" or "dukkering", as they call it, is not made by them at all (I will wager that no proper gypsy lady has ever made an inch of lace) but comes from the large factories in Nottingham.

USING A BOBBIN WINDER

Bobbin winders greatly speeded up the process of winding thread on to bobbins. The skein of thread was positioned around the pegs on the crossed blades and the end of it wound round the neck of the bobbin a couple of times to secure it. The neck was then placed in the spool of the winder and the fly-wheel turned.

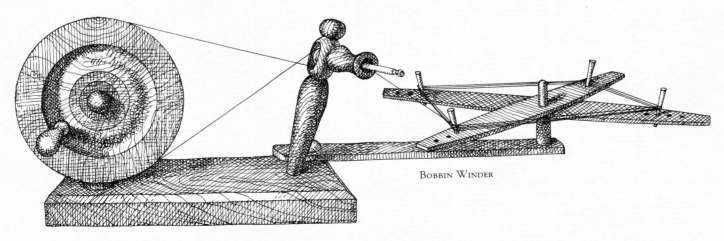

BOBBIN WINDER

CROCHET

VERY CHILD HAS AT SOME TIME made a chain of closed stitches out of a long piece of string. He or she makes two loops in the piece of string, and inserts the second loop through the first loop and pulls the latter tight. He continues in this manner until he has created a chain of closed stitches. Then comes the fun: the child pulls both ends of the chain at once and the chain miraculously disappears, so that he is left holding the ends of an ordinary piece of string again.

This is the basis of crochet. If the child had tied a knot in the end of his chain so that it could not unravel and then worked back along it, pulling more loops through the loops of the chain, he would have ended up with a piece of fabric. If he used a hook fashioned out of a piece of wood, he could do the job more quickly and more neatly.

VARIETY OF STITCHES

Needless to say, crocheters soon found ways to elaborate the basic crochet stitch and there is now a long list of crochet stitches, including: single, rose, Russian, ribbed, chain, picot, slanting, crossed, Russian crossed, counterpane, knotted and loop. In addition, elaborate patterns can be worked incorporating large holes.

So-called granny squares, or hexagons, can be crocheted out of left-over bits of coloured wool and subsequently sewn together to make bedspreads: a fine use of left-over yarn much employed by pioneering white Americans. In Tunisian crochet many stitches are held at once on a long crochet hook and then cast off in the same way as knitting. Perhaps this gave rise to the practice of working the stitches from one needle to the other. Not that I wish to incur the wrath of the crocheters of the world by implying that their skill is one whit less sophisticated than that of knitting: not a bit of it. The Victorians took crocheting to great elaborations, effecting lace-like crochet work with tiers of tassels. Victorian ladies tended to cover the nether limbs of tables and grand pianos with tasselled crochet work, as bare legs, whether belonging to humans or pieces of furniture, were considered most indecent.

CROCHET STITCHES
There are half a dozen basic crochet stitches; the long double crochet stitch is shown below. The basic stitches provide an endless variety of patterns for mats, ornamental laces and for fancy articles of clothing like shawls.

CROCHET EDGINGS
Many different crochet edgings can be used to finish off pieces of crochet, knitting or other fabric. When worked in fine cottons and with a small hook, crochet edgings look extremely pretty, often resembling old lace made with needles and bobbins. Edgings are worked directly on to the fabric or are worked separately as a strip and joined on.

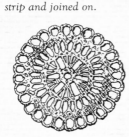

CROCHET EDGING

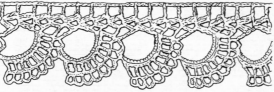

SCALLOP EDGING

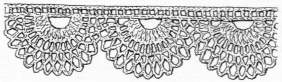

PLAIN PICOT EDGING

ARCH EDGING

PICOT ARCH EDGING

TATTING & MACRAME

OU NEED A SHUTTLE FOR TATTING. You simply wind the thread around the spool between the two pieces of boat-shaped wood or ivory. Then weave the shuttle in and out of the work, leaving a line of thread behind, much as a spider spins a web behind her as she goes. Tatting can be used for making quite fine lace-like fabrics.

THE ORIGINS OF TATTING

Like many arts, tatting found its way to Europe from the East. It is still practised in Arabic countries today, where it is called "makouk". In France it is called "frivolité" which a philistine might think just about describes it. Certainly it is not a useful art— you could not, for example, make a barge's mainsail with it—but it does create delightful borders on the collars of girls' pretty blouses and is often found decorating peasant costume. For peasants, perhaps the most practical people in the world, are nevertheless fond of decoration. Tatting had its heyday in the eighteenth century and would have died out if it hadn't been for the nuns, who carried on the craft to embellish church furnishings and vestments. It is now enjoying something of a revival.

MACRAME

Macramé is the art of tying knots in threads of string that hang from a horizontal string or strings. It is very easy to learn and quite useful, too, as practical items such as curtains and screens can be made using macramé, in addition to decorative fringes. Very complicated and often beautiful patterns can be created using the simplest of macramé knots. The half-hitch and the clove hitch are often used, and so, strangely enough, is the granny.

The granny knot, anathema to scout masters and girl-guide leaders, is a more decorative knot than the reef, which it is often mistaken for. It is also not a very good knot, which is why the granny knot is the one chosen by the gypsies for tying their neckties, or dicklos. If, in a fight, you grab a man's neckerchief and it is tied with a reef knot, it will not come undone and you might strangle the man. If it is tied with a granny knot, it will simply come loose in your hand and he will be free to counterattack.

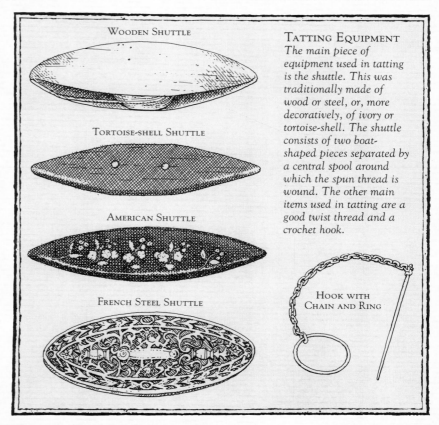

WOODEN SHUTTLE

TORTOISE-SHELL SHUTTLE

AMERICAN SHUTTLE

FRENCH STEEL SHUTTLE

TATTING EQUIPMENT
The main piece of equipment used in tatting is the shuttle. This was traditionally made of wood or steel, or, more decoratively, of ivory or tortoise-shell. The shuttle consists of two boat-shaped pieces separated by a central spool around which the spun thread is wound. The other main items used in tatting are a good twist thread and a crochet hook.

HOOK WITH CHAIN AND RING

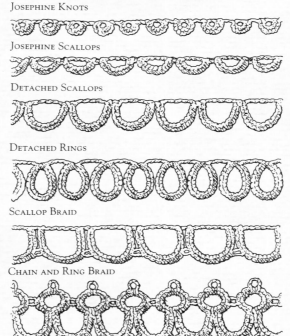

JOSEPHINE KNOTS

JOSEPHINE SCALLOPS

DETACHED SCALLOPS

DETACHED RINGS

SCALLOP BRAID

CHAIN AND RING BRAID

TWO-COLOUR BRAID

VARIETIES OF TATTING
Although tatting looks quite complicated, it is really made up of only one knot. The design varies, depending on the way the knots—or stitches—are combined. The picot is a loop between double stitches and is often used to join motifs.

MAKING A PICOT

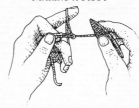

MAKING A JOIN

KNITTING

WHILE SOME OF THE MEN OF THE world have been posturing like peacocks, fighting with each other and flying to the moon, many of the women have been quietly engaged in an activity that is completely harmless, peaceful, non-polluting and, above all, useful. They have been turning woollen or other yarn into garments of the utmost utility and beauty with the help of nothing more complicated than a couple of pointed sticks.

This is not to give the impression that knitting is necessarily a restful pastime, although no doubt it is when performed as a leisure activity. In the past much knitting was done by hard-pressed women to help pay the rent. I have a photograph of the wretchedly poor inhabitants of the island of

A FAMILIAR SCENE
The once familiar scene of all the women of the household busily knitting is now relatively rare. Knitting is still a popular activity, even though ready-made woollen garments are so easily available, but it is now more likely to be a solitary one.

KNITTING SHEATHS
Knitting sheaths were first used at around the end of the eighteenth century. Women discovered that by using a stick to support their knitting needles, their fingers were left free to manipulate the wool. The knitting sheath was hooked into the wearer's belt and a needle was slotted into a hole at the end of the sheath. The more knitting needles being used, the more knitting sheaths were needed. Sometimes up to six sheaths were slotted into the knitter's belt at one time. They were about eight inches long, made of wood and were often elaborately carved. At one time, young men gave them to their sweethearts as love tokens.

CARVED WOODEN KNITTING SHEATHS

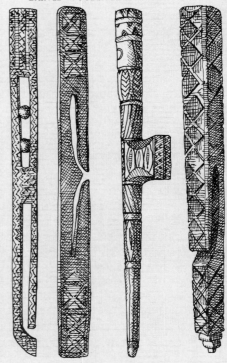

WORN ON THE BELT
The knitting sheath was so made that it could be hooked over a belt. This device allowed several knitting sheaths to be used at the same time without inconvenience to the knitter.

St Kilda, standing beside a perfectly enormous pile of knitted garments, which they were shipping to the mainland to pay the rent to some mainland landlord; surely, in all conscience, there should have been no rent to pay.

THE KNITTING GUILD

In the Middle Ages there was a guild of knitters in England. All the members were men: women were traditionally the spinners. In the late sixteenth century the guild members furiously turned away the inventor of the knitting machine and he had to flee to France. Possibly it was the invention of the stocking framing machine in 1589 that transformed hand knitting from a male-dominated activity into a female one and now, except for a few lightship crewmen and the odd man who might be considered slightly eccentric by his neighbours, knitting is the domain of women.

JERSEYS OR GANSEYS

Fishermen wear jerseys (which most of them call "ganseys") in Great Britain and, if you have ever tried hauling in any sort of a net at sea wearing a jacket with buttons on it, you will know *why* they wear jerseys! You spend all your time disengaging your net from your buttons and end up entirely bereft of the latter. Also, at sea, fishermen need the warmth and comfort of wool. So their wives and girlfriends knit jerseys for them.

Traditionally, fishermen's ganseys were knitted in the round—that is, as seamless tubes and not as shaped panels to be sewn together afterwards. Knitting in the round gives them a four-square look that is very becoming. Knitting shaped panels with two needles and sewing the panels together to form the jersey is a more modern and landlubberly practice altogether.

LOCAL KNITTING TRADITIONS

All around the coast of northern Europe there are local knitting traditions: cable knits, hearts and diamonds and herringbone patterns. Many of these patterns have stories attached to them and some have special meanings: one pattern represents true love, and another marital constancy. A Norwegian lady told me that if a young girl in her country is seen knitting a particularly elaborate and beautiful jersey, her parents wink and smile at each other knowingly, assuming that she has fallen in love. Wives and girlfriends used to knit special patterns

into their men's ganseys in case they ever had to identify their bodies if they were drowned (as far too many were) at sea.

EXPLOITATION

When I first went to County Donegal in Ireland, perhaps twenty years ago, Father McDyer, whose parish was Glencolumcille, had just come back from New York, having fixed up a deal to supply several shops there with locally knitted so-called Aran sweaters. He had secured £5 per sweater for the ladies who knitted the sweaters. Hitherto, merchants had been paying them a tenth of this price and selling them for forty times as much. Working four hours a day, it might take two or three weeks to knit one of these absolutely magnificent garments. The craft is still practised all along the west coast of Ireland and the hand knitters compete successfully with the machines, for their products are of infinitely better quality.

THE PEGOTTY
The pegotty or "knitting Nancy" was a wooden gadget that had pegs protruding, either all round it, or from its corners. It was used for knitting long,.tubular strips of wool.

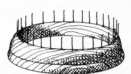

SHETLAND DRYING BOARD

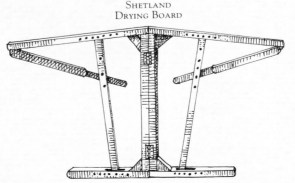

DRYING WOOL
When a Shetland sweater was finished, it was soaked thoroughly, rolled in a towel to remove the excess water and then left to dry on a drying board. As the wool shrank a little while it was drying, any unevenness in the knitting was unnoticeable once the sweater was dry.

MAKING & REPAIRING CLOTHES

PEWTER
THIMBLE

MID-VICTORIAN
THIMBLE

SILVER VIENNESE
THIMBLE

VICTORIAN SILVER
THIMBLE

NICKLE "FINGER NAIL"
THIMBLE

SILVER FINGER
PROTECTOR

CELLULOSE FINGER
SHIELD

HEN THE FIRST PALEOLITHIC LADY got a thorn and stuck it through a piece of hide and dragged a thread through the hole she probably didn't know what she was starting. There are people in Africa today who still wear only rawhide clothes and very nice they can look, too, although the material tends to be pretty stiff and inflexible.

Soft and flexible clothes came about with the invention of weaving. Indeed, it was the art of weaving that introduced the concept of straight lines and right angles, for a piece of woven cloth must start as a rectangle.

MAKING THE CLOTH

In the days before synthetic fibres the cloth that clothes were made of was woven from either animal fibres, such as wool or goat hair, or vegetable fibres.

In many temperate regions, beside making the best rope in the world, hemp made a tough and lasting cloth. It would again if people were allowed to grow it, but alas it is now grown only illegally and for quite other purposes. In the Middle Ages, nettles, a close relative of hemp, were cut and turned into a tough if rather coarse yarn for weaving into a strong cloth.

Flax, that marvellous gift of nature or God to humankind, besides giving us linseed oil, provided the fibres for the finest linen and the toughest sail cloth alike. As it requires hand labour to produce cloth made from flax, it has suffered a severe decline and is hardly produced at all these days.

Silk, originally brought from China in caravans of camels that wound their way along the Great Silk Road, was bound for the wealthy only until it began to be produced in France and prices fell. Its production there is happily now being revived.

Wool, that most noble of materials, clothed most of the population of Europe for most of its history. Cotton arrived in Europe from the East and the Americas in increasing quantities during the seventeenth and eighteenth centuries. Very cheap cotton, produced by slave labour in America, flooded into England, and other countries in Europe, and soon became the basis of the commonest fabric. It withstood block printing easily, and made gaily coloured cloth cheaply available for the first time.

THE COMING OF TROUSERS AND TUNICS

There can be little doubt that a Hindu gentleman of southern India would today feel more at home sartorially in the Athens of Pericles or the Rome of Vergil than he would in modern London. When men began to ride horses, trousers were invented. Herodotus described the Scythians, who lived on their horses (and so lacked cloth that they made handkerchiefs out of the scalps of their enemies), as wearing heavily embroidered trousers and padded jackets. The invention of the latter is, of course, hardly surprising in colder climates.

The simple tunic was a logical development to those who were physically active. For, it is extremely hampering trying to do hard work in a single rectangular garment. Sinhalese peasants today tuck their graceful sarongs up into their waistbands to enable

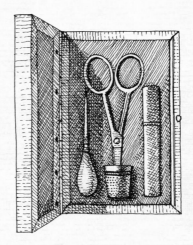

STORAGE AND CLAMPS
Basic sewing tools, such as scissors, needles and thimbles, were kept in special sewing cases or boxes, which were often highly decorated and given as presents. While sewing, it was useful to have a reel stand nearby which held reels of thread on short, wooden rods on a revolving base. Sewing clamps were used for holding pincushions, reels of thread and hemming birds, and could be clamped to the table.

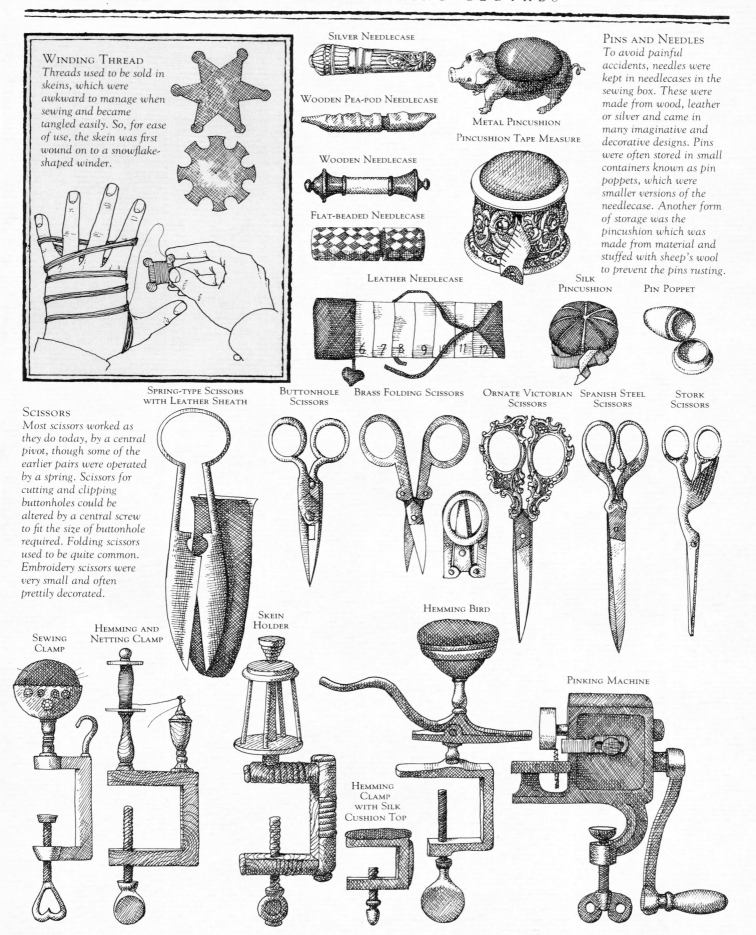

WINDING THREAD

Threads used to be sold in skeins, which were awkward to manage when sewing and became tangled easily. So, for ease of use, the skein was first wound on to a snowflake-shaped winder.

SILVER NEEDLECASE

WOODEN PEA-POD NEEDLECASE

WOODEN NEEDLECASE

FLAT-BEADED NEEDLECASE

LEATHER NEEDLECASE

METAL PINCUSHION

PINCUSHION TAPE MEASURE

PINS AND NEEDLES

To avoid painful accidents, needles were kept in needlecases in the sewing box. These were made from wood, leather or silver and came in many imaginative and decorative designs. Pins were often stored in small containers known as pin poppets, which were smaller versions of the needlecase. Another form of storage was the pincushion which was made from material and stuffed with sheep's wool to prevent the pins rusting.

SILK PINCUSHION

PIN POPPET

SCISSORS

Most scissors worked as they do today, by a central pivot, though some of the earlier pairs were operated by a spring. Scissors for cutting and clipping buttonholes could be altered by a central screw to fit the size of buttonhole required. Folding scissors used to be quite common. Embroidery scissors were very small and often prettily decorated.

SPRING-TYPE SCISSORS WITH LEATHER SHEATH

BUTTONHOLE SCISSORS

BRASS FOLDING SCISSORS

ORNATE VICTORIAN SCISSORS

SPANISH STEEL SCISSORS

STORK SCISSORS

SKEIN HOLDER

HEMMING BIRD

SEWING CLAMP

HEMMING AND NETTING CLAMP

HEMMING CLAMP WITH SILK CUSHION TOP

PINKING MACHINE

them to work better and Burmese men do the same with their lunghis. Such people understand better than Westerners the biblical injunction "gird up your loins"! They have to do it every time they enter a paddy field. The tunic is a practical working garment; it allows untrammelled freedom of the arms, just as trousers do of the legs. Tunics are made today, as they were made in Roman times, quite simply out of six pieces of rectangular cloth.

FASHION FOR RICH AND POOR

Breeches were almost universally worn by men up till the nineteenth century. They fastened just below the knee with buttons or buckles and were worn with stockings. Long trousers were worn only by sailors and poor shepherds until the Prince of Wales wore a pair of sailor's white trousers in 1807 while on holiday in Brighton. The trend was set: by the middle of the nineteenth century long trousers were the norm for all social classes. They were cut with a front flap, which was fastened at each side of the waist. While working trousers were made with front falls, fly fronts were fashionable for gentlemen. Until the end of the century, to accompany his long trousers, the average working man wore a wide-cut shirt and waistcoat with a neckerchief and, of course, a soft felt hat.

Working women, especially in rural areas, all wore the same basic costume up until the middle of the nineteenth century. It comprised a shift, an ankle-length petticoat, a low-necked overgown, a bibless apron and a large kerchief or shawl. From the 1820s it was no longer fashionable to wear a single, high-waisted garment and it was common for working women in rural areas to wear bodices and skirts at second, third or even fourth hand after they had gone out of fashion. They wore their skirts shorter than town or upper-class women, revealing sturdy boots or sensible shoes.

The practice of making clothes look beautiful with pattern and ornament was almost universal up to the first part of the nineteenth century. Then, although women's clothes continued to be ornamented, men's clothes became sombre and severe, and funereal black became the predominant colour. As G.K. Chesterton remarked, a Medieval prelate wore sackcloth next to his skin but cloth of gold on the outside, where it would be seen, whereas the Victorian rich man wore black where it could be seen and kept the gold next to his heart.

Women's clothes became more and more restrictive and less and less functional as the century wore on. This all changed with the First World War, when at last the female leg (or nether limb as the Victorians called it) became once again visible and the female waist was allowed to resume its normal proportions (although its position on the body tended to be unanatomical). However, in the 1920s a new fashion was universally adopted in the West by which the female mammary glands were made, by some alchemy, to disappear altogether.

FINE NEEDLEWORK

My own first experience of the needle and thread is limited to observation. I am old enough to remember the French lady's maid (yes, such beings did exist, although they are probably rarer in these days than French mermaids). It was generally allowed that they were consummately skilful with the needle. If you peer into old needlecraft books you will be surprised at the complexity the noble art of needlework attained.

DOMED BUTTONS
These were simple home-made buttons made from two circles of linen. Ravelling was placed in the centre of each circle, and the circle was then drawn up to form a "bag". The two bags were then sewn together to make the button.

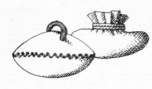

DORSET CROSSWHEEL BUTTON
This type of button was made from a curtain ring and thread. First the ring was closely wrapped in thread. Then six threads were wound round the ring, making twelve spokes radiating from the centre. The wheel was then filled in by weaving thread in and out of the spokes to finish the button.

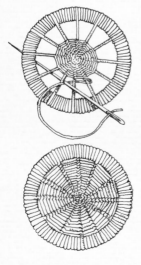

THE PAPER PATTERN
It was Ebenezer Butterick, a Massachusetts tailor, who first had the idea of cutting a paper pattern for his wife to follow, to make it easier for her to sew his shirts. Soon he was selling various shirt patterns locally and, in 1862, he made a pattern for the shirt worn by Garibaldi and his legion, which proved immensely popular. He started making paper tissue patterns for underwear, dresses and children's clothes along

DRESS PATTERN TRACER

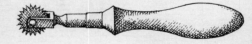

with men's shirts and was so successful that in 1865 he was able to buy a New York fashion journal and sell patterns by mail all round the world. Queen Victoria bought several patterns from him. It did not take long for others to follow his example and, in England, Mrs Beeton's husband's magazine, *The Englishwoman's Domestic Magazine*, was the first to offer paper patterns to its readers. At last, housewives could sew fashionable garments easily and be sure that they would fit.

MAKING & REPAIRING CLOTHES

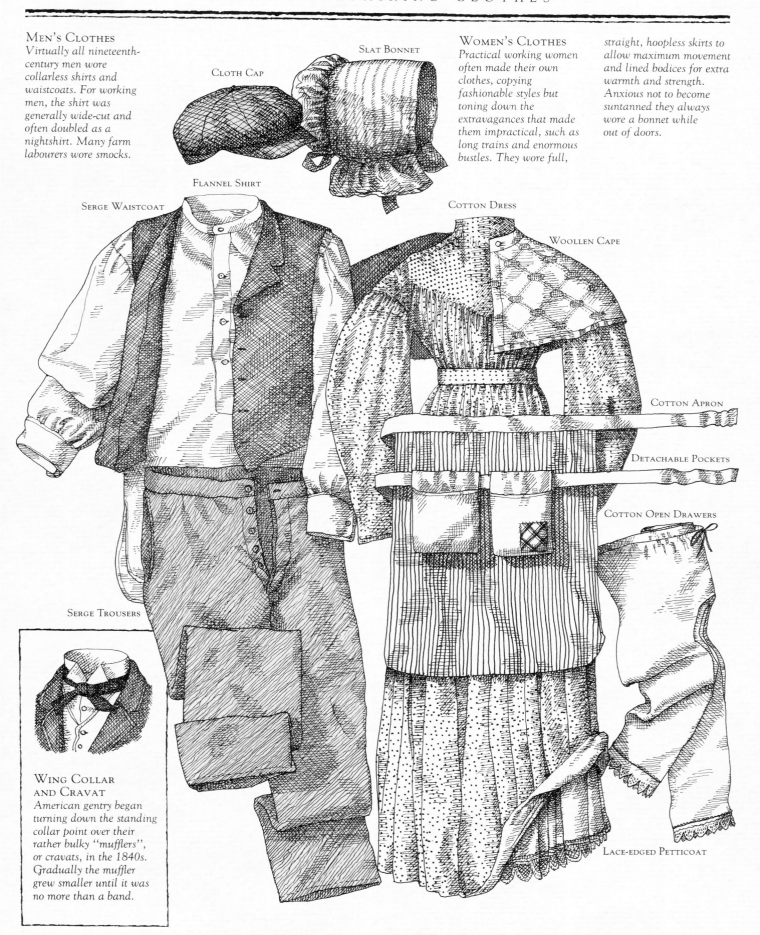

MEN'S CLOTHES
Virtually all nineteenth-century men wore collarless shirts and waistcoats. For working men, the shirt was generally wide-cut and often doubled as a nightshirt. Many farm labourers wore smocks.

CLOTH CAP

SLAT BONNET

FLANNEL SHIRT

SERGE WAISTCOAT

WOMEN'S CLOTHES
Practical working women often made their own clothes, copying fashionable styles but toning down the extravagances that made them impractical, such as long trains and enormous bustles. They wore full, straight, hoopless skirts to allow maximum movement and lined bodices for extra warmth and strength. Anxious not to become suntanned they always wore a bonnet while out of doors.

COTTON DRESS

WOOLLEN CAPE

COTTON APRON

DETACHABLE POCKETS

COTTON OPEN DRAWERS

SERGE TROUSERS

WING COLLAR AND CRAVAT
American gentry began turning down the standing collar point over their rather bulky "mufflers", or cravats, in the 1840s. Gradually the muffler grew smaller until it was no more than a band.

LACE-EDGED PETTICOAT

351

In France, the art of fine needlework did not die out as it did in England after the Edwardian era. The French have always been pre-eminent at this beautiful and most essential craft: by far the best book on the subject ever produced was written by Thérèse de Dillmont, a woman from the Alsace region of France.

THE HUSSIF

My next encounter with the needle and thread was in the Second World War via an object called the "hussif". We each carried a hussif, or little bag, in a little pocket sewn into our jungle battledresses, together with a first aid field dressing and a morphia syringe. The hussif contained a few needles, a thimble and some darning thread.

I was in the King's African Rifles and it was a stirring sight, back at base camp, during the period set aside for what was quaintly called internal economy, to see a thousand men, some of them self-confessed cannibals, squatting on the ground in parade formation all plying their needles and thread. Whether they were practising the French double seam, the antique or old German seam, the back stitch, the running stitch or just plain petit point I never found out. Certainly, we managed to keep our bottle-green battledresses hanging together until we went to Burma, where they rotted off our backs in the monsoon, thread and fabric alike; our boots went the same way. Replacement battledresses and boots were dropped to us from aeroplanes.

CLOTHES MADE TO LAST

In the nineteenth century every young girl, and many boys, of good households were taught the rudiments of sewing and mending. Over stitch, back stitch, running stitch, buttonhole stitch, chain stitch, cross stitch, whipping, darning, seaming and gathering were the basic stitches and sewing techniques taught. Despite this, it usually fell to the woman of the household to sew the clothing for all the family. This was an extremely time-consuming task, as she would probably have to manufacture the cloth first. Consequently, she made the family's clothes to last and patched and darned old clothes until they were truly beyond repair.

The clothes such women made generally bore little resemblance to the elegant silk gowns worn by the wealthy, who could afford to hire a dress maker or tailor to cut

DRESS MAKING
Most women could not afford to hire a professional seamstress and sewed all the family's clothes themselves. Their work was made much easier with the advent of the affordable domestic sewing machine and the paper pattern, which was often sold by, and sometimes even given away with, late Victorian women's magazines.

EXPANDING
SKIRT STAND
This was an early form of the tailor's dummy and was a very useful sewing aid. It expanded and folded to cater for all sizes. To ensure the skirt was a perfect fit, it was tried on the stand and altered accordingly.

SEWING BY MACHINE

MACHINE SEWING HAS SEVERAL ADVANTAGES over hand sewing, the main one being the increased speed of stitching. In 1845, Elias Howe promoted his invention, the sewing machine, which sewed 250 stitches a minute, by challenging five of the fastest seamstresses who could be found to a sewing race. He maintained that he could finish five seams in the time it took for any one of them to finish one. He won, and what was more, his machine-stitched seams were judged to be the neatest and strongest: two more advantages of sewing by machine.

The first machines were designed primarily for use in tailors' shops and factories and were very expensive. The first family machine was not designed until 1856 by Isaac Singer. Called the "turtle back", it was smaller and lighter than the industrial models and came in a wooden cabinet, which doubled as a table for the machine to stand on. Sales were slow to begin with, as most men saw no reason to purchase what was still quite an expensive

machine to do the work their wives and mothers had done, perfectly satisfactorily and at absolutely no cost to themselves, for years. And indeed, what would their wives do with the free time the machine afforded them? Newspapers printed letters, purportedly from women, who said they rued the day they finally persuaded their husbands to buy a machine, as they had tried and tried but found it impossible to operate successfully. But gradually the women and the sewing machine companies won the battle, with clever argument, hire-purchase schemes and decreasing cost, until the sewing machine became a standard item in virtually every household.

The basic lock-stitch sewing machine enabled the housewife to sew more complicated styles of dress than before, especially with the increasing availability of paper patterns (see p.350). The clothes she made were more sturdy, too, as the seams did not fall apart if a stitch was torn.

WORKING WITH THE MACHINE
Few women encountered any difficulty either in threading the machine or controlling the progress of the stitches along the cloth. As long as she guided the cloth gently under the presser foot with one hand, while turning the handle at a comfortable speed with the other, the housewife could run up clothes and stitch household linen in next to no time.

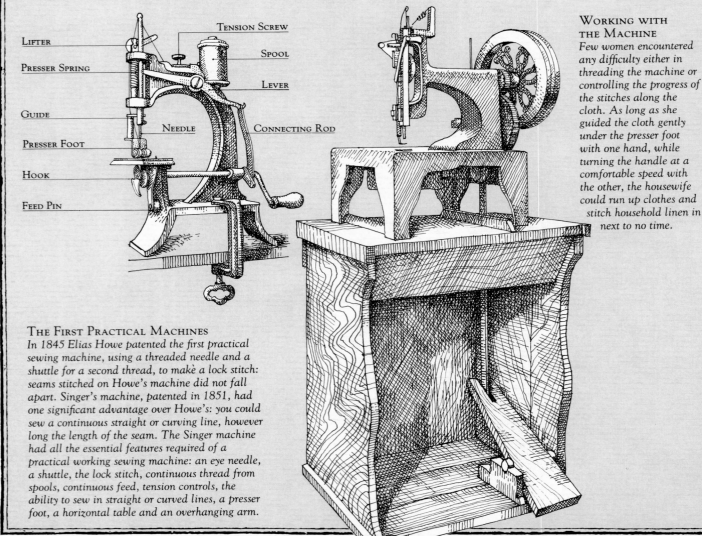

LIFTER

TENSION SCREW

PRESSER SPRING

SPOOL

LEVER

GUIDE

NEEDLE

CONNECTING ROD

PRESSER FOOT

HOOK

FEED PIN

THE FIRST PRACTICAL MACHINES
In 1845 Elias Howe patented the first practical sewing machine, using a threaded needle and a shuttle for a second thread, to make a lock stitch: seams stitched on Howe's machine did not fall apart. Singer's machine, patented in 1851, had one significant advantage over Howe's: you could sew a continuous straight or curving line, however long the length of the seam. The Singer machine had all the essential features required of a practical working sewing machine: an eye needle, a shuttle, the lock stitch, continuous thread from spools, continuous feed, tension controls, the ability to sew in straight or curved lines, a presser foot, a horizontal table and an overhanging arm.

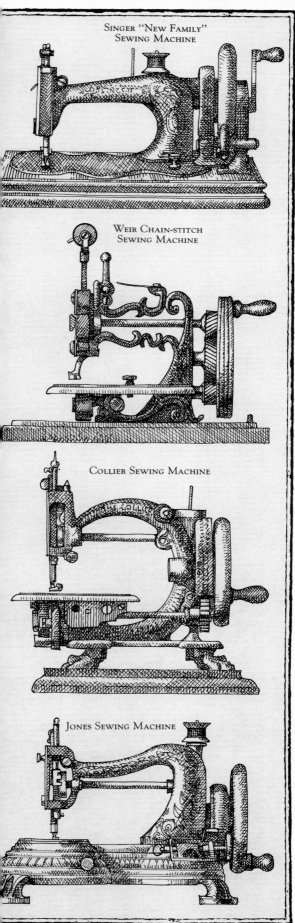

SINGER "NEW FAMILY" SEWING MACHINE

WEIR CHAIN-STITCH SEWING MACHINE

COLLIER SEWING MACHINE

JONES SEWING MACHINE

and sew their dresses and suits. However, they were neatly sewn, with wide seams so that they could be let out, if necessary! Even then, we are told, the mistress of the house could make eight shirts out of a piece of linen a yard wide, although we are not told how long it was.

Most women did not have the luxury of using patterns and simply cut the shirt or dress to the same size as the last shirt or dress made for that person, incorporating allowances for seams and changes in shape! Experienced sewers had no trouble cutting the fabric to the appropriate size, but novices were advised (if they could afford it) to go to a dress maker to get the person fitted for the item of clothing. Then, if it was a dress, to rip out one sleeve, half the waist, half the back and half the front and cut out paper patterns for each section. These were then used as a guide next time, when the sewer would not need to return to the dress maker but would be sure of a good fit.

SEWING EQUIPMENT
The mistress of the house always had a well-equipped work basket. In it would be needles of different sizes for wool and cotton, small and large darning needles, and a tin of pins. There would be fine scissors, common scissors and buttonhole scissors; tapes of all sizes and colours; spools of white and coloured thread; a bag for buttons and another for braid and cord. Two thimbles were generally kept in the basket in case one was lost, and if the basket was a large one a brick cushion might be found in it! This was simply a pincushion positioned on top of a covered brick for extra stability.

MENDING CLOTHES
Darning and patching were high arts until this age of factory-made, throw-away garments. Stockings worn thin at the heel were usually patched with hose before a hole appeared to save darning them. Trousers were often "reseated" when they became thin, and if the sleeves of a dress or shirt became worn or thin, they were ripped out and new ones sewn in their place. In every case, rather than discard a worn garment, it would be looked at carefully and if the worn area could be replaced, it would be, and often, you'd be hard put to see the join. Even if the garment was beyond repair the material was not thrown away, but thrown into the rag bag. Whole new garments were made from the contents of the rag bag.

EMERGENCY MENDING
The darning ball was dropped inside a sock or stocking to make a firm foundation for darning a hole. This gadget was later superseded by the darning mushroom which had a handle and was easier to hold. The darning stick served a similar function for the fingers of gloves that needed mending.

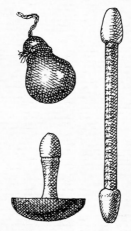

DARNING EQUIPMENT

QUILTING & PATCHWORK

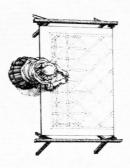

WADDED QUILTING WAS BORN OUT OF the practical need to provide warmth and is still made today. A layer of wadding is sandwiched between two layers of fabric and the top layer sewn with attractive stitch patterns or patchwork. Some clothing was made in this way, and today you can buy quilted waterproof coats, but the most commonly made quilted item was the bedcover, so much so, indeed, that it became known as the quilt.

STRETCHING THE FABRIC

For best quilting results, the layers of fabric and wadding are stretched on a frame. In this way, the layers are kept taut and together and the stitching appears in deeper relief when the finished quilt is removed from the frame, therefore emphasizing the pattern.

Women often gathered together to make a communal quilt, usually to give as a present. These gatherings were often known as quilting bees, especially in America, and the quilt was often given to a girl about to be married. Decorative cotton panels to commemorate special occasions, such as jubilees, were sewn into the centre of quilts and coverlets made as gifts. Such "friendship" quilts were very common around the middle of the nineteenth century.

DECORATIVE QUILTING

A later development from the practical wadded quilting was Italian, or cord, quilting. This was purely decorative and did not involve any wadding. Two layers of fabric are placed together and narrow lines of stitching are sewn to make mainly pictorial patterns. Cord is then threaded between the lines of stitching to raise the pattern.

Trapunto or padded quilting is purely decorative. Again, using only two layers of fabric, the pattern or motif is stitched through both layers and padding inserted from the back to raise the pattern.

Patterns for all varieties of quilting have been handed down from mother to daughter through the centuries.

QUILTING FRAMES
Quilting frames were about four feet long and made from strips of wood. The quilt was stretched between the sides of the frame, and held in place with quick stitches. This stretching ensured that the quilt did not become out of shape and baggy while it was being made. As each width was finished, it was rolled up.

MAKING NEW FROM OLD

Even today, wherever cloth is scarce and expensive, articles of clothing are conserved when partially worn out and the good parts cut out and used to make patchwork. Such thrift has always been practised in peasant societies. To begin with pieces of cloth of all sizes and very rough shapes were sewn together until the required size was reached, but gradually quite sophisticated designs were developed. Instead of simply sewing together large oblongs or squares of different sizes, identical diamond-, hexagon-, octagon- or square-shaped patches were cut out, using templates. This gave the patchworker much greater control over the look of the finished patchwork article.

Templates were usually made of wood, tin or card, but were sometimes made from more expensive material, such as pewter, copper, brass or even silver. The patchworker would place the template of the shape required on a piece of paper, draw round it and cut out the shape. She would cut out as many pieces as she needed for the patchwork and then pin them to the material and cut out the shapes in the cloth. Quite often the lining paper would be left on the inside of the quilt when it was finished.

HIGH ART

The early American colonists brought the art of patchwork to its highest expression. The American weaving industry was still in its infancy and most cloth had to be shipped from England. Consequently, all cloth was very expensive and none was wasted. My brother has a beautiful bed counterpane made from diamond shapes of two shades of blue. It was made by my great great grandmother before she got married, using scraps of material from the liveries of the household slaves of her husband and her own household, for she lived in the South before the days of emancipation.

Quilts were not the only articles decorated with patchwork: tea cosies, egg cosies and coffee pot cosies made of crazy patchwork were common. Pieces of brightly coloured cloth of all sorts of shapes, sizes and designs were arranged haphazardly and stitched along the edges to cover the raw edges of the fabric. People who amassed large drawers full of worn-out articles had a wide store of different fabrics and colours to draw from and were able to make beautiful patchwork counterpanes, chair covers and sometimes even curtains.

PATCHWORK AND QUILT DESIGNS

Traditional patchwork designs were made from templates arranged in an overall pattern, comprising a dominant centre with linked border and corner motifs. Early designs were usually symmetrical. A widely used motif was the tulip, as it was a popular flower and had the advantage of a simple outline.

Repeated block patterns, such as that used in the nine-patch design, produced a strong visual image. This design was made up of one-inch squares that formed a nine-patch block, hence its name. Mosaic patterns were created by repeating a geometric shape, such as a square, triangle or hexagon. The sunburst pattern was made entirely from diamond patches in shades of orange and brown. Diamond shapes were also used in the tumbling block pattern, the three-dimensional effect being created by the use of colours. The feathered star pattern was one of the classic patchwork designs—it was made from tiny triangles.

Some patterns were created with texture instead of colour. Wadding was placed between two pieces of fabric and then designs were sewn through the layers. Motifs included flowers, leaves and hearts. This was known as stuffed quilting and could be used in conjunction with other forms of quilting and patchwork.

ROSE OF SHARON   TREE OF LIFE   FRIENDSHIP

PRINCESS FEATHER   PENNSYLVANIA PINEAPPLE   TULIPS AND RIBBONS

STORM AT SEA   SUNBURST   TUMBLING BLOCK

FEATHERED STAR   MARINER'S COMPASS   NINE-PATCH

SMOCKING

N THE DAYS WHEN MEN AND WOMEN were contented with the station in life to which "they had been called" (as indeed they had to be), people could be identified as to the calling by their garments. Merchant sailormen really did wear bell-bottomed trousers and a coat of navy blue when ashore and coal miners were proud to wear the white silk neckerchief while out of the mine.

Countrymen such as farm workers used to wear smocked overalls. The smocking was usually overlaid with embroidered designs and made of tough linen. The patterns worked sometimes denoted the trade of the wearer. A design of shepherds' crooks and sheep hurdles meant that the wearer was a shepherd, while horse-shoes and sheaves of wheat indicated a ploughman.

SMOCKS FOR ALL OCCASIONS

There were two kinds of smock: the working smock and the ceremonial smock. The smocking on the working smock was functional; it was a simple way of shaping what would otherwise have been a purely cylindrical garment. Smocking at the bottom of the sleeves constricted them at the wrists and kept the weather out. The ceremonial smock was highly decorated and worn for special occasions, such as harvest suppers. It was handed down from father to son and often served four to five generations.

In considering the smock it must be remembered that linen, which could be produced in any parish in England and Wales from home-grown flax, was an absolutely splendid material. Heavy, dyed flax cloth, such as was used to make country smocks, would keep its wearer warm and dry in all but the hardest rain, and because it was a wide-skirted garment it was a cool and well-ventilated garment to wear in summer.

The art of smocking is on the increase today but mostly for women's garments. It would be nice to think that women will some day again be proud to make fine and decorative working smocks for their menfolk and that men would be proud to wear them. I certainly would.

DRAWING UP
THE GATHERS
First, several rows of even stitches are sewn over the area of the garment to be gathered. Then the threads are pulled gently by the loose ends to make evenly spaced gathers, and secured round a pin.

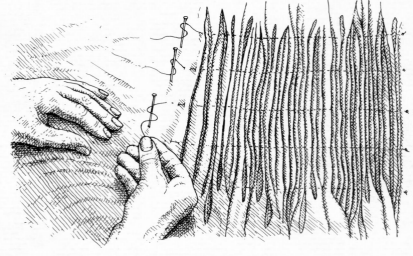

SECURING
WITH STITCHES
The gathers are held in place with various ornamental stitches. Basic stitches are outline stem stitch (top) and surface honeycomb stitch (bottom). The gathering threads are then removed and the smocking is complete.

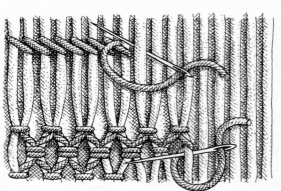

EMBROIDERY

MBROIDERY IS THE DELICATE ART OF drawing on cloth with stitches of thread. It is applied to cloth that is already woven and is quite distinct from tapestry. With tapestry, the designs are actually woven into the cloth as it is created on the loom. The warp threads of tapestry cloth are constant, but spaced fairly far apart so that they are not very prominent and the weft is dominant. Whenever the pattern calls for a different colour thread, the weft is interrupted during the weaving and the new colour woven in for the length required. In this way the picture is gradually built up within the weave and can be quite intricate if made by an accomplished weaver.

Embroidery is stitched on to already woven cloth. It is an embellishment of decorative stitches with thread of many colours. The Bayeux tapestry is not a tapestry at all but a piece of embroidery and a splendid piece, too, full of vigour and drama. Like all the best embroidery it is as good in its way as the best contemporary painting or drawing.

STRENGTHS AND LIMITATIONS

Good embroiderers understand the limitations of their medium and exploit them. They do not have the almost infinite range of colours that painters use at their disposal: their "palette" is much more limited. However, by using colours strongly and boldly this apparent defect can be turned into an advantage. Instead of trying to make natural-looking pictures, they create stylized or abstract designs.

Medieval embroidery, such little of it as remains in good condition—much has decayed and much was looted for its gold and silver thread—is magnificent and reveals a perfect understanding of the nature of the medium. *Opus Anglicanum*, Norman-English embroidery of the thirteenth and fourteenth centuries, was famous throughout Europe. Ecclesiastical garments and fabrics, horse-trappings (the cloth draped over horses when they went into battle), the jupons of their riders (garments worn over armour), ladies' gowns, bed-hangings and much more were all richly embroidered.

TAMBOUR WORK
This was so called because the frame resembled a tambourine. Crêpe or another fine cloth was stretched between two wooden hoops and looped stitches of gold thread were made in it, using a needle that looked similar to a crochet hook.

PATTERNS AND DESIGNS
Wooden stamps were used to print a pattern on to the material to provide guidelines for embroidering. Flowers and birds were common print designs. The designs were first worked out on a piece of paper. This paper pattern was glued on to the base of a flat wooden block and the design scored into the wood. Pewter or copper strips were then inserted into the scored lines. When the block was dipped in ink and stamped on the material, the image of the pattern was imprinted.

EMBROIDERY STAMPS

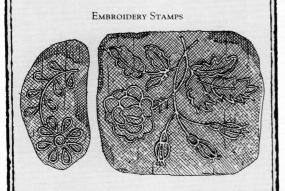

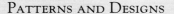

EMBROIDERY HOOP ON STAND

VICTORIAN STRAIGHT-SIDED EMBROIDERY FRAME

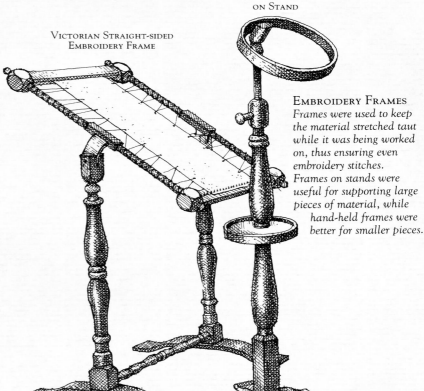

EMBROIDERY FRAMES
Frames were used to keep the material stretched taut while it was being worked on, thus ensuring even embroidery stitches. Frames on stands were useful for supporting large pieces of material, while hand-held frames were better for smaller pieces.

As time went on, more and more stitches were invented at home and imported from various parts of the world, and the art of embroidery became more and more sophisticated. It reached its peak in Tudor and early Stuart times but in the eighteenth century magnificent embroidery was still being stitched and was commonly found on clothing for both men and women, as readers of *The Tailor of Gloucester* will know.

It became seen as a duty that gentlewomen should learn fine embroidery. Many developed a lifelong interest in fine needlework and embroidered all the household articles it was practical to embroider: very little was missed even by the busiest of women.

DECLINE OF THE ART

In Victorian times the standard of embroidery fell as it was practised more widely. Every Victorian lady embroidered as though her life depended on it, and embroidered fabrics soon covered everything from tea cosies to crinolines. Books abounded on the subject of ladies' fancy work. Gentlewomen were urged to embroider initial letters on a corner of a gentleman's handkerchief, concealing the line of the letter with a drapery of stems, foliage and

fruit. As the nineteenth century wore on so taste declined (according to my taste at least) and embroidery reached perhaps its pit in Berlin wool-work, in which designs, generally of appalling sentimentality, were coarsely worked on canvas using garish wool.

On second thoughts, perhaps this was not the bottom of the pit, perhaps that has been reached today, when ready-to-embroider canvases are sold in the high street. Clumsy representations of the paintings of old masters are already painted on them and the coloured wool to create the picture is supplied with it. This is not what the high art of embroidery is all about.

A FINE ART

The fine art of embroidery can be found when wandering among the mountains of Crete. There you will find mothers embroidering household fabrics that they have woven beautifully themselves with strange and fanciful patterns, many of which have been handed down from mother to daughter since the Minoan civilization. These articles are then packed away in a bottom drawer, or a chest, and kept against the day when their daughter gets married, at which point they will form part of her dowry. She, in her turn, will hand it on to her daughter and so on.

There are signs of revival in the embroiderer's art in the rest of the world. The Embroiderers' Guild and the Royal School of Needlework in England are striving to improve standards. Perhaps a new school of *Opus Anglicanum*, or even *Opus Americanum*, is in the process of gestation. Let us hope that the skills developed over thousands of years will not be thrown away in a couple of generations.

EMBROIDERY SAMPLERS
Letters of the alphabet occurred frequently in embroidery samplers. Initial capital letters offered great scope for perfecting decorative and intricate stitchwork.

EMBROIDERY SAMPLER

AN EXTRAVAGANT DISPLAY
There were endless opportunities for displaying embroidery skills in the home. The covering of this eighteenth-century sofa was rather extravagantly embroidered with a decorative floral design in shades of green, pink and cream.

18TH-CENTURY SOFA

DECORATIVE CRAFTS

Before the Industrial Revolution every object made by man or woman was decorated fittingly and beautifully. In fact, the pre-industrial scientist would have found it hateful to work with apparatus unembellished by the work of the artist. Can you imagine a modern-day chemist asking a glass engraver to cut beautiful designs upon his test tubes? Farm machinery was one of the last classes of object to surrender to pure utilitarianism. Up until the 1950s farm machinery, even that designed to be pulled by tractors, was painted in the factory with panels and scrolls. Carts and wagons had chamfering carved on all their timbers, often skilfully "lined-out" in paint by the wainwright, and beautiful "fiddle-heads" were carved on projecting timbers. Today, no tractor manufacturer would consider doing such a thing. Objects manufactured for domestic use have suffered similarly but the living tradition of the decorative arts has not died out entirely and there is a growing number of craftspeople who are trying to revive the art of true decoration.

PAINTING & PAPERING

I F YOU GO INTO A PAINT SHOP nowadays you will find yourself surrounded by terribly expensive tins of undercoat, gloss and emulsion paint. The colours can be rather bright and garish, but the resulting painted walls are lacking somehow in character.

MIXING PAINTS

Up to the Second World War, when there was still a paint shop in every country town in England, you would find not tins of proprietary paints but sacks or wooden barrels filled with coloured powder. You bought the powder and mixed it yourself with water, linseed oil (obtainable from the same shop) or turpentine, depending on the sort of paint you required.

Going back even earlier, most country people made their own paints. They took coloured clays that they found in their locality, or bought from itinerant tradesmen just like the raddleman of Hardy's *Mayor of Casterbridge*, and mixed them with such unlikely substances as sour milk and lime. The acid sour milk and the alkaline lime (slaked lime) were mixed together in the correct proportions and neutralized one another.

Lime is mixed with water today to make limewash. In many Mediterranean countries there is almost a ritual whitewashing of houses where limewash is applied inside and out, once a year every spring. In Suffolk, England, red ochre is traditionally added to limewash to make that muted but attractive colour, "Suffolk pink".

In the middle of the nineteenth century an attractive paint finish became fashionable in living rooms of the middle and upper classes

in America, where stencilled walls (see p.364) were much more popular than in England, where wallpaper was all the rage. Where a bookcase ran all around the room, which was often the case in grand houses, an Indian red wash was often applied to the wall area above the bookcase and a dull gold stencil pattern applied on top to create the effect of a frieze.

GRAINING

A folk art or craft that has practically died out these days is graining. It might seem strange that anybody should go to the trouble of covering up the natural grain of wood, which looks pretty nice in itself, then laboriously paint a depiction of wood grain on it, but where the wood was cheap deal, and the craftsman knew his job, the result could be very pleasing. The cabins and fo'c'sles of sailing barges, the "snug" bars of country ale houses, and many a cottage kitchen were once "grained out". There is very little graining left now, and sadly today you would be hard put to find anyone who knew how to do it.

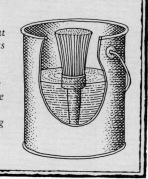

SWELLING BRUSHES
Before use, in order that the brush would keep its shape, it was first suspended in water, handle-down, up to the bristles. This caused the brush to swell in its binding without making the bristles flabby.

GRINDING PIGMENTS
Before the introduction of tinned paints, merchants sold paint in powdered form, consisting of ground pigments. Some machines enabled them to mix in the oil or water whilst grinding the pigment, but this was normally done at a later stage by the buyer.

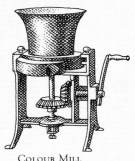

COLOUR MILL

DECORATING BRUSHES
Painting and decorating brushes came in a wide variety of shapes, sizes and qualities, as they do today. Early brushes ranged from inexpensive oval painters' dusters to flat, white-bristled wall brushes bound in brass.

WHITEWASH BRUSH

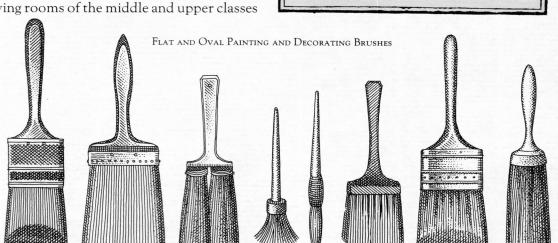

FLAT AND OVAL PAINTING AND DECORATING BRUSHES

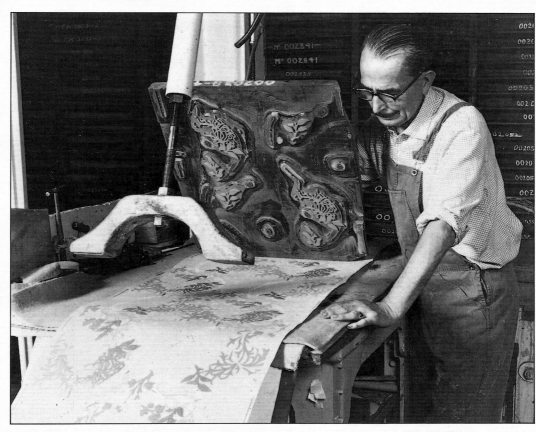

WALLPAPER BLOCKING

The first wallpapers were printed by hand and were labour-intensive. Once the pattern had been designed, it was separated into its component colours and each one carefully engraved on to a large pearwood block. Excess wood was then removed so that the design stood out in relief to hold the ink for printing. In early print shops the pressure required to transfer the paint on the block to the wallpaper was applied by human weight! Boys were employed to sit on cantilevered beams, which were positioned over the blocks. As in the William Morris design being printed here, some patterns required eight or nine blockings.

DECORATIVE PLASTERWORK

In the elegant Georgian times there was a wonderful development of decorative plasterwork created in England largely by Italian craftsmen. Staircases featured panels of exquisite pargeting, and intricate mouldings were created around fireplaces and doorways. Their brothers were doing the same sort of work, with far greater luxuriance and elaboration, for the Moghul emperors.

WALLPAPERING

The earliest wallpapers were hand printed with wood blocks and came in some attractive patterns. In the Victorian era printed wallpaper was mass produced and the standard of design fell swiftly to abysmal depths. It was the deplorable taste of the Victorian mass producers of wallpaper that caused William Morris to start designing wallpaper of his own. He set up a factory and employed dedicated craftsmen to make his elaborate intertwining floral designs: the first "designer" wallpapers.

The Victorians had a passion for wallpaper and applied it with vigour to every available wall. When one covering of paper got tatty they simply stuck another layer over the top of it: they did not bother with soaping the original layer off first. When I bought my farmhouse in Pembrokeshire I stripped six layers of wallpaper off the walls, each one more hideous than the previous one. Linoleum, too, was a terrible Victorian vice. In that same house I shovelled out five or six layers of lino, each progressively more rotten and infested with woodlice.

Different styles of wallpaper were advocated for different rooms. Complex designs of fruit, flowers and foliage with threads of dull gold running through them were recommended for the drawing room. Deeper tones but similar designs were considered appropriate for the library and dining room, while lighter coloured, less stylized paper was allowed in the bedrooms.

The model for many a trendy domestic interior of the 1920s and 1930s seems to have been the operating theatre. Patterned wallpaper gave way to bare, colour-washed walls and decorative plasterwork became extinct, not only because it was not desired but because there were no longer any craftsmen skilled enough to do it.

GRAINING

Cheap wood was often camouflaged by painting a wood grain over the original. The paint was applied and a graining comb dragged over the wet surface to achieve the desired effect.

GRAINING COMB

STENCILLING

T O STENCIL YOU SIMPLY CUT THE basic design out of a piece of stiff material, fix it on the wall, piece of furniture, book or material to be stencilled and then daub on your paint with a paintbrush. Stencilling is ideal for creating a repetitive design over a large surface and was used extensively on the inner walls of churches in many parts of Europe from Medieval times.

STENCILLING IN CHURCHES

Many church wall stencils imitate fabric by repeating a simple design on the background. In East Anglia in the east of England, in particular, there are some splendid stencilled wooden rood screens richly patterned in gold, black, white, blue, green, yellow and red. Some screens have stencilled backgrounds with hand-painted pictures of the saints on top. The church in the tiny village of Ranworth near the Norfolk Broads contains a very fine example of this, although the faces of the saints shown in the painting were touched up by a Victorian artist to look like local worthies!

STENCILLING WALLS AND FLOORS

Towards the end of the eighteenth century, journeyman artists began going about the villages seeking patronage. Instead of taking rolls of expensive wallpaper, as before, they took a stencilling kit of brushes, a selection of stencils cut from thick paper, dry colours and measuring tools.

For borders to outline windows, doors and mantels, they used stencils of flowers, leaves and stems and stencils of geometric designs. Friezes of swags, scattered flowers and festoons were often made to edge the ceilings and single motifs were repeated on the broad wall spaces.

Separate motifs were usually made with one stencil, as only one colour would be needed. For more elaborate motifs, a combination of stencils was used, the number depending on the number of colours used. Two colours were usually used for the bold pattern on large friezes: the painter would first go round the top of all four walls with one colour and then, when the paint was dry, go round again with the second stencil and the second colour.

Similar motifs were often used on the floorboards, and stencilled floors were popular in the eighteenth century, especially in America. Bold designs were favoured and some stencilled floors resembled mosaic tiling or marquetry.

STENCILLING FURNITURE

The traditional way of stencilling wooden furniture is first to apply a thin coat of size made of varnish and turpentine to the area to be stencilled. This acts as a binder for the bronze powders, which you apply with small velvet pads through the thin paper stencil, just before the adhesive dries. Pure gold powder was used on only the best furniture because it was so expensive.

WORKING UP
A PATTERN
Borders of repeating patterns were usually achieved with a combination of several stencils. In this example, there were two stencils—one for the leaf motif, which was stencilled first, and one for the vein markings, which was added when the paint was dry from the first stencil.

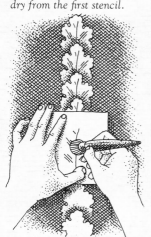

AMERICAN STENCILS
In the nineteenth century stencilled decoration was very popular in America. Stencil designs often depicted flowers, leaves and circular sunbursts, or else they were simply decorative shapes. The stencils were used in a repeating pattern on walls and floors, sometimes to decorate the entire surface, and often to highlight a particular feature, such as the skirting or a door frame. The simpler the design, the more effective the overall pattern.

FURNITURE & FURNISHINGS

 N THE MIDDLE AGES EVEN A RICH man's house was little more than a large farmhouse. Draughts were no doubt very prevalent at a time when glass was so scarce and expensive that kings carried glass panes in their baggage trains as they travelled from castle to castle. Decoration generally expressed itself in rich hangings, which also served the practical purpose of preventing draughts from entering the room. Such hangings were usually of heavy woollen cloth, sometimes beautifully embroidered. It was but a short step from draught-excluding hangings to beautiful tapestries that hung on the bare stone walls and provided decoration only.

INCREASING COMFORT

Most Tudor mansions had long galleries, which someone once told me were made long in order that the ladies could exercise in rainy weather. There was always a great fire in the middle of such rooms, before which were placed wooden chairs. In the seventeenth century it became the practice to upholster the chairs to make them more comfortable to sit on. Strong flax canvas was the material generally used for upholstering such chairs as it was hardwearing. Once the chairs had been upholstered, the ladies would decorate them with needlepoint.

With the invention of window glass, it became possible to sit still for longer periods during the winter and screens to confine the heat of the fire became common. These screens would be decorated elaborately with many kinds of embellishment, from woven tapestry to stencilled paint. Later, in Victorian times, young ladies would decorate wooden fire screens by pasting on pictures that they had cut out of magazines to create a picture patchwork.

BED-HANGINGS AND CHINOISERIE

The four-poster bed was so popular not only because of the privacy it afforded but also because the bed-hangings kept out the ubiquitous draughts! Bed-hangings, too, were lavishly embroidered. Even portable folding camp or field beds were usually fitted with curtains, so that the occupant could be completely enclosed. When not in use the curtains were held up by cords looped over a button. A simple arrangement for an

STENCILLED TALL CLOCK

METAL DECORATION
Punched tinplate was sometimes used to decorate furniture and household boxes. Pieces of metal were first cut to the right shape. Then the metal was punched from the inside so that a protruding hole formed on the outside. Intricate interlacings of patterns could be achieved with punched tinplate.

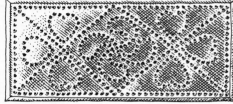
PUNCHED TINPLATE DECORATION

STENCILLED FURNITURE
Many items of furniture were elaborately ornamented with painted or stencilled designs. Wardrobes, chairs, clocks and pianos were all decorated, often with conventional designs of fruit or flowers. Some intricate and delicate designs contained a painstaking amount of detail, while other examples of folk art were whimsical in character, depicting homely village scenes, usually in bright reds, blues, greens, and yellows. Whatever the design, stencilled furniture was always cheerful.

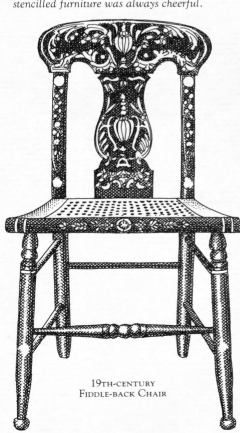
19TH-CENTURY FIDDLE-BACK CHAIR

ordinary static bed was to drape a curtain over a bracket positioned at the centre of the bed. Whatever the type of bed and curtain arrangement, it was considered good taste to match the bed-hangings as exactly as possible to the window curtains in the room.

In Regency times chinoiserie became rampant, to culminate in that absurd extravaganza, the Brighton Pavilion. Chinoiserie had a recrudescence in the 1920s and 30s, when it competed with art deco and art nouveau. I well remember friends of my mother who would not move without the disgusting little snuffling peke dogs that went with it.

RAMPANT DECORATION

In Victorian times the furniture that crammed every room was heavy and ornate. Made mostly of mahogany and stained even darker, the wood was concealed for the most part by a plentitude of tasselled fabrics. The upholsterer reigned supreme: everything that could be upholstered was upholstered. Any furniture made of a natural material was covered: nakedness, in things as well as people, was not allowed.

The work of keeping all this litter clean, let alone free from fleas, before the age of the vacuum cleaner was immense. But then that was done by the servants. When women of "the better sort" found that they could no longer afford to pay servants, all the clutter went out the door. It was the same with the huge tonnage of Victorian ornaments and knick-knacks: it took some time to get rid of them but they went.

Loose covers were being made in the seventeenth century. Chairs were often finished in coarse linen and covered with velvet

THE FIREPLACE
As the fireplace was the focal point of the room, it was often elegantly decorated. Gilt borders edged the fireplace itself, while ornamental tassels hung from the mantelpiece and heavy brocade drapes added the finishing touch.

GUARDS, SCREENS AND BOARDS
Fire guards were placed in front of the fire to prevent hot coals and sparks from flying out into the room. They were often made of brass or leaded glass and some had folding sides. Fire screens protected a person sitting too near the fire from fierce heat. They were elegantly decorated with embroidered needlework. Chimney boards served a practical as well as a decorative function. When the fire was not in use, the board was placed in front of the fireplace to hide the grate and block the draughts.

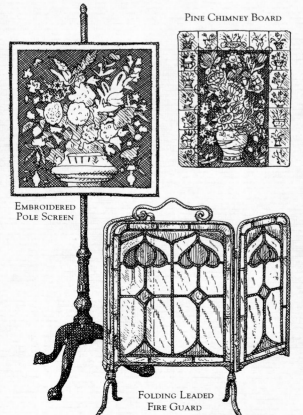

PINE CHIMNEY BOARD

EMBROIDERED POLE SCREEN

FOLDING LEADED FIRE GUARD

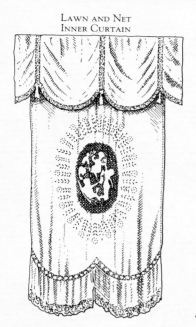

LAWN AND NET
INNER CURTAIN

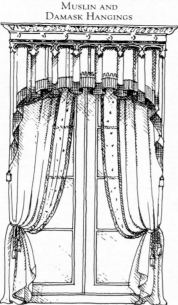

MUSLIN AND
DAMASK HANGINGS

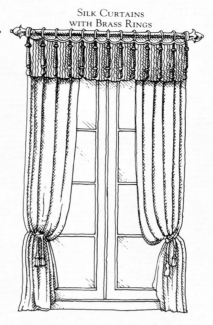

SILK CURTAINS
WITH BRASS RINGS

WINDOW CURTAINS
The quality of your curtain hangings was an indicator of your social standing. Handsome drapes of damask or silk lent an air of elegance to a room, and embellishments of tassels and valances added a touch of luxury.

LACED WINDOW BLINDS

BLINDS
Blinds were hung partly to protect curtains and furniture from strong sunlight, and partly to provide privacy from any passers-by. They were made out of stiff fabric and were often edged with crochet lace.

or damask slip covers of red and green. These handsome covers were removed for ordinary use. In the next century such costly materials were superseded by lighter, washable materials, which were left on all the time (apart from when they were being washed) and often concealed shabby, worn furniture. Red and green, and blue and white check patterns were exceedingly popular and window curtains were often made from the same material. Housewives often made up their own slip covers in the nineteenth century.

The anti-macassar was originally designed to prevent the upholstered backs of high chairs from being stained by the Macassar oil with which gentlemen plentifully anointed their hair. The anti-macassar became more and more elaborately decorated, usually with crochet work, and was always heavily betasselled. However, you could still remove it from the chair and launder it from time to time, as required.

Crocheted mantelpiece covers and cushion covers were common, as were lampshades, made in all sorts of ingenious ways—macramé and the rest. Lace curtains became beloved by the Victorians because they could hide behind them and peer through the window at the neighbours.

FOLK ART
Meanwhile, the labouring part of the population went on, in isolated pockets, creating their folk art. The cabins of narrow boats—those beautiful wooden craft that carried most of Britain's heavy freight traffic along

two thousand miles of canals—were magnificently painted with bold designs in bright primary colours. The pictures painted on the boats were of the same kind as those found on the famous watering cans and coal scuttles: roses and castles were the most popular. Of course, the fairy castles depicted standing beside lakes surrounded by mountains had never been seen by the canal boatmen, only imagined.

Vardos, or horse-drawn caravans, were similarly decorated, their interiors lined with brightly coloured curtain material, chamfering carved into all exposed timbers and fiddle-heads on their ends. Expensive Crown Derby china stood (and still stands) in the corner cupboard of the poorest vardo and there was brass everywhere.

RESTRAINED DECORATION
In Scandinavia, the Alps and any other region where wood was the chief building material, the art of wood carving was practised on all wooden furnishings. This beautiful but simple hand-carved furniture was the very antithesis of the dark, over-patterned furnishings so popular in England.

After the awful over-decoration of the Victorian period and the frightful aseptic sterility of the 1960s and 1970s, it is heartening to see people today decorating their houses with hand-woven cloth, good original paintings that really mean something, fine simple wooden furniture, either old or made by the new generation of craftsmen, hand-thrown pottery, and other articles of honest craftsmanship.

THE ANTI-MACASSAR
This was a piece of highly decorated crochet lace or cloth that hung over the back of a chair to prevent the upholstery being stained by men's hair oil, known as Macassar oil.

ORNAMENTING THE HOME

WEATHER VANES
As weather vanes had to be visible from a distance, their designs were fairly basic. Popular subjects were cockerels, archers, fish and angels. Early vanes were carved from wood and then painted in bright reds and yellows. The later metal vanes were usually left in an unpainted state but were sometimes gilded.

ICTORIAN AND EDWARDIAN YOUNG ladies, and no doubt Regency and Georgian young ladies before them, having absolutely nothing to do, invented an amazing variety of ways of making ornamental objects. Harmless wooden articles were attacked with red-hot pokers, to burn patterns into them, and boxes were covered with sea shells, arranged in tasteful patterns.

Actually, this is not a lost art: I know an old sailor who lives on the cliffs of the south coast of County Wexford, who has covered every inch of his house and out buildings with sea shells. Even the chimney has been decorated. He has also made a scale model of the Tusker light house.

ORNAMENTAL FASHION
Victorian ladies also made amazing pictures and objects out of feathers, pressed flowers, dead butterflies, beads and rolled-up paper. They worked tirelessly at their embroidery frames and at their tatting, crocheting and macramé: they were indefatigable. One

moment cutting out silhouettes was all the rage, the next it was making hideous paper beads out of scraps of paper. It almost seems as though genteel young ladies were prohibited from making anything useful.

USELESS OBJECTS
I am not old enough to remember the Victorian era itself but I am old enough to remember survivals from it. I remember the two Misses Weeley, who lived together in Weeley Hall in the village of Weeley in Essex, the nearest village to my own. Although desperately poor they were highly respected because they were gentry. Their house, in which I was always welcome and loved to go, was absolutely cluttered with useless objects. Every horizontal surface—and there were plenty—was crammed with china dogs, cats, cows, presents from seaside resorts and much much more. There is no way I could enumerate or describe the enormous variety of objects which these two dear old ladies considered absolutely essential to their well-being.

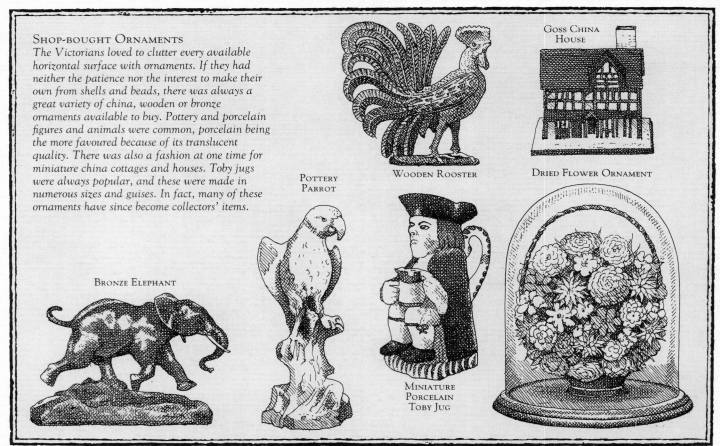

SHOP-BOUGHT ORNAMENTS
The Victorians loved to clutter every available horizontal surface with ornaments. If they had neither the patience nor the interest to make their own from shells and beads, there was always a great variety of china, wooden or bronze ornaments available to buy. Pottery and porcelain figures and animals were common, porcelain being the more favoured because of its translucent quality. There was also a fashion at one time for miniature china cottages and houses. Toby jugs were always popular, and these were made in numerous sizes and guises. In fact, many of these ornaments have since become collectors' items.

GOSS CHINA HOUSE

WOODEN ROOSTER

DRIED FLOWER ORNAMENT

POTTERY PARROT

BRONZE ELEPHANT

MINIATURE PORCELAIN TOBY JUG

HOME-MADE ORNAMENTS

Silhouette pictures provided popular ornamentation in the home. The silhouettes were usually of figures, either cut out of black paper or painted with black paint, and they were recognized by their shape. Fire papers, made from pieces of coloured tissue paper, were very simple to make. They were hung in the fireplace when the fire was not in use. Baskets of wax fruit, artistically arranged and trimmed with ribbon, were frequently displayed on the sideboard and in the fireplace during the summer months. Shells were used to decorate trinket boxes and pincushions, and even to cover up cracks on china bottles. They were also used to make borders for scenic paintings. Earthenware flower pots, considered too plain for general view, were often decorated with painted Egyptian figures, while brightly coloured motifs of birds, fruit and flowers were painted on tin kitchen boxes and pots.

PAPER SILHOUETTE PICTURE

SHELL TOILETTE BOX

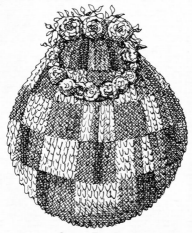

SIMPLE FIRE PAPER

HAND-PAINTED WOOD

Wooden articles were often decorated with painted designs. The wood had to be hard to stop the paint from running, and with a light grain—a heavy grain could spoil the design. First the outline was drawn on the wood in pencil. Then the design was painted in with watercolours or inks. Next, using a fine pen, the outline was inked over to give a crisp finish. Finally, when the paint and ink were dry, varnish was applied.

WOODEN SALAD SPOON AND FORK

PENNSYLVANIA COOKIE BOX

PAINTED COFFEE POT

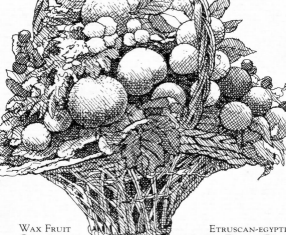

WAX FRUIT
ORNAMENT

ETRUSCAN-EGYPTIAN
FLOWER POT

FESTIVALS & DECORATIONS

HEREVER IN THE WORLD THERE ARE such things as calendars there are special celebrations. Even before calendars were invented mankind went to great trouble to establish such fixed points of the year as mid-summer and mid-winter in order to celebrate them.

It is not surprising that a celebration just after the shortest day should be universal in more northerly latitudes and should assume such great importance. As man worked his way northwards to occupy the lands being liberated by the retreating Ice Age he must have found it daunting that the days became shorter and shorter as well as colder and colder. As growth of vegetation lessened, he must have feared that the world was indeed about to die. At this point, perhaps, one of the more observant among them would have noticed that the days were lengthening again and that the sun was a fraction higher at midday. Naturally they would have greeted the change with great joy and celebrated!

CHRISTMAS

Christians are lucky in that the most splendid event in the calendar—Christmas—occurs just at the time when our spirits are cast down by darker and darker days and gloomy skies. Suddenly we are enjoined to make merry and rejoice, for the great universal principle of regeneration is vindicated.

The present-day orgy of rampant consumerism had not manifested itself by the time of my childhood. All I knew of the impending arrival of Christmas was that I was told to hang a stocking—a *large* stocking that was wont to adorn a much larger leg

THE CHRISTMAS CRACKER
The Christmas cracker was invented in 1860 by a man named Tom Smith, who, no doubt, wanted to make the most of the seasonal goodwill. His crackers proved to be immensely popular and, unlike their modern counterparts, generously contained all manner of goodies, from love messages, charms and toys to jokes, candies and trinkets.

THE CHRISTMAS TREE
The Christmas tree, bedecked with tinsel and baubles, is as much a part of Christmas today as roast turkey and plum pudding. Yet it was only in the last century that the Christmas tree became a part of the Yuletide festivities. There is a story that tells of Martin Luther originating the Christmas tree. While out walking one Christmas Eve, so the story goes, he was so moved by the night stars, glistening through the trees, that he rushed home to recreate the effect for his family, with candles and a small fir tree.

Traditional decorations for the tree consisted of fruit, nuts, gingerbread, candies, paper strips and lighted candles. An angel topped the tree, which was usually a spruce. Over the years, as commercialism took a firm hold, glass baubles replaced the fruit and nuts, multi-coloured electric bulbs replaced the candles, and the angel turned into a fairy!

than mine—at the foot of the bed. Then my mother would read a poem to my brother and me as we sat in front of the bright log fire. It began: "T'was the night before Christmas and all through the house not a creature was stirring, not even a mouse."

Then my brother and I would go to bed and fight to keep awake so that we should actually *see* that strange portly figure squeezing himself out of the small bedroom fireplace. We never did. We never thought of him as Father Christmas but always as Saint Nicholas; perhaps that was an Americanism.

Before daylight we would wake up to a new world. The whole house had been miraculously bedecked with holly bright with red berries (that was before most of the hedges had been bulldozed and there were tons of it), and a magnificent tree with *real* candles stood in the living room, tinsel-bedecked and beautiful with, and this was the most important part about it, a mound of intriguingly shaped parcels at the foot.

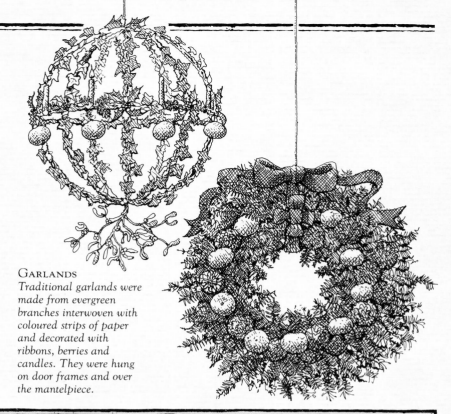

GARLANDS
Traditional garlands were made from evergreen branches interwoven with coloured strips of paper and decorated with ribbons, berries and candles. They were hung on door frames and over the mantelpiece.

BRINGING HOME THE TREE
Before the days of the reusable tinsel Christmas tree, spruce trees were chopped down from the local forest and taken home. Carrying a Christmas tree while riding a bicycle, with snow on the ground, cannot have been easy, but it was certainly no chore! After all, the arrival of the Christmas tree meant the festivities could start!

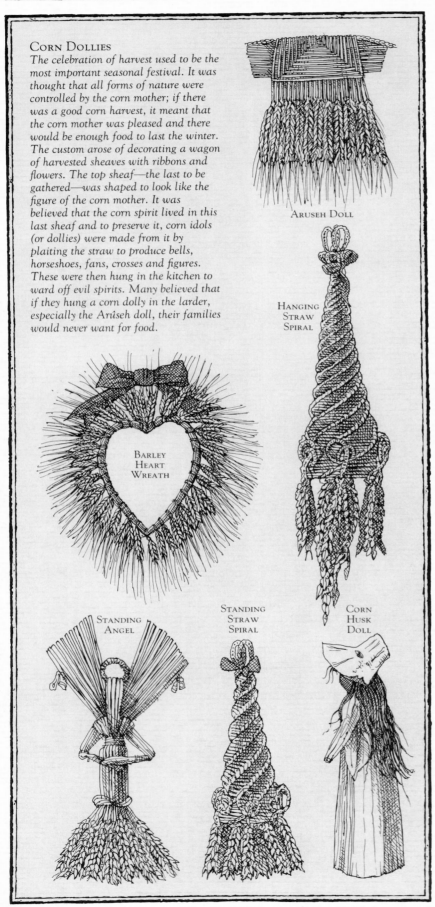

CORN DOLLIES

The celebration of harvest used to be the most important seasonal festival. It was thought that all forms of nature were controlled by the corn mother; if there was a good corn harvest, it meant that the corn mother was pleased and there would be enough food to last the winter. The custom arose of decorating a wagon of harvested sheaves with ribbons and flowers. The top sheaf—the last to be gathered—was shaped to look like the figure of the corn mother. It was believed that the corn spirit lived in this last sheaf and to preserve it, corn idols (or dollies) were made from it by plaiting the straw to produce bells, horseshoes, fans, crosses and figures. These were then hung in the kitchen to ward off evil spirits. Many believed that if they hung a corn dolly in the larder, especially the Arûseh doll, their families would never want for food.

ARÛSEH DOLL

HANGING STRAW SPIRAL

BARLEY HEART WREATH

STANDING ANGEL

STANDING STRAW SPIRAL

CORN HUSK DOLL

EPIPHANY

There are other ways of celebrating in wintertime. I stood once with my own children on the quay of a little Spanish fishing village and watched the customs launch, heavily disguised with coloured canvas and brilliant with whirling Catherine wheels, firing salvoes of rockets as she came steaming towards us to unload three gorgeously apparelled kings to be greeted by three equally gorgeously apparelled pages leading caparisoned horses. The kings mounted the horses, rather unsteadily as they were more accustomed to riding the waves, and were led to the town hall. There a huge pile of parcels awaited them, which the kings set about dispensing to every child in the village (mine, too) amid much rejoicing. This was not 25th December but epiphany.

I once celebrated epiphany with a couple of hundred Yugoslavs, refugees from their country, having fought on the wrong side during the war, who were living in a camp in England. Epiphany went on for three days and three nights: a large pig was roasted whole with an apple in its mouth, a small oak tree was dragged in decked with apples and toasted with a thousand glasses of slivovitz. We formed long human chains of dancing men, our arms around each others' necks, and were regaled with absolutely magnificent songs by three gorgeous Croatian folk singers, brought down from London specially for the occasion.

HARVEST TIME

On plough Sunday the instrument on which all civilized life depended was dragged in triumph around every English village, bedecked with ribands, and every householder was expected to contribute largesse. Largesse (in the form of money) was exacted too by the reapers in the harvest field. Corn reaping in the English countryside was accompanied by much badinage and ancient ceremony. The leader of the reapers was named "lord of the harvest" and his second-in-command, although equally a man, named his "lady". Any stranger who happened to pass by, who looked as though he might have some money, would be greeted by them with cries of "Largesse!" This meant one thing—he had to put his hand in his pocket. The cash collected would go towards providing beer for the thirsty reapers.

The subsequent harvest supper was a magnificent affair. The farmer's wife would provide a repast of great splendour, with

EASTER EGGS
The art of dyeing and decorating eggs at Easter was popular long before the advent of chocolate eggs. First the eggs were hard-boiled in water that contained a plant dye such as anemone or broom flowers. Then patterns were painted on the coloured shells.

huge barons of roast beef, roast legs of mutton and beer in lavish quantities. There would be much singing and playing of instruments during the evening and the telling of stories would go on far into the night.

EASTER

The celebration of the return of life after the winter, or Easter in Christian countries, was a great event. In Ireland, where I now live, it still is, for it ends the fast of Lent, which is still observed in this country. When I first came here thirty years ago I observed the melancholy fact that the front door of every pub was locked every day during Lent and the curtains drawn. It was some time before I discovered that the *back* doors were open, or would be opened in response to a discreet knock. Easter morning puts a glorious end to all these austerities, with the cry in church of "Christ has risen".

In Greece, Easter is the great event of the year. They have all-night vigils in the churches there, and there are no seats to sit down on. Young lambs, roasted whole, are eaten, washed down with wine and raki and the dancing which follows continues right the way through the night.

Besides Easter lambs, eggs and bunny rabbits are part of the Easter tradition. In Germany they paint pretty patterns on hard-boiled eggs, which they then hide all over the garden and the children have to hunt for them. This custom also prevails in America.

HALLOWE'EN

The Americans also make much of Hallowe'en, as do the Irish. The Welsh, Scots and English have rather forgotten this pagan survival in their celebration of the rather ghoulish Guy Fawkes' Day, during which the effigy of the man who was accused of trying to blow up the Protestant Houses of Parliament is burnt on a thousand bonfires. For fairly obvious reasons this event is not celebrated in Catholic Ireland and nor, of course, in North America.

FEAST DAYS

In Medieval times, the year was punctuated by numerous feast days in memory of various saints, and when people talk of the unremitting labour of the Medieval countryman they should remember that these "holy days" were indeed holidays—days of rest and jollification. It was not until the Industrial Revolution that the lives of working people became lives of unremitting toil. The idea that industrialism has relieved people of labour is an illusion. In those areas of the world in which there are still true peasants, excuses for spending the day in celebration are numerous. It does not, in fact, take many man or woman hours of labour a year for a family of subsistence peasants to make their living.

NEW YEAR'S EVE

The new calendar instituted by Pope Gregory in the sixteenth century has never been accepted in the Gwaun Valley of Pembrokeshire in west Wales, where I used to live. Although the people there have accepted the new date for Christmas, they still celebrate "Hen Nos Galan", or the Old New Year, on 13th January. On that day and night, "cwrw gatre", or home-brewed beer, is drunk in copious amounts and magnificent songs are sung in the Welsh language. In the same area, but more particularly in the southern half of Pembrokeshire (which is commonly known as "the English" because that language is spoken there), and in various parts of Ireland, too, a most peculiar ceremony is sometimes still performed. A wren is caught and put in a cage which is then hung on a pole. The caged wren is carried around the village on the pole by a gang of boys who sing particular songs outside each house, for which they are rewarded with cakes and home-brewed ale. In ancient times at the end of the evening the wren was brutally beaten to death. Fortunately that barbaric part of the ceremony is nowhere observed today.

HALLOWE'EN LANTERNS
Hallowe'en lanterns were made by hollowing out a pumpkin or turnip, cutting out a gruesome face from the remaining "shell" and then inserting a candle inside it. On a dark Hallowe'en night, these lanterns looked very menacing!

INDEX

ACKNOWLEDGMENTS

Part I: Forgotten Arts

Project Editor **David Lamb**   Art Editor **Flo Henfield**
Editor **Simon Adams**   Designer **Julia Goodman**
Managing Editor **Jackie Douglas**   Art Director **Roger Bristow**

Dorling Kindersley would like to thank Jonathan Hilton, Caroline Lucas, Moira J Mole, Steven Wooster, and Fred Ford and Mike Pilley
of Radius, for their help in producing *The Forgotten Arts*.

Many craftsman have given the author and contributing artists the benefits of their considerable experience and expertise. In particular, thanks
are due to William Brown, wheelwright and blacksmith, of Burwash, Sussex; Richard Carey, wheelwright, of Battle, Sussex; Mike Farmer, of G M
Catterall, saddler, of Tonbridge, Kent; F Hawkins & Sons Ltd, carpenters, of Tunbridge Wells, Kent; H J Phillips, shipwright and boatbuilder,
of Rye, Sussex; and Edgar and Trevor Stern, farriers and blacksmiths, of Maidstone, Kent.

Illustrations in Part I are by:

(Key: t = top, r = right, l = left, m = middle, b = below)

David Ashby: 25, 27t, 32, 33l, 34, 35, 37, 52, 53, 57, 59, 64r, 65, 68, 69, 73, 94b, 98, 104, 105, 110, 112, 113, 116, 117r, 122, 123, 127, 129, 131, 134t, 138, 140,
143t, 145, 146t, 147, 150, 151r, 152m&b, 154r, 155, 157m&b, 158, 159r, 162, 167, 175, 177tr&b, 178, 182, 183, 186, 187, 189, 190, 191

Brian Delf: 46, 47, 54, 55, 106, 107, 110, 111.

Peter Dennis: 26, 27b, 130, 133, 137, 143b, 151b, 152t, 153, 154t&l, 159b, 160, 161, 184, 185.

Robert Kettell: 2, 15, 16, 17, 18, 20, 21, 22, 23.

Peter Morter: 30, 31, 50–1, 82, 83, 117t&b, 118, 119, 121, 132, 134b, 135, 136, 144, 163,168, 169, 170, 171, 172.

Peter Reddick: 24, 48, 60, 72, 174.

Les Smith: 28, 36, 45, 58, 62, 63, 66, 67, 71b, 80, 81, 94t, 103, 108, 109, 125, 146b, 148, 164, 165.

Eric Thomas: 33r, 40, 41, 42–43, 64b, 71t, 75–5, 77, 78–9, 84, 85, 86–7, 88, 89, 90, 91, 92, 93, 96, 97, 100, 101, 114–15, 128, 157r.

Part II: Forgotten Household Crafts

Project Editor **Jane Laing**   Art Editor **Alex Arthur**
Senior Editor **David Lamb**   Editor **Heather Dewhursts**
Text and picture researchers **Valerie Janitch, Angela Murphy**
Illustrators **David Ashby, Brian Delf, Robert Micklewright, Donald Myall, Richard Phipps, Eric Thomas, John Woodcock.**
Indexer **Hilary Bird**

Editorial Director **Jackie Douglas**
Art Director **Roger Bristow**

Special thanks to: Sandra Archer, Lynn Bresler, Arthur Brown, Fiona Macmillan, Fraser Newman, Tessa Richardson-Jones, Jane Rollason,
Patrizio Semproni and Henrietta Winthrop for their help with the editing, design and production of *Forgotten Household Crafts*.

Dorling Kindersley would like to thank the following individuals and organizations for their invaluable advice, help and information: Brooke
Bond Oxo Ltd; Crosse and Blackwell; Monica Ellis for her book *Ice and Icehouses through the Ages*; Greater London Record office and History
Library; Mike Keeble, National Cattle Breeders' Association; Robert Lee (Bee Supplies) Ltd; Metal Box plc; David J. Parker; Rare Breeds
Survival Trust; Agnes Robertson, Glenesk Folk Museum; Ian Ross, City of Westminster Cleansing Dept.; Springwood Books for their book
Patons: A Story of Handknitting; Cecil Tonsley (editor), *British Bee Journal*; Eve Williams, Preston Library, Wembley, Middlesex.

Picture Credits

Dorling Kindersley would like to thank the following for their kind permission to reproduce their photographs:

(Key: t = top, r = right, l = left, b = below)

1 Farmers Weekly; 4–5 Hulton Getty; 10, 12–13 Hulton Getty; 14 Bernard Barton; 19 Jean Ribière; 25 Institute of Agricultural History and Museum of English Rural Life, University of Reading; 29, 31, 33, 34 Institute of Agricultural History and Museum of English Rural Life, University of Reading; 35 Farmers Weekly; 37, 40, 41 Institute of Agricultural History and Museum of English Rural Life, University of Reading; 44 Steven Wooster; 45 Kit Houghton Photography; 46 Jacqui Hurst; 49 Bryan and Cherry Alexander; 51 John Seymour; 55t Jacqui Hurst, b John Seymour; 57 Jacqui Hurst; 53 Michael Bussell Photo Library; 56l British Tourist Authority, r Steven Wooster; 58 Farmers Weekly; 59 Jean Ribière; 61, 63 Institute of Agricultural History and Museum of English Rural Life, University of Reading; 65 John Seymour; 68 Bernard Barton; 70 British Tourist Authority; 73, 76 John Seymour; 81 Farmers Weekly; 83 BBC Hulton Picture Library; 85 Kit Houghton Photography; 88, 91 Institute of Agricultural History and Museum of English Rural Life, University of Reading; 92 Farmers Weekly; 95 Jacqui Hurst; 99, 101 Institute of Agricultural History and Museum of English Rural Life, University of Reading; 102 Farmers Weekly; 104 Institute of Agricultural History and Museum of English Rural Life, University of Reading; 105 Welsh Folk Museum, St Fagan's, Cardiff; 106 Institute of Agricultural History and Museum of English Rural Life, University of Reading; 112 Kit Houghton Photography; 116, 117, 119 John Seymour; 120 The Sutcliffe Gallery, Whitby, Yorkshire; 123 Jacqui Hurst; 124, 126, 129 Institute of Agricultural History and Museum of English Rural Life, University of Reading; 135t John Seymour, b Kit Houghton Photography; 137 Farmers Weekly; 139 Institute of Agricultural History and Museum of English Rural Life, University of Reading; 140 BBC Hulton Picture Library; 141, 142 Jean Ribière; 145, 146, 147, 148, 150 Institute of Agricultural History and Museum of English Rural Life, University of Reading; 153 Cliché Musée des Arts et Traditions Populaires, Paris; 156, 157, 158, 161, 162 Jacqui Hurst; 164t Kit Houghton Photography, b Jacqui Hurst; 166 Farmers Weekly; 167 Kit Houghton Photography; 168 Farmers Weekly; 169 Kit Houghton Photography; 170 Farmers Weekly; 171 Jacqui Hurst; 173 Institute of Agricultural History and Museum of English Rural Life, University of Reading; 175 Andrew de Lory; 176 Doris Ullmann Foundation, Berea College, Kentucky, USA; 178 Topham; 179 J. Allan Cash; 180 Jean Ribière; 181 Ulster Museum; 182 Jean Ribière; 184 John Seymour; 185 BBC Hulton Picture Library; 186 Kit Houghton Photography; 187 BBC Hulton Picture Library; 188 Jean Ribière; 190 Topham; 191 John Seymour; 192–3 Corbis/Hulton Getty Collection; 196 Mrs J. Knock/Museum of English Rural Life, University of Reading; 204 Frank Meadow Sutcliffe/The Sutcliffe Gallery, Whitby, Yorkshire; 211 Pitstone Local History Society, Bedfordshire; 223 North of England Open Air Museum, Beamish, Durham; 227 Henry E. Huntington Library, San Marino, California; 234 Munby Collection, Trinity College, Cambridge; 242 Bruce Castle Museum, Tottenham, London N17; 251 Buckinghamshire County Museum, Aylesbury; 255–6 British Bee Journal; 258 The Beaford Centre, Devon; 263 Museum of English Rural Life, University of Reading; 264 North of England Open Air Museum, Beamish, Durham; 267 Cambridge and County Folk Museum, Cambridge; 269 North of England Open Air Museum, Beamish, Durham; 274 Birmingham City Reference Library; 278 Weybridge Museum, Surrey; 281 The Harry Ransom Research Center, University of Texas at Austin, USA; 287 North of England Open Air Museum, Beamish, Durham; 293 Frank Meadow Sutcliffe/The Sutcliffe Gallery, Whitby, Yorkshire; 297 Manor House Local History Department, Deptford; 310 Welsh Folk Museum, St Fagan's, Cardiff; 319 North of England Open Air Museum, Beamish, Durham; 322 Suffolk Record Office, Ipswich; 324 Mansell Collection, London; 326 Frank Meadow Sutcliffe/The Sutcliffe Gallery, Whitby, Yorkshire; 333 Doris Ullmann Foundation, Berea College, Kentucky, USA; 336 J. Allan Cash; 339 Doris Ullmann Foundation, Berea College, Kentucky, USA; 341 Buckinghamshire County Museum, Aylesbury; 344 North of England Open Air Museum, Beamish, Durham; 346 National Museums of Scotland; 347 Shetland Museum, Lerwick; 356 Minnesota Historical Society, USA; 358 Buckinghamshire County Museum, Aylesbury; 363 Arthur Sanderson & Co., London; 366 The Beaford Centre, Devon.